The Performance Improvement Toolkit

The Guide
to Knowledge-Based Improvement

Robert M. Gerst

The Performance Improvement Toolkit
Robert M. Gerst

Converge Consulting Group Inc.
Suite 200, 309 - 2nd Avenue SW
Calgary, Alberta
Canada
T2P 0C5

403 266 0061
www.converge-group.com
www.performanceimprovementtoolkit.com

ISBN 0-9688067-0-8

Printed in Canada

National Library of Canada Cataloguing in Publication Data
Gerst, Robert, 1954-
The performance improvement toolkit
Includes bibliographical references and index.
ISBN 0-9688067-0-8
1. Organizational effectiveness. I. Title.
HD58.9.G47 2001   658.4   C2001-911480-X

This book is dedicated to all those I have worked with over the years and who have so successfully demonstrated that real improvement can happen anywhere in the organization, at any level and at any time.

A special thanks to Barb and Marc, family members and friends, who managed to tolerate me while I was writing.

The Performance Improvement Toolkit

Contents

2. Improving Performance: Critical Components of Systems Thinking 35

3. Getting Ready: Planning and Organizing for Improvement 147

4. Creating Visual Models: Using the Tools of Depiction to Improve Understanding 189

Flowcharts 212
The Flowchart Symbol Set 213
Types of Flowcharts 214
Constructing Flowcharts 221
Basic Flowchart Analysis 226
Voice of the Process Tables 232
VOPT Part 1: Descriptive Analysis 236
VOPT Part 2: Preliminary Performance Analysis 236
From "As Is" to "To Be" 244
Cause and Effect (Ishikawa) Diagrams 246
What It Looks Like 246
Where to Use 247
How to Make an Ishikawa Diagram 248
Example: Examining Service Delivery Problems 253
Supporting Analytical Methods 257
Summary: Using Visual Models 269

5. Performance Measurement: The Basics of Gathering and Working With Numerical Data 271

The Science of Data 272

6. Analyzing Results: Tools for the Analysis of System Performance and Capability

7. Analyzing Relationships: Tools for the Analysis of Cause and Effect 513

9. Making Decisions: Tools for the Evaluation of Alternatives 627

10. Management & Planning Tools: From Intention to Implementation ...707

11. Organizational Alignment: The Tools and Techniques of Deployment ...769

12. Building Systems of Improvement: Key Considerations for Performance-Based Organizations 825

Introduction: The New Economics of Knowledge

Traditional economics teaches there are two factors of production: capital and labor. At times, technology is introduced as a third. Competitive advantage, we are told, can be gained by maximizing competitive position on one or more of these primary factors.

Yet some organizations defy traditional economics. Given similar positions in capital, labor and even technology, they outperform the competition – delivering products and services of better quality and with greater levels of productivity and profitability. They're able to do so because they leverage a far more important and fundamental factor of production – knowledge.

It may seem obvious, but some organizations outperform others simply because they *know how to*.

This, therefore, is a 'how-to' book. It is about how to improve organizational performance through application of standard tools and techniques designed to support learning and generate new knowledge. It is about using these tools to analyze products or processes, identify problems or improvement opportunities, make decisions on alternative courses of action, and implement solutions.

This book is not intended only for those in the front lines or middle management. Learning how to improve performance is relevant to everyone in the organization. The tools and techniques discussed apply from the shop floor to the executive suite.

It may seem obvious, but some organizations outperform others because they know how to.

A STORY OF FAILURE

Some years ago I was asked by a large oil and gas company to visit one of their plants and assist a team in their improvement efforts. Evidently, the team had bogged down and my task was to help get them moving again. This plant represented the company's initial efforts at what was to become a corporate-wide improvement initiative and they wanted some early successes.

I drove to the plant and met the team. They showed me the work they had done. The analysis of the process they were trying to improve had been summarized on a large cause-and-effect diagram – a tool designed to identify the causal effects of some performance problem. The diagram covered an entire wall and the various causal factors identified were written so small, they couldn't possibly be read unless you were within a few feet of the chart. There were literally hundreds of causal elements identified. To this day, I cannot recall anything like it – the most detailed analysis I have ever seen.

Unfortunately, it was also one of the most useless. The team had worked hard to identify all possible causes of problems in the process, but had so over-analyzed things they didn't know how to move forward. Why, I asked them, had they done the cause-and-effect diagram to such detail? Why had they continued to create the monster they had?

The answer – they had been told to! Equipped with two days of training on "Quality," including everything on the theory, tools and techniques of process improvement, the team had charged ahead following the prescribed eight-step process improvement model given in the training. Step two said the team should create a cause and effect diagram showing all the possible causes of process problems, so that's what they did. The model never really told them why they were creating this analysis or when to stop. And so, fearing they might have missed something and not really knowing what to do next anyway, the team continued to analyze possible causes, adding ever increasing levels of detail. They had fallen into an analysis-paralysis trap, never moving ahead to actually solving problems, generating alternative process designs or implementing solutions.

It took very little to move them forward. The list of possible causes was reduced to a few critical items and a measurement plan was developed and implemented. Within a few weeks the team had acquired the information necessary to make some intelligent decisions on improvements, which were quickly implemented.

But this is not a success story; it is a story of failure. The employees were told improvement was important and they believed it. They tried their best to bring this improvement about, to make the changes required and they worked hard at it. But no one really bothered to show them how. They were led to believe they had the training they needed, but they did not. In short, they were set up for failure from the beginning. Moreover, there was no one they could turn to for direction. The trainers had no idea. They were only teaching what they had been told to teach – they hadn't actually used this stuff. Senior management knew less. They had just purchased the program from a consultant.

THE BUSINESS OF IMPROVEMENT

Too often, organizational improvement efforts boil down to a two-day training exercise – with miracles expected upon completion. It's a sort of 'train them and turn them loose approach' to organizational improvement. When the exercises fail, and they almost always do, senior management can say they tried

that and it didn't work. Time to move on to the next management fad with its requisite two days of training for everyone.

But there is no room for fads in today's competitive environment. The tools, techniques and theory presented here are designed to support a scientific approach to improvement combined with a disciplined approach to change. Two days in the training room just won't cut it. To succeed, improvement must become part of the way things are done – by everyone. In short, improvement is everybody's business.

Improvement is about generating knowledge and applying it to yield performance gains and innovation

"There is no competitive advantage to ignorance"

that create competitive advantage. The process of performance improvement, therefore, is the process of organizational learning. The more you know, the more you can use knowledge as a source of competitive advantage. There is no competitive advantage to ignorance.

The lightweight approaches to performance improvement miss a fundamental truth – if you want improvement in anything, sooner or later someone has to do it. Someone has to make the changes that will produce performance improvement. To do the job, that person must be given the right tools and the training in how to use them.

This book provides a set of tools for analyzing and improving organizational performance. It also presents some of the theory behind the tools, to help those trying to make improvements understand why the tools work and the various ways they can be applied.

It is often said that employees must first learn the theory behind the tools before using them. But employees need not and could not learn *all* of the theory before attempting to use the tools. Theory and its practical application reinforce one another.

Which means sooner or later, we need to dive in, use the tools of improvement and experience our share of successes and failures. In so doing, we increase both our theoretical and practical knowledge of how to generate performance improvement. The same holds true for organizations. Organizational learning requires some theory, but it also requires the organization to try – to learn from failure and grow from success.

I hope this book helps.

The Way We Work: The New Model of Performance

Change is easy. Do nothing and things will change, although likely for the worse. Improvement, on the other hand, is difficult. It demands not only change, but change for the better.

Our organizations are awash in the culture of change. Consultants, professors, managers, and politicians preach the gospel of change as the key to economic and competitive salvation. Change has become a metaphor for all that is good. Organizations are counseled to manage at the speed of change, develop 'change leaders' or become 'change masters.' But change itself is neither good nor bad – it is notoriously neutral.

Change is only a measure of how different things are between yesterday and today or between today and what we believe tomorrow will bring. Producing change that hurts productivity or lowers product appeal is far easier than producing change that improves organizational performance. Indeed, some would argue our organizations display an uncanny ability for producing change that hurts. Those preaching change need to give direction to their efforts. Anyone can bring about change; the trick is to bring about improvement.

Improvement places more demands upon us because it requires knowledge. It is not sufficient for organizations to guess their way to performance improvement. Doing so is nothing more than applied ignorance. Organizations expecting to outlast and outperform their competition must constantly improve performance at rates exceeding those of their competitors. Continuous improvement in product and service, and in the processes that produce both, is the fundamental task of organizations.

Doing so, however, requires knowledge of how the relevant processes and systems function. It requires knowledge about how to bring about improvement and, most importantly, about how to continuously add to the organization's level of knowledge so the process of improvement can go on.

We Live in a New Economic Age: The Need for Improvement

People and organizations no longer exist in isolation of one another. Information moves across borders in an instant. Accessing the Internet, a young girl in Tokyo gathers information about life in Toledo. Information technology presents life in other lands to millions at a time. The morning stock market quotes include not just New York, but Tokyo, Hong Kong, London, Toronto and Berlin.

Products and services are becoming global as well. A Japanese company manufacturing cars in California uses transmissions assembled in Brazil, engines made in Germany and prepares the suspension system according to specifications detailed in England. Products and services move across national boundaries in ways and at speeds that would have been thought impossible only a decade ago.

The bottom line is, we live in a new economic age. Today's realities include:

▲ **The number and diversity of competitors is expanding.** The global marketplace means global competition as well. We no longer face simply American competition, but competition from Asia, Europe and South America. And all these competitors are seeking new and better ways of delivering new and superior products to our customers. Survivors will know their customers and know how to deliver what the customer wants, better than anyone else.

▲ **Widespread economic growth is no longer a given.** The post-war boom of the 50's and 60's is over. We can no longer rely on general economic growth to fuel the bottom line. Organizations today must generate their own growth by producing products and services that do a better job of meeting consumer demand. This in turn demands innovation in product and service design and development. In short, the task is to create new customers – customers that want to buy what we have to sell.

▲ **Quality, productivity and innovation are the new drivers of success.** Rapid innovation in product and service design, which enhances levels of productivity and delivers superior quality products to the customer, is the new driver of success. Organizations that know how to innovate in ways that create customers and can deliver this innovation at competitive cost, will lead the market.

▲ **Knowledge is the new key to competitive advantage.** The traditional factors of production, capital and labor, are becoming less important. Knowledge is emerging as the new critical driver of competitive advantage. Peter Drucker, the American management consultant, goes further. He argues knowledge is the only resource that can distinguish organizations – that an organization can truly call its own.[1] Short-term prosperity will come to those who do what they do better than anyone else. Long-term growth will come to those who know how to improve and innovate faster than the competition. Either way, knowledge and the ability to apply it is defining the winners and losers in the marketplace.

In the 1970's and 1980's, we learned the price of complacency – of failing to understand the new economy. One example was the rise of Japanese companies in what had been considered traditional American industries. The resulting decline in market share and the surrender of entire industries brought these lessons home. It was tempting to blame the Japanese for this decline. We cited their culture, newer factories, trade policies and a host of other differences. What we really produced was a long list of excuses.

At the time, those Japanese companies experiencing success in America and globally had a simple secret. They 'knew how' to do their work better.

> *"Other resources, money or physical equipment for instance, do not confer any distinction. What makes a business distinct and what is its peculiar resource is its ability to use knowledge of all kinds – from scientific and technical knowledge to social, economic and managerial knowledge. It is only in this respect to knowledge that a business can be distinct, can, therefore, produce something that has value in the marketplace."*
>
> **Peter Drucker, Managing for Results; p.5**

---

1. Peter Drucker, Managing for Results, Harper & Row, 1964, New York, NY, p.5

THE FORD TRANSFORMATION: THE NEW ECONOMIC AGE COMES HOME

No industry is more familiar with these lessons of complacency than the American automobile industry. In the 70's, the Ford Motor Company was the darling of American industry – a world leader. By 1980, Ford was no longer a world leader, it was a basket case. In that year, Ford lost more than $1.5 billion, the second-highest one-year loss in American corporate history. Market share was declining, customer disenchantment increasing and morale slipping. The basic design themes in Ford cars hadn't changed in a decade. Quality ratings were the lowest of the big three, and the Japanese were producing better quality cars at lower cost and gaining both market share and customer loyalty as a result. Obsolescence described not just Ford cars, but the company.

> *"Obsolescence need not be planned: it can just move in."*
> **Donald Peterson**

In 1980, Ford's president and chief operating officer, Mr. Donald Peterson, became convinced that a new approach was needed. He hired Dr. Edwards Deming to help bring this new approach to Ford. It was Deming who had been widely credited with helping the Japanese create the kind organizations that proved so successful on the global stage and Peterson wanted some of those lessons brought home to Ford.

To the surprise of many at Ford, Deming didn't emphasize the need for robotics or renegotiation of trade policy or even more chrome on the tailpipes. He emphasized building a culture of continuous improvement. This included bringing people together to work in teams, to use data and a scientific approach to increase knowledge of the product, the process that produced it and the customer that bought it.[2]

Within five years, ". . . Ford had emerged as the darling of the American auto industry. Earnings, for the first time since the 1920's, exceeded those of General Motors, and in fact exceeded GM's and Chrysler's combined. Ford's market share continued to increase at the expense of its two American rivals. Its new Taurus/Sable car line was an unqualified success commercially and in the eyes of Detroit's critics. *Consumer Reports* magazine, not usually a fan of American automobiles, called the new cars the best American cars it had ever tested and used

---

2. Donald E. Peterson, A Better Idea: Redefining the Way Americans Work, Houghton Mifflin Company, Boston, 1991, see pages 7 - 17

the Taurus as the standard by which to judge other domestic models."[3]

"Subsequent years confirmed that Ford's success was not a fluke as earnings continued to exceed GM's and Chrysler's. Ford announced profit sharing for its hourly employees of over $2,000 per worker in 1987 and $3,700 in 1988. Some estimates of Ford's cost advantage over GM ran as high as $600 per car. Not bad for a company that in 1980 was on the brink of disaster and seen as the basket case of the American car industry."[4]

THE TRANSFORMATION CONTINUES

Of course, the Ford experience is a convenient example if only because so many of us are familiar with how the automobile industry has changed over the past few years. But the lessons learned have now been applied in other industries, not only in America but in Europe, Asia and South America.

Perhaps the most current example is that of General Electric (GE). Jack Welch, Chairman and CEO of GE, leaves little doubt as to the importance of the new management to GE.

"We believe then and we are convinced today . . . that there is an 'infinite capacity to improve everything.' It's . . . quality, along with a culture of learning, sharing and unending excitement."[5]

SUCCESS: IT'S IN THE WAY WE WORK

The experience at Ford and other companies in similar circumstances teaches an important lesson. The past successes of Japanese companies (or any other company for that matter) are not so much about currency fluctuations, different cultures or singing company songs in the morning. It's about the way we work and our philosophy of management. When Ford, and now a host of other American companies from Motorola to Xerox to Harley Davidson, can successfully out-compete the Japanese,

3. Rapheal Aguayo, Dr. Deming: The American Who Taught the Japanese About Quality, Fireside Books, New York, NY, 1990, p.3
4. ibid.
5. As reported in Six Sigma Forum Magazine, Gregory H. Watson, "Cycles of Learning: Observations of Jack Welch", Vol.1, No.1, November, 2001, Wilwaukee, WI

we know the reasons are not due to differences in Japanese and American culture. They are due to differences in our organizations and the way in which we manage them. To paraphrase Shakespeare, the fault lies not in our stars, but in ourselves and the way we work.

THE OLD MODEL OF MANAGEMENT

So how do we work? Well to start, how do we think about it? When you think of how work is organized, what image springs to mind? If it's the image of the organization chart, you're not alone. The organization chart is the dominant metaphor we use to describe our organizations. It details where the individuals belong in the hierarchy, the reporting relationships and the accountabilities – identifying who is responsible to whom and for what. Anyone with access to the organization chart has a map of where they, and everyone else, stands on the corporate ladder.

The 'flows' represented by lines on the chart are essentially vertical, representing the movement of information. Informa-tion and reports flow up, while decisions flow down. For example, a problem occurs in production. This starts the upward flow of information – informing managers and executives as to what has happened. The job of the hierarchy is to decide who should be informed and who shouldn't, who has authority to deal with the problem and who is accountable. Once decisions have been made, they are transmitted downward through the hierarchy and eventually (hopefully) to the employees who follow the instructions to correct the problem. The organization chart, therefore, is really a description of the formal power relationships within the organization. There are other relationships within organizations. But so powerful is the metaphor of the organization chart, we have equated it with organizational reality in our thinking. In so dominating our thinking about how organizations work, the organization chart has also dominated our thinking about managing and improving organizational performance.

MANAGEMENT BY OBJECTIVES/ RESULTS

If the organization chart is the dominant metaphor of how we think about organizational structure, then 'Management by

Exhibit 1: Organizational Hierarchy

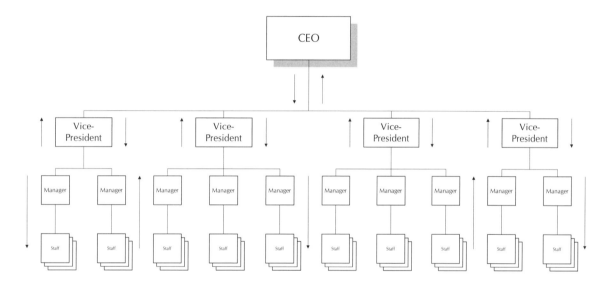

Objectives/Results' (MBO) is the operational glue that holds it together. MBO is the management method of the old way. Each individual in each little box in the organization chart is responsible and accountable for some task or job. Failure in that area means the individual failed. Success means the individual is somehow superior and needs to be rewarded. In essence, MBO emphasizes division and separation where each little box on the chart is seen as independent. Each individual is held accountable and responsible for the results in their little corner of the world. It is a management system defining who will do what and when and what will happen if they don't – a system of command and control.

YOU ARE HERE

CORPORATE LADDER

Command lies at the top of the hierarchy. The executive's job is seen as setting goals or objectives for the organization to pursue. It becomes the task of various departments or divisions to identify how these goals will be met and to set corresponding objectives for themselves. In turn, these goals are cascaded down through the levels of the hierarchy and ultimately to individuals who, through mutual negotiation with their superiors, set individual performance objectives.

Measuring performance, the control structure, then becomes 'easy.' We compare actual performance against the targets identified and reward or punish accordingly. We analyze departmental operations evaluating performance as we go. Departments failing to meet their targets are punished or worse, sold off and "*outsourced.*" We classify products as stars, cows or dogs and invest accordingly. Individuals, too, are measured, analyzed and ranked according to their performance. To the winners go the bonuses and promotions. To the losers, the "*unsatisfactory*" ratings and pink slips.

Unfortunately, there is far more myth than method in MBO.[6]

THE MYTH OF ENDS AND MEANS SEPARATION

The first of these myths is that the ends we want to achieve (expressed as goals, objectives or results) can be separated from the means to achieve them. The further up the hierarchy one goes, the more the job is seen as goal setting – identifying

---

6. I am in indebted to Raphael Aguayo and a series of conversations in a long automobile ride through the Canadian Rockies for these insights. His book, Dr. Deming: The American Who Taught the Japanese About Quality, is recommended.

what will be accomplished. The further down the hierarchy one goes, the more the job is seen as figuring out *how* to do it – identifying the means.

This view has mistakenly evolved to the point where ends (goals and objectives) are seen as separate from the process of identifying the means to achieve them. The manager's job is managing the targets. How employees are to achieve these tar-

gets is not seen as management's concern. Performance problems are boiled down to one of two things: either the goals were not communicated clearly or the subordinate responsible for achieving the targets failed.

Improving performance becomes a 'simple' exercise in raising the goal or objective. If an individual's sales were $6.0 million last year, the task of management becomes

"What we have here is a failure to implement!"

negotiating a performance increase to, say, $6.8 million for this year. Because the means by which this performance increase is to occur are missing, the goals and objectives become increasingly arbitrary and less connected to reality. Resulting plans emerge as simplistic, blue-sky pronouncements with little or no relevance to the real world conditions in which the company operates. In the end, the organization keeps functioning as it always has. The plans are tucked neatly away (or not so neatly disposed of), not to be disturbed again until the next planning session, where executive management laments the lack of progress. What a waste of time and energy! No wonder the constant refrain heard from executive management is, to paraphrase from an old movie, *"What we have here is a failure to implement!"*

The myth is that while ends and means are conceptually different, they are not separate in practice. It makes no sense to set lofty objectives without detailing how we plan to achieve them. When management says it wants to increase revenues 10 percent, this is at best honest intention and, at worst, empty rhetoric until a plan to accomplish the objective has been identified. Management that sets objectives is only doing half its job. MBO has become MBA (Management by Abdication) where management no longer feels responsible for getting its hands dirty with the details of how goals will actually be accomplished.

THE MYTH OF FUNCTIONAL INDEPENDENCE

Management by objectives takes the view that the operations of various functions or departments are essentially independent of one another. Each organizational unit has control over a certain area and a certain job to do. Departments have their unique objectives and are responsible for attaining them regardless of what happens elsewhere. Within departments, individuals have specific jobs and the job descriptions to prove it.

Sales people sell the product. Workers use materials and machines to build the product according to the design. Engineers create the design and so on. It's not just encouraging people to see the trees rather than the forest, it is essentially saying: "Here is your tree, now stick to it!"

What emerges is 'silo behavior.' Each department looking at things from its own perspective and working to its own advantage, jealously guarding its boundaries along the way. The silo keeps outsiders out and insiders in, so much so that some organizations spend more time arguing over the boundaries than accomplishing the work.

From an organizational perspective, departments or individuals within the organization are seen as contributing to overall organizational results in the same way bowling team members contribute to the results of the team – independently. Each individual contributes to the organization his or her 'score.' We even have a name for keeping individual contribution scores – performance appraisals.

If company results are poor, it follows that one or more of the contributors are to blame. A bad year or quarter usually results in a hunt for the guilty party with the inevitable politics (*"It is not our fault, it is those overly optimistic projections by the*

Exhibit 2: The Silo Phenomenon

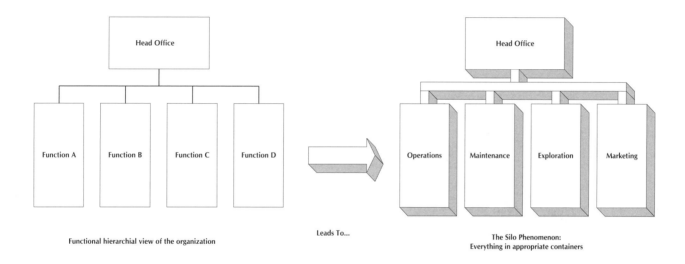

Functional hierarchial view of the organization

Leads To...

The Silo Phenomenon:
Everything in appropriate containers

marketing department that are to blame."), exposure of the guilty party, and eventual punishment.

But organizations aren't silos, or at least, they can't be operated efficiently as such. Every component of a company, including individuals within the organization, is affected by and related to other areas of the organization, often in ways that we cannot see, measure and in some cases, even imagine. Sales peoples'

ability to sell in any given year is affected not only by their own effort, but also by the quality, design, and usefulness of the product or service. Failure to improve the product relative to the offerings of competitors will contribute at least as much to sales decline (and likely a good deal more) than individual sales effort in any given year. Sales efforts, therefore, are affected by those who produced the product, the designers, by how much the product or service has improved this year over

last, and by all the strategy and capital investment decisions made by the organization. So it is with all departments. In any organization, whether we like it or not, we are dependent upon one another.

A better metaphor for organizations may be that of a symphony orchestra. The results of a symphony go beyond the results of each individual. The orchestra must 'play together.' It must produce an integrated whole from a number of players in a manner that demands interdependence. A high performance

organization is 'music to the ears' of all who work there versus the cacophony of sound represented by less successful organizations.

Businesses are not bowling teams. There is no such thing as independence in organizations – only interdependence. Management systems such as MBO and Personal Performance Planning (PPM), ignore this fundamental reality and so promote fractionalization and internal competition that similarly destroys the competitiveness of the organization. Put bluntly, effective organizations have got their act together, specifically the respective acts of the various functions within the enterprise.

Businesses are not bowling teams.

Exhibit 3: Different Levels of Interdependence[*]

[*]   Deming, Edwards W.; The New Economics, MIT, Cambridge, MA. 1994 p. 97 Reproduced with Permission

THE MYTH OF INDIVIDUAL EFFORT

The myth of individual effort is "a most seductive fallacy."[7] It seems to go to the very heart of the American value system that the individual is supreme and can triumph in any situation. To solve our problems, all we need is for each employee to try a little harder, to work a little more. If you give your best, give the company "110 percent," then the company will prosper and all will be well. Of course, if the company isn't doing well then it follows that some people must be contributing less (perhaps only 109 percent). They're lazy, careless or simply unmotivated.

Management practice is obsessed with individual performance. Think of all the things organizations do to get each person in each box to work a little bit harder. We have performance appraisal, performance coaching and performance management – all aimed at the individual. Throw in performance incentives, performance bonuses and pay for performance and you have a massive bureaucracy under the guise of a perfor-mance improvement system, working hard to get everyone *else* to work harder.[8]

These efforts are misguided. Business is a team effort. Indeed, we have organizations because we recognize the need to com-bine resources and talents to achieve more than we can as indi-viduals. How we organize ourselves (the system) has far greater impact on our success than pushing each individual to work harder. Dr. Deming estimates that 94 percent of the results of any system are a function of how the system has been designed and constructed, while only 6 percent are a function of the specific individuals working within the system.[9] The issue is not getting people to work harder but to change the way they work – to work smarter.

Working smarter means understanding and improving the pro-cess or system – the way we have organized our work. Most employees do not have the power to change the system; they are forced to work within it. Indeed, if individuals were entitled to change any part of the system they wanted at any time,

---

7. Rapheal Aguayo, Dr. Deming: The American Who Taught the Japanese About Quality, Fireside Books, New York, NY, 1990, p. 31

8. Everyone 'else' because I have never come across a performance manage-ment scheme designed to get those that designed the scheme to work harder.

9. Edwards Deming, The New Economics; MIT, Cambridge, MA. 1994, p. 33

chaos would ensue. Under these circumstances, the limitations and constraints the system imposes on individuals are far more important and have far greater impact on overall performance than the effort of individuals within the system. A systematic approach to improvement is required – one where processes and components of the system are analyzed and changed in a manner that maximizes the potential for gains in quality, productivity, service and cost.

Test for yourself how obsessed we are with individual effort. Think about your current performance management system. Most organizations have complicated and extensive performance review or performance coaching processes. They involve managers meeting with every employee, often up to four times a year. Detailed forms are completed, records kept and performance measurements documented. In large organizations, these reviews tie up millions of dollars in terms of managerial and employee time. Now think about the ongoing efforts in your organization focused on improving the performance of the system. Is there the same level of activity and documentation? Does every process have its performance reviewed regularly, and are development and improvement plans prepared?

Walk over to your supervisor or human resources department and ask to see a copy of your last performance appraisal. Chances are it's available, along with all your past appraisals complete with performance rating, training requirements, the works. Now ask to see a copy of the last performance appraisal of the process or system within which you work. Chances are you'll get a blank stare.

THE EFFECTS OF THE OLD MODEL

The traditional model of management has had profound effects on our organizations and our thinking about how to run them.

Short-Term Focus

In a system driven by measurable results, the first task is to find results to measure. Unfortunately, this is not so easy to do. Things like customer loyalty, employee trust and confidence in management are hard to define, harder to measure. Strangely then, we conclude they are too 'soft' to be measured. So we focus on what is easy to measure, the immediate or short-term financial results. These are important to be sure, but they aren't everything. We just behave as if they were.

Most of us have returned a defective product to a store. Have you ever run into a situation where the store refused to take the product back even though it was clearly defective? What was your response? It may have been a resolution never to buy anything from that store again. Within our traditional "bottom-line" thinking, the storekeeper saved the cost of replacing the product, so it appears to be a sound decision. In reality, it may have cost that store thousands of dollars in future business, something not measured in the financial statements or cost accounting reports.

If you're not sure whether short-term thinking dominates your organization ask the accounting department two questions. First, ask if they know the average cost to produce a product and then, for comparison, ask if they know the cost of a lost customer. Chances are they can answer the first question but not the second, and equally important, one.

Tampering & Tinkering

In a management system that rewards short-term results that are easily measurable, there is little incentive to make fundamental change, even when the need to do so is abundantly clear. Look how long it took General Motors to respond to the threat of Japanese competition. Long after the American consumer had embraced Nissans and Toyotas, General Motors was still arguing internally about the need for change. The people running General Motors weren't stupid – they were talented managers. But the system of hierarchical command and control and the need for short-term financial results simply constrained (if not eliminated) the possibility of action. The irony is that ultimately this management approach destroyed the very short-term results it was designed to preserve.

Not that organizations don't talk about fundamental change. Usually they do – endlessly! They just don't do it. They tinker here and tamper there. Symptoms of problems are attacked repeatedly but the root causes of those problems remain. Analysis of system-wide issues and the initiation of fundamental change simply do not occur. Management by objectives has become the institutionalization of the simple, and simple-minded, fix.

Game Playing

The traditional managerial model encourages individual employees to compete for promotion and pay. It shouldn't be surprising then when employees actively engage in game playing to win the competition. If the system makes meeting personal objectives paramount, you can be sure employees will focus their efforts at meeting those objectives even if it is at the expense of fellow employees or the company at large.

A good example concerns a large management consulting firm. Consultants were required to have so many chargeable hours in a year to qualify for a bonus. By mid-October many consult-ants had achieved the required level of chargeable hours – so now what do they do? There was no added benefit to getting more chargeable hours. Their response was simple. Although they were continuing to do chargeable work for clients they simply entered non-chargeable time on their time sheets for the remaining two months of the year. They sent out no invoices and charged all their time to "development" They met their year-end objectives and, at the start of the new year in January, had about two months of chargeable time saved to apply to meeting their next year's targets.

The system had clear, obtainable and objective performance standards. But all it did was encourage game playing and delayed cash flow in the last two months of the year. Evidently, a great many consultants were engaged in this game. Year end cash flow was a continuing problem for the firm and the start of every November was accompanied by a flurry of memos from head office encouraging consultants to "get those billings out." Right, and sacrifice next year's bonus in the process – not likely!

Organizations are awash in systems and processes designed to encourage employees to work harder or faster to accomplish some pre-ordained goal. Usually these systems encourage a "look out for number one" attitude, to the detriment of the company. There are few organizations where the employees do not have the system figured out and beaten.

Customer Confusion & Priority Perversion

Have you ever gone to a service counter where the employee is busy doing some administrative task and refuses to serve you until the task is finished? It happens in banks, airline ticket counters, and especially government offices. It drives me crazy! I don't care when they offer some excuse or apology: *"I'm sorry, I'll be with you in just a minute."*[10] There you stand, waiting for the particular service person to finally finish whatever it is they are doing and get around to actually providing some service. Of course the employee is serving a customer, it just isn't you. The customer being served is the boss, the hierarchy. You will just have to wait your turn.

When an employee's future in the organization is determined by ability to meet a set of objectives established between the employee and the supervisor, who is the customer for the employee's work? What does the employee do when the objectives conflict with the needs of the real customer? Right, forget

10. Good service may be defined as never having to say your sorry.

the real customer and meet those objectives! MBO encourages employees to believe that the next level of the hierarchy is the customer. That's priority perversion!

My first job out of university was with a major North American bank. I was to begin training for the position of Administration Manager. The existing branch manager had one simple rule for all staff: "No sitting down when there is a customer at the counter." Everything took a back seat to service. I didn't

know it at the time, but national surveys continually showed this branch as having the best reputation with customers. In fact, that's why we were training there – the bank wanted new recruits to learn whatever it was this branch manager was doing. What he did was to make sure we understood who the customer was and always put them first in line for service.

Linear and Local Thinking

Lastly, and perhaps most importantly, management by objectives/results encourages linear thinking patterns that emphasize simplistic cause-and-effect relationships. If something goes wrong, the first task is finding who had responsibility as defined by the organization chart and assigning the requisite blame. This process goes by the name of accountability. When something goes right, our concerns shift to how to reward the individual or unit responsible. Decision makers ignore more complex issues, such as problems with the system that produced the errors.

A perfect example of this simplistic thinking occurred in a major North American city a few years ago. A 911 emergency line dispatcher received a call from a women who was being attacked in her home. The dispatcher incorrectly routed the call, resulting in a delay in emergency response that conceivably could have cost the woman her life.

The dispatcher was disciplined and punished by the Emergency Response Department for his error. Part of the rationale for this punishment, offered to the media at the time, was the need to ***restore the public's confidence in the system*** (a similar situation had occurred just a few months earlier).

Simplistic thinking doesn't make the world any simpler.

Let's think about this. Do we really believe that any emergency operator would intentionally incorrectly route a call in these circumstances? Traditional management thinking says he was to blame because he was the one that handled the call. But could other causes have contributed? How about the level of training, human behavior in times of extreme stress, the design of the telephone equipment and so on? These types of explanations could have far greater impact on errors in call routing, yet was there any consideration of such factors? My faith in the system was not restored by the actions of management at the time, quite the opposite. The very fact management was punishing an individual convinced me they were not addressing real concerns at all nor had any real idea as to how to improve the system.

In emphasizing the separation of components making up the system, the existing management model encourages simplistic thinking about the organization, performance and improvement. A sales decline is a problem of the sales department. The effects of an outdated design, differing sales response in different sales territories, poor delivery performances and other systemic effects are ignored, to the detriment of the company as well as the sales department. Everyone loses.

Simplistic thinking doesn't make the world any simpler. The real world is a complex place. Results are influenced by many factors and the effects of our actions take place over longer times than are accommodated by simplistic linear thinking. We need to start thinking in terms that account for this complexity. That way we can be more effective in bringing about not just change, but actual improvements in organizational performance. We need to adopt systems thinking.

SYSTEMS THINKING: THE NEW MODEL OF PERFORMANCE IMPROVEMENT

The visual metaphor of the new management is not the organization chart – it is the Deming Flow Diagram. Dr. Deming first presented this to the Japanese Union of Scientists and Engineers (JUSE) back in the 1950's. It is as relevant now as it was then. It is a representation of the organization as a *system of production* – taking in inputs, transforming them in some way into products that are then delivered to customers.

The organization chart places the chief executive officer at the top. The Deming Flow Diagram places the customer at the end. In the organization chart, focus is on the information flows: reports up, orders down. In the systems view, the focus is on the production flow of taking in resources, transforming them and ultimately delivering some product or service of value to a customer. The systems view emphasizes:

▲ **Processes begin *with* suppliers and end *with* customers.** That's *with*, not *at*. The old view sees the organizational boundaries ending with those lowest on the organization

Exhibit 4: The Deming Flow Diagram[*]

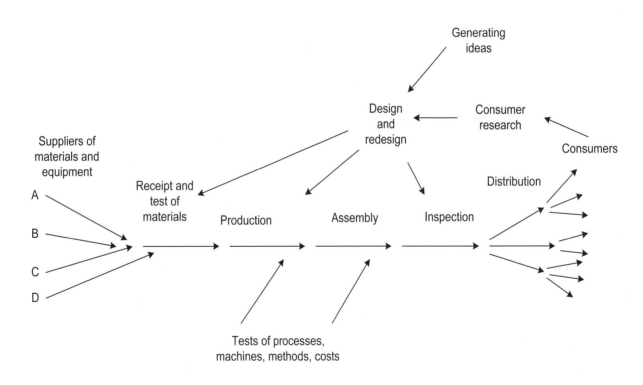

*   Edwards Deming, The New Economics; MIT, 1994; p. 58 Reproduced with permission.

chart. Customer and suppliers exist outside of the organization. But the new view of the organization is quite different. Customers don't exist outside the system, they are part of it. Trying to understand an organization without considering the customer is like riding a bicycle without any wheels. The view may be pleasant, even informative, but it is not likely to take you anywhere. Customers are part of the system because they determine the purpose of the system and pay for the results. Suppliers, too, are part of the system. Suppliers, after all, provide the organization with what it needs to function – the raw materials upon which the transformation process will be based.

▲ **Customer as opposed to hierarchically driven.** The old view sees the organization as driven by the positional power of the CEO. To answer why anyone does anything in the organization, one only has to look at the organization chart to understand: *"Because that is what my boss told me to do."* But the new view places the customer at the 'end,' representing the purpose or aim of the system itself. Improvement is driven by customer needs and requirements. Product or service flows to the customer, who in turn provides cash to the organization in return for the value received. This is reinvested in product design

and development using customer research to guide the reinvestment activity. The cycle repeats again and again, meaning improvement is a continuous process driven by the need to increase value to the customer.

▲ **Interdependency determines performance.** The old view emphasizes independence and individual effort. Increasing performance means targeting the specific problem area and raising the performance standards. But the new view emphasizes the flow of production traveling across departments, divisions and individual jobs. What happens in production affects sales, marketing decisions impact manufacturing and so on. Performance, therefore, comes from how the components of the system or process are designed and put together. Functional independence is recognized for what it is, a myth. To improve performance, we shift our focus from the individual boxes to the system or process that is actually producing value for the customer.

It is tempting to say this new view represented by the Deming flow diagram defines a radically different picture of what organizations are, and how to improve their performance. And to be sure, much of what the systems approach proposes is a very different way of thinking about organizations. But is the foundation of the approach really so new? Haven't we known all along that what is really important is producing quality products and services to customers and getting cash in return? Haven't we always known that maximizing the productivity of production is a key to success? And haven't we always known that doing so is more important than maintaining the paper flows up and down the organization?

I suspect we have. Perhaps we just lost sight of what's important, blinded by the image of the organization chart and its corresponding philosophy of independence.

CREATING A NEW ORGANIZATION CHART

It's time to create and accept a new view of organizations and how they work. We need a picture where work flow structures and hierarchical structures are combined, in a comprehensive view of organizational functioning.

We do need some level of hierarchy in our organizations, but productivity comes from process improvement, not power relationships. The flow of information does not produce anything

that customers pay for. These information flows may be important, but productivity comes from minimizing their impact on the process while maximizing the effectiveness, efficiency and flexibility of those process that deliver product or service to customers.

This view of 'organizations as systems' presents a new, more complex and realistic picture than the old view. The added complexity is necessary. Organizations, and the people within them, live and work in the real world. They are not a collection of discrete boxes on the organization chart, they are a part of the system and the means by which value is created.

ENDS AND MEANS ARE LINKED, NOT SEPARATE

A system without a purpose is not a system.[11] Neither is a system that has a purpose but no means of accomplishing it. In the new management, goals and the means to achieve them must be linked. This requires management and employees to work together in identifying goals, methods, and improvement opportunities.

_____

11. ibid. p. 50

Exhibit 5: A New Picture of Organizations

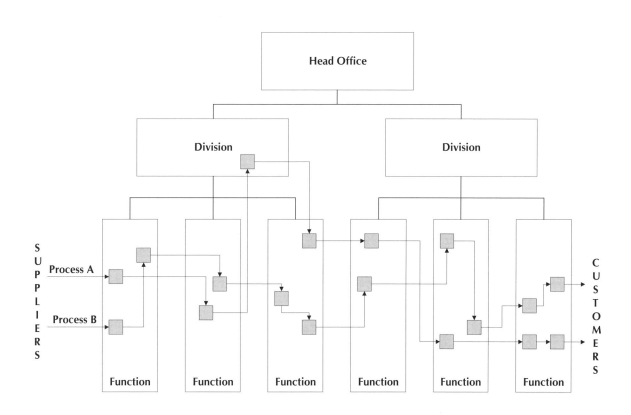

The information that flows up and down the organization chart is still important. What changes is the purpose and content of this communication. If information provided by the "lower" levels is used to assign blame and distribute punishment and rewards, then senior management must give up forever the notion of having good information suitable for performance improvement or sound decision making. Such information will always be modified, amended, delayed and otherwise 'influenced' by those having the most to lose or win by doing so.

In contrast, when the purpose of communication is knowledge transfer, to provide the facts required to better understand how the organization is functioning, performance improvement can take place and flourish. Only when fear is removed from the workplace can different levels in the organization be expected to communicate in the way required for real improvement to occur.

This means an open-book approach to sharing information. Employees cannot be expected to contribute meaningfully to goal setting if they do not understand how the organization measures performance or where it currently stands relative to those goals. Employees need to understand how their job contributes to the big performance picture. Nor can management

meaningfully contribute to identifying methods if employees are unwilling to share information on process problems. Employees must be free and feel free to communicate problems and issues if management is to understand the nitty gritty details of what really matters.

INTEGRATION, NOT INDEPENDENCE

Functional departments are not independent of one another. Systems and processes flow across departmental and functional boundaries. The more these functional areas integrate their activities, the smoother the flow. Often the key to improved productivity is nothing more than keeping different departments from getting in each other's way – encouraging them to support one another's efforts rather than working at cross purposes.

Integration includes customers and suppliers as well. Systems begin *with* suppliers and end *with* customers. Customers must be considered part of the system because they are the keys to value. No customers, no value added. The same holds true with suppliers. We have all heard of the expression *"garbage in, garbage out"* in relation to data processing. Well, it also applies to real world systems that manufacture product or deliver services. A system that relies on faulty inputs from suppliers will never maximize value, no matter how elegant or well designed the production process.

SYSTEM PERFORMANCE OVER INDIVIDUAL EFFORT

Estimates by Dr. Deming and fellow American consultant Dr. Joseph Juran indicate that between 85 percent and 94 percent of organizational results are a function of the system. The remainder is the portion owing to individual effort. In the new management, we focus on the area where we have the greatest leverage for improvement – the system.

Does this mean there is no role for the individual to make a substantial contribution to improved organizational performance? Of course not, it's just that the role has

> *In a fight between you and the system, bet on the system.*

changed. In the new management, the individual's role in improving organizational performance is contributing his or her brain power to improve the processes and systems within which all individuals work. We don't want people to work harder, we want them to work smarter.

In this respect, all jobs are knowledge jobs. Physical labor is important in many jobs, but its importance is small compared to the power of knowledge to transform work and make it more productive.

STAR QUALITY: PRINCIPLES OF THE NEW MANAGEMENT

Star Quality summarizes what we have learned about the new approach to performance improvement. It is not intended to be a complex model of managerial processes or of organizational functioning. It simply represents the fundamental principles that define and distinguish the systems approach to improvement from the more traditional approaches.

1. CUSTOMER DRIVEN

The primary function of any organization is providing what the customer wants. Doing so in a manner that is more productive or efficient than competing sources of the same product or service adds value. Management consultant Peter Drucker once noted that, "*The purpose of a business is to create custom-*

Exhibit 6: Star Quality

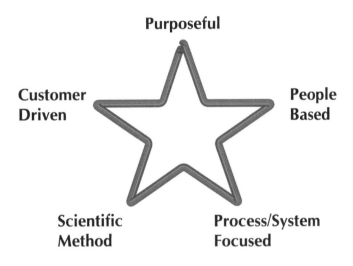

Purposeful

Customer
Driven

People
Based

Scientific
Method

Process/System
Focused

ers.[12] Customers define our success or failure, our product or service quality; ultimately they define whether our organization prospers or dies.

This holds true for internal customers as well as external ones. All too often, internal service departments assume they are above serving the customers within their own organization. By taking this attitude, they lose the loyalty and support of others within the company. What is surprising is the degree of amazement these same departments express when the organization decides to outsource their function.

The bottom line: "The most fundamental law of business is, without customers, there is no business."[13]

2. PEOPLE BASED

The real work of organizations is performed by people working together across functional boundaries to accomplish some task or goal. Improving the performance of any system or process requires people. There is no other way.

People are not objects of analysis or cogs in a huge industrial wheel. They are first and foremost individuals, with personal aspirations, beliefs and individual differences. The object of business is not to turn individuals into efficient little clones, but to get everyone contributing different perspectives to the long-term prosperity to the business. Organizations that understand

---

12. Peter F. Drucker, Managing for Results, Harper and Row, New York, NY, 1964, p. 91

13. ibid

this understand the true value of employees. They learn to respect the differences that define all of us and accept those differences as a source of strength. A people-based improvement effort is one that respects the individual.

It is also one that recognizes the necessity of teamwork. Improving process flow across organization boundaries requires an understanding of that flow from all perspectives. Maximizing improvement in organizational performance means improving the system and that, in turn, requires teamwork.

Teamwork maximizes something else – organizational learning. Employees in the organization represent an invaluable wealth of ideas but few organizations take advantage of this hidden asset. Separating responsibilities, through artificial organizational boundaries and levels, limits the ability of this resource to contribute effectively to improvement. Talent and ideas are wasted. Teamwork recognizes the value of this resource and, more importantly, provides an outlet for this experience and talent to be shared. "One Team"[14] is not an idealistic statement; it is a precondition for maximizing the

knowledge base within the organization and for maximizing the effectiveness of any improvement effort.

The bottom line: All improvement happens through people. Those organizations that understand what truly motivates people, and can best tap into the talents and ideas of employees, improve faster.

3. PROCESS AND SYSTEM FOCUSED

The new model understands organizations as systems. We move away from the localized, linear thinking of the past and identify the interdependencies linking the processes of production or service. The process becomes the focus of the improvement effort. To measure performance, we measure performance of the process, understanding its capability to deliver what customers need and want. Improving performance requires changing the process, not the people working within it.

Employees in an organization are not responsible for the systems within which they work. These have generally been designed by management. Management sets the rules, allocates the resources and gives the orders. Improvement will not come

---

14. Peter Scholtes, The Team Handbook, Joiner and Associates, Madison WI, 1988

from demanding everyone works harder, placing inspiring messages on the wall or holding out the prospect of bonuses or punishments for over/under achievers. Changing the system and using employees to help with this change is the key to real long-term performance improvement.

The bottom line: To improve performance, you must improve the process or system responsible for the existing performance level.

4. SCIENTIFIC METHOD

Scientific method links theories and ideas with empirical, real world results. The prediction inherent in theory is compared with observed results. If the results support the theory, we have evidence that our thinking is sound. If the results fail to support our theory, we must abandon it and look to new ideas and theories. Empirical evidence, then, is the acid test of our ideas and the foundation of scientific method.

We can only understand the systems and processes at work if we are willing to give up our biases and rely on data as the acid test of ideas. Moreover, we need a sound approach to working with data – applying statistics, *"the science of data"* – to enhance our understanding and learning. The word *"statistics"* tends to strike fear in the hearts of many managers and employees alike. But the basic methods used to analyze systems and processes are understandable to anyone.

Moreover, there is no viable alternative. Without scientific method and empirical data, we are left with gut feel, impressions, guess work, and bias. Improvement by guess work is expecting greatness to flow from ignorance – it won't happen. The scientific method is a learning model, grounding our understanding in empirical, real world information and building knowledge upon this foundation. Improving performance means we constantly test our ideas, conduct experiments, measure results and implement improvements where warranted.

The bottom line: Greatness doesn't flow from ignorance, improvement is dependent upon knowledge.

5. PURPOSEFUL

A system without an aim is not a system![15] To which we add that improvement without direction is an oxymoron. Improve-

---

15. Edwards Deming, The New Economics, MIT, Cambridge, MA. 1994, p. 50

ment, by definition, is purposeful activity.

Providing purpose is the first task of leadership. Leaders, at whatever level they exist in the organization, become leaders by defining direction and giving purpose to the activities of those they lead. Organizations all too often forget that the job of leadership is to lead. Management must demonstrate that leadership by clearly defining the aim and purpose of the system, as well as for each and every component of it.

Purposeful activity and the role of leadership, however, goes beyond simply identifying direction or providing purpose. Purposeful activity is also that which stays the course, seeing things through to completion. In short, purposeful activity demands discipline and focus.

With the new management, the role of manager as leader changes. It is no longer a "set the objective and forget it" approach. The role of management must become one of involvement – initiating and guiding performance improvement projects through to success. This in turn places new demands upon management. Managers must become more than figureheads bestowing blessings upon improvement initiatives. They become active participants, working with

improvement teams in supporting their efforts. Ultimately, showing leadership means demonstrating knowledge of the new management and the systems view of performance improvement.

The bottom line: If you don't know where you are going, any road will take you there. Improvement is a purposeful activity – it demands direction.

The five components comprise Star Quality. All five are required. Organizations promoting teamwork with one of the elements missing will succeed only in making decisions the same old way – except they will be doing it in groups. Focusing on the system with scientific methods, but without teamwork, will produce brilliant analysis but little actual change. Improving organizational performance requires that the improvement effort be:

▶ Customer Driven,

▶ People Based,

▶ Process/System Focused,

▶ Purposeful,

▶ and grounded in the Scientific Method.

Are You Ready? Of Termites and Top-Down

Individuals and teams seeking to improve performance in their organizations are often confronted with a dilemma. It is: how to begin changing to the new management when there is a lack of commitment at the top of the organization?

Organizations have paid a lot of lip service to quality, continuous improvement and process redesign. Improvement teams are charged with the responsibility of making change without having any real senior managerial commitment. In other organizations, middle managers or department heads see the need for change, but executive management does not.

Clearly, the best way to bring about the transformation represented by the new management is within a context of commitment at the top of the organization. The executive suite becomes the driving force of change, providing an environment where improvement is encouraged. Some companies, however, will die before this occurs. There is another pathway to change, albeit far less effective – the termite approach.[16]

The theory behind the termite approach is simple. It recognizes we can all take on a leadership role in our respective organizations. Whether we are a clerk in accounts payable, the supervisor of the mail room or the vice-president for production, we can adopt the new philosophy and apply it to our field of endeavor. In so doing, we demonstrate the leadership required without a top-down strategy. Change will be slower but at least it will occur. Moreover, as the new approach proves itself, it will gain the attention of others. It will gradually be adopted by greater and greater numbers – in effect, eating away at the old way of doing things. At some point, a critical mass will be established, the old philosophy will effectively be gone, and the new way will have become ***the way*** for the organization as a whole.

No matter what approach is taken to organizational change, leadership is still required. Individuals need to ask themselves if they ready to undertake the change.

If your answer is yes, read on.

---

16. I am indebted to the quality and performance improvement people at Shell Canada who first talked to me about the termite approach to change as an alternative to the more traditional change models.

Improving Performance: Critical Components of Systems Thinking

2

The key to improving organizational performance is systems thinking – focusing on the interactions and interdependencies among the various organizational components. To improve the way something functions, we need to understand it as a system.

Unfortunately, terms like process, system, improvement and performance are not well understood or the understanding is not widely shared within organizations. Many of these terms have evolved into motherhood phrases that tend to mean whatever the speaker wants them to mean. After all, who isn't in favor of improvement?

Some clarity and definition on the nature and scope of these concepts is therefore required. We need to understand what systems thinking is all about, how it creates knowledge, drives improvement and builds competitive position. This requires covering a lot of ground, including:

▲ **Understanding Systems:** The SIPOC (Suppliers, Inputs, Process, Outputs, Customers) Model
- ▶ System Structure: The Components of Performance
- ▶ System Characteristics: The Measures of Performance

▲ **Critical Concepts:** The Linkages Between Processes and Improvement
- ▶ Value
- ▶ Variation
- ▶ Complexity
- ▶ Control

▲ **Improving Performance:** Moving From Theory to Practice
- ▶ Dimensions of Performance Improvement
- ▶ Organizational Improvement Strategies
- ▶ Methods and Models of Improvement

UNDERSTANDING SYSTEMS AND PROCESSES

Processes are the verbs of work. This means that all results, from sales levels to production rates and staff turnover, are an outcome of the process or processes at work. They are physical manifestations of how the work has been structured – the way 'things are done around here.' The complete set of processes within an organization defines how the organization accomplishes everything and anything. But every process is also part of a larger system, and improving performance requires consideration of this system if improvement efforts are to be effective.

THE NEED FOR FRAMES

So how do we tell where processes stop and systems begin? What is the difference between a system and a process? The answer is largely one of scale and the frame of reference. Let's take a familiar physical example – the weather. Suppose we want to study global warming. Our frame of reference would be the planet and all the elements that contribute to global tem-peratures, such as levels of man-made pollutants and CO_2 emissions, long-term temperature cycles of the planet, evaporation rates, water vapor levels and so on. All these (and more) would be seen as underlying processes affecting the global system over many hundreds and thousands of years.

All results are the outcome of a process at work within a larger system.

But if we want to know whether it will rain tomorrow, we set a different frame of reference. Now the system is defined by our local geographical area and climate conditions, and the time frame is the next 24 hours. Underlying processes become the actions of various low or high pressure systems, and the impact of local conditions (nearby mountains or large bodies of water, etc.). The frame of reference, therefore, defines the system. The processes are the verbs, activities within the system that create the effects we are interested in.

When improving organizational performance, we must first define a frame of reference. How broadly the frame is defined determines the scope of the improvement effort, and the boundaries of the system to be analyzed.

Setting a frame of reference sounds arbitrary and it is. But it is also necessary. Without a frame of reference we expose ourselves to the possibility of endless "system or scope creep." This is where an improvement team responsible for addressing abnormally high inventory levels ends up arguing over currency exchange policy in Venezuela because it, too, is "part of the system." The simple fact is, we will never fix (or understand) anything if we insist on including everything.

The basic tool used for framing the system and providing scope to the improvement effort is the SIPOC model.

DEFINING THE SYSTEM: THE SIPOC MODEL

SIPOC stands for: Suppliers, Inputs, Process, Outputs, Customers – the five physical components of any organizational system. Because it is a representation of an organizational system, it is really nothing more than an elaboration of the Deming flow diagram presented in Chapter 1.

As a generic representation, however, the SIPOC model provides a useful way to structure our thinking when tackling improvement opportunities. Before diving in to some improvement initiative such as "fixing the inventory system," it makes sense to have a clear understanding and definition of what comprises this system. We need to know, for example, who the customers are, the specific outputs that are provided and so forth. In other words, an understanding of the various system components is essential to make an improvement in any area.

At the centre of the SIPOC model (literally and figuratively) is the process (or processes as the case may be). Process is the means by which inputs are transformed into outputs with some value (hopefully) being added along the way. The process **is** the work and the **way** we add value.

The physical components of a system give the SIPOC model its name and are represented in the upper part of the diagram presented in Exhibit 7: SIPOC Model - Suppliers, Inputs, Process, Outputs and Customers. Equally important are the informational components of the system, termed quality characteristics. They are represented in the bottom portion of the model. Any number of such characteristics may be associated with each of the physical components of the system.

Exhibit 7: SIPOC Model - Suppliers, Inputs, Process, Outputs and Customers

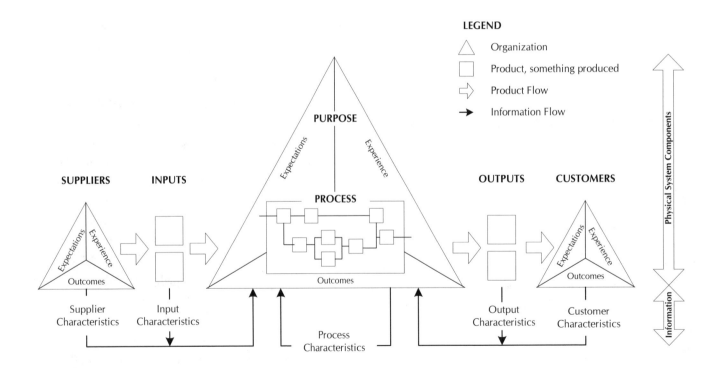

It is the physical components of the system that are 'real.' They transform inputs to outputs and add value in the process. It is the informational components, however, that allow us to understand the system. Information is our window on reality. We cannot understand or improve without information, without the quality characteristics that describe the various system components.

THE FLOW OF WORK

There are two work flows within the SIPOC model. The first is obvious; it is the flow of production that moves from left to right. However, production isn't the only job. Making things better – improvement – is also part of every job. And improvement tends to move in the opposite direction, starting with customers and moving from right to left.

Production Flow

The process takes inputs from suppliers and transforms these inputs in some fashion that produces outputs for which customers are willing to pay. This flow of production moves from left to right in the diagram. Suppliers, inputs, the process, outputs

and customers – all are part of the system and are presented in the order in which the basic production flow occurs.

The SIPOC diagram and the flow of production apply regardless of whether we are talking 'hard' products or the 'softer' services. Either way, the SIPOC model presents the components that must be defined and described before we can say we understand the system at work.

Improvement Flow

While the flow of production is from left to right, the flow of improvement tends to be just the opposite, from right to left. We start with the customer and work backward, moving upstream in the system until we reach the suppliers providing the inputs the process requires. In other words, improvement starts with the customer, be they internal or external to the organization. That's what being customer driven is all about.

For example, the focus of improvement may be increasing the efficiency of a given process. But the place to start is still the customer. Are there things our process produces that are of no use to the customer? If so, the simplest route to improved efficiency may be to simply stop producing those things. Unless we start with the customer, we will never have the full picture required for effective improvement activities.

The improvement flow doesn't stop there. We must continue to move upstream. Again, the focus may be on the process, but what about the inputs the process receives? Is the quality of input used for the old product sufficient for the new? Improvement and innovation cannot stop at product or process redesign; it must work its way back through the entire system to ensure it can and will be implemented.

SYSTEM STRUCTURE: THE PHYSICAL COMPONENTS

The physical structure of the system is represented by the suppliers, inputs, process, outputs, customers that lie above the informational feedback loops referred to as quality characteristics. It is these 'above the line' components that make up the 'real' part of a system. Real people doing real work. Like tellers taking deposits from customers and issuing receipts in return. Or police and emergency vehicles responding to a request for help. Or a manufacturer assembling digital switches from pre-manufactured components. Or suppliers shipping inventory, invoicing you and your accounts payable area responding with a payment. This the real stuff of work, with real value being added along the way. These 'real' components are represented by:

▲ **The Actors,** organizations and people represented by triangles in the SIPOC model. These are suppliers, customers and our own organization.

▲ **The Inputs and Outputs,** the physical set of products and services delivered or produced by one or more of the actors in the system. These are represented as boxes or squares within the SIPOC model.

▲ **The Process,** the means by which the organization has organized and performs the work.

THE ACTORS: CUSTOMERS, SUPPLIERS AND OUR OWN ORGANIZATION

Customers, suppliers and the organization that encompasses the process of interest are represented by triangles in the

SIPOC Model. These are the 'actors' in the system. What is common to all these actors are the three fundamental components that govern behavior. Specifically, these are each actor's unique set of expectations, experience and outcomes (see Exhibit 8: The Dynamics of Expectation, Experience and Outcomes).

Exhibit 8: The Dynamics of Expectation, Experience and Outcomes

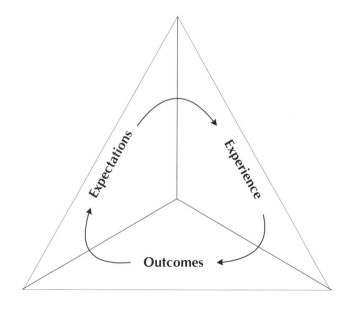

▲ **Expectations are the set of objectives, goals or standards relative to the system.** Every organization has expectations for the processes at work and the products and services those processes deliver. At times these expectations are explicit. Specific performance measures are identified and tracked, budgets are set in terms of either costs or revenue (sales) targets and so forth. However, these expectations may be implicit as well. In such cases, the performance expectations exist only in the minds of the various actors in the system and, therefore, will be more difficult to identify.

For example, customers have expectations of the product sold to them. Usually these expectations are implicit and some effort must be expended to find out what they are -- the primary purpose of customer research. But the expectations are still there whether we research them or not. Every customer has expectations of the product or service provided. Likewise, every supplier has expectations of our organization and, in turn, our organization has expectations of the processes it owns.

▲ **Experience represents the results arising from action or use of the product.** Sooner or later, customers will actually use the product they have purchased. This use represents their experience. How did the product perform? Did it do what it was supposed to do? Each interaction with the product represents what Jan Carlzon, former CEO of Scandinavian Airlines, called a "*moment of truth*"[17] – an interaction in which the customer experiences the product and then compares it to his or her expectations. Over time, these moments of truth build into a more collective experience for the customer.

The same holds true for organizations. Every organization has experience with the processes it uses to perform its work. How is the process performing? Is it doing what it is supposed to do? Over time, organizations build a collective experience of how their processes function. They make conclusions about those processes in much the same way that customers make conclusions about a product. Experience is compared with expectations and conclusions are drawn.

▲ **Outcomes are results; they represent the conclusions and actions resulting from the process of comparing experience with expectations.** When customers expectations are not met, satisfaction levels fall and sales levels decline. When large numbers of customers have their expectations met or exceeded, satisfaction levels climb, customer loyalty builds and sales improve.

Likewise, organizations continuously evaluate their processes, comparing their experience in terms of any number of factors (product quality, cost, productivity, profit, sales levels, market share) against their expectations. Dissatisfaction may produce a process improvement initiative, out-sourcing or some other activity designed to improve performance. These, too, are outcomes. Where experience exceeds expectations, senior decision makers may decide to leave well enough alone and focus on other improvement priorities. This is also an outcome of comparing expectations to experience.

Actors within the SIPOC model may represent any level or component of the organization, from the organization itself to major divisions and market segments, right down to the individual. All have expectations, experiences and associated outcomes.

---

17. Jan Carlzon, Moments of Truth, Harper & Row, New York, 1989

OUR ORGANIZATION (PROCESS OWNER)

Processes lie at the heart of the SIPOC model, but these processes exist within our organization – the process owner. Whether examining some process or redesigning a product, we can never lose sight of the process owner. Among the initial tasks for any team engaged in undertaking an improvement effort, therefore, is understanding what those organizational (owner) expectations, experiences and outcomes have been with the process. Doing so provides a context for the improvement activity. Understanding that context may be as critical to success as understanding the product or process that is the focus of the improvement effort.

Organizations Are the Sum of Their Processes

Processes are the means by which organizations accomplish things. Everything that happens, everything an organization accomplishes, happens through a process. Which means organizations are very much the sum of their processes.

To improve organizational performance, then, we must improve process performance. But organizations are complex. For any organizational performance issue, we may be confronted with having to address multiple processes, each of which interacts with other processes in different ways.

When engaged in broader organizational performance improvement issues, it is, therefore, useful to identify which processes are involved in the issue and which are not. Doing so helps ensure the improvement effort maintains a system/process focus that is so critical to success.

Organizational Resistance

Every process in the organization, and every part of every process, exists because someone thought it should. There is a reason for it being there. Someone, somewhere must have thought it was a good idea to do whatever the process is doing.

This means any team involved in making improvements or changes to the way things are done is also involved in making changes to what others in the organization

> *"Everything in this world has happened because someone thought it should."*
> **Malcolm Muggeridge**

---

probably believe shouldn't be changed. Process improvement demands change and change will produce resistance.

There is nothing wrong in any of this. After all, those resisting change may be right – proposed changes and improvements may prove to be no improvement after all. The point is that organizational resistance is to be expected. Those responsible for the improvement effort must be aware of this organizational reality and be prepared to address issues and concerns when and where they arise.

Processes Evolve Within the Organizational Environment

Organizations provide a rich environment for process evolution. Over time organizational structures change – new regulatory requirements are introduced, modified and then changed again, policies are amended, strategy reformulated and new technology is introduced. People come and go as do the jobs they performed. And in all this change are the processes, constantly adapting to the environment in which they are located.

Over time, gaps emerge between what the process is doing and what it is supposed to do. For example, organization expectations of the process (purpose) may have changed but the tasks

embedded in the process remain. The result is that some tasks are done simply because they were done before or because *"that's the way we've always done it."* Significant process improvements may arise from the discovery that the purpose behind some process activity has long since disappeared.

So improvement teams need to step back, take a look at the big picture and ask, "why?" Ask *why* something is done. For example, a simple process for managing employee expenses that existed 15 years ago evolved into a incomprehensible and complex monster that produced significant employee complaints and frustration. A review by a process improvement team revealed that many of the reasons behind this evolution, some of which were quite valid at the time, now no longer existed. The solution: eliminate those tasks that have no purpose. The result was a simple, streamlined and cost effective process that looked remarkably like the one that had existed some 15 years previously.

Multiple Expectations, Experiences and Outcomes Exist for Every Process

Because organizations are such complex environments, there is rarely a single clear set of expectations, experiences or outcomes associated with a process. Different people and different groups will likely have different expectations, experiences and ultimately different outcomes.

The accounting department, for example, may have a specific set of expectations for the inventory management process, but these expectations will likely be very different from those of the operations group. Likewise, other groups will have their own expectations of the inventory management process – human resources will have theirs as will production, sales and, of course, the inventory management group.

Improvement teams, therefore, will rarely have a nice simple set of well-defined expectations for a process. More often than not, a little investigation will reveal myriad expectations and experiences that exist for what may have appeared at first blush as a small, simple process. Within any organizational environment, there will be multiple expectations and experiences with the process.

Alignment is Required

The performance of any process is driven in large measure between the alignment of purpose (why the process exists) and process activity (what the process does and how it does it). The ends must be aligned with the means.

If this sounds familiar, it should. It reinforces a point made earlier in identifying a failing of traditional managerial approaches to improvement – separating ends and means. While ends and means can be separated conceptually, in practice they cannot. Alignment of both is a requirement for any real world improvement.

So how is this alignment achieved, especially in light of the various organizational expectations held for a process? There are some tools that can help teams in this regard (see Chapter 11: Organizational Alignment), but the first step is usually understanding the needs of customers and aligning process activity to met these requirements.

CUSTOMERS

At the end of it all is the customer. Every process has a customer and the purpose for any process (or organization) is to create and serve its customers. If there are no customers for a product, there is no need for a process to produce one.

Customer-In Thinking

The SIPOC model emphasizes the need to consider the customer as part of the system – a concept referred to as the 'customer-in' thinking. The idea here is simple. The customer must be thought of as an integral part of the system, not as some separate or nebulous component existing outside of what we are doing. The customer defines what it is we do, provides us with the priorities for improvement and determines whether we do a good job or not. The customer-in mentality is part and parcel of becoming customer driven.

The philosophy of product-out thinking: "Make it then sell it."

This is very different from how organizations traditionally view customers. The traditional view is dominated by a 'product-out' mentality, that sees the purpose of the process as producing a product (remember the lemonade stand). This product must then be sold, pushed upon the customer regardless of the customer's desire or need. The philosophy of product-out thinking: "Make it then sell it."

Becoming customer driven and developing a customer-in approach is not a philosophical position, it is a practical one.

Too often, change proceeds without including the customer in the equation. The result is vastly 'improved' processes producing things nobody wants. It's a waste of time and money, to everyone's detriment. When faced with some improvement problem or opportunity, start with the customer. Who is the customer? What does the customer want? What trade-offs is the customer willing to make and where does the customer place the greatest value? The answers to these questions need to drive the improvement effort, setting the priorities for change.

This holds true for internal customers as well as external ones. Not all processes deliver a product to some outside consumer. Sometimes the product is delivered to another department or unit within the organization. Human resources, marketing, finance, purchasing, inventory and a host of other functions all provide a product or service to some other internal process. But the rules of understanding the customer and becoming customer driven still apply. The customer may only be the next process, but that next process is still the customer.

Too often, organizational units fail to adopt a customer-in approach when the customer is internal. They fall into the product-out trap. The computer department that knows what is

Table 9: Differences Between Product-Out and Customer-In Thinking

Product-Out Thinking	Customer-In Thinking
We know what the customer wants. Organizations dominated with product-out thinking are typically convinced that they know what the customer wants. Usually, it is whatever the organization currently makes, a defense of the status quo. American automobile manufacturers, for example, were convinced they knew what the customer wanted long after the consumer had changed preferences.	**We need to know what the customer wants.** Customer-in organizations assume the needs of customers change and evolve over time. Continuous improvement does not mean just improving the process. It also means continuously improving our understanding of the needs, desires and requirements of the customer and constantly redesigning our product to meet those requirements. Moreover, it accepts that customers' desires and expectations change – what is expected now is a lot different than what was expected in the 1970's.
Sales declines are sales force problems. Product-out thinking equates poor or declining sales levels as sales force problems, with resulting organizational responses taking the form of sales force training, sales incentive programs or the replacement of sales staff with more aggressive personnel. None of these responses is capable of producing any more than short-term improvements.	**Sales declines are system problems.** Customer-in companies know that a sales decline may be attributable to the sales force, but they also know the decline may be due to product design, pricing and a host of other possibilities. The key is to understand why sales are declining, to find the root cause and fix the problem rather than jumping on the obvious and at times quite useless solutions.
We know best. Some product-out organizations go beyond believing they know what the customer wants. They believe the customer doesn't really know. The organization must tell the customer what they want – a "we know best" approach. Organizations producing a product of significant technical complexity often fall into this trap. They are, after all, the experts in the technology of the product – the customer really doesn't understand the technology.	**Customers know best.** Customer-in organizations understand that the customer doesn't really have to understand the technology or details behind the product. Customers care about what the technology can do, what value it can deliver. You don't have to be a brain surgeon to understand the benefits of surgery. Customers buy products to provide some benefit to themselves and the only person capable of determining the value of that benefit to the customer is the customer.

Table 9: Differences Between Product-Out and Customer-In Thinking

Product-Out Thinking	Customer-In Thinking
Simplified thinking about customers. Product-out organizations are typified by simplified thinking. A constant refrain is: "Customers want everything and they want it for free!" Even if this is true, so what? We know customers cannot get everything for free, from our organization or anyone else. The ability to define what is most important to the customer, what has greatest value, and deliver it in the most cost-effective manner is critical, but ignored by product-out thinking.	**Thinking about the relationship with the customer**. The customer-in approach emphasizes building relationships with customers and creating a sense of loyalty. Dr. Deming has emphasized that profits are generated not by just any customer but by the loyal customer. Loyal customers come back again and again; they require little or no marketing expense and only a little sales effort. Creating such relationships goes beyond the product-out mentality and simplified models of behavior. Customer-in thinking attempts to understand the motivations, expectations and all the other complex nuances of customers.
The purpose of customer research is to gather data relevant to increasing sales. Organizations dominated by product-out thinking believe the purpose of market research is to gather data that will help them sell more of their products. This research is often simplistic, focussed on product features or price alone. The result: data collection driven by what the organization wants to push.	**The purpose of customer research is to gather information relevant for improvement and innovation.** Customer-in organizations accept the fact that gathering data is just the beginning and easiest part of research. The whole point is to use this data to build a better understanding of the customer. To understand the customer, customer-in organizations go beyond the raw data to develop theories and ideas about what the customer is trying to tell us. No customer ever asked for the Sony Walkman or fuel-injected cars. These products came about from technological innovation combined with an understanding of the very real interests of the customer.

Table 9: Differences Between Product-Out and Customer-In Thinking

Product-Out Thinking	Customer-In Thinking
Customer research belongs to the market research department. Product-out organizations believe that customer research belongs to the market research department, a reflection of that functional silo approach to organizational behavior. The marketing function conducts the research and then acts as guardians to ensure no one else sees the data.	**Customer research belongs to all.** Customer-in companies know that good information can come from a host of sources. Sales people and other front-line staff may know far more about what is going on in terms of customer complaints and competitive features than any formal customer research could reveal. There is a wealth of customer knowledge existing within the organization that is tapped and unused by all. Moreover, once gathered, this information belongs to everyone.
If we don't hear anything, everything must be okay. Most customers don't complain – they simply take their business elsewhere. Product-out companies assume that no news is good news. But no news only means your customers are slowly migrating elsewhere. Product-out thinking adopts the ostrich approach – hide your head in the sand and hope for the best. Never, but never, go looking for problems. There is a reason for this logic – product-out companies know if they go looking for problems, they'll find all too many of them.	**Customer complaints are an excellent source of information.** Customer-in companies encourage customer complaints. They want to know if their customers are happy or not. Moreover, they give employees the power to fix things if the customer isn't happy. According to the Customer Satisfaction Institute, 30 - 46 percent of customers will switch vendors when their complaints are not handled promptly. In contrast, when complaints are handled quickly, only 5 percent will switch. Customer-in companies make the effort to hear from their customers and make changes when things don't function they way they should.

best for the organization, or the finance department with numerous bureaucratic rules that constrain customer service, are examples where product-out philosophy has become part of the organizational culture.

These same departments are surprised or shocked in realizing they have no internal support when they are targeted for down-sizing or out-sourcing. They are, of course, the only ones that are surprised. All their customers have been hoping, and possibly working toward this outcome for some time.

No Customer Ever Asked For the Electric Light Bulb[18]

"Wait," you say. Something doesn't quite ring true. No customer asked for or demanded electric lights or the fax machine or the telephone. No customer stood up in 1949 and said, "What we need here is a small desktop computer!" So what sense does it make to talk about listening to the needs of the customer when many great products were born without customer input at all?

The answer is fundamental to what is meant by *understanding the customer*. There is a big difference between simply asking customers what they want and truly understanding their needs, aspirations, motivations and requirements. Real understanding requires insight. Simply asking what customers want is by itself a cheap and relatively empty exercise. After all, we already know what customers want. Customers want it all, want it now and want it for free.

Phrased differently, we could say customers want more, and want it sooner and cheaper. There! Now that you know what customers want, there is no need to hire a marketing research firm to tell you. Good customer research, on the other hand, provides the insight and understanding that supports improvement and innovation.

The often told story of Bell Labs inventing the transistor deserves repeating here to make the point. Bell Labs invented the transistor in 1949. The inventors won the Nobel prize for its creation. Yet, in the years that followed, Bell failed to develop any products that made use of the invention. It wasn't until a group of touring Japanese engineers and business people saw the technology that its potential was realized. To these 'tourists' the transistor was a way of making radios smaller and consume less power, enabling them to be used almost anywhere, even in automobiles! The folks at Bell Labs had created a remarkable *device*. The Japanese had something else in mind – *a product*!

Moreover, it was a product borne of a deep understanding of the needs and desires of customers. In the great American marketplace, mobility had become the new reality, arising from the combination of a rapidly growing Interstate highway network,

---

18. Edwards W. Deming, The New Economics, MIT Center for Advanced Engineering Study, Cambridge, MA. p. 7

increasing disposable wealth and surging automobile sales. The Japanese visitors understood the potential. In this sense, it was the customers who identified the need for the transistor, even before they were aware of its existence.

Some years later, Sony would repeat the same trick. Recognizing the rising level of personal mobility (outside of the automobile) and the amount of activity occurring outside the home, Sony provided people with a product that would allow them to 'take their music with them.' The Walkman was born.

Customers Are Fast Learners

When it comes to a customer-in philosophy, remember that customers are fast learners.[19] So what if they didn't ask for the electric light. Look what they starting demanding once they got it. Everything! When the first desk-top computers appeared with the VisiCalc spreadsheet, people were delighted that a simple financial model could be run and solutions provided in a minute or so. Now they wait impatiently as highly complex computations complete with colorful graphics take two or three seconds. The Walkman started life as a radio. Within a few

years it had evolved through several generations including tape and CD players.

The point here is that while customers never asked for many of the innovations that are now commonplace, once those innovations appeared customers were quick to adopt not only the product per se, but its potential. This demand for innovation and improvement may quickly outstrip the organization's ability to keep pace or may take the product in a profoundly different direction than its creators originally envisioned.

SUPPLIERS

Suppliers, like customers, are part of the system. They provide the inputs that processes need in order to function. Traditional management practice, however, tends to look upon suppliers as outsiders. They are not to be trusted, but rather ruthlessly managed in a never-ending effort to squeeze out the best possible price. This attitude is evidenced in competitive bidding for services or product. More than one manager has justified competitive bids on the basis of "keeping the supplier honest." To which we reply, "Maybe you ought to keep better company!"

---

19. Edwards W. Deming, The New Economics, MIT Center for Advanced
     Engineering Study, Cambridge, MA. p. 7

Government, for example, typically has extensive policies on purchasing, usually emphasizing competitive bids and the awarding of contracts on the basis of lowest or near to the lowest cost. Many businesses still follow this practice. The entire supplier relationship is seen as an ongoing win-lose battle where each side tries to outdo the other. Specifications are written to ensure the company gets what it wants. Suppliers produce long lists of exceptions to the specifications as a way to raise the quoted price. Companies respond with tighter specifications and suppliers get better on meeting specifications but failing everywhere else. Is this any way to work together? Traditional practice encourages game playing and distrust between the two organizations having the greatest need to cooperate.

The Price of Input Specifications for Competitive Bid

There is a story of an oil company placing a major order for a specific piece of equipment for which extensive specifications had been written. The contract was awarded on competitive bid. Four months later, on schedule, the equipment was delivered to the field site and installed. There was just one problem, the equipment barely worked. It wasn't a problem for the supplier though, because for all the engineering specifications that had been written, the one specification missing was the requirement that the equipment would actually function.

The supplier noted that it knew the equipment wouldn't work well in the application and tried to point this out to the company. But the purchasing people didn't have the authority to change the engineering specifications. Discussions with engineering would have taken too long, putting the supplier behind schedule for which there were significant financial penalties. The company got what it asked for, and that's all it got. That's the price of setting rigid specifications and managing your supplier like the enemy.

No matter how the supplier is treated by the buyer, the supplier is still part of the system. That's not a statement of philosophy – it's a physical reality of every system. Traditional management approaches pit buyer against supplier in a win-lose negotiation and ongoing competitive bid. The economic losses attributable to this prac-

"All I could remember thinking was, 'My God, this thing was put together by the lowest bidder'."

Astronaut Scott Carpenter, on what he was thinking while waiting for launch of his Mercury spacecraft

tice are considerable. Competing against your competitors is hard enough. Competing with your suppliers is just added burden. Why fight battles with the very organizations you rely on? A different approach is required.

Creating Relationships With Suppliers

Organizations need to build relationships with suppliers in the same way they would like to build relationships with their customers. Effectively managing suppliers as part of the system means accepting the reality of suppliers as a vital component of that system. They become partners, not competitors. As partners, they share and take on at least part of the responsibility of keeping your customers satisfied. Managing suppliers as part of the system requires:

▲ **Forming relationships rather than formulating contracts.** The relationship between supplier and buyer cannot be managed on the basis of limited contracts specifying conditions, terms and time limits. A one-year contract barely gives the supplier time to get its own house in order let alone try and understand the specific needs of the buyer and its customers. Two years is hardly better. Time limits and terms should not be the focus of a business relationship any more than they should be the focus

of a marriage. Like it not, you and your supplier(s) are hitched. You must either learn to work together or find yourself new partners.

▲ **Sharing information and facilities, rather than "us versus them."** The us versus them mentality that turns suppliers into outsiders not only fails to recognize the reality of suppliers as part of the system, but is also a less efficient way of operating. Buyers often hold information close to the chest to keep suppliers in the dark. The result is that suppliers are forced to guess what it is buyers want, combined with the suspicion, all too often correct, that the buyers don't actually know what they want. Suppliers need to open up, too. Typically the last thing suppliers want to see is the buyer walking around the place. The fear is: "They'll find out how bad things are around here." Don't worry. If things are that bad, your customers probably already know. When a solid relationship is established between supplier and buyer, the two become a team and will actually work together to improve performance problems.

▲ **Building partnerships rather than playing bidding games.** You can't build a relationship on competitive bids or trying to play one supplier off another. The reality of partnership is having one supplier for each input required by the process. Then, as your business grows and profits rise, so do your suppliers. That's the way it should be – partners with the same interests and concerns involved in a win-win relationship. These points are not intended to be a simplistic analysis of supplier-buyer relations. Simply creating a single-source supplier relationship will not solve all problems. The relationship requires constant work to build trust and confidence.

Configurations of Supplier-Buyer Relationships

Conventional approaches to the supplier-customer relationship are often so ingrained in our thinking, we have difficulty breaking out of our traditional patterns. Won't the supplier take advantage of the relationship? How will we control costs? What happens if my single supplier goes out of business or has a fire and can no longer deliver?

These questions can be answered by examining the configurations of sole-supplier relationships. Some organizations have taken an extreme approach to the philosophy of sole suppliers, causing as much damage as traditional approaches. They embraced the concept but the supporting logic was forgotten.

Moving toward sole suppliers works because suppliers are part of the system. But if an organization has two different systems, two suppliers are just fine and may, in fact, be preferable to a single supplier relationship.

Exhibit 10: Configuring Supplier Relationships[*]

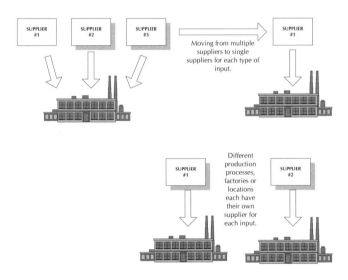

[*]   Adapted From William J. Latzko, David M. Saunders, Four Days With Dr. Deming, Addison Wesley, Reading, Mass. 1995, p. 60

For example, a company with two production facilities, one in California and one in New Jersey, may choose a single supplier if the supplier has local warehousing facilities or can efficiently deliver product to each location. But if no such supplier can be found, having different suppliers in each location is a better solution.

What holds true for different locations also holds true for different inputs. Structuring the system to optimize performance means moving toward a single supplier for each input, not all inputs. There needs to be an underlying logic to the design of the system, which identifies a single source for each input flowing into each process. This basic configuration is one in which suppliers and buyers can build a relationship to improve overall system and organizational performance.

INPUTS AND OUTPUTS

Inputs and outputs represent the physical set of products and services produced by suppliers (inputs) or the process (outputs). Our inputs are the outputs of our suppliers. Likewise our outputs are inputs to the customer. The difference between inputs and outputs is simply one of perspective.

OUTPUTS

Outputs are all those things produced by a process, what we generally try and sell to a customer. Not all outputs are intended, however, as every process produces both intended and unintended outputs.

Intended outputs are the goods and services the process is designed to produce and sell to a customer. But what do we mean by goods and services? The distinction between the two often causes confusion in teams seeking to improve performance. For the purposes of performance improvement, however, this is an empty debate. Effective performance improvement means focusing on the total set of outputs delivered to the customer. Instead of focusing on what constitutes goods versus a service, teams need to focus on the total product bundle[20]– the complete set of outputs and characteristics of the service received.

Think about buying a new car. Where does product end and service begin? Certainly the car itself would constitute the good but what about the warranty? What about the service you

---

20. M. H. Schwartz, "What Do the Words Product and Service Really Mean?", Quality Progress, June 1992, p.35

Exhibit 11: One Person's Output is the Next Person's Input - The Next Process is the Customer

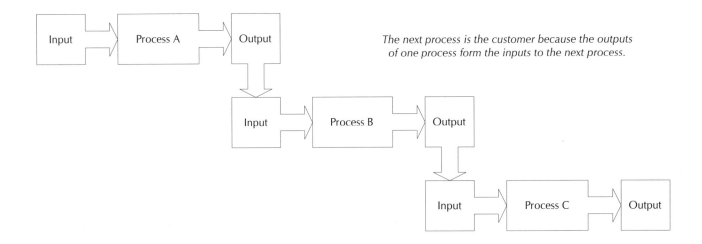

The next process is the customer because the outputs of one process form the inputs to the next process.

received at the local dealership? All these factors enter into the purchasing equation, all imply different levels of value from the customer's point of view and, therefore, all are components of the output or total product being delivered to a customer. Don't think of goods versus services. Think of the total product bundle.

This notion is detailed effectively in the Total Product Bundle Model. Goods and services are different in many ways. Goods are tangible, usually easily stored and can be moved from place to place. Services on the other hand tend to be intangible, cannot be stored or saved for use later and cannot be transported. Yet a pure product – a product that consists solely of a good or a service – is rare. Making a deposit to a bank may seem like a service only, but the receipt acknowledging the deposit "is no less tangible to a customer than a sheet of steel."[21]

---

21. ibid; p. 35

THE PRODUCT

The circles in the model represent the product – a combination of goods and services that, taken together, constitute the product of the process. This is far more reflective of the way customers actually see what it is we are selling – a combination of things that together create value.

At the center of the goods and services making up the product is the product kernel. The kernel represents the ability of the combination of the goods and services to satisfy the essential need, want or requirement of the customer. The product kernel for automobiles is personal and flexible transportation, but it is in the unique way the goods and services are combined that creates differentiation.

For example, Saturn makes cars but uses a unique way of selling them (no haggling, with the price clearly marked on the car) as a source of competitive differentiation and as proof they are "a different kind of car company." The service characteristics associated with selling the car has become part of the product.

Terms and Conditions of the Sale

The most important of the terms and conditions of the sale is price. Too high a price can drive consumers away in droves and a low enough price can compensate consumers for a host of problems. Price is very much a reflection of how well our product is received by customers. Products perceived as providing added value can command a higher price than those of the competition. Other characteristics of terms and conditions of the sale include delivery schedules, credit availability, interest charges, payment schedules and the like. The way these terms and conditions are defined or combined can be a real source of competitive advantage and differentiation. Banks, for example, have combined these various features in myriad ways to create different types of mortgages for various customers, despite the fact that mortgages are essentially a commodity with little apparent opportunity for differentiation.

Customer Service

Customer service, in the context of the Product Bundle Model, refers specifically to the after-sales service and support provided to the customer. This includes services such as delivery, installation, maintenance, ongoing information and advice, mechanisms for resolving problems and other forms of assistance. In the marketing of computers and computer software, characteristics of customer service may be the most important part of the purchase decision.

Exhibit 12: Total Product Bundle Model*

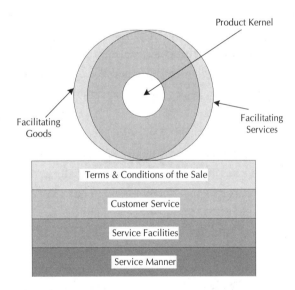

*   M. H. Schwartz, "What Do the Words Product and Service Really Mean?", Quality Progress, June 1992, Reproduced with permission

Service Facilities

Where does the customer buy the product? What are the facilities like compared to those of the competition? The characteristics of the environment within which the customer must buy the product may be as important to the customer as the product itself. In banking, for example, the availability of banking or cash machines is transforming traditional notions of retail branch banking.

For many companies today, the new service facility is the website. Differentiation in terms of ease of access, conducting business and transactions, obtaining support and the like has become a new and important source of competitive advantage.

Even in those cases where change has not been so dramatic, the facilities within which the customer must buy the product are still an important component of the product bundle. In a review of the competitiveness of a retail service outlets, a major gasoline retailer found that many of its service facilities were simply unsuitable for one of its target markets. It turns out that access and egress to many of their stations was difficult for medium- to larger-sized trucks – a function of poor design with inadequate spacing between pump aisles. You won't sell much product if customers can't even get in the door!

Service Manner

Service manner refers to the behavior displayed by service providers in the organization, including sales staff. Typical characteristics include degree of friendliness, politeness, courtesy, professionalism, promptness and so on. In short, it describes how the customer is treated when attempting to purchase a suitable product.

UNINTENDED OUTPUTS

Generally speaking, we use product and product bundle to describe or organize the characteristics of the outputs we are trying to sell to customers. Product and product bundles, therefore, describe the intended outputs of a process. But processes have unintended outputs as well. No one tries to make pollution, but it is a very real output of many processes.

A light rail transit system in a major North American city was designed to move people from the suburbs to downtown and home again. Because the system was built above ground, trains occasionally collided with pedestrians, with pedestrians generally faring worse in the altercation. Trains killed or seriously injured an average of about one person per year. Therefore, an output of the light rail transit system was about one death or serious injury per year. This is not an intentional output or a product being sold to the public, but it is a very real output of the process.

Teams seeking to improve process performance need to be aware of both the intended and unintended outputs – both in terms of seeing them as targets to improve and in terms of the implications of the improvement efforts. Speeding the trains up may improve system efficiency from the viewpoint of people moved, but it will also likely increase the likelihood of collisions with pedestrians.

INPUTS

Inputs are the raw materials, the resources that go into the process. If there are problems with the input the process receives, these problems will likely flow through the process right into the laps of your customers, or require a lot of rework. It is the old adage of "garbage in, garbage out." Processes cannot be fully understood without understanding the characteristics of the resources they use. A critical step to process improvement, therefore, is fully understanding the quality characteristics of the inputs that are flowing into the process.

These inputs usually take many forms. It can be easy to focus on the obvious and forget the not-so-obvious inputs to a process that may have a greater impact on performance. What are these inputs? Each process will have its own unique list, but some generic guidelines can be used to help teams think about the inputs flowing into and being consumed by a process. One such guideline is the 5 M's – men (people), money, material, machinery and methods.

1. People

These are the human resources that work within the process. Any system must ensure that adequate numbers of people are in place and that they are trained and capable of performing the tasks to which they are assigned. At times, the process may not be able to function because the people supporting the process, including management, have simply not been trained properly. They may lack the requisite skills or may simply have insufficient numbers to get the tasks completed correctly and on time.

2. Money

Every process will consume money. Organizations usually have detailed expectations of precisely how much money should and should not be consumed in production. Money is required to pay people, buy machines and purchase other inputs. Unfortunately, it is not always easy to gather financial data by process, because financial and cost-reporting systems usually organize data by organizational unit as defined by the organizational hierarchy (silos) rather than by process activities.

3. Material

Materials are the raw physical materials used by the system. It is not just the materials used to construct an output – more than steel is required to make steel pipe. You need everything from the natural gas to provide the heat, to the pencils (or computers) for the accounting staff. Teams need to ensure they have a comprehensive listing of the raw materials consumed by the process in its operation.

4. Machinery

Machinery comes in different styles. It can be brand new or out of date, well maintained or in a state of disrepair. It may be state of the art but misused or misapplied. It can be too large or too small. Machinery is usually a vital process input, especially as firms rely more on information technology to help get the job done.

5. Methods

These define how the process is supposed to function. Are the process methods being used causing problems? Are they out of date? Do the methods add unnecessary complexity and bureaucracy? A method can also be described as the way all the other elements are combined to build a process. Methods represent the knowledge of the organization. Organizations use a method of production because that is what they know how to do. Other organizations can use precisely the same inputs but produce better results from nothing more than superior methods – in other words, superior knowledge.

Each input to the process can also be considered using precisely the same model used in the analysis of outputs. As customers we are not only buying a good or service, but rather a total product bundle. Teams seeking to make improvement need to consider which inputs are important to the process and which are not. Some organizations may be purchasing more than a raw material. They may be using superior reporting provided by the vendor to help manage their input costs. These reports become part of what the organization is buying, part of the product bundle.

PROCESSES

At the core of the SIPOC Model is the process used to take the inputs provided by suppliers and transform them into outputs to be purchased by customers. A process is a "set of causes and conditions that repeatedly come together to transform inputs into outputs."[22]

A less formal definition is that processes are the verbs of work. Like the verbs in any language, they provide the action. Everything that happens in any organization – every product made, every employee behavior, every decline in financial performance – is a function of the processes at work. To understand what is going on in the organization you must understand its processes – those causes and conditions that have come together to produce effects or outcomes.

Processes are the verbs of work – they provide the action.

---

22. Ronald Moen, et all, Improving Quality Through Planned Experimentation, McGraw Hill, New York, NY, p. 14-15, 1991

PROCESSES CONSIST OF A SET OF CAUSES AND CONDITIONS THAT COME TOGETHER

Processes are constructed. They are made up of various causes and conditions including tasks, activities, rules, measurements, methods, people, policies, constraints, machines, materials and money, that all come together in a certain way to produce something. To make improvements, we need to focus not only on the causes and conditions – components of the process – but the way they come together or how the components are assembled.

The fact that all processes are constructed does not mean that all processes are designed, or designed well. Many of the causes and conditions that come together have evolved over time. New policies are added, new requirements identified and changes made to procedures. Such changes are often made with limited consideration to current process functioning – they are simply added on. As time progresses, the existing process bears less and less resemblance to the original. What may have been a simple, efficient, effective, and even elegant process gradually turns into an incomprehensible monster. Tagging on additions and changes without consideration to overall process design may fix some obvious problems, but it also creates its own hidden problems that can degrade performance.

PROCESS FUNCTION – TRANSFORMING INPUTS TO OUTPUTS

Between every input and output there is a process, transforming one into the other. Transformation, therefore, is about change – taking in one set of things and changing them into another set of things. This is the function of every process. It takes in labor, raw materials and money, it uses machinery and it transforms all these into some form of product that customers are willing to buy.

Teams seeking to improve the performance of any process must identify the specific function of the product or process under review. What are the inputs and outputs? Take an accounts payable process as an example. Invoices come in and checks go out. In the process, a lot of human effort and computer time may be consumed. What is the basic function of this process? Why do we do it?

Defining Functions: The Verb-Noun Technique

Defining the specific function of the process is not always easy. Teams may find themselves in endless debates about the function of some process or task.

A helpful approach in defining the function of a given process is stating the function using only two words, a single verb followed by a single noun. This technique is referred to, surprisingly enough, as the verb-noun technique. It is a good way of boiling things down to their basic function. In accounts payable, the function may be broken down as: pay bills (verb + noun).

Each sub-process, task or activity can likewise be broken down and its basic function described using the technique. You may not want to leave the defined function as a simple two-word (verb-noun) descriptor, but it does serve as a useful template for creating a concise definition of a function to improve understanding. In the accounts payable function of "pay bills," sub-functions or tasks could include:

- ▶ receive invoices
- ▶ verify amounts
- ▶ obtain approvals
- ▶ remit checks
- ▶ document payments

Each sub-function or task is defined using a single verb followed by a single noun. This approach to defining process functions, tasks and activities promotes clarity and discipline as to how a process is intended to add value.

THE PURPOSE OF EVERY PROCESS, AND EVERY PART OF EVERY PROCESS, IS ADDING VALUE

Defining the function of a process describes what the process is intended to do but not why we do it. The 'why' or purpose of every process, and every part of every process, is to deliver value to the customer.

It is the customer that determines how much any product is worth, what has value and what does not, because it is the customer that pays for it. Value, therefore, is whatever the customer says it is. No customer, no value added.

Process purpose, therefore, starts at the end – with the customer. This emphasizes the importance of understanding customers as part of any improvement effort. You cannot determine what is adding value, and what is not, if there is no understanding of the customer and what that customer is willing to pay for.

If the process hasn't added any value in the transformation or has consumed more value than it has added, then the process has done nothing other than destroy value. Destroying value is the production of waste. Organizations or processes failing to add value do not deserve to exist, nor will they for long.

Attempts to examine processes for value-adding or value-destroying steps too frequently take place in isolation from customers, outputs, suppliers and inputs. The SIPOC model emphasizes the need for analytical context to properly understand the process at work. Looking for non-value adding steps without consideration of value to the customer is likely to end up as an exercise in mindless cost reduction – reductions that reduce product appeal and, ultimately, demand. Likewise, examining non-value adding process steps without understanding the inputs flowing into the process will also be counter-productive. Process activities designed to control substandard inputs will never make sense unless they are understood within the context of the characteristics of the inputs flowing into that process.

TYPES OF PROCESSES

Because the purpose of every process is to add value, it is useful to classify the processes at work within an organization as to the specific role they play with regard to how value is added. Three basic types of process can be identified. These are:

▲ **Gemba Processes.** Gemba processes are those processes that directly contribute value to customers through the transformation of inputs to outputs. Essentially gemba means where the "heart and soul" lie. When we speak of gemba processes, then, we are referring to those processes that lie at the heart and soul of the enterprise, directly producing those products and services that are valued by customers. Many types of processes could be classified as gemba processes, depending upon the type of organization within which the processes lie. For example, paying bills is not a gemba process for a manufacturing company. But it is a gemba process for the accounting department. Gemba, therefore, is very much a relative term, depending on the specific organizational context (frame of reference) in which it is being applied.

▲ **Gemba Support & Development**. Other processes do not add customer value directly, but rather increase value by

Exhibit 13: Types of Processes

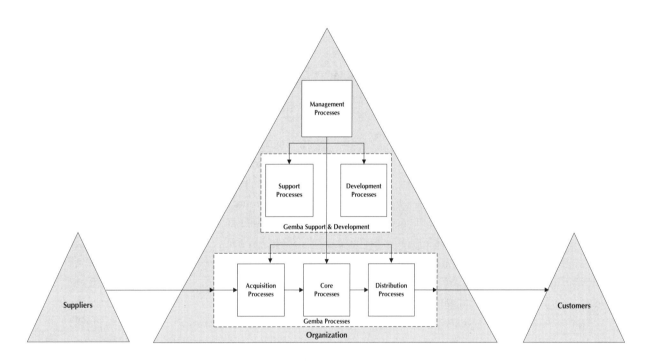

supporting, developing or improving the gemba. For example, customer research pertaining to service delivery is not a gemba process, but it does support the gemba by influencing the design of service delivery. Similarly, continuous improvement is not a gemba process, but it does support the gemba by improving how the gemba processes function. Most research and development and continuous improvement activities can be classified as gemba support and development activities.

▲ **Management Processes.** In contrast, we can also identify management processes that in and of themselves do not add any customer value. Most accounting and human resource processes can be identified as such. This does not mean to say that they are unimportant or that they do not produce value to the shareholders, in the form of required management direction and control. But they are not items customers are typically willing to pay for.

Management processes may not affect the gemba directly but have, nevertheless, a longer term impact on it. Inventory accounting may be a management process, but how it is done will impact the gemba processes of maintaining and managing inventory – something that will have an ultimate impact on how customers perceive the value of the product.

Classifying Process Types

Purpose is the distinguishing factor between various process types. Specifically, purpose defines who places or receives value from the process. If the process adds value for the customer, if it is something the customer is willing to pay for, it is gemba. Any process that exists for the purposes of managerial control (adding value to management) is non-gemba. If it will add value to the gemba, but is not something the customer is immediately and directly willing to pay for, it is a gemba support and development process.

In the real world, differentiating these process types can be difficult. The situation is made more complicated by the fact that employees typically want to be thought of as part of the gemba. Process improvement teams will quickly find that few want to be classified as involved in non-gemba processes (essentially saying they are not directly adding value for customers), leading teams to classify everything as gemba. It is a tendency that must be resisted.

Classifying process types accurately is essential to understanding what is truly important to customers and what is not, what adds value and how. It also provides a set of priorities for improvement initiatives. In short, classifying processes helps provide focus and discipline to the analytical and improvement efforts of any team.

Process Type is Relative to the Organizational Unit

Classification of gemba versus non-gemba processes also depends upon the organizational unit within which the analysis or classification is taking place. As mentioned, accounts payable is not a gemba process to an organization such as a manufacturing enterprise. It is a managerial processes. However, accounts payable is a gemba process to the Accounting Department within that enterprise.

The relativity of what is, and is not gemba makes it critical that improvement teams properly identify the scope of their improvement activities, by defining the organization in which they operate. For example, is the effort focused on improving performance of Human Resources or the organization within which HR is located? The answer will dictate much of the activity that follows.

The Need to Identify Gemba Processes

The importance of defining what is, and is not gemba is reinforced in the following case concerning a human resource department within a large oil and gas company. The department had decided to 're-engineer' itself as a means of improving its performance and perceived value to the larger organization. At the time, complaints about human resources were beginning to rise as were the costs of maintaining the function – a bad combination. The VP of Human Resources was coming under growing pressure to show where and how the department added value to the larger enterprise.

The approach taken by the department was to engage in a series of departmental planning and brainstorming sessions with a focus of "How can we add value?" This, of course, is precisely the wrong question to start any such activity. It is leaping ahead, asking people to generate solutions before obtaining any understanding or agreement of what is happening now. A much better question would have been: "***Where*** are we adding value right ***now*** and how do we do it?".

By asking the first question, however, what the department received in feedback was everything HR staff wanted to do or what seemed trendy at the time. This included supporting organizational change and change management, organizational development, performance management and human resource competency development.

This view was completely at odds with the rest of the organization who were, after all, HR's customers. They thought managing payroll, ensuring benefit and related programs were up to date, and assisting with the hiring of staff were the key value adding activities for HR. Indeed, paying people may not be seen as one of the 'leading edge' functions of HR. But if there is any doubt as to whether or not it is a gemba HR process, try not doing it for a while. The fact that an HR planning and improvement effort could take place, without considering that HR had a responsibility to pay people, shows just how misdirected some improvement efforts can get. Misdirected, because among other things, they had lost sight of the customer expectations and the impact of these on perceived value.

Examining in real terms where and how value is added *now*, and clearly identifying the gemba, gemba support and managerial processes, are critical steps in effective improvement. It ensures we stay focused not just on what we want, but on what customers demand and expect.

QUALITY CHARACTERISTICS: THE MEASURES OF PERFORMANCE

Think of any object. How would you describe it? Is it big or small? What color is it, what shape, what sound does it make? Is it animal, vegetable or mineral? The answers to these questions constitute a set of the object's characteristics. Quality characteristics then, are simply the descriptors for any object(s) in the SIPOC model.

In the world of process and product improvement, quality characteristics describe whatever it is we are trying to improve. They are the "measures of performance."[23] We can describe the operating characteristics of the process producing a product or the product itself. We can measure the characteristics of the customers that bought the product, or the suppliers providing the inputs or the quality characteristics of the inputs themselves. In short, and as the SIPOC Model indicates, these mea-

---

23. Ronald Moen, et al., Improving Quality Through Planned Experimentation, McGraw Hill, 1991, p. 14

Exhibit 14: Quality Characteristics on the SIPOC Diagram

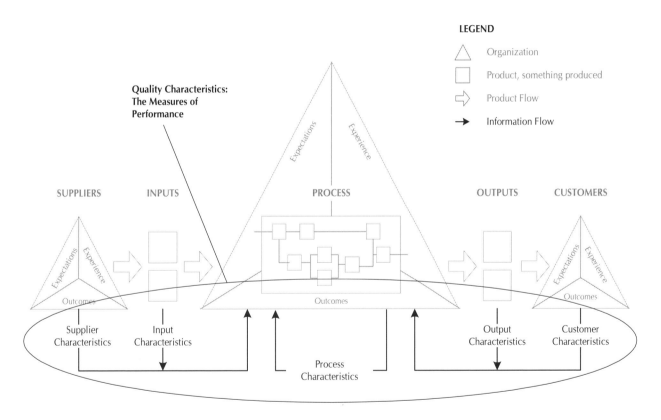

sures or quality characteristics apply to any component of the system.

TYPES OF QUALITY CHARACTERISTICS

The types of quality characteristics are classified by the component of the SIPOC model they are describing. Generally, quality characteristics can be used to describe any of the actors (suppliers, customers and our organization) within the SIPOC model, outputs and inputs produced or used by the process, and the process itself.

▲ **Customer Characteristics** are measures describing the customers purchasing the outputs produced by the process. In describing customers, or any of the other actors within the system, two dimensions are important:

▶ **Descriptive characteristics** are those used to describe or categorize customers for purposes of segmentation. These measures would include demographic measures, individual characteristics, volumes of purchase, benefits derived from the product being purchased and any other characteristic that can be used to describe customers generally or segment customers into identifiable groups.

▶ **Behavioral/outcome characteristics** are those measures that capture some element of customer behavior, the outcomes resulting from a comparison of experience with expectations. These include measures relating to customer satisfaction, loyalty, customer complaints, market share and repurchase behavior.

▲ **Supplier Characteristics** like customer characteristics, can be broken down into basic descriptive measures as well as behavioral or performance measures.

▶ **Descriptive characteristics** describe the supplier generally, including such measures as number of plants, distance to warehouses, safety and environmental performance, financial stability, service record, certifications and reputation.

▶ **Behavioral/outcome characteristics** relate to performance of the supplier in providing inputs to the process. This could include measures of order delivery times, responsiveness, reliability, warranty and service performance.

▲ **Output and Input Characteristics** describe the characteristics of a product or service. The measures used are essentially the same regardless of whether it is we who are doing the purchasing (inputs) or the selling (outputs). Generally we can define output or input characteristics into three broad categories

▶ **Quality,** which in the narrow sense of the word refers to the specific characteristics of the product or service being delivered to a customer. This includes measures such as purity, appearance, reliability, strength, dimensions, fit, response time, accuracy and fraction defective.

▶ **Cost,** which means characteristics related to profit including measures of productivity, defects, unit cost, selling price, margin, raw material cost and yield.

▶ **Delivery/Service**, which includes characteristics related to inventory, volumes, lead times, warranty and service costs.

▲ **Process Performance Characteristics** are divided into three general areas. These are:

▶ **Efficiency characteristics** describe the operating performance parameters of the process. Things such as cycle time, production volume, unit cost, inventory, yield rates, defect rate, throughput and productivity are all examples of efficiency measures

▶ **Effectiveness characteristics** describe the operating performance of the process relative to the organization, the owners of the process. This includes measures relating to value added, cash flow and return on investment.

▶ **Flexibility characteristics** refers to the ability to respond to changes in volume or outputs specifications. This includes measures such as die/tool changeover times, work in process levels and raw material inventory.

LEAD - LAG EFFECTS

The position of the various characteristics on the SIPOC model, or more appropriately their position in the real world of some actual system, means there will be some lead/lag effects when we attempt to measure performance. Consider, for example, customer behavioral or outcome measures. These outcomes lie with the customer – at the end of the process. Any change in performance at this location will be the result of changes occurring some time before, further upstream in the SIPOC model. How long before is dependent upon the specific process, but what is important is that there will be a time *lag*.

This fundamental reality of performance measurement should give pause to those arguing for the need to focus solely on outcomes. Organizations that do so will be measuring things after it is too late to do anything about it. The damage will have already been done. Certainly, measuring outcomes is important, but only when it is tied to other types of characteristics (output and process) that enable the examination of cause-and-effect patterns.

In contrast, output characteristics can be a *lead* indicator of customer outcomes. If the relationship between output characteristics and outcomes is known, measuring the output characteristics will enable the organization to know in advance what the outcomes will likely be. Moreover, problems detected in the output can be identified and corrective actions put into place before the problem hits the customer and affects outcomes.

Similarly, process characteristics are lead indicators to the outputs produced. By carefully monitoring process characteristics, changes and adjustments to the process can be made before errors or other forms of faulty output are produced.

CREATING A PERFORMANCE MODEL

Thus we are confronted with a paradox – or perhaps a challenge. The further to the right on the SIPOC model the characteristic is (further downstream), the more important it is, because it is closer to the customer. At the same time, however, the characteristic becomes less useful as a guide for action because of the time lag involved. In contrast, those characteristics residing further upstream in the process (to the left in the SIPOC model) are further from the customer and, therefore, less important to the business. However, they are relatively more useful for improvement because they can alert us to problems before those problems move down the line to the customer.

The challenge, then, is to not surrender to preconceived ideas about which characteristics should or should not be measured.

Guidelines such as 'focus on outcomes' or 'measure results' are misleading and, in fact, simply wrong-headed. Understanding what is going on in the system demands measurement of outcome, output and process characteristics (and input and supplier characteristics as well) in order to fully appreciate the dimensions of performance at work. No single or simple-minded approach to performance measurement will do. It involves not just paying attention to outcomes, but rather understanding how changes in output and process characteristics affect changes in outcome.

Start at the End – What is Important to the Customer

Quality characteristics cannot be developed in isolation; they need to flow from an understanding of the customer. This goes back to notions of value. We want to measure what is important to the customer because it is the customer that determines the value of the object we are trying to measure. In deciding what to measure, then, improvement teams need to first ask what is important to the customer and proceed up the SIPOC model (value chain) from there.

Unfortunately, this is rarely easy. Customers speak a different language. It is not their job to translate their requirements into our language; it is our job to translate their requirements into terms that can be understood by the product designer or shop floor supervisor.

For example, the market research department may find the most important quality characteristic of a car to the 18-25 year old male target group is 'sexiness.' Well how do you measure that and would an engineer understand it even if you did? Breaking down what the customer wants into measurable units that the organization, engineers or product designers can deal with can be a daunting task.

A first step in defining possible characteristics may be to think in terms of the Exhibit 15: What the Customer Wants to Measures Model. Quality demands of the customer, that is *what* is demanded, are usually measured in terms of quality attributes of the product/service and generally tie in to measures of effectiveness. Pricing concerns of the customer, that is *how much* is paid, are generally reflected in efficiency (including productivity and cost) characteristics of the organization. In the middle of the model are concerns regarding when the product/service is delivered, which tend to be measured in terms of cycle time characteristics.

Exhibit 15: What the Customer Wants to Measures Model

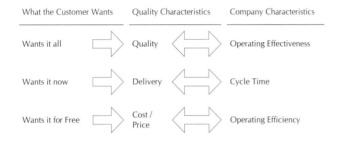

MOVING FROM MOTHERHOOD TO METRICS

In starting with the customer, the characteristics they express will be general in nature and difficult if not impossible to operationalize in measurement terms. These general quality characteristics need to be broken down into secondary and tertiary characteristics with greater and greater degrees of specificity. In so doing, the characteristics move further and further from the realm of the customer and more and more into the realm of the organization. This amounts to a process of translation – taking the words of the customer and translating them into the language of the organization.

For example, a particular customer group may prefer red cars. But what does 'red' mean to the paint shop? Very little. There are many of shades of red. We need to translate the general quality characteristic 'red' into something the organization can deal with – such as a specific paint formulation. Once this is defined, we have a specific quality characteristic and a metric for the more generalized characteristic of red.

All of which means we can think of quality characteristics in terms of different levels, depending upon the degree of specificity required by the function using the characteristic. These levels can be represented in a tree diagram. At the top is the specified customer need. From this flows a set of primary quality characteristics. Each primary characteristic may have a set of secondary quality characteristics and each of these may have a number of tertiary characteristics.

▲ **No matter how many characteristics are used, the description will never be complete – don't search for perfection.** No matter how many quality characteristics are defined for an object, they can never describe the object completely. Moreover, no set of secondary quality

Exhibit 16: A Hierarchy of Quality Characteristics

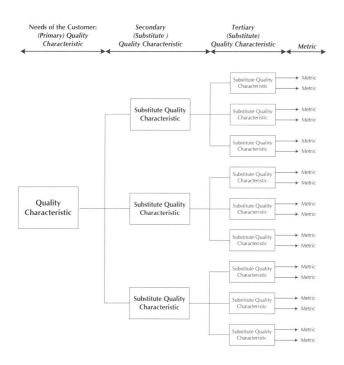

characteristics can fully describe the primary quality characteristic to which they are associated. Our knowledge will always be limited, we will never be able to fully describe and measure everything the customer wants or

management desires. The best we can do is try and identify what is important and use this as a basis for our measurements and our decisions.

It is important that organizations stop looking for perfection in their measurement systems and processes. Too many improvement initiatives become delayed over arguments of what constitutes the best measure of something. Such arguments may be driven by beliefs that the perfect set of measures exists 'out there somewhere.' It doesn't. The best set of measures and metrics for an organization is often the best set the improvement team can develop. Assuming there is a mix of skills, including team members with measurement and statistical knowledge as well as those with expertise in the systems and processes being measured, what gets defined will likely work well.

▲ **Metrics lie at the end of the characteristic hierarchy – they must be clearly defined.** At the end of this hierarchy are metrics, specific definitions of what is being measured. Characteristics are too general to measure as they are largely structured in the language of customers rather than the language of the organization. At some point, however, these characteristics must be brought to a level where they can be measured.

A metric is a characteristic that is sufficiently specific that it can be applied to gather data. As such, metrics must be clearly defined. There can be no doubt as to what is being measured. Variation here, in terms of what is being measured, will only degrade the accuracy and reliability of the measurement system.

DEFINE THE CRITICAL QUALITY CHARACTERISTICS

When we talk of using quality characteristics to describe a process or product, we are talking about the world of information. This world is always incomplete relative to the real world it attempts to describe.

For example, a great many quality characteristics would have to be defined to describe a car: basic style (sedan, hardtop, coupe, hatchback), color, size, engine type, transmission (manual or automatic), year, interior color, interior material, etc. The list could go on. The same holds true for even the simplest products and processes. A pencil is a pretty simple object, but we can still describe pencils in terms as being mechanical or not, lead hardness, length, weight, exterior shape, color of lead and so forth. In fact, for any product or process the list of characteristics is endless.

The real world is infinitely complex, which means to describe it perfectly we would require an infinitely complex measurement system – with infinite costs to go along with it! Those concerned with improving performance or performance measurement, therefore, must determine what is important to understanding system functioning. Specifically, the critical quality characteristics must be identified.[24]

Identifying Critical Quality Characteristics

What process characteristics have the greatest impact on output? What output characteristics have the greatest influence on customer outcomes? By analyzing these relationships, organizations can build understanding of what upstream improvements will have the greatest impact on the critical downstream elements such as customer satisfaction and value.

---

24. Critical Quality Characteristics are often referred to as CQC's or CTQ's (Critical to Quality Characteristics). Either way, the reader should be aware they refer to the same thing – characteristics that are critical to and affect outcomes, usually customer outcomes such as satisfaction and loyalty.

Think of this in terms of X and Y. Outputs are the X to the outcomes Y. To change Y (outcome), the X (output) must change. Likewise, processes are the X to the outputs Y. To change Y (output), a change must occur in the X (process). To change any Y, you must change X's that influence it. Building a performance model of an organization, therefore, requires definition of the Y's and their causal factors or drivers – the X's.

In focussing on a specific effect (Y), an improvement team may identify any number of potential factors or performance drivers (X's). At this point, the improvement team has a theory or hypothesis of which X's have the greatest impact on Y. Theory, however, is not fact. Just believing something doesn't make it so.

To build a valid performance model, improvement teams need to investigate to confirm or deny the theory. The critical connection between X and Y must be validated empirically, through analysis. Some X's will be shown to have a causal influence, others will be shown to have no influence at all. Either way, without empirical investigation it is all just opinion.

Exhibit 17: Performance Model

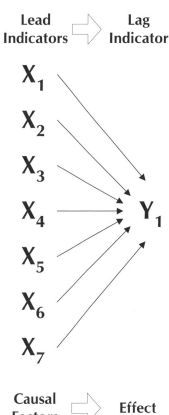

Lead Indicators ⇨ **Lag Indicator**

X_1

X_2

X_3

X_4 → Y_1

X_5

X_6

X_7

To understand performance, a model of the relationship between causal factors and effects (outputs or outcomes) must be constructed. This requires identifying what X's drive what Y's and to what extent.

Causal Factors ⇨ **Effect**

Making empirical connections between cause and effect does more than determine whether an X has a relationship or causal influence on Y. It also establishes the extent of this relationship. We are not just interested in how, but how much. Some X's will have an influence on Y, but the extent of this influence will be minor. Others will have a dramatic or profound effect on Y. These later factors are the critical quality characteristics to the system and represent the source of greatest improvement leverage.

From Description to Prediction

As the organization's knowledge of critical quality characteristics and cause and effect relationships increases, less focus can be paid to customer outcomes and greater emphasis on the factors (X's) that determine these outcome performance levels. The only organizations that place extensive focus on outcomes or lag indicators are those where knowledge of performance is so poor there is no choice but to measure here. Performance measurement is reduced to describing what happened.

As knowledge increases (what X's cause Y), the focus moves upstream in the SIPOC model and becomes inherently more predictive. Organizations with knowledge measure process

characteristics and know in advance what the results mean downstream for output quality and customer satisfaction. In short, organizations with knowledge know what is important and what isn't.

Moreover, the greater the knowledge and predictive capability the organization has, the more it is able to target performance improvement efforts. Critical quality characteristics represent areas of greatest leverage. Focussing improvement efforts on critical-to-quality characteristics will yield the greatest impact on customer satisfaction for our process improvement buck.

MEASUREMENTS, MEASURES AND METRICS

At this point, some definitions may be in order to clarify the distinctions between a measure, a measurement and a metric.[25]

▲ **Metric,** means a distinguishable characteristic with sufficient specificty to be measured, the definition of what is being measured. For example, the 'time to answer' metric for an emergency response department.

---

25. These definitions are adapted by those provided by Camille F. DeYong, Kenneth E. Case, in "Linking Customer Satisfaction Attributes with Process Metrics in Service Industries"; Quality Management Journal, Volume 5, Issue 2, 1998, p.79.

▲ **Measure,** is the scale used to evaluate a metric. Time, length, decibels are all measures. Related to this are the *units* of measure. Time, for example, can be measured in seconds, hours or years.

▲ **Measurement,** is the result of applying the measure to the metric. A measurement is the output of the measurement process – for example, six seconds.

An emergency response department may establish, as part of its performance measurement system, the time to answer (or average time to answer) metric, measured in seconds, producing the measurement of six seconds.

Some samples of possible metrics are provided in Table 18: Sample Metrics. These are meant to serve as examples only. The metrics to be used in each situation are unique depending upon specific circumstances – the nature of the customers, their expectations, the function of the process, nature of the product and so on. The critical consideration in defining the set of quality characteristics and resulting metrics, however, will rest upon what is important to the customer.

Ishikawa's Four Aspects of Quality

Kaoru Ishikawa, a respected leader of the Japanese quality movement, created his own classification scheme of quality characteristics. He identified four aspects or components of quality which, for any product, defines "good quality for the consumer."[26]

1. **Quality,** meaning quality characteristics in their narrow sense. They include performance, purity, strength, dimensions, tolerances, appearance, reliability, lifetime, fraction defective, rework fraction, non-adjustment ratio, packing method, etc.

2. **Cost,** meaning characteristics related to cost and price. They include yield, unit cost, losses, productivity, raw materials costs, production costs, fraction defective, defects, cost price, selling price, profit, etc.

3. **Delivery,** meaning characteristics related to quantities and lead times (quantity control). They include production volume, sales volume, change-over losses, inventory, con-

---

26. Kaoru Ishikawa, Introduction to Quality Control, 3A Corporation 1991, pp. 17-18

Table 18: Sample Metrics

Example	Outcome Metrics	Output Metrics	Process Metrics
Automobile Manufacturer	► *Percentage of customers indicating "satisfactory" or better satisfaction level with initial product quality* ► *Market share* ► *Brand recognition*	► *Fit tolerance of doors and hatches* ► *Number of finish blemishes* ► *Number of dealer adjustments per car* ► *Dollar value of dealer adjustments* ► *Factory warranty costs*	► *Units production per day* ► *Energy cost per unit* ► *Cost per unit* ► *Parts inventory holding costs* ► *Rework cost* ► *Number of finish defects per unit requiring re-work* ► *Scrap rate*
Police Department	► *Violent crime rate* ► *Incidents of physical injury during commitment of an indictable offence* ► *Rate of fatal traffic accidents*	► *Number and rate of police brutality claims* ► *Number of arrests per active officer* ► *Dollar value of stolen property recovered*	► *Conviction rate on indictable offenses* ► *Conviction rate on all offenses* ► *Police budget: dollars per 1000 population*
Regional Bank	► *Market share of new loans* ► *Market share of mortgages* ► *Percentage of customers stating 'favorite place to bank'* ► *Overall client satisfaction rating*	► *Number of new loans added* ► *Value of new loans added* ► *Loan default rate* ► *Number of new accounts opened*	► *Rate of return on assets* ► *Financial margin* ► *Number of new loans approved per loan officer*

sumption, lead times, changes in production plans, cycle time, etc.

4. **Service,** meaning problems arising after products have been shipped and product characteristics requiring follow-up. They include safety and environmental characteristics, product liability prevention, compensation period, warranty period, before sales and after sales service, parts interchangeability, spare parts, ease of repair, instruction manuals, inspection and maintenance methods, packing method, etc.

Such a listing or framework of possible quality characteristics serves as a useful starting point for defining the set of characteristics most appropriate for your own particular circumstance.

Kaplan's Balanced Scorecard

Another framework has been offered by Robert Kaplan. Whereas Ishikawa's framework is very much focused on the operational level of specific products and services, Kaplan's balanced scorecard approach is designed to be applied to the more strategic level of the overall organization or operating division. Kaplan's scorecard consists of:[27]

1. **Financial,** which measures such characteristics as return on capital, cash flow, project profitability and return on equity.

2. **Customer,** which includes levels of customer satisfaction, value for money measures, financial margin, etc.

3. **Internal,** meaning quality levels in the narrow sense, such as service characteristics, safety/loss control, employee satisfaction, etc.

4. **Growth,** which includes continuous improvement, innovation measures, new product introductions.

Kaplan's balanced scorecard approach is a good reminder that in any organization there is much more to pay attention to than the bottom line alone. Just as we can develop a number of characteristics for a pencil, so we can and should develop a balanced set of characteristics to measure the performance of the

---

27. Robert S. Kaplan, The Balanced Scorecard, HBS Press, Boston Massachusetts, 1996.

organization – or any other process or product. Financial performance is critical, but effectively describing the performance of the organization requires more than just financial measures.

Kaplan also suggests identifying lead and lag indicators in each of these categories. Again, this is essential if all components of the SIPOC model are to be understood and knowledge developed as to the relationship between organizational activity and customer satisfaction.

CONCLUDING REMARKS ON QUALITY CHARACTERISTICS

In describing anything we describe its characteristics. Deciding what characteristics to use should flow from an understanding of what is important to the customer. It is the customer that establishes the purpose of the process and the value of the product. No matter the circumstances, however, when attempting to improve performance, the characteristics or performance measures must be defined. That applies from improving the simplest of products to the overall functioning of the organization. In defining these characteristics, we define how performance will be measured.

Kaplan defines a set of characteristics for an organization. Ishikawa presents a set of characteristics more suitable for a specific product or service. Characteristics can describe outcomes, outputs, inputs or process efficiency. There are no predefined characteristics that will apply in every case. Teams seeking to define an operational set of quality characteristics must define their specific circumstances and what is important to their customers. Then, using their own knowledge, they must work from this foundation to build a reliable set of characteristics that will literally define performance.

CRITICAL SYSTEM CONCEPTS: THE LINKAGES BETWEEN PROCESS AND IMPROVEMENT

All the analysis of system components and measurement of performance characteristics cannot help teams improve without understanding the four most important concepts related to systems and processes. These four concepts provide the linkage between processes and improvement. They are:

▲ **Value.** Value is whatever people are willing to pay for. All systems and every component of every production process exist to produce value. Value, therefore, is what performance is all about – creating increasing value for our customers and shareholders. The closer a system comes to meeting the expectations of customers, the greater the value.

▲ **Variation**. All systems and processes produce variation in the quality characteristics being measured. When we manufacture any product or provide any service, our performance, no matter how defined or measured, will vary. The greater the variation, the less able the process is to meet customer or corporate expectations. Improving performance, then, means reducing variation.

▲ **Complexity.** Different systems, processes, inputs and outputs all have different levels of complexity. Some processes are simple, others are very complex. Everything else being equal, the more complex a system, the lower its performance. Improving a product or process, then, often means reducing complexity.

▲ **Control.** Control is the influence management or employees exert over a system. We cannot change or improve anything unless we can exert some element of control over it. The nature of this control will determine how effective and efficient our improvement efforts are.

There is an important relationship between these four concepts. Value is the purpose, what we are trying to create. Variation and complexity, in contrast, are the enemies of quality – they destroy value. The greater the complexity or variation, the lower the value added. Lastly, control is the means by which we reduce complexity and variation and thereby make improvement happen. The greater the control, the greater our ability to add value.

VALUE

Value is an economic concept. Processes add value when they transform inputs to outputs so that people are willing to pay more for the outputs than the organization paid for the inputs – including the cost of running the process. In short, if you get more out than you put in, you have created value.

The economic difference between inputs and outputs is the value produced by the process. The formula for any process 'p' would be:

Value Added$_P$ = Total Revenues$_P$ - Total Costs$_P$

Without getting into all the intricacies of managerial economics, the basic equation above defines performance for any process or system. The intent of any improvement effort, therefore, is improving or increasing the level of value.

Moreover, as the basic equation makes clear, there are only two ways to do it. Increasing the value added means either increasing total revenues or decreasing costs. Either approach will increase value.

It should be noted that revenues and costs are independent of one another. Revenue is essentially volume times price. The greater the value in the mind of the customer, the greater will be the volume sold or the price demanded or both, independent of the cost to produce the product. Likewise, cost is independent of revenue. Simply because it costs $20 to make something doesn't mean an organization can demand $20 for it in the marketplace.

VALUE AND PERFORMANCE

While value is easy to understand, it is much harder to generate. Part of the reason for this is that the relationship between the performance (product or process characteristics) and value is not a simple or direct one. At times, we can improve some product or process characteristic without affecting perceived value. Many organizations have been left confused and bewildered after improving some product significantly only to find the customer never noticed. So while all increases in value (expressed as customer satisfaction) require an improvement to product or process (expressed as improved process or product performance), not all improvements result in an increase in value.

Kano's Value/Quality Characteristic Model

Dr. Noriaki Kano recognized this and developed a two-dimensional model of the relationship between performance (expressed as internal performance measures) on the one hand, and value (expressed as customer satisfaction) on the other.[28] It should be considered a basic tool in the effort to overcome sim-

---

28. Noriaki Kano, et al. *Attractive Quality and Must Be Quality* in The Best of Quality, Vol. 7, ASQC, Milwaukee. 1996

plistic, linear thinking regarding the relationship between what an organization does and how this is perceived by the customer.

The model identifies three types of characteristics, depending upon the *type* of expectation the customer has for the product being delivered. The model defines *type* of expectation, because it recognizes that these differences go beyond differences in degree; they define different forms of the performance/value equation.

▲ **Basic Characteristics.** These are the characteristics we have come to expect, that we take for granted. Customers don't typically mention them, simply because they are so important or basic to the value equation.

In banking, for example, having accurate statements is a basic characteristic. People expect the bank to be able to count. No customer thanked a bank for getting their bank balance correct – it's expected. In the airline industry a basic characteristic is arriving at the destination – alive! In other words, don't crash the plane! No kudos from your customers for getting them there safely – it's expected.

No matter how well a company delivers these basic characteristics, the customer will never be more than neutral in terms of satisfaction or perceived value. But fail to deliver one of these characteristics and a great deal of dissatisfaction will be expressed. In other words, basic characteristics tend to be noticed only when absent.

This, by the way, is what so often underlies employees' complaint about customers: never a thank-you for doing a good job, but sure letting you know it when an error has been made. In these cases, the employee has just identified typical customer response to expected performance levels of a basic characteristic.

▲ **Satisfiers.** Satisfier characteristics are those that customers want as opposed to expect and are also referred to as 'more is better' characteristics. The more we deliver, the happier the customer will be. Doing well here allows us to create satisfied customers.

Satisfier characteristics include lower price, larger amounts, faster delivery, greater reliability, more convenient packaging and greater effectiveness.

It is interesting to note that most customer or market research is focused on satisfiers. This is because satisfiers are what most customers think of when asked questions about what is important. Rarely do fundamentals (basic

Exhibit 19: Kano Model of Quality Characteristics[*]

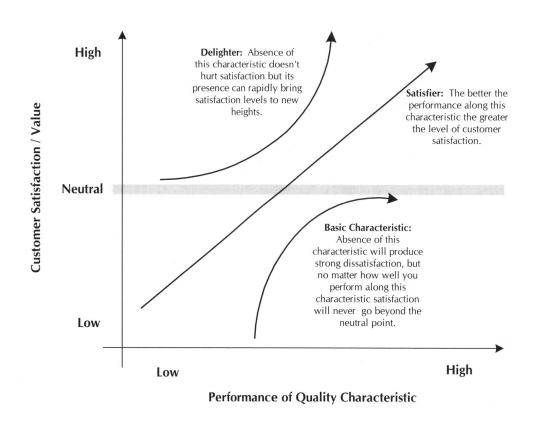

* Adapted from Kano, Noriaki; et al. *Attractive Quality and Must Be Quality* in The Best of Quality, p. 170, vol. 7, ASQC, Milwaukee. 1996, with permission.

characteristics) come to mind and delighters by definition represent the totally unexpected. The result can be research focused on the obvious – forgetting or omitting two-thirds of the customer satisfaction (value) picture.

▲ **Delighters.** Delighters are those characteristics that represent a positive surprise to the customer. They are totally unexpected. As such, if they are not present, they cause no dissatisfaction. Moreover, customers will not mention such things as important on customer surveys because they are, after all, totally unexpected by definition. But when delivered to the customer, delighters raise satisfaction and loyalty.

It is hard to describe delighters. There is no standard set of characteristics upon which to draw – every situation is unique. Perhaps the best way to understand is to ask yourself: have you ever experienced delight with a company?

Some years ago my wife and I were travelling extensively across the United States and flying with Delta Airlines exclusively. At the end of our travels were found ourselves in Los Angeles waiting to catch our last flight home. We were tired and generally fed-up with the world as people tend to be at the end of a lengthy trip. While waiting we were paged by Delta. Being an experienced traveler, I

immediately assumed the worst. Nothing could be further from the truth. One of the front line staff at Delta had noticed how extensive our itinerary had been. Reasoning we were tired of it all, she had paged to inform us that Delta would be upgrading my wife and I to first class as well as providing us with full access to Delta's lounge. To this day my wife books through Delta whenever she can. That is a delighter.

Determining What is Important to the Customer: Using the Kano Model

The Kano model provides insight into the specific dynamics of how players in a system arrive at some outcome (level of satisfaction, repurchase behavior etc.), by comparing expectations (basic, satisfiers or delighters) with experience (quality characteristic performance). It tells us that different quality characteristics will elicit different responses from the customer depending upon what the customer expects relative to that characteristic.

For example, consider airline baggage handling. We might consider measuring two quality characteristics:

▲ **The time it takes to unload luggage from the plane and have it appear at the baggage claim area of the airport.** Nobody likes waiting for their luggage. Clearly, the faster we can get it to the customer, the happier the customer will be. This is a classic satisfier.

▲ **The percentage of customers experiencing lost baggage.** Nobody likes having their luggage lost either. In this case, however, customers typically have a basic expectation that the airline will not lose their luggage, in which case any failure in this regard produces strong negative reaction from the customer.

Improving the unloading time of luggage by 10 percent will increase customer satisfaction. So will reducing the incidents of lost luggage by 10 percent. But what action will have a greater impact on satisfaction? At first blush, it might seem that by focusing improvement efforts on unloading time reduction, overall measures of customer satisfaction would likely rise more than if we reduced incidents of lost luggage, simply because we would be affecting a great many more people (just about everyone waits for luggage but the incidents of lost luggage are relatively rare). However, we would be improving performance in an area where the benefit to the customer is minor – having faster luggage unloading is nice but not funda-

mental. After all, would you notice if average baggage unloading time dropped from 15 minutes to 13.5?

Meanwhile, we would have ignored an area where the number of customers affected are few, but where the impact of each case is severe. Not losing luggage may be a fundamental or basic characteristic. As such, we may be wiser to reduce the incidents of lost baggage rather than reduce waiting times. The number of customers impacted will be fewer but the returns to the airline may be greater.

The bottom line here, and of the Kano model generally, is that all quality characteristics are not created equal. They are created in the mind of the customer and the customer not only has different expectations for each characteristic, but different types of expectations as well.

When identifying quality characteristics to measure, it is important to identify the type of expectation held for that characteristic by the customer. Doing so helps identify what characteristics should be measured and where priorities for improvement lie, and contributes to an improved understanding of the customer and how the customer perceives value. Identifying the type of characteristic may prove difficult, in which case some empirical customer research would be worthwhile. The research must be designed carefully, however, as customers will find it difficult to identify basic characteristics and nearly impossible to identify delighters.

Other Applications of the Kano Model

The Kano model, while originally designed to describe customer expectations of certain characteristics, is useful in describing the relationship between any actor in the SIPOC model and the expectations they hold. Other applications of the model include:

▲ **Examining the expectations of an organization for any process or product.** Our organization is also a player in the system and, like our customers, has expectations for the product or process. Similarly, these expectations can and should be classified by the type of expectation held. Is some characteristic a basic expectation or a satisfier? What would it take to delight the organization?

▲ **Examining the satisfaction levels of employees.** Organizations often survey employees to assess levels of satisfaction and morale. All too often, the approach is a simple set of questions about how employees feel about their salary, benefits, hours of work, relationship with supervisor, scope of work or other variables. This approach ignores the reality that employees consider these things differently. Fair salary, for example, would likely be a basic characteristic – we should not expect any employee to be satisfied simply because they are being paid the going rate. Allowing that same employee a little more say in how they do their job may be an example of a satisfier, or in some cases, a delighter.

▲ **Examining our relationship with suppliers.** Our suppliers also have expectations of their relationship with us. What do they require or expect of the relationship? What characteristics would improve the relationship? Understanding the nature of the expectations helps us improve levels of trust and build a win-win relationship with those we depend on for our inputs.

Beware Creeping Expectations

The Kano model depicts the relationship between performance as measured and as perceived. But things change, and first among the changes is how customers perceive value. This is especially true with delighters. Once delivered, the customer is delighted. But the customer's expectations are also modified.

Soon, customers come to expect those delighters. Thus, what was once a delighter evolves to become a satisfier or perhaps a basic characteristic.

This reinforces the earlier observations about adopting a customer-in philosophy. No customer asked for the electric light bulb, but the product delighted those that had it. Soon, electric lights became more than a delighter – they became basic requirement of every household in America.

Which means that when organizations speak of 'delighting the customer' they had best be careful. It may be easy to delight the customer once, perhaps even twice. But as expectations change, organizations will need to address issues of sustainability. Specifically, can the organization continue to deliver a delighter if it evolves into a basic characteristic?

VARIATION

All processes and systems produce variation in output. No system is perfect. This applies to all systems, natural and man-made. When the earth revolves around the sun it takes about 365.25 earth days to do so. But it is never exactly the same figure; sometimes it takes a little less and sometime it takes a little more. The 365.25 days we learn as school children is really the long-term average.

So it is with systems created by people. When we manufacture drive shafts of a specified diameter, what we produce are drive shafts with slightly different diameters, some a little larger and some a little smaller than the design. These usually minute differences make up the variation inherent in the process of manufacture.

> *"The central problem of management in all its aspects, including planning, procurement, manufacturing, research, sales, personnel, accounting, and law, is to understand better the meaning of variation."*
>
> **Dr. Edwards Deming**

This holds true in all manufacturing and service systems and processes. Profits rise one year and fall the next. Product cost rises slightly, then falls, then rises again. No matter how hard we try, no matter how much money we invest, systems will always produce some level of variation. Manufactured parts will never conform exactly to specifications, service levels will never be perfect. All systems and processes vary.

VARIATION CAN BE PICTURED AS A DISTRIBUTION

So what does variation look like? Let's take an example of the measurements resulting from a specific quality characteristic – emergency response time. In this case, it's the time it takes the fire department to reach the site of a fire once the call has been received by the fire station.

Typically, the fire department would keep statistics on how many minutes on average it takes and compare these figures to some standard or objective. In our example, let's assume the average response time last year was 7.5 minutes. However, it is clear that not every call took precisely 7.5 minutes. Sometimes the roads were empty or the fire was near the fire station. In such circumstances our response time would have been faster than 7.5 minutes. In other circumstances, the weather may have been lousy, traffic heavy and the fire in a difficult-to-access location. In these circumstances, response time would have been slower. We can begin to see that the figure of 7.5 minutes tells us very little about overall system performance.

If we examined every response and recorded the time it took and then plotted these on a graph, we might get something that

Exhibit 20: Picturing Variation: Fire Department Response Time

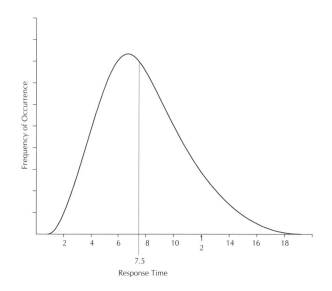

looks like Exhibit 20: Picturing Variation: Fire Department Response Time. What we are looking at is the variation inherent in the process as measured by this specific quality characteristic.

The bottom axis of the chart represents the quality characteristics being measured – in this case time. The vertical axis records the number or count of occurrences. We can see that the bulk of the responses took around six minutes with an average for the entire distribution being the 7.5 minutes indicated by the average line in the diagram. But look at the variation! At times, responses took close to 18 minutes. At other times, less than two minutes.

The distribution presents us with a picture of the variation inherent in the process. The average is an interesting and important statistic. But what it hides is the variation, an equally if not more important characteristic of the process. This is true for all quality characteristics, whether measuring revenues, costs, fraction defective, warranty rates, waiting times, customer satisfaction, market share, stock prices, inventory levels, scrap rates, response times, cycle times, unit costs, vacancy rates, inflation, crime statistics, employee satisfaction, international oil prices or any other characteristic you could name. When we use the average or any other single number to represent performance, we are doing a disservice to the process or product being described. We are summarizing all the detail into a single statistic (the average) and, as a result, producing a simplistic picture of what is going on.

Pictures like the one in Exhibit 20: Picturing Variation: Fire Department Response Time are said to present the "*voice of the process,*" because they present all the data produced by the process rather than hiding behind some measure of average. In this case, the process is telling us that while average response time may be 7.5 minutes, the system is capable of responding anywhere between one and 18 minutes.

TYPES OF VARIATION

Variation doesn't happen by magic, it is caused by something. When the earth goes around the sun a little more slowly than 365.25 days, there are reasons including the particular gravitational attraction of the planets and their alignment relative to the earth and the sun. When profits are down, there are reasons – usually attributed to the particular gravitational attraction of the planets and their alignment to the earth and the sun. Just kidding! Seriously though, determining the cause of variation is critically important.

If profits are down, we need to know why. The answers will determine the nature of our response – redesigning the product, cutting costs, etc. If the timing of the earth's rotation is slowing, we need to know why. Is it just the alignment of the planets or are we about to crash and burn? To take action, to undertake any form of improvement requires an understanding of the causes behind the variation we are experiencing. There are four types of variation defined by the nature of the cause producing it.[29]

1. Common Cause Variation

The most common variation is called common cause variation. Not because it is the most common type of variation, but because it is common to the system itself. Common cause variation is part of the system. The earth goes around the sun with as much variation as it does because there are nine planets, all influencing the earth's behavior. In other words, the variation is a function of the design of the solar system. In the same way, sales levels may go up one year and down the next. This is not due to profound changes in the competitive environment, but simply because of the random fluctuations in myriad causes and conditions that make up the system we call the marketplace. It is the cumulative effect of all these small causes that define common cause variation.

---

29. Brian L. Joiner, Marie A. Gaudard, *Variation, Management and W. Edwards Deming* in The Practical Guide to Quality, Joiner Associates, 1990 p. 38

Such variation cannot be attributed or attached to any one particular cause; it is simply the effects of a great number of relatively small causes combined. Common cause variation is also referred to as system variation (because it is inherent in the system) and random variation (because, you guessed it, it is inherently random).

2. Special Cause Variation

Special cause variation is assignable to specific events or factors that sporadically arise. Unlike common cause variation, these causes are not part of the system design but are generally thought to exist outside of the system proper or represent significant changes to the system itself. Because of this, the source of the variation can be tracked down and assigned to a specific cause.

For example, sales levels go up and down from year to year in a random but relatively stable pattern. This is common cause variation. But now consider the introduction of a new product with new features and sold at a remarkably low price point by a competitor. Our sales levels decline sharply. This is a special or assignable cause of variation – we can attribute the decline to a specific event in the marketplace. Something has changed or occurred that is special or different than the system we are used to. Expressed another way, there is a new and significant cause or condition that has been added to the mix of causes and conditions that have historically described the system.

Of course, this description begs questions. "Just how big of a sales decline does big have to be before it becomes a special cause?" "How can you tell if it is a special cause or just a pretty big common cause?"

Good questions. It was Dr. Shewart[30] who first realized the importance of this question and the need for a tool to provide an operational definition of when the change is big enough to be called special cause. That tool is the control chart.

It is the control chart that provides the operational definition of special versus common cause in virtually every field of endeavour. To see just how broad the field of application is, just think of all the times where a change in some number or statistic is used to bolster an argument or position. Crime is up, sales are down, customer satisfaction is down, employee satisfaction is up, the earth is getting warmer and the stock market

is trending down. Yet without control chart analysis applied to these numbers, there is little that can be said about what these changes mean. It may be something special happening, or it may be simply random fluctuations.

3. Structural Variation

Structural variation is regular or systematic variation that is usually the result of either cyclical changes or longer-term trends. Most managers are familiar with structural variation although they may not call it that. For example, sales levels may go up and down from month to month or year to year, but the long-term behaviour sees sales rise over time. There is a trend pattern, perhaps the result of a growing marketplace or the impact of inflation or both. This trend is structural variation.

Structural variation also describes the seasonal variation in the sales of home building supplies that tend to rise in the spring and decline in the winter. Similarly, North Americans are aware of the dramatic increase in retail sales that occurs during the Christmas season. This, too, is an example of structural variation.

---

30. Dr. Walter S. Shewart was a mentor of Dr. Deming and the originator of the control chart – the fundamental statistical tool of quality control.

4. Tampering

Tampering is the variation caused by inappropriate management or employee action. Specifically, taking action on common cause variation as if it were special cause variation.

If there was a single characteristic most favored by organizations in describing managers, it would have to be having a bias for action. You know, a "take charge," "grab the bull by the horns," "pitter-patter lets get at'er," "ready-fire-aim" type of person. Yet this bias for action may be the single largest cause of variation and waste.

Consider the following example. Sales go down in one year because of random fluctuations in the marketplace – common cause variation. But our bias for action tells us we must do something. So we make adjustments, demand reports, modify product design and generally make a nuisance of ourselves. None of this has any effect except to make even more work for the people on the front lines, increasing the variation in the process and generally making conditions worse. In short, we are tampering. The next year, when sales rise, not due to any of our efforts but again due to random fluctuations, we congratulate ourselves for a job well done, despite the fact we have done nothing but diminish performance. Sales probably would have been better if we had just left well enough alone.

DIFFERENT VARIATION, DIFFERENT IMPROVEMENT APPROACHES

The type of variation present in the quality characteristic measured determines the improvement strategy.

▲ **With common cause variation,** the variation present is common to the system, a part of the system itself. Reducing the variation, then, requires changes in the design and construction of the system. Using any other approach will only make things worse (tampering). Changing the design of the system means using the tools designed specifically for this purpose, such as flowcharts, cause-and-effect diagrams, histograms, run charts and control charts, all of which we will be discussing later. These tools make it possible for us to better understand the system, identify root causes of variation (problems) and develop pragmatic modifications to the process or product that can best improve performance. In short, to change common cause variation you must change the system that produced it.

▲ **Where assignable causes of variation are present,** the improvement approach does not lie in the design of the system, but rather in figuring out what specific problems or circumstances are producing the assignable cause. For example, the introduction of a competitor's new product leading to a large decrease in sales needs to be acted upon. We need to solve the problem, to remove the special cause. We could do this by repositioning or perhaps redesigning our product or product offering.

Special causes are not always negative of course. One sales person may be significantly outselling his peers – another special cause of variation. We need to learn why. It may be due to the make-up of the sales territory, or it may be this individual has some special talents or characteristics our customers identify with. If the later is the case, we should find out what the secret is and find a way of providing it to our other sales people.

In short, assignable causes of variation need to be acted upon not by altering the system, but by tracking down the cause and examining precisely how it impacts performance.

▲ **Management action relative to structural variation is usually limited.** The very fact it is structural tells us that removing the variation will be difficult if not impossible. What we can change is how we manage the business in light of this variation. Every retailer in the nation stocks up on product in the weeks preceding Christmas, when the bulk of sales occur. Immediately after Christmas, inventory goes on sale to reduce costs in the thin months ahead. These are the responses to the reality of structural cyclical variation in the retail industry.

▲ **The approach to improvement in cases of tampering is easiest of all to understand, the hardest of all to accept.** If it ain't broke, don't fix it. Stop trying to make things better. Your actions, despite all appearances, are making things worse.

VARIATION AND VALUE

Customers have expectations of the products and services they purchase. How well products and services meet these expectations is fundamental to the determination of value. But if all process and systems produce variation in output, then there are times our process will satisfy

"Variation is evil . . ."

Jack Welch

Table 21: Types of Variation and Implications for Improvement

Type of Variation	Location of the Cause	Improvement Approach
Common Cause	Myriad small random causes inherent in the design and construction of the system.	Change the design and construction of the system using process analysis tools – a process redesign strategy.
Special Cause	An identifiable cause outside of the system design.	Track down the cause and take the appropriate action – a problem-solving strategy.
Structural Cause	A large underlying cause that is part of the system, usually making itself apparent as a trend or cyclical pattern.	Usually too large to attack directly, but the process can be redesigned and made more flexible to accommodate and minimize the impact of the variation.
Tampering	The inappropriate actions of management, usually treating a common cause variation as a special cause.	Stop what you are doing.

customer requirements and at other times they will not or, at least, they will produce greater or lesser degrees of satisfaction depending upon the circumstances. As we vary further from what the customer wants, the value to the customer declines as does satisfaction. As we get closer to the expectations of the customer, satisfaction and value rise.

It is obvious, then, that variation is an enemy of performance. The less of it we have, the more reliable our process or product and the greater the value. But at the same time, we can never eliminate variation. So an important question is how much variation can be tolerated from a value or economic perspective? How much variation is too much?

Specifications: The Traditional Approach to Managing Variation and Value

Traditional approaches to dealing with this question have defined specification limits, to establish boundaries that control the degree of acceptable variation. Outside the boundaries lies the realm of the unacceptable, where the level of variation is great enough that value is deemed to be zero. Within the boundaries, the level of variation is deemed to be acceptable. A graphic representation of this approach is presented in Exhibit 22: Specifications - The Traditional Approach to Variation.

Take room temperature as an example. Suppose we know the temperature at which most people feel comfortable is 70 degrees. In practice, despite keeping the thermostat at this level, room temperature will vary somewhat. If temperature swings slightly, say to 72 degrees, should we call a technician to adjust the temperature settings? Probably not. But at what level should we call for a technician to adjust the temperature settings? Seventy-three degrees, seventy-four?

Specifications help us manage the situation by establishing a rule of thumb that guides decision making. We might specify that room temperature should be between 64 and 76 degrees.

Exhibit 22: Specifications - The Traditional Approach to Variation

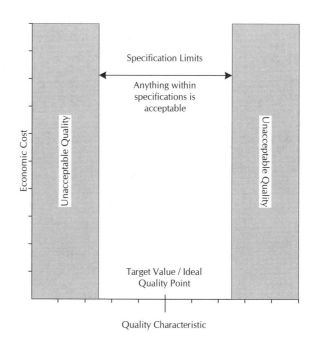

Anything within these specifications is deemed acceptable. Anything beyond, say 78 degrees, is unacceptable and a technician is dispatched to adjust the thermostat.

This approach accommodates variation by providing a range that defines the limits of action. Within the boundaries do nothing; outside the boundaries, fix it.

Unfortunately the traditional approach suffers from two problems. These are:

▲ **Its all or nothing nature.** Everything inside specifications is assumed to be perfect, everything outside is assumed to be useless. This assumption is rarely valid. A more accurate description of reality is that value declines as we move away from the target value.

▲ **The source of the specifications.** The traditional approach offers no real rational or logic for setting of specifications. Who should set them? Why set the upper specification at 78 degrees and not 77?

The Taguchi Approach to Understanding Variation and Value

The assumptions of the traditional approach to managing variation are indeed inconsistent with the way things actually work. Assuming 70 degrees represents the ideal or best all-round temperature for the comfort of employees, then people will become less comfortable as the temperature rises or drops from this ideal. At 75 degrees, for example, many people may be very uncomfortable despite the fact the temperature is still within specifications. This level of discomfort represents a decline in value.

Value can be lost, therefore, even when our products or processes are meeting specifications. In reality, economic loss is not an on-off function. Customer satisfaction doesn't suddenly become zero when the temperature hits 79, anymore than satisfaction is maximized when the temperature hits 75. Levels of dissatisfaction and, therefore, economic loss occur whenever there is any deviation from the ideal target.

A new approach to thinking about variation and value was first developed by Genichi Taguchi. He proposed that the relationship between variation and value was better represented by the curve in which value or customer satisfaction moves continuously and inversely with the degree of variation – the Taguchi Loss Function. See Exhibit 23: The Taguchi Loss Function (Quadratic). As the variation from the target value increases, we move up the curve and incur higher degrees of economic loss. As the variation decreases, we move down the curve and closer to the target value with its lower economic costs.

Exhibit 23: The Taguchi Loss Function (Quadratic)

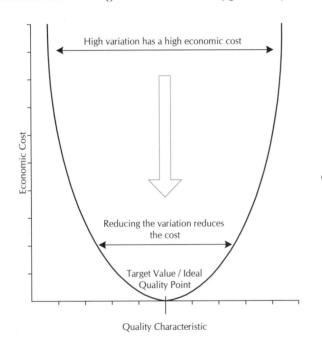

High variation has a high economic cost

Reducing the variation reduces the cost

Target Value / Ideal Quality Point

Economic Cost

Quality Characteristic

The bottom line here is that any variation from the target always produces an economic loss. Improving a system or process, therefore, means reducing variation. We say reduce rather than eliminate variation, because variation is a characteristic of all systems. It can never be completely eliminated. The best we can do is continuously improve, reducing variation and moving further and further down the curve.

World-Class Performance – Maximizing Value

The Taguchi Loss Function provides a far more realistic view of the relationship between variation and value. In essence, it defines what world-class quality or world-class performance really means: "***on target with minimum variance.***"[31] Any form of improvement comes down to moving the centre of the process closer to the target or objective and, secondly, reducing the variation around this target. This idea is represented graphically in Exhibit 24: Moving Toward World-Class Quality and Performance Levels. It is a way of saying performance measurement always has two dimensions – proximity to the target and the amount of variation.

VARIATION SUMMARY

Understanding variation is the key to understanding the performance of any process or system. Specifically:

---

31. Donald J. Wheeler, David S. Chambers, Understanding Statistical Process Control, SPC Press, Knoxville, Tennessee, 1992 p.146

Exhibit 24: Moving Toward World-Class Quality and Performance Levels

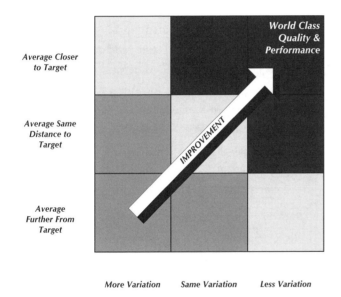

▲ The type of variation present in a process dictates the approach or strategy that should be taken toward improvement.

▲ Taking an improvement approach inconsistent with the cause of variation will invariably make things worse.

▲ Variation from the ideal represents a loss in economic value. This loss tends to increase exponentially as the distance from the ideal increases. Moreover, this variation and the economic loss which it represents are independent of existing specifications.

COMPLEXITY

Organizations, processes, inputs and outputs are all comprised of parts existing in both space and time. The number of parts and the amount of space or time serve to define how complex these things are. The complexity confronted by improvement teams will likely exist in one or more of four dimensions. These are:[32]

▲ **Number of components.** The greater the number of components or pieces involved, the greater the complexity. A process can have a great number of activities and tasks or

▲ Variation is present in every process. No matter what process is under examination, variation in the measured quality, quality characteristic or metric will always exist.

a few. A complex process adding the same value as a simple process will be less efficient than the simple process. A lot of the steps will not be adding value and should therefore be eliminated. Similarly, the more parts a product has the more complex it is. And the more complex, the poorer its performance or the more difficult (costly) its manufacture. Xerox improved the reliability of its copiers by redesigning them, making them simpler by reducing the number of parts involved. This not only increased reliability, it reduced manufacturing complexity and cost.

▲ **Volume/Space.** The greater the volume, the greater the level of complexity. It is one thing to manage a 500-square foot supply room, quite another to manage a 50,000-square foot warehouse. Sheer size presents its own problems including movement, transportation and storage. The bigger the volumes that must be managed, the greater the level of complexity and the higher the cost. Related to this is the concept of the space that a company must manage. Beyond warehouse size are the shear volumes of markets. A national or international company delivering products all over the world faces a profoundly more difficult and complex task than a company operating a corner grocery store.

▲ **Density**. Density is the relationship between the first two complexity dimensions, size and volume. The greater the number of components one tries to pack into a volume, the greater the density and, therefore, the greater the complexity. The modern desktop computer of today would not be possible without the ability of manufacturers to pack a lot of circuitry into a very small space – the microchip. The incredible amount of density makes the microchip a very complex product to manufacture.

▲ **Time.** The longer it takes to complete a transformation cycle – to make something, deliver a product or store something on a shelf – the greater the complexity. For every process, time is a critical component. It takes time to make something. The less time it takes, the more efficient the process, the more value added. The same holds true for inventory. While we recognize that the longer something is held on a shelf the greater the cost, we sometimes forget that the process used for keeping it on the shelf must become more complex as well. It simply takes more work to track something for a year than for a day.

---

32. Kenneth T. Delavigne, J. Daniel Robertson, Deming's Profound Changes; pp. 92-95; PTR Prentice Hall, Englewood Cliffs, NJ, 1994. The ideas presented here on complexity are derived from this excellent resource on Edwards Deming's management philosophy - recommended reading.

Complexity in all its dimensions may be considered the first enemy of performance. Our first approach to improving the performance, therefore, should be trying to make things as simple and straightforward as possible. Reduce the range of inputs and number of suppliers, remove steps in the process that do not add value, limit the amount of hierarchical interference in the process, design simpler products, reduce the size or volume of the process and so forth.

Unfortunately, processes and products tend to evolve in precisely the opposite direction; that is, they evolve towards greater levels of complexity rather than increased simplicity. The reasons for this are many. But they tend to be driven by the needs of the hierarchy to 'do something' for purposes of control, the need to accommodate variation and just our human tendency to meddle, usually in the form of tinkering and tampering.

Typical methods by which organizations add to the complexity of work are also identified by Delavigne and Robertson.[33] The descriptions have been adapted:

---

33. ibid

▲ **Nonlinear Flow of Work.** The more linear and straightforward the work flow, the lower the levels of complexity. However, all sorts of things crop up to destroy this linearity. First and foremost among these are the requirements of the hierarchy for information or approval. Each time a report must be filled out or the process flow must be halted to seek some new level of approval, complexity is added and performance declines. Many of these intrusions have arisen from a legitimate need to gather information required for effective management of the organization. Others have arisen out of curiosity and habit. Teams need to review where the intrusions are and confront the need – does the added complexity produce any real value added?

▲ **Working Around Missing Resources.** Complexity is added whenever organizations are forced to work to meet goals but where the resources required are not present. For example, when the delivery of certain parts is required for assembly of a product, but when delivery of these parts is uncertain, inventories are created as a buffer between the unreliable delivery time and the need to assemble the product. Partial completions or assemblies may also take place, further adding to the complexity of the manufacturing and inventory processes. Other types of resources that are frequently missing include time required to do the job, money or capital to purchase the right equipment, information about the real needs of customers. All these shortages increase complexity and reduce performance.

▲ **Tinkering and Tampering.** Traditional management emphasizes the need for action. When errors or mistakes happen, there is often overwhelming pressure to "do something." However, mistakes do happen and just doing something without considering the system as a whole is likely to add complexity without really addressing the underlying problem.

A good example concerns a mid-sized oil company seeking to improve a number of its administrative procedures. A process improvement team had just completed a process map of the expenditure claims process used by field personnel to recover their out-of-pocket expenses. The process was incredibly complex. When inquiries were made about the level of complexity, an interesting story emerged.

Years ago, the company had a simple employee expenditure reimbursement process. Field personnel would simply record their personnel expenditures on their time sheet and attach all receipts in excess of $20. It was simple, efficient

and most of all, it worked. However, in 1984, an employee was discovered to have abused the system to the tune of about $5,000. There were immediate demands to do something, to fix the problem. An investigation was soon launched with the aim of improving the level of control in the expenditure approval system. A new system was designed as a result, requiring all expenditures to have supporting receipts and approval signatures by field staff supervisors. A new part-time accounting position was introduced to implement 100 percent review of expenditure claims.

A year after the introduction of the new process, management decided to conduct a surprise audit 'to see how things were going.' The audit found lots of inaccurate paperwork, especially with supervisors failing to properly review expenditure claims of their field staff. (Some staff worked over 50 miles away from their supervisors). So more paper work was demanded to ensure the original paperwork was being completed properly. Within three years, the cost of controlling employee field expenses was greater than the level of reimbursable expenditures. Not only did the process increase cost with no value added, but it also affected employee morale, destroying the high trust levels between the company and its employees that had taken so long to build. And despite all this added effort, any employee could still figure a way around the new control system if desired. The new system added nothing and cost plenty.

▲ **Internal competition.** Many organizations encourage internal competition in the belief that this is the best way to improve performance. Individuals are pitted against individuals, departments against departments, usually under the guise of performance management system or some similar phrase. Promoting such competition as a means of encouraging performance really only increases the amount of complexity and waste occurring in the organization.

Consider this example. All the hospitals in a particular Canadian province were encouraged to compete with one another for budget allocation, based upon a sophisticated hospital efficiency measurement program. Some hospitals quickly found ways to play with the efficiency measures, 'admitting' the same patient over and over again in an attempt to build their performance numbers. Soon, hospital administrators were publicly accusing each other of cheating. Cooperation among hospitals, which had charac-terized this system earlier, effectively disappeared. The situation became sufficiently counter-productive that an inquiry was conducted to investigate the problems with the system. Soon after, the performance system was abolished and hospitals returned to the more substantive objectives of helping people (i.e. Customers!).

▲ **Ineffective Communication.** Complexity arises whenever employees, departments and other organizational units must guess as to what management wants. Fear of doing the wrong thing then takes the form of frequent checks and requests for management approval. Change proceeds hesitantly, time is wasted. And all this from a simple failure to communicate effectively.

Delavigne and Robertson cite some additional ways complexity is created within organizations. These include:

▲ **Building data collection, cost accounting and reporting systems where the purpose of the data is unclear and/ or where variation is ignored.** Organizations are often flooded with data, much of it of limited use. Often, the only criteria for collecting data is having the organizational or informational processing capability to do so.

▲ **Creating systems that are difficult to understand or apply in practice.** These include beautifully elegant processes that look great on paper but suffer from a reality gap. Real systems intended to do real work must live in the real world. That means the people working within the system must be able to comprehend it and apply it.

▲ **Working around problems instead of seeking out and correcting root causes.** Where no one has the ability to undertake change or improvement, no change or improvement will take place. Problems obvious to everyone remain problems for years.

▲ **Reorganizing frequently.** When all else fails, reorganize. Moving the boxes around will rarely improve the actual functioning of the processes that deliver value to the customer. Moreover, reorganizations tend to generate confusion and waste while everyone gets use to the new reporting relationships.

▲ **Making decisions on multiple levels.** When people are too frightened or inadequately trained to take responsibility, numerous signatures will sufficiently blur accountability so that soon no one is responsible for anything. The result is more steps, more forms, more time and a colossal waste.

THE GREATER THE COMPLEXITY, THE GREATER THE WASTE

The concept of waste is linked to the concepts of complexity and value. Anything that fails to add value is waste. Examples include: a process task that could be eliminated without harm, a useless approval step, product features the customer doesn't care about, rework or repair. These are all things containing little if any value and, therefore, all examples of waste. Wherever we find complexity, we find waste.

But identifying waste is not always easy. This is especially true when it comes to identifying process tasks that don't add value. Everything in a process, every step, task and activity, exists because someone thought it should. There are reasons for it being there, in theory at least. If we are lucky, the reasons behind the process step may have disappeared over time, and we can safely conclude the step or activity contributes nothing other than waste and eliminate it. More likely, however, some players in the organization will believe the step is still necessary. One person's waste may be another person's treasure – an absolute necessity. In such cases, improvement teams must carefully link customer requirements back to process functions, to justify removal or inclusion of the activity in the process.

One way to help identify waste is to use some basic lists of how other companies have classified different types of waste. Some examples are provided in Table 25: Types of Waste. There is duplication among the items listed and areas that have been overlooked. The intent is not to present a comprehensive model, but rather to provide some clues as to what to look for by examining how other organizations have looked at the problem. Use Table 25 to develop your own list and keep it handy.

Waste comes from the process we are using. To eliminate the waste, we must modify the process that produced it. This is critical and goes to the heart of applying systems thinking to management practice. Traditional managerial response is to blame the person or department most closely associated or nearest to the waste, as revealed by the organization chart. A large amount of wasted raw materials, for example, becomes the production department's problem. Pro-

duction management is encouraged to "do something" about the high level of waste in their area. Programs are introduced, employees are placed in improvement training, signs are posted with clever little sayings like "Watch Your Waste," and so on. None of these actions will have any impact if the levels of waste are simply part of the system design (common cause variation). The high levels of waste may be due to the quality of raw materials, scheduling problems or outdated infrastructure. To improve the situation, we must understand the root causes and change the process accordingly.

VARIATION AND COMPLEXITY

Variation and complexity are like two diseases, each feeding the other and destroying the health of our organization – destroying value. Variation produces complexity which in turn produces greater levels of variation. This increase in variation

Table 25: Types of Waste

Toyota's Seven Wastes	Cannon's Nine Wastes	
1. Waste of overproduction	1. Waste caused by work in process	
2. Waste of time on hand	2. Waste caused by defects	
3. Waste in transportation	3. Waste in equipment	
4. Waste of processing itself	4. Waste in expenses	
5. Waste of movement	5. Waste in indirect labor	
6. Waste of stock on hand	6. Waste in planning	
7. Waste of making defective products	7. Waste in human resources	
	8. Waste in operations	
	9. Waste in start-up	

Gerst's Top Ten Wastes	
1. Waste of labor	6. Waste of materials
2. Waste of production	7. Waste of time
3. Waste of space	8. Waste of movement
4. Waste of energy	9. Waste of customers
5. Waste caused by error	10. Waste of information/knowledge

produces greater levels of complexity and on it goes in an ever-expanding cycle of waste and lost value. This feedback loop is represented graphically in Exhibit 26: The Complexity – Variation Relationship.

So how does it work? Consider a customer service process. We know that no process is perfect and will produce variation. In this case, the variation takes the form of a service problem that leads to a customer complaint. Management decides that in being customer-responsive, it must find out who is to blame for the poor service. Some employee is singled out and punished, say in the form of a reprimand placed on the employee's file. Equally important, the process is changed in some way to ensure the error doesn't happen again – perhaps supervisory approval becomes a required part of the service. This is an added level of complexity.

Exhibit 26: The Complexity – Variation Relationship

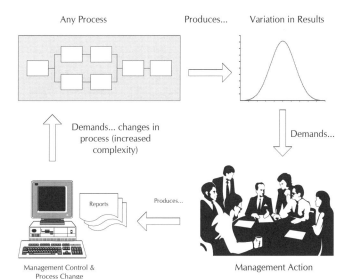

Any Process   Produces...   Variation in Results

Demands... changes in
process (increased
complexity)

Demands...

Reports   Produces...

Management Control &
Process Change

Management Action

Notice the positive feedback loop. A problem (common cause variation) has led to a new process step (increased complexity). This added step will increase the variation, response time will become slower for the types of transactions for which managerial approval is now required. This will lead to greater levels of complaints (variation) for which management will have to develop new process steps to control. And on it goes.

As process complexity increases, so does variation. This increase in variation produces a call to action – management is expected to do something. That something is usually some new report, form or procedure that represents a new layer of complexity that in turn will produce more variation.

The whole thing becomes a vicious cycle of declining productivity and performance. The very thing managers are taught to do (fix the problem) actually produces the opposite effect (increasing complexity and variation). No wonder so many employees constantly complain of fire-fighting. They are working as hard as they can creating new fires!

A principle task of process improvement is breaking this cycle. Teams must understand what is and is not contributing value and discard what is not. In short, the task is to continuously reduce complexity, making things as simple as possible for the task at hand.

CONTROL

Improvement means eliminating complexity and reducing variation. But this implies some level of control over the process – having the ability to affect some form of change. Control is what we need, but control comes at different levels.

CHAOS

The first of these levels is chaos. Have you ever experienced chaos in your organization? Many of us have. People racing all over the place, everyone in a hurry. There is no time to plan activities or coordinate tasks. Last-minute panics to complete a report, meet a filing date or similar requirements are commonplace. For many organizations this represents business as usual.

Chaos is defined as doing it differently every time. There is a complete lack of standardization. Every time a new task is presented or job is to be done, the organization reinvents the

Exhibit 27: Levels of Control

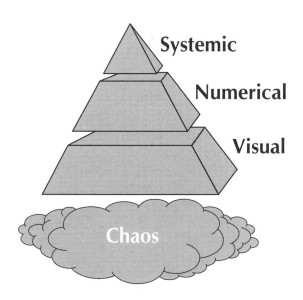

wheel, redefining requirements from scratch. The result is often panic, missed deadlines or overburdened staff. Chaos wastes time and resources, yet stems from nothing more than a lack of control – specifically a lack of standardization.

The excuses for such conditions are often self-serving – usually centering around pronouncements that there is no standardized approach to the job. *"Every job we do is unique, different." "You just can't standardize what we do!"* are the common refrains. It is a load of nonsense. All organizational units have missions or core purposes which they are expected to perform. Chaos represents nothing more than a failure in planning – in defining an organized approach (process) – for how this mission will be accomplished. Chaos isn't really a level of control, it is the embodiment of no control or no existing process.

VISUAL CONTROL

When confronted with chaos, you don't need detailed process analysis or measurement techniques because there is essentially no process to analyze or measure. At this stage we need to simply define a process, to standardize the way things happen. Don't spend time worrying if it is the right process. Just define something that makes sense on the surface and implement it. This is what we mean by visual control. It is a basic control level and requires nothing more than standardizing the way things are done.

But notice what happens when visual control is obtained – the complexity associated with doing it differently every time and the resulting variation are eliminated. While visual control may be simple, it yields significant improvement in process performance, especially when chaos is the order of the day.

We know we have obtained visual control because things look different. There are fewer people running around in panic as well as fewer panics. Things seem calmer, smoother. We have a sense that work is proceeding in an orderly way. This is the essence of visual control.

NUMERICAL CONTROL

While things look better with visual control, we still have made no efforts to measure or improve efficiency. We have only standardized the way things are done and the standardized approach may be very inefficient, ineffective or both. Numerical control consist of organizational attempts to improve performance through the use of measurements – numbers. Most of us are familiar with numerical control systems. Organizations are usually knee-deep in them. Budgeting systems, cost accounting systems, time sheets and punch cards, and performance appraisals are all forms of numerical controls.

Numerical controls are usually what organizations mean when they speak of control. It makes sense to know how much things cost, how much revenue we earned or how much cash we expended against budget. With numerical controls comes increased knowledge. We move from simple standardization and how things look, to measuring performance and economic benefit.

Numerical control is not the end-all and be-all of control, but it is, unfortunately, where many organizations have stopped. In such cases, improving control is seen as producing ever more elaborate and sophisticated numerical control systems (increased complexity). But numerical controls are limited in the knowledge they convey and the level of understanding they enable the organization to share. For example, knowing how much it costs to produce a product is important. But it is more important to know why it costs this much to produce, how competitive this cost is and how much the cost varies between production runs, factories and alternative systems of production. Numerical controls cannot answer these questions, no matter how many measures are taken or the size and sophistication of whatever enterprise-wide software is installed.

To answer these performance questions and provide the knowledge to see significant improvement take place, a different type of control is required – specifically, statistical or systemic control.

SYSTEMIC (STATISTICAL) CONTROL

Systemic or statistical control is the highest level of control we can have over any system or process. Systemic control is about understanding the physical reality of the systems or process we wish to improve, to a point where we can make reasonable predictions about how the process will behave in the future or if specific changes are made. It is a sophisticated understanding gained through empirical data, using scientific methods to analyze this data and making conclusions about how best to improve the performance of the process or system. Specifically, systemic control seeks:

▲ **To increase knowledge.** Statistical control allows us to understand the physical capabilities or limitations of the processes currently in use.

▲ **To predict.** By achieving statistical control we achieve predictability. We know what the process will do before it does it, and can track process performance to identify potential problems before they create significant loss to the organization.

▲ **To improve.** With our understanding and ability to predict, we can undertake initiatives to improve process performance with full knowledge of the likely impacts.

When we think of control, especially statistical control, words like knowledge, prediction and improvement rarely come to mind. But this is what statistical control really means. Consider a metaphor – a typical baseball game. The pitcher throws the ball to the catcher across home plate. Behind the catcher, the umpire calls each pitch as a ball or a strike. In the midst of it all is the batter, ready to pounce on a pitching error. In this metaphor, which of the actors represents the control system?

From the traditional management perspective, it would seem the umpire represents the control system. After all, the umpire is calling the balls and strikes in much the same way the budget system "calls" over- and under-project variances. The umpire even has a small counting device analogous to a computer system to keep a record of the count.

But in the real world, baseball fans knows better. If we ask, "Where is the control?" any baseball fan will tell you it lies in

the arm, in the skill and ability, of the pitcher. The catcher may call for a certain pitch, but only the pitcher can deliver it. Control in this sense exists in the ability to influence performance (throw a good pitch) **before** the fact. That ability rests solely with the pitcher. Indeed, the ability of the pitcher to throw what is called for, accurately and consistently, is the measure of pitcher performance.

The umpire, in contrast, can only make his calls **after** the fact.[34] This distinction between measuring after the fact, and influencing before the fact, is really what distinguishes numerical versus systemic control.

---

34. If you ever have any doubt as to where the *real* control lies, compare the average wages for major league umpires and pitchers.

When we speak of systemic control, we are speaking of our ability to influence or predict the performance of a process or system. That ability to predict, to know in advance of the fact, is what control is really all about. If you do not know what will happen in advance, you have only limited knowledge and limited control, regardless of how much data your measurement system has produced.

Equally important, with statistical control you can manage the changes and make those that have the greatest probability of yielding improvement. This is productive change born of knowledge and fact, as opposed to *any* change guided by guesswork, hunches and prejudice (all too commonly referred to as experience). Providing that knowledge is the purpose of statistical or systemic control.

A TYPICAL CONTROL SYSTEM

Regardless of the type of control, organizations need a system to apply it. A basic control system is presented in Exhibit 28: Performance Control System. These components of the control system are:

▲ **Object to be measured.** It may be an output of some process or the process itself. It may be a customer attitude, the

Exhibit 28: Performance Control System

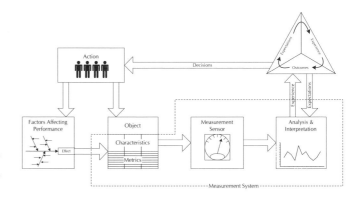

quality of some material to be used or one of our suppliers. Whatever it is, the first rule of any control system is that there must be some object we wish to control in some way.

▲ **Characteristics and metrics.** These are the things that describe the object and define what the control system will measure. In defining what will be measured, priorities must be set. For any real-world object there is virtually an unlimited number of potential metrics. Organizations need to specify what is important to measure for purposes of control and improvement.

▲ **Sensor.** The sensor is the device that creates data for each metric. There are many types of sensors. For example, an individual providing visual inspection of finishing blemishes on a manufactured product is acting as a sensor. Sensors may also be mechanical, electro-mechanical, electronic, a paper-based questionnaire or a single observation made by an individual. Whatever their design, their function is the same – generate data for each metric.

▲ **Analysis and interpretation.** This component organizes and summarizes the data generated by the sensor in a way that provides useful information to decision makers. The information generated represents the organizational experience with the object. This experience is compared to the expectations held for the object by the organization or decision maker.

▲ **Owner or decision maker.** It is the job of the owner or decision maker to compare performance (experience) with expectations and make decisions (outcomes) about the nature of improvement actions to be undertaken.

▲ **Action.** The purpose of a control system goes beyond measurement, it requires action to be taken based upon the decisions made by the owner or decision maker. In short, we are supposed to *do* something. The focus of this action may be on the object itself and/or the cause-and-effect system that produced the object. Either way, the intent will be to make some improvement to performance levels.

These components are required of any control system regardless of scope or application. For example, managing return on investment (ROI) performance of a large organization requires a clear operational definition of the metric (ROI), a sensor for gathering the data (accounting system), as well as a method of interpretation. It also requires an owner to understand this information, compare it with expectations and make decisions based in part upon these results.

The system used by a process operator to control product quality is really no different than that used by the corporation to manage ROI. The operator uses a sensor to track some metric and then makes decisions concerning process adjustments based on a comparison of expected and actual performance levels. Regardless of scale, then, all control systems require basic components identified in Exhibit 28.

Good and Bad Control Systems

Control and control systems exist at all levels of the organization in every department, function and division. They represent the way in which organizations gather information about the real world and interpret this data in order to draw conclusions and form a basis for action.

Like all systems, they will be of differing quality. Some will be accurate and reliable, providing a sound foundation for knowledge building and improvement. Others will be just the opposite, yielding poor information and ultimately destroying competitiveness and performance levels. An organization is only as good as the decisions it makes, and the decisions it makes will only be as good as the quality of information on which those decisions are based (garbage in - garbage out).

Table 29: Characteristics of Good and Bad Control Systems, provides a way to distinguish between the two types of control systems.

IMPROVING PERFORMANCE

Sooner or later, organizations and teams must face the task of making improvements. Three concepts of improvement are explored here. These are:

▲ **The Dimensions of Improvement.** Improvement to process or product will take place along one or more of three "dimensions." Teams need to know along which dimension improvement is required and have some of the tools and techniques to achieve this.

▲ **Organizational Improvement Strategies.** Organizations have different improvement strategies open to them. Different strategies are required for different circumstances and objectives of the improvement.

▲ **Methods and Models of Improvement.** Teams need to have a method of improving things. Improvement itself is a process. Agreeing on what this process should look like or how things will be done is a primary task of any team starting an improvement project.

Table 29: Characteristics of Good and Bad Control Systems

Control System Component	Bad Control Systems	Good Control Systems
Object to be Measured	Selecting objects to measure is haphazard, and no explicit consideration of sampling or its impact upon the measurements obtained is made.	The objects to be measured, and the means of selecting them, are spelled out, understood and rational given the nature of the metric.
Characteristics and Metrics	What is measured changes over time or from place to place. There is no organizational agreement as to what is important or how important it is.	What is measured is consistent over time and location. There is organizational consensus on what is important to measure and why.
Sensor	Reliability and accuracy of the sensor are not tested and few within the organization trust the data.	Constantly checked for accuracy and reliability. The organization has confidence in the numbers it produces.
Analysis and Interpretation	Long lists of numbers and data are produced. No graphical or statistical analysis is conducted. No identification of common or special cause variation. No one seems to know what the numbers mean, results are only fuel for further arguments and expression of opinions.	Long numerical reports are rare. Graphical analysis of data (using the standard data analysis tools) are commonplace. Control charts are used to track performance and provide signals of special cause.
Owner / Decision Maker	No clear owner of the data or information produced. Worse, there is no apparent connection between the data and the decisions or actions that are to be taken.	Every chart has an owner. Clear and explicit linkages between what is measured, and the decisions or actions that need to be taken, are made.
Action	Guidelines or standards for action are unclear. Decisions and actions do not take the types of variation into account.	Guidelines or standards for action are specified in advance. Improvement actions are based upon the nature of variation.

DIMENSIONS OF IMPROVEMENT

Improvement typically takes place along three dimensions. These are:

▲ **Efficiency,** the ability to convert inputs into outputs. (Are we doing things right?)

▲ **Effectiveness,** the degree to which the outputs meet the needs of customers and stakeholders. (Are we doing the right things?)

▲ **Adaptability/Flexibility,** the degree to which the process can change to suit required changes in input or output. (How easily can we change, can we improve?)

Any successful strategy for improvement will improve performance along one or more of these dimensions.

IMPROVING EFFICIENCY

Improving efficiency is what most people think of when it comes to improving process and organizational performance. Efficiency focuses on how well we do whatever it is we are doing, not whether we are doing the right things.

Exhibit 30: Improving Efficiency

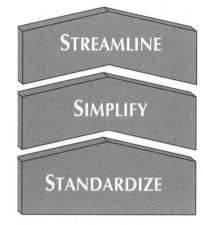

STREAMLINE
CYCLE TIME REDUCTION
VARIATION REDUCTION
INVENTORY & LOT SIZE REDUCTION
VALUE ANALYSIS OF PROCESS STEPS

SIMPLIFY
BUREAUCRACY BUSTING
DUPLICATION ELIMINATION
WORK FLOW SIMPLIFICATION
ERROR PROOFING

STANDARDIZE
PROCESS SELECTION & DEFINITION
SUPPLIER PARTNERSHIPS
DOCUMENTATION
PROCESS DEPICTION
STAFF TRAINING

There are three basic steps or levels of performance we can pursue when redesigning processes for improvement. We can:

▲ **Standardize the Process,** which means attempting to get the process under control by having it work the same way every time. When the same process functions differently from one time to the next, we have chaos. Nothing happens the same way twice. We face a barrage of meetings and phone calls from people trying to find out what is happening. Customer complaints are constant. Materials and other process inputs seem to constantly arrive at the wrong time or at the wrong place.

Standardization essentially creates a process where one did not previously exist in any meaningful way. We are not after great performance at this point. We are only trying to get things functioning the same way so we have a process we can improve.

Standardization does not usually require any real analysis of the process. After all, with things being handled differently each time around, we don't really have a process to analyze and improve. Rather, standardization may involve nothing more than a team or manager saying from now on and until further notice, this is the way we will do things. Block diagrams or flowcharts may be used after this decision is made to document the agreed-upon and standardized way of doing things.

In standardizing, however, we have achieved something. Not only does a well-defined process exist as a result, but the obvious special or assignable causes of variation within the process are removed which, in turn, increases value.

▲ **Simplify the Process,** which means attempting to remove complexity. This includes removing the hierarchical requirements that often constrain or impede process functioning. Processes may be awash in needless steps and forms, appeals to higher levels for approval and needless tasks that are done only because they always have been done. Simplification means breaking the bureaucratic chain and eliminating non-value adding steps that serve only to waste time, money and effort.

Simplification usually involves making use of block diagrams and flowcharts to identify non-value adding steps, time-consuming feedback loops, approvals and similar sources of waste. These tools are used as a means of analysis, whereas with standardization they were used simply as a source of documentation.

▲ **Streamlining the process,** which involves more sophisticated efficiency techniques. They include shortening the cycle time for the overall process or the sub-processes that support it, reducing inventories or production lot size requirements, and reducing the variation inherent in the system. Streamlining tends to make use of the various statistical tools such as Pareto charts, histograms, run and control charts, box and whisker plots and scatter diagrams (more about these later). The use of these tools to better understand the process, its operating characteristics and parameters, and the various sources or causes of variation, is at heart of statistical process control techniques.

Unfortunately, many process improvement efforts fail to get to the all-important step of streamlining and fall short of significant gains for this reason. Standardization is essential, but it is really nothing more than doing things the same way – regardless of how good this way may be. Simplification seeks to improve the process by removing complexity, but tends to address those things we can see easily or are obvious from analysis of flowcharts and other process-mapping tools. Streamlining, however, is the means by which improvement teams can move beyond the

plateau so often created when teams have standardized and simplified the process.

There is an order to the strategies outlined. Standardizing the process comes first. As a general rule, no process improvement should be initiated until a process has been standardized because until then there is no well-defined process to analyze or improve. Next comes simplification. With a standardized process as a foundation, simplification examines the components of the process (the now-defined activities, tasks, decisions, etc.) for their ability to add value. Those that do not are removed from the process, leaving only value-adding activity behind. Lastly, the functioning of these remaining value-adding steps are improved through streamlining.

IMPROVING EFFECTIVENESS

Effectiveness refers to the ability of the product or service produced by a process to meet the customer or stakeholder's expectations. Does it have the features the customer wanted, was it delivered on time and so forth. The organization also has expectations. Cost, profit, market share and growth may all be organizational expectations of the processes at work within the

organization. Additionally, our organization or the process also has expectations of the inputs received from suppliers.

As was the case with efficiency, then, we have three means of increasing effectiveness depending upon whose expectations we are trying to meet. They are:

▲ **Customer Fit,** which is redesigning the product, service or process to better meet the requirements and expectations of the customer. Doing so is a principle source of competitive advantage for any organization. In fact, failing here means failing, period.

Planning approaches such as quality function deployment (see Deployment Tools in Chapter 11) can be used to link the customer requirements with the design specifications of the product or service being delivered, and with the process that delivers it. It embeds the "voice of the customer" into the process itself. Statistical tools can be used to assess the ability of the process producing the product to meet defined customer requirements. The Kano model can be used here to link performance characteristics with different types of perceived value. And the Taguchi loss function can be used to assess the economic impact of different levels and types of variation.

▲ **Corporate Fit,** which means seeking to improve the effectiveness of the process relative to purpose or mission of the organization. Doing so is the process of organizational alignment. Processes in organizations exist because the organization needs to have the work done. Any moderate-sized organization will have literally hundreds of processes, sub-processes and tasks being conducted every day. Alignment or corporate fit is about ensuring these processes support one another and that, when taken together, they all work to support the overall aims or purposes of the organization.

Setting the vision and mission for the process, and ensuring they align with corporate goals and objectives, improves corporate effectiveness and fit. Policy deployment is a common approach to help ensure this alignment between different functioning components of the organization.

▲ **Cost or Value-Added Alignment,** which means examining the specific functions of each component of a product, service or process and determining the most economical way of providing that function. Cost or value analysis is concerned with the components or inputs to a process.

Basically, value analysis asks a series of four fundamental questions:

▶ What are the specific functions of a particular component of the product or process? Are they necessary? What are the alternatives to delivering this function?

▶ How does this component contribute to value added? What precisely does it provide to the customer? Why does the customer want this?

▶ What are the inputs used by this function or component? Are there alternatives? Can we standardize any parts of the product or process design to reduce input variation?

▶ Where is the waste in what we are doing now? How can this be reduced? Can changes in the process or product design influence the amount of waste produced or reduce the value or number of inputs?

As with strategies to improve efficiency, there is an order to the effectiveness strategies. Generally speaking, improving effectiveness starts with the customer fit. We start with the customer because it is the customer that defines value for the business. This usually involves targeting specific customer segments,

Exhibit 31: Improving Effectiveness

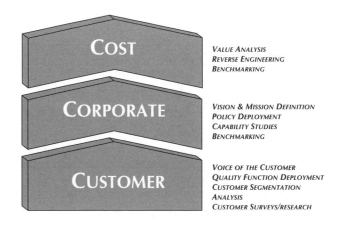

COST — *VALUE ANALYSIS / REVERSE ENGINEERING / BENCHMARKING*

CORPORATE — *VISION & MISSION DEFINITION / POLICY DEPLOYMENT / CAPABILITY STUDIES / BENCHMARKING*

CUSTOMER — *VOICE OF THE CUSTOMER / QUALITY FUNCTION DEPLOYMENT / CUSTOMER SEGMENTATION ANALYSIS / CUSTOMER SURVEYS/RESEARCH*

defining the set of customer requirements for each segment, and redesigning process and product to better align them with these requirements or expectations.

Next is corporate alignment or fit. With customer expectations being met at a process or product level, improvement teams can redesign to ensure the various processes at work align with one another and with the overall mission and purpose of the organization. The intent is to have process activities that reinforce each other rather than work in opposition.

But a word of caution here. Organizations too often examine corporate fit solely from the view of profitability. They may choose to eliminate a process or a product because it costs too much. This means the real problem is the efficiency of the process, not effectiveness. Effectiveness is concerned with what we are doing and the degree of alignment; efficiency is concerned with profitability.

Cost alignment comes last. This is because cost alignment is about the least costly way to provide certain functions. However, it is the customer and corporate fit that determines which functions must be delivered. The functions must be defined first, and the economics or cost effectiveness of providing them determined second.

IMPROVING ADAPTABILITY & FLEXIBILITY

Effectiveness and efficiency characteristics both assume, to some degree, that the world stands still while we improve or change our processes. Sometimes change happens the other way – the world changes and our processes are compelled to respond. A rise in the world price for oil produces increased demand for fuel-efficient cars. Collapse of the former Soviet Union shifts the Pentagon's demand for strategic weapons to more tactical systems. Changes in the world price of lumber tilts the balance of American home builders in favor of those using steel-frame versus wood-frame construction. All of these changes are, for the most part, beyond the control of the organizations affected. But the organization must respond to these kinds of change nevertheless.

A key to success, therefore, is the degree to which the process can effectively respond to or accommodate change. There are three basic ways to improve process response to change. They are:

▲ **Resiliency,** which means absorbing the impact of changes in demand volume. Here, the process is able to adapt to changes in the levels of demand as opposed to changes in what is demanded (responsive processes). Basically, resilient processes are capable of handling a wide variation in demand while maintaining performance levels. When demand increases, the process can pick it up and respond quickly. When it falls off, the process responds accordingly and operates efficiently despite the decline in throughput. Keeping inventories small or working on lot reduction are two methods of increasing resilience. Having flexible manufacturing process is another.

▲ **Responsiveness,** which means processes that change with changing customer requirements. These changes are not so much changes in levels of demand as they are changes in what is demanded. Responsive processes are sensitive to these changes in demand.

Often, such processes respond to the changing needs of the market or of the corporation seemingly "by themselves." Of course, nothing happens by itself. Strategies such as decentralizing decision making, empowering teams and employees, and establishing self-managing or directed teams all help improve the responsiveness of a process. Such strategies allow those most familiar and experienced with the process to make the changes required.

▲ **Robustness,** which means the capability of adapting to unanticipated change that goes beyond demand parameters or volumes. Such processes can undergo significant redesign with minimal retooling or cycle time. Modularized process design is a strategy commonly employed to make processes more robust. For example, the introduction of a new technology can be accommodated simply by replacing the modules affected by the technology – no other components of the process need be affected. Most soft-

Exhibit 32: Improving Flexibility

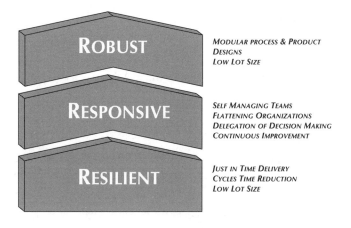

ROBUST — *MODULAR PROCESS & PRODUCT DESIGNS / LOW LOT SIZE*

RESPONSIVE — *SELF MANAGING TEAMS / FLATTENING ORGANIZATIONS / DELEGATION OF DECISION MAKING / CONTINUOUS IMPROVEMENT*

RESILIENT — *JUST IN TIME DELIVERY / CYCLES TIME REDUCTION / LOW LOT SIZE*

ware design today uses modularization to ease future developments and enhancements.

When we seek improvement, we seek to change our efficiency, effectiveness and/or our flexibility.

ORGANIZATIONAL IMPROVEMENT STRATEGIES

The strategies of process improvement differ in their scale, scope and timing. Organizations can adopt three basic strategies to improve business or production processes. They are:

▲ **Refining**, usually smaller-scale efforts aimed at improving the existing system within a single functional area or department.

▲ **Redesigning,** involving the reworking and reconfiguration of product or process, from a large- and cross-functional scale to moderately sized improvement efforts.

▲ **Re-engineering,** involving large-scale and usually cross-functional reworking of processes or product from the ground up.

REFINING

Process refinement is about making incremental improvement to processes that exist within a single department or function. The degree of interdepartmental impact of the process is seen as low, although the improvement effort must be careful to define the next process as the customer and to ensure customer requirements are met. While the intent of gaining incremental improvements to the process may seem small to the overall organization, they may be very large to the people working with that same process on a day-to-day basis.

The importance of process refinement should not be underestimated. The more dramatic approaches to process improvement all require an ongoing process of refinement. Rarely does a re-engineering effort, for example, produce a smoothly functioning process right out of the gate. While the change may be dramatic, such re-engineered processes still require ongoing refinement by those involved to actually achieve the benefits intended. For this reason, organizations should know how to refine processes on an ongoing basis before attempting more dramatic improvements, such as re-engineering.

Refinement is usually carried on by intact teams. These are simply the teams comprising all members of the functional unit or department. Because the processes are being improved on an ongoing basis, an intact team is rarely instructed by senior management to accomplish some task. Rather, the team exists for as long as the department does; ongoing improvement is seen as part of the job.

Table 33: Three Improvement Strategies

Nature of Improvement	*Discontinuous/Radical*		*Continuous/Evolutionary*
Improvement Strategy	**Re-Engineering**	**Redesigning**	**Refining**
Objective	Massive reconfiguration of existing system, usually reliant on technology	Understanding and resolution of process problems regardless of scale or technology	Incremental improvement within organizational units
Features	High-level project team, usually cross-functional	Cross-functional, multi-level project team	Single-function, single-level work group
Focus	How best to configure a new system using technology to maximize performance	Process performance at all three strategic levels: efficiency, effectiveness and flexibility	Workplace and process problems selected autonomously with guidance from management
Period of Activity	Disbanded after completion of the project	Disbanded after completion of project and once control established	Continuous
Formation	Directed by senior management	Directed by senior management	Voluntary
Assumptions	Technology critical to adding value Rapid and massive change is required	Enough time to study the problem Important to understand how things work now before making changes	Incremental change is sufficient Limited cross-functional impacts
Employee Involvement	Moderate to low	Moderate to high	High
Organization	Re-Engineering Team	Improvement Team	Improvement Circle or Intact Team

REDESIGNING

Redesign strategies tackle larger processes or process problems, usually focusing on those processes that have cross-functional impact. They flow across departmental, functional or divisional lines. The scope of the change or improvement effort is therefore greater than that of refinement strategies. This degree of difference can be minor or significant.

Redesign team composition usually reflects the various departments and operating levels affected. It is not unusual to have redesign teams with members from various levels of the organization, as well as all the departments that affect, or are affected by, the process under study. Also, unlike refinement teams, these cross-functional teams are disbanded once the issue has been resolved and the redesigned process is functioning as intended.

RE-ENGINEERING

Re-engineering has become a popular buzzword in management circles. Definitions of what is meant by re-engineering vary. We use the term to mean a massive redesign of a large cross-functional process, which usually takes advantage of technology to gain a step-change improvement in overall process performance. This is distinct from the "high risk," "bet-the-company," "start-from-scratch" definitions that have been used in some management circles. Such definitions imply that knowledge of the existing process is not important because the process will be replaced by a "re-engineered" process anyway. This "improvement from ignorance" argument seems more designed to sell consulting services than make any contribution to process improvement.

Used here, the term re-engineering is based upon the same basic model of process improvement as refinement or redesign. What differs are the time scales, scope and degree of technology needed to make improvements to the degree required. But a caution is warranted. People have a tendency to exaggerate the degree of change required or the urgency of improvement. Re-engineering should only be used when there is no doubt about the urgency of change. Where any doubt exists, there is no substitute for sitting down and spending a little extra time to fully study and understand a process before making dramatic changes. There is no substitute for knowledge.

METHODS & MODELS OF IMPROVEMENT

Improvement itself is a process, a process of acquiring knowledge we call learning. The ability of an organization to learn will determine its ability to improve performance. Organizations with learning disabilities will be forced to make improvements by guesswork, a hit-and-miss proposition. Those that learn, however, will continuously enhance their ability to improve. Failures become fewer and successful improvement efforts become the norm.

Generating knowledge allows the organization to make improvements, either through incremental or innovative change. The focus may be the product produced or the process that's producing the product. Improvement, either incremental or innovative, ultimately creates competitive advantage. The greater the rate of improvement, the greater the advantage.

LEVELS OF ORGANIZATIONAL LEARNING

Different organizations display various levels of ability to learn and to apply knowledge. This will be reflected in differing lev-

Exhibit 34: From Learning to Competitive Advantage

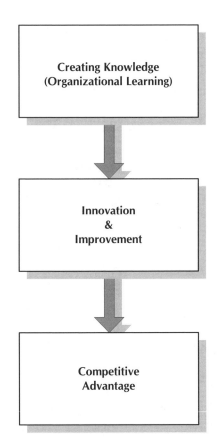

els of innovation and improvement and, ultimately, competitive position.

Delavigne and Robertson[35] have identified six levels of learning displayed by organizations. I have adapted these somewhat but the basic concept is theirs.

1. **Ignoring Problems.** Organizations are adept at convincing themselves that existing problems are being dealt with or are of such insignificance that they require little or no effort at solution. Some familiar refrains are: "We have always had that problem in production and always will." "There is nothing you can do about it." "Don't worry, it will get handled."

2. **Manipulating the Symbols of Solution.** Organizations fully admit they have some problem but, rather than deal with causes, they address symbols. Safety issues are infamous in this regard. A safety concern exists at a plant? Put up posters telling everyone to be safe. There are other examples. When profits take a dip, organizations often jump on the re-organization bandwagon, frantically rearranging the little boxes on the organization chart. Nothing of substance changes but it makes people feel better that at least "we're doing something."

3. **Solving Problems.** This is the first level at which some real organizational learning takes place. Problems are recognized and addressed. However, the problem-solving approach is loose and undisciplined. The organization is focused on the effects of the problem per se rather than the root causes. Fixes are made, but the problem typically resurfaces elsewhere in a different guise.

4. **Defining Problems.** The focus has now shifted away from the problem itself to the method by which such problems are addressed. A scientific problem-solving model is used, with extensive effort to gather and interpret data as a key to understanding opportunities for improvement. Problems are understood to be systemic/process problems and the solutions are structured accordingly, including identification of root (systemic) causes.

5. **Questioning and Organizing Problems.** The difference here is that the organization questions and orders problems in a broad organizational context that allows for clear pri-

35. Kenneth J. Delavigne, J. Daniel Robertson, Deming's Profound Changes, PTR Prentice Hall, Englewood Cliffs, NJ, 1994. pp. 61-80

Table 35: Levels of Organizational Learning

Learning Phase	Level of Learning Maturity	Description
1. Ignoring Problems	No Learning	Ignoring problems in the hope they will go away or denying that problems exist.
2. Manipulating the Symbols of Solution	No Learning	Acceptance of the problem but without applying any means of resolution. Organization reorganizes, adopts some latest fad and goes on a training "rampage," all in an effort to make it look like something is being done.
3. Solving Problems	Basic Learning Intermediate Step	Direct and narrowly focused efforts are made to solve problems as they arise. Localized thinking is usually applied.
4. Defining Problems	Learning (Passive)	Scientific method applied to problem solving, providing a clear definition of the problem within a systems context. Extensive use of data and analysis of process. Priority setting is still loose – efforts are directed at whatever is causing the biggest concern right now.
5. Questioning and Organizing Problems	Learning (Adaptive)	Intentional exploitation of the gaps or contradictions between organizational theories in use and observed phenomena in the real world. Improvement priorities are clear and are addressed in an organized fashion.
6. Active Experimentation	Learning (Active)	Organizations go beyond observing inconsistencies and try to create them so the knowledge gained from resolving them can be applied for purposes of improvement.

ority setting. A problem that arises may not be large on its own but, when examined against the set of organizational problems and issues, it may be one dimension of a much larger organizational dilemma. In short, the organization examines problems, places them in context and then establishes clear priorities for improvement.

6. **Active Experimentation.** Here, organizations literally try to create problems. Specifically, they conduct experiments on existing processes to find areas of weakness and opportunities for improvement. This is continuous improvement embedded in organizational culture. Processes are examined and improved even when there are no signs of problems or obstacles to overcome.

The higher the level of learning, the faster and more effective organizational improvement efforts become, and the more embedded in the culture of the organization.

ORGANIZATIONAL LEARNING METHOD

So how to improve? How to develop a learning process, a knowledge-generating process? The fundamental method is called the scientific method. Traditionally, the scientific method is seen as having three parts: hypothesis, experiment and observation.

The hypothesis represents what it is we believe to be true -- some idea, theory or belief. To test our theory we conduct an experiment. From this experiment we observe or study the results. These results may or may not confirm our theory. If

Exhibit 36: The Scientific Method

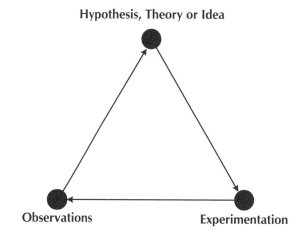

they do not, we must abandon our theory or at least modify it. If the data do confirm our ideas, we have found a new and useful model that can help us explain and predict real-world behavior.

It doesn't really matter where you start in the process. It may start with an observation, say an apple falling from a tree. From this observation a theory may be developed, in this case the theory of gravity, and a great number of experiments are per-

---

formed to see if the theory holds up. Or the process may start with an experiment that produces some strange observations. This may lead to the development of an entirely new theory or the modification of an existing one.

Regardless of where we start, we always move in the same direction. The order in which these events occur is important even if the starting point is not. It is the direction that makes the data the "reality test" of ideas. Data confirm or deny theory; theory does not confirm or deny data.

The scientific method is very much a process of passing judgment on our ideas. This can be an uncomfortable process. None of us like to have our ideas 'judged' or 'evaluated.' Fewer still like to admit to being wrong. At times, we may become so married to our ideas or our beliefs we cannot give them up. This is as true for organizations as it is for individuals. Improvement demands, however, that we test our ideas in the real world, accepting the often cold judgment of reality.

THE PDSA (PDCA) CYCLE

The world of organizations is a tougher place than the world of pure science. Science can be content with adding knowledge;

organizations, however, must apply it. Competitive advantage doesn't come just from knowing, but also from action. Dr. Shewart and Dr. Deming realized this close to half a century ago. They defined the Plan, Do, Check, Act (PDCA) Cycle as a learning model that incorporated management action (improvement) as part of its design. Dr. Deming later renamed it the PDSA cycle, replacing 'check' with 'study' to better reflect the intent of the model.

Exhibit 37: The PDSA Cycle

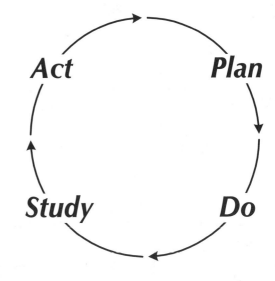

The four components of the model are:

▲ **Planning.** This involves identifying the processes to be improved, the key problems to be resolved and the objectives or basic goals we are seeking to achieve. This step corresponds to the hypothesis stage of the scientific method, except we are not so much creating a formal hypothesis as putting forward our ideas. We might believe a new advertising program is better than the old one or that a new machine will increase process performance. From this idea, we must plan how we intend to determine whether the idea has merit.

▲ **Doing.** This is the step where we actually try out the idea, preferably on a small scale. In other words, we conduct an experiment to see whether our improvement ideas have merit. Unlike the world of pure science, however, we will rarely have the opportunity to conduct controlled experiments. Companies, after all, can not usually afford to shut down operations to perform such experiments. Usually, they have to deal with the very messy world of reality (as opposed to the somewhat "cleaner," more controlled environment of the laboratory) and use analytical tools to help make their way through the confusion.

▲ **Studying.** This involves analyzing and studying the results of the experiment. What did we learn? Can it be applied to the bigger system under study? If so, how? Observations arising from our experiments must be studied. Success gives us ideas to build upon, but so does failure. Too often, organizations try out some new idea only to have things go wrong and then move on to some different idea. This is a waste of information. Studying means understanding "why," and using this understanding to add to our level of knowledge – knowledge that can be applied elsewhere.

▲ **Acting**. This is the new step added by Shewart and Deming to the scientific method. Management must not only learn but it must take action, applying what it knows to make things better. Remember, as much learning can come from failure as from success. Even when a new idea flops, there may be knowledge that can be adapted to existing processes or product designs to yield improvement.

As a learning and improvement model, the PDSA Cycle is designed to take us along an uphill path, from ignorance to knowledge.

As we gain knowledge or understanding, it becomes possible to improve our control of the process or system and therefore

Exhibit 38: PDSA – From Ignorance to Knowledge

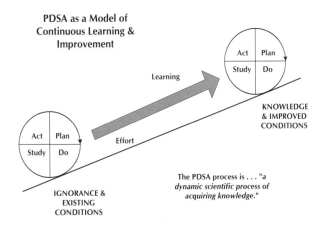

improve overall process or organizational performance. The faster we drive this process of "organizational learning" the faster we add value, the more innovative and flexible we become and the greater our competitive advantage.

ORGANIZATIONAL LEARNING DISABILITIES

Does your organization have a learning disability? Different organizations operate at different levels of learning maturity.

But some organizations are stuck, seemingly unable to advance their problem-solving and improvement capabilities.

Being stuck is often a function of failing to apply one (or more) components of the PDSA cycle. This happens when organizations fail to:

▲ **Plan.** The organization is all very action oriented but no real theory or idea drives improvement efforts. Thus, the organization is engaged in constant firefighting – so busy solving numerous problems that it never has the opportunity to address the root causes of those problems. Where the organization gets lucky and actually "fixes" some root cause, the broader knowledge is forgotten. The organization has to relearn the lessons again and again, often at great cost.

▲ **Do.** No experiment or data gathering is done before solutions or changes are implemented. Ideas or solutions that seem to make sense at the time on some "gut" level are readily adopted and implemented. Organizations operating with this learning disability are constantly changing the organization structure, product specifications, strategies, operating procedures – you name it – often with no significant positive impact. These organizations also tend to latch on to the latest management fads, introducing them with great fanfare, only to have them quickly fade – just in time for the next great thing to be introduced!

▲ **Study.** Data is gathered to study some problem or issue, but it turns out that nobody has any idea how to analyze or use the data gathered. Reports are produced, charts are created and lengthy verbal analysis is presented. Decision makers are left with an empty, "But what does it all mean?" feeling. The answer is: usually nothing. If you can't analyze the information you have, you can't learn. The result is decisions being made based upon gut feeling or personal preference, but with loads of pretense that "things have been studied in detail."

▲ **Act.** The organization does everything it should except implement what has been learned. An improvement team might study some problem, test out some solutions and even find a couple that work, but the organization is simply unable to implement the changes. Sometimes this is due to a lack of willingness. At other times, it is a simple inability to get the organization to change the way it does things. Organizations demonstrating this disability are often full of improvement reports, consultants' studies and

improvement teams. But nothing changes – initiatives die on the vine.

The Fifth Disability - PDSA in Reverse

Perhaps the most debilitating of all organizational learning disabilities is applying the scientific method or PDSA cycle in reverse. Instead of letting data be the reality test for ideas, some organizations let their prevailing theories of how to run an organization serve as the reality of test of data.

We can see the evidence of this learning disability in events that happened some 500 years ago. When Copernicus first determined that observational data on the movement of the planets made it clear the earth moved around the sun instead of the other way around, he was informed that his data must be wrong. Why? "Because everybody knows the sun moves around the earth!"

It may be difficult to imagine that some organizations operate in a manner equivalent to the methods of the 16th century, but that is exactly what happens. Organizations cling to their theories in use, their beliefs on how to do things or how things ought to work, while ignoring or dismissing empirical evidence.

Real learning involves risk. The price for advancing knowledge is that we may be wrong, that our ideas may not work out. Organizations can get stuck in a comfort zone, never allowing evidence to change their thinking. Getting stuck in this rut means being destined for last place among the competition. Sixteenth-century thinking shouldn't drive twenty-first century organizations.

THE SEVEN-STEP MODEL OF IMPROVEMENT

At the Converge Consulting Group, we use the *Seven-Step Model of Improvement* as a basic road map for teams seeking to improve process and organizational performance. It is essentially nothing more than an elaboration of the PDSA Cycle, with modifications to make it more accessible and applicable for teams working in organizational environments. The seven steps are:

1. *Planning for Improvement*
2. *Organizing for Improvement*
3. *Understanding the Current System*
4. *Redesigning the Current System*
5. *Implementing the Change*
6. *Learning From the Change*
7. *Acting on the Learning*

1. Planning for Improvement

This involves the basic goal- and boundary-setting activities that will frame the purpose of improvement team activity.

▲ **Select the process/product to be improved.** Not all processes can be improved at once. Organizations have resource limitations and constraints that will compel them to make choices. Generally, teams should start with where the biggest advantages can be gained. These advantages should be defined in terms of the potential for improvement as defined by the customer – remember, it is the customer that determines value. However, teams will often be assigned a focus, a specific process or a product that senior management wants improved.

▲ **Identify and frame current understanding of existing problems or issues.** Why is this problem a problem? What is happening that is undesired? What is the fundamental issue? What critical metrics define performance for this system? What is the extent of the performance gap?

Exhibit 39: The Seven-Step Method

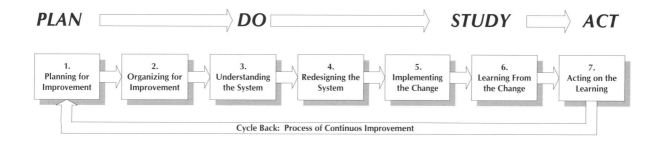

Answering questions like these provides for an improved understanding of what the team needs to do. We need to frame the issues to clarify the basic improvement opportunity and provide an appropriate context for understanding.

▲ **Define the project team charter.** The team charter provides a formal drafting of the purpose and mandate of the team. It details what the team will do and serves as a touchstone the team can refer back to help keep things on-track.

2. Organizing for Improvement

Once the basic purpose of the team is identified, work can begin actually creating and building the team.

▲ **Set the ground rules and team norms.** How will the team work together? What rules or guidelines of behavior do we wish to adopt? Teams need to address how they propose to work together.

▲ **Review and agree on all elements of the team charter.** Team members must have an opportunity to review and modify the team charter. All members must "buy in" to the charter, despite its initial creation by the team leader or senior management. The added perspectives presented by the team may improve the initial framing of the problem or the charter. With the charter now modified, a process of "catch-ball" begins, with the charter being returned to senior management for approval and then back to the team. This back and forth modification of the charter continues until both management and team members agree on charter content.

▲ **Agree on logistics.** Whenever teams are expected to work, there is always the mundane problem of basic logistics. When to meet, how often and where? As mundane as such questions are, they can prove to be the stickiest any team will have to deal with.

▲ **Select a team leader, facilitator and quality advisor (if required).** Different roles need to be fulfilled in the team. The team will require leadership. It will also require someone to take on the role of facilitating the group processes at work within the team. Meetings will proceed much more smoothly if there is someone assigned the task of helping them do so. Lastly, some expertise may be required in statistical methods, decision techniques and so forth. This may be the role of the quality advisor.

3. Understanding the Current System

Once organized, the team can begin identifying and analyzing the process or product. This first means understanding what is actually going on. Usually this involves a number of tools and techniques that include:

▲ **Process Mapping.** Creating maps of the process under review and developing detailed flowcharts to identify areas of complexity and waste.

▲ **Root Cause Analysis and Ishikawa Diagrams**. Detailing possible cause-and-effect relationships at work within the process and trying to clearly define these as likely candidates for improvement efforts.

▲ **Using Run & Control Charts.** Using these tools to better understand the performance level of the process or system, including process capability and the primary causes of variation.

▲ **Cause and Effect Analysis Tools.** Using histograms, Pareto charts, scatter diagrams and box and whisker plots (as well as other data analysis tools) to better understand the process or product and its performance drivers.

▲ **Experiments**. Intentionally altering process or product components to evaluate the impact of such change – taking an active approach to generating knowledge.

The application of these analytical tools is intended to help teams reach some conclusions about what is going on. Teams must look at the data, listen to the "voice" of the process and be prepared to make conclusions based upon the best evidence available at the time.

4. Re-Designing the System or Process

Once problems and root causes have been identified, the team can focus on solutions. A number of tools and techniques are useful. Whatever approach is used, however, the process of developing solutions is really the process of developing a new theory or idea about how to improve performance.

▲ **Prioritize the issues/problems.** Like organizations, improvement teams face constraints in terms of the resources at their disposal. Not all problems may be immediately solvable. The team may have to prioritize the issues, and focus in on those that will yield the largest potential gains.

▲ **Identify potential solutions.** If you're lucky, the solutions may have made themselves apparent in the process of understanding. If not, a number of creative techniques can be used to help the team identify potential solutions.

▲ **Explore potential solutions – will they work?** Not all ideas are practical or will generate the improvement desired. Once potential ideas have been generated, teams will have to reduce these to a select few. Eventually, one idea will need to be selected and implemented.

▲ **Identify objectives and expectations for change.** Once a solution has been adopted, the team needs to specify what it expects will happen. Will sales increase and, if so, by how much? Will the process operate faster? Providing answers here sets the expectations for the team's improvement recommendations.

▲ **Document the underlying assumptions or logic model.** It is not enough to identify **what** will change as the result of the improvement initiative, the team must also specify **why** it expects the changes to have the desired effect. The importance of this cannot be over-estimated. Learning cannot take place unless the logic of why 'X' will affect 'Y' is made explicit. Only by specifying the underlying logic can we go back and examine the results to see why things went right or wrong.

5. Implementing the Change

We never know if our ideas are really going to work. So, if possible, implement the proposed change on a small scale – that is, conduct an experiment.

▲ **Train employees affected.** If a change will mean a change in the process, in the way we do things, we must train the employees affected. Take the time to make sure people know what they are expected to do differently. The simple act of training can provide valuable feedback from front-line employees about potential problems with the new way. This allows further improvements to take place and helps ensure the changes have a fair chance of succeeding.

▲ **Communicate the changes to those that should know.** Others in the organization and occasionally outside it may have to be informed about what is going on. If the change will affect customers, better let them know. If it will affect other departments, they too will have to be informed.

▲ **Give the system time to settle down.** A new process or system will likely have many special causes of variation.

With every new change, there will be disruptions and problems. Employees involved in the process must be given time to work things out and bring things into control. Likewise, other departments must get used to the change as well. In short, be prepared for problems but don't let them panic you. Plan for possible disruptions – nothing new works perfectly at first – and address the unforeseen problems as they arise. This includes lending support to those in the front lines. Now is no time to abandon the people who are actually trying to make things work. Stay close, be supportive and be prepared.

▲ **Do it!** Outside of all the preparation and planning, at some point we must "turn the key" – that is start the new process. This can be a frightening experience. Whenever a new process, or some other change is introduced, uncertainty reigns. There is far more we don't know than we do. "Will it work?" "What new problems will be created?" "What happens if the whole thing crashes?" Because we don't know the answer to these questions at this point, the rationale for starting small and experimenting becomes clear. Experimenting or not, however, the only way we will get answers to these questions is by doing it.

6. Learning from the Change

Well, how did we do? Was the experiment a success or did we crash and burn? Teams have the responsibility to monitor the changes and develop the measurement system that will allow them to determine project success or failure.

▲ **Measure, measure, measure.** Don't be afraid of the numbers. The same tools used to help us understand the process can now be employed to help us understand the change. Track changes with run and control charts. Use scatter diagrams and box and whisker plots to assess changes in the cause-and-effect relationships. We must use the experiment to generate the data required to confirm or deny our theory.

▲ **Document learning as you go.** Is our theory correct? Our assumptions? This is where the logic model comes in. It is not enough to know how things are going. If we are to learn, we must know why they are going that way. We may be generating improvement, but we may be doing so for completely unexpected reasons.

▲ **Modify the experiment as you go – this is learning in real time.** In the real world of improving organizations, controlled experiments are rare – this is real time learning.

As the experiment continues, staff, team members and others may have ideas to further enhance the process. The very act of conducting the experiment may generate new ideas. Let the team examine and evaluate these ideas, and where appropriate, test them out. If they make things better, great; if not, we have still learned something.

▲ **Evaluate the changes.** Where they a success or failure? Did we achieve our objectives? Why did things go the way they did? Sooner or later, we must stop the experiment and be prepared to reach conclusions about our improvement idea. To be sure, success is more fun than failure. But if failure comes, accept it, learn from it, and move on.

7. Acting on the Learning

If the experiment is a success then it should be expanded to a full-scale change. Not all experiments are a success but they all provide valuable lessons. The team should be prepared to document these so that other teams can benefit.

▲ **Expand the changes if appropriate.** If we were successful, we need to ensure we understand why so the results can be applied in a broader context. These changes must then be implemented. If the experiment is a failure, there are likely some lessons that can be applied to make some modest improvements.

▲ **Standardize the new way of doing things.** The new way of doing things, once implemented, must be standardized. It must become the new "way things are done around here." Training staff is one way to ensure this standardization occurs. But there are others – the new process should be documented, affected departments will need to be briefed, policy and procedure manuals will need to be modified and so on.

▲ **Organize and close the files.** Once the new process has been implemented it's time for the team to wind things down. Make sure the work done by the team is documented. Where the team has used various performance improvement tools, document how they were applied and include this information in the files. Ten years from now, someone in the organization will be asking why things are the way they are, why certain decisions were made. This, too, is central to organizational learning. By documenting what was done now, the team creates the knowledge base that some day will be useful to someone else.

▲ **Publish.** Before those documented lessons are filed away, however, they need to be shared with the rest of the orga-

nization. Organizational learning requires that such sharing, be it of successes or failures, takes place. There is a reason why scientists must publish their studies in peer-reviewed journals – because it is through sharing information that learning occurs which others can build upon. Story-boards, corporate newsletters and, recently, electronic web-based story-boards are among the organizational communication tools that can be employed here.

▲ **Have a party and celebrate.** Take some time out and celebrate your successes!

▲ **Start on a new project**. Improvement never ends. So after the party, get back to work and begin looking for new improvement opportunities.

USING THE 7-STEP MODEL

The 7-step model is intended to be a guideline for improvement activity built upon the PDSA cycle. As teams work their way through the various steps of the model, the nature of the tasks to be accomplished change along with the tools required to do so. Table 40: The 7-Step Model of Improvement presents each of the steps, along with the basic focus of the activity and the tools that can be used to help support the tasks involved.

Table 40: The 7-Step Model of Improvement

	PLAN		DO			STUDY	ACT
	Step 1: Planning for Improvement	Step 2: Organizing for Improvement	Step 3: Understanding the System	Step 4: Redesigning the System	Step 5: Implementing the Changes	Step 6: Learning From the Change	Step 7: Acting on the Learning
Goal or Focus	To define the improvement project's purpose and scope.	To ensure the team is organized and capable of addressing the project's purpose.	To understand how the system works including its current performance levels and the root causes of problems.	To develop alternative solutions and select those most capable of delivering improvement.	To implement the solution, preferably but not necessarily on a smaller scale.	To evaluate the results of the change initiative.	To take action based upon the learning, including standardizing the new approach and identifying critical lessons learned.
Basic Questions to be Answered	What is the purpose of this project? What is the performance problem to be addressed? What is the performance gap? What are the expectations concerning this project? How will success be determined? Why is this project important?	Who should be on the improvement team? What skills and levels of interest are required? Are there people outside of the team that need to be involved? What principles will guide the teams efforts? Who will serve as leader of the team? What are the roles and responsibilities of team members? Are the resources (time, money, people) available sufficient?	What are the problems or issues concerning this system? What is the current design of the system? How does the current system function? What are the possible causes of performance problems? Who is responsible for what? How is performance measured? What is the current performance level of the system?	What alternatives are available? What criteria should be used to evaluate alternatives? What are the strengths and weaknesses associated with each alternative? Which alternative should be selected? Can we run a pilot project to test alternatives?	What will be the new method? Who will be involved? Have employees been trained in the new approach? How will results be monitored? Is process documentation and other reference material in place? Are there any cultural or related conditions that need to be addressed?	How do results compare with expectations? How do results compare with the previous performance levels? How do results compare with best practice comparisons? What recommendations can be made? Are there opportunities for further improvement?	What are the implications arising from our learning? What other improvements can be made? What specifically was learned from this project? How can this knowledge be best communicated? Are learnings here applicable to other processes or products? How can the gains be standardized? Go back to step 1 for the next task.

Table 40: The 7-Step Model of Improvement

	PLAN		DO			STUDY	ACT
	Step 1: Planning for Improvement	**Step 2: Organizing for Improvement**	**Step 3: Understanding the System**	**Step 4: Redesigning the System**	**Step 5: Implementing the Changes**	**Step 6: Learning From the Change**	**Step 7: Acting on the Learning**
Tools and Techniques Used	Critical Process Mapping; System Definition Diagram; Gap Analysis; Run & Control Charts; Matrix Diagrams; Deployment Diagrams; Preference Decision Techniques; Evaluative Decision Tools	Team Charter; Team Norms; Role and Responsibility Matrix; GANTT Charts; PERT Analysis	Process Mapping; Mind Mapping; Cause & Effect Diagrams; Relationship Diagrams; Histograms; Pareto Charts; Scatter Diagrams; Box & Whisker Plots; Run and Control Charts	Process Mapping; Brainstorming; Preference Decision Techniques; Evaluative Decision Tools; Affinity Diagrams; Tree Diagrams; Quality Function Deployment	Force Field Analysis; GANTT Charts; PERT Analysis; Role and Responsibility Matrix; Matrix Diagrams	Cause & Effect Diagrams; Histograms; Pareto Charts; Scatter Diagrams; Box & Whisker Plots; Run and Control Charts; Affinity Charting	Force Field Analysis; GANTT Charts; PERT Analysis; Role and Responsibility Matrix; Preference Decision Techniques; Evaluative Decision Tools; Process Mapping
Comments	A large number of tools and techniques are used in the planning function. It should be remembered that planning is a process of making decisions. Ultimately, we need to decide where to focus the improvement effort.	Teams must first get themselves organized to take on the task at hand. This requires attention to people as well as other vital resources such as time and money.	Understanding can have numerous levels. Visual models using mapping techniques can be followed by numerical models that lead to a deeper level of understanding. Run and control charts create a predictive model representing the deeper level of understanding.	Redesigning is largely a creative process. However, the creativity must be grounded in reality – the data and information that have been developed through an improved understanding of the system.	Whenever possible, implementation should be done or piloted on a smaller scale to see whether our theories about how to improve things actually work. Small-scale implementation is not always possible, however.	Learning from change demands that effort has been put into understanding the system. If you don't know how the system performed before, knowing how it performs now is of little use for evaluation.	Improvements developed must become they way things are done throughout the organization. They must become standardized.

THE PERFORMANCE IMPROVEMENT METHOD

Using the 7-step model for team-based improvement as a framework and linking it with the various tools and techniques available to teams, we can outline a general improvement method. The outline of the method is presented in Exhibit 41: Performance Improvement Method.[36]

The method outlines where to apply the various tools in the improvement process. We start at the top with the physical system – the real world. It is from this real world we recognize problems and opportunities for improvement. From here, we plan and organize the improvement effort using tools such as the system definition diagram and the team charter to help scope and provide direction to those people assigned the task of making the improvement happen.

With the project in place, we begin the process of increasing our understanding of the system – of what is going on. Block diagrams and flow charts are used to map the system while critical characteristics are identified, metrics defined and data gathering undertaken. This culminates with the nature and extent of the performance gap being determined.

If the performance gap is verified, the control chart is used to determine the stability of the system or process. If stable, the improvement strategy must focus on changing the process – reducing the common cause variation. If unstable, the strategy must focus on solving or fixing the problem(s) – removing special causes of variation.

Each approach proceeds in its own way but both culminate with the improvement team identifying what it believes lies at the root of the variation being experienced. Recommendations are made and changes implemented to the physical system where the problems and opportunities were first identified. At this point, we continue to monitor to see if the changes made had the desired effect.

---

36. This diagram and the approach it represents is a result of combining and modifying ideas in two excellent sources. Ronald Moen, et al, Improving Quality Through Planned Experimentation, McGraw-Hill 1991, p.45 and ASQ Statistics Division, Galen C. Britz, et al, Improving Performance Through Statistical Thinking, Quality Press, Milwaukee, Wisconsin 2000 pp. 83, 99

2. Improving Performance: Critical Components of Systems Thinking

Exhibit 41: Performance Improvement Method

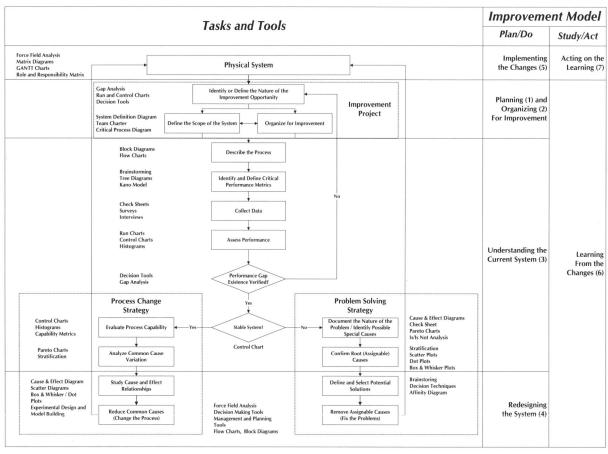

Getting Ready: Planning and Organizing for Improvement

3

PLANNING FOR IMPROVEMENT

If you have ever had to write a report at work or an article for a newsletter or even an angry letter to your local newspaper editor, you know that just getting started is often the hardest part. So it is with improvement. Getting started requires overcoming organizational inertia – the tendency to accept the status quo and to keep doing things the way things have always been done.

RECOGNIZING THE NEED

So how do we get started? Usually it starts with someone, somewhere, believing that a problem must be fixed, an issue

addressed or some performance characteristic improved. Recognizing the need is the first step in any improvement effort.

With Ford in the early 1980s, the need for change was recognized throughout the organization, including the top of the house with Chief Operating Officer, Mr. Donald Peterson. Describing the situation at Ford, he writes:

"The situation was so bleak that people in many of our organizations naturally started getting together to talk about what was happening. Talking was going on everywhere, more or less ad hoc. The discussions ranged widely, but what the conversations kept coming back to was "Why are we doing so badly? Why are our results so poor? What's wrong with us?" We had to do something to regain our footing, to keep pace with the

Japanese, and we could see we had to get back to the basics of running a business well."[37]

From this basic recognition of the need, Ford took the steps required to fundamentally change the way in which it managed itself and conducted its business. The need to first recognize that a problem exists is true for any organization or organizational level. It need not be so dramatic as a widespread corporate malaise. A supervisor in the shipping department may be experiencing too many addressing problems, a branch manager may perceive employee morale as being low, or an accounting manager might believe that month-end closing procedures take too long. The realization that change is required may occur with the Finance VP, the Manager of Marketing, the Director of Human Resources, the Supervisor of Customer Service or an assembly worker in the front lines.

Recognizing the need for change may occur anywhere people work. Relying on employees to recognize the need and demonstrating the leadership to initiate improvement is an informal process. It is, nevertheless, fundamental and important to ensuring that improvement happens at all levels of the organi-

37. Donald J. Peterson, A Better Idea, Houghton Miffen Company, Boston, 1991, p. 5

zation. It is not the only way organizations can highlight issues or improvement opportunities, however. More formal problem recognition processes can be constructed and used as well.

PROBLEM RECOGNITION PROCESSES

Some organizations rely on more formal processes in which areas of organizational performance are systematically analyzed as part of an early detection system of performance problems. In such circumstances, the need for change is developed within a system of organizational analysis and planning. This approach has the advantage of treating and analyzing the organizational unit as a system. When this is done, the often conflicting and competing priorities for change can be considered together. Cross-functional impacts can be examined and more systemic and effective improvement initiatives can be implemented.

However the problems or opportunities for change are recognized, one method should not be seen as superior to another. Rather, formal and informal approaches need to be viewed as complementary. Formal planning allows us to have a well defined and systemic approach to identifying issues that require improvement. But such approaches can always miss something. Meanwhile, employees may be aware of other fundamental problems affecting performance. These informal methods, however, can become focused on immediate or localized issues while missing the bigger picture presented by more formal planning approaches. Organizations that manage to blend informal and formal approaches create a robust system of identifying the issues and problems at work in their specific organizations.

PERFORMANCE GAP ANALYSIS

To be meaningful, data or information must be compared to something. Corporate profits might have been a million dollars last year, but what does this say about the company? Is this a good or poor level of performance?

There is no way to tell from the million-dollar figure alone. The company would be faced with very different situations if investors expected a $100,000 profit than if they expected a $10 million profit. If expectations had been $100,000, stock price would be soaring, management would be smiling and the shareholders meeting would be smooth sailing. But the seas would certainly be choppy had $10 million been the expectation!

Standards

The things we compare performance to are called standards. Standards come in a variety of forms and go by various aliases. Budgets, quotas, specifications, schedules, goals, objectives and targets are all different names to describe standards.[38]

In our example, we compared the million-dollar profit to investor expectations. The interpretation of good or bad performance depends upon the expectation or the level of the standard held by investors. There are other bases of comparisons, we needn't restrict ourselves to investor expectations. We could have compared profit to other companies of similar size in similar industries, or to the level of investment, or to profitability levels in previous years. The basis of comparison and the standards used depend upon what you want to know.

---

38. J. M. Juran, Managerial Breakthrough, McGraw Hill Inc., New York, NY , 1995, pp. 256-257

Problems are Performance Gaps

The distance between the standard and the level of performance defines the extent of the performance gap. The greater the gap, the more the situation is perceived as a problem to be resolved. The process of problem recognition, then, is one of comparing performance with standards.

It is the nature of the standard used that defines the type of performance gap. Four types of gaps can be defined depending upon the basis of the standard (empirical or expectation) and where the standard is located relative to the organization (internal or external).

▲ **Basis of Standard.** Standards can be expectation- or empirically based. Expectation-based approaches compare the performance level of a characteristic with the performance expectations (goals or objectives) held for that characteristic by some individual or group. Differences between an expectation and a given performance level are gaps in capability. In contrast, empirically based approaches compare measured performance levels with other measured performance levels. Here, we are not comparing performance data with expectations but rather with other data.

Table 42: Alternative Gaps and Problem Recognition Processes

		Basis of Standard	
		Empirical	**Expectation**
Focus of Comparison	**External**	Gap 1: Competitive Performance Competitive Benchmarking	Gap 3: Customer Capability Customer Research
	Internal	Gap 2: Organizational Performance Statistical Process Control	Gap 4: Organizational Capability Capability Analysis

▲ **Focus of Comparison.** The focus of the comparison deals with where the standard is located. It can be classified as being either internal or external to the organizational unit using the analysis. For example, an external focus can be placed on customers or competitors – both of these are external to the organization. In contrast, an internal focus may compare existing performance with previously

---

obtained levels of performance or with some goals or objectives.

Gap Analysis 1: Competitive Performance

A competitive performance gap is a difference between the performance of our organization and that of our competitors. Perhaps the gap is one of profitability or product quality or even customer satisfaction. None of these involves the use of expectations such as goals or objectives. Rather, the performance characteristic for one organization is being compared with the same performance characteristic of another organization or organizations. The comparison is strictly empirical – our return on investment (ROI) for example, may be 9.5 percent and that of the competition may be 14.7 percent.

This comparison of competitive performance is often referred to as performance benchmarking. Any characteristic can be benchmarked – it may be financial performance, inventory levels or turnaround time. Regardless of the characteristic, benchmarking can help us better understand our position relative to other organizations or 'best in class' performers.

Competitive gap analysis has natural appeal. The basis of comparison is, after all, competitive in nature. We are asking how our performance stacks up relative to someone else's and this basis of comparisons fits well with the general competitive nature of business organizations.

There are, however, issues involved with using external organizations as the basis of comparison. While efforts are made to compare apples with apples, no organization is identical to another. They come with different histories, strategies and circumstances – all of which can influence the performance comparison and the resulting size of the performance gap. In short, there are a great many confounding factors that can affect the basis of the comparison.

Gap Analysis 2: Organizational Performance

Organizational performance gaps, like competitive performance gaps, are also empirically based. But rather than comparing the performance of a characteristic with some external organization, the focus of comparison is with internal performance levels achieved previously or elsewhere in our own organization. Here we do a better job of controlling for those apples and oranges problems associated with competitive gap analysis; after all, the comparative data is coming from us.

A number of techniques are used to help identify organizational performance gaps. Statistical process control is one of the more common where ongoing process performance is tracked and analyzed through tools such as the control chart. By plotting performance levels over time, the control chart is making comparisons across time periods which allows for the identification of trends, sudden changes and the like, all of which can signal a problem. For example, in producing silicone we notice that the purity level that was once stable at 99.98 percent has dropped slightly but steadily over the past two weeks to a level of 99.95 percent. This may still be well within specifications, but it is a signal of a problem requiring attention.

Other comparisons other than over time are possible. The performance of two or more production lines can be compared, or two different factories. Such comparisons can highlight problems in performance in one or more of any number of organizational components.

Gap Analysis 3: Customer Capability

With customer capability, we move from empirical to expectation-based comparisons. Customer capability problems are those where our performance fails to live up to the expectations held by the customer.

All customers have expectations for the products and services they purchase. Sometimes customers are explicit in their declarations of what their expectations are, sometimes they are not – but the expectations are still there. The gap between what the customer expected and the customer's perception of what was received will determine the level of customer satisfaction and, ultimately, customer loyalty to the product.

The extent of the gap between customer expectation and experience can be established empirically through product testing, prototyping and customer and market research. This doesn't make for an empirically based comparison – the basis of the comparison (empirically verified or not) is still the expectation held by the customer. Empirical measurement can only quantify the extent of the gap between what the customer expects and what we have delivered.

Gap Analysis 4: Organizational Capability

Organizational capability is the comparison of performance with the expectations held by the organization – usually senior management or owners/shareholders. Where we fail to meet these expectations, we have an organizational capability problem.

While the extent of this performance gap can be measured empirically (the difference between expectation and performance), the basis of the comparison or type of standard – management expectation – is not in itself empirical in nature. In fact, management can hold any expectation it wants, from realistic and obtainable to outlandish and impossible to attain.

This is the fundamental problem with any expectation-based standard of comparison – the standard can emerge from thin air. With customers, even if the nature of the expectation is outlandish, firms may take a certain comfort from the fact that their competitors are no more likely to meet the customers expectations than they are. If, on the other hand, some competitors are able to meet these outlandish expectations then the expectations were not so outlandish after all. In short, with customer capability there is a built-in competitive regulator to the expectations held.

With management expectations, however, there is no such built in regulator. If management has the expectation of producing $1 million of profit at the end of the year and the firm fails to meet this objective, was the problem with the performance of the firm or in the expectation? There is no empirical way to tell. Setting objectives doesn't change reality. Unrealistic objectives are usually identified early on in the trenches where considerable effort is expended preparing for the predictable year-end disappointments.

Nevertheless, it is important for organizations to set objectives. They detail what the organization wants to accomplish, the direction. When performance falls short of these expectations, there is one of two options available – modify expectations or improve performance. In either case, we have an organizational capability problem or gap.

Getting a Handle on Performance Problems

The performance gap model highlights the four basic means by which we recognize and begin to define performance problems. Two critical points:

▲ **Organizations need to continuously monitor all four gap areas.** High-performing organizations continuously monitor for problems in all four potential gap areas. Moreover, there are formal processes in place to do so. Problems may arise in any one of these areas or in a combination of areas.

▲ **Organizations need to define the nature of the performance problems.** When problems are first recognized, leaders need to define the nature of the problem – is it a customer capability problem or one of competitive performance? Perhaps the problem is one of organizational capability. Placing the problem (or challenge if you prefer) into one of these four categories helps provide some clarity on the fundamental nature of the problem at hand.

CREATING COMMITMENT

Once the need for change has been identified, the next task is usually one of soliciting support. The individual may bring subordinates together, carry on informal discussions with like-minded people or simply begin some informal discussion among peers. Whatever the approach, it amounts to building a consensus on the need for change – in short, creating commitment.

A critical mass needs to be reached before the organization, at whatever level, decides to take on the issue at hand - people must buy in to the problem, accept it as their own. There are three basic strategies or means by which this buy-in or commitment is achieved.

TALK ABOUT IT – SHARE WHAT IS KNOWN

You would think this would be obvious. After all, how can you achieve buy-in and commitment without giving people a chance to even talk about the issue or problem? Yet all too often, the organizational instinct is precisely the opposite. When problems are first recognized, there is an immediate reaction to keep the problem close to the chest, hiding the information from employees, shareholders, suppliers, customers or anyone else who might be affected. This is a "We will fix it before anybody finds out!" kind of thinking. It is also nonsense.

Chances are that if you have detected these problems, your customers, suppliers, shareholders and employees have already detected them as well. If they haven't, they soon will, and are probably already suspicious. Either way, hiding the truth will likely fool no one and only delay the organization's ability to gain support for change.

In the worse-case scenario, the problem(s) becomes so secret that the organization fails to address the issue at all. The organization literally fools itself into believing it doesn't have a problem because it never talks openly about the problem(s) it has.

There is power in recognizing the problem, in stating what is on people's minds. The leadership of an organization rarely maintains or gains power by trying to keep things quiet. Quite the opposite. Power can often be derived by showing the leadership to state the issues boldly and encouraging involvement through discussion.

DEFINE THE PROBLEM

Of course, just talking about a problem has never solved anything. Beyond just sharing information, the discourse must move toward problem definition.

With Ford, the survival of the organization was at stake. But again, circumstances need not be so dramatic. It may be a growing customer satisfaction problem, continued defects arising from a particular assembly line, growing staff complaints at

an operating facility, or declining profitability of a popular product.

Whatever the nature of the problem, someone in the organization must move people from just talking about it to making a commitment to fix it. So the purpose might be saving the organization, but it also might be improving profitability, increasing customer satisfaction or lowering costs. That purpose must be clearly stated and communicated to the organization. In doing so, the organization also defines the mission for the improvement initiative.

PAINT A PICTURE, ESTABLISH A VISION

The last point to be made about building commitment to a change or improvement initiative is the need to make things concrete. Improving quality may be a noble purpose, but it alone is a difficult thing to commit to. It is too vague and fuzzy. We need to make the end state more concrete, to give people a sense of destination by painting a picture of what success will look like. In so doing, we move from "improving quality" to "no more than six parts per million defective and recognition as the most reliable components in the industry." The purpose or mission is improving quality, but the picture or vision is the most reliable components in the industry with no more than six parts per million defective.

Establishing a vision or aim provides not only the picture of what we hope to achieve, but is in itself a measure of success. It defines what success will look like. This is the kind of thing people can buy into.

A REAL WORLD EXAMPLE

The power of defining purposeful action, detailing a vision and communicating both is perhaps best illustrated by the actions of a very famous leader – Napoleon. After his disastrous Russian campaign and subsequent defeat at the Battle of Nations, Napoleon retreated to Paris only to be removed from office and imprisoned on the island of Elba. France was broken apart by the monarchies of Europe and the Congress of Vienna saw to it that France or democracy would never again be allowed to threaten Europe's existing order.

But Napoleon escaped from Elba and managed to return to a remote coastal area of France by hiding on a fishing boat. The story goes that he came, penniless, upon a village and still in prison garb. When asked who he was, he told them but he did

more. He told them he meant to take France back. He would remove the monarchy and restore the Republic. He would drive the foreign powers out of France and restore the country to its rightful place as a leader of nations.

Okay, so Napoleon was a little less than honest. You have to give him credit, though – these are pretty big objectives for a recently escaped convict with no visible means of support and few prospects. The villagers, however, didn't laugh. They picked up their pitchforks and whatever else would serve as a weapon, and started marching on Paris with Napoleon as their leader. As the small group marched through the countryside, each village they came to contributed volunteers as Napoleon shared his purpose and his vision of a new France.

Word of Napoleon's escape, however, got back to Paris and the king quickly set out the troops to recapture Napoleon and return him to Elba. The two groups, Napoleon's rag tag volunteers and the King's army, met a short distance from the French capital. Napoleon's volunteers were outnumbered and outgunned. It didn't matter. Napoleon walked alone and unarmed to the opposing commander and shared his dream of a new France for all to hear. Napoleon then challenged the opposing commander to strike him down – to kill not only a true patriot, but this vision of a new France. The opposing army didn't dare. Instead they joined the rabble and participated in the march on Paris. A few days later, Napoleon took Paris and control of France without ever having fired a shot.

Never underestimate the power of clear intentions, purposeful action and a powerful vision.

THE PROJECT

The process of problem recognition, combined with building commitment to do something about it, usually culminates in a project. A project is a temporary, organized effort to effect change – to make an improvement. It is also the way organizations formalize their intentions – projects are created when the organization is ready to commit.

With Ford in the 1980's, the project was to redesign the way the entire company operated, and accountability lay with the Chief Operating Officer. But a project might be as basic as redesigning data entry procedures in the accounts receivable department or reducing staff turnover at a construction site. Regardless of scale, the creation of a project indicates that three things are true:

▲ The organization recognizes a problem – there is an opportunity to effect improvement and create an increase in value.

▲ A sufficient 'critical mass' has been established for the organization to commit to pursuing the improvement opportunity.

▲ The organization is signalling that it recognizes the first two points and is making operational its intentions to pursue the improvement opportunity.

By organization, we mean any organizational unit, from the largest company to the smallest workgroup.

NO TRIVIAL PROJECTS, ONLY DIFFERENCES IN SCALE AND SCOPE

From changing the culture of a major multi-national corporation to improving the data entry procedures at clerical stations, it needs to emphasized that there are no trivial projects, only differences in scale. Redesigning data entry procedures may appear trivial when viewed from the lofty heights of the corporate boardroom, but it may represent a significant initiative to the department head with immediate accountability for this function. Indeed, the manager responsible may not sleep for days prior to implementation, even though executive leadership is completely unaware of the initiative.

Such initiatives should not be discouraged. Continuous improvement demands constant pursuit of improvement opportunities at all organizational levels and in all functions. In turn, this implies project teams continually forming, disbanding and reforming as opportunities are pursued, improvements made and new opportunities identified.

Moreover, while small local improvement projects may appear trivial from the boardroom, their cumulative effect may be significant at any level. Having a hundred small improvement projects on the go may produce greater levels of improvement, and with lower levels of risk, than a single major improvement project.

There is another reason why smaller projects cannot be seen as trivial – they may be required for the success of larger initiatives. A corporate initiative of a major railway to reduce load-handling costs over three years will in turn require any number of smaller improvement projects, which in turn may be comprised of any number of projects that are smaller still. Success

or failure of the major initiative may depend on the success or failure of one or more of these smaller projects.

IMPROVEMENT PROJECT FUNDAMENTALS

Teams assigned a specific improvement project are often filled with enthusiasm. There is a natural tendency for people to 'dive in' and fix whatever needs to be fixed. Before doing so, however, there is a need to slow down and consider the four fundamentals of an improvement project.

1. There are two purposes to every project

Every project has two purposes: the technical purpose and the systemic purpose.

▲ **Technical Purpose.** The technical purpose of a project is defined by the results to be accomplished within a specific scope. For example, the technical purpose of an inventory management improvement project at our Kansas plant is improving inventory management. We may want to be more specific in our technical definition, to provide a vision that details specific target inventory levels or carrying costs, for example. But the technical purpose nevertheless is linked directly to results.

▲ **Systemic Purpose.** In contrast, systemic purpose is not directly linked to specific results at a particular time and place. The systemic purpose of an improvement project is identifying those things that can effect improvement in different areas or at different times. We may, in our efforts to improve inventory management in Kansas, have learned lessons that can be applied to our plants in California and Texas or that can be applied to the design of new plants still on the drawing board. These lessons represent the systemic learning that has occurred as a result of our project.

The technical purpose changes with every new project team as it is defined by the specific improvement initiative the team is pursuing. Systemic purpose, however, is constant. It is always to maximize the general learning that may prove a benefit elsewhere in the organization.

2. The technical purpose must be (re)defined by the team

Typically, the technical purpose of a project is assigned by senior or executive management. Usually this results from some form of problem recognition process where the resulting project purpose is formulated as some variation of 'fix the problem.'

Team leaders, and the team generally, need to work and rework the technical purpose of the project. The purpose must be reconsidered in light of team knowledge and experience and, ultimately, must be meaningful to both the team and the leadership that assigned the project. In practice, this usually takes the form of back and forth negotiations or "catchball" between the team and the leadership, clarifying the scale, scope and mission (technical purpose) of the project team.

Usually, the very process of catchball (back and forth discussions on purpose or mission of the project team) contributes to shared and improved understanding of the issues at hand. By the time executive leadership and the team have reached agreement, the purpose and scope should be sufficiently defined to provide real direction to the team's efforts.

For this process to occur, however, the leadership of the team needs to be willing to push back when assigned a mandate. Simply accepting the mission as given only delays, usually to the most inconvenient time, the need to clarify and define the purpose of the project – and only after resources have been expended to some degree. Challenge and clarify the technical purpose up front, to the point where it is shared and understood by all.

3. Change has its enemies

Robert Kennedy has been quoted as saying: "Progress is a nice word. But change is its motivator and change has its enemies." Project teams exist to effect a change. If change has its enemies, so too will the team.

> *"Progress is a nice word. But change is its motivator and change has its enemies."*
> **Robert Kennedy**

In the midst of project activity, especially as the team begins to define proposed changes, levels of enthusiasm may rise to the point that the notion of someone else opposing the proposed changes never occurs to team members. Yet surely someone will be opposed. This gives rise to two basic considerations:

▲ **Change must be managed.** Not everyone will agree with the changes proposed by the improvement team. Specific strategies will be required to address these concerns. The strategy may be to try and convince those opposed or to build a critical mass of those in favor. Either way, however, teams need to recognize that no good idea sells itself; change issues must be identified and addressed if improvement is to come about.

▲ **You can't please everyone.** While agreement among all is desirable, it is rarely achievable. Using different levels of decision making (consensus versus unanimous for example) or different decision tools may help to some degree. But at the end of the day, organizations will have to decide to move forward or not. In such circumstances, this always presents the possibility that some will disagree and disagree strongly with the decisions made.

4. Making improvements is its own set of skills

Making improvements, specifically the managing of project improvement teams and the ability to work within and contribute effectively within such teams, requires its own set of skills. Technical skills and knowledge is vital, but so will be the ability to work with others as well as independently, to communicate clearly, to integrate the work of others into our own work and to coordinate and cooperate. How well the team brings all these skills to the table will in large measure determine project success or failure.

Here again, proper application of management and planning tools may help. Especially as improvement projects increase in scale or scope, tools such as GANTT charts, role and responsibility matrices and PERT may help the team manage its resources to best effect. This is not the total answer, however. Project team leaders need also to carefully consider who is to be invited to become team members – technical ability is one thing, ability to improve another.

ORGANIZING FOR IMPROVEMENT

Improvement initiatives and projects usually involve some form of team coming together to solve the problem or make the improvements. Working in teams is not a requirement of improvement, however. We are all individuals working in our respective jobs and many of us have made improvements here and there to the way in which we do our work. So if teams are not a prerequisite to performance improvement, why use them?

WHY USE TEAMS?

Anyone who has worked in a team probably has a variety of positive and negative experiences. The reasons are likely many, but we can never forget that 'teamwork' is just that -- work! It takes a lot of time and effort to get and keep a team functioning as it should. So why bother? Why not give someone the responsibility to fix the process and get on with it? Isn't that a more efficient way to go? The quick answer is no. A number of advantages can be identified to using teams.

BUILDING COMMITMENT

Assigning an individual to the task of process improvement only looks more efficient. More often than not, it is much slower and far less effective. To see why, remember we are seeking to actually make an improvement to a process or product, not just make a decision as to what changes should be made. Individuals can make quick decisions, but they do so without the involvement or commitment of those affected. The result is fast decisions but slow or non-existent implementation.

Using teams to solve problems, on the other hand, builds involvement and commitment of those affected by the impending changes. Building this commitment takes time and energy – meaning the team will get off to a slower start than an individual working on a problem. The catch-up comes when it is time to implement. By stressing involvement, individuals affected by the decision become committed to it. They make the changes work! With the individual approach, once the recommendations have been made, time and effort must be spent on selling the solutions. This inevitably leads to internal conflict and politics. Some areas of the company fight the changes or work subversively to ensure they never come about.

The individual approach, therefore, puts little time and effort into reaching the decision. But it puts plenty of time into trying to convince, cajole or otherwise force people into accepting or supporting the changes proposed. In contrast, the team approach puts a lot of effort into reaching a decision that all can accept, so little energy needs to be expended on the actual implementation.

EFFECTIVE FRAMING

Team decisions also tend to be more effective. The reason for this lies in the diversity teams bring to the problem solving/improvement equation.

Individuals tend to see problems or opportunities from their own points of view. Accountants see problems as failures of control or proper budgeting, marketing people see problems as marketing driven, production people see them as production driven and so forth. Defining a problem from a particular viewpoint is called *framing*.

A frame defines the boundaries of the improvement effort. Before any process problem can be addressed, it must be defined or framed. But when framed by an individual, the problem is defined in a way that accommodates the bias of the individual, constraining innovative thinking and solutions that could prove useful. In contrast, teams bring a mix of perspectives and different ways of seeing the problem to the problem-solving process. With representatives from different functional areas of the company as well as different hierarchical levels, teams have a wealth of knowledge and a diversity of perspective no individual can possess. When the team frames the problem, this diversity must be accommodated. The result is frames that are more comprehensive, less biased and more likely to accommodate innovation.

BARRIER BUSTING

Teams also encourage barrier busting, the communication and sharing of information across functional and hierarchical barriers existing within organizations. Since processes tend to flow across these functional and hierarchical divisions, getting information from these different sources is important if we are to gather a sound understanding of how the process functions and where problems exist.

But will marketing tell someone from production about its problems? Will information services discuss slow processing times with operations? Not likely! Years of living within the hierarchy has taught managers the value of holding on to information and ensuring outsiders never know what's going on inside. It's part of that silo thinking mentality discussed earlier.

Teams help overcome the barriers between departments and levels by including a mix of representatives, drawing individuals from diverse backgrounds and skill sets. The intent is to provide representation, ensuring all areas affected have some form of presence within the team. Using a charter to provide the team with a common mission or purpose may also help overcome the barriers and get team members working together.

KNOWLEDGE GENERATION & SHARING

Beyond representational diversity, teams bring with them a diversity of knowledge as well. Put simply, a group of people from various areas of an organization 'knows' more than a single individual. Knows more about what? About the way things are done in various departments, specific problems, attitudes and concerns of those with which they work and so forth. In short, all individuals on the team bring with them their tacit knowledge of the way things work.

Tacit and Explicit Knowledge

It is useful to distinguish between tacit and explicit knowledge, if only to better understand how knowledge is developed within organizations. Tacit knowledge is personal. It tends to arise out of practice and is, therefore, very context specific and difficult to codify or communicate. Explicit knowledge is public or shared knowledge. By definition, it is knowledge that has been codified and communicated across the organization. Tacit knowledge is the knowledge of the craftsman; explicit knowledge is the knowledge of the scientist.

When we talk of knowledge, we tend to focus on the explicit knowledge shared within the organization, but we forget the tacit knowledge held by individuals. Effective teams tap into the tacit knowledge held by members and use it to their advantage in designing and making improvements. In so doing they convert tacit knowledge held by members into explicit knowledge shared by the team and, later, the organization. Tacit knowledge can only be made useful in a broader context if it is converted into explicit form. Otherwise it remains the sole (intellectual) property of those that have it.

TYPES OF TEAMS

Teams differ primarily by the nature of the improvement task at hand. A team established to re-engineer a manufacturing process will look very different from a team whose mission is ongoing improvement within the Human Resources department. Basically four types of teams are identified: Executive Leadership Teams, Corporate Task Force, Cross-Functional Teams and Intact Teams.

Exhibit 43: Types of Teams

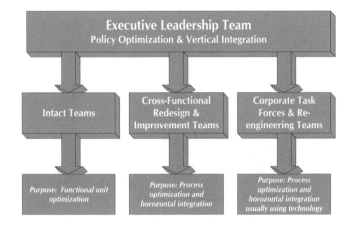

EXECUTIVE OR LEADERSHIP TEAM

Executive Leadership Teams (ELT) are really a special case of team whose task is not so much to tackle specific problems or process improvement activities, but rather to provide guidance to the other types of teams and clear away the hurdles preventing them from accomplishing their objectives. Specifically, the tasks and functions of an Executive Leadership Team are:

▲ **Identifying the Priorities for Improvement.** There are always more improvement opportunities than resources capable of addressing them. One function of leadership, then, is deciding what is most important to the organization and committing the resources required to see improvement made in this area. At the same time, this means that other areas will not have the resources they require. This comes down to providing focus and discipline.

If there is any area where executive improvement teams fail, this is it. Usually, problems result from a lack of focus or discipline. Instead of picking one or two priorities and focusing organizational efforts accordingly, numerous priorities are identified. The improvement effort gets spread too thin and, in an attempt to fix everything, nothing changes.

▲ **Securing the Resources.** Improvement efforts and the teams that direct them require the resources to do the job. Too often, improvement assignments are simply added on to the existing workload of the employees involved. The result is team members with divided loyalties, one for the improvement effort and the other for the day-to-day

requirements of their job. This does not mean that team assignments are an all or nothing affair. It is certainly reasonable to divide an employee's time, reserving a portion for the day-to-day activities and a portion for the improvement effort. What is not reasonable is a continual process of adding to the workload.

Time is not the only resource to be secured. Money, machinery, methods and the like are all valuable resources to the improvement effort. As was the case with time, it is the Executive Leadership's Team's job to secure the resources required to ensure the improvement effort is accomplished. Resources, after all, are not only a requirement of the improvement initiative, they are also a measure of commitment. Organizations that are 'committed' to some form of improvement, but have not allocated any resources to the effort, are not committed at all.

▲ **Integrating the Efforts.** Once the corporate priority for improvement has been established and the resources secured, various teams may be formed to resolve or address different dimensions of the problem(s). It is the function of the ELT to keep these various teams aligned so their efforts support one another rather than work at cross purposes. Doing so is the process of ensuring horizontal integration.

▲ **Clearing the Path.** Improvement efforts never go as smoothly as we envision. Problems always creep in. A problem turns out to be a lot more difficult to tackle than originally anticipated: an improvement team encounters resistance from some operating area of the company; a proposed solution requires agreement from two areas of the company that haven't agreed to anything since the American Civil War. All of these complications and more can bog down and/or destroy an otherwise well-functioning improvement team.

In such circumstances, it becomes the function of the ELT to "clear the path" or "plow the road." This entails dealing with the inevitable hierarchical concerns that emerge with any improvement effort, and dealing with them so they do not become a serious impediment to the improvement effort.

Creation of executive leadership teams reinforces the notion that meaningful improvement requires leadership. As such, the ELT needs to be as familiar with the tools, techniques and approaches of process improvement as anyone else in the organization. Process improvement cannot, or at least should not, be considered a requirement of employees that excludes the higher levels of the organization. If executive managers don't know how to do process improvement, they cannot guide it.

The first task of an ELT, therefore, is to learn. Learn the methods of data analysis, teamwork, process analysis and change. In short, learn the requirements of improvement. Only when this is accomplished should ELT's begin the effort of guiding and helping others.

CORPORATE TASK FORCE

Corporate task forces are generally high-level teams comprised primarily of senior officers and managers whose task is the significant redesign or re-engineering of core or primary business processes or products. The problem or issue to be resolved is usually of strategic importance to the organization, requiring significant levels and breadth of expertise. There is usually representation from various departments and functions because the processes involved are of sufficient scale to flow across or impact numerous areas of the organization.

Exhibit 44: Corporate Task Force

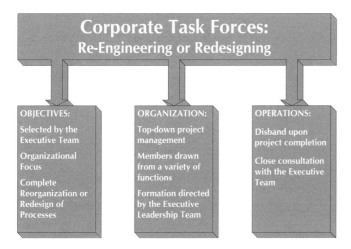

The corporate task force is the usual vehicle in re-engineering applications. It can also be used in process redesign strategies, where the process or problem is of significant scope and importance to the organization.

Corporate task forces distinguish themselves from the cross-functional teams (discussed next) in terms of the nature of the issue to be resolved. Task teams are usually focussed on significant problems often of a strategic nature combined with a high level of perceived immediacy. As such, they are often concerned with pursuing a problem-solving strategy to address a significant special cause of variation. Some examples of typical applications for a corporate task force:

▲ **A competitor introduces a new product with significant technological improvements over existing designs.** The organization creates a task team to reverse-engineer the new product, analyze it and design a competitive product within six months that matches or improves upon the various characteristics of the competitor's entry.

▲ **An organization realizes that product quality has declined to the point where it is beginning to affect sales.** Never mind how we got into this situation, the organization must quickly address the quality problem. A task force is assigned to re-engineer the production process, retrain staff and perhaps even redesign the product to provide for easier manufacturing, and all within a limited time period so that sales declines do not become a major financial problem to the organization.

▲ **A product suffers a catastrophic failure and the product design is called into question.** A task force is quickly assembled to determine the cause of the failure and if that cause is with the product design, to modify the design as quickly as possible.

As the examples above indicate, the Corporate Task Force is usually reserved for those high-level applications where the organization is confronting some new and usually unanticipated development. This is why technology usually plays a key role in re-engineering applications. Rapid advances in technology, including information technology, often present organizations with a whole new set of game rules. When this happens, the organization must typically respond quickly to take advantage of the new operating realities. The Task Force is the improvement team designed for such purposes.

CROSS-FUNCTIONAL IMPROVEMENT TEAMS

Cross-functional improvement teams are the most versatile and widely used of the team types. They are the structural backbone of organizational improvement efforts and differ from task forces only in the circumstances under which they are created. Usually the issues facing a cross-functional improvement team involve less dramatic circumstances. But less dramatic doesn't mean less important. Generally, the cross-functional improvement team simply has more time to carefully study the

situation, understand what is going on and make improvements.

Membership tends to be drawn from more numerous layers of the hierarchy than the task force, and from whatever functional areas are involved with the problem or process under examination.

Exhibit 45: Cross-Functional Teams

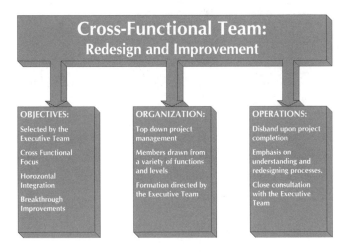

Cross-Functional Team:
Redesign and Improvement

OBJECTIVES:
Selected by the Executive Team
Cross Functional Focus
Horozontal Integration
Breakthrough Improvements

ORGANIZATION:
Top down project management
Members drawn from a variety of functions and levels
Formation directed by the Executive Team

OPERATIONS:
Disband upon project completion
Emphasis on understanding and redesigning processes.
Close consultation with the Executive Team

For the cross-functional improvement team, the issues can be large or small, of importance to a specific department, or of strategic importance to the entire organization. Cross-functional teams, then, generally find themselves pursuing a process redesign strategy in order to improve performance – usually through reduction of common cause variation. Some typical applications include:

▲ **An organization wants to develop a world-class manufacturing process.** The organization creates a cross-functional team to analyze the current process and redesign it to achieve superior quality and cost-operating performance that is beyond that of competitors.

▲ **A company wants to reduce the number of accidents or errors occurring in a process.** A cross-functional team is created to analyze an existing process and locate and eliminate the root causes of a performance problem. Examples could include reducing the number of billing errors, lost time accidents, manufacturing flaws, main line derailments, mailing and packaging errors, late time arrivals, surface paint flaws, high scrap rates and manufactured parts outside of specifications.

▲ **The Human Resources department wants to improve its hiring process.** The application is not strategic but a cross-functional team is created because of the implications for the rest of the company.

Be Innovative: Consider Your Customers

The flexibility of cross-functional teams is reflected in the novel way in which many companies choose to use them. An oil field engineering company created a cross-functional team to *"improve service and product quality to the customer."* Three of their largest customers were members of the team. They provided direct input as to what was and was not important to them and participated directly in the setting of priorities and guiding the improvement initiatives. The result was not only an improved engineering process but unparalleled levels of customer loyalty.

Similar situations exist with suppliers. Suppliers are part of the process. Organizations seeking to improve some aspect of process or product performance should consider making their suppliers part of the improvement effort by making them members of the improvement team. Often, they can identify cost savings that simply would never have occurred to the organization operating in isolation.

Note, however, that such innovative use of cross-functional teams requires 'customer-in' thinking combined with a 'suppliers as partners' mind-set. Organizations that play suppliers off against one another in a 'win-lose' competition, for example, should not expect a lot of cooperation. In such circumstances, suppliers will use the occasion to maximize their own profits at the organization's expense.

INTACT TEAMS

Intact teams differ significantly from other types of teams in that their membership is not established by management and they are not designed to handle cross-functional issues or concerns. Rather, intact teams exist within single functional departments or organizational units, and membership of the intact team is drawn from the membership of the department. Membership is voluntary and processes selected for improvement are established by the team. The focus of improvement activity is largely the processes that exist within the department or function (the frame establishes the departmental boundaries as the point of input and output of the process).

Intact teams do not disband. As they turn their attention from issue to issue and from project to project, however, their mem-

Exhibit 46: Intact Teams

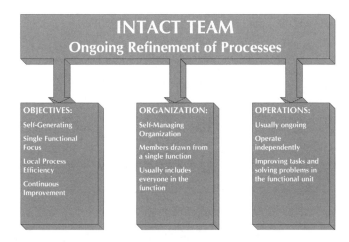

bership may change depending upon the ability of different department members to contribute, the time they have available and related factors. The existence of intact teams is a signal that the organization has reached a certain level of maturity in moving from the old methods of management to the new. Employees feel free to identify process performance issues without attaching blame; they form and reform project teams to study and resolve the problems and have the tools, training and authority to do so.

Self-Generating Teams

In organizations where the culture supports continuous improvement, teams form and disband in a continuing process of identifying, analyzing and resolving process problems. We call these 'self-generating' teams because they appear to come together spontaneously in response to process performance issues. This is particularly true with intact teams whose membership is constantly changing in response to changing issues or problems.

Of course, their formation is not spontaneous at all. It just looks that way because individuals within the organization have the power to decide whether something needs improvement and to gather the resources, in terms of people, time and money, to do something about it.

This makes for highly responsive organizations, but there is a tendency for these teams to take a "We don't need anyone else!" attitude. An intact team at a lower level of the organization can suffer from the same framing bias as a team framing an issue in the executive suite. Even when teams are self-generating, therefore, it is a good idea to solicit feedback and obtain guidance from stakeholders of the process, including senior management. Remember, the next process is the cus-

tomer. What is changed in one department will likely affect another department. It is the responsibility of any self-generating/organizing team to ensure improvement efforts are customer driven and take into account the overall functioning of the system of which the process is a part.

Examples of Intact Teams

Some typical examples of intact team applications are:

▲ **The production department undertakes an initiative to reduce scrap rates.** The focus of the improvement effort is on the existing manufacturing process within the department. Employees informally assign four departmental employees to examine existing methods and devise a plan to reduce the losses owing to scrap rate.

▲ **Tellers at a small bank come together to discuss closing-out procedures.** The closing procedures seemed to take longer than they should. The tellers came together to discuss the closing procedures used at other banks, as well as what tasks of the closing procedure seemed to have little purpose or value. They changed what they could and forwarded their additional recommendations having an impact other departments to management for consideration.

▲ **The call center of a telecommunications company reviews ways to reduce the wait time experienced by customers.** The departmental manager asks for eight people from the department to examine all the current processes affecting the total time it takes for a customer to "get through" to a service representative. The team is provided two hours per day to deal with the problem and come up with some immediate and longer-term solutions for the department.

PLANNING & ORGANIZING

When first brought together, the team must reassess any initial framing that was done by the individual that first recognized the need for change or improvement. As part of this process, the team will need to set objectives and discuss membership.

For example, in reassessing how the issue was framed, the team may change both the definition of the issue, the scope of the project, and as a result, the membership of the team. In the end, the team must have clear and agreed upon definition of what is to be done, how and by whom.

While conceptually different, therefore, planning and organizing are inter-related in practice. Some planning must precede the creation of the team and, once created, the team must do some planning and examine its own membership and structure.

ASSIGNED TASKS

In many instances, problem recognition occurs at senior levels of the company. The 'problem' is then assigned to someone in the organization, complete with an initial team and deadlines. There is a tendency, in such cases, for teams to skip over the planning and organizing tasks, accepting them as given by senior management and move immediately to fixing the problem. Don't!

When such assignments occur, the preliminary planning and organizing suffers from all biased framing described earlier. When senior management frames issues, there is a natural tendency to see the issue as existing outside the system or in spite of it. This occurs because the existing system reflects past decisions made by this same senior management. After all, it is difficult for any of us to see the problems with the things we create and take pride in – senior management included.

Take, for example, a safety issue. Management may be concerned about a rise in the number of accidents on the job. A team is formed to resolve the issue. But the issue as framed by senior management may be "getting employees to follow the safety policy." The underlying assumption is that the problem is with the employees not doing what they are told, whereas the problem may in fact be with the safety policy itself.

When teams simply accept the assignment as defined by others they are setting themselves up for failure. Problems or issues are generally caused by the system itself, in the way the work has been structured. If the team must resolve an issue or problem, but where the system is untouchable, frustration and failure are the usual end results. For this reason, teams and team leaders should be prepared to play a little catchball with those chartering the team.

Which means some negotiation and discussion will be required for all parties to come to agreement on the team mission or purpose, scope and membership. When this agreement is reached, the team and the organization will be in a good position to tackle the improvement opportunities at hand.

SELECTING TEAM MEMBERS

Team membership should be kept as small as possible while ensuring the representation requirements as dictated by the nature of the project or improvement effort are maintained. As a guideline, try to keep team size to below 10 members. In selecting specific membership, keep in mind the need for:

▲ **Diversity**. Representation from different levels and different functional responsibilities is necessary to ensure the problems are framed in the most productive way possible, and to ensure the team has members with sufficient exposure in different parts of the business to effectively discuss and resolve issues.

▲ **Skill & Knowledge**. Members must have the skills and knowledge required to address the process improvement issues at hand. In the name of representation, organizations may nominate members to teams that have neither the training nor the capability to handle the nature of the discussions or activities. This is neither fair to the team nor to the individual.

▲ **Willingness.** Not everyone wishes to be part of an improvement team or has the interest in participating. The reasons for this reluctance may be many, but regardless of the reason, team leaders need to respect individual wishes and desires. In some cases one individual possesses the specific breadth of skill or experience required by the team, but whose willingness to participate is limited. In such cases, the team leader needs to probe the reasons behind the reluctance and attempt to remove the barriers that stand between the individual and enthusiastic participation.

TEAM RESPONSIBILITIES & DUTIES

Whatever task the team has been assigned or it has assigned itself, it is important that it have the authority to act. The whole purpose of teams is to frame problems broadly, break down the barriers that separate departments and levels, analyze issues using a scientific approach, and implement solutions that have or can gain broad organizational acceptance. In short, the objective is improvement. But little of this will be accomplished if team members are expected to gain executive or senior management approval at each and every stage. Organizations are notoriously efficient at derailing improvement efforts. Failing to give teams authority is a way to guarantee improvement never happens.

With the authority comes the responsibility to ensure that implementation occurs – not simply recommendations being made. Too often, teams are disbanded at the point of making recommendations or at the point of having implemented the changes. Both these points are too early in the improvement process for disbanding. Teams need to be kept functioning, not only to the point of implementation, but through to the point where early operating problems arising from the change are resolved and a standardized process is in place.

Project Team Charter or Mandate

A team charter is a good starting point for process improvement teams. It is a written document, agreed upon by all members of the team and providing a brief description of what the team is expected to do.

Those experienced in working on improvement projects, either in teams or as individuals, know the importance of maintaining focus. It is too easy to get halfway through things only to begin drifting. The focus shifts from what was originally intended to some new recently evolved objective. In teams, you reach this point when team members begin asking questions like "What are we supposed to do?"

The team charter acts as a touchstone, a point one can return to and regain bearings. In short, it is a reminder to the team about why they are here and doing what they are doing.

What Does it Look Like?

The project team charter should simply be a single-page document describing team purpose, key result area(s), project scope and constraints, fundamental principles, and timing and wind-up criteria. It need not be some fancy scrolled masterpiece. Rather, it should be a working document, something team members can use for guidance when considering the purpose and limits of the work.

Creating a Charter

Getting all the members of a team to agree on lunch is hard enough; getting them to agree on the team charter can seem impossible. The following process for creating a charter may be helpful.

1. Why are we here?

This will likely be the first meeting, so team members will not have had a chance to discuss what the project is all about or even meet one another. Now is the time. Arrange for introductions and make sure people know one another. Then ask team

Exhibit 47: Sample Team Charter Template

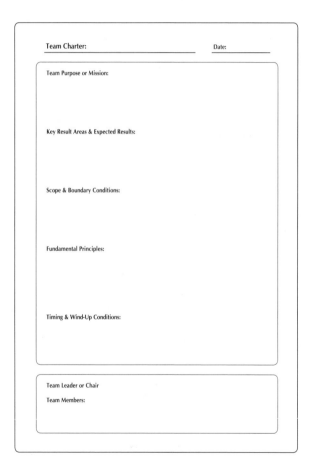

members to answer the question "*Why are we here?*" This essentially requires each individual to define the team purpose. Allow for and guide any discussion designed to increase the team's understanding of the problem, the processes at work and other project components.

2. Let ideas percolate

Let people sit with their thoughts for awhile. Ask them to privately write down their ideas or points to be included in the team charter as they think of them. Timing is flexible, but as a rough guide give people at least 20 minutes. While the first 10 minutes produces the greatest quantity of ideas, the last 10 minutes usually provides ideas of greater quality.

3. Solicit ideas from team members

With everyone having had time to think about and write down their specific points, go around the table soliciting individual ideas and recording them on flip chart paper and posting the paper on the wall as you go. Continue to go around the table until everyone's ideas on purpose have been recorded. Then move on to key result areas, fundamental principles and so on. Do not attempt to refine or discuss each category at this point.

Table 48: Team Charter Components

Charter Components	Definition	Examples
Team Purpose or Mission	Why the team exists and what end it is expected to accomplish. Purpose may also define the team's purpose in terms of the objectives of some larger team or the organization as a whole.	▶ *The purpose of the safety team is to reduce accidents in the plant, improving morale and reducing workers' compensation rates.* ▶ *Our mission is to improve efficiency at the teller stations, enhancing customer satisfaction by reducing wait times.*
Key Result Areas	Areas where we want to see some demonstrable improvement. These are often areas of high leverage where improvement is likely to have its greatest impact, or areas simply thought to be critical to organizational performance. The team may cite specific targets for these areas such as *reducing cost 15 percent,* or may choose more general performance improvement indications such as *improving staff morale.*	▶ *Reduce lost time accidents by half.* ▶ *Develop a reliable accident reporting system.* ▶ *Maximize customer throughput at the teller station reducing average wait time from 8 to 3 minutes.* ▶ *Reduce customer complaints of slow service by 25 percent in the first year and by an additional 25 percent in the second year.*
Project Scope & Boundary Conditions	What areas will come under the team's activities and any specific limitations that constrain improvement activities. Limitations are often defined in terms of budgets, timing or product design. Constraints that are defined in terms of conforming to corporate policies or procedures are to be avoided since these policies may be the cause of poor performance.	▶ *All safety processes used by the plant to reduce accidents, including safety training, safety reporting, safety audits and on-site procedures.* ▶ *All recommendations must meet federal and state regulations.* ▶ *The customer service process begins at the front door and is not completed until the customer has left the branch satisfied with his or her transaction.*

Table 48: Team Charter Components

Charter Components	Definition	Examples
Fundamental Principles	Describe the basic values and beliefs to which the team subscribes and that guide team and team member behavior.	▶ *We believe all employees have the right to know what our team is doing and the kind of results we are generating.* ▶ *We believe all team members deserve to be treated with respect and dignity.* ▶ *The team will use process analysis tools to analyze and describe processes.* ▶ *We will emphasize the use of knowledge and facts over opinion and gut feel.*
Timing and Wind-Up Conditions	Every team should know what constitutes completion of their efforts. This is the purpose of the timing and wind-up conditions. They state how long the team has to complete its task and at what point the team should disband. Teams should avoid the temptation to wind-up once a change has been implemented. Rather, team mandates should extend until the effects of the change have been measured and some reasonable estimation of success or failure can take place.	▶ *The project must be completed and a standardized process implemented by May 1.* ▶ *A report detailing process performance will be presented to the Executive Improvement Team by September 1.* ▶ *The team will wind-up after process changes have been monitored for 6 months.* ▶ *A report assessing overall success or failure, as well as key learnings, will be completed at that time.*

Simply make sure you are getting everyone's ideas up and before the team.

4. Define each charter component

Once everyone's points are up for each charter component, return to the team purpose. Attempt to combine similar ideas, refine wording and generally move towards a consensus. Don't belabor the issue, we are moving toward a consensus not perfection. Once the team loses energy for one component (i.e. team purpose) move on to the next. After you have gone through all the components of the charter in this manner, the team will have what is essentially a first draft of its charter.

5. Let the draft incubate

With the rough draft completed, team members will be drained, so let things incubate for a couple of days. Besides, other items may have to be addressed before the charter is finalized – adding team members for example. This time can also be used to type up and circulate the draft, complete with any controversial areas or issues to be resolved. The draft charter should be circulated within 24 hours of the meeting to make sure things are still fresh in everyone's mind.

Circulation of the draft should not be restricted to team members. If members of senior management were responsible for originally bringing the team together, they should also receive the initial draft. In addition, the team may be aware of potential impacts their activities may have on other departments not represented on the team, or on other improvement project teams.

In either case, these groups should also receive copies of the initial draft.

6. Reconvene the team and finalize the draft

After everyone has had time to reflect, reconvene the team to finalize the charter. Remember, the team may be slightly different than originally defined so don't be afraid to review past discussions, accomplishments and remaining issues. With this review of the past completed, the objective becomes consensus – everyone must agree to accept and support the final draft as written. There is no room for holdouts or conditional approvals.

7. Gain other approvals as required

Once the team has come to agreement, approval may have to come from the Executive Leadership Team or some other group. The team needs to gain this approval. As mentioned earlier, the way the team has framed the issue, the resources and the membership it thinks it requires may not be the same as senior management originally had in mind.

In such circumstances, the team should have its case ready and be prepared to present it to obtain the scope it thinks it requires to effectively address the issues. Having senior management sign the charter once agreed upon is a good way to symbolize the commitment of all parties to the success of the team.

Don't be afraid to accept some outside help. A process facilitator can help keep the group on track and free up the team leader to discuss issues of substance. Once a final draft has been completed, circulate to key stakeholders for comment.

HELPFUL HINTS

Some helpful hints to facilitate the process are:

▲ **Don't bog down.** Some teams argue endlessly over minor points or wording. Perfection is a concept, it doesn't exist in the real world so don't try to create it. When the team is close enough that all can accept and support, move on.

▲ **Create passion.** Successful teams have missions or purpose that create passion and excitement. Okay, that's a tall order if your tackling something that seems boring, like reducing the shipping time on telephone orders or reducing material scrap. Can anyone get passionate about scrap? Sure! Keep in mind these three pathways to passion:

▶ *Make it challenging.* Don't just try to make it better, try to make it outrageously better. A 10 percent improvement would be great, but what level of improvement is required to make us among the best in the world or the very best in the company? Challenge fires the imagination and the passion.

▶ *Make it specific.* People respond better if they know what success looks like. General goals are fine, but the more specific and concrete the goal, the easier it is to picture the end result. Remember the mission of Lexus: '*Beat Benz.*' It's specific, it's challenging and, frankly, it's fun. Who doesn't want to knock off the market leader?

▶ *Make it real.* There is excitement in the challenge, but goals need to be realistic and achievable too. That's one of the benefits to comparing yourself against other parts of the company or against competitors – if they have achieved it, maybe you can too.

▲ **Involve customers and stakeholders.** The team creates the charter, but it shouldn't be frightened of involving key stakeholders and customers in the process. Customer especially bring a unique and vital perspective to process improvement. After all, if we make improvements in a manner that doesn't suit the customer, we haven't achieved much. This includes outside consumers of the product or service as well as internal customers.

▲ **Recognize the role of the charter.** Make sure team members understand the importance of what you are creating. The team will be expected to live (and die) by its charter.

SYSTEM DEFINITION (SIPOC) DIAGRAM

It's all very well for a team to talk about improving system performance, but do we know what we are talking about? Do we agree on what the frame of reference is – on what constitutes the system?

The system definition diagram is designed to help here. It is nothing more than a SIPOC model with specific areas the team is required to detail to properly define the system. Doing so adds clarity, including the identification of key process suppliers and customers, inputs and outputs and major system components.

This is not intended to be a formal analysis tool; that's the function of process mapping and other related tools detailed in the next chapter. The system definition diagram is only intended only to provide some basic definitional parameters of the system. In short, the diagram can help frame or scope the system as it will be examined by the team.

The diagram identifies the 10 basic components of a system. These mirror the components presented in the basic notion of a system with a few additions relevant to teams assigned the task of some level of improvement. These 10 components are:

1. **Process Description,** a basic description of the process and its purpose. What is the name of the process involved? What does this process do – how does it add value?

2. **Customers,** a description of all the customers of the process, including various customer segments. Each of these in turn has a set of expectations, experiences and outcomes relative to the process and its outputs. These, in so far as practical at this early stage, should be identified.

Exhibit 49: System Definition Diagram

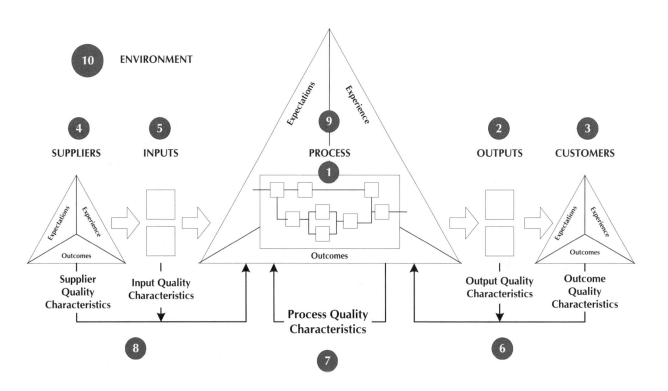

Exhibit 50: Sample Process Definition Template

Process Definition Worksheet (1/4)   Date:

1. Process Description: What is the purpose of this process and how does it accomplish this purpose – in other words, what is this process supposed to do?

2. Outputs: List all the outputs associated with the process. Be sure to include relevant intended and unintended outputs.

3. Customers: List all the customers for the outputs produced by the process. Some customers will be internal to the organization while others will be external. Some will be direct, the essential purchasers of what we are producing, while others will be indirect, essentially purchasing the by products of the process. For each of these, customer expectations, experience and outcomes should be identified.

Customer	Direct or Indirect	Internal or External	Expectations	Experience	Outcomes

---

Process Definition Worksheet (2/4)   Date:

4. Suppliers: List all the suppliers providing some form of input to the process. Like customers, some suppliers will be direct, providing what the process needs to function now, others will be more indirect, providing longer term or supportive inputs. Similarly, some suppliers will be internal while others will be external. For all of these, different suppliers will have different expectations, experiences and outcomes.

Supplier	Direct or Indirect	Internal or External	Expectations	Experience	Outcomes

5. Inputs: List all the inputs provided by each supplier. If you are having trouble or if you want to test for comprehensiveness remember the five M's: Men (people), Machines, Materials, Methods, Measures.

Exhibit 51: Sample Process Definition Template (Continued)

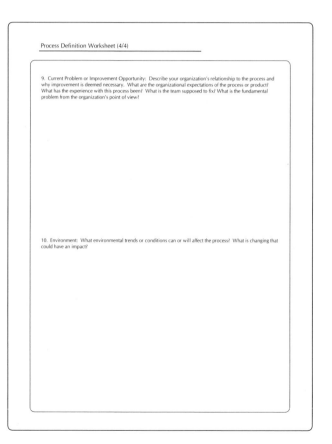

Process Definition Worksheet (3/4)   Date:

6. Outcome/Output Characteristics: What measures are used to analyze the effectiveness of the process? Are outcome measures (sales levels, customer satisfaction, market share, etc.) gathered and/or available? Are output measures (percentage of defects delivered, turnaround time, percentage conforming to specifications, etc.) gathered and/or available?

7. Process Performance Characteristics: What measures are used to analyze the effectiveness and efficiency of the process? Metrics such as cycle time, defect rates, cost per unit, delivery time, scrap rate, etc. are typical.

8. Input Quality Charatersictics: What measures are used to analyze inputs to the process, including our relationships with suppliers?

Process Definition Worksheet (4/4)

9. Current Problem or Improvement Opportunity: Describe your organization's relationship to the process and why improvement is deemed necessary. What are the organizational expectations of the process or product? What has the experience with this process been? What is the team supposed to fix? What is the fundamental problem from the organization's point of view?

10. Environment: What environmental trends or conditions can or will affect the process? What is changing that could have an impact?

3. **Outputs,** the specific services or products provided by the process. Each and every output of a process can and should be mapped to a specific customer or customer segment.

4. **Suppliers,** all the individuals or organizations that supply inputs to the process. As actors in the system, suppliers also have a set of expectations, experiences and outcomes associated with the process. What are these?

5. **Inputs,** the specific materials and resources provided to the process. Each and every input should be mapped to a specific supplier.

6. **Customer Feedback/Measures**, how we measure customer satisfaction and the results of these measures. What do we know about the effectiveness of our products or services?

7. **Process Performance Feedback/Measures,** how we measure process performance and the results of these measures. What do we know about how the process performs?

8. **Process Input Characteristics and Measures**. What types of resources does this process consume? How much of these resources does it consume? What are the characteristics of these resources?

9. **Understanding of Current Problem or Improvement Opportunity.** What we know about current process and functioning as well as the specific "felt needs" or performance gaps that led to the creation of the team. Is there something we are supposed to fix? If so, how bad is the problem? Where are the opportunities for improvement?

10. **Key Environmental Considerations,** a description of key drivers or environmental elements deemed to likely affect process performance now or in the near future. This could include proposed legislative changes, trends in consumer demands, technological change, etc.

USING THE SYSTEM DEFINITION DIAGRAM

Out of the 10 components of the diagram, the system/ process definition diagram has only one item concerned with the process itself. This is because the diagram is not an analytical tool designed to understand how the process works but rather a planning tool designed to help teams understand the scope and focus of the improvement effort.

As such, the process definition diagram is a good first step for teams undertaking an improvement effort. It is a long way from all the work that needs to be done, but it is a foundation for further work.

TEAM NORMS: OPERATING GUIDELINES

Operating guidelines are a translation of fundamental principles to the day-to-day functioning of the team. They provide a formal description of team norms, the specific acceptable and non-acceptable behaviors of team members. Without this formal description, the habits of individuals become the norms of the team by default. Rarely do such habits translate into effective team behavior. Team norms:

▲ establish a common set of behaviors describing how team members will treat one another;

▲ provide a touchstone against which the team can regulate the behavior of members in a non-threatening and non-confrontational way;

▲ prevent individual habits from becoming the operating norms by default;

▲ foster trust and openness in team settings.

It's important to keep in mind that effective team norms are:

▶ *clear,* use simple language in a simple way to communicate a clear and easily understandable message;

▶ *concise,* keep it short and to the point; this is not the place for lengthy exposition as to why the norm is there;

▶ *comprehensive,* they cover off behaviors in all the circumstances in which members will find themselves. This usually takes fewer norms than you might think. The trick is to use principles that guide behavior, not rules that dictate behavior.

EXAMPLE SET OF TEAM NORMS

Some examples of team norms include:

▶ We will respect each other's time, allow others to state their piece and keep our own speeches short and to the point;

▶ Meetings will start on time and all will be present;

▶ Decisions will be team decisions and based on consensus;

▶ We will attack the issues and not each other;

▶ Having fun is permitted, but not at others' expense.

CREATING TEAM NORMS

Team norms should be one of the first orders of business for any team. Creating the norms is a straightforward process consisting of three steps:

1. Gather the team

With the team together, the leader or advisor/facilitator should review what team norms are and their purpose. Discussion to clarify these what norms are should be encouraged.

2. Brainstorm the guidelines

On a flip chart, record team members' ideas for basic norms. As each page becomes filled, post it on the wall. Continue until there are no more fresh ideas.

3. Revise the list

Combine ideas and amend until a workable list is completed. Remember the three criteria for effective norms: clear, concise and comprehensive.

Once completed, the entire set of norms should fit on two sheets of flipchart paper, with large enough print when posted on the wall they can be easily seen by all team members. In fact, the norms should be posted on the wall in every team meeting. This itself can become quite the norm. Some teams will not consider the team meeting to have started until the norms have been carried into the room and posted on the wall by the team leader.

As the team is modified over time, the norms may also be modified to reflect changes in make-up or purpose. They are very much a living thing, reflecting the team to which they apply.

3. Getting Ready: Planning and Organizing for Improvement

Creating Visual Models: Using the Tools of Depiction to Improve Understanding

Performance in organizations, and any measure of it, depends on the process used to generate the output delivered to the customer. It doesn't matter what that output is, from policing services to the provision of health care to building automobiles or creating a new airliner. All these activities use some process to generate the intended output. A critical foundation of any improvement effort, therefore, is getting some idea of just what that process is.

There is a problem, however. Processes are largely invisible. They don't exist on the organization chart. You can't really see them when you're an outside observer. We see people working, product moving from one location to another, things being created, customers being served and so on. But the overall process, how all these things are organized – how they come together to "*turn inputs into outcomes*" – remains difficult to see.

Processes are likewise difficult to see to those working within the process. You can see yourself or others working, paper moving here and there, or perhaps some operator adjusting a machine. But you can't really see the whole process, those causes and conditions that all come together. You can see activity – pieces of the process – but not the process itself.

To overcome this problem and improve our understanding of how the process works, we can depict the process through a visual representation or model. We can draw a picture.

Pictures are powerful. The very act of creating a visual image of a process is definitional in nature. In drawing the process, an improvement team must first define its boundaries. This in itself goes a long way to defining the scope and focus of the improvement effort. Pictures can also help take the "fuzziness" out of our verbal descriptions. Like some dramatic newspaper photograph, visual representations of the process can make a statement about how we, as an organization, have structured the work. Lastly, making the relationships and structure visible allows teams to examine and evaluate the process design. Do things actually happen they way they are drawn? Is the design efficient? Do all tasks add value? Is there unnecessary waste?

For all their power, visual models – the tools of depiction – may be some of the least used tools in the Performance Improvement Toolkit. People seeking to improve performance often want to jump to numerical methods. But charging ahead with detailed measures of performance before depicting what is being measured is like jumping off the high diving board before ensuring there is water in the pool – the trip may be exhilarating, but the end result is likely to be messy! Before diving in to numerical methods, it is important to ensure you understand what is being measured. Visual models are the key tools for doing so.

TWO TYPES OF PICTURES

There are two basic types of visual models we can use to help represent a process. They differ in terms of what is being represented. They are:

Exhibit 52: Process Map and the Cause & Effect Diagram

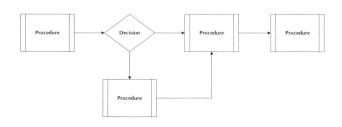

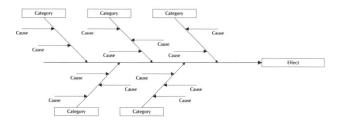

▲ **System & Process Maps**, which depict the physical activities or tasks involved in the process and how we have organized these various activities into a set of 'causes and conditions that come together.' System and process maps are commonly used when seeking to improve performance related to physical process design, such as process efficiency, productivity and reduction of complexity and resulting waste.

▲ **Cause-and-Effect (Ishikawa) Diagrams,** which depict the set of causal factors affecting some quality characteristic or outcome. The cause and effect diagram is not concerned as much with the physical design of the process as it is with the resulting cause-and-effect relationships that impact performance. These diagrams are most often used when investigating the root cause of a specific problem such as a decline in sales levels, recurring defects in a manufactured product, production of non-conforming product or delays in delivery.

SYSTEM & PROCESS MAPS

System and process maps attempt to present the underlying physical reality of the process or system. They depict the various process components, activities and tasks and show how they have been organized to work together.

WHY USE SYSTEM & PROCESS MAPS?

While they may lack a certain excitement (who can get excited just depicting what is happening?), process maps can often point the way to significant improvement. As the old saying goes, "*A picture is worth a thousand words.*" Process maps provide the picture. Few, if any, tools are better able to cut through the often bewildering array of policies, procedures, opinions and perceptions, to communicate to an improvement team or anyone else what is actually going on. Making the process visible:

▲ **Forces the definition of process boundaries.** If you are going to draw the process, you must decide where it begins and where it ends. Process maps force teams to decide where the boundaries will be, what will be included and excluded in the analysis.

▲ **Provides an understanding of the whole.** While individuals in organizations are aware of their own job situations and requirements, they are often unaware of how their job affects the overall picture. Process maps show how the individual 'parts' fit together and how they contribute to the production of a product or service and, ultimately, to customer satisfaction.

▲ **Leads to discovery of new customers and suppliers.** Because processes begin *with* suppliers and end *with* customers, mapping processes often leads to the discovery of 'new' customers or suppliers that had not been previously considered. The simple act of drawing the picture may lead to improved effectiveness, as the process is re-configured to serve these newly discovered players.

▲ **Disciplines our thinking.** Carefully documenting what is actually occurring within a process requires disciplined thinking. We have to cut through fuzzy definitions and operational uncertainties. This can be tedious, but the result is increased clarity in our understanding of what is actually going on. This is coupled with greater precision in the language used to communicate with one another about problems and opportunities.

▲ **Identifies opportunities for process improvement.** You don't need a control chart or fancy statistical methods to identify and make process improvements. Process maps are ideal tools for identifying problem areas or highlighting opportunities for improvement. For example, in flowcharts (a type of process map we will discuss shortly),

areas of delay, storage or loops are prime targets for elimination. Inability to agree on what is happening with certain parts of the process indicates areas where a standardized approach does not exist and chaos reigns – another prime target for improvement. Simply completing a process map may yield the response: "Well, no wonder things were screwing up!" In other words, making the process visible can also make the solutions apparent.

SOURCES OF PROCESS MAPS

Who actually creates the process maps? There are three generic strategies for process map creation. They are:

▲ **The expert.** This approach uses an expert trained in systems analysis to conduct the interviews, review the documentation and actually create the process map. It is a valuable approach when time is of the essence, but it suffers greatly from individual bias and a lack of team agreement.

▲ **Those most familiar.** A second approach is to ask the individual most familiar with the process to draw a flowchart or map the process under review. Again, this has significant advantages especially in terms of time. But these people are often under pressure to map things as they are supposed to be, rather than the way they are. Like using an expert, this approach suffers from individual bias and lack of team agreement.

▲ **Improvement Team.** This approach gets members of the improvement team involved in mapping the process. Different assignments are often made, but the emphasis is on agreement in order to produce a shared understanding of the process and how it functions. This does not mean that the team should exclude experts as part of the team, nor that the team should ignore the help and opinions of those most familiar with the process. It only means that agreement and understanding are the operating rules. This is a more time-consuming approach, but it also produces a more useful result.

TYPES OF PROCESS MAPS

For most business-process analysis, there are three types of process maps. These are:

▲ **Critical Process or System Maps**, which are used to identify what processes are actually at work within the organization, as well as the role these processes play relative to the overall organizational mission.

▲ **Block Diagrams**, which represent the first step in breaking down identified processes into manageable-sized "blocks" that can be targeted for further analysis. Block diagrams provide a breakdown of the basic structure of the processes at work within the organization.

▲ **Flowcharts**, which represent the workhorses of process mapping. They detail the activities and tasks associated with each major block of the process. Flowcharts use a more complex set of symbols than either system maps or block diagrams, and are used to communicate additional information about the various types of activities and tasks within the process.

Each type of process map has its own application and can be used independently where appropriate. However, the maps can also be used together to form a comprehensive system of process mapping. Critical process maps are used to identify the processes at work within the organization. Block diagramming can then be used to break down these critical processes into

Exhibit 53: A System of Analysis Using System & Process Maps

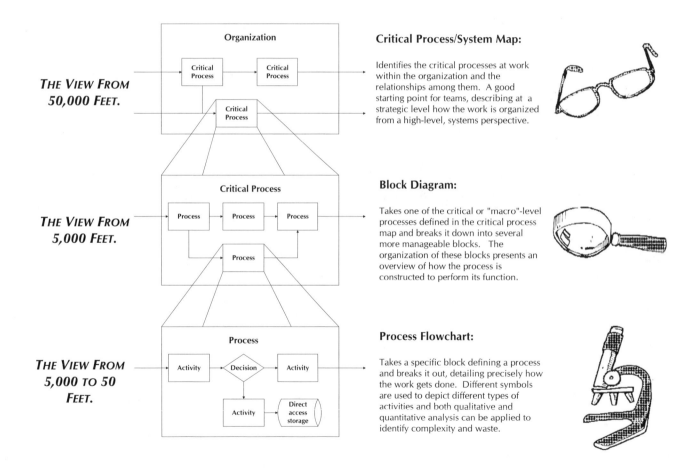

THE VIEW FROM 50,000 FEET.

Critical Process/System Map:

Identifies the critical processes at work within the organization and the relationships among them. A good starting point for teams, describing at a strategic level how the work is organized from a high-level, systems perspective.

THE VIEW FROM 5,000 FEET.

Block Diagram:

Takes one of the critical or "macro"-level processes defined in the critical process map and breaks it down into several more manageable blocks. The organization of these blocks presents an overview of how the process is constructed to perform its function.

THE VIEW FROM 5,000 TO 50 FEET.

Process Flowchart:

Takes a specific block defining a process and breaks it out, detailing precisely how the work gets done. Different symbols are used to depict different types of activities and both qualitative and quantitative analysis can be applied to identify complexity and waste.

sub-processes or more manageable 'blocks' of analysis. Priorities can then be set as to which of these blocks needs to be addressed first. Flowcharting is then used to detail the inner workings of each block, showing what types of activities are done, where and by whom.

Using the three primary-process mapping tools together provides organizations and teams with a powerful mechanism for effectively and efficiently depicting what is going on in the organization. It is effective because there is no better first step in an improvement effort than making visible what is to be improved. It is efficient, because the different tools provide varying degrees of analytical detail, and they can be selected and applied depending upon the circumstances and the need for information. If considerable detail is required, a flowchart can be used. If detail is not required, a block diagram can be used instead, saving considerable analytical effort.

CRITICAL PROCESSES/ SYSTEM MAPPING

Critical process mapping represents the highest level in the hierarchy of mapping processes. This is because the basic purpose of the critical process or system map is different than other types of maps. With block diagrams and flowcharts, the intent is to depict *how the process functions* by identifying *critical activities*, decision points and the like. With a critical process map, the intent is to depict how the *organization functions* by identifying the underlying *critical processes*.

For this reason, critical process maps are most commonly used in the initial stages of organizational planning and improvement efforts. If the organization has not yet identified its basic or critical processes, it is difficult if not impossible to be process-focussed in the improvement effort. Before initiating a crusade to improve, organizations need to define themselves in terms of their critical process, to provide focus and direction for what is to follow. Critical process maps are an ideal starting point of a performance improvement effort.

This is true regardless of the organizational level at which the improvement effort has been initiated. The effort may apply to the overall organization or entire company, or it may apply to a single department. The critical process map outlines the process at work within an organization, regardless the nature or scope of that organization.

A DIFFERENT KIND OF PROCESS MAP

Critical process maps are very different from other forms of process maps. We are not seeking to analyze and improve a system. Rather, we are seeking to better understand our organization by clearly depicting the processes at work within it. Critical process maps represent the ultimate top-down view of the organization and its supporting processes.

Creating the critical process map accomplishes several things. The task:

▲ *Compels management to identify the processes essential to the organization in accomplishing its mission.* Our thinking is too often dominated by the hierarchical image of the organization chart. This image prompts us to focus on departments or other organizational units when, in fact, we should be focusing on processes. A focus on organizational units often leads to simplistic solutions such as corporate rationalization and downswing efforts that chop "unnecessary departments." Instead, the focus should be on the processes within the organization – identifying those that do, and do not, add value and developing improvement strategies appropriate to each. The critical process map can help shift our focus away from the organization chart towards the critical processes that are actually at work creating and, in some cases, destroying value.

▲ *Provides a focus for improvement efforts.* Identifying critical processes provides an immediate focus for future process improvement efforts. In a corporate-wide strategy of process improvement, different teams can be established for each of the processes identified in the critical process map. Where resources are harder to come by, the critical process map can establish priorities for which processes need to be addressed first.

▲ *Highlights linkages between critical processes.* The critical process map highlights linkages between processes, and enables a global review of these relationships. This helps management avoid simplistic solutions to problems and emphasizes a more global, systematic approach to corporate strategy and organization performance improvement.

▲ *Segments types of critical processes.* Creating the critical process map compels management to segment the various critical processes into:

▶ **gemba processes,** which are those processes at the very center of the organization's mission and which have a direct impact on product and service quality that affect the customer. Conducting these processes effectively and efficiently is at the core of competitive advantage and corporate survival. These are placed in the middle of the critical process map.

▶ **supporting and management processes,** which are those processes that support or facilitate the conduct of gemba process activities. While clearly not core processes, they are nevertheless required to ensure core processes function to their maximum potential. These are placed at the bottom of the critical process map.

▶ **innovation and development processes,** which are those processes that are essential to the long-term viability of the organization. These may include processes used to identify customer requirements and translate them into new or improved products, as well as processes involved in the research of new product designs. These are placed at the top of the map.

CHARACTERISTICS OF A GOOD CRITICAL PROCESS MAP

What makes for a good critical process map? Basically, there are four characteristics:

▲ **It emphasizes connections with customers and suppliers.** The critical process map follows the rule that processes begin *with* suppliers and end *with* customers. Most, if not all, critical processes that are identified should connect directly with outside customers or suppliers, or at least be connected with another critical process that makes this 'outside' connection.

▲ **It emphasizes processes over organizational boundaries.** The critical process map identifies the processes at work, as opposed to the various departments or divisions within the organizational hierarchy. Sometimes, it is hard to tell them apart. When this happens, use the 'state change' test. Organizational units tend to manage components. Processes, on the other hand, convert inputs to outputs in a manner that adds value. This requires a state change from one thing into another. Try and apply this when creating a critical process map. Ask yourself: "What has changed?" What were the inputs and what were the resulting outputs?" If nothing has changed, then you're probably talking about organizational units, not processes.

▲ **The number of critical processes identified is kept to a manageable level.** Few organizations have more than 15 critical processes essential to the accomplishment of their mission. For the purposes of creating a good critical process map, this represents an operational maximum. Nor should too few processes be identified. Experience indicates that somewhere between five and 15 processes will produce useful results.

A sample critical process map is presented here. It demonstrates the general format and appearance of the map – at least in its initial draft.

Exhibit 54: Basic Critical Process/System Map

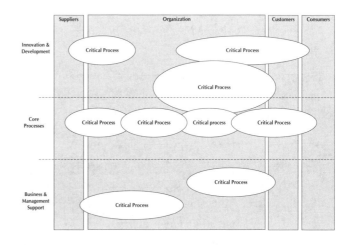

Circles, ovals or boxes – usually hand drawn in actual team planning sessions – represent the critical processes and are labeled with the process name. Overlaps represent points of connection where one process is dependent upon another. A process positioned to the right of another, and connected to it, is a customer for the process that is positioned to the left. Conversely, the process to the left is a supplier to the process on the right. Together, these linkages form a chain of processes connecting suppliers to the organization, and the organization to its customers and ultimate consumers of the product.

CREATING THE CRITICAL PROCESS MAP

The process of creating critical process maps is generally divided into two stages. These stages are:

▲ **Identify critical processes.** The hard part of creating the critical process map is agreeing on just what the critical processes are. Brainstorming techniques combined with affinity charting can be used to facilitate this process. This means gathering individual perceptions and discussing them in a team setting, and ultimately agreeing on what constitutes the operating processes of the organization. These processes are translated, roughly at first, onto a map with each critical process labeled and represented by an oval.

▲ **Depict the relationships between these critical processes.** Once the critical processes are identified and agreed to, a more sophisticated process map can be created that highlights not only the critical processes, but the fundamental relationships between them. Teams may decide not to proceed to this second phase if all they require is a definition of critical processes

The underlying assumption with critical process mapping is that everyone knows and accepts the core mission of the organization for which the critical process map is being created. The mission, however, may be changed after the map is completed. Often, the identification of critical processes motivates teams to modify the organization's mission – making it more realistic and reflective of the organization's activities and customers. This is especially true whenever the mission is more 'motherhood and apple pie.'

Eight steps are used to create the critical process map. The first six steps define the processes. Steps seven and eight provide a more detailed drawing that highlights the key relationships among the critical processes.

1. Review the organization and its mission

In a team setting, the team leader reviews the organization mission and the organizational boundaries. The mission should be customer-driven to some degree, so discussion of the mission should naturally include discussion of customers and their various requirements.

2. Individual listing of critical processes

Once there is general agreement on the mission of the organization, team members are asked to list what they believe are the critical processes at work in the organization. If required, some preliminary discussion around the definition of a process and characteristics of a good critical process map can start this step. Team members list these critical processes on sticky-notes. Usually, the number of critical processes each member can identify is unlimited, so the facilitator or leader should impose some restrictions. For example, people may be directed to limit the number processes identified to 15 as a means of retaining focus on the big picture, macro-level processes at work. To aid thinking, the facilitator may also ask individuals to write down separately core processes, supporting processes and development processes after carefully defining each.

3. Post individual results

When all team members are finished, the sticky-notes are placed on a large white board or piece of paper mounted on the wall. This can be done by all team members at once or in turns. As these notes are posted, team members should try to group notes that are similar.

4. Hold group discussion and rework

Once all the notes have been posted, the team is free to discuss, move or change any of the notes on the wall. Usually it is easiest to nominate a team member (not the facilitator or team leader) as the controller of the map, the only individual allowed to actually move or change the sticky-notes, ensuring that changes have the support of the group. There are no points for speed. The grouping of sticky-notes may go through numerous revisions before there is team-wide agreement.

5. Classify the critical processes

The next task is to classify the resulting critical processes as either core processes, supporting processes or developmental processes. In addition, the team may want to complete written definitions for each of the processes identified.

6. Draw the process map

With the critical processes identified and classified, the actual map can be constructed. Use a critical process map template as is or on an overhead, or reconstruct a similar template on the white board, so that all team members can see the emerging

Exhibit 55: Initial Critical Process Map

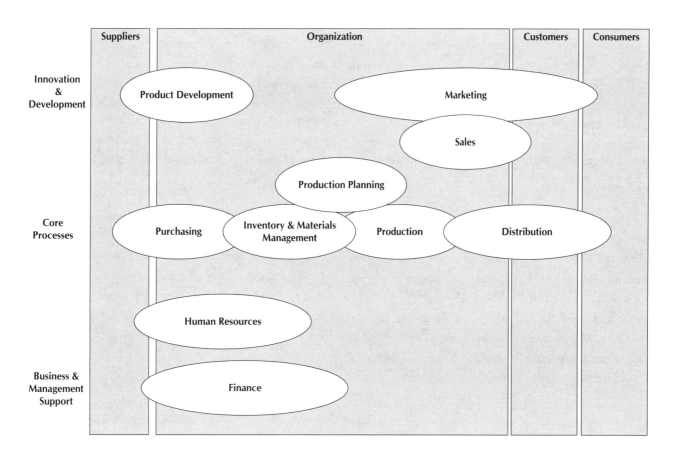

map. Here again, there is no prize for speed. The team should take its time and be prepared to discuss issues of concern

With this initial map created, the team can then move forward to create a more detailed version highlighting the relationships among the processes.

7. Identify the key or critical relationships

Team members can now discuss the critical relationships between the various processes. These relationships are best defined in terms of the products or services one process provides to another. In the example above, what does Human Resources provide to the rest of the organization? What does Inventory and Materials Management provide to Production? All these relationships need to be defined so critical inputs and outputs for each process are identified. The key here is to keep things at a high level. Recall the notion of the gemba, the kernel that describes the essence of what we are doing. During the discussion, the team leader or facilitator can use the initial chart as a worksheet to identify these relationships.

8. Redraw the final critical process map

Once the team has agreed on the relationships (inputs and outputs) linking the critical processes, the map should be redrawn using blocks to identify critical processes and arrows to indicate the nature and direction of the relationship.

Critical process maps have particular value in compelling organizational leadership to look at the organization differently, as a set of inter-related processes rather than a set of functional stand-alone silos.

The sample critical process map provided is a complex version – about as complicated as you would ever want of such a map. It nevertheless depicts the processes at work within the organization, and the relationships between them expressed in terms of inputs and outputs. It is, therefore, a systems-focused representation of the organization and a sound foundation for moving forward in analyzing organizational performance issues.

EXAMPLE: DESCRIBING CHEVRON CANADA

A good example is the critical process map created by Chevron Canada. At the time the map was created, Chevron was in the

Exhibit 56: Completed Critical Process/System Map

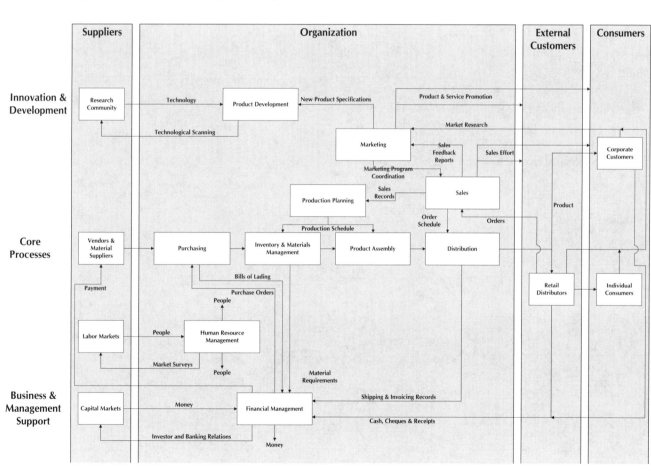

midst of redesigning itself – seeking to better understand the organization in order to achieve significant performance improvements. The executive, under then-President Donald Paul, created the critical process map presented in Exhibit 57: System Map at Chevron Canada.

The map is not complicated, but it is radical. This is a very different way of understanding an oil company. It allowed Chev-

ron to focus on its critical processes and better understand its core competencies. This diagram provided the basis of Chevron Canada's successful improvement efforts at the time by giving definition and focus to those efforts.[39]

---

39. Donald Paul, from a presentation given to the American Society for Quality Control, Calgary Chapter. My thanks to Mr. Paul for providing the diagram.

Exhibit 57: System Map at Chevron Canada

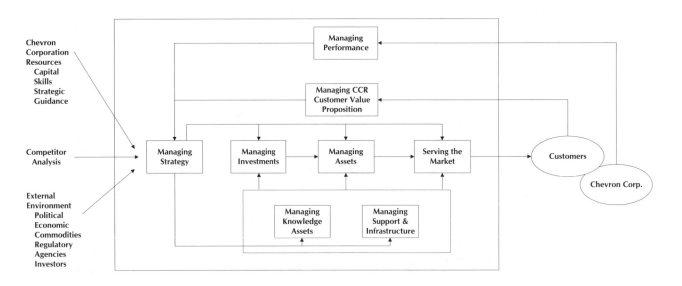

Critical process maps reflect not only the critical processes at work, but also how the organization thinks about itself. There is no such thing, therefore, as a definitive critical process map for any organization in any industry. Every critical process map is specific to the organization that created it, because it is intended to make visible not only the critical processes at work but also how the leadership chose to think about those processes. The critical process map created at Chevron Canada is as much a map of processes as it is a depiction of how Donald Paul and his team chose to think about their business and their organization.

BLOCK DIAGRAMS

Critical process maps are used to identify and define the critical processes within the organization. Block diagrams are the first tool to help teams analyze those processes. Block diagrams are simple and straightforward tools that can be used to break down any identified process into a logical, visual representation of the various activities and tasks that comprise the process. A sample block diagram is presented in Exhibit 58: Basic Block Diagram.

Three symbols are used in creating block diagrams. These symbols are:

▲ **block or rectangle,** representing an activity, task or other process component;

▲ **arrow,** representing the process flow or the relationships between the blocks;

▲ **an elongated circle,** to mark the beginning and end of the process.

The simplicity of block diagrams is their strength. They provide a quick overview of a process and can be used to simplify large or complex processes by breaking them down into more manageable, easier-to-understand 'blocks.'

Block diagramming is also a good intermediate step between critical process maps and the more detailed flowcharting discussed next. Flowcharting each block of the block diagram separately breaks down an extensive flow charting effort into several smaller, more manageable components. That way, the flowcharting effort can be better prioritized, focussing only upon those blocks likely to yield the greatest benefit from more detailed analysis.

Exhibit 58: Basic Block Diagram

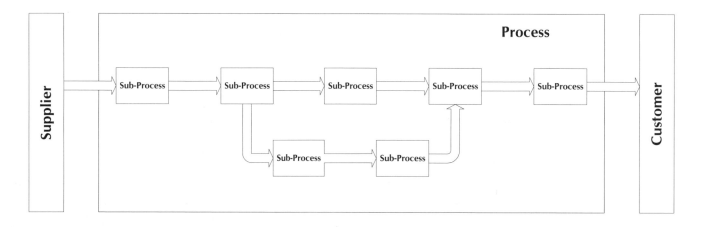

TWO BASIC TYPES

There are two basic types of block diagrams. These are:[40]

▲ **The Block Boundary Diagram.** The block boundary diagram is intended to make the boundaries of the process as explicit as possible. No attempt is made to detail the pro-

cess itself. Rather, the intent is to clarify who the customers and suppliers are, as well as other elements that define the context for process operations. In short, the block boundary diagram helps by defining the scope of the improvement effort.

▲ **The Block Flow Diagram.** The second step involves diagramming the basic building blocks of the process itself. Here we move away from analyzing the boundaries of the

---

40. The basic idea of separating block diagrams into these two distinct parts comes from James H. Harrington, Business Process Improvement, McGraw Hill, 1991

process and focus on how the process itself is organized and constructed – the internal operations.

BLOCK BOUNDARY DIAGRAM

In the block boundary diagram, the process itself is represented by a single block. Blocks outside the process usually describe, with a noun, the object the block represents. The objective here is to be exhaustive, detailing all the inputs, outputs, suppliers and customers that are in some way connected to the process.

Exhibit 59: Block Boundary Diagram

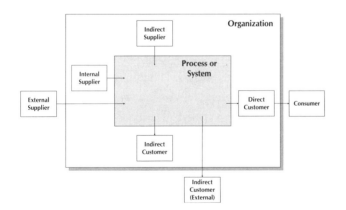

If the system is already well understood or is relatively simple to begin with, this initial boundary-definition stage can be skipped. However, experience suggests that process problems are as often due to a lack of clarity around the customer and suppliers, as they are to a lack of clarity on the process per se. For this reason, proceeding with the process definition and block boundary diagrams is often a useful exercise, even when the team believes it already has a good understanding of the suppliers and customers.

BLOCK FLOW DIAGRAM

The block flow diagram focuses not on the boundaries of the process, but on the depiction of what is happening inside the process. Creating the block flow diagram within a team environment is often most effective using affinity charting. Team members write down their individual perception of the activity components of the process on sticky-notes. These are then placed on a white board or large piece of paper mounted on a wall. The team discusses, moves and groups the pieces until there is agreement on the basic flow.

In contrast to the block boundary diagram, the block flow diagram is about activities rather than objects. The various blocks

---

Exhibit 60: Block Flow Diagram

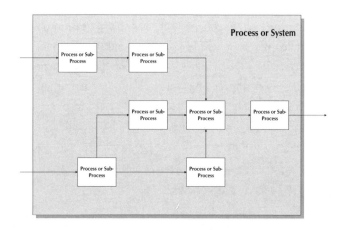

of the diagram are therefore usually described by a verb followed by a noun, (as opposed to just the noun in the block boundary diagram). This verb-noun technique ensures the description is of activities, tasks and sub-processes rather than products or organizational units. The block boundary diagram describes 'what' and 'who' are involved in the process. The block flow diagram describes 'how' the organization gets the work done.

The block flow diagram and the block boundary diagram can be combined, to show the relationships between activities inside the process and various suppliers and customers that define the boundary of the process. Teams are often surprised by the complexity that emerges from what was believed to be a very simple system.

CREATING THE BLOCK DIAGRAM

Whether creating block boundary or block flow diagrams, teams can use the following four-step procedure:

1. Brainstorm the components

The first step is getting team members to identify all the various components of the diagram. With a block boundary diagram, this will include customers, suppliers, inputs and outputs. Each of these is best described by a noun. With the block flow diagram, the components are the activities and tasks that make up the process. Each of these is best described by a verb followed by a noun.

In either case, the requirement at this stage is not agreement or analysis, it is comprehensiveness. The brainstorming process allows people to identify everything they see as being part of the process. Remember, the team should be focused on the "as is," not the "should be," of the process.

The results of the brainstorming are either captured on flip-chart paper or on sticky-notes. Posting results on flip-chart paper makes it easier for everyone on the team to see what has been mentioned so far, but capturing results on sticky-notes make it easier to organize the results in step 2.

2. Organize the results of the brainstorming

Once the brainstorming has produced what the team believes is an exhaustive list, the next step is organizing these results. Affinity charting is an ideal tool to do this. This basically involves organizing the sticky-notes into groups that logically fit together. For example, several identified tasks may be grouped together into a single activity. As the grouping exercise continues, the team may:

▲ **discard duplicates of tasks.** Be careful: make sure that the two tasks are, in fact, talking about the same thing. Seek clarity before discarding anything.

▲ **set aside tasks that the team agrees lie beyond the scope of the process.** These tasks should be set aside rather than

discarded, because the definition of the process and its boundaries may change as the block diagram progresses. Tasks that at one time are considered outside the process may later be considered as part of it.

3. Create the block diagram

Using the affinity chart groupings to define the blocks, create a first draft of the block diagram. The diagram may be drawn vertically or horizontally. By convention, the process will move from top to bottom on a vertical diagram and from left to right on a horizontal diagram. Whatever the format, each task, activity or component of the diagram is represented by a rectangle and is connected to other blocks where appropriate by an arrow.

The very act of drawing the block diagram will likely remind team members of other steps or components missed in the original brainstorming exercise. These should be dealt with as they arise and included in the diagram if all team members agree. If not everyone agrees, save the idea on the side – there will be time to reconsider it later.

4. Review and complete the diagram

With the first draft of the diagram created, now is the time to sit back and review the finished product. Are there gaps? Is anything missing? Do the arrows connect the blocks properly? Is this how things really happen? All these questions need to be addressed by the team in reviewing the diagram. New blocks can be added, others removed.

The team needn't restrict itself to team members. Outside feedback can be encouraged. Walk around and reality test the basic diagram. Because the block diagram maps things at a high level, this reality testing and feedback will likely take the form of questions such as "Where is the assembly function?" or "Did you include the government agency as a customer for our compliance reporting?" If you have answers to these questions, great. If not, they represent areas that are missing and that need to be addressed.

The first draft only represents the team's initial approximation of how things are, as a foundation to additional brainstorming, data gathering and modifications. These modifications are then made to the block diagram and a finalized version is completed.

CHARACTERISTICS OF A GOOD BLOCK DIAGRAM

No matter what type of block diagram is used – whether block flow, block boundary or a combination of the two – all block diagrams:

▲ **Simplify the Process,** by breaking it down into more manageable "chunks" that can be better understood by employees and teams. Avoid excessive detail. When too much detail emerges, consider combining blocks. These blocks may be worthwhile targets for future flowcharting efforts.

▲ **Make the Boundaries Visible,** by specifying where the process begins and ends. This is true even when a block boundary diagram is not used. The specific start and end points must be clearly identified and understood, to provide focus and a clear scope to any performance improvement effort.

▲ **Highlight Activities,** by using verbs as the first word of block flow diagram descriptions. This helps prevent falling into the trap of describing organizational units rather than the process flow.

Exhibit 61: Redesigning with the Use of Block Diagrams

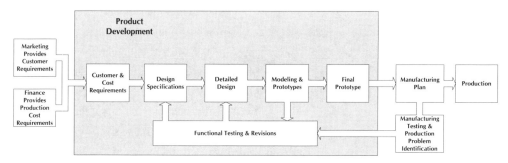

Block Diagram Depicting a Product Development Flow

The block flow diagram, by highlighting the re-work loop, makes it clear that manufacturing should have its requirements identified up front in the process.

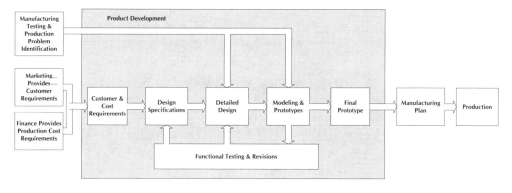

Redesigned Process

Manufacturing testing and requirements identified earlier, new product development cycle time reduced.

▲ **Are Well Documented,** indicating the process name, who was responsible for drawing the diagram and the date when the diagram was finalized.

With these characteristics in place, improvement teams will have a clear 5,000-foot view of the process they are seeking to improve.

FLOWCHARTS

Flowcharts are the work-horses of process mapping tools. They are invaluable for detailing the flow and inner workings of any process through the use of standard graphic symbols that represent different types of process activity. The introduction of these different graphical symbols distinguishes flowcharts from block diagrams. It also allows flowcharts to depict a process in considerably greater detail than is possible with block diagrams, and provide greater analytical power.

This greater analytical power makes flowcharts an ideal tool for improving understanding of how the process works, with the intent of analyzing opportunities for improvement. From this perspective, flowcharts should be used for purposes of:

▲ **Analysis.** Flowcharting is used to identify and analyze the specific tasks, steps or activities inherent in an existing process. The objective of this analysis is reducing the occurrence of loops, delays and other situations that increase process complexity and thereby reduce performance. Moreover, the flowchart allows the team to *see* what is going on. Doing so is the best first step in attempting to improve understanding. It is also, therefore, a good first step to take before any serious effort is expended at measuring process performance.

▲ **Documentation/Communication.** Flowcharts are not only a superb analytical tool, but also a powerful communication tool. As James Harrington put it, if *"One picture is worth a thousand words,"* then *"A flowchart is worth a thousand procedures."*[41] Any attempt, therefore, to standardize procedures or policies should include flowcharts as an aid to understanding what is trying to be communicated in the text.

▲ **Re-Design and Re-Engineering.** The flowchart, beyond considering what exists and analyzing potential problems or documenting current procedures, is an ideal tool in

---

41. James Harrington, Business Process Improvement, McGraw Hill Inc., 1991, p.40

Exhibit 62: Sample Flow Chart

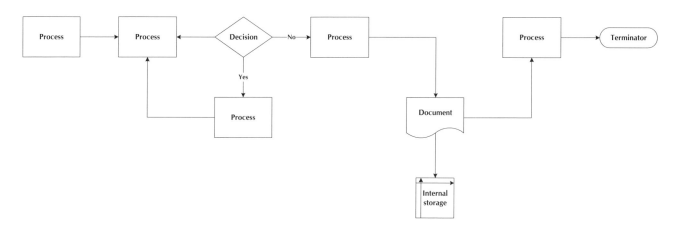

helping teams redesign existing processes or design entirely new processes. Again, the visual representation allows teams to see how the new or redesigned/re-engineered process will work before it is implemented. This allows teams to assess the level of complexity as well as likely effectiveness and efficiency. Moreover, the flowchart provides an opportunity for the improvement team to compare the proposed process with the existing one, making a direct comparison between how the proposed alternative will work with how things work now.

THE FLOWCHART SYMBOL SET

The flow chart symbols in Exhibit 63: Basic Flowchart Symbol Set, are the 10 most commonly used in depicting business and production processes. There are many more, but these 10 form the backbone of effective process documentation. Additional symbols can be used, but beware of introducing complexity at the expense of clarity.

Exhibit 63: Basic Flowchart Symbol Set

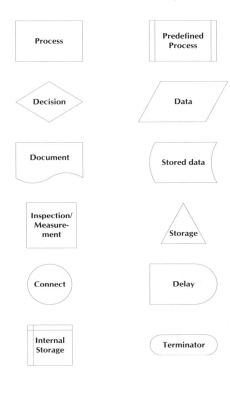

These symbols represent a partial set of symbols available for process analysis. However, like many things, the greatest value comes from the basics. Resist the temptation to create or apply different symbols for everything. The basics provided should cover just about any real world flowcharting application.

TYPES OF FLOWCHARTS

For process improvement purposes, all flowcharts use the same set of symbols and are laid out in basically the same way. Types of flowcharts are differentiated on the basis of the type enhancement added to the basic flowchart template. Generally, we can identify four basic types of flowcharts:

▶ the basic flowchart

▶ hierarchical flowchart

▶ deployment flowchart

▶ annotated flowchart

1. BASIC FLOW CHART

The basic flowchart is the most widely used of all flowchart types. It is called a basic flowchart because it does not add information beyond the basic symbol set.

In the example provided, a basic order-entry process has been flowcharted. It starts with a phone order being received (at the top of the diagram) and proceeds through a number of steps, including confirming customer status, setting up as a new customer if required, confirming credit, inventory of items ordered, entering into the production scheduling system if not in inventory, and so on.

You might see some items here that strike you as odd, inefficient or illogical. That's the kind of thinking a flowchart is intended to stimulate. More on flowchart analysis later.

2. HIERARCHICAL FLOWCHART

Hierarchical flowcharts are simply a group of basic flowcharts, each reflecting a different level of detail in the analysis. The top chart is generally referred to as the macro-process flowchart. Subsequent charts may be referred to as process flowcharts, sub-process flowcharts and so on. The idea is essentially the same as using critical process diagrams, then block diagrams and finally flowcharts to provide greater levels of detail. In this case, we are using flowcharts throughout to provide the detail required to effectively analyze the production or business process.

Hierarchical flowcharts are efficient. They allow the team to flowchart in detail only those areas that would benefit from additional analysis or where an opportunity for improvement is

Exhibit 64: Basic Flowchart

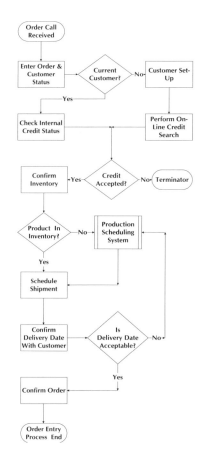

Exhibit 65: Basic Concept of Hierarchical Flowcharts

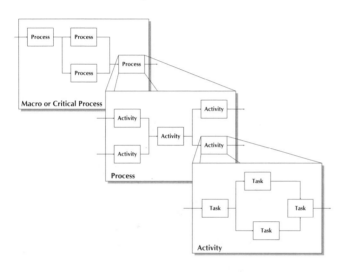

believed to exist. In short, we spend our analytical time where it will do the most good.

Hierarchical flowcharts also make big flowcharting tasks easier to handle, by breaking them up into more numerous smaller tasks. Each of these smaller tasks can then be assigned to individuals or team members to be brought back together and incorporated into the larger picture at a later date.

Lastly, hierarchical flowcharts can reveal the complexity behind what is perceived to be a simple process. Too often, people not familiar with a process bring a certain bias to the analysis. Questions like "How much work can it take?" or "What takes so much time to get this done?" reveal ignorance about what is happening behind the scenes. Hierarchical flowcharts make the activities behind the scenes visible.

3. FUNCTIONAL OR DEPLOYMENT FLOWCHART

Functional or deployment flowcharts divide the flowcharting workspace into sections that represent different organizational units. Symbols of the flowchart are mapped in the usual way, but placed in the space associated with the organizational unit that has responsibility for the specific task or activity represented by the flowchart symbol.

Functional flowcharts provide an additional level of analysis to the basic flowchart, by detailing how process responsibilities are deployed across organizational units. Obviously, in situations where the scope of the improvement effort is narrow – say, limited to a single department or area – the usefulness of the deployment flow chart will be limited. In other applica-

Exhibit 66: Hierarchal Flowchart

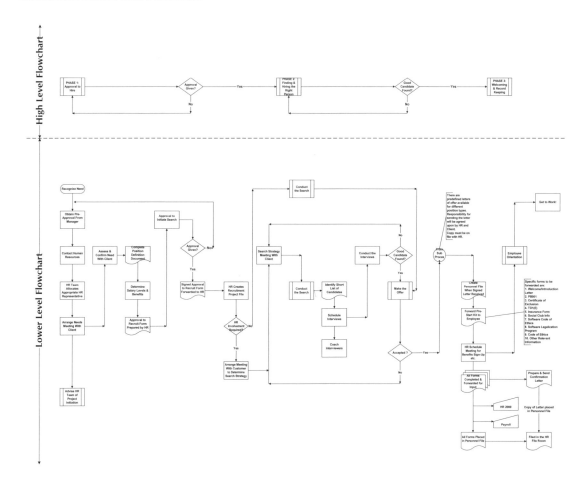

There is a Lot of Detail Down There!

At this level, the flowchart outlines a basic hiring process.

At this level, however, all the detail and complexity is there for everyone to see. This provides a focus for improvement. With the complexity exposed, teams can begin to target areas adding little or no value.

Exhibit 67: Basic Deployment Chart

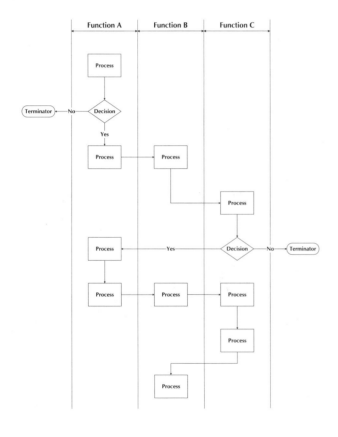

tions, however, the improvement effort is on processes that work across functional or organizational boundaries. For these applications, few tools are better able to convey who does what than the deployment flowchart. Indeed, it would be difficult to conceive of any cross-functional improvement effort that couldn't benefit by representing process flow as it occurs within and across the functional organizational design.

The more organizational boundaries the process must cross, the greater the complexity in the relationship between process and organization. Moreover, crossing organizational boundaries usually implies formal requisitions, memos or other forms of bureaucracy so deadly to process performance. These may not always be captured in the initial flowchart, but they should be looked for in subsequent revisions.

Despite the additional work they require – which isn't much – functional flowcharts should be used more than they are. Not only do they aid analysis, they are a real asset to process re-design where clear understanding of assigned roles and respon-sibilities is important. It is hard to imagine a situation, outside of a narrow within-function improvement, where deployment flowcharts should not be used, given the added value for the extra amount of effort.

Exhibit 68: Detailed Deployment Flowchart

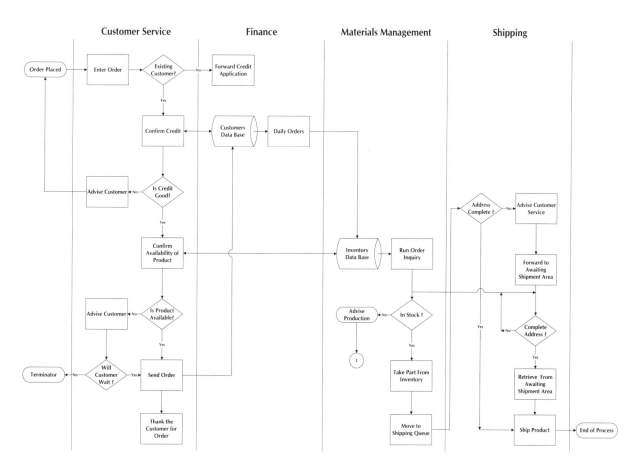

Deployment flowcharts can also be combined with hierarchical flowcharting. This entails creating a high-level deployment flowchart first, then providing additional detail with lower-level flowcharts in those areas where the team sees value in doing so.

4. Annotated Flowchart

Annotated flowcharts are flowcharts that contain or have notes attached to the various activities depicted. Usually these notes are in the form of a narrative that provides additional detail to the text attached to the flowchart symbol.

With this type of annotation, more detailed directions or enhanced explanations can be given than would otherwise be possible, making this type of flowchart ideal for purposes of process documentation and standardization. These flowcharts can be used for:

▲ **analysis**, depicting the way things function now, with notes detailing specific highlights including issue areas requiring improvement;

Exhibit 69: Annotated Flowchart

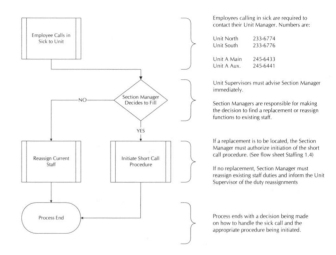

▲ **documentation,** explaining how things are to function and providing additional information to staff to help ensure the process as depicted is followed or adhered to;

▲ **re-design/re-engineering,** depicting a proposed improvement in how the process functions, to identify and remove potential problems before the new process is introduced.

CONSTRUCTING FLOWCHARTS

Critical process maps and block diagrams can be constructed solely by the team that's investigating process problems or seeking opportunities for improvement. There is no requirement to seek out opinions and knowledge of others outside the team, although doing so is recommended. Such is not the case with flowcharts.

A good flowchart is a data-gathering and organizing tool. The data is qualitative in nature but it is still data. It is used to accurately depict how a process is organized. Constructing a good flowchart requires members of the improvement team to seek out those employees engaged in the process, and to gather the facts about what is going on or how things are done. This requires interviewing employees, talking to them in a way that encourages honesty and understanding.

We can list five basic steps in flowchart creation. They are:

1. Define the process

Before employees can describe how the process works, the improvement team needs to define the process they are work-ing on. Completing the process definition diagram, as well as basic scoping work through block diagrams will go a long way to providing this definition. Don't try and flowchart a process without doing this preliminary work. The likely result will be wasted effort, as those doing the flowcharting struggle to define the boundaries and scope of their efforts. Define boundaries first, flowchart second.

2. Gather the data

Gathering data is the hardest part of creating the flowchart. The team must deal with a number of tricky elements, including bias of individual perspectives as well as the fear element. People will wonder why the flowcharting is being done and about its impact on them. Equally challenging is to understand the way people talk about things. We tend to use vague terms when describing activities or conditions. "This is always a problem," we say. What is meant by 'always'? What exactly is the problem?

Team members responsible for interviewing employees need to be specific – they need to "sweat the details." Never accept vague descriptions. The interviewer needs to come away with a precise description of exactly how the work gets done.

For help, see the section, Data Gathering: Some Helpful Notes on Interviewing immediately following this section. Another useful tool is using Voice of the Process Tables. These provide a basic data-gathering structure focused on the essential descriptive facts – namely the what, where, why, when and who and how of various process tasks.

3. Draft the flowchart

Sticky-notes can be a real help in building the flow chart. They allow teams to easily make changes and move things about. Tape a large sheet of paper on some wall space. The amount of paper you will need will depend upon the process and the size of the sticky-notes you are using. No team has suffered from having too much space to work on, but many have had problems when trying to move things about on too small a work surface. When in doubt, make it big!

Building the flowchart is easiest using a step-by-step approach, focusing first on tasks and decisions. From the interview notes, list the specific tasks of all those involved in the process on sticky-notes. Other team members can then begin posting these on the working space. Decisions also can be listed, with the symbol for a decision drawn onto the sticky-note. These sym-bols are roughly arranged into the order in which the process flows, from left to right or from top to bottom.

After the tasks and decisions are posted, other symbols are added to the flowchart. Delay and inventory symbols, as well as symbols for reports or data entry and data bases can also be added.

Once things start coming together, missing components will begin to make themselves apparent – places where a decision is required or some task is being performed. The team should feel free to add these missing components as the work is progressing.

4. Reality test

Once the flowchart is complete, a reality test of the completed diagram is needed. This is usually a two-step procedure.

▲ Follow the process through, ensuring it covers off all the elements gathered from the interviews. The flow chart needs to be comprehensive, capturing all the details of the process.

▲ Review the flowchart with those interviewed. Be prepared to sit down with those interviewed and take them through the flowchart. Move slowly, constantly checking accuracy: "Is this what happens?" "Does it happen this way every time?" This is not a session to show how great your flowchart is. It is an opportunity to gather additional data and ensure that what you have on paper accurately reflects the reality of the process under review.

5. Finalize

With the reality test complete, the flowchart will have to be updated and finalized. Explanations, notes and other elements can be added to help the reader and the team proceed with the analysis. Make sure to date the flowchart, list who was interviewed, and note the team members responsible for its creation.

DATA GATHERING: SOME HELPFUL NOTES ON INTERVIEWING

Because the flowchart is intended to reflect reality, data must accurately describe current conditions. This requires a good interviewing technique. Interviewers must strive to:

▶ Eliminate Bias

▶ Overcome Fear

▶ Clarify Fuzziness

Eliminate Bias

Whenever someone is interviewing for a flowcharting task, there is always a potential for bias. We all tend to see things from our own unique perspective. The sources of this bias are twofold:

▲ **Normative Bias** is the tendency to show things as they are supposed to be or as they soon will be "*as soon as we fix it next week.*" Modern organizations often function in spite of the policies and procedures in place. To get things done, employees regularly "*bend the rules.*" This is widely known but is not readily admitted (especially when something goes wrong). Asking employees to detail how things actually work, therefore, is asking them to detail exactly how and when they break the rules.

To overcome normative bias, the interviewer needs to stick to the facts. Document only what is happening right now rather than how policy says they should happen. Interviewing different people about the same process or process step also helps. The different perspectives should be reconciled by those creating the flowchart, to try and arrive at the reality that so often lies between conflicting viewpoints.

▲   **Centric Bias** is the tendency to see things from the point of view of your own department or organizational unit. Someone working in Accounts Payable is likely to detail activity in Accounts Payable, but is unlikely to be able to detail activities in other departments that may also have significant impact on the process. This is why the team needs to gather data from all those involved. The problem may be seen as an Accounts Payable problem, but additional data from other parts of the system can be invaluable in allowing the team to see the big picture.

Overcome Fear

Assigning blame is an essential characteristic of hierarchical thinking and the old model of management. Process improvement efforts can often imply that blame is about to be allocated. This is hardly conducive to effective process mapping.

Economic times in which organizations have "right sized" and restructured have not helped. These efforts have often left employees demoralized and untrusting of improvement initiatives. Many organizations have cut themselves off from the most important source of performance improvement information, their own people.

Overcoming fear is obviously easier said than done. Process improvement teams need to carefully consider the historical context of their organizations and develop tailor-made strategies to try and address this issue. There are no simple answers, but a little communication can go a long way. Specifically, improvement teams should explain their charter and the reason for analyzing the specific process(es), as well as explaining the intent and nature of the flowcharting technique. These are not perfect responses, but they can help lower the defensive barriers that often arise when employees hear that something is being reviewed for its efficiency.

Clarify Fuzziness

Getting to the facts during an interview can be a difficult, even irritating process. We all love to give our opinions on what is wrong with the company and what someone else should be doing better. But describing specifically what is actually happening is something else altogether.

Part of the problem is the way we use everyday language. Fuzziness – a lack of clarity – is typical and to be expected. Statements such as "*I feel just awful about it*" or "*That project really bombed*" convey meaning suitable for everyday conversation. But this language is totally unsuitable for flowcharting a process or conveying information usable for improvement. Here are some traps to look out for – the eight factors of fuzziness:

▲ **Universal Quantifiers.** Words like *never, all, always, everyone,* are broad generalizations that rarely stand up to analysis. Try to get the respondent to be specific or identify possible exceptions.

▲ **Implied Necessity.** Words such as *must, cannot, should,* imply a lack of choice. The most important follow up question here is "*Why?*" (i.e. "*Why must something be done this way?*")

▲ **Unspecified Nouns.** To depict a process, we need to be specific on what nouns are being discussed. If "*forms are arriving late,*" we need to know which forms are arriving late.

▲ **Unspecified Verbs.** Processes are concerned with verbs because processes are made up of actions. In fact, we can describe processes as the verbs of work. It is very important, therefore, that the interviewer drill down for specifics when general verbs are used. For example, if a respondent says something is "*moved*" during the process, the immediate response should be "*How is it moved?*"

▲ **Omissions.** Simple omissions of information need to be filled in if the statement by the respondent is to make sense. This is not as obvious as it might sound. For example, "*It costs too much*" is an omission. Compared to what?

▲ **Rules.** These are usually judgmental generalizations. For example, the phrase "*We do it the best way right now*" avoids examining the question of *best* for whom? It also avoids answering what constitutes *best*.

▲ **Nominalizations.** Words that have been changed from verbs to nouns are called nominalizations. Going from *relate* to *relationship, recognize* to *recognition, confused* to *confusion* are examples of nominalizations. If a respondent says "*We have a poor relationship with the customer.*" the interviewer should convert the noun back to a verb: "*What can be done to improve the way we relate to the customer?*" The whole idea here is to gather specific information.

▲ **Implied Cause & Effect.** Random variation in systems and processes is often to blame for errors. But people have a tendency to assign blame or point fingers. When respondents say one thing is caused by another, the interviewer should pursue specifically how the item or activity caused the change. For example, *"Employees are causing the high error rate"* could produce the follow-up question: *"Precisely how are the employees causing these errors?"*

A tool used to help support this type of data gathering is Voice of the Process Tables (VOPT), especially Part 1. These tables provide a structured approach to gathering information. They are designed to help remove fuzziness and provide the clarity required to understand process functioning. They are discussed in detail in the next section.

BASIC FLOWCHART ANALYSIS

So what can a flow chart tell us about the operation or process being examined?

Basic flowchart analysis focuses on the flowchart itself and what the patterns and symbols tell us about the design and functioning of the process. A comprehensive analytical review of the completed flowchart consists of 10 steps. They are:

1. **Examine All Decision Points.** In any process, there are points where decisions must be made. But every decision represents a point where the process must essentially stop, or at least slow down so a decision can be made. Eliminating decision points, therefore, can improve the efficiency of the process and streamline the process flow.

Processes tend to evolve towards greater complexity, and the creation of decision points within a process indicates the presence of this increased complexity. Decision points arise because of historical circumstances, curiosity in one area about what is happening in another area, and a lack of clarity concerning who is responsible for what.

Usually, the more bureaucratic an organization is, the more decision points there are (usually at multiple levels). In this way, no individual or group is required to take responsibility for the outcomes of the process. Teams need to question:

▶ How many decision points are there and does this

Exhibit 70: The First Eight Steps of Qualitative Flowchart Analysis

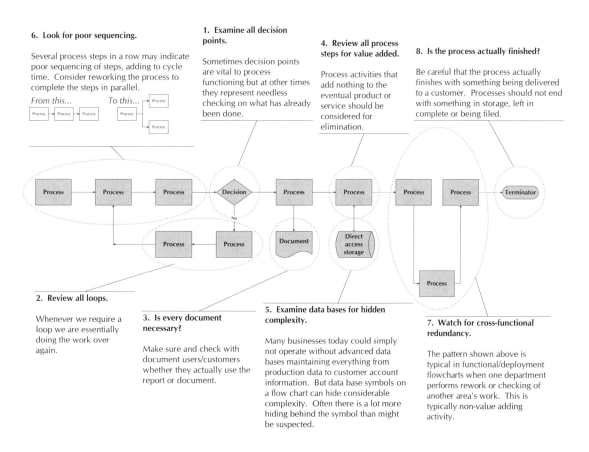

6. Look for poor sequencing.

Several process steps in a row may indicate poor sequencing of steps, adding to cycle time. Consider reworking the process to complete the steps in parallel.

1. Examine all decision points.

Sometimes decision points are vital to process functioning but at other times they represent needless checking on what has already been done.

4. Review all process steps for value added.

Process activities that add nothing to the eventual product or service should be considered for elimination.

8. Is the process actually finished?

Be careful that the process actually finishes with something being delivered to a customer. Processes should not end with something in storage, left in complete or being filed.

2. Review all loops.

Whenever we require a loop we are essentially doing the work over again.

3. Is every document necessary?

Make sure and check with document users/customers whether they actually use the report or document.

5. Examine data bases for hidden complexity.

Many businesses today could simply not operate without advanced data bases maintaining everything from production data to customer account information. But data base symbols on a flow chart can hide considerable complexity. Often there is a lot more hiding behind the symbol than might be suspected.

7. Watch for cross-functional redundancy.

The pattern shown above is typical in functional/deployment flowcharts when one department performs rework or checking of another area's work. This is typically non-value adding activity.

seem too many?

▶ Who is the process owner and is this individual making the decisions? Or is someone else and, if so, why?

▶ Why is a decision required at each point? What specifically is the added value being delivered?

▶ Are we actually making a decision or are we engaged in some form of checking?

▶ Can this decision point be made earlier, upstream in the process?

▶ What would happen if we eliminated this decision point?

2. **Review All Loops.** A loop is basically a rework of what was done previously – a potential waste of both time and effort. When loops are encountered, the reasons they exist must be explored. An assessment must be made as to the extent to which they add value to the product or service being delivered to the customer. Some key questions to be asked are:

▶ Are we performing this loop because of errors upstream and, if so, can we eliminate these errors?

▶ Does this loop do anything to prevent errors from happening or does it exist to accommodate errors? If the loop permits errors to recirculate, why not fix them once and for all?

▶ How many resources does this loop consume? (This is the cost of poor quality and should be identified.)

3. **Is Every Document Necessary?** Computers promised the paperless society. Instead, they have allowed us to produce more paper than ever before. Too often the question today is not "Do you really need this?" but "How many copies would you like?" Unfortunately, paper has its own cost, most of it hidden. Paper must be produced by someone, it must be read or at least reviewed by someone else, it must then be filed and the filing must be maintained – all for a piece of paper that the reader may not have wanted anyway!

The evolution toward greater complexity shows up in paper as well – with a vengeance. A report that someone required years ago continues to be produced, either out of habit or because someone thought it would be "nice to have." Over time, many if not most of the documents and reports produced by a process may fit into this category.

The bottom line is we end up producing a lot of paper. We go through a lot of work in the process, all for something no one really needs or wants.

Wherever the process produces a report or some other form of document, teams should review whether the piece of paper has any value. They should ask who it has value for and who it does not. This often requires interviewing recipients of the various documents produced by the process to ensure the paper is actually used for something other than filling up filing cabinet space.

4. **Review Process Steps for Added Value**. The purpose of every process is to add value. This means that every step or task within the process should do likewise. Teams need to review process or tasks in the flowchart and ensure the activity actually adds value.

Properly constructing the flowchart helps here. Use the proper labels for various types of process steps. The verb/noun technique especially helps team members understand precisely what the function of each step is, so they can better determine its value to the process and, ultimately, to the customer. Some specific questions teams should ask:

Value Added Classifications

There are different definitions or classifications of value added versus non-value adding activities. The two most useful approaches present either a two-part or a three-part classification scheme. The basic two-part approach is:

VA: Value Adding process step. This is an activity that produces something the customer (internal or external) is willing to pay for.

NVA: Non-Value Adding step. This is an activity that does not add value; it does something but nothing that would elicit additional perceived value from the customer.

The three-part scheme keeps the definition of *NVA* but divides Value Adding activities into two parts:

RVA: Real Value Added. These are process steps or activities that produce additional value to the customer – they provide value the customer would be willing to pay for.

BVA: Business Value Added. These are process steps the customer would not be willing to pay for, but nonetheless are required for the successful management of the company or the process itself.

▶ What exactly does this step contribute to the process?

▶ How does performing this task add value; that is, what does this step add that customers are willing to pay for?

▶ How does performing this step reduce the cost of the process, and is this cost saving greater than the cost of the task itself?

Check the specific activities identified in the flowchart for non-value adding activities. Value is not being added (or is being destroyed) whenever:

▶ The work step repeats an activity or task that has already been done elsewhere.

▶ The work step involves nothing more than movement from one storage situation to another. For example, transferring an item from one inventory location to another.

▶ Any activity that is really storage of an item.

▶ Activities that are reviewed and approved but have already been approved by someone else (multiple levels of approval).

5. **Examine Data Bases for Hidden Complexity.** Organizations would find it difficult if not impossible to function without advanced computer systems and data bases maintaining everything from production data to financial records to customer account information. There is a tendency to put 'everything' on the computer because the obvious costs are relatively low – things like storage costs and the cost of new machines. But more often than not, the hidden costs are far greater than the cost of additional hardware. Data base symbols can hide considerable complexity and waste. Maintaining information, like producing documents, incurs its own hidden costs. Information must be gathered by someone, it must be entered into the computer, it must be reviewed in some regular fashion to ensure accuracy, and the data base must be maintained and secured. All this implies costs which are often hidden from view.

6. **Look for Poor Sequencing of Tasks.** Several tasks in a row indicate a very linear, step-by-step approach to production. This linear sequencing may be due to a dependency – one step cannot begin until the previous one ends. However, the dependency may be more myth than reality; the next step may in fact be initiated before the previous

process task ends. If this is the case, parallel processes can be introduced.

Parallel processing involves different tasks being done concurrently, or nearly so, by different individuals or departments. This reduces the overall or elapsed time required for the process to produce a product.

7. **Watch for Cross-Functional Redundancy.** Deployment flowcharts are powerful because they allow an analysis of "who is doing what," not just "what is being done." This enables a team to analyze cross-functional redundancy. This is where one department performs re-work or checking of another area's work. It is indicated where the flow chart shows a jump in the process from one department to another and then back again, especially with no state change or value being added along the way. Some key questions teams should ask in this regard are:

    ▶ Why is this department involved?

    ▶ What is the nature of this involvement? Does the department actually add something of value to the process or does it simply need to be informed of what is happening?

    ▶ What is the value added of this process step; is it something the customer is willing to pay for?

    ▶ What is the cost of this additional step in terms of process time; does it speed things up or does it slow things down?

8. **Is the Process Actually Finished?** Processes end with something being delivered to a customer. Be careful in reviewing the flowchart that the nature of the thing being delivered, and to whom, is documented. Processes do not end with something being placed in a filing cabinet, in storage or in inventory. This is another way of saying the process isn't finished because, as yet, nothing has actually been delivered to the customer.

    If a process flowchart ends in some unproductive fashion, the team needs to inquire or revisit the output of the process, as well as the customers for that output. The process needs to end with a product or service in the hands of an internal or external customer.

9. **Delay.** Delay activity has its own flowchart symbol, but it is not always to be found in flowcharts. Two types of conditions can cause a delay.

▶ **A supply push** is where deliveries from suppliers pile up faster than the next stage in the process can handle. In this case, the net effect is stockpiling of resources (work in process) and excessive inventory. The delay is with whatever inputs are to be used in the next part of the process as they wait in inventory.

▶ **A demand pull** is where the next stage of the process is requesting input faster than the supplying area can provide it. Here, the delay is with the process as it waits for the resources it requires.

In either a supply push or a demand pull, there is a problem of imbalance between two processes or process tasks. Supply and demand need to be better aligned with one another.

10. **Storage.** Any storage condition is a waste of resources. It ties up capital and slows down the process, necessitating tracking systems to monitor the storage condition, administrative/bureaucratic requirements to release the items from storage and so forth. Like delay, the problem of storage is usually related to timing. Look for root causes that impact the timing of things, including inaccurate forecasts, a lack of production or service delivery planning, poor scheduling and generally poor levels of process reliability.

VOICE OF THE PROCESS TABLES

Voice of the Process Tables (VOPT) are useful guides or templates to support the information-gathering process for building flowcharts, and the analytical process of identifying process design issues.

Voice of the Process Tables consist of two parts. They are:

▲ **VOPT Part 1: Descriptive Analysis** is designed to gather essential descriptive information related to the process. To do so, an elaboration of the 5W-2H technique is used (See Box). Asking "Who?" "What?" Where?" "When?" "Why?" "How?" and "How Much?" gathers the basic 5W-2H data detailing the process steps – removing fuzziness and providing clarity.

▲ **VOPT Part 2: Preliminary Performance Analysis** involves a preliminary analysis of performance, gathering

Exhibit 71: Voice of the Process Table: Part 1

Process:

ID	Process/Task Step	Purpose	Description					Value Added Classification:
	What	Why	Where	When	Who	How	How Much	RVA BVA NVA

Prepared By: Date:

Exhibit 72: Voice of the Process Table: Part 2

Process:

Process Task ID	Inputs	Outputs	Process Characteristics / Measures		
			Reliability	Cycle Time	Other

Prepared By: Date:

data on specific inputs, outputs as well as reliability and cycle time of process steps.

5W-2H Technique

The 5W-2H technique is a useful approach to ensure a problem, issue, customer demand or some other situation in which we find ourselves is adequately described. The name is derived from the seven questions to be answered: "Who?" "What?" "When?" "Where?" "Why?" "How?" and "How Much?" People will recognize this as an elaboration of the five "W's" of good reporting often taught in grade school.

The technique serves as the basis for three tools discussed in this book. They are:

▶ *Voice of the Process Tables: designed to elicit a complete description of the process and its constituent tasks or steps.*

▶ *Variance Analysis Tables: designed to help identify the set of causes and conditions that come together to produce process variances or exceptions. These are discussed in this chapter as supporting tools to Cause and Effect Diagrams.*

▶ *Voice of the Customer Tables: designed to detail the demands or requirements that various customer groups have for a product or service. These are discussed in Chapter 11 as supporting tools to deployment matrices.*

Apart from its application with these tools, the 5W-2H technique is helpful whenever the task is to describe circumstances or conditions. It serves as a useful test of our understanding. Unless we can answer all seven questions, our description, and therefore our understanding, is likely incomplete.

VOPT PART 1: DESCRIPTIVE ANALYSIS

Using VOPT in the data-gathering process provides the interviewer with a valuable tool to help ensure descriptive information is clear, specific and as objective as possible. During the interview, the interviewer notes any task identified by those being interviewed by placing the task in the "What" column of the table – that is *what* is being done. The table then provides a guide for the follow-up questions to be asked. "Who does this task?" "When is it done?" "Where is it done?" "Why is it done?" In addition, the interviewer asks "How is it done" and "How much?" The later question, "How much?" is usually expressed in such contexts as "How often?" or "How many?"

If these questions cannot be answered or filled in on the table, then there is still some fuzziness in our depiction of the process. The team, or some member of it, should go back and gather additional information to provide the clarity. In this regard, the Voice of the Process Table serves to test the thoroughness of our process description.

The use of Voice of Process Tables continues as subsequent interviews are conducted. When the data gathering is completed, the analyst will have a well-documented record of how employees see the process functioning. These notes and observations will then have to be combined into a single VOPT.

The answers to the 5W-2H questions also provide insight for the analysis that is to follow. Answering *why* a task is done, for example, offers insight into the value adding nature of the task. There should be some reason or requirement demanded by a customer (internal or external) for the task being done. If there is no customer demand, there is no value being added and the organization should consider eliminating the task from the process.

VOPT PART 2: PRELIMINARY PERFORMANCE ANALYSIS

Voice of the Process Tables also serve as useful guidelines for analysis. Asking the improvement team to document the inputs to and outputs of the process, the basic process or task reliability, and the cycle times ensures that the fundamentals of performance are being examined.

INPUTS

The first column of the VOPT Part 2 is for listing the inputs required by a particular process step. What resources are consumed by the process? Usually we can classify these resources as:

▲ **People.** How many individuals are involved in this activity? Does it take one person to do this or 50? Is it a full-time job or is it a part-time function? The efforts of people are a fundamental input to any process. Determining just how many people are involved is a good first step in evaluating the extent of this effort.

▲ **Materials.** What is the extent of material consumed by the process step? In service activities, materials will likely be minimal; in manufacturing, extensive.

▲ **Machines.** When products are manufactured, they "consume" some amount of the machine doing the work in the form of wear. Such concerns are not limited to manufacturing environments. Service activities also may consume considerable amount of machine time, usually in the form of computer processing.

▲ **Money.** Activities may also involve the direct or indirect expenditure of money. In other words, how much does it cost us to perform this activity?

OUTPUTS

Outputs define the entire set of things, intended and unintended, produced by the activity under analysis. Outputs are difficult to pre-define because they depend on the nature of the activity. What needs to be done in this column is to list what, in fact, is produced.

For example, a credit check activity would produce a confirmation of credit rating and a specific classification, either acceptance or rejection. Likewise, a fabrication procedure would produce a specific part with specific dimensions.

For each output, however, at least one quantifiable characteristic can always be captured – **volume**. How many units are produced or how many credit checks are performed? Other measures may be available, but the simple measure of volume assures us we have a sense of scale.

RELIABILITY (EFFECTIVENESS) ANALYSIS

Reliability means the quality (in the narrow sense of the word) of the outputs produced by the process or activity under analysis. Usually reliability focuses on the number of errors produced by the process, the level of waste, or the amount of re-work.

For example, a billing department may mail about 275 invoices per week – an output volume measure. But how many of these invoices are incorrectly posted and fail to reach the customer being billed? Posting errors can involve sending an invoice to the wrong customer or stuffing two different invoices into the same envelope or any number of possibilities. The error rate – or more appropriately the success rate – with posting would be the reliability of the process.

If the reliability of the invoicing process is 90 percent, about 28 invoices per week are failing to get to the customer for which they were intended. This, in turn, would cause considerable pressure on cash flow to say nothing about customer satisfaction or the added effort required within the billing department to perform or process the re-work. In the world of reliability, high numbers like 90 percent that would sound pretty good if we were still in grade school are rarely good enough. For this reason, measures of reliability usually deal with errors per thousand, per hundred thousand or per million.

CYCLE TIME (EFFICIENCY) ANALYSIS

Time is the one constant characteristic for all processes – it takes time to do anything. Moreover, the longer it takes to do it, the less efficient the process or activity. Analyzing time, therefore, is critical to understanding just how well or efficiently any process is functioning.

When analyzing the amount of time used or consumed by a process, two types or measures of time are used. These are:

▲ **Processing Time** is the time it takes to conduct the process step. When the processing times for each task or step are added together, we have the shortest possible time in which the entire process could be completed.

▲ **Cycle Time** is the elapsed time between a step being started and completed to the point where the next step in the process can be started. Adding all the cycle times gives the actual elapsed time it takes the process or activity to complete its cycle.

There is usually a considerable difference between processing time and cycle time. For example, a document may require only a minute to be reviewed and approved by a manager (processing time) but the same document may wait a week in that same manager's in-basket (cycle time) before it in fact gains approval.

These concepts of processing and cycle times can be applied to a flowchart. This creates an annotated flowchart where the annotations are the average processing and cycle times for each step. Alternatively, each step on the flowchart can be numbered in some way and used as a reference to a calculation worksheet in which processing and cycle times are listed for each step.

The Opportunity for Improvement: The Processing to Cycle Time Ratio

To extend the analysis, we could calculate the processing to cycle (P/C) time ratio. This ratio is simply the processing time divided by the cycle time.

$$\text{P/C Ratio} = \frac{\text{Processing Time}}{\text{Cycle Time}}$$

The larger the ratio, the greater the efficiency of the process. The maximum that can be achieved is 1.0 – where the time to process is equal to the cycle or elapsed time used to accomplish the task. This is the case where there are no delays of any sort. World-class process performance, therefore, translates into processes that have P/C ratios that are near to 1.0.

It should be noted that the processing-to-cycle time ratio is essentially an efficiency measure. There is no consideration of whether the steps should be done – only the time required to complete these steps is being measured.

The Value Added Cycle Time Ratio

Value added cycle time attempts to address effectiveness issues. Processing time is not included in the analysis at all. What is examined is the different types of cycle times.

Value added cycle time analysis first classifies the steps within the process as value added or non-value added. The cycle times associated with these steps are then obtained. The total of all the cycle times is equal to the total cycle time for the entire process. This forms the denominator.

The numerator in this ratio is the total cycle time for the value added steps. When this numerator is divided by the total cycle time ratio we obtain a proportion – specifically the proportion of total cycle time actually comprised of value adding activities. The specific equation would appear as follows:

$$\text{Value Added Cycle Time Ratio} = \frac{\text{Value Added Cycle Time}}{\text{Total Cycle Time}}$$

USING VOPT TO SUPPORT FLOWCHART ANALYSIS

Using VOPT to support flowchart analysis requires a basic numbering scheme, to link flowchart elements with VOPT descriptions and analysis. The numerical system usually takes the form of:

▲ **Numerical hierarchy;** especially when hierarchical flowcharts are being developed. A numerical hierarchy scheme takes the form of:

    1.0
      1.1
        1.1.1
          1.1.1.1
    2.0

▲ **Alphanumeric;** especially where deployment flowcharts are used. In these cases, the first letter represents some division or department, whereas the numeric portion represents the specific activity. An alphanumeric scheme looks like this:

    A.1
    A.2
    B.3.a.1

The first example would represent the first activity in Division "A." The second example represents the second activity in Division "A." The third example represents the third activity in Division "B" and the first activity in department "a" (within Division "B").

Whatever approach is used, the numerical identifier must be unique for each and every component identified on the flowchart. This identifier is then entered into the "ID" column of the VOPT.

The two tools may be developed sequentially (usually flowchart first and the VOPT second), or concurrently with the VOPT detail being added as the flowchart is developed. Either way, linking the two tools provides an enriched level of analysis and understanding.

Example: VOPT Analysis of Order Processing

An example of linking flowcharts and the VOTP tables is provided in Exhibit 74: Descriptive VOPT (Part 1) and Exhibit 75: Analytical VOPT (Part 2). It is based upon a high-level sales order processing flowchart presented in Exhibit 73: Sales Order Flowchart. Despite the relatively high level of the flowchart, the analysis was sufficient to identify some critical process problems. The flowchart and connected tables are presented in the exhibits on the following pages.

The numbering system was kept simple here, using integers to identify each of the major high-level process elements. These link directly to the VOPT, detailing basic process descriptions and analysis. Value added assessments were based solely on the opinions of the process improvement team and obtained using the Value Added Assessment Guide presented earlier.

Exhibit 73: Sales Order Flowchart

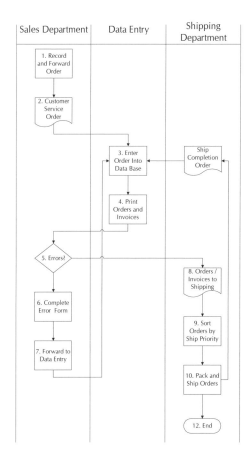

Exhibit 74: Descriptive VOPT (Part 1)

Process Task		Purpose		
Task ID	Task Name/Description	Why	Where	When
1	1. Record and Forward Order	Essential details of sale must be captured	Sales Department	At time a sale is received or closed
2	2. Customer Service Order	Service order is the basic form used throughout the rest of the process	One copy forwarded to Data Entry and a second copy maintained within Sales	At time a sale is received or closed
3	3. Enter Order into Database	Database used to track customer orders	Data Entry	As orders are received
4	4. Print Out Orders & Invoices	Used to drive the actual shipping of product	Data Entry	Printed at 2:30 pm. daily
5	5. Errors?	Ensure accurate entry of the order	Sales Department	All orders reviewed by Sales upon receipt from Data Entry
6	(If Yes) 6. Complete Error Correction Form	Corrections highlighted for database	Sales Department	Upon finding any errors within the sales orders
7	7. Forward to Data Entry	Forwarded to Data entry department to ensure data base and orders are accurate against sales records	Sales to Data Entry	Errors usually forwarded at about 4:00pm
8	(If No) 8. Orders & Invoices to Shipping	Shipping needs to know what to ship	Sales to Shipping	Correct orders forwarded at about 3:30 daily
9	9. Sort Orders by Ship Priority	Rush and standard orders are separated to ensure rush items are addressed first	Shipping	orders sorted immediately upon receipt
10	10. Pack & Ship Orders	Orders are prepared	Shipping	Priority orders usually shipped by 5:00 Balance of orders shipped the next day
11	11. Forward Order Completion	Order completion ensures database has accurate shipment status	Shipping to Data Entry	Order completion forms completed when shipped and forwarded twice daily 5:00 pm and 3:00pm
12	End			

Exhibit 75: Analytical VOPT (Part 2)

	Prcoess Task	Purpose		
Task ID	Task Name/Description	Why	Where	When
1	1. Record and Forward Order	Essential details of sale must be captured.	Sales Department	At time a sale is received or closed
2	2. Customer Service Order	Service order is the basic form used throughout the rest of the process	1 copy forwarded to Data Entry and a second copy maintaned within Sales.	At time a sale is received or closed
3	3. Enter Order into Database	Database used to track customer orders.	Data Entry	As orders are received.
4	4. Print Out Orders & Invoices	Use to drive the actual shipping of product	DataEntry	Printed at 2:30 pm. daily
5	5. Errors?	Ensure accurate entry of the order	Sales Department	All orders reviewed by Sales upon receipt from Data Entry, usually about
6	(If Yes) 6. Complete Error Correction Form	Corrections highlighted for database	Sales Department	Upon finding any errors within the sales orders
7	7. Forward to Data Entry	Forwarded to Data entry departmet to ensure data base and orders are accurate against sales records.	Sales to Data Entry	Errors usually forwarded at about 4:00pm
8	(If No) 8. Orders & Invoices to Shipping	Shipping needs to know what to ship	Sales to Shipping	Correct orders forwarded at about 3:30 daily
9	9. Sort Orders by Ship Priority	Rush and standard orders are seperated to ensure rush items are addressed first	Shipping	orders sorted immediately upon recept
10	10. Pack & Ship Orders	Orders are prepared	Shipping	Priority orders usually shipped by 5:00. Balance of orders shipped the next day.
11	11. Forward Order Completion	Order completion ensures database has accurate shipment status	Shipping to Data Entry	Order completion forms completed when shipped and forwarded twice daily 5:00 pm and 3:00pm.
12	End			

Numerical data was derived solely from conversations with staff. They are, therefore, opinion data as opposed to empirical data. Nevertheless, these estimates were deemed sufficient to better understand how the process operates. For example, how many service orders does a Data Entry Clerk process in a day? Answer: look at the Input and Output columns of the VOPT. In step 3, it takes two Data Entry Clerks to enter about 350 orders, or 175 orders per clerk per day. Each order takes about two minutes to process (see Cycle Time column). Lastly, about 80 percent of orders are entered correctly (see Reliability column. Determined as 70 out of every 350 have errors).

Processing-to-cycle time ratios can also be calculated for these process steps. These are provided in Table 74.

In this example, we can identify areas where time is literally being wasted. In step 7, for example, processing time is about a minute as this is the time it takes to forward the daily errors to Data Entry. The error list, however, often sits around in Sales for upwards of one hour. The processing to cycle time ratio, therefore, is 1 divided by 60 or 0.02 as presented in the table. The reason these orders sit in sales for the time they do turned out to be a simple one: it was too late to do anything about these orders the same day, so there was no motivation for Sales to move the listing along to Data Entry. A similar situation exists in step 11, Forwarding Completion Orders to Data Entry. This task is a low-value concern to the Shipping Department, which is far more focused on packaging and shipping orders than completing paperwork for Data Entry.

FROM "AS IS" TO "TO BE"

Application of visual models such as block diagrams and flow-charts is not limited to analyzing the current state of affairs. These models are also useful in mapping the way things should be as part of a redesign effort. We move from mapping the process 'as is' to mapping the process as it is 'to be.' This provides a valuable visual representation of what it is we are trying to achieve, which helps gain approval for change and improves the ability to communicate intentions with those impacted.

In the sales order example, the process improvement team focused on eliminating paper and reducing the movement of information and the amount of rework. These typically non-value adding activities tend to consume organizational effort and resources.

Table 76: Calculating Processing-to-Cycle Time Ratio

Process Steps/Tasks	Processing Time (1)	Cycle Time (2)	Processing to Cycle Time Ratio (1)/(2)
1. Record and Forward Order	6	8	0.75
2. Customer Service Order			n/a
3. Enter Order into Database	2	2	1.00
4. Print Out Orders & Invoices	30	40	0.75
5. Errors?	35	40	0.88
(If Yes) 6. Complete Error Correction Form	2	5	0.40
7. Forward to Data Entry	1	60	0.02
(If No) 8. Orders & Invoices to Shipping	5	15	0.33
9. Sort Orders by Ship Priority	10	15	0.67
10. Pack & Ship Orders	350	400	0.88
11. Forward Order Completion	5	20	0.25

Simply reviewing the flowchart along with the VOPT gave rise to a number of important questions. For example, "Why do Sales Representatives capture the information on paper and then forward everything to someone else to enter on the com-puter? Why don't they just enter it themselves?" There is always an answer to these types of questions by those interested in maintaining the status quo. In this case, the response was: "Sales Representatives are not computer people, they do not like using the system and don't know how." Such a response may or may not be valid, but the VOPT analysis can give a first-cut empirical indication of the cost of the status quo – that is, the cost of not making changes. This can go a long way to having people reconsider their opinions and their options.

Other questions arose as well. "Why do we use paper to communicate everything to do with the order? Do we really need three different forms to communicate the single idea that a customer wants something? Why does Sales check Data Entry work and why is the reject rate 20 per cent?"

In the end, the process improvement team pursued a strategy of "vigorous simplification," based on only moderate enhancements to existing technology. Using this strategy, they redesigned the existing process, created a new design and used a basic high-level flowchart to capture how it would work. The redesigned 'To Be' process is presented in Exhibit 75. This

Exhibit 77: "To Be" Sales Order Process Flowchart

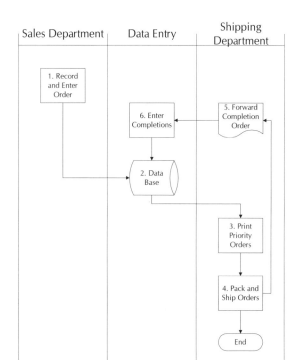

chart was then used by the team to communicate the proposed changes and build support for the effort.

CAUSE AND EFFECT (ISHIKAWA) DIAGRAMS

Cause and effect (C&E) diagrams are also called fish-bone diagrams because of their appearance, or Ishikawa diagrams, after their inventor Kaoru Ishikawa. They are intended to illustrate the relationship between a performance characteristic or outcome and those factors or causes that affect it. Think of the diagram as a theoretical map of all the possible causes affecting a performance characteristic. It is theoretical because the cause and effect diagram is usually the result of a team's brainstorming effort. It is, therefore, based on opinion and theory – not empirical evidence.

WHAT IT LOOKS LIKE

A quick glance at the cause and effect diagram reveals how it got the "fish-bone diagram" description. A performance outcome or characteristic is presented in a box at the right of the diagram. Connected to this box is a long horizontal line – the backbone of the "fish." Attached to the backbone are numerous other "bones" or lines representing causal groups. In turn, other

Exhibit 78: Basic Cause and Effect Diagram

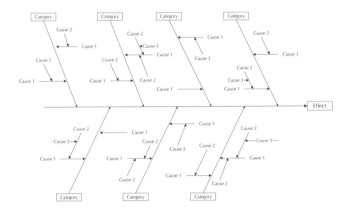

lines are attached to these, representing elements further up the causal chain. A generic C&E diagram is presented in Exhibit 78: Basic Cause and Effect Diagram.

The diagram essentially breaks down possible causes into main groups or categories. These are the primary causal characteristics. These are broken down into smaller and smaller potential causes of variation – secondary and tertiary causal characteristics. The result is a comprehensive map of all causal factors that could affect some result.

WHERE TO USE

Cause and effect diagrams are most commonly used when some performance problem has arisen. Examples include: an organization is experiencing a sales decline, material costs suddenly rising, increasing employee turnover and falling morale or a sudden increase in the number of customer complaints. These represent rather unique situations that require the improvement team to tackle the problem. As a map, cause and effect diagrams provide teams with guidance on where to look for root causes.

The diagram is also useful when preparing to gather data or building a measurement plan. Each arrow on the Ishikawa diagram represents a point at which some measurement could or should be taken; that is, where a measurement sensor could be placed. The relationship between cause and process performance can then be examined to see if there is a correlation between the effect and the suspected cause.

Ishikawa diagrams, then, should be used in conjunction with data analysis tools such as Pareto charts, histograms, scatter diagrams and run and control charts. These tools help move the performance improvement effort from the visual to the mathematical, and from the theoretical to the empirical. In these instances, the cause and effect diagram becomes a visual map of the measurement plan.

Ishikawa diagrams should be used:

▲ **Whenever teams are faced with unique or unstructured problems**, usually in the form of a problem or issue related to some performance outcome. The diagram is used to help identify potential causes, and to seek out likely root causes to the performance problem at hand.

▲ **Prior to initiating any data gathering or measurement initiative.** By identifying likely causes affecting a performance characteristic, the Ishikawa diagram identifies the best potential areas for empirical investigation. The diagram represents the current state of our theory as to why some problem exists. As such, it also pinpoints where we should look for empirical evidence to verify these causes.

HOW TO MAKE AN ISHIKAWA DIAGRAM

Ishikawa diagrams are intended to be used in a team setting. The greater the representation from the organization, the more comprehensive the result. It is this comprehensiveness we are looking for in creating the diagram. The cause and effect diagram does not represent the actual causes affecting the quality characteristic, it represents a consensus or group theory as to possible causes. These possible causes must then be combined with other data analysis tools to confirm or deny the theory. Specific steps to creating the Ishikawa diagram are presented below.

1. Gather the team

People from the various departments that have an interest in the process being examined need to be brought together. They may likely go beyond improvement team members to include customers, suppliers, those involved in the process itself, and those working outside of the process but having some stake in or relationship to it. Remember, the objective is comprehensiveness – building a map that encompasses a diverse set of perspectives and ideas.

The session should be understood as an open and free exchange of ideas, with everyone given the opportunity to express their opinions without fear of evaluation. Empirical tools will be used to confirm or deny theory later. At this point, the cause and effect diagram is intended to present a comprehensive picture of the possibilities – that is, the root causes and drivers of performance.

2. Decide on the performance quality characteristic or problem

What is it that concerns us – the yield of a process, errors made during hospital admissions, cracks in a solder joints? Perhaps we're concerned about a specific yet unstructured problem – declining sales in a particular region or a drop in employee morale. The more specific the performance characteristic or problem, the greater the usefulness of the Ishikawa diagram. General statements can be interpreted by various people in different ways. In larger team settings, this means some members may provide or offer causes to effects that are completely different than the effects on which the team needs to focus. The improvement team needs to provide focus by defining the problem carefully and by being specific in establishing the improvement objective.

Once the performance quality characteristic has been decided upon, draw a big horizontal arrow pointing to the right on a large piece of flip chart paper posted on a wall. The arrow represents the process under examination. At the right end of this arrow, write down the effect or problem as defined. This provides the backbone of the fishbone diagram and the foundation on which to build the causal structure.

3. Build the causal structure

Use brainstorming or related techniques to develop a list of possible causes (see "Brainstorming" on page 584). Generally, the more the merrier. We are not necessarily after quality at this point, simply quantity – as many likely or potential causes as possible.

Arrange the results of the brainstorming exercise into major groupings. Affinity charting is an ideal tool for this purpose ("Affinity Diagrams" on page 609). These major groups then become the major headings for the cause and effect diagram. An alternative procedure is to use a data reduction technique –

simple voting or rating methods to identify the major headings (see "Preference Decision Tools" on page 631). Ideally, there should not be too many or too few major headings – between two and 10 are good limits to keep in mind. These major groups or headings are then marked on the diagram, again in the form of arrows pointing to the major process arrow or backbone of the diagram.

Continue building the diagram by linking basic causes, obtained through the brainstorming, to the major headings. Continue adding causes where appropriate by linking them to major branches, sub-branches, sub-sub-branches and so on. By the time this initial draft of the diagram is finished, all the results of the brainstorming exercise should be a part of the diagram.

4. Fill it out – use the 5-Why Technique

As team members add the results of the brainstorming session to the diagram, the diagram itself can and should be used to help drive additional ideas. As each new cause is added to the diagram, the facilitator or team leader asks why this cause occurs. This elicits identification of additional and more basic causes, which are then added to the diagram as arrows con-

nected to the higher-order cause they are believed to influence. This is repeated for each new cause. The question 'why' is posed to the group in an effort to identify even more basic causes which are then added to the diagram.

This technique is referred to as the "5-Why Technique," because of the general advice that the process should be repeated five times to tunnel down to the root cause driving the performance effect or outcome. The five times is arbitrary. It is simply a guideline designed to help drive thinking down to root, as opposed to apparent, causes.

This process continues across the entire set of causes initially identified until the team is satisfied that every branch of the diagram begins with root causes.

5. Check and amend for logical consistency

Once completed, the cause and effect diagram needs to be checked for logical consistency. The causal chain presented on the diagram needs to make sense. Do the smallest branches cause the effect in the larger branch to which they are connected or is the reverse true? For example, do errors on hospital emergency room admitting forms cause errors in priority setting or vice versa?

Exhibit 79: The 5 Why Technique

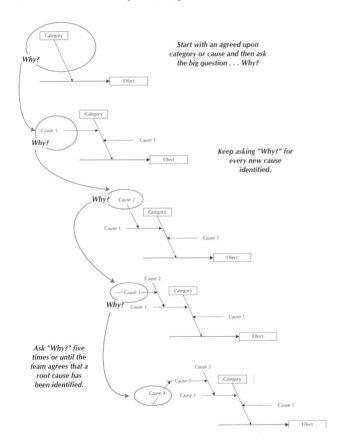

Exhibit 80: Checking for Logical Consistency

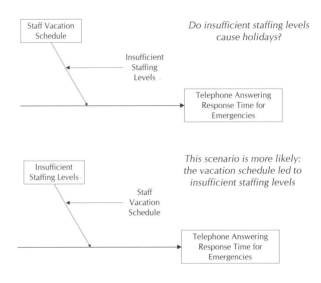

Beware of vague items in the causal chain. Causes may appear to make sense only because they are so vague they can mean anything, or at least different things to different people. Comments like "lack of training," "insufficient resources," "low staffing levels" are examples of vague comments that should be looked at in greater detail. For example, if staffing levels are low, what constitutes low and how does this impact or affect the cause to which it is connected? Searching for clarity will help later on when data analysis tools are used to measure the cause and effect relationships. It will also help ensure the team is working from a common framework or understanding.

The logic check can be tedious but it is essential. It is important to remember that the intent is more than simply organizing brainstorming data – it is creating a logical causal map of a process. Such a map demands a logical causal chain throughout.

6. Record the preparation specifics

Always record the date and team name as well as date of revision if applicable. The cause and effect diagram can be used as a living document, constantly under revision as the team learns more about the cause and conditions that do, and do not, lead to problems or effects.

HELPFUL HINTS

Here are some hints will help in preparing the Ishikawa diagram:

▲ **If identifying major categories is a problem, use the 6 M's.** These are People (Men), Material, Machines, Methods, Money and Measurements. Remember, any result is a function of the process characteristic being measured and the measurement system used. As such, it is wise to include a measurement section in the analysis. Other standardized categories can be used as well, especially if there is a logical technical flow to examination of the problem.

▲ **Revise constantly.** Cause and effect diagrams are not intended to be static tools. As causes are examined using data analysis, their influence on the quality characteristic can be confirmed or denied. If it is the latter, this "cause" should be removed from the cause and effect diagram. This is the process of constantly updating the diagram in light of new knowledge. Another source of revisions is the employees who did not have a chance to participate in the original session that created the chart. Some improvement teams post their cause and effect diagrams on hallway walls, to invite additions from the staff at large. This in effect broadens participation in the brainstorming effort.

▲ **Make a diagram for each quality characteristic or performance issue.** Any number of cause and effect diagrams can be prepared, each one corresponding to a different quality characteristic. Single diagrams that attempt to describe the entire process with all possible outcomes are too general in nature. They produce vague generalizations rather than a theory of causal connections or chains. If the process has a number of key quality characteristics, create a cause and effect diagram for each one. The added effort will be worth it.

▲ **Act on the obvious.** During the construction of the diagram, there may be some elements or causes that everyone agrees can be addressed and addressed now. If this is the case, don't wait – take action.

EXAMPLE: EXAMINING SERVICE DELIVERY PROBLEMS

An oil field service firm was having difficulty getting the correct parts to the proper well sites at the right times. Failure had significant consequences. A well site is costly to operate and maintain. When a part is needed, it is often needed now. The longer the delay, the greater the costs to the owner of the well.

Competitive advantage accrues to the company that can get the right part out to the well site as quickly as possible. In this case, however, the company just couldn't do it, at least not in any reliable way. Drivers were forever delivering the wrong parts and then having to return all the way to the warehouse (sometimes over 300 miles away) to pick up the right part and drive all the way back to the well site.

All this created a rather large and ingenious 'underground inventory' of parts hidden in the backs of delivery trucks. This informal approach to the problem was only partially successful in resolving the delivery of incorrect parts, but was very good at driving up inventory holding costs and shrinkage.

Moreover, delivery was slow. Even when the right part was delivered, it seemed to take longer than it should and definitely longer than competitors serving the same customers.

In response to the problem, the organization decided to deliver a one-day course on effective communication skills to its order processing and warehouse employees. This was coupled with numerous posters designed to support the training, emphasizing the need to: *"Listen actively," "Get it right the first time"* and *"Fulfill your promises."* This is a classic case of seeing all problems as people problems as in *"They just won't listen"* or *"Can't they read the labels?"* To add insult to injury, this same group was required to complete accountability agreements, essentially promising to get the correct replacement part to the right location quickly.

When this program failed to have the desired effect, the company decided to "get serious." It brought together a small group of employees directly involved with the process, to help identify what could be going wrong – defining the potential causes of the problem. Once this initial problem identification took place, the team used a basic cause and effect diagram to help structure their ideas. The results of this initial causal analysis are presented in Exhibit 81: Initial Cause and Effect Diagram: Shipping Problems. The initial diagram combined pre-defined major branches with other classifications that seemed to emerge from the data.

The team, armed with the initial diagram, then redrew the cause and effect diagram paying special attention to a logical causal flow. The diagram woke a lot of people up. It had been all too easy to blame those in the front lines for the problem. After all, what could possibly go wrong in shipping beyond

people just not paying attention? The cause and effect diagram had the answer: "Plenty!"

Using the diagram as a causal map, the team identified those causes it believed to be major drivers of the overall effect – the shipping errors generally. It did this by classifying the causes as chronic, periodic or sporadic (See "Supporting Analytical Methods" on page 257). The team then picked their top three and easiest-to-fix causes among those classified as chronic and implemented some fairly simple solutions. As it turned out, all three dealt with causes on the labelling branch of the diagram. In essence, the team had defined a labelling improvement initiative as the improvement strategy likely having the greatest leverage on shipping errors and delays. Within three weeks of making the changes, errors had dropped by just over 20 percent. Using the diagram as a road-map, the team continued to identify problem priorities for the next 14 months. Not all the solutions were successes. However, the net effect was a continuous process of improvement evidenced by an ever-declining rate of shipping errors.

Exhibit 81: Initial Cause and Effect Diagram: Shipping Problems

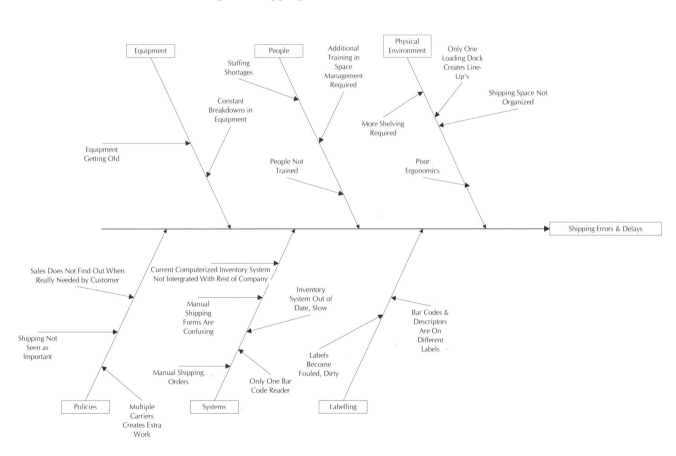

Exhibit 82: Revised Cause and Effect Diagram

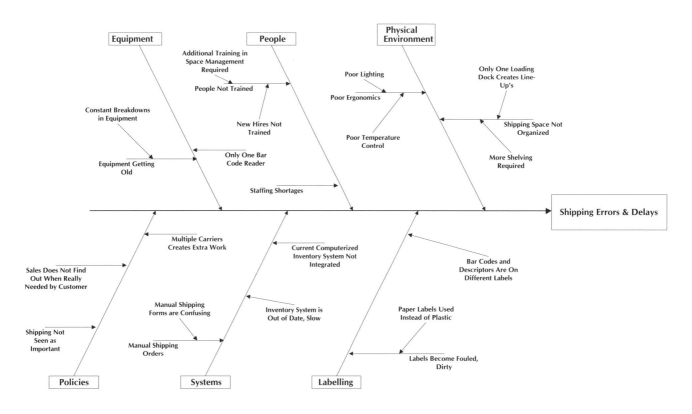

SUPPORTING ANALYTICAL METHODS

The cause and effect diagram is supported by a number of analytical methods that can help teams find the root causes of performance problems. First and foremost among these is performance measurement. As already mentioned, the cause and effect diagram can serve as a measurement plan – identifying areas where measurements can take place. In the process, suspected causes (as detailed in the diagram) can be confirmed or eliminated depending upon the empirical findings arising from the measurements. If eliminated, these causes are removed from the diagram or at least given a special marking to indicate they are not as significant as first thought.

The cause and effect diagram can also be used directly as a problem-solving tool. In such circumstances, it provides a map of what likely problems exist and how they influence performance outcomes. The supporting analytical methods that follow use the cause and effect diagram as a foundation for analysis and identification of potential solutions.

CLASSIFYING FREQUENCY OF OCCURRENCE

A good first step when attempting to locate the cause of some problem is to classify the frequency of occurrence. A three-part scheme is used, with effects and causes classified as sporadic, periodic or chronic.

Some problems occur all the time. These are chronic problems likely due to excessive or unacceptable levels of common cause variation. Others problems may be periodic, returning with regular frequency, such as at month's end. This is likely structural variation. Lastly, some problems are sporadic, occurring infrequently and without any correlation to time or place. These may be signals of special or assignable causes of variation.

To help set priorities on which causes the team will examine first, match the classification of causes to the type of performance problem experienced. If customer complaints are the quality characteristic we are seeking to understand and complaint levels rise periodically at month's end, we may want to examine causes related to that same period as the first priorities for improvement.

Table 83: Classification of Causes and Likely Associated Variation

Classification	Description	Associated Variation
Chronic	Cause would likely produce ongoing or chronic problems in the effect.	This cause is likely producing common cause variation.
Periodic	Cause would likely produce occasional changes in the effect at identifiable times.	Likely structural variation associated with elements beyond managerial control.
Sporadic	Likely to produce changes in the effect at unpredictable times without any predictable pattern.	Likely special causes of variation.

IS/IS NOT (VARIANCE) ANALYSIS

Variance analysis involves identifying and locating the cause of performance problems by localizing the circumstances in which the problems do, and do not, occur. To achieve this localization, a variation of the 5W-2H Tables described earlier is used.[42]

With Voice of the Process Tables, the initial 'What' referred to a particular process step or task. With variance analysis, however, the initial 'What" refers to a specific problem or performance issue.

For each descriptor of the 5W's, separate listings of "Is" and "Is Not" are complied to localize the problem and find the root cause. In the first column of the table, what "Is" happening is specified. Below this, what "Is Not" happening is spelled out. In the last row, any unusual observations related to what is happening are noted. This process is repeated for each of the columns, moving through where, when and so on.

---

42. Is/Is Not Analysis builds upon an approach to problem solving first defined by Charles H. Tregoe; Benjamin B. Kepner, The Rational Manager, Kepner Tregoe Inc. 1976

Exhibit 84: Is/Is Not Analytical Table

Problem or Variance:

Status	Variance or Problem What is Happening?	Description Details of the Problem	Analysis				
			Where	When	Who	How Much	How is this Possible?
IS							
IS NOT							
ODD?							

Prepared By: Date:

For example, a problem may be occurring with the dimensions of a component manufactured at a particular plant. The first question to be answered, then, is "What is happening?" For example, what is the error? Perhaps it is specified diameters being considerably beyond specifications. While the diameters may be too large, the part's length may be just right. So the problem "Is" the diameter of the part, but "Is Not" its length.

Continuing such an analysis, we may find that only parts coming off a particular line of the plant are affected and not any other line. This points to a specific machine or operation rather than the design or nature of the process itself. Perhaps we discover that these errors only occur on the night shift. Now we know more. Not only is the problem traceable to a particular machine but is also tied to a specific time of day.

If the company uses rotating shifts, the next question would be 'who.' Does the problem occur with only a specified shift, or does it move with a specific group of people as they rotate through the shift? If it rotates with the people we have a training or operating problem on our hands. If it is constantly occurs on the night shift, regardless of what shift rotation is working, the problem is more likely due to the specific operat-

ing conditions of that particular line at that specified time of day.

By asking the right questions and separating what is, and is not occurring, we slowly tunnel our way down to the root cause of the problem.

Example: Emergency Room Waiting Lines

This approach to finding the root cause has applications beyond manufacturing. A major hospital had recently experienced an increase in demand at its emergency ward. Unprepared for the change, and unsure of whether this was just a "blip" or some significant shift, hospital management did not know how or even if they should respond. Should they add more nurses and doctors to the emergency room staff, or should they treat the change as an unusual occurrence that would soon pass? In the meantime, waiting lines in emergency were growing as was the frustration of staff.

To compound the situation, everyone had an opinion about the problem and what to do about it. Some people were convinced that this had been a growing trend for some time. They believed the hospital management was just now noticing the effects of a growing population and an increasing demand for service. Others saw the situation differently, believing the change had occurred only recently. Still others had additional explanations, including the fact the moon had recently been full! They pointed out that the problems were worse at night than during the day.

After a particularly gruelling night, a small group of emergency room staff decided to try to figure out just what was going on. Staff members, when they had a spare minute, were requested to step into the "war room" (actually a corner of the coffee room). They were asked to write down ideas and observations on sticky-notes adding these to either the cause and effect diagram or the variance analysis worksheet. What they thought the cause *could be* – their opinions – were placed on the cause and effect diagram. What they *knew* to be true – the facts – were placed on the Is/Is Not analysis.

This separation of fact from theory was important. Everyone had pet theories as to what was going on. The purpose of the Is/Is Not analysis was not to elicit opinions, but rather to gather basic facts that could be used to analyze or identify which of the causes highlighted on the cause and effect diagram was at the root of the problem.

Within only a few short hours, the analysis had progressed toward some conclusions. First, a review of log sheets at emergency admitting made it clear that increases in demand started about three and a half weeks ago. In fact, a quick tally done by the admitting clerk on the back of a scrap piece of paper indicated that the emergency room was now handling about 15 to 20 percent more cases than it had in the weeks previously. This was definitely not a trend or a gradual build up but rather a sudden jump.

Secondly, staff agreed the increase in demand was occurring at night and not during the day. Lastly, staff reported that the demand consisted of more elderly people than usual – a fact confirmed by a quick review of emergency room admitting records.

Although these facts were relatively scant, the team compared what they had to the cause and effect diagram. What likely cause on the diagram was most consistent with the facts they had? The sudden nature of the increase was inconsistent with an increasing population or changing demographics. It was always possible that the increase was due to internal changes at the emergency room. In other words, what was being experienced may not be an increase in demand but rather a decrease

Exhibit 85: Sample Is/Is Not Analysis

Problem or Variance: Emergency room demand has increased.

Status	Variance or Problem	Description	Analysis				
	What is Happening?	Details of the Problem	Where	When	Who	How Much	How is this Possible?
IS	Increase in emergency room demand	Increasing demand in emergency room is putting added strain on the staff. Mostly general ailments	Emergency room	About 3 and a half weeks ago. A rather sudden increase	Appears to be a greater proportion of the elderly	Case load up on average 18% over the last three weeks compared to the previous 3.	Some sudden change occurring about 3.5 weeks ago. Facility closure? Physician changes?
IS NOT		Not accidents or similar trauma cases	Any other areas or wards of the hospital	A continual build up. Hasn't really increased over time.	Not broken out by any other demographic group; i.e.; gender	Continuing to grow. Caseload has been relatively constant over the past three weeks.	Not increase in population or general growth -- too sudden
ODD?		No other elements noted					

Prepared By: Emergency room staff shift NX56.   **Date:**

in the ability of the emergency room to handle the work-load. But this was inconsistent with the review of admitting records that had indicated a 15 to 20 percent increase in admissions. Some thought the full moon could be the cause. Although the increase in volume started with the full moon, it didn't decline with the moon's phases. So this explanation too, was inconsistent with the data.

All this analysis led to the conclusion that the likely culprit was a sudden change outside of the hospital. But what? During the war room discussions, one nursing attendant had recalled reading about a clinic closing or reducing hours recently, and the attendant had placed this as a potential cause on the cause and effect diagram. Could this be at the root of the problem?

The details emerged during a quick trip to the library. A nurse decided to go through the newspapers, starting about four weeks past to see if a little more information could be found. Sitting in the reading room, she came upon a notice published by a local clinic that it was suspending its 24 hour-a-day service in favor of an 8:00 a.m. to 8:00 p.m., 12 hour-a-day service. The timing was right on the mark. The last day of 24-hour service was the Friday, three and a half weeks ago.

The clinic was small compared to the hospital, but it was located in the heart of an older neighborhood with a very high proportion of seniors. When it reduced its hours, the people living nearby began to use the hospital emergency room as a replacement clinic. After all, it was open 24 hours a day and, while not quite as convenient to the neighborhood, it was considerably closer than any other clinic.

The response by the hospital management was immediate and appropriate to the findings. They didn't add additional staff to the emergency ward. Rather, they negotiated an agreement with the clinic to extend its hours, returning it to a 24-hour service. The rationale was straightforward. The cost of compensating the clinic was far less than the cost to the hospital of processing all the new patients. Emergency wards are designed – and their cost structure reflects – a bias toward the severely injured patient requiring a high degree of attention and care. Such operations are not particularly well suited for comparatively minor concerns of a specific population – in this case, the aches, pains and medication requirements of the elderly.

The bottom line is that Is/Is Not Analysis can be used wherever unique issues arise with the performance of some system or process. This is especially true when there is a need to separate the 'opinion' from the 'facts' in order to reduce the confusion that so often surrounds performance issues.

CEDAC/SEDAC

CEDAC, and its newer cousin SEDAC, are both enhancements to the basic cause and effect diagram. The enhancement comes in the form of cards. In fact, CEDAC stands for Cause and Effect Diagram with the Addition of Cards. SEDAC stands for Structure for Enhancing Daily Activity through Creativity.[43] The techniques are essentially the same. The name change to SEDAC was intended to better reflect the function of the technique as opposed to any changes in method.

Building the SEDAC diagram

The SEDAC diagram makes extensive use of cards, placing them on a skeletal version of the cause and effect diagram. It is the use of cards that allows the cause and effect diagram to be more of a living document – highlighting problem areas, indi-

---

43. CEDAC was first developed and used by the Standardization Study Group of Sumitomo Electric Industries. In 1978 the group published an article about the technique in the journal, Standardization and Quality Control. See, Fukuda, Ryuji, Building Organizational Fitness, Productivity Press, 1997.

cating what problems are currently being analyzed and identifying implemented solutions. The current state of knowledge regarding the problem, as well as the status and effectiveness of various solutions, is communicated through a combination of symbolic codes and colors.

There are five basic steps in building the diagram and applying the SEDAC technique. They are:

1. Define the effect

First, define the effect or problem the team wishes to address. This may be reducing waiting lines at a hospital, increasing shipping accuracy or improving profits. Any problem that needs to be addressed can be analyzed with this technique.

Part of the requirement here is specificity. The basic measure to be used and how often measurements will be taken to assess performance must be clearly defined. SEDAC is an active, ongoing technique intended to link a continuous program of improvement with results. Assessing the results in terms of measuring the net effect must be done regularly, and at a frequency consistent with the pace of the improvement effort, to ensure the connection between improvement activity and result.

Exhibit 86: Generic SEDAC Diagram

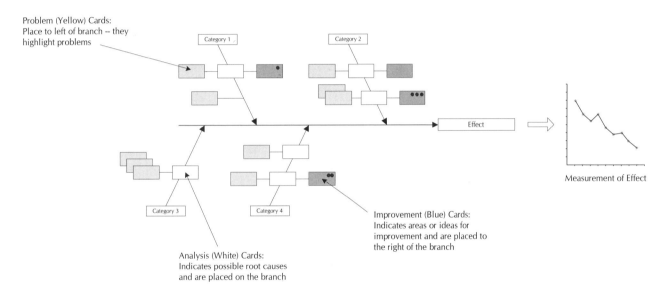

Once this effect has been defined, a skeletal cause and effect diagram is created on a large piece of paper. This starts with the effect plotted on the extreme right hand side of the paper. The backbone of the cause and effect diagram is drawn as it is for the standard cause and effect diagram.

2. Brainstorm the problem cards

Next, all the potential problems that could be influencing the effect are brainstormed by the team. As you might suspect, the results of the brainstorming are captured on cards. Traditionally, yellow cards are used.

The actual structure of the brainstorming exercise may vary. It can be a group endeavor where the entire team works together in identifying problems. Or it may be a process where team members, working as individuals, write down their ideas on the cards (again, sticky-notes work great in this application). If a group brainstorming is conducted, the output of the brainstorming is transferred to cards or sticky-notes for eventually mapping the skeletal structure of the cause and effect diagram.

No matter how the set of problem cards is created, a set of rules applies to what is placed on each card. Specifically, each card:

▶ May have only one problem written upon it

▶ Must be very specific and concrete

▶ Must quantify the problem where possible

▶ Must be dated and initialed by its originator

3. Develop the causal analysis

Once the problem cards have been completed, they are grouped using affinity charting techniques. The groupings define the main branches of the cause and effect diagram. Like with regular cause and effect analysis, if grouping proves to be difficult

for the team, pre-defined categories may be used, including the 6 M's.

With a large structure of the cause and effect diagram posted on a wall where all team members can see it, the problem cards are added. They are always posted to the left of a major branch and connected to it by a straight line. Some problem cards may be stating much the same thing or identifying a set of problems that are closely related. If this is the case, these cards can be grouped together and connected to the major branch by a single line.

At the point of intersection of the main branch and the line connecting it to the problem cards, a white analysis card is created as an option. Usually, these analysis cards are developed by the entire team. The purpose of the white card is to identify methods or means of analyzing the problem, to the point of being able to reach some conclusion as to the root cause or extent of the problem. Usually, where the team decides an analysis is warranted, selected members of the team are assigned to pursue the analysis and verify the nature of the problem.

4. Identify possible solutions/improvements

Next, a third set of cards is prepared. Using either group or individual idea-generation techniques, sets of possible solutions are identified for all the various problems and issues identified. These solutions or improvement cards, usually blue, are then posted to the right of the major branches of the cause and effect diagram – opposite the problem they are intended to address.

What results, is a comprehensive map of all the potential problems or causes (yellow cards), leading to some overall effect linked directly to areas requiring additional analysis (white cards), and a set of possible solutions (blue cards). Moreover, all of this is mapped in a way (using the cause and effect diagram) that indicates the possible causal chain connecting problem to effect.

In defining the solution cards, the same set of rules applies that applied to problem cards – namely that a single, concrete and well defined idea is mapped out per card. This rule ensures that specific items for action are identified, rather than vague conceptual solutions that are too abstract to be acted upon.

5. Prioritize improvements

Once solutions are identified for all the various problems, some prioritization is required. The team will be unable to pursue all possible solutions and certainly not all at once. This next step, therefore, involves the team making some assessment of the value or likely success of the various ideas identified.

This is not a matter of deciding which solutions are good ideas and which are poor. Reality will be the ultimate judge. This is only a prioritization process that defines which solutions will be tried first, second and so on. In short, we are soliciting the experience and expertise of the team to identify where to first focus our improvement efforts.

Any number of voting and rating techniques can be used for this purpose. Generally, a three-point prioritization score is created:

▲ **No interest** – solution cards judged to be likely ineffective or inappropriate in addressing the problem.

▲ **Of interest** – solution cards that may be effective or appropriate, but are not an immediate priority either because of resource constraints or uncertainty as to likely effectiveness.

▲ **Immediate interest** – solution cards that have an immediate interest to the team because the ideas are judged to be likely effective, and feasible given resources constraints including time.

The results of the prioritization are recorded on the solutions cards using small glue-backed dots typically used for coding files (although a felt-tipped marker works just as well). Immediate interest solutions are coded with two dots, of interest cards are coded with one dot and solution cards of no interest are left without any coding.

6. Identify and standardize best practices

Once priorities are identified, this last step involves moving from the world of what we think we should do to the actual application of ideas. We reality test. Ideas that are to be tested in the field are marked with a third dot. Team assignments for the experiment are made and a trial or test is conducted.

* Adapted from *Building Organizational Fitness* by Ryuji Fukuda. Copyright 1997 by Productivity Press. Adapted and reprinted with permission.

Exhibit 87: Coding the Cards[*]

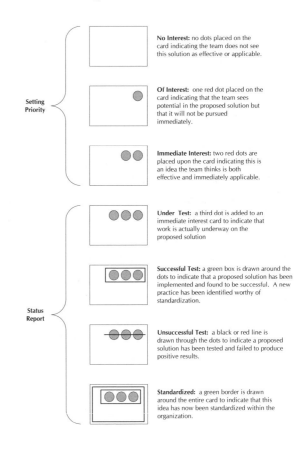

No Interest: no dots placed on the card indicating the team does not see this solution as effective or applicable.

Of Interest: one red dot placed on the card indicating that the team sees potential in the proposed solution but that it will not be pursued immediately.

Immediate Interest: two red dots are placed upon the card indicating this is an idea the team thinks is both effective and immediately applicable.

Under Test: a third dot is added to an immediate interest card to indicate that work is actually underway on the proposed solution

Successful Test: a green box is drawn around the dots to indicate that a proposed solution has been implemented and found to be successful. A new practice has been identified worthy of standardization.

Unsuccessful Test: a black or red line is drawn through the dots to indicate a proposed solution has been tested and failed to produce positive results.

Standardized: a green border is drawn around the entire card to indicate that this idea has now been standardized within the organization.

Setting Priority

Status Report

Like any test, there are two basic outcomes: success and failure. Successes are recorded on the SEDAC diagram by drawing a square around the dots on the card. Failures are recorded by drawing a line through the dots.

Lastly, when success is experienced in the field, the lessons learned must be deployed in practice. The new way must become the standard practice for the rest of the organization. This is what is meant by standardization. Learning is great but it won't pay the bills (ask any college student!) To be effective, new learning must be shared and applied in the field.

SUMMARY: USING VISUAL MODELS

Making something visual, creating a map of some sort, communicates a tremendous amount of information in a very concise and workable format. Maps of all types communicate not only 'what is' but also reveal the relationships between the elements pictured.

With process maps, the physical tasks and activities are charted, along with the physical input/output flow relationships among those activities. In the cause and effect diagram, the potential causes contributing to some effect are charted, as are the causal relationships among those causal factors. In both cases, the visual model presents elements and relationships that are directly relevant to the specific problem-solving activities of the improvement team.

The power of visual models to communicate a lot in a small package makes them useful for more than analysis. As important as they are in this role, they can also be used to help document or standardize a process – clearly defining what gets done, by whom and when.

In summary, visual models are among the most useful tools for any group engaged in an improvement effort. They are so useful in that regardless whether the task is analysis, redesign or documentation, creating a visual representation or model is among the most valuable of first steps. Pictures really are worth a thousand words.

Performance Measurement: The Basics of Gathering and Working With Numerical Data

5

Numerical facts make up an increasing part of the information we need to understand our world, including our organizations and the sphere in which they operate. Rates of inflation and growth, costs per unit, market share, customer satisfaction levels, average incomes, cycle time, unemployment rates, value of the dollar, oil prices – it seems we are overwhelmed with data. It shouldn't be surprising, then, that the organizational problem today is not so much obtaining data. Rather, it is getting good data and separating the wheat from the chaff.

Getting good data is critical. Data is the window through which we gain understanding and insight about what is going on in the world. It keeps us grounded and in touch with reality. If our data is suspect or of poor quality, it is likely that our understanding of reality and the decisions that flow from this understanding will likewise be flawed.

Unfortunately, few organizations understand how to gather or use data. Too often, information is incorrectly gathered or gathered only to support current biases and beliefs. Interpretations are often suspect, proper analytical tools are not used and variation is neither understood nor appreciated. The result is that the window to reality becomes opaque or blurred.

Organizations that fail to use data soon lose touch with reality. They begin operating according to tradition and prejudice. Things are done they way they are because that's the way they've always been done. The organization fails to apply the reality test and therefore leaves its prejudices and problems unchallenged and intact.

Organizations that fail to use data lose touch with reality.

If data is our window to reality, it is important that we understand how to properly gather and interpret data so our vision remains clear.

THE SCIENCE OF DATA

Making sense of numerical data is the function of statistics or statistical practice. There is a tendency for many to run for cover upon hearing the word 'statistics.' The reason may be math phobia, bad experiences at high school or general disillusionment after years of hearing conflicting statistics quoted to support competing positions. Perhaps it is the 'geek' factor where anyone good with numbers is presumed to be odd, or at least, not normal.[44] (A statistician is someone good with numbers but who didn't have sufficient personality to become an accountant.)

Whatever the reason for fearing statistics, organizations are best advised to 'get over it.' The practice of statistics is simply the scientific means by which we interpret and give meaning to data. In short, no statistics – no organizational learning and haphazard improvement. Here's a good definition of the practice of statistics:

> *"Statistics is the science of data – of gathering data, organizing the data into clear and usable form and then interpreting the data to draw conclusions about the empirical world."*[45]

Three observations need to be made about this definition.

▲ **Statistics is a science.** Specifically, it is the science of data – how we gather and analyze data to produce information and ultimately knowledge about the 'real world.' Statistics does not consist of mechanical mathematical operations or some practice where you can "prove anything." As a science, there are certain rules and procedures to be followed as well as limits as to what can be accomplished. If we want to be scientific in our methods, we must use the tools of science to analyze our data.

---

44. For those that remember the normal curve from some previous statistical experience let me simply say that normality is over rated. Try to become exponential instead!

45. This is a definition I came across some years ago although I have never been able to track down the source.

▲ **Statistics relies on data.** Statistics is data driven. The data drives us, not the other way around. Sound statistical practice, therefore, is about listening to what the data has to say and being fair in the interpretations. It is not about us driving the data and torturing it to the point where it will "tell" us anything.

Failing to gather and use data appropriately is just another manifestation of an organizational learning disability.

We are attempting to gather and interpret data in a manner that is fair to the world we are trying to describe.

▲ **The purpose of statistics is to make conclusions about the real world.** Statistics is not a numbers game where analysts play with the numbers until they get the answer they want, although this may describe statistical practice in many organizations. The purpose of statistics is to make conclusions – to say one method of production is better than another, or that changes in marketing strategy have had some desired effect, or to identify whether incidents of violent crime are increasing or decreasing.

In short, statistics is the science of making the data work. Anyone or any team wanting to make improvements to anything needs to know a little statistics. Not a lot. But enough to adopt some sound statistical (systemic) thinking, gather data appropriate to the improvement effort and know which analytical tools to use to help turn the data into information.

FOUR THINGS YOU CAN DO WITH DATA

There are only four things you can do with data, and statistical procedures will generally fall into one or more of these four categories. If the purpose of statistics is to make meaningful conclusions, then we can say these are the four basic steps to making data meaningful. These are:

▲ **Gather the Data**. Before you can work with data, you must have data to work with. Gathering data is about getting the data you need. Two areas that organizations need to pay attention to when gathering data are:

  ▶ **the measurement process**, the specifics of how measurements or counts will be taken, including the specific operational definitions and metrics to be used.

  ▶ **sampling,** the process by which units to be measured are selected.

▲ **Organize the Data**. Once gathered, you must organize the data in some rational way that is reflective of the real world from which the data is drawn and which the data will be used to represent. This comes down to doing one of two things:

▶ **sorting the data**, placing the data in some logical or rational order.

▶ **grouping the data**, placing 'like' data together in groups that reflect real world conditions.

▲ **Summarize the Data**. Once organized, the data must be summarized to provide some overall picture – allowing us to see the forest for the trees. With numerical data, this usually involves the calculation of 'summary statistics.' Two types of summary statistics most useful in performance improvement work are:

▶ **summaries of location** or central tendency, the most commonly used of which is the average.

▶ **summaries of dispersion** or how spread out the data is, the two most common of which are the range and standard deviation.

Exhibit 88: Working With Data

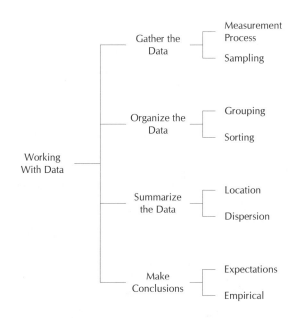

▲ **Make conclusions**. To make conclusions, the data and their corresponding summaries must be compared to something. Generally, we can identify two primary bases of comparison:

▶ **comparisons with expectations**, comparing the data and summaries with the expectations held by decision makers.

▶ **empirical comparisons**, comparing the data and summaries with other data.

It doesn't matter if the data is measured or counted, quantitative or qualitative, the basic steps of gathering, organizing, summarizing and comparing the summaries with something to draw conclusions are the means by which we create information from data.

Sound statistical analysis really isn't so difficult. The basics of gathering, organizing, summarizing and comparing information are understandable by anyone.[46]

---

46. In fact, I find that the four steps serve as a useful framework by which to evaluate the opinions or evidence offered by anyone in support of some conclusion. Ask yourself, or those offering the argument, "How did you get your data?" "How has the data been organized?" "How has the data been summarized?" and lastly, "What is the data being compared with to make conclusions?"

CRITICAL DATA GATHERING CONSIDERATIONS

Before initiating a data-gathering process, two critical considerations need to be kept in mind. These are:

▲ **Purpose of the Analysis: W*hy*** are we collecting data? What is the nature of the question we hope to answer?

▲ **Stratification: *What*** critical conditions or factors can or could influence the results of the measurement process?

PURPOSE OF THE ANALYSIS

The first and most important data-gathering consideration is the purpose of the analysis. There are two fundamentally different purposes for any data-gathering or statistical analysis. We may want to determine how many objects exist or determine the performance of a cause and effect system. These two purposes distinguish the two primary types of statistical studies – enumerative and analytic.[47]

Enumerative Studies – to determine how many

Enumerative studies are those where the purpose is trying to describe, at a particular point in time, the characteristics of a finite larger population (lot), usually but not necessarily from a smaller data set (sample). The focus of an enumerative study and any resulting action is on the larger finite population or lot.

An example is a public opinion poll where the purpose is estimating some characteristic of the larger population from a smaller sample. Determining what proportion of the population of the United States will vote for the Democratic nominee from a much smaller sample, or estimating the proportion of the population watching a particular television program from a sample of households, are two examples.

In organizations, enumerative studies are usually limited to basic consumer research (where a small sample is used to estimate some characteristic of the market) or to the purchase/ acceptance of materials (where a sample of some material, say grain, is used to judge the quality of the overall shipment). In virtually all other cases, improvement teams will be concerned

---

47. The importance of this distinction is emphasized by Edwards Deming and others. See Edwards Deming *Out of the Crisis*, MIT Press, 1986 pp. 132, 182 and *The New Economics*, MIT Press, 1994, pp. 100-101.

not with determining how many but with determining the level of performance and seeking ways to enhance it – the purpose of analytic studies.

Analytic Studies – to determine or compare performance and answer 'why?'

Analytic studies are those where the purpose of the study is determining the performance level of some process, or understanding why the performance characteristics are the way they are. The focus of the study is on the cause and effect system that produced the results, rather than on a specific lot. Examples include analyzing problems in a production process, establishing the performance of an emergency response department or comparing the efficiency of two alternative delivery techniques.

Improvement teams are usually concerned with either determining the level of performance or understanding why performance is the way it is with the intent of making improvements. So they are generally engaged in analytic studies. However, people with statistical training tend to be more familiar with enumerative studies or at least the tools and techniques of enu-

Exhibit 89: Enumerative vs. Analytic Studies

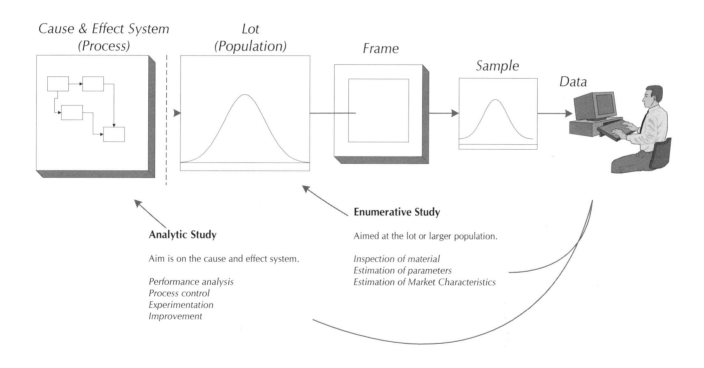

Cause & Effect System
(Process)

Lot
(Population)

Frame

Sample

Data

Analytic Study

Aim is on the cause and effect system.

Performance analysis
Process control
Experimentation
Improvement

Enumerative Study

Aimed at the lot or larger population.

Inspection of material
Estimation of parameters
Estimation of Market Characteristics

merative approaches. For this reason, it is worth noting some of the differences between analytic and enumerative studies.

▲ **Enumerative studies require random probability samples – analytic studies are more dependent on judgment.** The primary source of uncertainty in an enumerative study is with the sample. By using appropriate random sampling techniques, this source of uncertainty can be quantified and controlled. This is not true with analytic studies. The major sources of uncertainty here are with confounding factors and extrapolation into the future. This uncertainty is not quantifiable and cannot be controlled or quantified with sampling techniques. Analytic studies are more reliant upon judgment samples in which expertise in the subject matter is more important in determining what objects need to be sampled.

▲ **There are limited application of statistical tests in analytic studies.** Statistical tests such as calculation of standard error, confidence intervals and hypothesis tests – vital in an enumerative study – are not particularly useful in an analytic study. This is primarily because such statistical tests tend to hide the most useful part of the information – the order of production.

Consider the average of a data set. It makes no difference in what order the data appears, the average will be the same. But the order of the data is critically important in an analytic study. For example, machine performance trending downwards is vital to know. So are the trends in crime rates, sales levels and costs. The average (a descriptive statistic) doesn't care if there is a trend. But we do. The same holds true for other statistical tests. The order in which the data appear is largely irrelevant to tests of significance, confidence intervals and *t* tests. But few things are more important in analytic studies, where it is important to know if sales are trending up or down, or whether a machine is experiencing wear.

▲ **Analytic studies emphasize graphical techniques in understanding the data.** Graphical techniques capture

"Analysis of variance, t-tests, confidence intervals and other statistical techniques taught in books, however interesting, are inappropriate because they bury the information contained in the order of production"
Edwards Deming, Out of the Crisis, p. 132

Table 90: Enumerative and Analytic Studies[*]

	Enumerative Study	Analytic Study
Purpose	Description & Inspection	Prediction & Improvement
Focus	Population	Cause & Effect System
Method of Accessing Data	Frame	Models of the Process such as Cause & Effect Diagrams and Flowcharts
Major Source of Uncertainty	Sampling Error	Extrapolation into the Future and Confounding Factors
Is Major Source of Uncertainty Quantifiable	Yes	No
Environment of the Study	Stable	Dynamic

[*] Ronald D. Moen, et al. *Improving Quality Through Planned Experimentation*, McGraw Hill, 1991 p. 57. Reproduced with permission

and present the variation occurring within the data including variation in the order of production. This is essential to understanding the cause and effect system at work (the causes and conditions that make up all processes), and being able to provide some prediction about process performance. Graphical techniques allow us to see what is going on.

The use of these graphical techniques, combined with statistical analysis appropriate to the analytic problem at hand, helps ensure that the work of improvement teams conform to Shewhart's rule:

"preserve, for the uses intended, all the evidence in the original data."[48]

Distinguishing between the two types of studies

A helpful way to think about and distinguish between enumerative and analytic studies is to consider what would happen if

48. As reported by Edwards Deming, *Some Contributions to Statistical Inference and Practice,* in Eugene I. Burdock, Abraham Sudilovsky, Samuel Gershon, The Behavior of Psychiatric Patients: Quantitative Techniques for Evaluation, Marcel Dekker Inc. New York and Basel, 1982 p. 519

we were to take a census or measure response from the entire population rather than take a sample. In an enumerative study, doing so would essentially provide us with 100 percent certainty in our estimate of the characteristic. But a census wouldn't help at all in an analytic study. After all, taking a census of all units coming off the production line today won't help us estimate or improve what will happen tomorrow. With enumerative studies, the uncertainty is in the sample. With analytic studies, the uncertainty lies in the future and the range of confounding factors that can influence results.

STRATIFICATION

Stratification is the separation of data into logical groups. Identifying what those groups should be requires knowledge of whatever process, product or outcome is being studied. Familiarity with the object of analysis is essential because the stratification must be logical – it must reflect some real world operating factors or conditions.

For example, a study of customer service processes at a bank may want to stratify the data by branch. Separate branches may have different processes at work or face varying operating realities, including different market profiles. Being able to analyze

the data by branch will likely reveal far more than lumping all the data together. Similarly, a study of part specifications may want to stratify by the machine on which the part was manufactured, the source of raw input material, day of manufacture, shift or time of manufacture and so forth. Stratification applies to anything that logically could impact performance: seasons, weather, working conditions, different locations, time of day, different suppliers, types of material, customer segments. The intent is to capture and group the data in logical categories, so the information reveals more about the underlying processes and root causes of problems than would otherwise be possible.

Failing to stratify – a multi-million dollar mistake

Failing to understand stratification can have devastating consequences. A gas station owned by a major oil and gas company in Canada had three underground storage tanks – one for premium gas, one for mid-grade and one for regular. Safety regulations required the station operator to take daily readings and calculate the percentage of loss in the tanks weekly. Any loss over a specified percentage had to be reported and investigated as a potential leak.

Unfortunately, both the company and government regulators failed to specify that the readings and calculations were to be stratified by tank. (Note: This is a failure to provide a sufficiently clear operational definition of the loss percentage.) The operator of the station added the data from all three tanks together before conducting his percentage loss calculations. Had he not done so, his calculations would have shown his premium fuel tank to be leaking. Because the data from all three tanks was added together, however, the amount of the leak in the premium tank was never sufficient to exceed warning levels.

Over a few years, the amount of gasoline lost was substantial, eventually migrating under a nearby seniors' apartment building. The result was a multi-million dollar lawsuit.

The more data is lumped together, the more it reveals about general conditions, but the less it reveals about specific problems or improvement opportunities. Plan in advance how the data should be grouped or stratified. Make sure the basis of stratification is rational. Its roots must lie in the real world operating conditions upon which the improvement effort is focused.

How to stratify

In practice, the cause and effect diagram is a key tool for identifying areas of stratification. Different causal factors identified on the cause and effect diagram will provide the clues. For example, when attempting to understand variation in product quality for some manufactured product, a causal factor identified on the cause and effect diagram may have been 'supplier' – the supplier of the raw material. Here is an obvious application of stratification. The question begging for an answer is "How many suppliers do we have for this raw material?" If the answer was, say 'three,' we would want to set up three check boxes with the suppliers name clearly labeled beside each on the data collection form.

To stratify, first create a cause and effect diagram for the characteristics being measured. Go through the diagram to check for completeness, and then gather feedback from those in the field or others with a high degree of familiarity with the system under analysis. From this point, two steps remain: identifying the relevant stratification variables and establishing the categories for each variable.

1. **Identify the stratification variables.** Stratification variables are those where the data needs to be separated to

reflect underlying real-world conditions. For example, in a study of emergency medical service response times, driving conditions at the time of the emergency could be an important stratification variable. Driving conditions would likely have an impact on the time it takes an emergency medical vehicle to reach a person in need. Day of the week could be another stratification variable, as could nature of the emergency, time of day and so forth.

When preparing to collect or gather new data, pay careful attention to the possible stratification variables. Take the time to create a good cause and effect diagram that identifies possible causal factors as sources of stratification, because it will be impossible to add them afterwards. Another caution: Don't create or identify stratification variables just for the sake of it. Different groupings or stratifications must be grounded in the reality of the process or product under analysis. This is what is meant by logical categories – they must represent the underlying reality from which the data will be drawn.

If using existing data, the selection will be constrained by the data available. Having data that can be stratified in such circumstances is more good luck than anything else.

There is good news, however. Often existing data that find their way into management reports and the like is the summarization of detailed source data buried deep within some computer. Finding this source data may permit the improvement team to stratify information that seemed impossible to analyze from printed reports.

2   **Establish categories for each stratification variable.** A category is a value or a range of values of a stratification variable. Take the example of the response time for an emergency medical service. A stratification variable may be the time at which the emergency was reported. The theory of the improvement team may be that more demand is placed upon the emergency response system at night. Time of the call may be categorized as morning (6 a.m. to 12 noon), afternoon (12 noon to 6 p.m.), evening (6 p.m. to 12 midnight) and night (12 midnight to 6 a.m.). Calls could then be grouped into these categories and analyzed to see if greater problems occur during a particular time interval.

If a checksheet is used to gather the data, make sure the various categories are identified on the form so that those gathering the data can easily 'check-off' the category. This approach is safer and less prone to error than having an observer write in the data.

GATHERING DATA

Organizations typically have all kinds of measurement systems in place, producing all sorts of data. In some cases, the data produced by these systems will be just what the team needs. More often than not, improvement teams will find the data is not appropriate for purposes of process or product improvement.

Why? Because existing management information systems are usually designed to address information concerns of organizational hierarchy. They satisfy the vertical information requirements of the organization, usually in terms of financial control, responsibility and accountability. In contrast, improvement tends to be more concerned with the physical system. This includes the quality characteristics of goods or services as they move from one stage of a process to another – the cycle time of production, number of errors, physical characteristics, levels of customer satisfaction and the like.

People seeking to make improvements can become frustrated with the lack of information required to make the kind of decisions they want to make. Often comments like *"Our accounting system is hopeless!"* surface in team meetings. The real problem is that these information systems were never designed to capture information that supports process or product improvement. Remember, different measuring systems exist for different purposes. More often than not, improvement teams must establish their own (and often temporary) measurement systems to gather the type of data required.

So how do we go about gathering data? How do we know what data to gather? What things should be measured? Proper gathering of data is the essential first step to drawing useful conclusions about the world in which we are operating. It starts with the measurement process.

THE MEASUREMENT PROCESS

Some years ago, Sir Isaac Newton said; *"If you don't know how to measure it, then you don't understand it."* For better or worse, the current management wisdom has adopted this sentiment and rephrased it into the popular phrase; *"If you can't measure it, you can't manage it!"* Organizations seem to place considerable importance on measurement. It is surprising, therefore, the degree to which organizations remain so ignorant of basic measurement principles.

People seeking to improve performance, however, do not have the luxury of ignorance. If performance improvement is to be achieved, change initiatives had better be based on an understanding of real world operating conditions – that is, on sound data.

> **"If you can't measure it, you can't manage it."**
> **Current Management Wisdom**
>
> **"Measure the meaningless and misinterpret what is measured."**
> **Current Management Practice**

Having data to analyze requires having a data-gathering system or measurement process. Every numerical fact is the result of a measurement process that's designed to extract the data from the real world.

What do we mean by measurement process? We do not mean specifically going out with a ruler and measuring something, although doing so is indeed a measurement process. We can define a measurement process as any process in which a sensor is applied to an object or objects, in an effort to classify, order or establish the dimensions of the object(s).

This is a broad definition of measurement and covers a lot of ground, including terrain usually not thought of as measurement. But that is exactly what makes the definition useful. We make measurements every day of our life, although we tend not to think of them as such.

For example, what happens in deciding to purchase a tie? We apply some internal standard of what looks good (our opinion or judgment as to what constitutes good taste) against some objects (a selection of ties) and reach a conclusion (this tie looks really good!). Others may reach a different conclusion, but that is only because they have applied their own standards and come to a different result or measure. Anyone receiving a tie as a present knows just how varied those internal standards of good taste can be! This type of measurement system is a special case we usually refer to as judgment, but it is a measurement system just the same.

The human resource professional who is counting the number of people attending a training program is also engaged in a measurement process. So is the salesperson calculating the daily sales totals, the engineer reading a meter on a pipeline and the teacher administering a spelling test to the grade three class. All are attempting to learn something about their respective worlds that only a measurement of some sort can provide.

NO TRUE VALUES OF ANYTHING

So was the tie I received in good taste or bad taste? Well, it depends. That is, the conclusion is dependent upon the standard used to make the judgment. This 'it depends' answer holds true even when we talk about more quantitative or 'hard' forms of measurement.

The measurement process is a function of the measuring 'stick' or sensor being used, the object being measured and the process of comparing the stick to the object. If a measurement is a function of these three things, changing any one of them will affect the result. For example, measuring the same object using a different measuring stick will yield different results. Likewise, a change in the way in which the standard is applied to the object will also affect the result. There is no 'true' value resulting from a measurement, only a particular result of apply-

ing a certain measuring stick in a specific way. Let's look at an example.

How long is the coastline of England?

Let's ask a relatively simple question: "How long is the coastline of England?" At first, this may seem to be a rather trivial question; after all, can't we just go out and measure it?

Okay, how? First, what measurement stick would we use? Typically, a survey would be done using some form of sighting system. But how often should we sight? Ultimately, we are forced to measure in a series of straight lines but how long should each of these lines be? The shorter we make them, the longer the coast line and the more expensive the measurement process. The longer the sight-lines, the shorter the coastline but the measurement process decreases in cost. This is represented in Exhibit 91: Measuring Coastlines, where differences in measuring in three-mile and one-mile lengths is highlighted.

So while the coastline is infinitely complex with its curves, nooks and crannies, our measurements are restricted to straight lines. So how long is the coast of England.? The answer, as you might have guessed, is "it depends." It depends upon the measurement system – in this case the length of the measuring segments used.

Exhibit 91: Measuring Coastlines

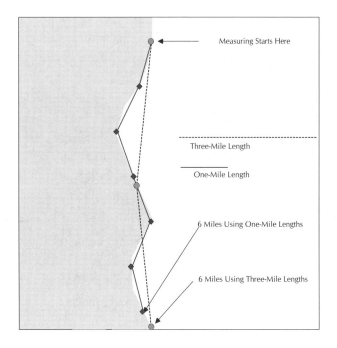

Measuring Starts Here

Three-Mile Length

One-Mile Length

6 Miles Using One-Mile Lengths

6 Miles Using Three-Mile Lengths

There is, therefore, no *true* answer to the question "How long is the coastline of England?" There is only a quantitative result arising from the application of a specific measurement standard at a certain time. Fortunately, 'philosophical' truth is not required for the conduct of science or for the improvement of product or process performance.

What is required, in this case, is agreement among nations having coastlines on how their length will be measured. If everyone uses the same standard and the same process, we can make objective statements about the length of coastlines and compare coastlines across nation states. Without such agreements, comparisons of national coastlines is simply meaningless. Such agreements are called operational definitions.

For Those of You Who Must Know

When Britain's coastline is measured in line segments of 100 kilometers, the length of coastline is about 3800 kilometers. When measured in line segments of 50 km., the coast line expands to approximately 6000 km. in length.[*]

---

[*]   John L. Casti, *Complexification,* Harper Collins, 1994, New York, NY, p. 230

All measurement systems have their limitations. What is true for measuring coastlines is true for measuring everything else – reality is always more complex than our ability to measure it. For this reason, there is no 'true' value resulting from any measurement process. There is only the result of an operational definition applied.[49]

OPERATIONAL DEFINITIONS

For purposes of process improvement (or any other scientific endeavor) we need operational definitions. They define not only what will be measured, but also how the measure is operationalized – how we will go about measuring. Specifically, if any measurement is a function of the thing being measured, the measuring stick used and the measurement process, an operational definition must clearly define:

▲ **The thing to be measured.** What objects will be selected and what specific characteristic(s) and metrics pertaining to the object(s) under examination will be measured?

▲ **The standard to be used.** What unit of measure will be most worthwhile and produce the most useful results? What tool will be used to gather the data and to what level of detail?

▲ **The process to be used to obtain the measures.** Applying the standard in different ways to the same object will produce different results. The operational definition must define how the data will be gathered, including who will gather it, where it will be gathered and when.

Clearly defining these three items and coming to agreement among interested parties creates an operational definition. Operational definitions then, are agreements between individuals or organizations explicitly defining how they intend to extract data from the world.

What Does "On Time" Mean?

Organizations of all types promise "on time" service or delivery, yet do we really know what they are promising? In the airline industry, it is common practice to have "on time" defined as whether the plane left the boarding gate when scheduled, but only after making allowances for a host of factors such as weather, airport problems, scheduling delays, control tower

---

49. See Edwards Deming, *The New Economics* MIT Press 1994 pp. 104-106 for a discussion on this. See also *Out of the Crisis* also by Edwards Deming MIT Press 1986 pp. 276-308 for a detailed discussion on operational definitions and their importance to industry.

delays and so forth. From the customer's perspective, on time means whether the plane left when scheduled without all the excuses. It is, therefore, possible for an airline to have a 100 percent on time record despite never having left the gate on-time by the customer's watch. What is missing in such circumstances is an operational definition shared by both airline and customer.[50]

Operationalizing the Measurements

Failing to operationally define characteristics produces disagreements, bickering, controversy and disputes. What would company meetings be without ongoing arguments about levels of customer satisfaction, comparative product quality or on time delivery rates? Yet how many companies ever take the time to develop shared definitions of what these terms actually mean?

This is also true for relationships among organizations. For example, government regulations, laws and rulings *"are notorious for lack of clarity in definitions and costly confusion."*[51]

---

50. From a speech delivered by Mr. Kevin Bensen, President of Canadian Airlines, at the Quality Council of Alberta Conference, Calgary, 1995
51. Edwards Deming, *Out of the Crisis*, MIT Press, 1986 p. 287

Teams responsible for improving performance, therefore, must first define performance. How is it measured? What data is used and how is it gathered? At what point does performance become good? At what point does it become bad? What other things affect performance? How do we measure these? Operational definitions must be created for all the measurements we will be making – before the data itself is gathered.

MEASUREMENT QUALITY: THREE QUESTIONS TO ASK ANY MEASUREMENT SYSTEM

The preceding examples demonstrate the limitations of measurement systems and the need for operational definitions. But even with an operational definition, improvement teams need to be able to asses how good the measurement system is. The measurement system is like any other system. It comes with varying degrees of quality. Answering three fundamental questions will help determine this quality level.

1. Is the measurement system accurate?

The accuracy of a measurement system is defined as how close the value produced by the measurement system is to some accepted standard. Note that accuracy has nothing to do with how close the result comes to the 'true value' since *"truth"* has no operational definition. After all, how would you determine the true value of something? You would have to measure it, but no measurement system can produce a true value. The only thing we can do is compare how our measurements compare with some reference standard and use this as a basis for establishing accuracy.

The degree of accuracy is usually expressed in terms of the amount of error relative to the total size of the measurement (error divided by average measurement), expressed as a percentage. A worn gauge, for example, may produce results that are eight percent larger than those measures produced when using the reference standard. Accuracy, or the lack thereof, is a function of systemic bias in the measurement system. Moreover, such errors typically grow over time as the physical measurement tool, a gauge in this example, continues to wear.

2. Is the measurement system precise?

Variation is a product of any process or system – including the measurement system. If we were to measure the same thing again and again under the same conditions, would the resulting measurements be the same or at least close enough to give us

confidence in the reliability of the measurement system? If the answer is no, then there is too much variation in the measurement system for the data produced to be considered reliable. A lack of precision tends not to reflect systemic bias, but rather a "looseness" in the measurement process that produces variation in results.

Exhibit 92: Measurement Accuracy and Precision presents a visual representation of accuracy and precision. The reference standard is represented by the two circles (target) and the actual measurements arising from the measurement system are represented as dots against the reference standard. The greater the accuracy of the measure, the closer to the very center of the target it will be. Four situations are depicted:

a) **The measurement system is both accurate and precise.** The average value produced by the measurement system is very close to the reference standard (accurate) and there is limited variation around this average (precise).

b) **The measurement system is accurate but not precise.** Now the average is still close to the reference standard but there is much greater dispersion of

Exhibit 92: Measurement Accuracy and Precision

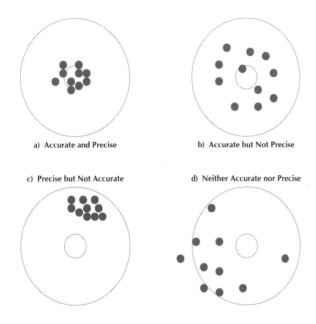

a) Accurate and Precise

b) Accurate but Not Precise

c) Precise but Not Accurate

d) Neither Accurate nor Precise

results around the average. In fact, it is quite possible that the average of these results is closer to the reference standard than the average result obtained through system (a). However, despite this accuracy, the individual measures are significantly dispersed indicating a lack of reliability or precision.

c) **The measurement system is precise but not accurate.** Now the results are tight around the average produced by the measurement system, but that average is no longer near the reference standard.

d) **The measurement system is neither precise nor accurate.** Not only are the results loose – widely dispersed from the average produced by the measurement system, but that average value is not close to the reference standard.

3. Is the measurement system valid?

This is the bottom line and most important question we can ask of the measurement system. Are we measuring what we think we are measuring? For example, when we measure the production cost of a widget, are we measuring the economic cost of the widget or are we also measuring the impact of the cost allocation systems and the way this system distributes overhead? Our measurement system may be precise and accurate, but the thing actually measured may not be what we think we are measuring.

At times, our operational definitions may look good, but they may be measuring things that are unrepresentative of the process or product we want to improve. The measurement system must not only have clear operational definitions, be precise and accurate, but what we are measuring must make sense.

Statistical expertise alone cannot address this last concern. The logic behind a measure, must come from a partnership between those with statistical knowledge and those with knowledge of the process or product that is the focus of the measurement process and the improvement effort.

IMPACT OF MEASUREMENT SYSTEMS ON PEOPLE

A final consideration in designing a measurement system is the use to which the data will be put and the resulting effect on people. When measuring the flow of gas through a pipe or the diameters of transmission shafts or the output of a generator, we do not have to concern ourselves with what these objects 'think' of the measurement process. But people do care. If we are taking measurements to ensure or improve the quality of product, that is one thing. But if we are taking measurements to reward or punish employees, that is very clearly another. In the later case, there will be a reward to some for fudging the figures.

The Importance of Validity

Some years ago a man by the name of Alfred Binet was trying to find a way to determine what students in the French educational system needed additional help. He devised a crude test for doing so. Today we call this the Intelligence Quotient or IQ test. Given the name, you might think that this test measures intelligence. It does not.

Yet the use of the IQ test as a measure of intelligence is widely accepted. It continues to find application in schools, the workplace and even academia (including many psychology departments which, of all groups, should know better). The harm done, and that continues to be done, from the failure to understand validity is immense. It was not long ago that failure on the IQ test resulted in people being sterilized against their will, in a misguided effort to improve the intelligence of society at large.

Perhaps we should have listened to Mr. Binet more closely when he said: *"The scale, properly speaking, does not permit the measure of intelligence."*

You can use the data to punish or reward employees or you can have good data. You can't have both!

If data will be used or is being used to reward or punish employees, then the data will likely be useless for improvement. The reason is simple. People whose future depends on the results of a measure will spend a lot of time trying to influence the measure. It is hard enough trying to obtain meaningful data without having to contend with that data being manipulated by those gathering it. The choice is simple. You can use data to punish or reward employees or you can have good data. You can't have both.

SAMPLING

If there is anything that can throw the fear of statistics into the average employee (or statistics student), it is the subject of sampling. Sampling has been the subject of extensive academic volumes and the topic could never be fully dealt with here. However, teams that need data are going to have to obtain a sample and while the topic can be daunting, the fundamentals are straightforward and easily understood. By adhering to some basic methods and principles, improvement teams should be able to draw a sample and get the data they need for improvement.

WHAT IS SAMPLING?

Sampling is the process of selecting a limited number of objects to measure, from a much larger universe of possible objects. We do so either because measuring everything in the universe is simply too costly (in the case of enumerative studies) or impossible (in the case of analytic studies).

"All scientific observation, whether statistical or not, is based on sampling."

F.F. Stephan, "History of the Uses of Modern Sampling Procedures," Journal of the American Statistical Association, 43, 12-39

The purpose of sampling is to ensure the units selected for measurement fairly represent the real world about which conclusions will be drawn. In short, we want to eliminate, or at least limit, possible sources of bias in the measurement process.

All of us engage in some form of sampling everyday. Consider purchasing strawberries from the local market. If your market is like mine, the strawberries are presented in baskets covered in some form of transparent plastic wrap. We can't undo the plastic, so we are forced to select a particular basket, based upon our observations on the quality of those few strawberries that lie at the top, within view. In short, we are taking a sample. The strawberries at the top are the sample. We are compelled to act, to select one basket over another, based on this sample. How representative the sample is of the strawberries is another question. There is more than one consumer out there believing that some employee is putting all the good strawberries on top to induce some purchasing.[52]

FRAMES: EVERY SAMPLE NEEDS ONE

Frames are the means by which we access the units for study. If we are conducting a telephone survey of households in the United States, we might draw our sample, or select the households to be phoned, from a list of telephone numbers or the phone book. A frame, therefore, is the way we operationalize the sample.

Notice that the frame is not equivalent to the population of interest. Not every household has a phone, nor does every household have a listed number. No frame is perfect. It is a matter of judgment and expertise in the subject matter that will determine the suitability of the frame given the universe to be studied.

In an enumerative study, the frame will be a tangible list of objects that can be selected. It may be a listing of waybills, telephone numbers, invoice, customers or part numbers. It is from this list that the sample is selected.

In an analytic study, there is no finite population and, therefore, no list of units is possible. We need a different means of accessing the data – a different type of frame. In analytic studies, we use models of the cause and effect system such as process maps and cause-and-effect diagrams, combined with expert judgment, to help select the units for measure.

SAMPLING METHODS

If sampling is the process by which objects are selected for measurement, then different sampling methods are defined by

---

52. By the way, and for those who are curious, this is an example of an enumerative study. Action is being taken on the lot, not the cause and effect system that produced and delivered the strawberries.

the way in which units are selected. There are four basic sampling methods.

Census

A census is a sample where all the units in a frame are selected for measurement. This method of sampling is a lot more common than typically presumed. In many manufacturing applications, for example, every unit off the production line has some critical quality characteristics that are measured and recorded. The same holds true for many social statistics (i.e. accident rates, on-the-job accidents, etc.) and administrative data where all occurrences or measures are recorded.

Random Sampling

A random sample is one where every object in the frame has an equal probability of being included in the sample. This usually requires every sampling unit to be assigned a number. Then a random number table, or random number generator in a computer, is used to identify the selected candidates for measurement.

Essentially, the purpose of random sampling is to 'mix' the units sufficiently so that the sample will fairly represent the larger population – will eliminate bias. Using our purchase of strawberries example, random sampling ensures that all the good strawberries are not on top.

Consider conducting a study of employee attitudes. We might have 30,000 employees, but may wish to survey only 1,000 in order to keep survey costs down. A random sample would be the appropriate here. We would assign every employee a number (they might already have one as part of human resources' record-keeping system) and then randomly select 1,000 employees using a random numbers table or a random selection routine within a computer.

The selection by random number ensures that the sample is sufficiently mixed so that sources of bias are removed. For example, we can't select only those employees known to be happy with company policies. Similarly, we can be assured that the employees selected won't all come from just one or two of the company's 20 manufacturing facilities. The 'mixing' that occurs as a result of the random sampling pretty well assures us we will have employees in the sample from all 20 locations.

Systematic Sampling

Systematic sampling simply takes a sample or measurement at a pre-specified time or interval. Examples include measuring every tenth item produced off an assembly line, or gathering customer satisfaction data from every third customer that purchases an item, or sampling every fifteenth shipping record. The start point – the location or time at which we begin measuring – is usually decided randomly.

Because of this last point, systematic sampling is often passed off as random sampling. It isn't. The systematic approach can produce significant bias, especially when there is some cyclical factor at work that roughly corresponds to the sampling interval. Imagine sampling retail sales of stores every 12 months starting in December. Yearly estimates based on these figures would be grossly inflated.

Systematic sampling, however, has found wide application in analytic studies. Measuring every fifth item off an assembly line, for example, is a practical approach to sampling in manufacturing applications where taking a census would be too expensive. Problems of corresponding cyclical factors still apply, yielding the potential for bias. Actual design of the sample, especially defining the sampling interval, must be done in concert with those having knowledge of the system so that this potential for bias can be minimized.

Cluster Sampling

In cluster sampling, the objects to be sampled usually exist in large clusters or chunks. The sampling procedure selects the clusters rather than the individual objects within them. For example, if we had 50,000 customers across the country associated with some 100 sales office locations, we might randomly select five locations and sample all the customers associated with each. The random selection of office locations eliminates some bias by ensuring we don't arbitrarily select those locations we know to have a particularly good (or bad) reputation. If the number of objects in each of the clusters is rather large, a random sample of objects within the selected cluster could be applied to reduce sample size.

In enumerative studies, cluster samples are done as matter of convenience and cost. For example, think of surveying households in a major city. We might cluster the households into blocks, assign random numbers to each block, and then draw the random numbers to identify which blocks will participate in the survey. Every unit or household in the selected block would then be sampled. This approach greatly reduces interview costs as well as the cost of preparing the sampling frame.

In analytic studies, cluster samples are used frequently. Virtually all medical trials (testing a new drug, for example) or agricultural testing (testing a new seed or fertilizer) use clusters. For example, in testing a new blood thinner designed to reduce the size of blood clots, a hospital selects current patients known to have clots. The hospital is its own cluster. No attempt is made, nor is it practical, to use a random sampling procedure where the sampling frame is everyone in the world with a blood clot – it simply isn't possible. In a manufacturing application, a company might sample the first five units that come off the assembly line for the day. This, too, is a cluster sampling approach.

Stratified Samples

Stratification is the separation of data or, in this case, the separation of objects to be sampled into rational groups that correspond to some factor of interest. These 'strata' may be any real world condition we believe will have some significant impact on the outcomes of the study. The critical condition is that whatever groups or strata we define, they must be mutually exclusive. This means an object in strata A cannot also be an object in strata B, and likewise an object in strata B cannot also be an object in strata A.

Stratification can be applied to random, systemic and cluster sampling. Thus, we can have stratified random, stratified systemic and stratified cluster sampling.

▲ **Stratified Random Sampling.** Stratified random sampling first partitions the population into groups or strata, and then draws a random sample from each strata. For example, a survey of customers may be stratified by the amount of business the customer does with us – perhaps classifying the customers as major, large, moderate and small. Once these strata are identified, a frame is defined for each and a random sampling of units within the frame is conducted – as if each strata were a separate population. We may want to conduct a census of major customers and a random sample of other classifications. In stratified random sampling, it is the units within each strata that have an equal opportunity for selection.

▲ **Stratified Systemic Sampling.** Here, the population is stratified by the factor of interest, and then a systemic procedure of selecting units at designated intervals is applied.

Usually, a random start procedure is used for each of the strata, meaning the sampling will begin at different times or locations for each of the strata. For example, a factory may be 'stratified' by different production lines to see if there any important differences between these lines, or whether certain problems affect one line more than another. Once stratified, every tenth item is sampled from each line. In one line, every tenth item is selected starting from the first unit produced. For another line, it may be every tenth unit starting from the sixth unit produced.

▲ **Stratified Cluster**. Stratified cluster sampling usually begins by identifying the clusters to be sampled. Once these have been identified, the strata within the clusters are defined and a census or random sampling of these strata is applied. Take, for example, testing a new fertilizer on different types of grain crops. We may conduct our experiment on three different fields (clusters) and stratify by type of fertilizer and type of crop.

However, the procedure may also be applied in reverse. We could identify the strata first, and then take a randomly selected cluster within each strata as the sample.

ENUMERATIVE AND ANALYTIC STUDIES DEMAND DIFFERENT SAMPLING METHODS

The two basic types of studies we can undertake – enumerative and analytic – each demand different sampling methods.

Enumerative studies require the use of random sampling – either simple or stratified. Properly applied, random sampling eliminates or minimizes bias in the sample relative to the sampling frame. This allows estimates to be generated that will, within some margin of known error, describe the larger population within the frame. All this is possible because the population of interest is of fixed size, allowing a random selection procedure to be applied – effectively mixing up all the elements in the frame. The quality of an enumerative study, therefore, is often determined by the quality of the random sampling procedure used.

But in analytic studies, we are interested in the cause-and-effect system producing the units, not the units that have been produced. In fact, what we are really interested in is improving performance. This means the units we are interested in have yet to be been produced – they will be produced in the future. So we have no defined population by which to carry out a random sampling procedure. Rather, there is a process continually producing new units.

Moreover, in analytic studies we are not just interested in estimating some parameter, but rather in looking at how a specific system behaves over time or how its behavior changes across different stratification classifications. The mixing that occurs with random sampling would only muddle our results to the point of making them useless. In analytic studies, therefore, random sampling is not possible, nor would it be useful even if it were possible.

Table 93: Types of Studies and Sampling Method[*]

	Type of Sample	
Type of Study	**Random**	**Non-Random/ Judgment**
Enumerative	Good	Poor
Analytic	Fair	Good

[*] Source: Ronald Moen, et al., *Improving Quality Through Planned Experimentation*, McGraw Hill, 1991, p. 57. Reproduced with permission.

Performance improvement teams will, therefore, likely be relying on some form of judgment sample – systemic or cluster sampling with some degree of stratification. It is the quality of the judgment used that will be a critical factor in determining the quality of the analytic study. This requires the involvement of those with knowledge of the system to be improved, combined with some statistical expertise. It is these two skill sets that are required to reduce bias and other sources of error in the sample in an analytic study.

A second difference in sampling methods employed by enumerative and analytic studies is how stratification is employed. Stratification, prior to sampling, is hardly ever necessary in an enumerative study. Its usefulness is restricted to improving the efficiency of the study or the precision of the estimates.

But stratification prior to data collection is frequently essential to an analytic study. Often, the whole purpose of an analytic study is making comparisons between one strata and another – comparing two treatments, for example, or two processes or two set-up procedures. Prior stratification for the selection of units in these circumstances is absolutely required. After all, if you want to compare two treatments, you have to identify the two treatments you will be comparing.

So performance improvement teams will likely be working with judgment samples, using the experience and expertise of those close to the process or product to help select the units to be studied. Moreover, careful stratification will likely be required before the sampling process begins. The specific stratifications used will depend on the research question at hand, and will be based in large measure on the opinions and judgments of the improvement team.

PROBABILITY AND JUDGMENT

All this talk of random versus judgment samples and the limited applicability of random sampling to analytic studies may leave some a little uneasy. It tends to run contrary to what most people with some statistical training believe to be the case. After all, anyone who has taken a statistics course in college or university will remember something about the importance of random sampling and how important it is to avoid judgment samples.[53] This is reinforced by media reporting of the latest poll results – assuring the public that the poll was based on a

random sample of Americans and is considered accurate to some level of precision.

However, much of what is taught in introductory statistics courses concerns tools and techniques applicable to enumerative work, not analytic. Unfortunately, this small bit of information often goes missing during these introductory courses.

The fact is, all samples have some element of judgment about them. Even a random sample relies upon the expertise and judgment of the statistical expert, and the expert in the subject matter at hand, as to the best way to define and operationalize the sample. This constitutes the frame to be used in accessing the data. The results of any enumerative study are conditional upon the quality of the frame used, and that frame is created through expert judgment. There is no perfection in sampling or in anything else.

Likewise, judgment samples may use random procedures to help mix the sample and eliminate bias. When testing a new drug, for example, a factor to be controlled is the placebo effect. For this reason, one study group is given a treatment, the other group (called the control group) is given a placebo, say in the form of a sugar pill.[54] There must be people in each group

---

53. That is assuming anything at all was remembered from the introductory statistics course. Perhaps it is better stated that if anything at all was remembered from an introductory statistics course, it was the importance of a well-designed random sample.

(so we can compare the effectiveness of the new drug against sugar pills), and the people in each group must have whatever condition it is we are hoping to improve. For these reasons, there is no point in trying to create a random sample. We need to identify those individuals at our hospital that have the condition. This is a cluster sample based totally on expert judgment (a doctor had to diagnose who has the condition).

But how to decide which people go to the control group and which go to the group receiving the treatment? Here we use a random process to make the assignments. Why? Because if we didn't, those wishing to prove the drug works might assign people most likely to get better regardless to the group receiving the treatment. In short, they might introduce bias into the measurement process. Making the assignments randomly helps ensure that all the confounding factors that could influence the results are sufficiently "mixed up," so they will not bias results between the two groups one way or the other.

GOOD SAMPLING LEAVES NOTHING TO CHANCE

After all this talk about sampling and statistics, the statement "Good sampling leaves nothing to chance"[55] may seem a little surprising. But this is the bottom line of sampling method. The purpose of sampling is to deliver the data you need to analyze a problem and provide some answers. Collecting good data can be expensive and time consuming. This is no time to roll the dice and hope for the best. That's why good sampling should leave nothing to chance.

Suppose you are conducting a study of your customers to determine their level of satisfaction with your product – an enumerative study. You may have 2,000 customers, of which 35 are major customers – collectively accounting for over half of all sales. Use a random sample of all customers? No way!

The two customer groups should be stratified. Then conduct a complete census of the major customers and a random sample

---

54. This is an example of the need to pre-stratify a sample in most analytic studies.

55. For more on this idea, see Edwards Deming, *Sample Design in Business Research.*, John Wiley & Sons, 1990 The book is not for the uninitiated; however, the introductory chapters are a gold mine for those with more than a casual interest in sampling theory and design.

of everyone else. The results can later be combined and adjusted if determining some overall satisfaction measure is required. What is important here is that the sampling design did not leave the selection of major customers to chance. Making sure you get the data you need is the first objective and fundamental purpose of sampling.

The same holds true in analytic studies but is more difficult to deliver. The challenge of analytic studies is the number of unknowns – all the confounding factors, current and future, that could impact system performance. All of these can never be accommodated in an analytic study. A balance is required, carefully stratifying units where appropriate while randomizing to minimize bias of all these background conditions.

The bottom line is the same in both cases. The purpose of sampling is to help give you the data you need to take action.

THE PROCESS OF GATHERING DATA

So how to gather the data? What is the process to be used? Obviously, the specifics of gathering data will vary with the application and purpose of the analysis. But we can define a generic process to help ensure all the bases get covered. There are seven basic steps in data gathering.

1. DEFINE THE PURPOSE OF THE DATA OR RESEARCH

Step one is to clearly understand what it is we are trying to do. What is the focus of the research question? Is it some process or product? Are we trying to estimate some parameter? The team must have a clear idea of the fundamental purpose of the study.

The critical word here is fundamental. We are not so much concerned with the phrasing of an appropriate or precise research question, as we are with agreeing on the basic issue or problem to be resolved. For example, some issues might be:

▶ Does the basic quality of our product compare well with the competition?

▶ How good is the service we deliver?

▶ Is our inventory process cost-effective?

▶ Is our response time adequate?

Exhibit 94: Seven Data Gathering Steps

▶ How many of our customers like dealing with us?

These are the types of fundamental questions or issues that concern improvement teams. They set the context and scope of the problem the team must address.

The improvement team should be able to write down this issue and agree on it. This may take some discussion and debate. But agreement is required. Don't proceed with gathering data unless the basic, fundamental issue at hand is defined and shared among team members.

Once the fundamental issue is clear, the team must also agree on what the fundamental issue has to say about the nature of the study required. Specifically, will we be conducting an enumerative study or an analytic one? If the purpose of the study is to establish or analyze some level of performance or examine likely causal relationships, an analytic study will be required. In contrast, if the purpose comes down to estimating some parameter in a lot or population, an enumerative study will be required.

2. DEFINE THE CRITICAL PERFORMANCE CHARACTERISTICS AND METRICS

With the basic purpose established, the team can move on to refining the basic performance it is concerned with into a more definable set of characteristics. These quality characteristics are the means by which the team will define performance. A simple question such as "How does our quality compare?" needs to be distilled into the specific set of characteristics that define what we mean by "quality."

Take an emergency 911 response service for example. The job of the service is to take calls from people in trouble and relay this information to the appropriate responding department – the police, fire or ambulance service. The emergency response service is there to get help to where people need it. In a project concerned with improving responsiveness of the system, responsiveness must be defined through a set of characteristics that specify what we mean by this term. Teams may use such tools as the tree diagram to refine the concept to a point where the measurable characteristics are clear.

Note how the tree diagram breaks down responsiveness into two fundamental characteristics: how fast the call is handled

Table 95: Tree Diagram: Responsiveness of 911 System

Customer Requirements	Quality Characteristic	Metric
Gets help to where people need it.	Fast	Time to Answer
		% Calls Abandoned
	Reliable	% Accurate Relay
		% Accurate Nature of Emergency
		% Address Accurate

and how reliably. The first deals with speed, the second with whether the right information is forwarded to the right department. These two characteristics, however, are not precise enough to gather measurements, so they are further refined. 'Fast,' for example, is broken down into the elapsed time to answer (the time between the caller connecting to the system and the time at which the emergency response operator actually answers the call) and the percentage of calls abandoned (the percentage of callers who hang up while waiting for an operator to respond). Now we have something approaching a specific performance metric.

In some cases, only one measure will need to be identified. In other cases, the fundamental research issue will be sufficiently broad that several specific measures will have to be defined to create an adequate research program. Using tree diagrams and related techniques can often help teams build a consistent and comprehensive measurement plan.

3. CREATE A MEANS FOR ACCESSING THE DATA, THE FRAME

The means by which the data will be accessed needs to be created next. In an enumerative study, this requires defining the frame – the method by which units in the universe will be selected for inclusion in the sample. For example, if we are conducting a telephone survey, the frame might be a list of telephone numbers of the target population and a random sample will be drawn from this frame.

With analytic studies things are not so straightforward. We must rely on some model of the process we are hoping to analyze. Such models are ultimately based on expert judgment of what is and is not important to understanding of how the process functions. In most process or performance work, the best

tool to capture, organize and present the collective judgments of those familiar with the issue is the cause and effect diagram.

Recall that the cause and effect diagram provides a visual representation or model of our shared theory about what factors are likely to cause changes in the quality characteristics we are measuring. The diagram is, in fact, a measurement road map of all the things we could measure or might be important to the analysis of the performance characteristic. A cause and effect diagram, therefore, should be prepared for each response variable or metric.

In practice, however, this can lead to producing mountains of cause and effect diagrams and, ultimately, analysis paralysis. Teams usually employ some priority-setting techniques to identify areas of highest leverage, where teams feel the greatest benefits will result from their actions. They attack those areas first.

The cause and effect diagram is a visual theory of what things (factors or causes) have an effect on some characteristic we consider important. But it is still just a theory. Data is required to confirm our expectations. Specifically, we need to identify and gather data on:

▲ **Response Variables.** Response variables are the specific performance measure associated with some performance quality characteristic. A complete set of response variables defines performance for whatever fundamental issue the improvement team is working on. A change in the response variable indicates a change in the performance of the process. Exhibit 95: Tree Diagram: Responsiveness of 911 System lists the set of response variables for an emergency response (911) service. Measurements are gathered for each response variable that together define the overall responsiveness of the system.

If, for example, the percentage of accurate relays rises, we can say the performance of the system is improving. At the same time, the percentage of dropped or abandoned calls (these are the calls where the caller simply hangs up) may be rising. If they are, it indicates the performance of the process (as measured by this characteristic) is becoming worse. There are no guarantees that measures of performance will always move neatly in the same direction. Finding these apparent discrepancies and differences can be the first step to improved understanding and, ultimately, action.

▲ **Explanatory Variables (Factors).** What are all the things that could affect whatever it is you are measuring? What are all the things that could affect, in our example, time to answer? We could list telephone system design, training of staff, time of day, staffing levels, call volume and a host of other variables. These and many more are all examples of explanatory variables – measures representing factors that could cause some changes in our response variable of time to pick up the phone. On the cause and effect diagram they are represented by the causal branches and can be broken down into finer levels of detail. To make improvement, we need to understand the mechanics of performance. The cause and effect diagram provides a theoretical listing of all the variables that can explain changes in process performance.

Once identified, we can then use empirical methods to explore and validate these theoretical relationships. Explanatory variables are analyzed relative to performance or response variables. Where there is correlation, we can begin to infer causal relationships that, in turn, can help guide the improvement effort. Where there is no such correlation, the explanatory variable can likely be removed as an effective cause or factor influencing performance.

The real world is a complex place. Things do not always present themselves in a nice, neat and linear fashion. At times, we may have to shift our theories a little. Sometimes, response variables can be treated as explanatory variables and vice

versa. Take our emergency response example. Time to pick up the phone and percentage of calls abandoned are both response variables. However, we may suspect that the percentage of calls abandoned is dependent upon the time it takes the system to answer the call (time to pick up). To test this idea, time to pick up becomes an explanatory variable affecting abandoned calls.

Exhibit 96: Using the Cause & Effect Diagram to Define Possible Explanatory Variables for a Specific Quality Characteristic

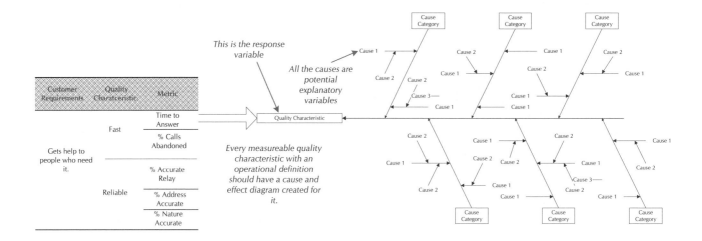

Similar changes occur as we move upstream on the cause and effect diagram. We might find, for example, that a single causal element is responsible for almost all of the changes in the response variable. In progressing up the causal chain to find the root cause of changes in performance, we might establish this cause as the new response variable and begin examining all the causal factors connected to it as explanatory variables.

In short, the cause and effect diagram is the start of thinking about what is going on in the real world and how this gets reflected by the data. Those involved in the improvement effort should feel free to move things around a little, to explore and play with the research design to ensure that data needed to answer the research question is actually gathered.

One last point on using the cause and effect diagram to help create a means for accessing the data. It is important that one of the major branches be labelled "Measurement" on the diagram. The various branches connected to this branch should identify how the measurement or data-gathering process itself can cause some effect on the final result.

4. OPERATIONALLY DEFINE THE MEASURES AND METRICS

With the creation of the cause and effect diagram, the team will have a clear set of response and explanatory variables to measure. Two things must be accomplished at this point. First, the range of possible measurement will likely have to be reduced. Second, specific operational definitions will have to be defined for each metric.

At times, the range of things that can be measured will be overwhelming. The team will have to decide which of myriad variables needs to be studied. Not all can be, not unless we want to spend the rest of our lives measuring! Priorities must be set. Team members must decide, based upon their judgments, what causal factors identified likely have the largest or most important impact upon the response variables of interest.

Once decisions have been made as to what will and will not be measured, operational definitions are created. Establishing the operational definition requires careful consideration of the details of the measurement process. We must get to a level of detail where, for each metric, there are clear definitions of what will be measured, how it will be measured and the specific measurement tool to be used.

Returning to our example of responsiveness of an emergency response service, when do we start to measure response times and when do we end? Do we start measuring when the 911 operator picks up the phone? If so, some people could be waiting on the phone for some time before an operator comes on the line and their wait times would not be captured. When do we stop measuring? Do we stop when the 911 operator forwards the call to the appropriate department or when the emergency vehicle leaves the station? Perhaps we should stop measuring response time when the emergency crew actually begins delivering aid to the party requesting help. Deciding these issues is the process of creating the operational definitions we need, to have a reliable data set arising from the data gathering effort.

5. DESIGN THE DATA-COLLECTION STRATEGY

How are we going to get the data? Answering this involves answering two other questions:

▶ How are we going to select the units we want to measure?

▶ How will the data be gathered?

The first of these questions concerns the sampling plan. In turn, the nature of the sampling revolves around the purpose of the research. If the nature of the research is enumerative, a detailed sampling plan that ensures a random approach in the selection of units from the population is required. If the study is analytic, judgment of those involved is required to ensure the process is represented fairly in the data collection effort.

Once the sampling plan is known, the team can focus on where the data is best gathered and who will do the collecting. This is not as easy as it sounds. Complexity in work flow – such as rework paths, multiple processes and the like – can all mean problems for those interested in gathering good data.

This is why completing a good process map early on in the improvement effort is so important. A map of how and where things move in the process can highlight obvious data-gathering points, or at least aid the process of deciding where to focus the data collection effort.

Deciding how the data will be gathered also means deciding who will collect it. Generally, the data should be gathered by those having easy access to the data required. But caution is warranted. Gathering data can also mean more work for those who are busy enough doing other things – such as serving customers. Tellers in a bank may have easy access to information about line-up times or other data. But operationalizing the data collection effort with tellers may be difficult, especially if there is a long line of customers anxiously waiting for service.

This emphasizes the need to keep data collection forms and methods simple. Data collection forms need to facilitate the process of gathering valid data – not make it more difficult. Take the time to design the form carefully.

Good data collection forms include these characteristics:

▲ **The template or check sheet should be designed to reduce the chance of error.** If categorical data is to be gathered (i.e. gender), the check-sheet should clearly spell out the options (male/female). Do everything to keep the form as unambiguous as possible. Use visual clues to help data gatherers with interpretation. If a computer is being used for data input, use data-evaluation techniques to ensure the right type of data is being entered in the correct locations.

▲ **Capture information for future analysis and reference.** When taking a measure or a count, ensure the time and date are recorded, who took the measure, the specific machine or type of product, and other data that could prove important when analyzing for root causes. There is always a trade-off between the amount of data teams would like and the costs of collecting the data. But it is better to gather the data needed the first time out than have to repeat the data-gathering process because key data was missing.

▲ **Keep it simple.** Complex forms usually translate into errors, frustration or both. Don't be afraid to involve those in collecting the data with the data-collection form or template design. It should be clear, concise, easy to read and as self-explanatory as possible.

6. PRE-TEST

Conduct a test before finalizing the form design and other elements of the data-gathering process. Results arising from the test can then be assessed. We are interested in answering two basic concerns through the pre-test:

▶ Will our data-gathering method work?

▶ Will we get the data we need to answer the questions we have?

▲ **Pre-testing the data-gathering method.** Pre-testing the data gathering method is usually done on a small scale. The intent is to see if the basic set of data-gathering forms and methods work in a real world setting. They may not. Not everyone reads data collection forms the same way, nor does everyone have the time to read through things that may be confusing or unclear. In conducting the pre-test, try and replicate the same conditions that will be in place when the data collection effort is rolled out. For example, don't provide any special instructions that wouldn't otherwise be available.

After the pre-test of the data gathering, conduct a debriefing with those involved. Identify what worked and what didn't, what was difficult to do, and any other issues that arose. Did some data gathers do things one way while others did things differently? Now is the time to get all this out and make the modifications necessary to ensure the data collection effort goes smoothly.

▲ **Pre-testing analytical approach.** Next is testing the proposed method of analysis. Here, we conduct an analysis of the information gathered during the pre-test of the data-gathering effort. We will not have enough data to make any conclusions. But we will have enough to see if the information we will be getting back is suitable to the analytical task at hand. This means using the tools of analysis on the data we have, and ensuring that the application of these tools will address our basic research questions. If they do not, then different data will be required.

This may seem like an odd time to decide upon the appropriate data analysis tool. After all, so little data has actually been collected. But, in fact, now is the perfect time. Teams should have a clear vision of how they will be organizing and comparing the data (analysis) before they start to collect it, if only because the data gathered can have such a large impact on the applicability of the various tools.

The range of data-analysis tools includes:

▶ Histograms

▶ Run Charts

▶ Control Charts

▶ Pareto Charts

▶ Scatter Diagrams

▶ Box & Whisker Plots

▶ Dot Plots

Pre-testing the data collection and analysis permits the team to answer some important data-gathering questions. Does the tool provide you with the kind of output the team needs to draw its conclusions? What kinds of questions does the analysis still leave you with? Do additional data need to be gathered? Is a different tool more appropriate? Pre-testing the analysis not only helps answer these questions, but does so when there is still time to make changes.

7. IMPLEMENT

The last step in the data-gathering process involves implementation. It's never quite as simple as "just do it" – to borrow from a popular slogan. At the very least:

▲ **Train those involved.** The people responsible for collecting the data will need to be trained on precisely how to accomplish the task. Data collection may seem simple, but the problems faced by those in the field or on the front lines can often add a whole new layer of complexity to the task. Take the time for training. Not only will it improve the confidence of the data collectors, it will improve data quality as well.

▲ **Ensure understanding.** Check with those who will be doing the work to see if things make sense and they fully understand the task. Just because you are doing the training doesn't mean those in the field have nothing to teach. At times, those gathering the data may be aware of problems that pose a real threat to data validity. Be prepared to listen and accommodate feedback.

▲ **Validate the effort and revise where appropriate.** Assuming the steps just described have been followed, problems should be few – but they won't be eliminated. Someone on the project team responsible for data collection should be available to answer questions as they arise in the field (real time, on-line problem solving). Taking the time to simply walk around and ask how the data collection effort is going can help as well.

▲ **Standardize.** Once implemented, the data collection process must become standardized for the term of the data collection effort. This means that once the best way of gathering the data has been decided upon, it needs to be 'hard-wired' into the way things are done generally. Data gathering cannot be allowed to unconsciously evolve over time as this will impact the measures or data gathered.

DATA GATHERING TOOLS

The tools used to gather data are virtually endless and they are as varied as the nature of the data being gathered. Market research departments gather customer satisfaction measures through questionnaires and from purchasing/sales records. The accounting function uses various forms such as purchase orders and expense statements, while operations has inspectors record finish blemishes on a computer screen.

However, it may be useful to focus on at least two basic data-gathering tools: the check sheet and the data documentation template. The first is used to provide a means of gathering data and the second defines what data is required (the data that needs to be gathered and why).

CHECK SHEETS

Numerical data is such a large part of our world that improvement teams may often find themselves overwhelmed with data.

Rather than having to go out and gather more, the first job may be deciding what is useful and what is not. Nevertheless, there will be occasions where teams will have to gather their own data. The primary tool for doing so is the check sheet.

Check sheets, unlike most of the tools in this book, are not necessarily analytical tools – they are data-collection devices. They can be used to gather the data required for histograms, Pareto charts, scatter diagrams and other analytical tools. However, many check sheet designs attempt to embed data analysis within the design. Most of the examples presented here do this. It is often useful to encourage real-time analysis as the data is being collected, especially in field applications.

But why do we need check sheets at all? There are three basic reasons:

▲ **Data collection should be driven by the nature of the problem under examination, not the availability of data.** This may mean gathering new data, because organizational information systems are not typically designed to gather the type of data useful for process or product improvement. Check sheets provide a simple and straightforward means of gathering the data we need in a format that supports the use of analytical tools.

▲ **Data collection and analysis efforts in organizations are typically oriented to corporate decision making at a very high level**. Far less often are they focused on gathering process or field data geared to analyzing the actual work being conducted. If such data is collected, it is usually summarized before it moves up the corporate ladder, making it difficult to apply. Check sheets provide a means of gathering the raw data in the field, directly from the people doing the work.

▲ **Check sheets simplify the data-collection process and limit errors.** If a process team is going to gather data directly in the field or in the factory, then some effort should be made to ensure the data is of sufficient quality to be used in subsequent decision making. Check sheets provide a convenient way of detailing precisely what the improvement team is looking for, and structuring the input process in a way to limit the possibility of error.

In practice this means check sheets are usually, although not necessarily, a temporary device to gather data that the improvement team needs to analyze some aspect of performance. Once sufficient data has been obtained, the need for more data and the check sheet itself is gone.

Types of Check Sheets

Check sheet types are as numerous as the problems organizations seek to improve. There is no one template guaranteed to work for the all the various problems different organizations face. However, as an aid to custom-designing data-gathering tools, some basic types are presented.

▲ **Check Sheet to Produce a Run Chart.** This captures the data by time period, allowing for the creation of a run chart in real time – as the data is gathered.

▲ **Frequency Distribution Check Sheet.** This combines histogram creation with a check sheet, in effect allowing staff to create a histogram in real time, right at the job site.

▲ **Defect Frequency Check Sheet.** When there are various types of defects, workers can place check marks against appropriate items, which creates a basic Pareto chart – again in real time right at the job site.

▲ **Defect Location Check Sheet.** Widely used in manufacturing, location check sheets provide a map of the object being produced and allow the worker to highlight the location of defects by placing a check mark on the map.

Some samples of the various types of check sheets are provided on the following pages.

Design considerations

As mentioned, the purpose of the check sheet is to simplify and error-proof the data collection process. Some general considerations that support these objectives are listed below.

▲ **Good check sheets list the specifics of what is being looked for (problems, types of errors, and so on) and restrict data entry to these options.** Data entry choice is then restricted to these options, to reduce ambiguity and error in recording the data. For example, when gathering data related to the gender of customers, provide two alternative check boxes – one for female and one for male. These are the only options and the check box eliminates the possibility of confusion related to poor handwriting.

▲ **When designing the template, use illustrations where appropriate.** This makes the check sheet easier to use and can reveal patterns during your later analysis. For example, to collect data on damaged packages, include a sketch of the package and have data collectors put an X where they see the damage. If you are studying where errors

Exhibit 97: Defect Check Sheet to Produce a Run Chart

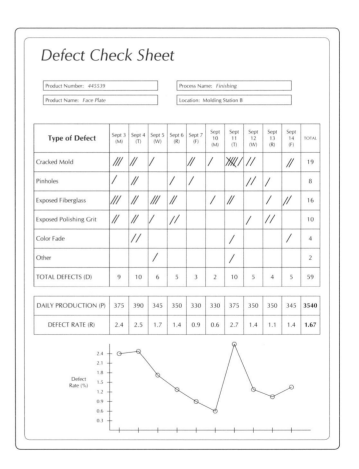

Exhibit 98: Frequency Distribution Check Sheet

Exhibit 99: Defect Frequency Check Sheet

Measurement Check Sheet (Histogram)

Date: September 12, 1997

Product Number: 33582

Characteristics: Thickness

Product Name: Wire

Process: Stranding

Thickness	10	20	30	TOTAL
301 - 305				
306 - 310	//			2
311 - 315	////			4
316 - 320	///// ///// /			11
321 - 325	///// ///// ////			14
326 - 330	///// ///// ///// ///// ///			23
331 - 335	///// ///// ///// ////			18
336 - 340	///// ///// //			12
341 - 345	////			4
346 - 350	///			3
351 - 355	/			1
356 - 360				

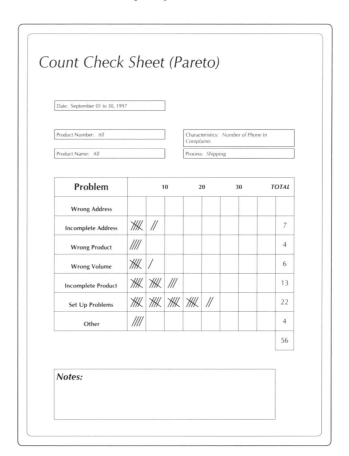

Count Check Sheet (Pareto)

Date: September 01 to 30, 1997

Product Number: All

Characteristics: Number of Phone In Complaints

Product Name: All

Process: Shipping

Problem	10	20	30	TOTAL
Wrong Address				
Incomplete Address	///// //			7
Wrong Product	////			4
Wrong Volume	///// /			6
Incomplete Product	///// ///// ///			13
Set Up Problems	///// ///// ///// ///// //			22
Other	////			4
				56

Notes:

Exhibit 100: Defect Location Check Sheet

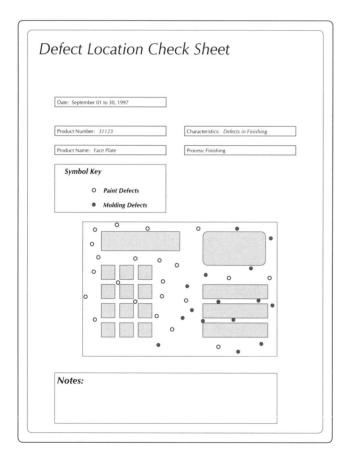

occur in a report, put check marks on a sample of the report.

▲ **Keep separate check sheets for stratified data.** An example is using separate check sheets for gathering data on damages to packages shipped by different companies. A separate check sheet would be set up for each company, ensuring the data could be analyzed by the shipper at a later date.

▲ **Keep the check sheet near the action.** For example, if monitoring telephone interruptions experienced by tellers at their stations, don't put the check sheet in the branch manager's office. Place by the tellers.

▲ **Check sheets should support preliminary analysis.** The very process of collecting data should support the analysis of the same data. For example, many data collection sheets, including the first three examples provided here, gather the data in such a way that the very process of entering the data builds a histogram or Pareto chart of the data. This allows for immediate, real time analysis without having to enter the data in a computer or calculate complex statistics.

DATA/INDICATORS DOCUMENTATION TEMPLATE

Data documentation templates are used to document what data is being gathered and why. From defining the rationale behind a corporate scorecard measure to documenting why an improvement team is gathering data on invoice errors, the data documentation template is a useful way to help standardize the data gathering effort. A sample of a typical template is provided in Exhibit 101: Data Documentation Template.

1. **Indicator Name**. This should be a relatively self-explanatory name of the measure or indicator.

2. **Measurement Purpose**. This describes why we are gathering data. The reason may be straightforward, even obvious. For example, the importance of measuring profit is relatively straightforward. There may also be downstream logical/rational connections to the measure. For example, measuring staff turnover has impact not just on the cost of hiring and training, but may also impact customer service or some other downstream area.

Exhibit 101: Data Documentation Template

1. Indicator Name

2. Measurement Purpose (Why)
a. Direct

b. Downstream

3. Who Needs to Know

4. Relates to Which Business Objective(s)

5. Data / Measurement Elements

5.1 Numerator	5.1.a Definition	5.1.b Source	5.1.c Collected By	Data Collection Frequency
5.2 Numerator	5.2.a Definition	5.2.b Source	5.2.c Collected By	

6. Sampling

6.1 Numerator — 6.2 Denominator

7. Reporting & Analysis

6.1 Compiled By:

6.2 Reporting Frequency

6.3 Basis of Analysis

6.3.a Basis of Comparison	6.3.b Description	Method/Tool
☐ Target / Goal ☐ Competitive Performance ☐ Previous Performance		

8. Action

8.1 Action Will Be Taken When — 8.2 Action Taken By: — 8.3 Comments

3. **Who Needs to Know.** Who needs the data or indicator? Try to be specific – identify job or function that requires the information or that is requesting it be gathered.

4. **Relates to Which Business Objectives.** The specific business objectives the measure or indicator relates to need to be identified here. There may be one or more such objectives.

5. **Data / Measurement Elements.** For both numerator and denominator (if some form of ratio or proportion is being calculated), the data being gathered needs to be clearly specified and defined. Equally important, the source of the data (specific computer file, data collection sheet, etc.) needs to be specified, as does the person or job responsible for gathering the data and the collection frequency.

6. **Sampling.** If appropriate, the specific sampling method should be documented here. This includes the basic sampling method and supporting rules for staff who may be gathering data in the field. In administrative applications where the data is being taken from computer records and the like, this may not be relevant, although the source of the data, the time period etc. should still be included.

7. **Reporting and Analysis.** In this area, the individual responsible for preparing the analysis, and the frequency at which this is done, are specified. In addition, the basis of analysis is also detailed. This refers to what the data is being compared to. Target or goals represent expectation-based comparisons established somewhere within the organization. The basis of comparison may also be competitive performance (benchmarking) or previous performance (statistical process control). A description is also required of the specific comparison and the method or data-analysis tool that would be used. For example, if a comparison to goal or target is being used, this where the target level would be documented – staff turnover target of 8.0 percent, for example, or a process capability index of less than 1.33.

8. **Action.** In this area, who does what and when, depending upon the results of the indicator, are specified. It may be that we have a staff turnover target of 8.0 percent, but that no action will be taken unless the turnover exceeds 10.0 percent. This threshold value and the action to be taken are specified here.

The data documentation template is useful in documenting and standardizing measurements and data collection efforts. Teams or organizations setting up a measurement system and performance model are advised to adopt the template or some version of it, to ensure the reasons, underlying logic or rationale and the methods of data collection are not lost as time goes by.

OTHER DATA-GATHERING TOOLS

There are many data-gathering tools and methods and it is beyond our scope here to deal with all of them. They include:

▲ **Focus Group** is a data-gathering technique designed to elicit a large amount of qualitative data on some well-defined topic or interest area. A small number of people, usually less than 10, is brought together and led through a facilitated discussion on the topic of interest. The resulting conversations are recorded and later analyzed.

▲ **Questionnaires** gather data from any group of people including customers, employees, suppliers and stakeholders. They may be paper-based, administered in person, over the phone or more recently, over the Internet. They can gather both quantitative and qualitative data.

▲ **Internal Records** of all kinds represent what is often the most overlooked source of data – the company's own records. They may be filed away on paper or buried deep within a computer's hard drive. Diving in to the organization's own files in search of data is often one of the most inexpensive and fruitful exercises in a performance improvement initiative.

ORGANIZING AND SUMMARIZING DATA

Once gathered, the data must be described in some succinct way. We need to organize and summarize it in order to make sense of it. In short, we need to describe it in a way that helps us draw conclusions about whatever is being studied.

The first issue in providing these summary descriptions is dealing with different types of data. This may come as a surprise to many. Aren't all numbers the same? No, they're not. Remember that the data gathered is a function of the thing being measured, the measuring stick used, and the process employed to compare the stick to the thing being measured. Different measuring sticks produce different types of data.

TYPES OF DATA

We can distinguish between two basic types of data: data that arises from a measurement (called measured or variables data), and data that arises from a count (called counted or attribute data).

1. MEASURED (CONTINUOUS OR VARIABLES DATA)

When we measure, we are basically answering the question: "How much?" For example, when measuring response time, we ask "How much time?" We answer with a specific measurement, say in seconds. If the characteristic is weight, we ask "How much weight?" We answer with a specific measurement, say in pounds or ounces.

With measured or variables data, a specific measuring 'stick' with a continuous scale is used. Because of this, it is always possible for any form of measured data to produce a fraction.

An item can weigh 24.44 kilograms, for example, or be 37.116 inches in length. Whenever it is logically possible to have some fraction in the data gathered, the data resulted from measurement as opposed to a count.

2. COUNTED (ATTRIBUTE OR DISCRETE DATA)

Not all products or services are measured on a continuous scale, however. Many times we look to see if a sample has a characteristic or not. For example, did the student pass or fail? How many students in the class failed? Does the order form have an error or not? How many errors are there? In these cases, we are counting rather than measuring across a scale. The question is not "How much?" but rather "How many?"

Determining the number of errors occurring on a form or the number of scratches on a painted surface are examples of data resulting from a count. Data produced in this way is referred to as attribute or discrete data. It is easy to determine if something is attribute data or not since attribute data produces only integers, or whole numbers. A painted surface cannot have 1.5 scratches nor can there be 2.3 errors on a form. Errors, scratches or anything else that is counted consists of whole numbers only.

Note that if we take averages or compute other statistics, fractions can be created with attribute data. For example, counting 35 scratches on 13 body panels yields an average of 2.69 scratches per panel. However, we couldn't count 35.7 scratches. The fraction with attribute data is created by computing a statistic, as opposed to arising from the data collection itself.

The fact that no measuring stick is used with counted data does not discount the impact of the measuring system on the item being measured. While there is no 'yardstick,' there is still a system of measurement (the counting process) that will impact the final result. There is no truth with counted or any other type of data. There is only the result of a particular data-gathering process applied to a specific characteristic.

3. COMPOUND DATA

People, being what they are, have a tendency to make things a little more complicated than they would appear at first blush. So it is with types of data. In the real world we often combine numbers to create ratios, proportions, etc. What happens if we combine a piece of measured data with a piece of counted data. Then what do we have?

Exhibit 102: Types of Data attempts to provide an easy to follow guideline. If a measured value is in the numerator, then it is measured data regardless of what is in the denominator. If a counted value is in the numerator, then it is counted data regardless of what is in the denominator. In short, the numerator rules.

There is a need to be careful when using compound data. Most organizations use various forms of compound data to relate one thing (numerator) to another (denominator) in an effort to control for differences in scale or changes over time. This is especially true in the definition of performance indicators. For example, one measure of crime would be to simply count up the number of crimes committed. But typically, and indicator is developed such as crime per 100,000 population.

This works well when there is some rationale (real world) connection between the numerator and denominator. We would expect, for example, that as the denominator goes up there would be a tendency for the numerator to rise as well. When

Exhibit 102: Types of Data[*]

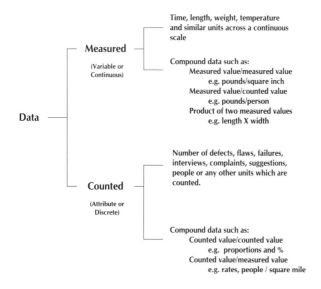

*   Kazuo Ozeki and Tetsuichi Asaka, *Handbook of Quality Tools*, Productivity Press 1990, p. 119. Reproduced with Permission.

this is true, we are dealing with a proportion or a rate and all is well. But with another form of compound data, the ratio, the rational connection between numerator and denominator isn't

required. For this reason, ratios are to be used with caution in empirical data analysis.

Proportions

Proportions usually arise when both the numerator and denominator are count data and where the objects in the numerator form a physical subset of the objects counted in the denominator. The physical connection between numerator and denominator in this case is clear – both arise from a count of the same set of objects. Proportions can usually be expressed as percentages. For example, we could count the proportion of people attending a conference that are male or the proportion of yesterday's production failing to meet specifications.

Rates

Rates are typically produced when the numerator is counted but the denominator is measured. Typical rates include things such as: miles per hour, violent crime per hundred thousand population or the production level per worker-hour. With rates, the denominator is an area of opportunity that is still directly connected to the numerator. For example, it makes sense that the number of crimes would increase with population simply because the greater number of people provides a greater area of opportunity for crimes to occur. Likewise, increasing worker-hours should provide a larger area of opportunity to increase production.

Ratios

With ratios, however, the rational connection between numerator and denominator is sometimes missing. For example, one company calculated a 'rebate percentage' with the dollar value of rebates given to customers in a particular month (numerator) divided by the revenues earned in the month (denominator). But the value of rebates given in a particular month isn't a function of the revenues earned in the same month; it arises from problems experienced in previous months. So in this case, there is no physical connection between numerator and denominator. For all intents and purposes, any analysis using this ratio is pretty much meaningless.

This is typical of ratios that compare re-work arising from some previous time period with current production or related data. Beware of using ratios where numerator and denominator are not physically connected in some way. They can lead to seriously misleading conclusions.

IMPLICATIONS

Generally speaking, the higher order the data, the more we can do with it from an analytical perspective. When we measure how much or to what extent a characteristic varies from unit to unit (variables data), we know more than when we examine whether or not an attribute is present or absent in a unit (attribute data). Measured data, then, is of a higher order than counted data. So teams should make every effort to obtain measured data where possible.

This is especially true when dealing with overall performance measures – response variables. The use of measured data here allows for the use of variables control charts and other analytical tools that are easier to use and more powerful than those associated with counted data.

Of course, nature doesn't always allow teams to use measured data. In some instances, there may be advantages to using attribute or counted data.

▲ **Not all quality characteristics can or should be measured and expressed in a measured value.** The entry of a social security number on an application, for example, is either right or wrong. The quality characteristic is accuracy, and the characteristic is either present or absent. Although you might argue that some measurement of degree or accuracy could be devised, you must ask yourself if knowing "how wrong" will help you manage the process. Probably not. It such circumstances, attribute data may simply be a more appropriate and useful type of data to gather.

▲ **When a process is stable, a single counted value can replace a lot of measured values.** A product may have several quality characteristics that are important to the customer. With a stable process, measuring and tracking each and every characteristic would take considerable time and resources. In such a circumstance, simply tracking the number of non-conforming or returned items may make more sense and save money. So a single count value could replace several measurements. Caution is warranted, however. Tracking the process in this fashion will mean you will not detect problems until defects are being produced and delivered to customers. Measurement data may have been able to detect a shift in quality and provide feedback in time to properly adjust the process before defects occurred. Teams must constantly assess the value of infor-

mation, weighing the costs and benefits with different data-collection strategies.

▲ **The counted data may already be available.** When the attribute data you need already exists, it may be a cost-effective choice. For example, many companies maintain data on the number of returned items, number of customer complaints and the like. This data can be quickly gathered and analyzed.

▲ **Attribute data may be more relevant to senior decision-makers.** Teams must deal with the issue of communication if they want their analysis to be accepted and their solutions adopted. Measurement data sometimes conveys less bottom-line meaning to decision-makers. For example, saying that on average, customers reported a satisfaction level of 4.3 out of a possible 5 points uses a measured scale. But it is vague and difficult to grasp. In contrast, saying that 20 percent of customers are dissatisfied with our service and do not plan to buy our products again paints a more concrete and meaningful picture that decision-makers can easily relate to.

SCALES IN MEASUREMENT

To add to the mix of data types, there are also different types of data depending upon the nature of the scale used in the measurement process. These basic types are:

▲ **Ratio & Interval Scaled Data.** Interval scaled data is what we usually think of when we talk of measured data. Interval scaled simply means that the distances between the scales of the measuring stick are the same distance apart. Temperature is an example of interval scaled data. The distance on any thermometer between 34 degrees and 35 degrees is exactly the same as the distance between 35 degrees and 36 degrees. The intervals along the scale are the same distance.

Ratio scaled data is essentially the same as interval scaled data, except that ratio scaled data has a natural zero point. This natural zero point means we can use a ratio to describe various measures – for example, a four is twice as large as a two. This describes the case with measures of length, weight or time. But it is not the case for temperature, where zeros fall at arbitrary points for different types of scales. Zero degrees on the Celsius scale is different than zero on the Fahrenheit scale. It is because of this that it makes no sense to speak of 80 degrees being twice as hot as 40 degrees.

Despite the fact it is not measured and so no measurement scale is used, attribute or counted data is naturally ratio scaled. In any count, there is a natural zero point and four objects are always twice as many as two. The 'scale' in these cases is the objects being counted.

▲ **Ordinal (Rank) Data.** We do not always have the type of 'rulers' where the scale is so well defined as to produce interval scaled data. Often, the ruler is capable of saying one object is bigger than another, but not capable of saying how much bigger. Now there is no interval scale – only a rank ordering of small objects to big ones. Rank ordered data is often generated when we are dealing with the measurement of people's attitudes. Individuals often have difficulty saying precisely how much they prefer one thing to another, yet they can easily say they do prefer it. This would produce rank ordered data. Another example is measures of hardness which are generally done on an ordinal scale.

▲ **Categorical or Nominal Data.** At times, the yardstick consists of classification categories into which objects can be placed but where these categories imply no reference of scale or rank order. Gender is a perfect example. Some people are male and some are female, but it makes no sense to order either of these groups let alone imply some scale of difference between them. They are simply different categories. Assigning numbers to different product models or jobs is another example of categorical or nominal data.

As is the case for the type of data (measured or counted), the scale of measurement used will also have an effect on how the data can be analyzed and interpreted. Improvement teams should understand the implications of the data-gathering decisions they make. Higher-order data is preferred to lower-order data, especially with response variables. As such, ratio scaled data is preferred over interval scaled data, interval scaled data is preferred over ordinal data. Reality, however, can impose its own considerations on the type of scale used.

ORGANIZING THE DATA

There are only two ways to organize data: sort it and group it. Sorting is the process of arranging things in some order, such as lowest to highest. Grouping is the process of placing like

data together, creating sub-groups of data sets. The two approaches can be combined. For example, we can first group the data and then sort the data within each sub-group.

Let's work with an example. We choose to test the set-up procedure on a particular machine. In the morning we use one procedure, in the afternoon another. A critical performance characteristic is the purity of product produced. Over a period of five days we gather the following data.[56]

The data-gathering effort has captured the day on which the data was gathered, whether the data was gathered in the morning (set-up procedure a) or in the afternoon (set-up procedure b). A Sample ID number has also been attached to ensure the precise order in which the data was captured is clearly identified. Presented last is the performance characteristic we are

---

56. The search for examples that are relevant to the reader is always difficult. If the idea of two set-up procedures on a machine seems too manufacturing-oriented, think of all the other possible examples where we might wish to compare the performance of two alternatives. We could be talking about the success of two alternative sales techniques, employee satisfaction with two training delivery options, the testing of a new drug, or satisfaction with two different customer service processes. The list is virtually endless. It is these kind of comparisons, by the way, that go to the heart of analytic studies. In fact, Dr. Deming gave consideration to calling analytic studies, comparative studies.

Table 103: Machine Set-Up Data

Day	Time	Set Up	Sample ID	Purity
Monday	Morn.	a	1	88.8
Monday	Aft.	b	2	92.1
Tuesday	Morn.	a	3	91.1
Tuesday	Aft.	b	4	90.5
Wednesday	Morn.	a	5	89.7
Wednesday	Aft.	b	6	92.3
Thursday	Morn.	a	7	89.8
Thursday	Aft.	b	8	89.8
Friday	Morn.	a	9	90.4
Friday	Aft.	b	10	90.8

interested in, the purity of output. The higher the purity, the better.

SORTING THINGS OUT

The first way to organize is to sort the data, to arrange it according to some order. If you were looking at the purity measures presented in Table 103: Machine Set-Up Data, you might think the data is not yet sorted. But this isn't true, it is sorted. Specifically, it is sorted in the original time order in which the measures were obtained, starting with Monday morning (Sample ID #1) and ending with Friday afternoon (Sample ID #10).

However, we can also sort the data by the values obtained; that is, by the purity level. Doing so would produce data as presented in Table 104: Machine Set Up Data – Sort by Purity Level. Sorted by time, the data tells us one thing – namely how our little experiment in set-up procedure unfolded. Sorted by purity level, the data begin to tell us something else – the range of purity values produced. In this case, the lowest value was 88.8 percent and the highest was 92.3 percent. This sort also allows us to examine for patterns. For example, are the purity values distributed more or less equally across the range from 88.8 to 92.3 percent or are they bunched on one end of the range or the other?

So simply sorting the data creates information. Depending on the basis of the sort, we can look for ranges of values and patterns within the data.

GROUPING THE DATA

Another data-organization strategy is grouping the data – putting like data together. By 'like' data we mean that the data

Table 104: Machine Set Up Data – Sort by Purity Level

Day	Time	Set Up	Sample ID	Purity
Monday	Morn.	a	1	88.8
Wednesday	Morn.	a	5	89.7
Thursday	Morn.	a	7	89.8
Thursday	Aft.	b	8	89.8
Friday	Morn.	a	9	90.4
Tuesday	Aft.	b	4	90.5
Friday	Aft.	b	10	90.8
Tuesday	Morn.	a	3	91.1
Monday	Aft.	b	2	92.1
Wednesday	Aft.	b	6	92.3

should be grouped on some rational basis that reflects the real world conditions from which the data was drawn. Usually, these groupings reflect some underlying factor(s) we believe may have an impact on the numbers.

With the machine set-up time example, the first most obvious choice is to group the data by set-up procedure. After all, it is the different set-up procedures we are examining in this experiment, so it makes sense to put the set-up '*a*' data together in one sub-group and set-up '*b*' data together in another sub-group. Doing so would produce the data presented in Table 105: Machine Set-Up Data – Grouped by Set-Up Procedure.

With grouping, the grouping variable is usually categorical in nature. There is no scale implied with set-up procedure *a* versus set-up procedure *b*, just two categories. However, again, simply by grouping we create information. A quick review of the data in each of the sub-groups reveals that the purity values in sub-group *b* seem to be higher than those in sub-group *a*. This isn't a rigorous statistical test, but it is information – information created by simply grouping the data.

Notice, too, that in Table 105, the data has been sorted by purity level (lowest to highest) within each sub-group. This allows for immediate comparison of high and low values as well as examination of data distribution patterns within each sub-group.

Other groupings of the data are possible. For example, we could have grouped the data by the day the data was gathered. In that case, each day would be a sub-group. Grouped in this manner, we would be looking for differences or patterns among the various days. For example, the purity values might be get-

Table 105: Machine Set-Up Data – Grouped by Set-Up Procedure

Day	Time	Set Up	Sample ID	Purity
Monday	Morn.	a	1	88.8
Wednesday	Morn.	a	5	89.7
Thursday	Morn.	a	7	89.8
Friday	Morn.	a	9	90.4
Tuesday	Morn.	a	3	91.1
Thursday	Aft.	b	8	89.8
Tuesday	Aft.	b	4	90.5
Friday	Aft.	b	10	90.8
Monday	Aft.	b	2	92.1
Wednesday	Aft.	b	6	92.3

ting larger with each passing day, indicating that a trend might be present.

So by sorting and grouping the data differently, we create new information about the impact of different factors of interest. Group by set-up procedure to see if the two procedures differ, group by day to see if there is a trend in the data. Different groupings reflect different factors of interest and answer different questions.

SUMMARIZING THE DATA:
CALCULATING SOME STATISTICS

In summarizing quantitative data we produce what most people think of when they hear the word 'statistics.' In this sense, statistics are used to summarize the basic characteristics of the data set. There are three basic characteristics of any data set:

▲ **Location or central tendency,** the middle of the data set. The average (mean) is the most common summary statistic used to describe the location or middle of the data. In addition to the average, two commonly used statistics or measures of central tendency are the median and the mode.

▲ **Dispersion,** how spread out the data is to either side of the middle. Range, variance and standard deviation are the most common statistics used to describe dispersion.

▲ **Shape,** the degree to which the dispersion is skewed to one side or the other, or is relatively 'tall' or 'flat.' Shape, therefore, is an enhancement of dispersion that details how the data are dispersed as opposed to what degree. Kurtosis and skewness are the commonly used statistics to describe the shape of a distribution.

MEASURES OF LOCATION: FINDING THE MIDDLE

Measures of location or central tendency find the middle of the data. Measures is plural because there is more than one measure of 'the middle,' depending on the type of data being analyzed and what your idea of 'middle' is. Here are three basic ways to finding the middle:

▲ **Mean.** The mean is typically referred to as the average and is the most commonly used measure of location and likely the most commonly used summary statistic generally. The mean is probably best described as the 'center of mass'[57] for a data set. The mean is calculated by adding up all the values in a data set and dividing by the number of values that were added up. The mean of 6, 9 and 4 is 6.33 ([6+9+4]/3 = 6.33).

---

57. I first came upon this characterization of the mean in Donald J. Wheeler and David S. Chambers, Understanding Statistical Process Control, SPC Press, Knoxville, Tennessee, 1992

▲ **Median.** The median is the point dividing the values in a data set into two equally sized halves. That is, 50 percent of the values lie above the median and 50 percent lie below. Calculating the median requires ordering or sorting the values within the data set and selecting the middle value. The median of 6, 9 and 4 is 6, because 6 is the value that divides the data set into two equal halves with one number (4) below it and one number (9) above.

▲ **Mode.** The mode is simply the value that occurs most often in the data set. Using the three data points of 6, 9 and 4, no calculation of the mode is possible. If another measure was taken and the result was a 9, then 9 would be the mode of the data set as it occurred most often (twice).

Different types of data require different measures of location. Table 106: Different Types of Data - Different Measures of Location/Central Tendency details the types of data and the associated measurement of the middle.

There is a hierarchy implied in the table. The higher forms of data are interval and ratio scaled. With this type of data, the usual measure of average is the mean. However, other measures of average can also be used. There is nothing preventing

---

Table 106: Different Types of Data - Different Measures of Location/Central Tendency

Type of Data	Measure of Central Tendency	Example
Interval and Ratio Scaled Data: data about objects measured against a common scale. Length, weight, and time are all examples of interval scaled data. Interval scaled data with a natural zero point are referred to as ratio scaled data.	**Mean:** what most people think of when calculating a summary statistic describing location. It is calculated by adding up the measurements taken of all the objects and then dividing by the number of objects. Median and mode can also be used.	Suppose you wanted to know the average number of points scored by teams in the NBA. You now have a scale – number of points. Add up all the points scored by all the teams and divide by the number of teams. This will give you the 'average' or mean score for NBA teams.
Rank Ordered Data: data about objects ordered from smallest to largest, but that makes no assumption about the scale or amount of difference between objects.	**Median:** measures the middle of the distribution by finding the point that equally divides the number of objects. Mode can also be used on rank ordered data depending upon circumstances	You list from best to worst, all the teams of the NBA according to your general assessment of their ability. The median is whatever team lies in the middle of the list.
Categorical Data: data about different classes of objects that cannot be added together without creating a mix of 'apples and oranges.'	**Mode:** uses the most common observation as the measure of average.	50 men and 250 women enter a particular store on a certain day. Who or what is the average customer? Gender is a category – you can't place values on it and sort or calculate results. Using the mode, we could summarize by saying that generally the store's customers are women since they are the most frequent customers (250 to 50).

the analyst from using the median on interval scaled data; indeed, there may be very good reasons for doing so.

The reverse, however, doesn't hold true. With ordinal data, the median or mode can be used to describe the middle of the data set, but the mean cannot. Likewise with categorical data, the mode can be used, but the mean and median cannot. In summary, lower orders of central tendency can be applied to higher orders of data. But higher-order measures of central tendency cannot be used on lower orders of data.

Because the mean is what people usually think of as the average, it tends to be over used. Using the mean on rank ordered data or on categorical data is all too common and all too wrong. Although a tendency to use the mean exists, make sure that the nature of the data supports its use.

SAMPLE CALCULATIONS OF LOCATION

To provide some sample calculations of location or central tendency, we can use the same data from the machine set-up procedure example used earlier in discussing sorting and grouping data. This data is presented in Table 107: Machine Set-Up Data – Sorted and in Exhibit 108: Machine Set-Up Data – Grouped.

Calculations are done on both the overall data set and for each of the sub-groups.

Table 107: Machine Set-Up Data – Sorted

Sorted by Purity Data	
Sample ID	Purity
1	88.8
5	89.7
7	89.8
8	89.8
9	90.4
4	90.5
10	90.8
3	91.1
2	92.1
6	92.3
n (count)	10
Sum	905.3
Mean	90.53
Median	90.45

Calculating the Mean

The mean, our first measure of central tendency, takes the sum of the values and divides by the number of observations being summed. For the 10 observations in the overall data set, we total or sum all the values (which turns out to be 905.3) and divide by 10. This gives an average or mean purity level of 90.53. This calculation is expressed mathematically below.

$$Mean = \bar{x} = \frac{\Sigma x}{n} = \frac{905.3}{10} = 90.53$$

The process is the same for calculating the mean for each of the sub-groups. In each sub-group we have five observations. In sub-group *a*, the sum of purity values is 449.8. This divided by five (for the five observations) yields a mean of 89.96 percent. Likewise, the calculation for sub-group *b* proceeds by calculating a total, in this case 455.5, and dividing this by five to yield a mean of 91.1 percent.

Notice how calculating a summary statistic like the mean makes it easy to compare data. We can see immediately that the mean purity level for set-up *b* is greater than the mean set-up procedure for set-up *a*. We even know by how much – 91.1 versus 89.96 percent. Keep in mind, however, that the mean is

Table 108: Machine Set-Up Data – Grouped

Grouped by Set-Up Procedure *a*		Grouped by Set-Up Procedure *b*	
Sample ID	Purity	Sample ID	Purity
1	88.8	8	89.8
5	89.7	4	90.5
7	89.8	10	90.8
9	90.4	2	92.1
3	91.1	6	92.3
n (count)	5	*n (count)*	5
Sum	449.8	*Sum*	455.5
Mean	89.96	*Mean*	91.1
Median	89.8	*Median*	90.8

only one summary statistic – there are others. Just because we see a difference here doesn't mean that this is the end of the story. We only know that the mean purity level for two set-up procedures over the five-day period examined.

Median

The median is quite a different animal than the mean. With the mean, the data is totalled and divided by the number of observations. In contrast, the median simply tries to find the middle of the data set. Doing so requires that the data be sorted. This is not the case with the mean. It doesn't care if the data are sorted or not – the nature of calculation removes this from consideration. But the median is not so much concerned with the actual values in the data set as it is with the relative position of the values – and this means having to sort the data.

Looking at Table 107: Machine Set-Up Data – Sorted, the second column presents the sorted purity levels for all 10 observations. The median, by definition, is simply the middle point of this data set. In other words, it is the value that divides the data set into two equally sized halves.

However, there's a problem. Because we have an even number of values (10), there will not be a single value that represents the middle (as there is with an odd number of values). Therefore, we identify the fifth value down and the sixth value down and take the half-way point (mean) between these two values. The fifth value down is a 90.4. The sixth value down is 90.5. The middle ground (mean) between the 90.4 and 90.5 is 90.45. This is the value of the median.

Notice that this is not the same value calculated for the mean of the overall data set (90.53). The two different measures of central tendency yield two different results. The mean, because it is based on the values, tends to be influenced or reflect extreme values – either very large or very small relative to the data generally. The median, which uses the position of the values rather than the values themselves, tends to give the extreme values less weight.

Calculating the median for the two sub-groups is easier as there are an odd number of values in each sub-group. Once the data is sorted for each sub-group, as it is in Table 108, we simply have to locate the middle value. With five observations in each sub-group, this would be the value with two observations above and two observations below. For sub-group *a*, this is 89.8 percent and for sub-group *b* it is 90.8 percent.

Mode

The mode is perhaps the simplest measure of the middle to determine – it is simply whatever value occurs most. Referring to Table 107, we can quickly see that none of the values is repeated. This means that calculation of the mode on this data is impossible.

If, however, two of the measures were the same, this would represent the mode. For example, if the two highest observations (Sample ID's #2 and #6) were both 92.3, then the mode of the data would be 92.3 percent.

So there we have three different measures of average and three possible results. Sometimes these results will agree with one another, other times they will not. The trick is to ensure you understand the differences between the various measures and apply them appropriately.

DISPERSION

The middle is only one way to describe a set of data. Another description is how spread out the data is, which is called dispersion. When we measure dispersion we are in fact measuring the amount of variation. Variation is present in every system, which means the data will always be dispersed to some degree. Determining the dispersion is as important as understanding the central tendency.

Exhibit 109: Differences in Dispersion contrasts two data sets with identical middle points but very different levels of dispersion. The mean of the data is represented by the line through the middle of both distributions. The fact this line is located in the same position on the bottom (x) axis of the chart indicates the respective means are the same. But the variation in the lower distribution is much greater than the upper distribution, indicated by the degree of horizontal spread.

It is easy to see why variation is an enemy of performance. Suppose the distributions pictured in Exhibit 109 represent the results of two different production processes measured by the same performance characteristic. The average value is the target value for both, say the density of photographic film. The target value will produce film that produces the best results for photographers. Which process would be more effective at meeting the needs of the customer?

The process represented by the upper graph produces film very close to the target density value. It is not perfect – there is still variation. But there is far less variation than the levels recorded in the second process represented by the lower graph. It produces film with a great deal of variation around the target density value. This greater variation around the target represents an economic loss. The process represented by the upper distribution will be far more effective and implies much lower levels of economic loss that the lower distribution.

Exhibit 109: Differences in Dispersion

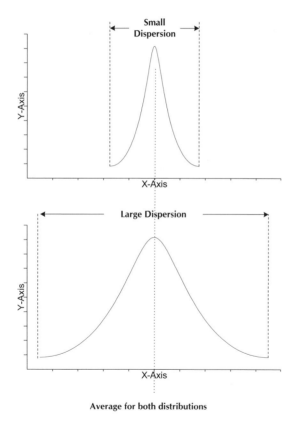

As with central tendency, there are different measures of dispersion. Three of these measures commonly used are:

▲ **Range.** The range measures the difference between the highest and lowest values in a data set. Subtract the smallest number from the largest and that's it. Range is generally used with smaller data sets, say when there are fewer than 10 data points. The range is expressed mathematically below.

$$Range(R) = x_{max} - x_{min}$$

▲ **Variance.** The range uses only two values to assess the amount of variation. This is a big simplification when the data set might contain 20, 30 or 100 values. In contrast, the variance uses all of the data to establish the amount of dispersion in the data.

The variance is the sum of squared differences between observed values, and the mean of the data set, all divided by the number of values less one. This is expressed mathematically below.

$$Variance(v) = \sigma^2 = \frac{\Sigma(x - \bar{x})^2}{n - 1}$$

▲ **Standard Deviation.** Like the variance, standard deviation is a more sophisticated measure of dispersion than the range. It is simply the square root of the variance. Recall that the variance was dependent upon the sum of squared deviations from the average. The standard deviation, by taking the square root of the variance, provides a measure of dispersion in the same units as the original observations – making interpretation easier and the resulting number more relevant for most improvement teams and decision makers. For this reason, the use of standard deviation is more common than the variance. The formula for standard deviation is:

$$\text{Standard Deviation (s)} = \sigma = \sqrt{\frac{\Sigma(x - \bar{x})^2}{n - 1}}$$

SAMPLE CALCULATIONS OF DISPERSION

Application of the formulas is made a little more understandable with an example. Using the same example of the purity of product produced by two machine set-up procedures, we can calculate the range, variance and standard deviation of the overall data set as well as for each of the sub-groups. The overall data set, along with some calculations for the variance, is

Table 110: Machine Set-Up Data with Variance Calculations

Sorted by Purity Data		Calculations of Variance	
Sample ID	Purity (x)	1 $(x - \bar{x})$	2 $(x - \bar{x})^2$
1	88.8	-1.73	2.993
5	89.7	-0.83	0.689
7	89.8	-0.73	0.533
8	89.8	-0.13	0.017
9	90.4	0.57	0.325
4	90.5	-0.73	0.533
10	90.8	-0.03	0.001
3	91.1	0.27	0.073
2	92.1	1.57	2.465
6	92.3	1.77	3.133
n (count)	10		
Range	3.5		
Mean (x̄)	90.53		
Sum			10.761
Variance (v)	*The sum of column (2) divided by (n-1)*		1.196
Std. Dev. (s)	*The square root of the variance*		1.094

presented in Table 110: Machine Set-Up Data with Variance Calculations. The same data but grouped by set-up procedure is presented in Table 111: Machine Set-Up Data – Grouped with Variance Calculations.

Range (*R*)

The range is the largest value less the smallest value observed in the data set. The largest or maximum value recorded (max.) was a purity level of 92.3 percent. The lowest or minimum purity level (min.) was 88.8 percent. The range is the difference between these two values, or 3.5 percent.

With the grouped data, we use the maximum and minimum values within each sub-group. This makes the range for set-up procedure *a* 2.3 percent (91.1 - 88.8), and for set-up procedure *b* 2.5 percent (92.3 - 89.8).

This is as easy as it gets. The range is most often used when the number of values in the data set is small. When the number of values increases, variance or standard deviation tend to be used.

Variance (*v*)

Table 110: Machine Set-Up Data with Variance Calculations presents some of the calculations required for determination of variance. The columns to the right of the data essentially present the various stages of the calculations in the variance formula numerator.

Column 1 presents the first set of calculations in the variance formula, specifically the difference between the observed value and the overall mean for the data set. The mean purity level was 90.53 percent. The first measure in Table 110 is 88.8 percent. Subtracting this value (88.8) from the mean (90.53) yields -1.73 percent. It is this value that is presented in the first row of Table 110 under column 1. This process is repeated for all the values in the data set.

Notice that the sum total of all these differences is zero. This is always the case and serves as a nice check to ensure the calculations are proceeding correctly.

The next step is squaring all the calculated differences in column 1. This removes all the negative values, since a negative number squared results in a positive number. This means that in calculating the differences from the mean (column 1), it

Table 111: Machine Set-Up Data – Grouped with Variance Calculations

Grouped by Set-Up Procedure Sub-group A			Variance Calculations		Grouped by Set-Up Procedure Sub-group B			Grouped by Set-Up Procedure	
Sample ID	Sub-Group	Purity	1 $(x - \bar{x})$	2 $(x - \bar{x})^2$	Sample ID	Sub-Group	Purity	1 $(x - \bar{x})$	2 $(x - \bar{x})^2$
1	a	88.8	-1.16	1.3456	8	b	89.8	-1.3	1.69
5	a	89.7	-0.26	0.0676	4	b	90.5	-0.6	0.36
7	a	89.8	-0.16	0.0256	10	b	90.8	-0.3	0.09
9	a	90.4	0.44	0.1936	2	b	92.1	1	1
3	a	91.1	1.14	1.2996	6	b	92.3	1.2	1.44
n (count)	5				*n (count)*	5			
Range	2.3				*Range*	2.5			
Mean ($\bar{x}$)	89.96				*Mean ($\bar{x}$)*	91.1			
Sum				2.932	*Sum*				4.58
Variance	*The sum of column (2) divided by (n-1)*			0.733	*Variance*	*The sum of column (2) divided by (n-1)*			1.145
Std. Dev.	*The square root of the variance*			0.856	*Std. Dev.*	*The square root of the variance*			1.070

doesn't matter if you take *x* away from the mean or the mean away from *x,* the negative values will ultimately disappear regardless.

For the first item in the table, the difference from the mean was -1.73 percent. To create the squared difference, this value is multiplied by itself. The result is 2.993. This is the value recorded in the first row of the squared differences column (column 2). Again, this process is repeated for all the values in the data set.

These squared differences are then summed (added up). The result, presented at the bottom of column 2 in the table, is 10.761. To calculate the variance, this sum of squared differences is divided by the number of values less one (n-1). We have 10 observations so the divisor would be this less one, which is 9. The variance is, therefore, 10.761 divided by 9 or 1.196.

A similar procedure is carried out when working with sub-groups. As was the case with the range, we are calculating the variance within each sub-group. The mean within each sub-group is subtracted from each of the values in the sub-group (column 1), squared (column 2), then totaled and divided by the number of observations less 1. This results is a variance of 0.733 for sub-group *a*, and a variance of 1.145 for sub-group *b*.

Standard Deviation (*s*)

With the variance calculated, calculation of the standard deviation is easy. It is simply the square root of the variance. So enter 1.196 into your calculator, hit the square root function and you've got it – 1.09 percent. Likewise for the sub-group calculations. For sub-group *a*, the variance was 0.733, the square root of which is 0.856 percent. For sub-group *b*, the standard deviation is the square root of variance 1.145 or 1.07 percent.

Standard deviation has the advantage of converting the variance back into the original units of measure. Because the differences between the mean and the observed values were squared in the variance calculation, the result is in units squared. In our example, the variance was 1.196 percent squared (whatever a square percent is). By taking the square root of the variance, standard deviation returns the squared percent to percent, making for easier interpretation.

SHAPE

Shape of a data set is described by two basic measures: skewness and kurtosis. Together, they help describe *how* the data is dispersed. Skewness deals with the degree to which the data is skewed to one side of the middle or the other. Kurtosis deals with whether the distribution is tall or flat.

These notions are detailed in the Exhibit 112: Skewness and Exhibit 113: Kurtosis.

Exhibit 112: Skewness

Exhibit 113: Kurtosis

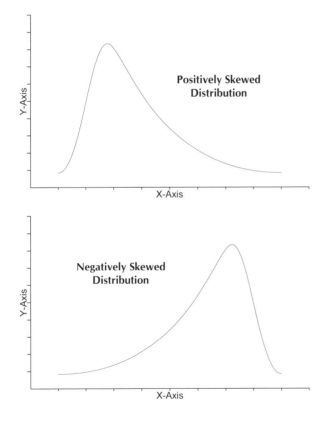

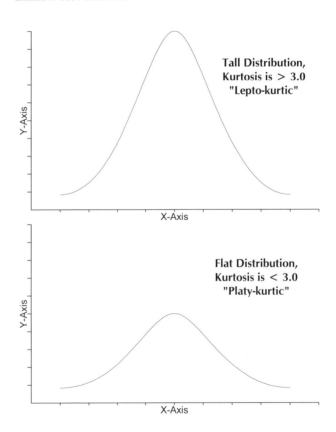

In practical application, measures of skewness and kurtosis are of limited usefulness. It is far easier and more direct to simply examine the distribution of the data (using a histogram) to draw some inferences about what the pattern of the data reveals. Moreover, knowing the central tendency and dispersion is all that is required to produce effective analysis – actual measures of skewness and kurtosis are not required.

Skewness (*sk*)

Different measures of the central tendency will have different values, depending on how skewed the distribution is and whether it is skewed positively or negatively. Exhibit 114: Effects of Skewness on Measures of Average, details these effects. When a distribution is skewed positively, as in Exhibit 114, the mode, the median and the mean will spread out as depicted. The reverse order will occur with a negatively skewed distribution. This is why different measures of central tendency will produce different results. There is no true value of central tendency or anything else!

This tendency for the various measures of average to yield different results in a skewed distribution can be used to provide a shortcut method of calculating skewness. As mentioned, the

Exhibit 114: Effects of Skewness on Measures of Average

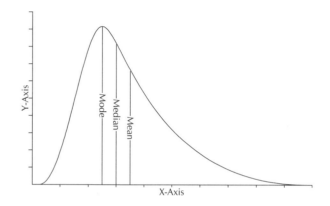

actual calculation of skewness is of limited usefulness. Nevertheless, for those who would like to see a formula, it is provided below.

$$sk = \frac{3(\bar{x} - \tilde{x})}{\sigma}$$

Skewness then, is equal to three times the difference between the mean and the median all divided by sigma or the standard deviation. (*x-bar* represents the mean while *x-tilda* represents the median).

Kurtosis

The measurement of kurtosis is more complex than measuring skewness and arguably of even less value in practical application. Again, however, for those that must know, the formula is provided below.

$$Kurtosis = \frac{(\Sigma fx^4)/N}{((\Sigma fx^2)/N)^2}$$

A normal distribution would have a kurtosis of 3.0. A kurtosis above this value indicates a relatively tall distribution and is referred to as being lepto-kurtic. A kurtosis of less than 3.0 indicates a relatively flat distribution and is referred to as platy-kurtic.[58]

---

58. This existence of this term should dispel forever the notion that statisticians have no sense of humor. Anyone who could name something platy-kurtic has a sense of humor. The options beyond platypus, it seems to me, are endless.

MAKING CONCLUSIONS

The last of the four things you can do with data is make conclusions based on a comparisons of the data or its summaries with something else. Generally, there are two routes we can take here. We can compare the data with expectations or compare it with other data.

EXPECTATIONS

Expectations exist in the mind of people. They may be customers or shareholders, engineers or accountants. The process of evaluating performance is often one of comparing an individual's own internal standard (expectation) with actual demonstrated levels of performance.

In our example, purity levels ranged from a high of 92.3 percent to a low of 88.8 percent. How good this is depends on the expectations of the customer. If our customers are demanding a minimum purity level of 95.0 percent, it doesn't really matter if we use set-up procedure *a* or *b*, we will not be keeping our customer for long. On the other hand, if the customer requires a purity level of 80.0 percent, we are in pretty good shape no matter what set-up procedure we use. Either way, the data and its associated summary statistics only has meaning when compared to something – in this case the expectations of the customer.

OTHER DATA/EMPIRICAL

Comparisons needn't be made to expectations, they can also be made to other data or the data gathered can be compared to itself (by comparing the summary statistics of various sub-groups). Again, using the purity level data as an example, if the purity level obtained by our competitors is 75.0 percent, we are producing a better quality product. At this point, it doesn't matter that the customer would prefer 95.0 percent – the customer can't have it.

The fundamental comparison here is our purity level versus those of our competitors. This is comparing data with data – a comparison with an empirical basis. We can, of course, compare our data with itself, specifically comparing the performance of set-up procedure *a* with that of set-up procedure *b*. This, too, is an empirically based comparison. We might, for example, compare the sub-group means. Set-up procedure *a*

had a mean purity level of 89.96 percent and procedure *b* had a mean purity level of 91.1 percent (see Table 108 on page 333). Of course, we could have based the comparison on median values or measures of dispersion such as variance or standard deviation.

LIMITATIONS OF SUMMARY STATISTICS

Whenever we seek to make conclusions, either through comparisons with expectations or with other data, we are faced with two problems. These two problems are:

▲ **The devil is often in the details.** Statistics such as the average are valuable in their ability to summarize the values in a data set. Like any summary, however, they hide as much as they reveal. Unfortunately, for those engaged in performance improvement activity, the devil is often in the details.

▲ **There are two dimensions which must be compared.** World-class performance means "*on target with minimum variance.*" This means when analyzing and trying to understand any data, we must be concerned with both its location or central tendency and its dispersion.

Which means that summary statistics, while important, are usually insufficient for purposes of improvement. To understand the data and what, if anything, it is trying to tell us, we need to complement summary statistics with graphically based methods of analysis.

Statistics, especially those concerning central tendency and dispersion, are still important. The calculation of median, mean and standard deviation in particular, will accompany most if not all the graphical tools of data analysis. It is just that alone, these statistics are not sufficient. The seven basic graphical tools (see Table 115 on page 349), properly applied, give a clear presentation of the data in a manner that supports analysis, understanding and action.

THE THREE LAWS OF PERFORMANCE MEASUREMENT

The use of descriptive statistics such as average and standard deviation is important in understanding the characteristics of what is being measured. Their use is widespread, from the latest opinion polls to the management and financial data typically used in organizations. We speak of average costs, average return on investment, the crime rate (average for the year) and the current performance rating of the president from the latest opinion poll.

In using these numerical summaries of data, we must keep in mind the three fundamental laws of performance measurement and analysis.

LAW #1: HALF OF EVERYTHING IS BELOW AVERAGE

The average represents the middle of a distribution or data set. For there to be middle, there must be stuff on either side. You can't have all your stuff on one side of middle. Think of the line running down the middle of the road – it equally divides the lanes to either side (and a good thing too!). Neither side is good or bad – they simply lie to either side of the line.

But things change when we talk about any form of performance data. What would be your reaction if you were told your performance is below average? Has anyone ever told you had below average talent at something – how did you feel? All of a sudden we become concerned, our blood pressure rises, we want to do something! In these cases, the average moves from being a simple middle point to some profound shortcoming, at least when you are on the 'wrong' side of the line.

I have bad news. Half of all the people reading this book right now are 'below average'. It doesn't matter at what – pick something. Half of you are worse at math than the other half, half are less musically inclined. One-half of readers are better looking than the other half (the author generously includes himself here!). None of this is relevant to anything other than the definition of the average.

Yet organizations will launch benchmarking exercises where some performance characteristic is compared with nine other organizations. Half of all participants shriek in horror upon discovering they are below average. The other half confidently cite their superior management for the results. (Well, they must be superior managers; after all, their results are above average.) Schools grade on the curve, performance appraisals rank employees to discover 'above average' performers, and accountants fret over last month's costs rising slightly above the average for the year. What a waste of time and money! All this effort to prove the obvious, that about half of everything will be above the average and the other half, below.

The tyranny of the average

We refer to this over-reliance and undue focus on the average as the "tyranny of the average." A tyranny, of course, is a state where a single ruler has absolute power. The tyranny of the average is our uncritical acceptance of this single summary statistic to represent all the complexity of the data. We forget that for there to be an average there must be points to either side. We move from the average representing the middle of the data, to believing that each and every data point should be as good as the average, if not better. This is, of course, pure nonsense. Unfortunately, it describes the way the average is used and interpreted in many organizational and performance measurement applications.

LAW #2: PERFORMANCE MEASUREMENT HAS TWO DIMENSIONS

To describe data and understand it, we must understand its center or middle point expressed though some measure of central tendency. But we must also understand the degree to which the data is dispersed, and to some extent, its overall shape. The average, by itself, is quite useless for fully understanding any real world data set because the average hides far more than it reveals. Specifically, it hides the variation and the order in which that variation occurs.

Think of an executive or board meeting in your organization. The issue under discussion may be current production costs, say the costs to produce a particular type of widget. Figures from accounting reveal that costs run $6.40 per unit. Discussions, arguments and plans center on what can be done to reduce these costs to something more in keeping with what we believe are our competitor's costs.

But what about that $6.40 figure? Does every unit cost $6.40? Are there times when production costs are higher or lower? Of course there are, because variation is a characteristic of every process. How large is the range of this variation? Isn't having an average cost of $6.40 with a range of plus/minus $4.00 different from a situation where the range is plus/minus $0.50? And what about trends? Perhaps our $6.40 figure consists of earlier units that cost over $9.00 to make, as well as units that currently cost around $4.80. Where is that fact reflected in the average? The answer is, it isn't reflected. It is buried within the average and, as a result, hidden from view.

The $6.40 figure is in many ways an illusion – a computational fiction. It is dangerous because, once used, we tend to forget about all the variation and complexity that hides behind that figure.

The average can drown an army

To drive home this point, consider that an army can drown crossing a river with an average depth of three feet. If you want to know where to cross a river, knowing its average depth is as useless information as you can have. It's good information if you are conducting academic studies of rivers generally. But the minute you are required to take action, to change or improve something, you need more information than the average can provide.

At a minimum you need the range (which would give you maximum depth). Better still, an actual picture of the cross-section of the river (called a histogram – one of the seven essential graphical tools of data analysis) would clearly indicate where it was safe to cross and where it isn't. Which leads us to our last law.

LAW #3: TO UNDERSTAND THE DATA, YOU MUST USE THE TOOLS DESIGNED FOR THAT PURPOSE

To understand a system and address issues of performance, the right tools must be used. There are only seven basic data analysis tools: histograms, Pareto charts, scatter diagrams, box and whisker plots, dot plots, run charts and control charts. Reports that convey measures of central tendency and dispersion, without showing a picture of the data through one of these tools, should be viewed with the utmost suspicion. Never accept the statistical summaries by themselves.

Why these tools?

Why? First, because these tools organize the data in the right way. By organizing the data correctly and displaying it in an appropriate format, the tools maximize the informational content in the data. They ensure that messages within the data are not lost or obscured. When sorted data is displayed on a histogram, for example, and the histogram has been properly prepared, you know you are using a tool that will allow you to see any special patterns in the data – if indeed any special patterns are there to be seen. Likewise, control charts, properly pre-pared, will ensure appropriate comparisons of sub-grouped data, allowing teams to identify real differences among groups.

Secondly, these tools present a picture of the data with all its variation. As essential as mathematical summaries are, they are not enough. In the real world of managing and improving processes, there is no substitute for actually seeing the data. In this regard, it is wise to remember the Yogi Berra adage:

"You can see a lot just by looking!"

The data-analysis tools allow those involved in improvement efforts to do just that. It is not just that these tools organize the data correctly; it is that once organized, the tools display the data appropriately, allowing the analyst to see special causes and patterns if any are there to see.

There is a more formal description of this fact. It's called the ITT. ITT stands for the Inter-ocular Trauma Test, which means the message of the data should hit us right between the eyes. It is the most important significance test of all. Not a test of statistical significance, but one of business significance – the importance of our findings for purposes of performance improvement.

Table 115: Summary of Quantitative Data-Analysis Tools

Analytical Tool	Purpose	Data Type	Comments
Histogram	Analysis of performance through a single response variable or effect.	Measured.	Used to represent the "voice of the process" and support process capability analysis. Presents the 'performance profile' of a process.
Pareto Chart	Analysis of performance or of cause and effect depending on the nature of the categories used.	Counted.	Most often used to identify the most prevalent problems affecting performance.
Box & Whisker Plot	Analysis of relationship between response variable and causal factor.	Measured response variable and any form of stratified/categorical causal variable.	Particularly useful in comparing response characteristics when data has been stratified into categories.
Dot Plot	Analysis of relationship between response variable and causal factor.	Measured response variable and any form of stratified/categorical causal variable.	Used in place of the box and whisker plot (and sometimes histograms) when number of measurements (sample size) is small.
Scatter Diagram	Analysis of relationship between response variable and causal factor.	Measured response variable and measured causal variable.	If histograms are the workhorses of process improvement, the scatter diagram is the workhorse of cause and effect analysis.
Run Charts	Analysis of system performance over time as well as possible cause and effect relationships.	Measured or Counted.	Presents the 'running record' of process performance.
Control Charts	Analysis of system performance over time as well as possible cause and effect relationships.	Measured or Counted.	Can be used to determine process or system stability as well as the type of variation present in a process.

Exhibit 116: The Data Analysis Tool Set

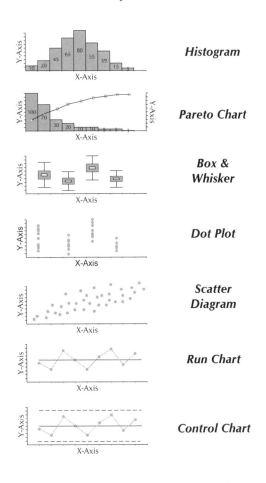

Histogram

Pareto Chart

Box & Whisker

Dot Plot

Scatter Diagram

Run Chart

Control Chart

Table 117: Tools and Typical Summary Statistics

Tool	Typical Measure of Location	Typical Measure of Dispersion
Histogram	Mean	Range Standard Deviation
Pareto Chart	Mode	Typically no dispersion statistic is used
Box and Whisker	Median	Range
Dot Plot	Median	Range
Scatter Diagram	Median For non-metric quadrant analysis.	Range
Run Chart	Median	Typically no dispersion statistic is used
Control Chart	Mean	Standard Deviation

ITT: The Inter-ocular Trauma Test

The term Inter-ocular Trauma Test was first coined by Dr. Joseph Berkson, an M.D. with a Ph.D. in statistics who worked at the Mayo Clinic. ITT emphasizes that a lot can be gained from just looking at the data. If the message hits you right between the eyes, you don't need a lot of fancy statistical analysis to tell you something is going on – you already know! The whole purpose behind all the data analysis tools, including scatter diagrams, histograms, Pareto charts, box & whisker plots and run charts, is to allow teams to observe the data with all its variation and peculiarities. In other words, these tools allow for the application of ITT.

Types of Quantitative Analysis Tools

There are seven basic data analysis tools. They have different applications depending upon the intent of the analysis and the type of data gathered.

▲ **Intent.** Data-analysis tools differ in their basic analytical intent. Recall that measures of performance can be differentiated as to whether they are the performance characteristic we wish to describe (response variable) or some other measure we believe may have a causal affect on the performance characteristic (explanatory or causal variable). Is the intent of the analysis to establish the performance of the process – to analyze the performance characteristics? Or is the purpose to explore the possible causal effects that different factors have upon process performance? Different intent will require different analytical tools.

▲ **Data Type.** Data can be measured or counted. The type of data gathered will affect which tool can be used. Generally speaking, measured data is preferred, especially when dealing with response variables that describe the overall performance of the process. However, it is not always possible to gather measured data. In these cases, counted or attribute data is used, and with such data a different type of analytical tool is necessary.

Table 115: Summary of Quantitative Data-Analysis Tools details the seven basic data-analysis tools available to teams, along with the data type and purpose of each. No matter the tool, the purpose remains the same – to help us see better what is going on with the system and, by doing so, improve our understanding and the quality of our actions.

As different tools are used with different types of data it should not be surprising that different measures of location and dispersion are typically associated with each. Table 117: Tools and Typical Summary Statistics lists each of the seven basic tools and the measure of location and dispersion that is typically applied. There are exceptions to this listing of course. For example, there are control charts that use the median rather than the mode and there is nothing preventing the calculation of the median with the histogram. The table simply lists the summary statistics most commonly applied when using the various data analysis tools.

Analyzing Results: Tools for the
Analysis of System Performance and Capability

How fast do we process orders? How many errors do we make in delivering our service? What is the return rate on our product? What is our cost of production? How long does it take us to deliver a product? Is the crime rate decreasing or increasing? What is the response time of our computer software? How does it compare with the times of our competitors? What is the level of impurity in our product? What is the level of exhaust emissions? How satisfied are our customers? ***What is our Performance?***

These are important questions for organizations. There are thousands more questions just like them, all relating to the performance of some system or process. When we gather data to answer questions like these, we are dealing with the analysis of response or effect variables. The response in this case is the measured performance of the system. We are not yet looking for potential causes that produced the effect, only for some measure of overall performance in the system's day-to-day functioning. Doing so provides us with the measure of performance for a given quality characteristic.

So how do we answer questions of performance? Too often, the answer is some single measure – the tyranny of the average. Cost of production is $6.40. Response time is 3.0 seconds. Impurities are 0.65 percent. Exhaust emissions are 6.8 parts per million. Ninety-four percent of customers say they are satisfied with our service. All these responses are in some way averages or some other empty 'statistics' which, by themselves, tell us little about the underlying process performance that produced these results. To get the big picture, to see how the process actually behaves, we need to use the tools designed for this purpose.

In the analysis of performance, three basic tools are used:

▲ **Run Charts** are typically used with time-oriented data regardless of whether the data has been measured or counted. It is a robust tool that benefits from ease of preparation.

▲ **Control Charts** are essentially run charts in which additional statistics (the upper and lower control limits) are calculated and plotted. The control chart is the core or central tool in data analysis for performance improvement.

▲ **Histograms** show the distribution of the data gathered and illustrate the 'performance profile' of the system. They allow the team to see the shape of the distribution with time or non-time oriented data.

RUN AND CONTROL CHARTS

In the realm of performance improvement, no data analysis tools are more fundamental to understanding process behavior than run and control charts. This is because run and control charts not only display the variation in the data, they preserve the time order of the data. This allows improvement teams to:

▲ examine system or process performance over time;

▲ evaluate the impact of change and determine if improvement initiatives actually produced improvement;

▲ determine the performance capability and behavior of a process.

Moreover, run and control charts also identify and distinguish different types of variation. This is essential in determining the improvement strategy. Where special causes of variation are present, initial improvement efforts need to focus on identifying and eliminating these. In contrast, the system may be operating under a set of chance causes (common cause variation). If this is the case, then improvement must focus upon the design and redesign of the system itself.

HISTOGRAMS

Histograms do not preserve the time order of the data, but they do display the variation inherent in a data set. This makes the histogram a useful tool when:

▲ summarizing the performance of a process or system over some specified time interval;

Exhibit 118: System Performance Measured by the Response Variable

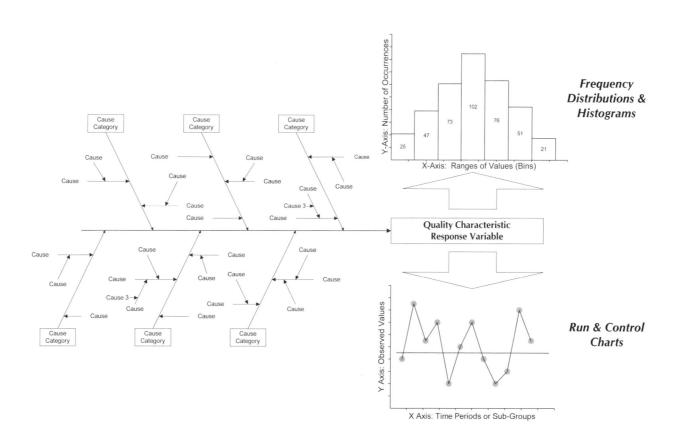

▲ the data being analyzed has no time component to it. This may include data arising from different locations, product lines or customers as opposed to time periods;

▲ it is important to understand or see the performance profile of a process, such as when comparing performance to expectations.

These three tools provide the basis for analyzing system performance and behavior. No matter what the nature of the characteristic of interest is, analysis can and should be conducted using the run chart, control chart or histogram.

RUN CHARTS

Run charts are basically simple line graphs displaying the measurements from some quality characteristic as they occur over time. Few data analysis tools are simpler to prepare. Time is represented along the bottom (horizontal or x) axis and values of the characteristic being measured are presented along the side (vertical or y) axis. This conforms to standard practice where the assumed causal factor or factor of interest is presented along the horizontal axis. With run charts, the causal

factor – the area we want to examine as having a potential effect on the quality characteristic – is time.

Exhibit 119: Basic Run Chart

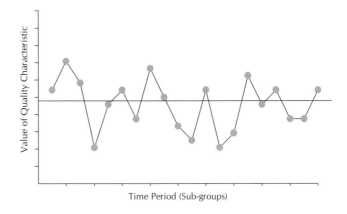

We want to know how the measurements of some quality characteristic change or vary with time. Do these changes present some pattern? Do they violate probabilities of random behavior so that we can conclude some special cause of variation is present? These are the types of questions run charts are intended to answer.

ADVANTAGES OF RUN CHARTS

The simplicity of run charts is often interpreted as a weakness in analytical capability. As a result, run charts are often passed over by improvement teams in favor of their more advanced and sophisticated cousins, control charts.

Doing so is a mistake, however. The simplicity of run charts provides some real advantages over control charts.

▲ **Run charts make no assumption as to the type of data.** Control charts require the analyst to understand differences between attribute and variable data, as well as different types of data within these categories. Differences in data type and sample size require different control charts. In contrast, there is only one type of run chart and any type of data can be plotted on it – measured, counted, interval scaled and ordinal data. Little knowledge of the data type or sampling method is required. If the data is reliable, it can be plotted and analyzed through the run chart.

▲ **Run charts require no mathematical calculations.** Different control charts require the application of different formulas to properly determine the control limits on the chart. Run charts require no such calculation. All that is required is an ability to plot points on graph paper and an ability to count.

▲ **Run charts make it easier to look beyond control limits to see the underlying patterns in the data.** Control chart interpretation relies on where data points lie relative to the control limits. This is how the state of statistical control is determined. Run charts help us avoid mechanistic interpretations of the data, encouraging teams to look for patterns and underlying root causes of variation.

The simplicity of run charts is their strength. Teams wanting to analyze time-based data, but where there is uncertainty about the type or nature of this data or the appropriate control chart to use, are well advised to use the run chart as the analytical tool. Moreover, teams not yet comfortable with control charts or their calculations can use the run chart and still have confidence in their analysis.

The bottom line is that run charts can be used with any form of data. Teams working to improve processes should feel free to experiment in applying run charts to data produced by the processes under examination.

APPLICATIONS OF RUN CHARTS

Production levels, customer complaints, number of defects, costs, revenues, weight, size – you name it and measure it, and it can be plotted on a run chart.

Whenever data is being collected or tracked over time, the first data-analysis tool that comes to mind should be the run chart. Applications might include:

▲ **An emergency response department of a major city uses run charts to track response time.** Average time required to reach a person in distress is tracked and recorded on a weekly basis. Run charts are used to present and analyze the data. Patterns are quickly identified, and an improvement effort is undertaken to address controllable sources of variation that increase these response times.

▲ **A major oil company uses run charts to track inventory levels.** The old inventory reports used to be pages filled with numbers that few people looked at and fewer understood. These reports have now been replaced with just a few run charts that neatly summarize over a year's worth of data, providing a sound analytical tool for identifying trends and patterns in inventory levels.

▲ **A metropolitan police department uses run charts to present crime statistics.** Using run charts to provide both monthly and yearly crime statistics has enabled the department to avoid the annual and wasteful exercise of developing massive reports that attempt to explain why crime was up (or down) in the latest year. By making the variation visible, run charts have allowed the public and the department to better understand the patterns of crime and to develop more systemic responses.

▲ **A manufacturer uses run charts to track production volume.** Under the old system, operations management had to explain production variances from target that were as small as 5.0 percent. This resulted in lots of reports and little improvement (the number of reports explaining the variances never decreased over the years). Dissatisfied with the old way of doing things, the company began tracking production volume on run charts. These charts made it immediately apparent how much variation there was in the production system.

CREATING THE RUN CHART

The advantage of run charts is their ease of construction. Once data have been gathered, producing a run chart is a four-step process. These steps are:

1. Determine the axes

The first step is determining the x- and y-axes on the chart. The x-axis is easy because it represents the time periods under review. If you have monthly data starting in June in 1994, the axis will extend from June 1994 to the present. The y-axis is slightly more difficult. The lowest and highest values of the data to be plotted need to be identified. These will basically represent the bottom and top of the scale. To provide a little 'headroom,' add about 25 percent to the top value to make the top of the scale. Where possible and practical, make the bottom of the scale zero. If this is not practical, subtract about 25 percent from the lowest value to create the bottom of the scale.

2. Plot the dots (data points)

With the scales set up, the data points are plotted on the chart in the proper time sequence. If there are 30 data points to plot, there should be 30 time periods along the bottom x-axis. Start with the first time period and plot the data point at the corresponding y-axis level. Then move to the second time period along the x-axis and plot the second data point and so on until all the data have been plotted.

3. Connect the data points

Connect each of the data points with a line, again moving in the proper time sequence. There is no calculation here – a ruler is the perfect tool to connect the data points. This line is intended to communicate the time-oriented nature of the data. Connecting the dots represents a kind of flow occurring between the times the measurements were taken. Some people prefer working without a line connecting the data points; however, the choice is one of personal preference. I find it easier to interpret the chart when the dots have been connected.

4. Construct the median line

Remember the definition of the median. It is a measure of central tendency dividing the data points into two equally sized halves – half the data points lie above the median and half below. Constructing the median line, then, is simply drawing a line parallel to the bottom axis of the chart to divide the data

Exhibit 120: Constructing the Run Chart

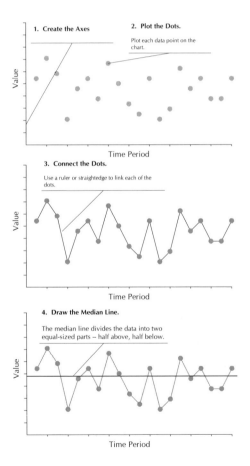

points into two equally sized halves. Half the points are above the line and half are below. A calculator or computer can also be used to determine the median if they have a median function. However, using a ruler works just as well.

Constructing the run chart is about as easy as analytical tools get. Four steps, no calculations required and the result is a useful analysis of any reliable data set where the measurements occur over time.

RUN CHART ANALYSIS

So what does this chart tell us? How do we analyze it? Like its construction, run chart analysis is straightforward. It is a three-step process:

▶ Analyze run length.

▶ Analyze the number of runs.

▶ Analyze the patterns presented by the data.

1. ANALYZING RUN LENGTH

A run is defined as a series of points on the same side of the median line. A minimum run length is always equal to one since this is the smallest number of points that can lie on one side of the median line or the other. But statistical theory tells us there are some maximum run lengths above which a run should not go. If run length goes above these maximum values, we can suspect that some special cause of variation is at work.

Exhibit 121: What is a Run?

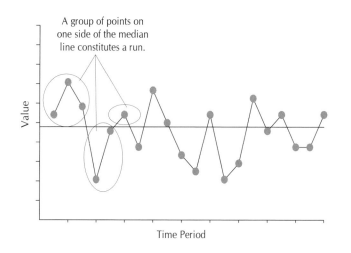

Exhibit 122: Determining Run Length

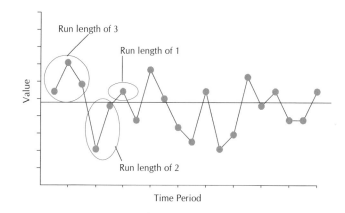

The maximum run lengths we should see in a process are dependent upon the number of observations in the run chart. Table 123: Maximum Run Length Table provides the values teams should look for. It indicates the longest run length we would expect to see if no special causes of variation are present. If a run length exceeds the value in the table, we can conclude that some special cause of variation is indeed present.

Table 123: Maximum Run Length Table

Number of Observations or Data Points	Maximum Run Length
10	5
15	6
20	7
30	8
40	9
50	10

In the example provided, there are a number of runs that are only one point in length. But there is also one run where the run length is three – three consecutive points lie on one side of the median line. Does a run of this length (three points) indicate that a special cause of variation is present?

In the example, the number of observations was equal to 20. The maximum run length that should be observed if the process is reliable with no special causes of variation apparent, is seven (from Table 123). Since the longest run observed in the example was three, we can conclude that no special causes of variation were detected by the run length test. Had a run in the chart had a length longer than seven, we would conclude that some special cause of variation was present.

2. NUMBER OF RUNS

The second step in analyzing the run chart is determining the number of runs that occur above or below the median line. A process in statistical control (no special causes of variation) should have neither too many nor too few runs.

Exhibit 124: Determining the Number of Runs

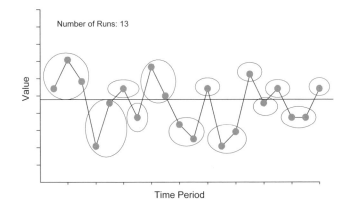

The number of runs is determined simply by counting. In the example, there are a total of 13 runs – six runs below the median line and seven above the line. But does 13 runs indicate the process is in or out of control? The answer can be found using the Table 125: Allowable Number of Runs.

Table 125: Allowable Number of Runs

Number of Observed Values	Smallest Number of Runs	Largest Number of Runs
10	3	8
12	3	10
14	4	11
16	5	12
18	6	13
20	6	15
22	7	16
24	8	17
26	9	18
28	10	19
30	11	20
32	11	22
34	12	23
36	13	24
38	14	25
40	15	26
42	16	27
44	17	28
46	17	30
48	18	31

The table details the minimum and maximum number of runs that should be present for a given number of observations if the

process is a state of control. If the number of runs exceeds these limits, then we should begin to suspect the existence of some special cause of variation.

The example has 20 data points or observed values. According to the table, if the process is experiencing only common cause variation, it should have no fewer than six runs and no more than 15. In fact, the process has 13 runs (see Table 125). So we can conclude that this test, too, has not detected any special causes of variation.

Notice that the two tests, run length and number of runs, are related. As the number of runs increases, the run length will tend to decrease and vice versa. The first two steps of run chart analysis, therefore, are really analyzing much the same thing from different perspectives.

3. RUN CHART PATTERNS

The last stage in run chart analysis is looking for patterns in the data. Some of the more common patterns displayed by run charts are presented in Exhibit 127: Basic Run Chart Patterns.

Freaks & time correlations

Freaks are spikes – a sudden increase or decrease occurring in a single time period. They are essentially anomalies that show up infrequently in otherwise relatively stable data. There are a host of potential causes for freaks, not the least of which is faulty measurement or inspection. But measurement is not always the cause.

If we believe our data to be reliable, the basic question becomes: "What special causes may be producing these spikes?" If only one spike has been observed among 25 or more observations, it is fair to conclude that the occurrence was an isolated event. However, if more than one spike shows up, the critical question becomes: "What do these spikes or freaks have in common?" Because run charts present data by time period, the first place to look to answer this question is along the x-axis of the run chart. Look to see if these spikes occurred during the same time period – the same day of the week or same month of the year. If they do, then we have a time correlation that indicates something special is happening during these time periods to cause the spikes.

Repeating patterns & cycles

The data presented on a run chart can also display repeating patterns or cycles. For example, a constant up and down pattern may indicate the presence of a special cause of variation. Or the up and down pattern may be more subtle, occurring over longer time periods. This indicates the presence of an underlying cycle in the data.

In both cases, the presence of repeating patterns and cycles may be detected through the analysis of runs. Constant up and down patterns will likely lead to a violation of the maximum number of runs test. Longer-term cycles will likely violate maximum run length rule or present too few numbers of runs. In either case, don't be mechanistic in the analysis. Just because run length or number of run rules are within established limits doesn't mean the pattern is not there. However, the violation of run rules certainly adds to the certainty of the interpretation.

Shifts

Shifts are sudden changes in the data where the run line suddenly breaks to a higher or lower level. An example could be order time taking a sudden tumble when a new order-taking system is implemented. Shifts can also reverse themselves, moving back to their original position. Whatever the direction, the shift indicates a special cause of variation.

A shift will often make its presence known through a violation of the maximum run length rules. Because the data shifts suddenly up or down, and then follows a random pattern centered around this new level, most if not all this new data will tend to lie to one side of the overall median line or the other.

Trends

Trends are often the easiest signs to pick up from a run chart. A trend indicates that the process being examined is in a state of drift. Drift can be the result of wear in a machine or the consumption of a resource that produces a general decline in process performance. Of course, process drift is not always a negative sign. A decline in the assembly time required for a small electrical part, for example, is a sign of continuous improvement. Perhaps it results from employees moving along the learning curve as they become more experienced with the assembly process.

Determining whether a trend exists or not is aided by statistical theory. Only a certain number of consecutively increasing or

Table 126: Trend Test Table

Total Number of Observations	Maximum Number of Consecutively Increasing or Decreasing Points
5 to 8	4
9 to 20	5
21 to 100	6
Over 100	7

decreasing points are expected under the assumption of random variation. If more than these maximums occur, it is likely that a special cause of variation is present in the form of a trend. Table 126: Trend Test Table, presents these maximum numbers of consecutively increasing or decreasing points for different numbers of observations.

Typically, performance improvement teams will be dealing with between 21 to 100 observations. Basing analysis and decisions on less than 21 data points is dicey, and having over 100 is often expensive overkill. As such, a general guideline is that seven or more consecutively rising or declining points is a good indication of a trend. If you don't have at least seven consecutively increasing or decreasing points, you haven't got a trend.

Some Comments on Trends

Put two points on a graph and somebody will see a trend. I was listening to a radio program where the commentator was discussing the latest crime statistics. Over the past three years, the city where I live had experienced a decline in the rate of household break-ins. But last year, it seems, the rate increased.

"What is behind this disturbing trend?" asked the commentator, soliciting a variety of responses from lay people and professionals alike including our chief of police. One is apt to respond: "Commentators without the foggiest notion of what a trend is!"

Equally as bad, a data analyst, no less, claimed that after three consecutive months of production increases at a gas plant, the plant had ". . . . turned a corner and is now *trending* toward meeting its production quota for the year." Nonsense. There was no trend. The plant didn't meet its production quota. In fact, production dropped the very next month.

A final observation: consider the number of now 'dead' oil companies that based their early 1980's capital spending on predictions of $100 per barrel oil. Everyone was fitting fancy regression (trend) lines to oil prices, but no one it seemed used the trend test table. If they had, they might still have their oil companies today. (Try it yourself. Do the run chart on world oil prices from 1970 to 1984 and see what happens). As one oil production engineer remarked: "What do you call any two data points? An executive trend!"

The trend test is as much a test to discourage people from labelling everything as a trend as it is a test for trends per se. People have the habit of seeing trends everywhere (See Box: "Some Comments on Trends" on page 366). The trend test table provides a mechanism to prevent such premature labelling of the data.

Exhibit 127: Basic Run Chart Patterns

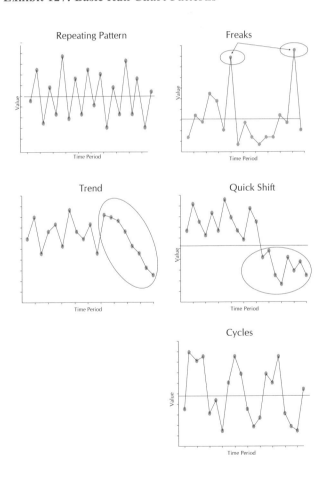

TESTING THE SIGNIFICANCE OF RUN CHART PATTERNS

In examining run chart patterns, teams may become uncomfortable with the subjective nature of the exercise. Outside of determining trends, for which there is a statistical table to aid interpretation, there are no easy-to-follow rules or guidelines for confirming a specific pattern is present. When is a freak a freak and when is it a point just slightly higher than the others?

The critical statistical test in these cases is the ITT. Remember the ITT stands for the Inter-ocular Trauma Test; that is, the message within the data should hit you right between the eyes! Statistical analysis, like that used by the control chart, is certainly very useful. But don't let these tests blind you to the obvious. Remember, one of the advantages of the run chart is that it allows us to move beyond mechanical interpretation.

The ITT also implies direction – the data hits you, not the other way around. The message of the data should be obvious. If team members have to argue, debate, look at the graph sideways and under ultraviolet light to see the message, the message isn't there. Remember the statistician's old rule – if you torture the data long enough, it will tell you anything. The intent is not to torture the data, but to let it speak of its own accord.

RUN CHART EXAMPLE 1: CHILDREN UNDER PROTECTION

A major government department, responsible for protecting children in cases of physical abuse, is trying to deal with an increasing caseload. Changes in both legislation and programming introduced in October of 1994 are being cited as a cause of rising case load levels. To help analyze the situation, the department gathered the caseload data and placed it on a run chart. (Table 128: Children in Protection Caseloads and Exhibit 129: Run Chart of Children in Protection Caseloads.)

 The run chart presents a clear picture. Caseloads have gone up. There is an insufficient number of points that continuously increase to argue that the increase is a trend, but enough points lie on one side of the median line to indicate a special cause.

The pattern is that of a shift. There was a rise in caseloads, but the caseload level appears to have stabilized over the past few observations. In absence of any other explanation, it would be

Table 128: Children in Protection Caseloads

Month	Cases	Month	Cases
Jan. 94	7,400	Jan. 95	8,091
Feb. 94	7,506	Feb. 95	8,175
Mar 94	7,573	Mar 95	8,484
Apr. 94	7,581	Apr. 95	8,445
May 94	7,588	May 95	8,884
Jun. 94	7,591	Jun. 95	8,951
Jul. 94	7,411	Jul. 95	8,749
Aug. 94	7,472	Aug. 95	8,755
Step 94	7,579	Step 95	8,663
Oct. 94	7,512	Oct. 95	8,662
Nov. 94	7,864	Nov. 95	8,683
Dec. 94	7,939	Dec. 95	8,653

reasonable to conclude that legislative and program changes have indeed had an impact. Remember, however, that this alone does not constitute proof – only that the empirical data supports our theory. There could be other theories and confounding factors influencing our results as well. However, the correlation between the timing of legislative changes and caseload increases is likely too great to be ignored. The ITT would definitely lead us to believe that changes in legislation were responsible for increased demands.

Exhibit 129: Run Chart of Children in Protection Caseloads

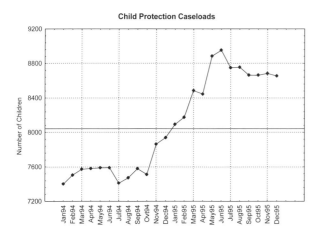

course. We have no evidence that a trend will continue upwards, placing ever increasing strains on the system. Rather, if our interpretation of a shift is correct, the agency can begin to plan for caseload levels of about 8,700.

In situations such as this, there is apt to be a lot of rhetoric from various political interest groups, each with their respective axes to grind. The same holds true in corporate settings, where the latest sales, cost or other figures are hotly debated. A simple plot and five minutes' worth of analysis could save everyone considerable heart burn!

RUN CHART EXAMPLE 2: ANALYZING SALES LEVELS

Also notice that the pattern of change violates our number of runs and run length rules. We have two years of monthly data or 24 data points but only two runs, each with a run length of 12. This further supports that a special cause of variation has impacted the system – likely the change in legislation.

The conclusion that the pattern is one of a shift would support our theory that the increases in case loads have likely run their

A small regional bank is attempting to better understand the pattern of consumer loan demand. The common wisdom is that loans tend to peak in the summer and in December. But how strong are these peaks? What kind of increases should the bank expect? Management reports used to be filled with columns of numbers, comparing current loan sales to budgets as well as current month's sales with sales levels for the same month last year.

The bank is now changing its reporting structures, using run charts to convey the information and enable for improved interpretation of the data. Table 130: Loan Sales details new consumer loans written monthly for a small branch.

Table 130: Loan Sales

Loans	Month	Loans	Month
55	Jan. 94	48	Jan. 95
52	Feb. 94	50	Feb. 95
36	Mar. 94	39	Mar. 95
49	Apr. 94	42	Apr. 95
56	May 94	50	May 95
77	Jun. 94	69	Jun. 95
69	Jul. 94	79	Jul. 95
96	Aug. 94	81	Aug. 95
75	Sept. 94	69	Sept. 95
62	Oct. 94	50	Oct. 95
70	Nov. 94	62	Nov. 95
90	Dec. 94	84	Dec. 95

The accompanying run chart (Exhibit 131: Run Chart of New Loans) tends to display a rising and falling pattern consistent with the summer vacation and pre-Christmas periods. This type of analysis can be combined with other techniques to further 'mine' the data to improve our understanding.

The standard run chart shows the data from the beginning of 1994 to the end of 1995. Presentation in this manner is excellent to see if trends, quick shifts or other patterns are evident over this time period.

Exhibit 131: Run Chart of New Loans

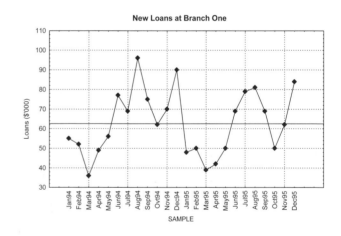

The same data can also be examined by plotting two different lines, one for 1994 and one for 1995 (Exhibit 132: Run Chart New Loans - Stratified Run Lines). Using run charts in this fashion – that is, stratifying the data, and preparing different lines for each strata, may contribute significantly to an increased understanding of the processes at work. In this case, the primary area of interest is cyclical patterns, specifically a monthly pattern of variation that sees loans sales rise in the summer months and in December.

Exhibit 132: Run Chart New Loans - Stratified Run Lines

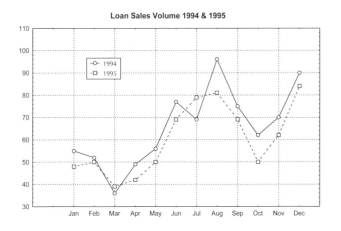

As the run chart indicates, this is precisely the pattern displayed. In this case, no run tests are required – the data hits you right between the eyes.

CONTROL CHARTS

Control charts are likely the most important of the data-analysis tools in the Performance Improvement Toolkit. The reason for this is straightforward. The type of variation in a system determines the most appropriate improvement strategy, and it is the control chart that identifies the type of variation. In other words, control charts are the critical process-analysis tools, determining the type of variation present and the resulting improvement strategy.

DESCRIPTION

Control charts are really an extension and enhancement of the basic run chart. Like run charts, control charts are a plot of data, usually but not necessarily organized in time sequence. Time (or factor of interest) is represented along the bottom (horizontal) axis. The values of the characteristic being measured are presented along the side (vertical) axis, just like the run chart. Also like the run chart, there is a center or average line, although in control charts the center line tends to be represented by the mean rather than the median.

The differences in outward appearance between run and control charts is simply that control charts contain two additional lines: an upper control limit (*ucl*) and a lower control limit (*lcl*). These control limits are, in fact, a calculated statistic. They represent a distance of three standard deviations or three sigma from the mean – in essence, a measure of the inherent variation in the data.

Exhibit 133: Typical Control Chart

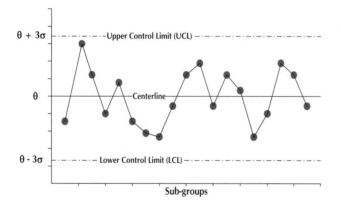

It is the calculation of these control limits that adds to the complexity of the control chart. Just as there are different calcula-

tions for the average with various types of data, there are also different calculations for the control limits for various data types. Preparing a control chart, therefore, requires knowledge of the type of data as well as the specific formulas to apply with each.

This added complexity makes the control chart a more difficult tool to use than the run chart. But the added difficulty has a payoff in greater analytical capability.

ADVANTAGES AND USES OF CONTROL CHARTS

So when and where to make use of this greater analytical capability? The first applications of control charts were in manufacturing, for analyzing the physical properties of parts and materials. Unfortunately, because of this, their use has largely been restricted to manufacturing applications.

Control charts, however, can and should be used wherever the performance and capability of a process or system is of interest, or where the performance and capability of different systems need to be compared. Specifically, use control charts when:

▲ **Determining the stability of a system or process.** Control charts provide the operational definition of system stability. If the system is stable, it is in a state of statistical control, operating under a system of chance, rather than special, causes. Such a system has a defined capability. Making improvements to it will require making changes to the system itself. Other systems lack stability – special causes of variation are present. Improvement here requires the removal of these special causes to create a stable system. Stability is important because without it, we cannot speak in any meaningful way of system or process capability.

▲ **Defining the capability of the system or process.** What is our system actually capable of? When special causes of variation have been removed and the system is stable, we can speak about the specific capability of the system. This capability is defined through the statistics presented in the control chart – the process mean and standard deviation. Discussion of average product cost, historical levels of demand, average number of defects in delivered product and other characteristics only have real meaning if deter-

mined through the control chart. That's because they only have meaning when the system has a defined capability.

▲ **Predicting expected behavior of the system.** A stable system, where the capability has been determined by the control chart, can be expected to continue to behave as it has. That is, providing there are no changes to the system and that no new special causes of variation emerge. Establishing these performance expectations allows teams to compare predicted performance with actual performance to identify emerging performance problems.

▲ **Evaluating the impact of change.** Does the new process function better than the old? Is the new advertising campaign having an effect? The control chart can be used to compare the effects of any change on system performance as measured by some quality characteristic. If the change produced a substantial benefit (or loss), this will show up as a special cause of variation in the chart.

▲ **Comparing the performance of different organizational or production units.** Rather than evaluating the performance of a system or process over time, the control chart can also be used to evaluate different processes over a specific time period. How do the safety records of the various trucking companies compare? Are some plants generating more pollution than others? If no special causes of variation are detected by the control chart, we can assume the cause and effect systems in these different organizational entities over the time examined are essentially the same – or at least have the same capability.

The control chart may be the most powerful and useful tool in the Performance Improvement Toolkit. So why isn't its use more widespread? There are three possibilities:

▲   Early manufacturing applications have 'typecast' the control chart as something only to be used in production or plant applications.

▲   People are unaware of the control chart as a powerful tool capable of analyzing the performance of a variety of processes and systems.

▲   Fear. Control charts provide answers as to whether or not improvement initiatives had an effect. Not everyone wants these answers, especially organizations where fear or unwillingness to change rules over improvement.

Control charts are simply too valuable in understanding system performance and capability to be ignored. In contrast to typical beliefs about statistics ("You can prove anything with statis-

tics"), control charts give us definite answers. They tell us whether something 'special' is going on or not, and dictate the best improvement strategy to pursue based upon the results.

FUNDAMENTAL CONTROL CHART CONCEPTS

The proper application and interpretation of control charts depend on understanding two basic concepts:

▶   control limits

▶   rational sub-groups

1. CONTROL LIMITS

The presence of the calculated control limits on the control chart distinguishes it from its simpler cousin, the run chart. But what are control limits?

Control limits are the result of a specific calculation performed on the data used in the chart. This calculation produces a statistic that represents three standard deviations or three sigma from the mean or average of the data. These control limit lines are plotted on the chart in the same way the center line is plotted. So the charts has a line representing the middle of the data, an upper control limit line three sigma above this center line, and a lower control limit three sigma below the center line.

The fact that control limits are a calculated statistic has created the impression that these limits represent probabilities of occurrence or measures of significance. This is incorrect. Control limits are a set of guidelines or rules, designed to minimize the economic loss resulting from decisions based upon incorrect assumptions about the nature of variation occurring within the system. In other words, they reduce management error in decision making.

There are two basic types of errors we can make in trying to improve the performance of any system or product. We can:

▶ Make a change where no change is warranted.

▶ Fail to make a change when a change is required.

It is easy to avoid making one type of mistake or the other, but you can never avoid both.

For example, if we never make changes we will never experience mistake number one. Let's call this the conservative

approach. Unfortunately, for the conservative manager, this strategy will produce an abundance of mistake number twos. Change never happens, even when it is desperately required, so there can never be improvement. The organization struggles along, as it always has, soon to be overtaken and surpassed by the competition.

Conversely, we can make all sorts of changes all the time. Every little thing produces a management reaction. Let's call this the aggressive approach. Here, management never makes mistake number two but, unfortunately, is constantly demanding change where none is required or warranted. This is not just fire fighting – it is creating the fires and then fighting them!

Both types of mistakes entail significant economic costs to the organization. It was Dr. Shewhart who recognized the need for a set of rules to guide management action – rules that would minimize the economic loss resulting from mistakes. These rules are the upper and lower control limits found on the control chart.

"They provide under a wide range of unknowable circumstances, future and past, a rational and

economic guide to minimum economic loss from both mistakes."[59]

Control limits are the rules that guide performance-improvement decisions. They do not eliminate mistakes. They provide a rational basis of decision making that minimizes economic loss.

Control limits are the data speaking, not management

The most important point to make about creating control limits is that they are calculated from the data. In a very real sense, they represent the "voice of the process."[60] The calculations for control limits are derived from statistical theory and the application of specific formulas depending upon the type of data. They are, therefore, empirical and exist independent of any wishes, desires or expectations.[61]

This is a critical point, because there is considerable confusion about control limits on the one hand and specification limits or targets on the other. Management sets specifications, but no one sets control limits. Specification limits have no place on the control chart. To move the position of the control limit or narrow the spread between the upper and lower control limits, physical changes to the system or process must be made in the real world. These physical changes, if they have any impact, will be reflected in the resulting data and, ultimately, in the control chart statistics arising from the data.

Control limits are not tests of significance or of hypothesis

It is important to note for those with some statistical training that the three-sigma control limit is not a statistical test of significance or a hypothesis test. Statistical significance concerns itself with levels of confidence that a small sample represents the larger population from which it was drawn. This is important in enumerative studies where the goal is to determine what the larger population looks like. Remember, a typical enumerative study is a poll in which citizens are asked for whom they will vote. In such an application, it is important to know our degree of confidence that the study reflects the population at

---

59. Edwards W. Deming.; *Out of the Crisis*, MIT Press, 1986. p.319
60. See description of control limits as "the data speaking to us" attributed to Irving Burr by Edwards Deming, *Out of the Crisis*, MIT Press 1986
61. Edwards W. Deming.; *Out of the Crisis*, MIT Press, 1986. p.333

large. This degree of confidence is presented through figures of statistical significance.

However, performance improvement tends to require use of analytic as opposed to enumerative studies. The purpose of an analytic study is to understand why things are the way they are, to understand the cause and effect system with an aim to predict and improve performance. Because improvement can only happen in the future, the units we want to study haven't been produced yet. There is no universe or population to study; therefore, no statistical tests of significance are applicable.

What does apply are rules to guide our decision making. Control limits are a set of rules, albeit very special rules which, when followed, minimize economic loss.

Control limits do not establish probabilities

Control limits do not set or establish probabilities of occurrence. There is no equating the control limit with a theoretical probability of a point going beyond these limits. Beware of presentations placing a normal curve beside a control chart with the 'appropriate' probabilities labeled. In such presentations, the control limit may also be described as a hypothesis test that the system is stable.

While it is true that control limits are calculated on the basis of statistical theory, it is wrong to consider them as tests of hypothesis.[62] The reason is simple. In the real world (the world we are concerned with in performance improvement), no process produces nice, neat and perfectly stable normal distributions. The real world is simply too 'messy.' Machines wear out, customers tire of product design, advertising approaches wear thin with consumers, competitors enter and exit markets, complexity sneaks in to processes, and resource inputs to the process change. Control charts were designed to provide a guide to action in this uncertain and 'non-normal' world. Control limits are simply the rules for playing the game to maximum economic benefit.

2. RATIONAL SUB-GROUPS

Control charts require the definition and creation of rational sub-groups. These sub-groups define how the data will be organized in the control chart, specifically along the x-axis. The notion of sub-groups here is the same as has been used elsewhere when discussing the organization of data. However,

---

62. Deming, Edwards W.; Out of the Crisis, MIT Press, 1986. p334 See also: *Understanding Statistical Process Control,* by Donald J.Wheeler and David S. Chambers.

the importance of creating rational sub-groups is critical in control chart construction, because statistics derived from the sub-groups will be used to determine the upper and lower control limits.

Two critical factors guide the process of defining rational sub-groups. These are:

▲ **The purpose of the control chart**, what it is we want to know about how the process works.

▲ **Separating variation**, ensuring that the sub-groups capture only common cause variation so that special cause variation is left to show through between sub-groups.

Purpose of the control chart

The most important consideration in determining rational sub-groups is the purpose of the control chart. Typically, the purpose of the control chart is to detect changes as they occur over time. In such cases, time is the factor of interest – we want to see how process performance varies with it.

Consider conducting a study of sales levels. We might want to examine how sales levels change over time. To do so, we would group sales data by time period – say monthly. Each

month, then, becomes a sub-group and the control chart is created with months located along the x-axis of the chart (see first chart in Exhibit 134: Some Rational Sub-groups).

But there may be other factors of interest as well. In our study of sales levels, we may also want to know how sales vary among our various sales locations. Sales data would be grouped by each location, and each location would be represented as a sub-group along the x-axis of the chart (see second chart in Exhibit 134: Some Rational Sub-groups).

In a study of sales levels, the list of potential factors of interest is virtually endless. Beyond examining sales over time and by location, we could also examine sales levels by sales person, market territory, customer segment, product line, advertising campaign and different sales promotions. Each of these could be used to define the sub-groups within the control chart.

Take another example. Suppose we are selecting a construction company from among 20 potential candidates to act as a sole source supplier to our firm. An important selection criterion is the safety record of the candidate firms, measured by man-hours lost due to accidents. In this case, our factor of interest is not time at all, but the various companies under consideration.

Exhibit 134: Some Rational Sub-groups

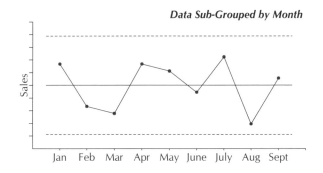

Data Sub-Grouped by Month

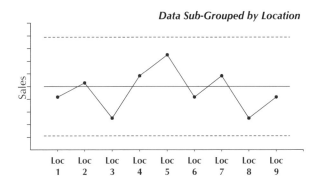

Data Sub-Grouped by Location

To understand if there are any real differences in safety performance of each company, each company would treated as a sub-group and represented along the x-axis of the chart.

The sub-grouping of data, then, is dependent upon what we want to know about the system – the purpose of the control chart. But it is also dependent upon our existing knowledge. The sub-grouping of data should be reflective of the real world from which the data is derived. We can't throw just any old data together and call it a sub-group. We must have a rational, real world basis for grouping the data together.

Separating variation

The second of our two factors guiding the definition of rational sub-groups is separating variation. Separating variation is the aim of rational sub-grouping. Specifically, the intent is to capture only *common cause* variation *within each sub-group,* so that *special cause* variation is left to emerge *between sub-groups*.

Suppose we have grouped production data on a daily basis (daily sub-groups). The data set in this example is the accuracy of holes made by an automatic drilling machine. As the machine wears over time, the accuracy of the holes drilled declines. We may test the accuracy four times a day, and combine these measures or tests to create the daily sub-group. Our understanding of the process is that the machine wear occurring in a single day of drilling is minimal. So any variation in drilling accuracy we see in a single day should be due to common cause variation. However, as the days pass, we should see variation creep in among the days. In other words, variation between days (rather than within individual days) may show signs of a special cause of variation (machine wear).

The same logic holds when comparing the accident rates of different construction companies. In this case, each company is a rational sub-group. Because each firm has its own set of safety regulations, methods and procedures, it makes sense to believe that variation within the sub-group (within a single company) will represent common cause variation. We are looking for special causes of variation among the various sub-groups – differences among the various construction companies.

The bottom line of rational sub-groups

Appropriate sub-grouping of data requires an underlying logic or rationale supported by practical understanding. There must be a reason why we are creating the sub-groups we are. Specif-

ically, we must have good reason to think the sub-groups will capture the common cause variation, leaving the special cause of variation to emerge between the sub-groups.

This understanding or logic must come from experts or people with experience in working with the process – not from statistical experts alone. No amount of statistical expertise can determine the appropriate time periods to use in measuring sales levels, accident rates, wear rates of machines or any other characteristic. This requires the combined efforts of those with some statistical knowledge and those with familiarity with the process or system under analysis.

CONTROL CHART INTERPRETATION

How do we analyze the control chart? In general, we can think of a three-step analytical procedure. The first of these is examining the control chart for any points beyond the upper or lower control limit. This is the classic rule for concluding that a special cause of variation is present within the process or system. The second step is analyzing the 'runs' in the control chart, in the much the same way we analyzed the run chart. Lastly, we can divide the spread of the control limits into zones and examine the pattern of the data relative to these zones.

1. THE CONTROL LIMIT RULE

Examining the control chart for any point lying above or below the upper and lower control limit is the classic rule for identifying a special cause of variation. If any point falls outside these limits, a special cause of variation is deemed to be present.

What this means is dependent upon the number of observations outside the control limits. A single point may be an isolated event. It still is a special or assignable cause, but may not be prevalent in system. This source of variation should be sought out and identified, but interpretation will demand familiarity with the process under examination. Depending upon circumstances, you may consider removing this data point from the analysis if you wanted to get at least a hypothetical idea of how the system would likely behave without the impact of this special cause.

On the other hand, if two or more points show up beyond the control limits, there is a lack of a standardized process and the system cannot be considered stable or reliable. Under these cir-

Exhibit 135: Basic Control Limit Rule

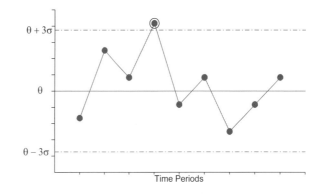

cumstances, the process has no real defined capability. So measures of average and the control limits themselves are really quite meaningless, at least in terms of describing system performance. The most that can be said of such a system is that it is unstable and unreliable, and that is not saying much. Removing these special or assignable causes from the analysis will not produce anything of value. There is simply too much special cause variation to try and estimate what a stable system might look like.

Stated differently, when a process produces numerous points outside the control limits there is no well-defined process at work. In these circumstances, the improvement task becomes removing these special causes of variation from the system itself to bring the system into a state of control.

2. RUN RULES

The control chart is an enhanced version of the run chart. The run rules and patterns that apply to the run chart also apply to the control chart, including run length, number of runs and trends (consecutively increasing or decreasing runs). This is only true when analyzing time-oriented data – the sub-groups along the x-axis represent time periods.

Because the minimum number of sub-groups analyzed on the control chart tends to be over 20, we can identify the following two run rules for special causes of variation:

▲ **A run of eight or more points to one side of the center line or the other** is a signal of a special cause of variation, usually some form of shift in process performance.

▲ **Seven consecutive points increasing or decreasing** is a signal of a special cause of variation, namely a trend.

Exhibit 136: Run Rules for Control Charts

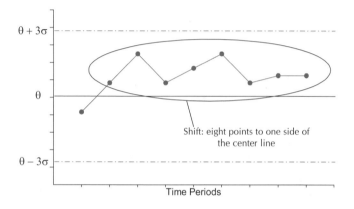

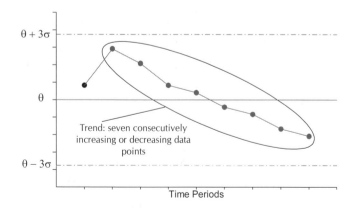

Like the run chart, a review of the data for patterns is also appropriate for the control chart. Once again, the primary tool here is the Inter-ocular Trauma Test (ITT). Look for patterns that hit you right between the eyes. If a pattern is apparent, you may want to use some of the other tests to help confirm that a special cause of variation is present. In these cases, the zone tests presented next, as well as the various run rules, may prove useful.

Comments about the interpretation of trends in run charts also apply to control charts. People tend to see trends everywhere – any two points will do. Remember, you need seven to make a trend.

3. ZONE RULES

The classic control chart format contains a center line as well as upper and lower control limits drawn at a distance of three sigma from the center line. A zoned control chart adds lines at one and two sigma distance from the center line, to create a set of three zones on either side of the middle. How the data falls within these zones can provide a signal of a special cause. Caution is warranted, however. Like the run rules, zone rules are

Exhibit 137: Basic and Zoned Control Chart Formats

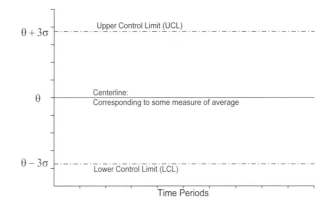

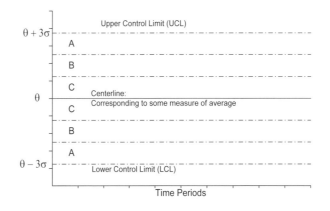

generally to be applied with time-oriented data – time periods compose the sub-groups along the x-axis.

These zones are labeled A, B, C with zone C closest to the center line and zone A next to the upper and lower control limits. With these zones, we can identify four additional rules for guiding our considerations as to whether a special cause of variation is present in the system.

▲ **Upper limits rule.** When two out of three points fall in zone A or above, beyond the two-sigma limit line, we can suspect a special cause of variation is present.

▲ **Middle limits rule.** The middle limits rule detects a special cause when four out of five observations lie in zone B or more than one-sigma distance from the center line.

▲ **Limited range rule.** When 15 points in a row lie within zone C on either side of the center line, or within one-sigma distance from the center line, a special cause of variation may be present. The data is not displaying as much variation as it should. This is often a signal that problems exist with the measurement process.

▲ **Extended range rule.** In this case the data is displaying too much variation. If eight points in a row lie beyond

Exhibit 138: Upper Limits and Middle Limits Rules

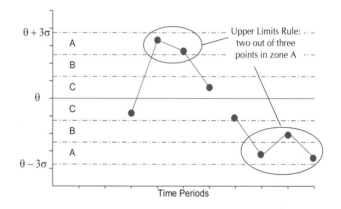

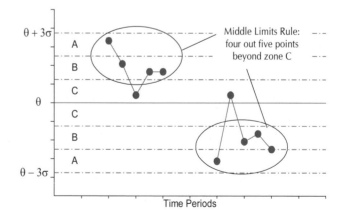

Exhibit 139: Limited Range and Extended Range Rules

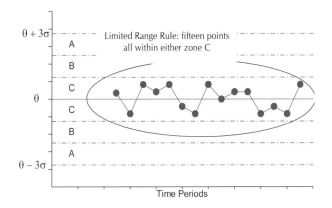

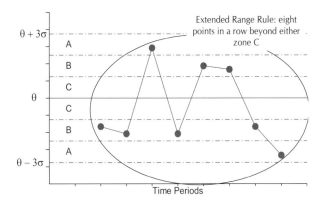

either side of zone C, or beyond one-sigma distance from the center line, then a special cause of variation is assumed to be present This is a pattern common when data from two different sources are combined. Look for the source of the differences, stratify the measurements when found and then plot on two separate control charts.

IMPORTANT CONSIDERATIONS WHEN INTERPRETING ZONED CONTROL CHARTS

The first thing to keep in mind regarding the rules used to identify special causes of variation is that they imply nothing about whether the special cause is desirable or undesirable. For example, a trend may indicate improving performance or declining performance. A special cause is just that, something special or assignable.

A second consideration is the number of rules. So far, we have identified the classic control limit rule, two run rules and four zone rules. If all these rules are applied to every control chart, the problem of finding something multiplies.

For this reason, teams should be explicit about which rules will be applied and why, before conducting a control chart analysis.

Ultimately this decision is based on the team's knowledge of the process and what they are looking for when using the control chart. This knowledge can only come from a familiarity with the process, combined with experience in using control charts. Statistical expertise alone cannot provide guidance.

A CONSISTENT INTERPRETATION STRATEGY

Try to apply no more than four or five rules. Applying every possible run and zone rule to a specific chart amounts to torturing the data.[63] Better to apply a few simple rules to gauge the stability of a process. When unsure of which rules to apply, a good strategy is to use the following package of four:

▲ **Classic control limits test,** to look for any point(s) going beyond the upper or lower control limits.

▲ **Run length test of eight or more points to one side of the center line or the other**, as a signal of a shift.

▲ **Upper limits test of two of three points in zone A,** where some cause appears to be pushing the process to some new level.

---

63. If you torture the data long enough, it will tell you anything.

▲ **Trend test of seven consecutive points trending up or down,** if only to prevent the labelling of trends for any two or three increasing or decreasing data points.

Again, the assumption with the zone rules is that the subgroups are based on time. So time periods are represented on the x-axis of the control chart. If this is not the case, only the classic control limits test should be used. Other tests such as the trend test, run length test, etc. have no meaning with non-time based sub-groups.

CONTROL CHARTS AND PERFORMANCE MATURITY

Control charts are considered to be the most important of the performance measurement and improvement analysis tools. Indeed, performance improvement and control charts are inseparable in practice. Why is this so? It is because control charts provide us with an operational definition as to the type of variation we are experiencing. Knowing the type of variation, in turn, is essential to effective improvement activity.

The nature of improvement and the type of variation we experience with a process tends to vary with the maturity level of

Exhibit 140: Maturity Stages

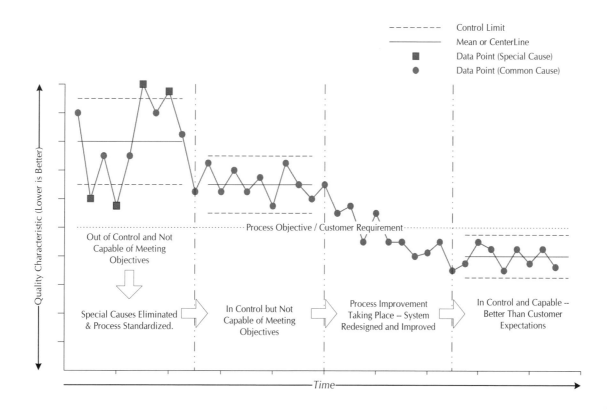

the process. New processes, for example, are likely to have numerous special causes – the result of a lack of standardization, employee familiarity or environmental impacts not being fully considered at the time of implementation. This might be termed the first phase of the performance life-cycle.

Through analysis and elimination of the various special causes, however, the process becomes standardized over time. It evolves from a process without any clear capability to one where the capability is well defined. This is the second phase of the maturity curve – having a standardized, reliable process. It is important to note that just because a system is in statistical control (reliable) doesn't mean that it is performing well. It only means that the system now has a defined capability, meaning it is predictable.

With the capability defined, the process may or may not be capable of meeting the objectives set for it. Improvement that is designed to ensure expectations are met brings performance into the third stage of evolution – reliable and capable. Now the performance of the system is in line with expectations.

These phases from one stage of performance maturity to the next are pictured in Exhibit 157: Maturity Stages. It presents how the control chart appears for performance characteristics representing systems at different levels of maturity.

TYPES OF CONTROL CHARTS

There are many types of control charts. For the most part, they look pretty much the same. They differ in the calculations required to determine the control limits, which in turn depends on the type of data being analyzed.

There are basically two different types of data – measured data and attribute data. These two data types define the two basic classifications of control charts.

VARIABLES (MEASURED) DATA CONTROL CHARTS

Measuring along a continuous scale produces measured or variables data. For this reason it is also referred to as continuous data. Examples include measuring weight, length or time. To determine if you are dealing with variables data, ask yourself if it makes sense to have decimal places in the data. If it does, you are using variables data. For example, it is logical to have something 2.6 inches long or weigh 23.7 pounds, so each of these are variables data. In contrast, it is illogical to have 2.3 persons responding to a poll – which means this would be counted data.

The type of control chart used with variables data depends upon the sample size associated with each sub-group. There are three basic types of control charts used with variables or measured data:

▲ **Individuals Chart or X, Moving R Chart (*XmR*).** This is used when the sample size for each sub-group on the chart is equal to one. Some types of data simply do not allow for multiple measures to be taken. For example, apartment vacancy rates, oil prices and monthly sales figures. In these cases, it is difficult to see how a rational sub-group could incorporate multiple samples. *XmR* charts are most often used in the analysis of administration, general management, service industries and strategic applications, where the existence of natural sub-groups with a single measure is most common.

▲ **X-Bar, R Chart ($\overline{X}$, R).** This chart is used when the sample size for each sub-group is between two and 10. This is the most widely used control chart, especially in manufac-

turing applications. This is because it is easier in these types of environments to measure four or five manufactured pieces per day, or within some other sub-grouping, and analyze the data. Sub-group size can usually be held constant in practice, with three to six samples per sub-group being the most common.

▲ **X-Bar, s Chart ($\overline{X}$, s).** This is used when sample size per sub-group is greater than 10 or where the sample size within each sub-group varies considerably. Because it is usually practical to hold the sample size within each sub-group constant, this control chart is used infrequently in practice. Its interpretation, however, is the same as the *X-Bar, R* chart.

ATTRIBUTE (COUNTED) DATA

Attribute charts deal with data that is produced by *counting* rather than measuring along a scale. Usually, the attributes being counted are errors, mistakes or flaws in product or service. But they needn't be so negative. Recovery rates, levels of acceptable product, and the like, can also be counted.

Because we are counting, the data is not continuous but rather discrete – it consists only of whole numbers. It is impossible to count 1.8 errors. We can have one error, two errors, three errors or more, but never 1.8. This is in contrast to variables control charts where the data is a result of a measurement. In these cases, it is reasonable to have decimals or fractions in the data.

Decimals will appear on the attribute control chart, however. That's because attribute control charts plot whatever is being counted relative to some sample or area of opportunity. For example, in analyzing circuit boards, the number of boards with defects are counted relative to the total number or circuit boards in the sample. Thus, a count of 22 defective circuit boards out of a sample of 300 boards yields a proportion defective of 0.073.

Likewise, when analyzing the occurrences of violent crime, the count of incidents is relative to the population in the community at the time. A count of 235 incidents of violent crime in a community with a population of 450,000 yields a violent crime rate of 0.52 per thousand population.

These proportions and rates will be plotted on the attribute control chart. So decimals will be found on attribute control charts despite the fact that during the counting, only whole numbers are possible. For this reason alone, care needs to be taken by those constructing the chart to ensure the correct chart is being used with the right data.

Unfortunately, the situation becomes more confusing still. There are different types of attribute control charts that make different assumptions about what is being counted and the size of the sub-group samples. To determine the appropriate type of attribute control chart, then, we need to distinguish what is being counted as well as the size of the sample.

What are we counting: occurrences or units

We can count one of two things: occurrences or units. When counting units, the objects being counted are classified into one of two categories. They either belong to one class or another: good or bad, defective or not defective, within specifications or not. Counting occurrences, in contrast, is counting the number of things within a broader area of opportunity, such as counting the number of crimes committed within a community or the number of defects occurring on a specific product.

A good way to tell the difference between occurrences (counts within an area of opportunity) and units (counts classifying units as belonging to some class or another) is to reverse what is being counted. With units, good units can be counted as well as bad. We can count the number of bills with errors or the number of bills without errors. If 23 percent of the invoices have errors on them, then it is logical that 77 percent of the units are error-free. But you can't count the number of non-occurrences. It is impossible to count the number of non-errors on a invoice or the number of non-crimes in a community.

For example, consider that a single printed circuit board may have eight defects. If counting occurrences an eight would be recorded. If counting units that are defective, however, a one would be recorded since the circuit board is defective, and it can only be defective once regardless of how many defects occur on it. Another circuit board might have one defect, in which case a one would be recorded whether counting occurrences (defects in this example) or defective units.

Nature of the sample or area of opportunity: fixed or variable

Now for sample size. With attribute charts, the sample size or area of opportunity can be either fixed or variable. As the name implies, a fixed sample size is one where every sub-group has the same number of units or the same area of opportunity.

For example, a process improvement team studying the number of incomplete waybills may decide to draw a sample of 50 waybills for each week of the previous three months. These 50 waybills will be examined for completeness. The number of incomplete waybills in each week will be the focus of the control chart, with each week being the sub-group. In this example, the sample size for each sub-group is fixed at 50.

In contrast, a manager wanting to examine the number of shipments made by premium freight as opposed to regular freight is faced with a varying sample size. This is because the total number of shipments made changes from month to month. In this case, a different type of control chart will be required, one that recognizes a variable sample size.

Types of attribute control charts

We have two possibilities for what we are counting (occurrences or units) and two possibilities for the nature of the sample (fixed or variable). As a result, we have four different types of attribute control charts.

▲ *NP-Chart.* This is used when counting units and the sample size is fixed. It is particularly useful in situations such as the examination of waybills, where an improvement

Table 141: Types of Attribute Control Charts

		What is Being Counted	
		Units Proportions	Occurrences Rates
Sample Size	Fixed	*np*-chart	*c*-chart
	Variable	*p*-chart	*u*-chart

team has an opportunity to set the sample size, say drawing a standard sample of 50 waybills each week.

▲ **P-Chart.** This is used, like the *np*-chart, when the focus is upon units or classification of things. Unlike the *np*-chart, however, the *p*-chart does not require a constant sample size. In a study of waybills, suppose the team did not draw a set sample of 50 waybills each week, but rather examined all the waybills issued for the week. The *p*-chart would then be used, because the total number of waybills occurring each week would likely be different – meaning, in effect, a different sample or sub-group size for each week.

▲ **C-chart.** This is used when counting occurrences and where the sample size is constant. Again, using a waybill example, the sample drawn each week was 50. But the focus of interest is the number of errors occurring on each waybill as opposed to the number of incorrect waybills. In this situation, the *c*-chart would be used.

▲ **U-Chart.** This is used when dealing with occurrences but where the sample size or area of opportunity for the count varies. Again, using the waybill example, suppose the total number of weekly waybills was drawn as the sample or area of opportunity (as was the case with the *p*-chart) but the focus was the total number of errors (as was the case with the *c*-chart). Then the *u*-chart would be used.

The charts differ from one another based upon what is being counted and whether the sample size is fixed (same size for every sub-group) or variable (each sub-group has a different sample size). The charts requiring fixed sample size are essentially special cases of the charts used for unequal sample sizes.

▲ **The *np*-chart, then, is a special case of the *p*-chart.** Both deal with the analysis of proportions.

▲ **The *c*-chart is a special case of the *u*-chart.** Both deal with an analysis of rates. With the *c*-chart, the denominator is essentially ignored as the sample size (area of opportunity) is fixed.

There are some advantages to the constant sample size, the main one being that only a single set of control limits needs to be calculated. With unequal sample sizes, separate control limits are usually calculated for each sub-group.

Calculating separate control limits is no problem when using a computer, but it is sheer drudgery when computing by hand. If a computer with some form of statistical analysis program or spreadsheet is not available, take the time to design a data-collection scheme that produces constant sample sizes for each sub-group. The time saved in calculation will be worth it.

Summary: Basic Types of Control Charts

Table 142: Summary of Basic Control Chart Types provides a basic outline of the different charts to use under different circumstances – type of data and sub-group size. A summary of the various control charts, the basic formulas used in construction and other pertinent data are presented in Table 143: Variables or Measured Data Control Charts and Table 155: Attribute or Counted Data Control Charts.

Table 142: Summary of Basic Control Chart Types

Type of Data		Sub-group Sample	Control Chart
Measured (Variables)		Sample size is 1	Individuals Control Chart (XmR)
		Sample size is between 2 and 10	Control Chart for Averages ($\bar{X}, R$)
		Sample size is over 10 and/or variable	Control Chart for Averages ($\bar{X}, s$)
Counted (Attribute)	Units	Sample size is fixed	Control Chart for Proportional Counts (np-chart)
		Sample size is variable	Control Chart for Proportions (p-chart)
	Incidents	Sample size is fixed	Control Chart for Counts (c-chart)
		Sample size is variable	Control Chart for Rates (u-chart)

CONSTRUCTING VARIABLES (MEASURED) CONTROL CHARTS

Measured control charts are the foundation of performance improvement. They are robust tools for identifying special causes of variation within a process as well as for determining the degree of stability within a process. Their use should be far more widespread.

ISSUES WITH MEASURED CONTROL CHARTS

There are two issues of concern with measured control charts that may be at least partly responsible for the lack of wide-spread use. These issues are:

▶ Normality of data

▶ Auto correlation

NORMALITY OF DATA

It has been argued that when confronted with a process or system producing non-normal data, the *XmR* chart cannot be used – it is the *X-bar, R* chart or nothing.[64] The argument has been that employing the X-bar, R chart requires multiple measures per sub-group and these multiple measures take advantage of the central limit theorem.

The central limit theorem is an important idea in statistics. It states that the larger the sample from a population, the more the sample will be normally distributed even if the underlying population from which it is drawn is not normal. Using the $\overline{X}, R$ chart, it is argued, ensures the sample is normally distributed as it require more measures than the *XmR* chart. The result is a more accurate chart.

Some authors have gone further and recommend testing data for normality before using any control chart, *XmR* or $\overline{X}, R$. If

---

64. Those with some training in statistics may recall that normally distributed values will form a symmetric 'bell curve' when plotted as a histogram. Non-normally distributed data will form any number of odd-looking distributions when similarly plotted.

the data proves to be non-normal, the advice is to not use any control chart at all.

The underlying assumption in all these arguments, however, is that control charts require normally distributed data in order to work. They don't.

While control limit calculations were originally derived based on an assumption of normally distributed data, control charts – *all variables control charts* – are insensitive to this assumption. Control charts are robust tools for working with real world data, regardless of the nature of the underlying statistical distribution.[65]

The bottom line is that the underlying nature of the distribution is not a critical consideration with measured data control charts. Feel free to use them more often.

AUTO CORRELATION

Auto correlation is said to occur when successive values tend to be similar – a measure in period 1 is very close to a measure in period 2. This is a way of saying that measures in one period are dependent upon measures in the previous period.

Auto correlated data does affect the control chart – the greater the degree of auto correlation, the tighter the control limits become. From this, it is argued that the data need to be tested for auto correlation before using the control chart.

While auto correlated data may be a concern, for the most part, the concern is a limited one. Impact on control limits occurs only when the data is very strongly auto correlated – a rare occurrence. Even so, while such data will impact the control limits, it has limited impact on actual control chart interpretation. In other words, the usefulness of the control chart is only marginally diminished.[66]

Concerns about auto correlated data are, therefore, misplaced. Improvement teams should have every confidence in measured

---

65. There is no better argument for why this is so than in Donald J. Wheeler and Davis S. Chambers, *Understanding Statistical Process Control*, SPC Press, 1992. For those with a need to understand the theory, read pages 55 through 88 for clear and comprehensive analysis of the "whys and wherefores of control charts." Worth the time and effort.

66. ibid. pp. 80-82

control charts, as robust tools, to work in a variety of applications and circumstances. As John Wheeler notes:

> *"Control charts have worked with auto correlated data for over 60 years!"*[67]

BASIC FORMULAS AND CONSTANTS

As their names suggest, measured or variables control charts actually consist of two control charts that are used together. One chart is used for plotting the measures of location (either x or $\bar{x}$) and a second for plotting the measures of dispersion (either R or s). For each chart, calculations are required to determine the centerline as well as the upper and lower control limits.

The three basic types of variables control charts, along with the respective formulas for calculating the various statistics required, are presented in Table 143: Variables or Measured Data Control Charts.

The formulas presented in Table 143 make use of several factors. The various factors used with control charts are presented in Table 144: Control Chart Factors.

THE *XmR* CHART

X, Moving Range or Individuals (*XmR*) control charts are most often used for clerical, accounting, business/management or general industry data where multiple sampling on the basis of rational sub-groups is not possible or practical. The *XmR* chart is used when:

▲ each data point is already a natural, rational sub-group.

▲ it is simply not possible to gather multiple samples – published data, for example.

▲ the cycle time of the process is long enough that single measures are appropriate – a batch process taking two weeks, for example.

CONSTRUCTION STEPS

Construction of the *XmR* chart initially mirrors that of the run chart. The following 10 steps outline the procedure.

---

67. ibid. p. 81

Table 143: Variables or Measured Data Control Charts

Chart Name		Center line (mean)	3 Sigma	Sample	Data	Distribution	Chart Example
XmR	X	$\dfrac{\Sigma x}{k}$	$2.659 \times \bar{R}$	1 measure per sub-group	measured or attribute	based upon normal/ robust in practice	
	mR	$\dfrac{\Sigma mr}{k-1}$	$3.267 \times \bar{R}$				
$\bar{X}$, R	$\bar{X}$	$\dfrac{\Sigma \bar{x}}{k}$	$A_2 \times \bar{R}$	2 to 10 measures per sub-group	measured	based upon normal/ robust in practice	
	R	$\dfrac{\Sigma r}{k}$	$D_4 \times \bar{R}$ $D_3 \times \bar{R}$				
$\bar{X}$, s	$\bar{X}$	$\dfrac{\Sigma \bar{x}}{k}$	$A_3 \times \bar{s}$	over 10 measures per sub-group or variable sub-group size	measured	based upon normal/ robust in practice	
	s	$\dfrac{\Sigma s}{k}$	$B_4 \times \bar{s}$ $B_3 \times \bar{s}$				

Table 144: Control Chart Factors

Sub-Group Size (n)	Individuals (*XmR* Chart)		Control Chart for Averages ($\overline{X}$, *R* Chart)			Control Chart for Averages ($\overline{X}$, *s* Chart)			Bias Correction Factors	
	3 sigma of *X*-chart	Upper control limit of *R*-chart	3 sigma of $\overline{X}$-chart	Lower control limit for Ranges chart	Upper control limit for Ranges chart	3 sigma for $\overline{X}$-chart	Lower control limit for *s*-chart	Upper control limit for *s*-chart	*R*	*s*
			A_2	D_3	D_4	A_3	B_3	B_4	d_2	c_4
1	2.659	3.267	-	-	-	-	-	-	-	-
2	-	-	1.880	-	3.268	2.659	-	3.267	1.128	0.7979
3	-	-	1.023	-	2.574	1.954	-	2.568	1.693	0.8862
4	-	-	0.729	-	2.282	1.628	-	2.266	2.059	0.9213
5	-	-	0.577	-	2.114	1.427	-	2.089	2.326	0.9400
6	-	-	0.483	-	2.004	1.287	0.030	1.970	2.534	0.9515
7	-	-	0.419	0.076	1.924	1.182	0.118	1.882	2.704	0.9594
8	-	-	0.373	0.136	1.864	1.099	0.185	1.815	2.847	0.9650
9	-	-	0.337	0.184	1.816	1.032	0.239	1.761	2.970	0.9693
10	-	-	0.308	0.223	1.777	0.975	0.284	1.716	3.087	0.9727

1. Collect and organize the data

The team must identify the appropriate time period or sub-groups and the data to be collected. The very fact that an *XmR* chart is being used may indicate there are some restrictions in sampling. For example, the data may already be published. Some basic tasks to be done:

▶ **Decide what to measure.** Decide what to measure and provide an operational definition. Are you measuring absolute size or deviation from a target? What is the scale to be used? Is everyone measuring in the same way?

▶ **Design the sample.** Because the data tends to be already organized into existing natural sub-groups, actual design of the sample is often a minor issue with *XmR* charts.

▶ **Set up data-collection forms.** Make sure clear and concise data collection forms or check-sheets are established, and that those doing the data gathering know how to use them. Again, this tends to be less of a concern with Individuals charts, as often the data has already been published or is contained in some form of management reporting.

Be sure to record the data in the order in which the sample occurs. If the sub-groups represent time periods, using a minimum of 20 periods is a good guideline. But familiarity with the process is still the most important factor in determining the actual number of data points. There must be sufficient samples that possible special causes of variation have the opportunity to make themselves apparent.

2. Create the axes for the *X* chart and plot the data

This is done in the same way as the run chart was created. The horizontal axis will be used to represent the logical sub-groups, usually time periods with the earliest time period to the left and the latest time period on the right side of the axis. The vertical axis will be the scale against which the observations will be plotted. Remember to add a little headroom above and below the maximum and minimum values observed. The data points are then plotted on the chart and connected with a line.

3. Calculate and plot the centerline for the observations

For the average of the observations, total the observations and divide by the number of observations totaled. This is the basic calculation of the mean.

$$Centerline(\bar{x}) = \frac{\Sigma x}{k}$$

Where:
x = individual sub-group values

k = number of sub-groups

Notice the symbol for the mean of the x's is an x with a bar over it. This bar represents the mean and is usually pronounced 'x-bar.' The number of sub-groups is represented by k. The centerline is then drawn on the control chart.

4. Calculate the moving ranges (*mR*)

The moving range is simply the absolute difference between each successive observation. Start with the first value and subtract the second to determine the difference. We are interested in the absolute value, so make the number positive even if the actual calculation produces a negative number. Continue on through all the data, taking the third number away from the second, the fourth away from the third and so on.

5. Create the axes for the moving range chart and plot the data

This is done in the same way as the X chart was created, except now we will be plotting the moving range values calculated in step 5. The horizontal axis will be the same as for the X chart, but the first sub-group will have no moving-R value (the calculation of the moving range will always produce one less value

than was used to create the X chart). The vertical axis will be the scale against which the observations will be plotted. Remember to add a little headroom above and below the maximum and minimum values observed – 25 to 30 percent usually provides sufficient space for the plotting of control limits. The data points are then plotted on the chart and connected with a line.

6. Calculate and plot the centerline for the moving range

Add up all the moving ranges calculated in step 5 and divide by the number of moving ranges. This is simply calculating the mean for the moving ranges. Note, the number of moving ranges should be one less than the number of observations or sub-groups used to calculate X-bar.

$$Centerline(\bar{R}) = \frac{\Sigma R}{k-1}$$

Where:
R = moving ranges
k = number of sub-groups

The resulting value of *R-bar* is then plotted on the chart as a center line for the R's.

7. Calculate the control limits for the moving ranges

This calculation is done by multiplying $\bar{R}$ by a factor, in this case 3.267. The result is the upper control limit for the *mR* chart. Notice that no lower control limit is required since the moving *R* chart cannot be less than zero. The specific formula is:

$$UCL_R = 3.267 \times \bar{R}$$

Where
UCL_R = Upper Control Limit for the ranges
3.267 = a standard control chart factor
$\bar{R}$ = the mean of the moving ranges

Again, because we are dealing with the Individuals chart, the value of factor used to calculate the upper limit for the ranges is always the same – 3.267.

8. Interpret the ranges chart

Examine the *mR* chart. Look for points along the chart that lie above the upper control limit. These are indications that a special or assignable cause of variation is present in the process. This may be a single outside event or some significant change occurring within the process itself. It is possible to have special causes on the *mR* chart but not on the *X* chart. For this reason, it is advisable to prepare both the *mR* and *X* charts.

9. Calculate the control limits for the x-values

The upper and lower control limits are determined by multiplying the centerline value (mean) for the moving ranges (*R-bar*) by a factor, in this case 2.659. The resulting figure is then added to, and subtracted from, the average for the observations to create the upper and lower control limits. The basic formulas for the upper and lower control limits are provided below.

$$Control\ Limits = \bar{x} \pm (2.659 \times \bar{R})$$

Where:
$\bar{x}$ = mean for x's or individual values
$\bar{R}$ = average for the ranges
2.659 = a standard control chart factor, often rounded to 2.66

Notice that in the formula a constant of 2.66 is used. This is obtained from Table 144: Control Chart Factors. Because the sub-group size is always equal to '1' with the *XmR* chart, this factor is always the same – 2.659 or 2.66. Once calculated, these values can be plotted as the control limit lines onto the control chart for the observations.

10. Interpret the results

Using the control chart interpretation guide presented earlier, interpret the results of the chart. Is the process in control? Are there special causes of variation? If so, when and where do they occur?

EXAMPLE 1: MONTHLY SALES LEVELS

A major company is reviewing its sales levels of a specific division. The executive committee is of two opinions. Some say sales are declining and the company must act to reverse the trend. A review of the performance of its sales people has been discussed, along with the possibility of bringing in 'some new blood.'

Not all share this view. Some members of the executive don't see any evidence of a decline. Yes, they argue, sales have been lower the past few months, but this is just the way things go. They are confident things will bounce back.

Notice that the discussion at the executive committee is essentially a version of arguing for or against the presence of special causes. Those arguing that things will bounce back on their own are essentially arguing that the variation in sales is common cause variation – part of the system itself. Those arguing for a change are essentially arguing that recent sales numbers reflect some special cause of variation that needs to be addressed by specific management action.

Doing the math

The monthly sales level data is presented in Table 145: Monthly Sales Level Data. Some of the basic calculations have already been done. For example, the moving ranges have already been calculated (Step 5). The moving range is simply the difference between successive values of x, in this case sales levels. The first moving range value is 227, which is the difference between sales levels in month 1 (1,115) and month 2 (888). Likewise the next moving range is 57, the difference between month 2 (888) and month 3 (945). Notice this means there will always be one less moving range than the number of observations.

The average monthly sales level or *x-bar* has also been calculated (Step 4). It is the total of all sales ($18,519) divided by the number of observations or sub-groups (19) or $974.68.

Table 145: Monthly Sales Level Data

Month (Sub-group)	Sales (x)	Moving Range (mR)
1.	1115	
2	888	227
3	945	57
4	1040	95
5	922	118
6	912	10
7	982	70
8	992	10
9	1018	26
10	1130	112
11.	1010	120
12	999	11
13	1110	111
14	905	205
15	972	67
16	1018	46
17	912	106
18	792	120
19	857	65
Sum	18519	1576
Average	974.68	87.56

The average of the moving ranges or *R-bar* has also been calculated (see Step 7). It is the total of the moving ranges (1,576) divided by the total number of moving range values (18) to yield 87.56. Remember that the number of moving range values will always be the number of sub-groups less one.

The control limits for the *X*'s or values (Step 8) are simple to calculate. They involve multiplying a standard factor, 2.66, by *R-bar*. *R-bar* is 87.56. So 87.56 times 2.66 is 232.91. This amount added to *X-bar* (232.91 + 974.68) is 1207.59, yielding the upper control limit for the Individuals chart. The lower control limit is 974.68 - 232.91 or 741.77. These are essentially the same as the values produced by computer on the control charts in the Exhibit 146: Individuals, Moving-R Chart on Sales Data. The differences are due to the rounding of factor values.

The control limits for the Moving *R* chart also use a factor, in this case 3.267 (see Step 9). This, multiplied by *R-bar* of 87.56, yields 286.06. Again, this is close to the limit calculated for the moving-*R* chart by the computer. Note that only an upper limit is required for the chart.

In short, the control limit calculations for the *XmR* chart are

Exhibit 146: Individuals, Moving-*R* Chart on Sales Data

driven by *R-bar* (the mean of the moving ranges). For creating the upper and lower control limits for the *x*'s, *R-bar* is multiplied by the factor 2.66. The result is then added to, and subtracted from, *x-bar* to yield the control limits.

For the moving ranges, the factor is 3.267 and this is multiplied by *R-bar* to yield the value of the upper control limit for the moving ranges chart.

Interpreting the results

With the charts plotted and the calculations completed, the resulting control charts can be interpreted. First and foremost to note, all the data lies within the control limits. Further, the data does not violate any of the run or zone rules (see Table 147: Run & Zone Tests on Sales Data).

As a result, we can conclude that the empirical evidence does not show any signs of special causes being present. The variation we see is common cause, simply part of the random fluctuations to be expected in sales. Management will be well advised to wait things out before taking any action. In other words, the best action to take in these circumstances is no action at all.

Table 147: Run & Zone Tests on Sales Data

Run & Zone Tests	Status
8 samples on same side of center	OK
6 samples in row increasing/decreasing	OK
14 samples alternating up & down	OK
2 of 3 samples in Zone A or beyond	OK
4 of 5 samples in Zone B or beyond	OK
15 samples in Zone C	OK
8 samples beyond Zone C	OK

EXAMPLE 2: COMMUNITY CRIME RATE

Control charts can be used to analyze the performance of any system across some measurable characteristic. Take the example of crime. We can use control charts to examine crime rates and draw conclusions about whether crime is increasing, decreasing, out of control or whatever.

Take the example of a medium-sized city concerned about the levels of violent crime. Statistics are gathered with the aim of first establishing what the rate of crime is in the community and whether it is rising or falling. Table 148: Community Crime Rate Data presents the reported incidents of violent crime per thousand households for the past 19 years.

Most of the math used to calculate the control limits has already been done and is presented at the bottom of the table. The average rate is 4.8. This is the value of *x-bar*. *R-bar* is the mean under the Moving Range column or 1.09.

Next, we apply some basic factors. The upper control limit for the moving ranges will be *R-bar* (1.09) times the factor 3.267. This yields 3.56. This is close to the value of 3.57 the computer calculated in Exhibit 149: XmR Chart of Incidents of Violent Crime.

The control limits for the x's use a factor of 2.66. This, too, is multiplied by *R-bar* (every control limit calculation with measured data control charts involves multiplying some factor by R-bar). The figure is then added to and subtracted from *x-bar* to arrive at the upper and lower control limits. (2.66 times 1.09 is about 2.9). This, added to *x-bar* of 4.8, gives an upper control limit of 7.7. The lower control limit would be 4.8 minus 2.9, or 1.9. Simple!

Table 148: Community Crime Rate Data

Year (sub-group)	Incidents of Violent Crime (per 1000) x	Moving Range mR
1977	3.7	
1978	4.1	0.4
1979	3.9	0.2
1980	5.8	1.9
1981	3.1	2.7
1982	3.0	0.1
1983	2.3	0.7
1984	5.4	3.1
1985	4.3	1.1
1986	3.5	0.8
1987	4.6	1.1
1988	5.7	1.1
1989	6.6	0.9
1990	6.5	0.1
1991	7.3	0.8
1992	6.1	1.2
1993	5.4	0.7
1994	6.2	0.8
1995	4.2	2.0
Sum	91.7	19.7
Average (mean)	4.8	1.09

Exhibit 149: XmR Chart of Incidents of Violent Crime

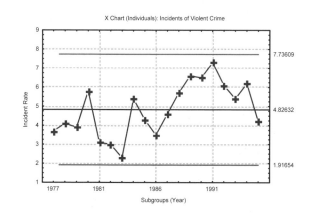

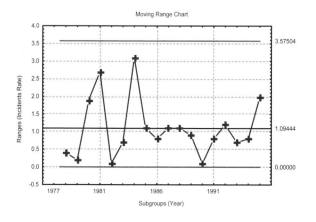

And what does the control chart tell us about the crime rate in the community? Well, first of all it is stable. There is no evidence that crime is rising or falling. Note that this is not to say whether residents feel crime is too high or not. That is a separate issue. What we can say, based upon the empirical data, is that the rate of violent crime is stable. It is not likely to change much unless there is some significant change in the structure of the system.

This means if the residents would like the crime rate to fall, some structural changes in the system will have to take place.

EXAMPLE 3: INVENTORY LEVELS

Management of inventory provides a good example of the effectiveness of control charting techniques. A typical report to support management of inventory is provided in Table 150: July Inventory Management Report. It compares this month's inventory levels with last July's inventory levels, year-to-date averages and plans. But what does it convey about the performance of the system? Nothing!

The historical data, analyzed through a control chart, provides a much more detailed and comprehensive picture of the performance of the inventory system. The data is presented in Table 151: In-Process Inventory Levels. The resulting control charts (*XmR*) follow in Exhibit 152: XmR Charts of In-Process Inventory.

Table 150: July Inventory Management Report

	This Month			% Diff. This Time Last Year	Year to Date		% Diff. From Plan	% Diff From Last Year
	Actual	Monthly Plan	% Diff From Plan		Avg. Year to Date	Plan		
In Process Inventory	28	19.7	+42	+12	21.6	19.7	+9.6	+5.9

Table 151: In-Process Inventory Levels

	Year 1	Year 2	Year 3
Jan.	19	20	20
Feb.	27	22	15
March	20	19	27
April	16	16	25
May	18	22	17
June	25	19	19
July	22	25	28
August	24	22	
Sept.	17	18	
Oct.	25	20	
Nov.	15	16	
Dec.	17	17	

Exhibit 152: XmR Charts of In-Process Inventory

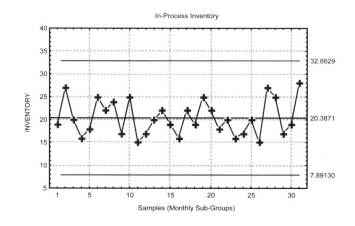

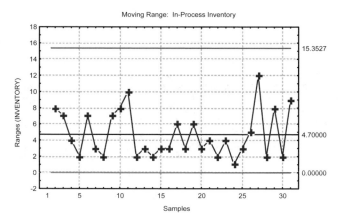

The control charts present a clear picture. In-process inventory levels are stable. The current system is capable of producing in-process levels anywhere from zero to roughly $32.9 million. Any in-process inventory levels within this range are simply the normal functioning of the system.

The management report presented in Table 150 implies that management should do something. After all, inventory levels this month are 42 percent above plan. Likewise, year-to-date levels are 9.6 percent over plan. The fundamental question is: "What should be done?"

The control charts make it clear that improving performance in this case requires redesign of the in-process inventory management and production system. This is because the control chart indicates that the system is operating under chance or common causes alone. The variation is part of the system. This means if you don't like the variation you see, you will have to change the system that produced it. Management action directed at "*getting those numbers down*" will likely have only the shortest-term effects (if any effect at all).

THE *X-BAR, R* CHART

With the *XmR* chart, there was a natural single measure for each sub-group. In contrast, with the *X-bar, R* chart, there are multiple measures for each sub-group. Instead of plotting these multiple measures, however, the average for each sub-group is plotted. If four measures or samples for each sub-group were taken, for example, these values would be added up, divided by four and then plotted. On the ranges chart, the difference between the highest and lowest values for each sub-group is plotted, rather than the moving range like with the *XmR* chart.

As was the case with the *XmR* chart, there are really two control charts at work here. They are the *X-bar* ($\overline{X}$) chart for the sub-group averages and the *R* chart for the ranges. Both the *X-bar* and *R* charts are control charts. The *X-bar* chart is looking for special causes of variation between the sub-groups. The *R* chart is looking for special causes of variation within the sub-group measurements. If the *R* chart is not in control or stable, the results for the *X-bar* chart will not be valid.

The reason for this goes back the to original definition of a rational sub-group. Recall that the intent of rational sub-grouping is to capture common cause variation within the sub-group, exposing the special or assignable cause variation between sub-groups. If special cause variation is showing up within sub-groups, then we have a problem that needs to be resolved before attempting to analyze the *X-bar* chart.

GUIDELINES TO USAGE

The *X-bar, R* chart plots sub-group averages (means) and sub-group ranges and is the most commonly used chart for the analysis of measured data, especially in manufacturing environments. Some important considerations for where to use the chart:

▲ **Creating rational sub-groups must be both possible and practical.** The $\overline{X}$ chart plots averages for the sub-groups, and the R chart plots ranges within each sub-group. The control chart assumes that Shewhart's principle of grouping like data within sub-groups in a rational way has been adhered to. (Remember Shewhart's principle that sub-groups should reflect some real world conditions.) The sub-group size and sampling method should be chosen to minimize the chance of special cause variations occurring within the sub-group, and to maximize the chance of special cause variations occurring among the sub-groups. Remember, like data is required in each sub-group.

▲ **How many observations are enough?** Each sub-group should contain the same number of observations (measurements) – the sample size should be constant. A sample size of between three and six per sub-group is most common and usually adequate. There are no absolute rules dictating sample size. It will depend upon the process being ana-

lyzed and other considerations, including the time and money involved in the data collection effort.

▲ **What if your sample size is not constant?** At times, it is simply not possible to hold sample sizes constant. Measurements obtained through automatic measuring devices typically measure every occurrence (hold time for every call as an example) but where the sample size varies considerably in each sub-group (time period). There are three solutions. First, take a random sample from the data of four or five from each sub-group and then use the *X-bar, R* chart to analyze the data. Second, analyze the overall average for each sub-group using the *XmR* chart. Third, use the *X-bar, s* chart.

CONSTRUCTION STEPS

Construction of the *X-bar, R* chart is somewhat more complicated than the *XmR* chart because of the multiple measures per sub-group. However, as was the case with the *XmR* chart, creating the *X-bar, R* chart comes down to a 10-step process.

1. Collect and organize the data

The team needs to determine what it wants to accomplish with the chart and the nature of the rational sub-groups. Moreover, for each sub-group, the team needs to decide how many measurements will be taken – the sample size needs to be determined. Generally, 20 sub-groups should be created if the data is based on time periods. If there are 20 sub-groups and the sample size for each sub-group is five, there will be a total of 100 measurements. This data should be organized into a table that clearly defines the sub-groups and the sample logic. Like the *XmR* chart, some basic tasks are:

▶ **Deciding what to measure.** Decide what to measure and provide an operational definition. What will be measured? How is the metric defined? What is the measuring stick used? What does this metric represent; that is, what is the quality characteristic we are after?

▶ **Design the sample.** Decide how those taking the measurements will decide which object will be measured. Refer back to the data-gathering principles if necessary. There must be a clear and objective way of selecting the objects to avoid individuals influencing the results, such as selecting only those objects that "look good."

▶ **Set up data-collection forms.** Make sure clear, concise data-collection forms or check-sheets are established, and those doing the data gathering know how to use them. Because we are taking measurements, it is important to record additional information that may affect the measurements taken. Who took the measurement? When was the measurement taken? Were there any special circumstances? This data needs to be captured along with the measurements themselves.

▶ **Perform the sampling and record measurements.** Be sure to record the data in the order in which the sample occurs. If the sub-groups basically represent time periods, a minimum of 20 periods should be analyzed. However, familiarity with the process being analyzed is still the most important factor to consider when determining the actual number of data points.

2. Calculate the sub-group averages

With the data gathered and organized, the next task is to compute the averages for each sub-group. This is what will eventually be plotted on the *X-bar* chart. Add the measurements within each sub-group and divide by the number of measurements (sample size). Continue calculating the average for every sub-group, recording the results on the sheet or form containing the data.

3. Calculate the centerline for the sub-group averages

The overall mean of the sub-group averages will form the centerline on the *X-bar* chart. Add up the sub-group averages and divide by the number of sub-groups to get this overall mean or centerline value. The result would be the same if you added all the observations and divided by the number of observations.

$$Centerline(\bar{x}-bar) = \frac{\Sigma\bar{x}}{k}$$

Where:
$\bar{x}$ = sub-group mean
k = number of sub-groups

This overall mean is referred to as bar-x-bar or x-bar, bar.

4. Determine the ranges

The ranges are the difference between the largest value and the smallest value in each sub-group. The result will always be positive and should be entered on the form with the data and sub-group averages. It is these values that will be plotted on the *R* (range) chart.

5. Calculate the centerline for the ranges (*R-bar*)

Simply add up all the ranges you calculated for each sub-group and divide by the number of sub-groups to get the mean range or *R-bar*. This will determine where the center line for the *R* chart is placed.

$$Centerline(\bar{R}) = \frac{\Sigma R}{k}$$

Where:
R = sub-group range
$\bar{R}$ = the mean of the subgroup ranges
k = number of subgroups

6. Create the scales and plot the data

The scales need to be set up for both the *X-bar* chart and the *R* chart. Traditional practices place the two charts on a single piece of paper, with the *X-bar* chart above the *R* chart. Remember to add some head room to the vertical axis to accommodate all the data plus the calculated control limits. Once set up, plot the data points and connect the points with a line.

7. Plot the center lines for both charts

Using the overall mean for sub-group averages (step 3), plot the centerline line on the *X-bar* chart. Similarly, using the mean for the ranges (step 5), plot the centerline on the *R* chart.

8. Determine and plot the control limits for the ranges

Always calculate the control limits for ranges first. If these are not in control there is little point in proceeding further. Calculating the control limits requires use of a special table of control limit factors presented in Table 144: Control Chart Factors.

Calculating the control limits for the ranges, the formulas are:

$$UCL_R = D_4 \times \bar{R}$$

$$LCL_R = D_3 \times \bar{R}$$

Where:
LCL_R = Lower Control Limit for the ranges

UCL_R = Upper Control Limit for the ranges
D_3 = A standard control chart factor
D_4 = A standard control chart factor

As was the case with the *XmR* chart, calculating control limits for the *R* chart involves using a factor and multiplying this factor by *R-bar*. The result is a control limit. In this case, the value of the factor (D_3 or D_4) depends on the size of each sub-group.

9. Interpret the statistical control for the ranges

If none of the ranges is beyond the control limit, then the ranges are in control and calculation can begin on the control limits for averages. If two or more ranges are outside the control limits, then there is simply too much special cause variation within the sub-groups for any meaningful analysis of the control chart. This again goes back to Shewhart's principles about sub-grouping – the sub-groups should contain common cause variation so that special cause can show through between sub-groups. If special causes are within the sub-groups, this principle has been violated, and resulting control limit calculations for the sub-group averages cannot be relied upon.

If only one of the ranges is beyond the control limit, you may want to eliminate this sub-group data and recalculate. If upon recalculation one or two points are out of control again, then the ranges are out of control and examination of the averages would not be productive. If the out-of-control condition disappears, it may well be reasonable to continue with the analysis and treat the one range as an isolated event.

10. Determine control limits for averages and interpret

If the ranges are in statistical control, then calculate the control limits for the averages. The formula are:

$$UCL_X = \overline{\overline{X}} + \left(A_2 \times \overline{R} \right)$$
$$LCL_X = \overline{\overline{X}} - \left(A_2 \times \overline{R} \right)$$

Where:
X-bar, bar = Overall mean for the data set (average of the averages)
A_2 = A standard control chart factor
R-bar = The mean of the ranges

Again, the value of A_2 is determined from the table of control limit factors and will vary with sub-group size. With the control limit values calculated, they can be plotted on the *X-bar* chart and interpretation of the results can proceed.

EXAMPLE OF CONSTRUCTION STEPS: SERVICE TURNAROUND TIME

The computer department of a major company is attempting to measure its performance and service levels to internal customers. A key performance characteristic is turnaround time. This is defined as the time between the processing request being made and the report being delivered to the client.

Step 1: Collecting the data. The department processes hundreds of requests every week and measuring the turnaround time on all reports would be simply too expensive. They decide to take a sample of four reports each day, with the requests arriving closest to 8:45 a.m., 10:30 a.m., 1:45 p.m. and 3:30 p.m. being selected for the sample. As such, the sample size is four. They continue taking the sample for 20 days, making 20 sub-groups. The results are presented in Table 153: Data From Processing Time Study.

Step 2: Calculate sub-group means (averages). These have also been detailed in Table 153. The sub-group means are simply the average of the four samples recorded for each sub-group (sub-groups are organized on a daily basis – each day is a sub-group). In this case, Day 1 has a sub-group average of

Table 153: Data From Processing Time Study

Day (Sub-Group)	Sample 1	Sample 2	Sample 3	Sample 4	Sub-Group Sum	Sub-Group Mean (X-Bar)	Range
1	40	18	50	38	146	36.5	32
2	19	22	22	52	115	28.75	33
3	35	23	35	37	130	32.5	14
4	32	43	38	29	142	35.5	14
5	41	10	18	44	113	28.25	34
6	35	29	21	35	120	30	14
7	23	27	25	40	115	28.75	17
8	33	33	45	16	127	31.75	29
9	24	30	29	16	99	24.75	14
10	15	27	44	26	112	28	29
11	25	29	34	13	101	25.25	21
12	30	36	42	50	158	39.5	20
13	16	27	37	32	112	28	21
14	34	24	49	11	118	29.5	38
15	35	41	39	21	136	34	20
16	29	33	30	33	125	31.25	4
17	40	34	44	18	136	34	26
18	32	44	16	28	120	30	28
19	15	33	11	27	86	21.5	22
20	33	39	29	12	113	28.25	27
Sum						606	457
Grand Mean.						30.3	22.85

36.5. This is simply the sum of values for that day (totaling 146) divided by the number of samples (4).

Step 3: Calculate the overall mean for sub-group means. The overall average is 30.3. This is simply the sum of all the sub-group averages divided by the number of sub-groups. In this case, 606 divided by 20 which equals 30.3.

Step 4: Determine the ranges. The ranges are the largest values less the smallest values recorded in each sub-group. For sub-group 1, this is 32 (40 minus 12). This is the range recorded for Day 1. These calculations are made for each sub-group are shown in Table 153 in the Range column.

Step 5: Calculate the mean for the ranges (*R-bar*). Once the ranges for all the sub-groups are determined, they are totaled and then divided by the number of sub-groups to yield an average for the ranges. In this case the total was 457 which, divided by 20, yields an average of 22.85. This is *R-bar*.

Step 6: Create the scales and plot the data. With basic statistics calculated, the *X-bar* and *R* charts can be created and the data points plotted. Remember, for the *X-bar* chart we are plotting the sub-group averages. In the *R* chart, the ranges for each sub-group are being plotted.

Step 7: Plot the average lines. Once the data is plotted, the average lines can be drawn in. For the *X-bar* chart, this will be

30.3, the value calculated in step 3. For the *R* chart, the value will be 22.85, the value calculated in step 5.

Step 8: Determine the control limits for the ranges. The control limit for the ranges is the factor D_4 times *R-bar*. In this case, the factor D_4 is equal to 2.28 (see Table 144: Control Chart Factors with a sub-group size of 4). 2.28 times *R-bar* (22.85) equals 52.098 or about 52.1. This is the upper control limit for the ranges and it is drawn on the *R* chart.

Step 9: Interpret the statistical control for the ranges. As is detailed in Exhibit 154: The 10 Steps of Creating the X-bar, R Chart, the *R* chart is in statistical control. None of the sub-groups displays values greater than the control limit.

Step 10: Determine control limits for the averages, plot and interpret. Again a factor is used to calculate three sigma. In this case, the factor is A_2. Multiplying A_2 (0.73) by *R-bar* (22.85) we get 16.68. This value is then added to *x-bar* and subtracted from it to get the upper and lower control limits. This would make the upper control limit 30.3 + 16.68 or 46.98, and the lower control limit 30.3 - 16.68 or 13.62.

As detailed in Exhibit 154: The 10 Steps of Creating the X-bar, R Chart, all the sub-group averages are within the upper and lower control limits, meaning the system is stable, reliable and operating under chance causes alone. It has a defined operating performance level.

THE *X*-BAR, *s* CHART

Construction of the $\overline{X}$, *s* chart is conceptually the same as the construction of the $\overline{X}$, *R*. With the $\overline{X}$, *R*, ranges are calculated for each sub-group, $\overline{R}$ is calculated and a suitable factor applied to $\overline{R}$ to determine the three sigma limits. With the $\overline{X}$, *s* chart, standard deviation is calculated for each sub-group rather than the range. The sub-group values for *s* are used to calculate $\overline{s}$. Again, appropriate factors are applied to $\overline{s}$ determine the three sigma limits for both the $\overline{X}$ and *s* charts.

With the $\overline{X}$, *s* chart, however, we are calculating sigma directly. The factors applied to determine the three sigma limits are essentially bias correction factors adjusting for small sample (sub-group) size. As sub-group sample size grows, the bias correction factors approach 1.0 and the calculation of three sigma limit consists of multiplying $\overline{s}$ by three and adding this

Exhibit 154: The 10 Steps of Creating the *X-bar, R* Chart

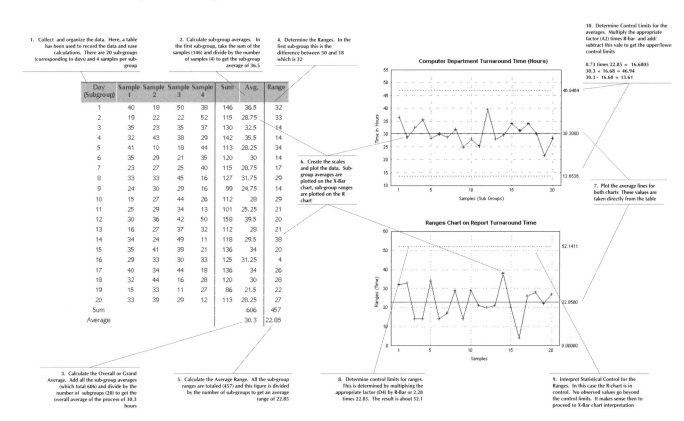

1. Collect and organize the data. Here, a table has been used to record the data and ease calculations. There are 20 sub-groups (corresponding to days) and 4 samples per sub-group

2. Calculate sub-group averages. In the first sub-group, take the sum of the samples (146) and divide by the number of samples (4) to get the sub-group average of 36.5

4. Determine the Ranges. In the first sub-group this is the difference between 50 and 18 which is 32

10. Determine Control Limits for the averages. Multiply the appropriate factor (A2) times R-bar and add/subtract this vale to get the upper/lower control limits

0.73 times 22.85 = 16.6805
30.3 + 16.68 = 46.94
30.3 - 16.68 = 13.61

Day (Subgroup)	Sample 1	Sample 2	Sample 3	Sample 4	Sum	Avg.	Range
1	40	18	50	38	146	36.5	32
2	19	22	22	52	115	28.75	33
3	35	23	35	37	130	32.5	14
4	32	43	38	29	142	35.5	14
5	41	10	18	44	113	28.25	34
6	35	29	21	35	120	30	14
7	23	27	25	40	115	28.75	17
8	33	33	45	16	127	31.75	29
9	24	30	29	16	99	24.75	14
10	15	27	44	26	112	28	29
11	25	29	34	13	101	25.25	21
12	30	36	42	50	158	39.5	20
13	16	27	37	32	112	28	21
14	34	24	49	11	118	29.5	38
15	35	41	39	21	136	34	20
16	29	33	30	33	125	31.25	4
17	40	34	44	18	136	34	26
18	32	44	16	28	120	30	28
19	15	33	11	27	86	21.5	22
20	33	39	29	12	113	28.25	27
Sum						606	457
Average						30.3	22.85

6. Create the scales and plot the data. Sub-group averages are plotted on the X-Bar chart, sub-group ranges are plotted on the R chart

Computer Department Turnaround Time (Hours)

46.9464

30.3000

13.6536

7. Plot the average lines for both charts These values are taken directly from the table

Ranges Chart on Report Turnaround Time

52.1411

22.8500

0.00000

3. Calculate the Overall or Grand Average. Add all the sub-group averages (which total 606) and divide by the number of subgroups (20) to get the overall average of the process of 30.3 hours

5. Calculate the Average Range. All the sub-group ranges are totaled (457) and this figure is divided by the number of sub-groups to get an average range of 22.85

8. Determine control limits for ranges. This is determined by multiplying the appropriate factor (D4) by R-Bar or 2.28 times 22.85. The result is about 52.1

9. Interpret Statistical Control for the Ranges. In this case the R-chart is in control. No observed values go beyond the control limits. It makes sense then to proceed to X-Bar chart interpretation

to, and subtracting it from, $\overline{X}$ to determine the three-sigma limit.

APPLICATIONS

The $\overline{X}$, s chart has traditionally found limited application in performance measurement. This is because of the wide applicability of the *XmR* chart or the ease of holding sample size constant and relatively small in most manufacturing applications. However, the $\overline{X}$, s chart is finding growing application in service and technology industries, where large amounts of data are often maintained in corporate data bases. Some typical analytical examples include:

▲ **Analyzing customer or employee satisfaction data over time.** Typically, each year or application of the survey is treated as a sub-group, with an important consideration being whether the performance characteristics (some measure of satisfaction or loyalty) are improving. Literally hundreds or thousands of measures are taken in each sub-group (respondents) and these likely vary with each survey.

▲ **Analyzing performance of a network.** For example, call switching over time. A switch or other network device might handle thousands of calls daily (sub-group), and a critical monitoring function is establishing how the switch is functioning over time to assess the likelihood of a crash.

▲ **Assessing the performance of call centers.** Call centers typically sub-group their operating day into 15-minute intervals. Thousands of calls are handled within each 15-minute segment, but the volume of calls within each segment is never the same (sample size is greater than 10 and unequal). Performance is measured within these sub-groups across a number of metrics – time to answer, call drop-off rate, time to completion and call volume. Data on these metrics is automatically recorded within the call handling system. $\overline{X}$, s charts are used to analyze the data and provide superior tracking of system performance and identification of special and common causes of variation.

In summary, the $\overline{X}$, s chart is finding broader application in those areas where large amounts of data are automatically captured. In these circumstances, the $\overline{X}$, s chart is often the perfect tool to reduce the complexity of these large data sets and provide decision makers with meaningful analysis of the data at hand.

CONSTRUCTING ATTRIBUTE CONTROL CHARTS

Attribute control charts are trickier to use than measured control charts. The reasons for this have to do with the nature of counted data. Some of the specific issues are:

▶ Sample Sizes

▶ Operational Definitions

▶ Distributional Assumptions

SAMPLE SIZE: TO ANALYZE COUNT DATA, YOU MUST FIND SOMETHING TO COUNT

For attribute control charts to work effectively, sample sizes must be large enough to find occurrences or units to count. There are two basic guidelines to use in determining whether the sample size is large enough. These guidelines are:

▲ The sample should be large enough to find occurrences or units with the characteristic of interest in at least 90 percent, and preferably 100 percent, of the sub-groups. In other words, essentially every sub-group should have a unit or occurrence of interest in the sample.

▲ The average count per sample should be at least one. If it is less than one, the control chart will be insensitive, meaning sample size will have to be increased significantly for the chart to differentiate special and common cause variation.

If the sample size is too small and defects are rarely found, the attribute control charts will reveal little. There will be many points plotted at zero; the average line will be near zero as will the control limits. The first point where some defect(s) actually shows up will likely show up as a spike, rising above the upper control limit and so indicating a special cause of variation where none in fact exists.

Unfortunately, this means there is a price to be paid for having a well-performing process. This is because the better the process, the fewer defects produced. And the fewer the defects, the larger the sample will have to be to find them.

OPERATIONAL DEFINITIONS: WHEN IS A BLEMISH A BLEMISH?

The second issue with attribute control charts is the difficulty in establishing clear operational definitions. Consider counting blemishes on a painted surface. When does some minor variation in the finish stop being a minor variation, and become a blemish? Or a scratch? Would all operators or inspectors see it the same way?

Establishing operational definitions for attribute data, then, may be difficult. With measured data, the issue is relatively straightforward – specify the gauge or measuring stick, and the way it is to be applied to an object, and you have a basic operational definition. But the operational definitions of an attribute may evolve over time, as inspectors or operators develop an improved understanding of just when a blemish is a blemish and when it is not. In short, definitions of attributes may take time to develop.

DISTRIBUTIONAL ASSUMPTIONS: THE DATA MUST BE THE RIGHT TYPE OF DATA

Unlike measured or variables control charts, attribute control charts assume an underlying statistical distribution. If the data being analyzed in the attribute control chart doesn't conform to the appropriate distributional assumptions, the chart will not work effectively.

For p- and np-charts (proportions) the assumed distribution is the binomial distribution. A binomial distribution is simply one where values can only take on one of two possible values. Recall that p- and np-charts deal with classifications of units. Typically, the classification is of the unit being defective or not This fits with the binomial distribution since only two possible classifications exist – the unit is defective or it isn't.

The critical assumptions for p and np are:

▲ **Sub-group samples are consistent.** The probability that any item in the sub-group has the attribute being counted must be the same for all items in the sub-group.

▲ **The likelihood of an item possessing an attribute is not affected by whether the preceding item possessed the**

attribute. This means it is assumed that the attribute being counted doesn't occur in bunches.

Likewise, *c*- and *u*-charts also assume an underlying statistical distribution, although in this case it is the Poisson model. The Poisson distribution describes those situations where counts of objects or occurrences are made within an area of opportunity (rates), and where the number of occurrences is relatively rare compared to what might be. This is the case with both *c*- and *u*-charts.

The critical assumptions for the *c*- and *u*-charts are:

▲ **Sub-group samples are consistent.** The likelihood of an attribute occurring is proportional to the area of opportunity for the specific sub-group.

▲ **The attributes in question are rare.** They are rare, relative to the area of opportunity or what might be.

It is important, in the proper application of attribute control charts, that the relevant statistical distributions hold in each case – binomial distribution with *np*- and *p*-charts and Poisson distribution with *c*- and *u*-charts. If the assumptions made by these statistical distributions don't hold, the attribute control chart should not be used.

I'm not sure if the assumptions hold, now what?

At times, you will have attribute data but the assumptions for their use will not hold or the team is unsure if they hold or not. What do you do?

The good news is there is a solution. When unsure about the applicability of an attribute control chart, convert your counts to a common base (a proportion or a rate) and use the Individuals, Moving R (*XmR*) chart to analyze the results.[68] Because this chart makes no assumption about the underlying distribution of the data, (or is robust to distributional assumptions), it can be used to analyze attribute data. It doesn't matter if you are analyzing incidents or units, the *XmR* chart will provide a good analysis of the data.

What about ratios?

All count data arise from an area of opportunity or sample – meaning count data is inherently compound data. For example, we don't just count defective units, but rather, we count the

---

68. See: Wheeler, Donald J. and Chambers, David S.; Understanding Statistical Process Control, for a detailed discussion of this approach and why it works. For those who don't care why it works but are thankful it does, you don't have to worry about it.

number of defective units out of the total number of units produced. The attribute charts described deal with proportions and rates – compound data where there is a physical or rational connection between numerator and denominator. Where this rational connection exists, attribute control charts work effectively.

However, we may be confronted with ratios, especially those ratios where numerator and denominator are not connected in some rational way. In these circumstances, use of attribute control charts is not appropriate. With ratios, use the *XmR* chart and if unsure about the degree to which the numerator and denominator are connected, chart the data for numerator and denominator separately again through the *XmR* chart.

BASIC FORMULAS

Measured or variables control charts always came in pairs, one chart for the x-values or variable of interest and a second chart for the dispersion. However, only one chart is required for attribute control charts – there is no separate chart to present the dispersion. Whatever proportion, count or rate is being pre-

sented is simply plotted on the chart and the centerline and control limits are calculated and plotted.

Nevertheless, attribute control charts throw in their own peculiar wrinkle here. While only one chart is required, there are two different types of charts – those with a single three-sigma value (the upper or lower control limit is represented by a straight line) or those with different three-sigma values for each sub-group (multiple control limits are plotted).

Generally, multiple control limits are used when the sample size in each sub-group varies as is the case with *p*- and *u*-charts. Single values control limits are used when the sample size remain constant as is the case with *np* and *c*-charts.

The different types of attribute control charts along with their respective formulas are presented in Table 155: Attribute or Counted Data Control Charts.

Table 155: Attribute or Counted Data Control Charts

Chart Name	Center line (mean)	3 Sigma	Sample	Data	Distribution	Chart Example
np	$\frac{\Sigma np}{k}$:	$3\sqrt{\overline{np}\left(1-\frac{\overline{np}}{n}\right)}$	constant sub-group sample size	count of units	binomial	
c	$\frac{\Sigma c}{k}$	$3\sqrt{\overline{c}}$	constant sub-group sample size	count of incidents	Poisson	
p	$\frac{\Sigma p}{k}$	$3\sqrt{\frac{\overline{p}(1-\overline{p})}{n}}$	variable sub-group sample size	proportion of units	binomial	
u	$\frac{\Sigma u}{k}$	$3\sqrt{\frac{\overline{u}}{n}}$	variable sub-group sample size	rate of incidents	Poisson	

COUNTING THE NUMBER DEFECTIVE – THE *NP*-CHART

The *np*-chart is used to analyze the proportion of units having a certain characteristic. Usually, this characteristic is in the form of a 'defective' unit. Examples include the number of units failing inspection, the number of products returned under warranty, or the number of customers expressing dissatisfaction with the service provided.

In all of these cases, it would be reasonable to believe that each unit has an equal chance of being 'defective.' Under these circumstances, the np-chart can be used to analyze the performance of the system. The unit characteristic analyzed with the np-chart doesn't have to be of negative quality. It could also be used to analyze the number of customers expressing complete satisfaction with a product or service. The basic requirement is that we are dealing with a situation that is 'yes' or 'no', on or off, and where it is reasonable to believe that each unit stands the same chance of having the characteristic we are looking for.

The *np*-chart is used only when sample sizes are held constant. Therefore, the chart is more commonly used when improvement teams have the opportunity to design the data collection procedure from scratch. Rarely will teams come across existing data where a constant sample size has been controlled and is sufficient to gather observations of interest to the team. If the sample size is not constant, use the *p*-chart.

CONSTRUCTION

Construction of the *np*-chart consists of five basic steps.

1. Gather and organize the data

Determine what to measure and give it an operational definition. Are you counting defective units? Great, but what constitutes a defective unit? Do all those doing the counting interpret a defective unit the same way? Those collecting the data must have this clear. Once we know what to measure, then we need to:

▶ **Design the sample.** Remember the requirements of lot size when dealing with the attribute chart. It must be large enough to find something. Because constant sample size is required, some care is needed to ensure there is a reasonable chance that a unit of interest will be observed in each lot.

▶ **Set up data-collection forms.** Make sure clear, concise data-collection forms or check-sheets are established, and those doing the data gathering know how to use them. Because the sample size is constant, you need to only record the number of units of interest observed in each lot or sub-group. But the sample size still needs to be recorded somewhere on the form, because it will be needed when analyzing the data.

▶ **Perform the sampling and record measurements.** Be sure to record the data in the order in which the sample occurs. The number of lots or sub-groups is largely dependent upon the nature of the data being gathered and studied. For example, with data gathered daily, consideration should be given to having the number of sub-groups exceed the number of days in a month. This is just in case some special causes of variation creep in to the process at certain times of the month. Decisions of this nature need to be based on the experience of those most familiar with the process. They are decisions best made by the improvement team in consultation with employees. At a minimum, however, collect 20 lots when sub-groups represent time periods.

2. Determine the axes and plot the data

Once the data is gathered, the size of the axes can be determined. The sub-groups are marked along the horizontal axis. The vertical axis is used to plot the number of units with the characteristic of interest. Setting up the vertical axis, therefore, requires finding the smallest and largest value in the data and adding a little headroom. Usually, the minimum is set at zero. The maximum of the axis is usually about 25 percent higher than the largest value observed. Once the axes are set up the data can be plotted and the points connected with a line.

3. Calculate and plot the average

Next, the average or the value of $\overline{np}$ is calculated. This involves adding up the values in the data and dividing by the number of values – the simple calculation of the mean. The formula is:

$$Centerline(\overline{np}) = \frac{\Sigma np}{k}$$

Where:
$\overline{np}$ = the mean for np
np = number of defective units in each sub-group
k = number of sub-groups

Once the value of $\overline{np}$ or the average number of defective units is calculated, the centerline on the control chart can be drawn.

4. Calculate and plot the control limits

The calculation of the control limits is often seen as a more daunting task than calculating the centerline, if only because the formula appears much more complex. The formulas are:

$$LCL_{np} = \overline{np} - 3\sqrt{\overline{np}\left(1 - \frac{\overline{np}}{n}\right)}$$

$$UCL_{np} = \overline{np} + 3\sqrt{\overline{np}\left(1 - \frac{\overline{np}}{n}\right)}$$

Where:
LCL_{np} = Lower Control Limit for np
UCL_{np} = Upper Control Limit for np
$\overline{np}$ = the mean of np values (the average calculated in step 3)
n = the sample size (number of values in each sub-group)

Don't let the formula scare you – it is not as complicated as it looks. There are only two numbers in the formula, $\overline{np}$, which is the average you have already calculated, and *n*, which is the sub-group sample size. Detailed calculations are shown in the examples provided. Note the presence of the number three in

the calculation. Everything under the square root sign is multiplied by three. This is because you are creating a three-sigma limit. Once the values for the control limits are calculated they can be plotted on the control chart.

5. Analyze the chart

The standard set of interpretive procedures can be applied to the np-chart. Observing the chart for the basic control limit test (any points going beyond the control limits) is the first step. Equally important, however, is analyzing the chart for runs and specific patterns. As mentioned, it is important that the team identifies the basic rules it will apply before interpretation, because applying all the rules all the time is bound to find 'something.' Understand what you are looking for before you begin interpretation.

EXAMPLE OF NP-CHART: CUSTOMER SATISFACTION

A utility company is measuring its in-home service through a telephone-based customer satisfaction survey. Each month 100 homes are surveyed. Each customer is asked the degree to which he or she was satisfied along a five-point scale. Those respondents indicating a satisfaction level of '1' (completely dissatisfied) or '2' (dissatisfied) along this scale are treated together as service 'failures.' It is the proportion of service failures the company tracks as part of its performance measurement system. Therefore, there are only two possible conditions, a service success (where the level of satisfaction expressed was a '3', '4', or '5' along the five-point scale) or a service failure (with a expressed level of satisfaction being '1' or '2').

The *np*-chart is used here because we are dealing with a constant sample size (100) and we are concerned with each unit (customer), identifying them as satisfied or not. The number or proportion of dissatisfied customers is tracked and analyzed through the *np*-chart. The data for the past 20 months is provided.

The calculations here are straightforward. It boils down to calculating the average number of complaints and then calculating the control limits. The average number of complaints is easy. We simply add up the total complaints for the 20 months and divide by the number of months.

$$Centerline(\overline{np}) = \frac{\Sigma np}{k} = \frac{121}{20} = 6.05$$

Table 156: Customer Satisfaction Data

Month	Sample Size (*n*)	Not Satisfied (*np*)
1	100	4
2	100	12
3	100	3
4	100	8
5	100	0
6	100	9
7	100	6
8	100	10
9	100	8
10	100	4
11	100	2
12	100	3
13	100	6
14	100	4
15	100	8
16	100	0
17	100	8
18	100	6
19	100	8
20	100	12
Sum	2000	121
Mean	100	6.05

Now for the upper and lower control limits. The average number of customers not satisfied $(\overline{np})$ was 6.05. The sample size or *n* was 100. These values are substituted in the basic *np*-chart control limits as follows:

$$Control\ Limits\ =\ \overline{np} \pm 3 \sqrt{\overline{np}\left(1 - \frac{\overline{np}}{n}\right)}$$

$$Control\ Limits\ =\ 6.05 \pm 3 \sqrt{6.05\left(1 - \frac{6.05}{100}\right)}$$

$$Control\ Limits\ =\ 6.05 \pm 3 \sqrt{6.05(1 - 0.0605)}$$

$$Control\ Limits\ =\ 6.05 \pm 3 \sqrt{5.68}$$

$$Control\ Limits\ =\ 6.05 \pm 7.15$$

The basic steps are: divide 6.05 by 100. Take this result and subtract it from 1.0. This leaves you with 0.9395. Multiply this by 6.05 (giving you 5.68). Then take the square root which leaves you with about 2.38 which is one sigma. Multiply this by three (to get three sigma) and you have 7.15. This is the amount that is added to, and subtracted from, the centerline to obtain the upper and lower control limits.

So the upper control limit is 13.2 (7.15 added to 6.05). The

lower control limit is 6.05 less 7.15 which is less than zero, so the control limit is simply set at this natural limit of 0.0.

Exhibit 157: *np*-chart of Customers Expressing Dissatisfaction

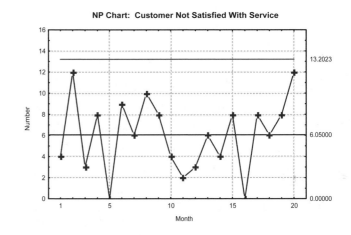

The final result? The system of service and delivery has a defined capability, in terms of the level of customer satisfaction as measured by the survey, because the system is operating under common causes only. For every 100 service calls, the system will produce about six dissatisfied customers. On a monthly basis, this may rise as high as 13 out of 100, or fall to as low as zero.

ANALYZING PROPORTIONS: THE *P*-CHART

A p-chart plots the percent or fraction of units with a specific characteristic. We are dealing with the fraction of units because the p-chart is used when sample sizes are unequal. Reporting the simple number of units (as was the case with the *np*-chart) would be misleading if the sample sizes producing these counts varied. The *p*-chart takes the varying sample sizes into account. It takes the number of units of interest in each sub-group, and divides these by the sample size in each sub-group to get a proportion of units per sub-group. These sub-group proportions are plotted rather than the physical counts. For this reason, the values plotted on the *p*-chart must always be between zero and one.

CONSTRUCTION

Because the sample sizes vary, the *p*-chart requires separately calculated control limits for each lot or sub-group. However, from a practical standpoint, if the sample sizes do not vary by more than 20 percent, a single set of control limits can be calculated. Therefore, two construction procedures are presented. The first is for when the sample size varies by more than 20 percent, requiring separate control limits. The second procedure is for when sample size varies by less than 20 percent.

Procedure 1: Unequal sample sizes

1. **Gather and organize the data**. Decide what to measure. This requires the team to decide on what is important. What will be the characteristic of interest and what will be the operational definition of this characteristic so that data can actually be gathered? After this the team must:

    ▶ **Design the sample.** Remember the requirements of lot size when dealing with the attribute chart. It must be large enough to find something – preferably in every sub-group. Even though constant sample size is not required, teams should still pay careful attention to the sampling method. Even the smallest samples should stand a reasonable chance of finding a unit of interest.

▶ **Set up data-collection forms.** Make sure clear, concise data-collection forms or check-sheets are established, and those doing the data gathering know how to use them. Because the sample size varies, you must ensure there is an opportunity to record the number of observations of interest in each sample, as well as the size of each sample.

▶ **Perform the sampling and record measurements.** Be sure to record the data in the order in which the sample occurs. If the sub-groups basically represent time periods, a minimum of 20 periods should be analyzed. The advice for the *np*-chart also applies here. Familiarity with the process being analyzed is still the most important factor to consider when determining the actual number of data points.

▶ **Calculate the proportion for each lot.** As data is collected, the proportion should be calculated. This is done by taking the number of units of interest observed in each sub-group and dividing by the sample or sub-group size. It is good practice to calculate these proportions at the time the data is gathered. Such calcula-

tions are required if those in the field are plotting the data in real time, as opposed to having things calculated and plotted somewhere else. Moreover, calculating proportions at the time the data is collected introduces some redundancy in case a figure becomes smudged or there are problems interpreting an individual's handwriting.

2. **Set up the axes and plot the data.** Axes are set up as discussed with other control charts. The data plotted is the proportion data, not the actual counts. Be careful to plot the correct data set. Because you are plotting proportions, you should have no result above 1.0 or 100 percent. These values express the practical limits of the "y" axis of the *p*-chart.

With the chart set up and the proportions calculated for each sub-group, the values for p can now be plotted on the chart. This is done precisely the same way as for the run chart. Once the data is plotted, connect the dots with a line.

3. **Calculate and plot the mean of *p* (*p-bar*).** Now the mean (average) of *p* can be calculated. This is done by adding up all the units of interest in all the samples and dividing by the total of all sample sizes. As an alternative, the *p* values for all sub-groups can be totalled and then divided by the

number of sub-groups. Either calculation will give you the same result. The formula is given by:

$$Centerline(\bar{p}) = \frac{\Sigma np}{\Sigma n} \; or \; = \frac{\Sigma p}{k}$$

Where:
np = number defective or classification of interest for each sub-group
n = number in each sample for each sub-group
p = proportion for each sub-group
k = number of sub-groups

4. **Calculate and plot the control limits.** The formula used for the p-chart control limits is similar to that used for the *np*-chart. This is not surprising since both charts are based on the same theoretical distribution – the binomial. The primary difference with the p-chart is that we are calculating separate control limits for each sub-group. For each sub-group, the control limit is determined by:

$$Control \; Limits = \bar{p} \pm 3 \frac{\sqrt{\bar{p}(1-\bar{p})}}{\sqrt{n}}$$

Where:
$\bar{p}$ *= mean for p*
n = number in each sample for each sub-group

Note that $\bar{p}$ is used for every sub-group. The only unique number used in each calculation is the value of *n*, the sam-

ple size for that sub-group. Once the set of upper and lower control limits have been calculated for each sub-group, they can be plotted on the chart itself.

5. **Interpret the chart.** Interpretation of the p-chart is similar to that of other control charts and attribute charts specifically.

Procedure 2: Sample size varies by less than 20 percent

1. **Gather and organize the data.** The procedure for gathering the data is the same as that used for varying sample sizes, except the team must ensure the sample size does not vary by more than 20 percent. To determine this, find the largest sample size and subtract the smallest. Take this amount and divide by the smallest sample size. If the value you get is less than 0.20, the sample size variation is less than 20 percent.

2. **Set up the axes and plot the data.** Again the procedure is the same as for varying sample sizes. Remember, as a proportion the value of p will always be between zero and 1.0. This range should be a good enough for a first draft of your chart, so if unsure about an appropriate range for the vertical (y) axis, use zero to 1.0.

As was the case with unequal sample sizes, the data will likely be gathered not as pre-calculated proportions, but as numbers of units of interest and total number of units. The proportion for each sub-group (*p*) is calculated by dividing the units of interest by the total number of units.

3. **Calculate and plot the mean (average) proportion defective.** The average, too, is calculated as it was in the first procedure. Divide the total number of units of interest observed by the total of all the samples. Alternatively, divide the sum of the *p*'s for all sub-groups by the number of sub-groups.

$$Centerline(\bar{p}) \ = \ \frac{\Sigma np}{\Sigma n} \ or \ = \ \frac{\Sigma p}{k}$$

Where:
np = number defective or classification of interest for each sub-group
n = number in each sample for each sub-group
p = proportion for each sub-group
k = number of sub-groups

4. **Calculate and plot the control limits.** The formula used to plot the control limits is essentially the same as the formula used in the first procedure. Because we are calculating a single set of limits, we use the average or mean value of n (sample size) in the calculations rather than the spe-cific sample size for each sub-group. The specific formula is given by:

$$Control \ Limits \ = \ \bar{p} \pm 3 \frac{\sqrt{\bar{p}(1-\bar{p})}}{\sqrt{\bar{n}}}$$

Where:
$\bar{p}$ = mean for p
$\bar{n}$ = mean or average number in each sample for each sub-group

In the first procedure, the calculation is performed for each sub-group. Here once is enough. It is now easy to see why designing a data-collection effort that keeps sample sizes constant (or nearly so) is worth its weight in gold in terms of computational ease.

5. **Interpret the chart.** The chart is interpreted in the same manner described earlier for control charts. Some caution is warranted, however. This approach to the *p*-chart is basically a handy short-cut. If some observation is just outside the control limit, you may want to recalculate a separate control limit rather than jump to the conclusion that a definite signal of a special cause of variation has been detected. Exercise judgment in interpretation.

EXAMPLE OF *P*-CHART: ON-TIME DELIVERY RECORD

A company wants to examine its on-time delivery record. The president has received a number of phone calls from disgruntled customers complaining about late deliveries. At the president's request, a process improvement team has been set up to examine how to improve the on-time delivery record.

But how big is the problem? The team decides to pull all of the shipping records for the past 19 months and record the number of items shipped and the number arriving late. Their research produced the data presented in Table 158: Late Shipping Data and Calculations.

The *p*-chart was used because the improvement team was focused on units "defective" (the delivery is either late or it isn't), and the sample size (the number of units shipped) varied from month to month.

Individual control limits need to be created for each sub-group because the size of the sample varied by over 20 percent. This requires quite a bit of hand 'crunching' of the data. Statistical programs and spreadsheets help the process considerably.

First, the proportions need to be calculated. This is done by dividing the number of late shipments (*np*) by the total number shipped (*n*). For the first month, this means dividing 13 by 78 to produce a *p* value of 0.167. This is done for all the months for which data was collected. These points can now be plotted on the actual attribute control chart.

The next step involves calculating the overall average of *p* or $\bar{p}$ that will make up the center line on the control chart. At the bottom of the table, the total number of units shipped and the total number of units late are totaled. Dividing the total late (232) by the total shipped (1807) gives an average for *p* (*p-bar*) of 0.128.

Because the values vary by over 20 percent, individual control limits need to be calculated for each month (sub-group). The basic formula is used as described earlier. To remind you, it is:

$$Control\ Limits\ =\ \bar{p} \pm 3\frac{\sqrt{\bar{p}(1-\bar{p})}}{\sqrt{n}}$$

It looks harder than it is. It is really comprised of two parts. The first is used to calculate sigma. The second then multiplies this by three to obtain three sigma and adds it to, or subtracts it from, $\bar{p}$ to get the upper and lower control limit.

Table 158: Late Shipping Data and Calculations

	Data Collected		Calculations				
Month	Number of Shipments (*n*)	Late Shipments (*np*)	Proportion of Late Shipments (*p*)	Sigma (*s*)	Three Sigma (3*s*)	Lower Limit (*lcl*$_p$)	Upper Limit (*ucl*$_p$)
1	78	13	0.167	0.038	0.1136	0.0148	0.2420
2	96	9	0.094	0.034	0.1024	0.0260	0.2308
3	79	7	0.089	0.038	0.1129	0.0155	0.2413
4	104	16	0.154	0.033	0.0984	0.0300	0.2268
5	68	15	0.221	0.041	0.1217	0.0067	0.2501
6	79	11	0.139	0.038	0.1129	0.0155	0.2413
7	46	8	0.174	0.049	0.1479	-0.0196	0.2764
8	67	6	0.090	0.041	0.1226	0.0058	0.2510
9	133	17	0.128	0.029	0.0870	0.0414	0.2154
10	156	24	0.154	0.027	0.0803	0.0480	0.2087
11	189	23	0.122	0.024	0.0730	0.0554	0.2014
12	140	12	0.086	0.028	0.0848	0.0436	0.2132
13	109	8	0.073	0.032	0.0961	0.0323	0.2245
14	56	8	0.143	0.045	0.1341	-0.0057	0.2625
15	78	11	0.141	0.038	0.1136	0.0148	0.2420
16	103	18	0.175	0.033	0.0989	0.0295	0.2273
17	78	10	0.128	0.038	0.1136	0.0148	0.2420
18	50	3	0.060	0.047	0.1419	-0.0135	0.2703
19	98	13	0.133	0.034	0.1013	0.0270	0.2298
Sum	1807	232					
Average	95.105	12.211	0.128				

So for month 1, the calculation would be:

$$Control\ Limits\ =\ 0.128 \pm 3\frac{\sqrt{0.128(1-0.128)}}{\sqrt{78}}$$

$$Control\ Limits\ =\ 0.128 \pm 3\frac{\sqrt{0.116}}{\sqrt{78}}$$

$$Control\ Limits\ =\ 0.128 \pm 3(0.038)$$

$$Control\ Limits\ =\ 0.128 \pm 0.113$$

Note that it is the average for p ($\bar{p}$) that is used in the calculation for the first month. The only number specific to this sub-group is the sub-group sample size or n, which in this case is 78. Using the formula, sigma is calculated to be 0.038. You will see this number under sigma for month 1 of Table 147. Multiplying this number by three provides the three-sigma spread.

Add this three-sigma spread to $\bar{p}$ (0.128) to get the upper control limit, and subtract it from $\bar{p}$ to get the lower control limit. This process is repeated for each and every month until a complete set of upper and lower control limits has been calculated. These, too, can then be plotted on the control chart and interpretations initiated.

The resulting *p*-chart is presented in Exhibit 159: p-chart: Late Shipping. The first point to notice is that none of the data points goes beyond the control limit for each month. What does this tell us about the shipping system?

Exhibit 159: p-chart: Late Shipping

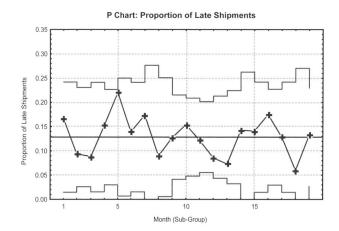

To begin with, the system is operating under a system of chance causes with no special causes of variation present. In short, the system appears stable. The system has and will likely continue to deliver about 12.8 percent of all its deliveries late.

We could turn this around and state the system will generally deliver 87.2 percent of all deliveries on time (12.8 percent is simply the proportion of 0.128 multiplied by 100).

If this is not acceptable to customers or to management, some physical changes to the shipping process will have to take place to see improvement occur. No amount of training, incentives or bullying will improve shipping time performance.

EXAMPLE OF *P*-CHART: EMPLOYEE ABSENTEEISM

A large company has become concerned with employee absenteeism rates. Management feels that too much time is being lost. A recent meeting of the management committee revealed that while everyone agrees absenteeism is too high, no one could agree on what the absenteeism rate is or why it is occurring.

The human resources department was given the responsibility of analyzing absenteeism and making recommendations to the management committee. The first step in the human resources department's efforts was providing an analysis of absenteeism rates over the past two years.

Personnel records going back some 24 months were used to gather these rates. The data as collected is provided in Table 160: Employee Absenteeism Data Table.

The good news is that because the sample sizes (employee days) did not vary by more than 20 percent, separate limits for each sub-group were not required. This makes the calculations simpler.

First, as was the case in the previous example, the proportion of absenteeism must be calculated. For each month, the number of absent days (np) must be divided by the total number of employee days (n) to determine the proportion absent (p).

Next, $\bar{p}$ or the overall average of absenteeism is calculated. This is done by taking the total number of absent days (143) and dividing by the total number of employee days (58,551) to get an average ($\bar{p}$) of 0.00244 or 0.244 percent.

Table 160: Employee Absenteeism Data Table

	Data Collected		Calculations				
Month	Employee Days (n)	Absent Days (np)	Proportion (p)	Sigma (s)	Three Sigma (3*s)	Lower Control Limit	Upper Control Limit
1	2300	4	0.00200	0.00100	0.00300	-0.00056	0.00544
2	2330	12	0.00500	0.00100	0.00300	-0.00056	0.00544
3	2401	3	0.00100	0.00100	0.00300	-0.00056	0.00544
4	2410	8	0.00300	0.00100	0.00300	-0.00056	0.00544
5	2390	0	0.00000	0.00100	0.00300	-0.00056	0.00544
6	2410	9	0.00400	0.00100	0.00300	-0.00056	0.00544
7	2415	6	0.00200	0.00100	0.00300	-0.00056	0.00544
8	2500	10	0.00400	0.00100	0.00300	-0.00056	0.00544
9	2490	8	0.00300	0.00100	0.00300	-0.00056	0.00544
10	2450	4	0.00200	0.00100	0.00300	-0.00056	0.00544
11	2430	2	0.00100	0.00100	0.00300	-0.00056	0.00544
12	2430	3	0.00100	0.00100	0.00300	-0.00056	0.00544
13	2430	6	0.00200	0.00100	0.00300	-0.00056	0.00544
14	2435	4	0.00200	0.00100	0.00300	-0.00056	0.00544
15	2430	8	0.00300	0.00100	0.00300	-0.00056	0.00544
16	2380	0	0.00000	0.00100	0.00300	-0.00056	0.00544
17	2390	8	0.00300	0.00100	0.00300	-0.00056	0.00544
18	2370	6	0.00300	0.00100	0.00300	-0.00056	0.00544
19	2470	8	0.00300	0.00100	0.00300	-0.00056	0.00544
20	2500	12	0.00500	0.00100	0.00300	-0.00056	0.00544
21	2550	10	0.00400	0.00100	0.00300	-0.00056	0.00544
22	2540	3	0.00100	0.00100	0.00300	-0.00056	0.00544
23	2550	8	0.00300	0.00100	0.00300	-0.00056	0.00544
24	2550	1	0.00000	0.00100	0.00300	-0.00056	0.00544
Sum	58551	143					
Average	2439.63	5.96	0.00244				

The next step is calculating sigma and the three-sigma spread to be added to, and subtracted from, the average for p. The control limit formula and the calculations are:

$$Control\ Limits\ =\ \bar{p} \pm 3\frac{\sqrt{\bar{p}(1-\bar{p})}}{\sqrt{n}}$$

$$Control\ Limits\ =\ 0.0024 \pm 3\frac{\sqrt{0.0024(1-0.0024)}}{\sqrt{2439.63}}$$

$$Control\ Limits\ =\ 0.0024 \pm 3(0.001)$$

$$Control\ Limits\ =\ 0.0024 \pm 0.003$$

The only tricky step in calculating the control limits is determining what value of n to use. In this case, simply use the average n or 2439.63 (the total number of employee days for the 24 months divided by 24).

The calculation only has to be done once because sigma and the three-sigma spread is the same for all months. Here again, the lower control limit is calculated as a negative number. Since the smallest number possible with proportions is zero, the lower control limit is simple set to this value.

Exhibit 161: *p*-chart: Absenteeism

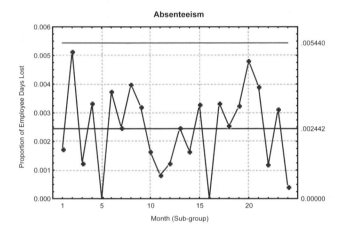

The interpretation here is that whatever the set of causes and conditions that together account for absenteeism levels, the system is stable. We would expect absenteeism rates to vary around the 0.2 percent of employee days worked and not exceed 0.54 percent of employee days.

COUNTING OCCURRENCES: THE C-CHART

What the *np*-chart is to units, the *c*-chart is to occurrences – both require constant sample sizes and both make the job of calculating control limits a whole lot easier. Like the *np*-chart, the requirement of constant sample size means improvement teams will likely make more use of this chart when there is an opportunity to design the data-gathering approach rather than rely on existing data.

Unlike the *np*-chart and the *p*-chart, the *c*-chart counts occurrences of some characteristic as opposed to units. Usually, but not necessarily, these occurrences are expressed in the form of a defect or problem to be addressed. Examples would include the number of typos per page, number of errors on each invoice, the number of flaws on a painted surface, the number of faulty solder joints per circuit board, or the number of crimes committed in a community where the population is essentially constant.

CONSTRUCTION

Like with the other attribute charts discussed so far, five basic steps are involved in constructing the *c*-chart.

1. Gather and organize the data

Before the data is gathered, decide what to measure. What held true for the *np*- and *p*-charts holds here as well. The team must decide what is important to measure, and then give this meaning with an operational definition. If we are counting the number of defects, do we have a definition of what constitutes a defect and what does not? Do those gathering the data understand these definitions and can they apply them consistently? With definitions set and the procedure operationalized, the team must also:

▶ **Design the sample.** Remember the requirements of lot size when dealing with the attribute chart. It should be large enough to find something and in the case of the *c*-chart, must be of constant size.

▶ **Set up data-collection forms.** Make sure clear, concise data-collection forms or check-sheets are established and those doing the data gathering know how to use them.

▶ **Perform the sampling and record measurements.** Be sure to record the data in the order in which the sample occurs. If the sub-groups basically represent time periods, a minimum of 20 periods should be analyzed. What was said for the *np*- and *p*-charts also applies here. Familiarity with the process being analyzed is still the most important factor to consider when determining the actual number of sub-groups.

2. Determine the axes and plot the data

Once the data is gathered, the chart needs to be created. The horizontal axis will mark each sample collected and needs to be clearly labeled. The vertical axis will present the number of occurrences of the characteristic of interest. The process is basically the same as for all the other control charts. Remember to add some head room for the numbers – adding and subtracting 25 percent to the highest and lowest values recorded should do the trick.

3. Calculate the mean and plot the centerline

Next, the mean or average value of *c* is calculated ($\bar{c}$). This simply involves adding up the values in the data and dividing by the number of values – the simple calculation of the mean. The formula is:

$$Centerline(\bar{c}) = \frac{\Sigma c}{k}$$

Where:
c = count of occurrences
k = number of sub-groups

With the value of $\bar{c}$ determined, the centre line for the control chart can be plotted.

4. Calculate and plot the control limits

The calculation of the control limits for the *c*-chart is the easiest calculation of all the attribute control charts. Simply take the square root of $\bar{c}$ (the mean calculated in step 3) and multiply by three. The formula is given by:

$$Control\ Limits_c = \bar{c} \pm 3\sqrt{\bar{c}}$$

Where:
$\bar{c}$ = mean for c

Once the values for the control limits are calculated they can be plotted on the control chart.

5. Analyze and interpret the chart

The standard set of interpretive procedures can be applied to the *c*-chart. Observing the chart for the basic control limit test (any points going beyond the control limits) is the first step. Once this is done, the chart can be analyzed for runs and specific patterns. As mentioned, it is important that the team identifies the basic tests it will apply before interpretation, as applying all the tests all the time is bound to find 'something.' Understand what you are looking for before you begin interpretation and use the chart to confirm (or deny) your theory.

EXAMPLE OF C-CHART: PUMP FAILURES

A process improvement team is trying to improve plant efficiency. A key area of loss is downtime – the amount of time the plant cannot operate because of equipment failure. A Pareto analysis reveals the major source of downtime is due to pump failure. Pumps are just about everywhere in the plant, and the team is beginning to think that improving the maintenance on these items alone may have some significant benefits.

The team gathered monthly data on the number of pump failures going back almost two years. The plant has not undergone any major changes over this time so the number of pumps in use has remained relatively constant. The data gathered is presented in Table 162: Pump Failure Data.

The *c*-chart was used to analyze the data, since sample size or area of opportunity for failure (number of pumps in the plant) was constant and the focus was on the number of incidents -- that is, the number of failures.

With the data gathered and plotted as a run chart, the next step was calculating the mean monthly number of pump failures or *c-bar*. Notice that each month is treated as a sub-group. The formula is straightforward:

$$Centerline(\bar{c}) = \frac{\Sigma c}{k}$$

Where:
c = the count of incidents
k = the number of sub-groups

Given this, the calculation for $\bar{c}$ is:

$$Centerline(\bar{c}) = \frac{\Sigma c}{k} = \frac{125}{23} = 5.43$$

Table 162: Pump Failure Data

Month (sub-group)	Pump Failures (c)
1	5
2	3
3	9
4	3
5	3
6	6
7	5
8	3
9	4
10	10
11	3
12	4
13	7
14	6
15	8
16	3
17	5
18	7
19	9
20	6
21	8
22	5
23	3
TOTAL	125

The formulas for the calculation of the control limits are just as easy. Specifically, they are equal to three times the square root of *c-bar*. The calculations for the upper control limit are:

$$Control\ Limits_c = \bar{c} \pm 3\sqrt{\bar{c}}$$

$$Control\ Limits_c = 5.43 \pm 3\sqrt{5.43}$$

$$Control\ Limits_c = 5.43 \pm 6.99$$

Because the number of incidents cannot be less than zero, the negative value calculated in the formula is simply set equal to zero.

The interpretation of the control chart is that the current system is designed to produce anywhere from about 13 to zero pump failures per month, with an average of about 5.43 such failures monthly. Because the system is operating under a system of chance causes, similar performance in the future is to be expected. Redesigning the maintenance system is, therefore, a reasonable approach to reducing plant down time and one likely to meet with success.

Exhibit 163: c-chart: Pump Failures

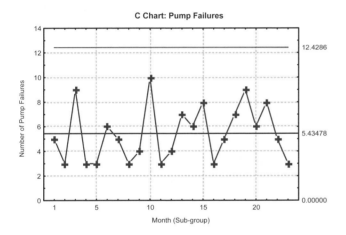

with occurrences, so it is possible that multiple occurrences of the characteristic of interest can or could appear on each unit. For example, crime rates, traffic accidents, number of errors per document, incidents of disease and the number of defects per unit can all be analyzed using the *u*-chart.

The fact that different sample sizes are permitted presents the team with the same advantages and disadvantages as the *p*-chart. The downside to different sample sizes is that different control limits for each lot or sub-group need to be calculated. This is a tedious process when having to calculate the control limits by hand. As was the case with the *p*-chart, however, a short-cut calculation can be performed when the variation between samples is less than 20 percent.

RATES OF OCCURRENCE: THE *U*-CHART

The upside to accepting different sample sizes is the ability to analyze data in situations where the team has not had an opportunity to design the data-gathering effort, or where the data simply does not avail itself to standardized sampling – such as published data.

The *u*-chart is to occurrences what the *p*-chart is to units. When the requirements of constant sample size cannot be met and the team is interested in counting occurrences rather than units, the *u*-chart is the tool to use. Like the *c*-chart, we are concerned

An example is crime statistics. A community-based improvement team may be interested in knowing whether crime is actually increasing or decreasing in a community or neighborhood.

Various crime statistics would likely be available from the local police and would apply to a community whose population (sample size) is changing. Or, the team could compare the crime statistics of their community with other communities of different populations, to see if rates are higher or lower than elsewhere and if any special causes of variation are present.

The charts for tracking occurrences (*u-* and *c-*charts) are based on the Poisson distribution. To use these charts, the data should reflect the characteristics of the distribution. This means that the area of opportunity for an occurrence to happen is large, while the actual probability of an occurrence is relatively small. Take the entries in the human resource database, for example. There are many possible mistakes that could be made in completing an entry in many different fields – meaning there are many opportunities for a defect to occur. But the chance that a mistake will occur is usually small.

CONSTRUCTION

Because the sample sizes vary, the u-chart requires separate calculated control limits for each sub-group. However, from a practical standpoint, if the sample sizes do not vary by more than 20 percent, a single set of control limits can be calculated.

Like the *p*-chart, two construction procedures are presented. The first is for sample sizes that vary by more than 20 percent (requiring separate control limits). The second procedure is used when sample size varies by less than 20 percent (requiring only common control limits across sub-groups).

Procedure 1: Unequal sample sizes

1. **Gather and organize the data**. As always, the first step is deciding what to measure. This requires the team to decide what is important. What will be the characteristic of interest and the operational definition of this characteristic so that data can actually be gathered? After this the team must:

    ▶ **Design the sample.** Remember the requirements of lot size when dealing with the attribute chart. It must be large enough to find something. Because the u-chart is being used, there is a good possibility the team itself did not design the sample but is using published or preexisting data. This is fine, but make sure to reference the source of the data.

    ▶ **Set up data-collection forms.** If the team is designing the sample, make sure clear, concise data-collection forms or check-sheets are established and those doing the data gathering know how to use them. Because the sample size varies, you must ensure there is an opportunity to record the number of observations of interest in each sample, the size of each sample and the rate represented by dividing the objects of interest by the area of opportunity.

▶ **Perform the sampling and record measurements.** Be sure to record the data in the order in which the sample occurs. If the sub-groups basically represent time periods, a minimum of 20 periods should be analyzed. As is the case with all attribute control charts, familiarity with the process being analyzed is still the most important factor to consider when determining the actual number of sub-groups.

▶ **Calculate the rate for each lot.** As data is collected, the rate (u) should be calculated. This is done by taking the number of occurrences of interest observed in each sub-group and dividing by the sample size or area of opportunity. It is good practice to calculate these rates at the time the data is gathered. The rates are required if those in the field are plotting the data in real time as opposed to having things calculated and plotted some-

where else. Also, calculating the rate at the time the data is collected introduces some redundancy in case a figure becomes smudged or there are problems interpreting an individual's handwriting.

2. **Set up the axes and plot the data.** Axes are set up as with other control charts. Again, make sure to add some head room. Remember, too, the data plotted is the rate data, not the actual counts, so be careful to plot the correct numbers. As the points are plotted, connect them with a line.

3. **Calculate the mean ($\bar{u}$) and plot the centerline.** The overall average can be calculated. This is done by adding up all the occurrences of interest in all the samples and dividing by the total of all sample sizes. The formula is:

$$Centerline(\bar{u}) = \frac{\Sigma c}{\Sigma n} = \frac{\Sigma u}{k}$$

Where:
c = count of occurrences in each sub-group
n = area of opportunity for each sub-group
u = rate for each sub-group
k = number of sub-groups

Once the mean of u ($\bar{u}$) is calculated, the center line should be plotted.

4. **Calculate and plot the control limits.** The formula used for the u-chart control limits is similar to that used for the c-chart. This is not surprising since both charts are based on the same theoretical distribution – the Poisson. The differences with the *u*-chart are the requirement of calculating separate limits for each lot or sub-group, and the inclusion of sample size (*n*) in the calculations. The formula is:

$$Control\ Limits_u\ =\ \bar{u} \pm 3\frac{\sqrt{\bar{u}}}{\sqrt{n}}$$

Where:
$\bar{u}$ *= mean occurrence rate*
n = area of opportunity for each sub-group

Once the upper and lower control limits have been calculated for each sub-group, they can be plotted on the *u*-chart.

5. **Interpret the chart.** Interpretation of the *u*-chart is similar to that of other attribute charts.

Procedure 2: Sample size varies by less than 20 percent

1. **Gather and organize the data.** The procedure for gathering the data is the same as with varying sample sizes, except the team must ensure the sample size does not vary by more than 20 percent. To determine this, find the largest sample size and subtract the smallest. Take this amount and divide by the smallest sample size. If the value you get is less than 0.20, the sample size variation is less than 20 percent.

2. **Create the chart and plot the data.** Again the procedure is the same for that with unequal sample sizes.

3. **Calculate and plot the average defect rate.** The average is calculated as it was with unequal sample sizes. Divide the total number of occurrences observed by the total size of the samples. Again, this is the same formula used in the first procedure.

$$Centerline(\bar{u})\ =\ \frac{\Sigma c}{\Sigma n}\ =\ \frac{\Sigma u}{k}$$

Where:
c = count of occurrences in each sub-group
n = area of opportunity for each sub-group
u = rate for each sub-group

k = *number of sub-groups*

4. **Calculate and plot the control limits.** The formula used to plot the control limits is essentially the same as the formula used with unequal sample sizes. Because we are calculating a single set of limits, however, we use the average sample size ($\bar{n}$) in the calculations rather than a separate n for each sub-group.

The specific formulas are:

$$Control\ Limits_u = \bar{u} \pm 3\frac{\sqrt{\bar{u}}}{\sqrt{\bar{n}}}$$

Where:
$\bar{u}$ = *mean occurrence rate*
$\bar{n}$ = *average area of opportunity for all sub-groups*

The differences in the formula compared with those in the first procedure is the little bar over the *n*. This, as you may recall, is statisticians' parlance for the mean. Average *n* is used because we are creating only one upper and one lower control limit for all the sub-groups.

5. **Interpret the chart.** The *u*-chart is interpreted in the same manner employed earlier for control charts. Caution is warranted, however. This approach to the *u*-chart is basically a handy short-cut. If some observation is just outside the control limit, you may want to recalculate separate control limits rather than jump to the conclusion a definite signal of a special cause of variation has been detected. Exercise judgment in interpretation.

EXAMPLE OF *U*-CHART: BENCHMARKING COMPARATIVE ACCIDENT RATES

A government department is in the process of selecting a construction company as a sole source supplier on a highway bridge refurbishment and construction program. A key selection criterion is the accident rate of the various firms competing for the contract. The specific measure of interest to the government is the number of man-hours lost due to accidents.

Each firm has submitted its workers' compensation record of lost time accidents over the past two years and the total number of man-hours worked. The government wants to know if there are really any differences on how the various firms conduct their business, as measured by the levels of accidents. This is just another way of asking if we can see any special causes of variation among the safety systems of various trucking firms.

Not only does the sample vary but the factor of interest is not time. Instead, the factor of interest is each of the competing companies involved in bidding for the contract. Each company, then, will be a sub-group. The data submitted by the 12 companies competing for the contract is provided in the first three columns of Table 164: Man-Hours Lost Data and Calculations.

Table 164: Man-Hours Lost Data and Calculations

Company	Man Hours Worked '000 (n)	Number of Lost Time Accidents (c)	Accident Rate (u)	Sigma (s)	Three Sigma (3s)	Lower Control Limit (lcl_u)	Upper Control Limit (ucl_u)
A	910	21	0.0231	0.0043	0.0128	0.0037	0.0293
B	415	7	0.0169	0.0063	0.0189	-0.0024	0.0354
C	958	23	0.0240	0.0041	0.0124	0.0040	0.0289
D	786	14	0.0178	0.0046	0.0137	0.0027	0.0302
E	211	5	0.0237	0.0088	0.0265	-0.0100	0.0430
F	869	13	0.0150	0.0044	0.0131	0.0034	0.0296
G	426	9	0.0211	0.0062	0.0187	-0.0022	0.0352
H	507	14	0.0276	0.0057	0.0171	-0.0006	0.0336
I	920	5	0.0054	0.0042	0.0127	0.0038	0.0292
J	698	7	0.0100	0.0049	0.0146	0.0019	0.0311
K	850	10	0.0118	0.0044	0.0132	0.0033	0.0297
L	577	6	0.0104	0.0053	0.0160	0.0005	0.0325
Sum	8127	134					
Average	677.2500	11.1667	0.0165				

First step in the calculation is determining the overall average of lost time accidents or *u-bar*. This is simply the total number of lost time accidents (134) divided by the total number of man hours worked.

$$Centerline(\bar{u}) = \frac{\Sigma c}{\Sigma n} = \frac{134}{8127} = 0.0165$$

The calculations for the control limits are the square root of $\bar{u}$ (0.0165) which is 0.1284, divided by the square root of *n* for each sub-group. For the first company 'A', square root of the number of man-hours worked (910) is equal to 30.166. This divided into 0.1284 is equal to 0.0043. This is the figure under the sigma column for company 'A' in the Table 164.

For the second company 'B,' the same figure of 0.1284 is divided by the square root of the number of man-hours worked (415) at that company. So the square root of 415 is 20.371. This, divided into 0.1284 is equal to 0.0063, which again is found under the sigma column for company 'B.'

Sigma figures are then multiplied by three to get the three-sigma spread. This figure added to, and subtracted from, $\bar{u}$ to obtain the upper and lower control limits

Exhibit 165: u-chart: Lost Time Accidents

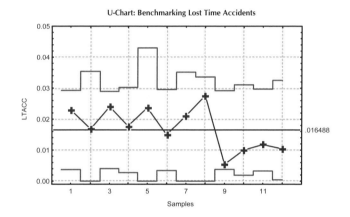

Interpretation of the control chart in this case would lead us to conclude that there is nothing substantially different in the safety systems of the various firms competing for the contract. This is because no special causes of variation are present in the control chart. The various firms submitting bids are operating under a system of chance causes. In other words, their respective safety systems are essentially the same – as least as assessed by their respective performance, measured as the number of lost time accidents per thousand man-hours worked.

EXAMPLE OF *U*-CHART: CRIME RATE

At a recent police commission meeting, the new police chief confidently told the review committee that household break-ins were going down – a clear result of the new anti-robbery unit incorporated only a year ago. The 'law and order' lobby is outraged. They say crime is rising and people don't even feel safe in their own homes anymore. They are calling for a new get-tough policy and a tougher police chief to implement it.

To help resolve the debate, the police commission contracts a review of household break-in rates in the community. The community in question is a prosperous residential community near a larger metropolitan center. Population has not increased by more than 10 percent over the past seven years. The police commission decides to look at the past two years' worth of monthly data to see if the number of break-ins has, in fact, gone up or down over the period and what the source of any changes might be. Note that asking whether we see any significant changes over the past two years is just another way of asking if any special or assignable causes of variation are present in the data.

The data gathered is presented in Table 166: Household Break-Ins. The rates have been calculated for every thousand homes in the community. The short-cut method of creating the u-chart can be used, because the household count (area of opportunity) has not varied by over 20 percent.

To calculate the mean or average value for u or $\bar{u}$, the number of break-ins (2,566) is divided by the area of opportunity or the number of households (2,979). The formula and calculation are:

$$Centerline(\bar{u}) = \frac{\Sigma c}{\Sigma n} = \frac{2566}{2979} = 0.8614$$

Note here that this is the rate per thousand households.

Next is the calculation of the control limits. The respective formulas and calculations for the control limits are:

$$Control\ Limits_u = \bar{u} \pm 3\frac{\sqrt{\bar{u}}}{\sqrt{n}}$$

$$Control\ Limits_u = 0.8614 \pm 3\frac{\sqrt{0.8614}}{\sqrt{129.52}}$$

$$Control\ Limits_u = 0.8614 \pm 3(0.0816)$$

Table 166: Household Break-Ins

Month	House-holds ('000) (*n*)	Break-Ins (*c*)	Rate (*u*) (*c/n*)
1	125	125	1.0000
2	125	87	0.6960
3	125	130	1.0400
4	125	125	1.2480
5	125	112	0.8960
6	130	89	0.6080
7	130	125	0.9620
8	130	133	1.0230
9	130	100	0.6000
10	130	140	1.0770
11	130	103	1.0150
12	130	121	0.9310
13	130	118	0.9080
14	130	89	0.6850
15	130	97	0.7460
16	130	111	0.8540
17	132	131	1.0980
18	132	122	0.9240
19	132	110	0.5680
20	132	85	0.6440
21	132	119	0.9020
22	132	101	0.7650
23	132	93	0.7050
Sum	2979	2566	
Average	129.5217	111.5652	0.8614

$$Control\ Limits_u = 0.8614 \pm 0.2446$$

So the upper control limit for *u* or ucl_u is 1.106 (0.8614 + 0.2446) and the lower control limit or lcl_u is 0.6168 (0.8614 - 0.2446). The resulting *u*-chart is presented in Exhibit 167: U-Chart: Incidents of Break-Ins.

Exhibit 167: *U*-Chart: Incidents of Break-Ins

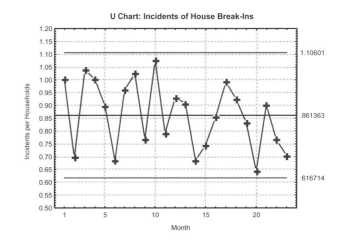

So what does the chart tell us? It defines the capability of the system that produces break-ins. Specifically, we should expect about one (0.8614 to be more exact) break-in for every thousand homes each month. We may also expect this rate to be as high as 1.106 and as low as 0.6168 break-ins per thousand homes per month. Any more or less than this and we should suspect some special cause of variation at work – a cause creating a sudden and significant change in the break-in rate.

As it is, however, the level of break-ins recorded to date has been relatively stable, with no special trends or causes of variation readily apparent. This means neither the police chief nor the law and order lobby is correct. Crime, as it turns out, is neither going down nor up in this community – it is rolling along at the rate it has been for the past two years.

HISTOGRAMS: THE PERFORMANCE PROFILE

Histograms are often considered the workhorses of process improvement. They belong to a class of data-analysis tools called frequency distributions. Histograms and frequency distributions generally are simple, yet powerful tools used to present a comprehensive profile of how the data within a data set are distributed. The central tendency, dispersion and shape – virtually all we need to know about the distribution of the data – are presented in the histogram. In short, the histogram presents the data in a manner that preserves the complexity so easily hidden with statistical or numerical summaries of the data.

If a process characteristic is important enough to be measured, then the results are probably important enough to be presented in the histogram. The very use of histograms destroys that 'tyranny of the average' and opens our eyes to the variation inherent in process performance.

DESCRIPTION

The histogram, like all frequency distributions, is basically a bar chart. It shows how often (how frequently) measurements occur at each value or range of values. It is used when the performance data is measured data, resulting from the application of a standardized scale as opposed to a count.

Basically, the histogram has three parts. These are:

▶ **X-axis.** The horizontal or x-axis shows "measurement opportunities," the range of values within which any given measurement may occur. These measurement opportunities are grouped into "bins." Each bin is a range of values encompassing the same number of measurement opportunities – so the width of each bin is the same. In the basic histogram example provided, the range of each bin is five seconds. So we have one bin from zero to five seconds, a second from five to 10 seconds and so on.

▶ **Y-axis**. The vertical or y-axis is the scale for reading the heights of the bars, to determine the number of observations in each bin. In some cases, the y-axis is labeled "count," and in others it is labeled "frequency."

Exhibit 168: Basic Histogram

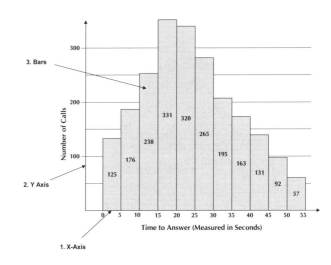

In the basic histogram example, the y-axis measures the number of calls answered. It starts at zero and goes to above 300.

▶ **Bars or Bins.** The heights of the bars represent the number of measurements (observations) that occur at a given value or range of values. In the example, the first bin indicates that 125 calls were answered within five

---

seconds. The next bin indicates that 176 calls were answered in between five and 10 seconds, and so on across the time range experienced.

Notice how the histogram quickly conveys all the basic information one needs to know about a process. Yogi Berra was right – you can see a lot just by looking! Just looking at the basic histogram we can see that the middle or average is about 20 seconds, that the mode (peak) is between 15 and 20 seconds, and that the distribution is skewed slightly to the right. We also know that for the time period in which data was collected, it never took us less than zero seconds to answer a call. Well, no kidding! More importantly, it never took longer than 55 seconds.

Notice, too, that had some standard been in place, such as all calls will be answered within 45 seconds, the histogram indicates immediately the degree to which the process is capable of meeting the expectation. This is significantly different than assessing such a standard by observing the average response time of 20 seconds. Using the average would give the impression the process is capable of meeting the 45-second standard. The histogram, however, presents a far more detailed and different story, namely that the process will fail to meet the standard from time to time and, indeed, has failed to meet that standard 149 times in the past (92+57).

WHERE TO USE HISTOGRAMS

How often do you see histograms presented in response to questions of process performance? When someone inquires about the cost of a product, do we give them a single number or a histogram? If we ask about the current level of customer satisfaction, do we quote the latest percentage of respondents indicating 'satisfied' to some survey or do we hand out the frequency distribution of responses? More than likely, we quote a single number, leaving the histogram – if it has been created at all – in the back room.

So where should histograms be used? The quick response is: use histograms whenever numbers are used. Specifically, whenever data is used to represent performance, that data should be depicted in a histogram. Moreover, whenever an average or other single statistic is presented to convey some information about performance, a histogram of the data that yielded that statistic should be completed.

Use histograms for:

▲ **Reporting.** Averages and other single-point measures by themselves mean little. Histograms present us with the data we need to begin understanding the response of some quality characteristic. Histograms should be used wherever numbers are used in a report. In market surveys, replace those averages with a histogram. Likewise for management reports presenting accounting data, cost figures, inventory levels, warranty costs, error rates and delivery times. Toss out those single numbers (statistics), and show those who need to know what is going on in the detail behind the numbers.

▲ **Analyzing Processes.** Histograms present the 'voice of the process.' They allow the process to tell us exactly how it performed and in what manner. Analyzing this voice is called process analysis. We are searching to understand how the process performs as measured across some characteristic. In the basic histogram example, the process told us where the middle was (about 20 seconds), what its range was (from zero to 60 seconds), and what kind of shape it had (skewed slightly to the right). This is the way this process behaves, at least as measured across this particular quality characteristic. Histograms, therefore, should be used whenever teams are seeking to profile process behavior.

▲ **Determining Capability.** Management has expectations of every process. But is the process capable of meeting those expectations? The ability to meet expectations is referred to as process capability. Histograms are used whenever it is important to understand the ability of the process to meet some expectation – that is, when comparing the voice of the process with the voice of the customer or management. In the basic histogram example, managerial or customer expectations were set at the 45-second mark. The histogram clearly revealed the process as incapable of meeting this expectation. This tells us right away that the process must be redesigned in some fashion if this expectation is to be met consistently.

LIMITATIONS OF HISTOGRAMS

For all their analytical power, histograms do have certain limitations.

▲ **They do not show changes over time.** Histograms represent a snapshot of the process. While the data gathered on

---

a process may have been acquired over a day or a year, the data is pooled together in a manner in which the time component is lost. This shortcoming can be addressed by stratifying results by time or linking histograms with run and/or control charts.

▲ **They require a lot of data.** Usually, a minimum of 50 observations is required to produce a good histogram and 100 values are preferred. At times, there may not be enough data or enough resources to gather a sufficient number of measurements. When the number of measures is less than 50 use with caution, or use another tool such as the box and whisker plot or the dot plot.

▲ **They display only a single distribution at a time.** The histogram displays the data distribution for a single characteristic. At times, however, the interest may not be in the distribution of a characteristic by itself, but in how the distribution compares with another distribution gathered for the same characteristic. Examples include comparing response time of one fire station with another, or examining the distribution of response time before and after some change in design has occurred. The nature of the histogram makes it difficult to deal with these types of situations – the greater the number of comparisons to be made,

the clumsier the histogram becomes. When more than three comparisons are to be made, it is time to use box and whisker plot.

CREATING A HISTOGRAM

Creating a histogram is as easy as following the seven steps listed below.

1. Collect the measurements

Collect the data either directly from the field or from historical data from organizational records. This will almost always involve considerations of an appropriate time period. Do you want the last year's data or last week's or last month's? Make sure the data being collected and the time periods involved are relevant for the type of process decisions being made.

2. Calculate the range

This involves finding the largest and smallest numbers in the data set, and subtracting one from the other. This is the standard definition of range, the difference between the biggest and smallest numbers in the data set. The problem in determining the range is rarely one of calculation – after all it's easy to subtract one values from another. Rather, the problem is usually in finding the two values required. Look carefully – they're in the data somewhere.

3. Determine the number of bars (bins)

The trickiest part to creating a histogram is determining the number of bars that will be used in the graph. Each bar is like a bucket or bin that captures data points falling within its dimensions. But how many of these buckets should be created?

Table 169: Determining the Number of Histogram Bars

Number of Data Points or Measurements	Number of Histogram Bars or Bins
Under 50	5 to 7
51 to 100	6 to 10
100 to 250	7 to 12
Over 250	10 to 20

The number of intervals used should be based on the number of observations or measurements occurring within the data set. A good rule of thumb is to use the square root of the number of measurements. So, for example, if you have 100 measurements, try using 10 bars. Table 169: Determining the Number

of Histogram Bars can also be used to help determine the appropriate number of intervals or bars. Rarely would the number of bars exceed 20, because after this point, preparation and interpretation become problems.

4. Determine the interval of each bar

Once we know how many bars or bins to create, how large should each bin be? To determine the width of each bar, divide the number of bars (step 3) into the range of the data set (step 2). The result should be rounded to some convenient figure. For example, if we had 100 values and the process range was 75, we would calculate the number of bins (approximately 10 since this is the square root of 100) and divide this into the range to produce 7.5. This is a little inconvenient so we would round up to eight. Each bin would be eight units wide.

5. Determine the frequencies

Tally the data for each bin or class frequency. Simply count up the number of observations occurring within each bin determined in step 4. Usually, this is done using a frequency table. The first column of the table describes each bin, and the next column records the number of observations associated with that bin.

6. Draw or plot the histogram

Using standard graph paper, draw the resulting histogram using the tally figures calculated in step 5. Each bar of the histogram represents the tally or frequency of occurrence.

7. Interpret the histogram

Examine the histogram for patterns using the interpretation guide following.

SOME BASIC RULES OF PREPARATION

▲ *Always ensure the intervals are of equal width.* Unequal interval widths will distort the distribution and give you incorrect results.

▲ *Do not use open-ended intervals.* Intervals must have a beginning and an end. Never use open-ended intervals such as "64 and above."

▲ *Do not break the scales.* This can cause misinterpretation as well as data being overlooked.

▲ *Keep it simple*. Don't try and put too much information on a histogram. Keep it simple; prepare a histogram for each quality characteristic except when you are deliberately trying to compare distributions. In these cases, try to keep the number of distributions limited to two. If more distributions need to be compared, try using a box and whisker plot.

▲ *If there is a special standard in use, make this standard a boundary of one of the classes*. For example, if there is an arbitrary acceptance limit, make this limit a boundary point of one of the bins or bars. This will help identify those situations where the measurement system may be affected by existing standards or limits.

HISTOGRAM ANALYSIS AND INTERPRETATION

Analysis of histograms consists of two basic types. These are:

1. **Qualitative Analysis.** This involves analyzing the performance profile presented by the histogram. We are seeking insight into the behavior of the process by examining the patterns and peculiarities produced and exhibited by the histogram.

2. **Quantitative Analysis.** This entails analyzing the data by calculating the basic descriptive statistics associated with the histogram. This involves calculation of both average and dispersion statistics, usually the mean and standard deviation.

QUALITATIVE ANALYSIS

With process analysis we are attempting to understand how the process behaves. What do the results or process outputs look like? How are they distributed? Is the distribution skewed to one side or the other? Is the distribution "tall and skinny" or is it "flat and spread out?" Are there gaps in the histogram? Are there outliners?

In analyzing the process, we look for patterns in the histogram. Some of the more common are:

1. **Bell-shaped or normal.** This is the pattern most people recognize when they think of histograms. The bell-shaped or normal distribution is a balanced distribution, where the number of points occurring on one side of the peak (mode) are about the same as the number of observations occurring on the other side of the peak. In a normal pattern, the mode, median and mean (remember the three measures of

central tendency) are all located at about the same place – that is, they are essentially equal. This is a classic perfor-

Exhibit 170: Bell-Shaped or Normal

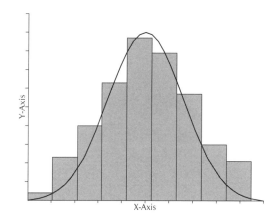

mance profile when the process or system is operating under common cause variation.

2. **Skewed.** A skewed distribution has a relatively large number of observations tailing off to one side or the other. There could be a number of reasons for this. It might be due to the nature of the process itself – the process is not 'normal,' but follows some other distributional pattern.

Exhibit 171: Skewed or Lopsided

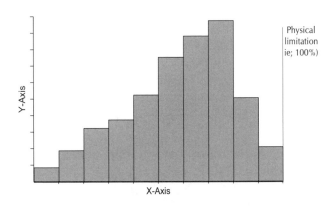

Just because a distribution is called the normal distribution doesn't mean every process produces the 'normal' pattern. The pattern may also be skewed because of physical limitations that define the type of data used. For example, the time to answer the telephone has a physical limitation of zero seconds – it can't take any less time than this. In such circumstances, process behavior may be skewed away from this boundary. In other words, the observations or values look as though they are piled up against the boundary or limitation.

3. **Double-Peaked (Bi-Modal).** The double-peaked or bi-modal histogram resembles a double-humped camel. Usually, this condition is created when the data from two different processes have been combined into one histogram. The solution – stratify! Separate the data into logical groups and then create two different histograms, one for each of the groups.

Exhibit 172: Bi-Modal

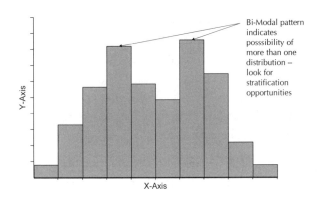

4. **Plateau.** Plateau distributions are flat, at times resembling a rectangular box more than a bell shaped curve. Usually, plateau-shaped distributions result when data from multi-

ple processes are combined. This is essentially the same problem as with the double-peaked distribution. But instead of having combined two processes, we have combined data from more than two. The flatness is created when the multiple peaks from all these various processes are combined into a single histogram, creating the plateau-like appearance. The first solution in such cases is to stratify the data. See if separating the data along some logical line will create more recognizable patterns.

Exhibit 173: Plateau

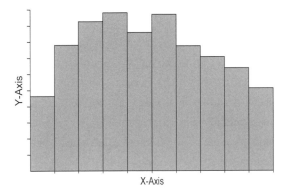

5. **Comb Distribution.** The comb or gap-tooth pattern describes a histogram where alternating high and low bars present a comb-like pattern. The most common cause of this is incorrect construction – usually using too many bars for the amount of data involved. Go back to the histogram construction steps to ensure the appropriate number of bars are used and that intervals are of equal width. If the comb-like pattern cannot be removed, there is a very good chance you are dealing with a process that has numerous special causes of variation. This may result from a failure to standardize a process, allowing things to be done differently each time.

6. **Edge-Peaked.** The edge-peaked distribution resembles the normal distribution, except there is a large peak at one end or the other. The most common cause of this type of distribution is faulty histogram construction, usually involving an open-ended category, i.e. a histogram of age where the last category is 65 and over. Remember that there are no open-ended categories in a properly constructed histogram.

7. **Truncated.** Truncated distributions appear to have been 'cut-off' at some point. The usual causes are artificial intrusions in the process, usually in the form of a specifi-

Exhibit 174: Comb or Gap-Tooth

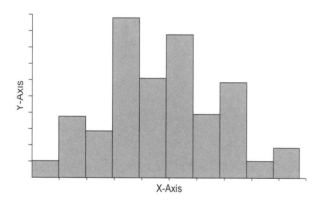

Exhibit 175: Edge-Peaked

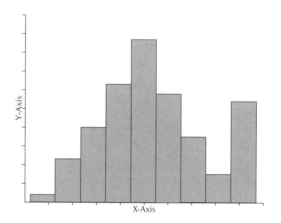

cation limit. For example, a process will yield a truncated distribution if the measurements came from parts that have been inspected against some standard and the non-satisfactory pieces removed. In this case, the data is not from the process itself, but rather from an amended process that includes some form of audit and adjustment. Unfortunately, the only option is to go back and redo the measurements prior to the inspection taking place.

8. **Isolated Peaks (Outliners).** Isolated peaks or outliners resemble normal distributions, but they have a small number of observations or a single observation lying to one

side of the bulk of the distribution or the other and separated by a gap. Assuming the histogram has been properly constructed, such outliners may be an assignable or special cause of variation in the process. Process improvement teams should investigate these outliners to see what can be learned from this special cause, and amend the process accordingly.

Exhibit 176: Truncated

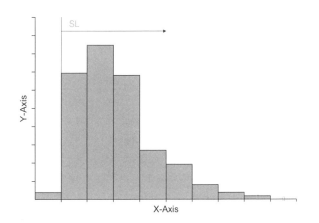

Exhibit 177: Outliner

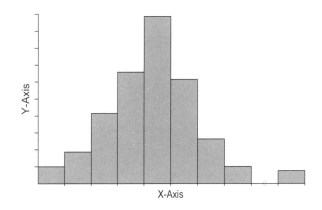

Comparing histograms

Another task facing performance improvement teams is comparing two or more distributions – that is, comparing two or more histograms. The need to do so occurs when the data has been stratified in some way. Examples include: comparing emergency response times in the day to those experienced in the evening; specifications of some manufactured part coming off two different production lines; the gas production volumes coming from two or more different wells; customer satisfaction from two different customer segments.

Comparing histograms can be a messy and confusing business. This has become all the more problematic with recent advances in desktop computer software that can produce brilliant and colorful three-dimensional graphics that are visually appealing, but impossible to decipher. Histograms are simply not designed to compare multiple distributions.

When comparing histograms, arrange each distribution above the other on the page while maintaining common scales for the x- and y-axes. The proper presentation format is presented in Exhibit 178: Comparing Histograms. This presentation method

Exhibit 178: Comparing Histograms

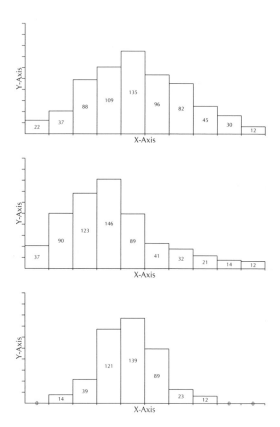

will allow you to see different patterns in the distributions, and will make it easier to see differences and similarities in the distributions.

In Exhibit 178, the differences between the three histograms are immediately apparent. The first, relative to the others, is flat with a good deal of variation. The second distribution is positively skewed (tails off to the right), while the last demonstrates less variation than the other two.

Even this correct approach of histogram comparison tends to get confusing when more than three histograms are being compared. In these cases, where the primary purpose is to compare distributions rather than to analyze a single data set, consider using the box and whisker plot. They make the comparisons far more accessible, although the information content about the performance of a specific data set is reduced.

QUANTITATIVE ANALYSIS

Quantitative analysis with histograms usually involves calculating some measure of central tendency (typically the mean) and measures of process variation (range and standard deviation). The range needs to be calculated to develop the histogram (see step 2 in histogram creation), and therefore is known at the time the histogram is prepared. Standard deviation is a more complex calculation, but it is a statistic that captures all the variation inherent in the data set being analyzed.

Exhibit 179: Process Quantifiable Characteristics

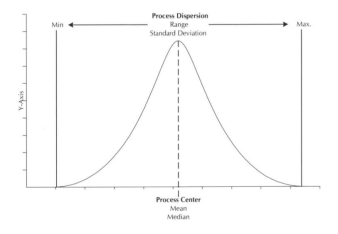

Also, simply noting the *Max.* or maximum value recorded and the *Min.*, the lowest value recorded, can provide useful information about the data set.

The formulas and methods of calculation of all these 'statistics' have been detailed in the previous chapter.

HISTOGRAM EXAMPLE 1: TIME TO ANSWER FOR EMERGENCY RESPONSE

An emergency response department wants to improve its current functioning. A critical performance measure is response time – including the time it takes to answer a call once a connection has been made. To analyze its performance, the department reviews the response times as recorded by the automatic call-detection system. Time is captured as the number of seconds between the time the call is connected until the emergency operator pick up the call to respond to the user's request.

Table 180: Time to Answer Data in Seconds presents some of this data. Eighty-five data points have been captured. With 85 data points, about nine bins or bars would be created (the square root of 85 is very close to nine). The minimum value is two and the maximum value is 11. This results in a range of nine seconds. Dividing nine seconds by the number of bars (nine) yields a bar width of one. In other words, we will have a bar representing one second, two seconds, three seconds and so forth.

Table 180: Time to Answer Data in Seconds

Data Points (Time in Seconds)				
3	5	4	6	6
3	7	5	8	11
3	4	7	9	7
4	6	8	6	6
8	9	6	6	4
7	2	4	7	9
3	7	6	8	6
8	9	8	5	7
10	8	7	7	5
7	2	4	5	10
6	7	6	8	5
4	4	7	4	3
6	5	5	4	5
5	9	7	4	
6	7	7	9	
2	7	7	6	
7	6	2	7	
5	6	3	7	

The data is then placed or tallied in each of these bins. This is best done using a frequency table. The frequency table simply tabulates how many values fall into each of the bins. In this case, how many times a response took two seconds (four

times), how many times the time to answer took three seconds (six times), and so forth. The complete frequency table for the data is presented in Table 181: Frequency Table of Time to Answer Data.

Table 181: Frequency Table of Time to Answer Data

Number of Seconds	Frequency	Percentage of Total
2	4	4.71
3	6	7.06
4	11	12.94
5	11	12.94
6	16	18.82
7	20	23.53
8	8	9.41
9	6	7.06
10	2	2.35
11	1	1.18
Totals	85	100.00

The frequency table can also be enhanced. Adding a column that represents the percentage of the total recorded in each category or bar is the most common such enhancement. In the example, the total number of observations is 85. So to calculate the percentage of calls answered within two seconds, the number of observations in this category (four) is divided by the total (85) to get the percentage. The result is the 4.71 percent presented in the table.

Exhibit 182: Histogram of Time to Answer Data

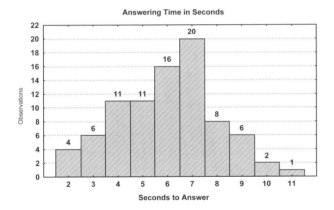

The results of the table are then plotted on the histogram. A bar on the histogram corresponds to a category in the frequency table. A histogram could also be prepared for the percentages calculated in the same table. However, such a presentation should always be done as an addition to the histogram on fre-

quency, never as a replacement for it. The frequency counts on the actual data represent the process without any modifications. Converting to percentages provides some additional information, but also loses something in the process – namely the size of the sample from which the percentages were calculated.

Quantifying: Calculating a few statistics

We can also calculate some statistics to provide a quantitative description of the data. These could include the mean of the data, range and standard deviation. All of these statistics are calculated as described in Chapter 5.

The mean of the data is calculated by adding together all the values of interest and then dividing by the number of values there are. In this case, the data adds up to 510. This, divided by 85 (the number of values or measures we have), comes to 6.0. So the average time to answer is six seconds.

The dispersion in the data is measured by the range and the standard deviation. The range was determined at the time of creating the histogram. The shortest time (*min.*) was two seconds and the longest time (*max.*) was 11 seconds. The range is simply the difference between these values or nine seconds. The standard deviation is a more complex calculation (details are also provided in Chapter 5). For the time to answer data the standard deviation is 2.0.

HISTOGRAM EXAMPLE 2: DAYS REQUIRED TO FILE REGULATORY COMPLIANCE DOCUMENTS

A company operating a potentially dangerous plant must file regulatory compliance documents with a government agency within 14 days of month-end. The government agency involved has notified the company that the required compliance documents are not arriving as required by legislation. The regulator has demanded changes to the company's reporting system.

The company has responded that its reporting systems are adequate, but human error and other unexpected factors are causing occasional delays. Nevertheless, the company undertakes a review of its procedures. The first step in this review is analyzing past performance.

The plant has operated for five years. The full five-year compliance reporting record of the plant is presented in Table 183: Days Required to File Regulatory Compliance Doc-

Table 183: Days Required to File Regulatory Compliance Documents

Days	Mon.	Year	Days	Mon.	Year	Days	Mon.	Year
14	Jan.	1993	18	Jan.	1995	9	Jan.	1997
13	Feb.	1993	11	Feb.	1995	16	Feb.	1997
14	Mar	1993	12	Mar	1995	15	Mar	1997
15	Apr.	1993	11	Apr.	1995	11	Apr.	1997
13	May	1993	10	May	1995	10	May	1997
13	June	1993	13	June	1995	10	June	1997
14	July	1993	14	July	1995	10	July	1997
20	Aug.	1993	14	Aug.	1995	19	Aug.	1997
12	Sept.	1993	17	Sept.	1995	16	Sept.	1997
17	Oct.	1993	13	Oct.	1995	18	Oct.	1997
15	Nov.	1993	14	Nov.	1995	17	Nov.	1997
12	Dec.	1993	14	Dec.	1995	12	Dec.	1997
13	Jan.	1994	17	Jan.	1996			
14	Feb.	1994	12	Feb.	1996			
12	Mar	1994	16	Mar	1996			
15	Apr.	1994	15	Apr.	1996			
9	May	1994	14	May	1996			
12	June	1994	19	June	1996			
15	July	1994	10	July	1996			
11	Aug.	1994	11	Aug.	1996			
11	Sept.	1994	19	Sept.	1996			
13	Oct.	1994	15	Oct.	1996			
11	Nov.	1994	15	Nov.	1996			
20	Dec.	1994	17	Dec.	1996			

uments. With five years worth of monthly data, this amounted to 60 records. These values were initially analyzed using the histogram. The fastest turnaround time was nine days in May 1994, repeated again in January 1997. The longest time took 20 days in August 1993, and again in December of 1994. The range, therefore, is 11 days (20 days minus nine days). With 60 measurements, the number of bars should be about seven or eight since the square root of 60 is between seven and eight. A range of 11 days with seven bins produces a bin width of about 1.6 days. Since the data is recorded as whole numbers, using a bin width of 1.6 would be awkward. A bin width of one or two days would be more appropriate; however, a width of a single day would likely produce too many bins or bars creating a gap-toothed histogram. In this case, the team decided to go with a bin width of two.

Notice that the data in this case is counted data, not measured. Histograms are usually applied to measured data, but this example shows that they can also be used for counted data. However, as was the case here, creating the appropriate bin width is often more difficult with counted data as we are forced to stick to whole numbers.

An added complication is presented by the reporting requirement of 14 days. Reports are to be received in less than 14 days; 14 days or more is deemed to be a late report. Generally, it is useful to use this demarcation point as the boundary of one of the bins to determine if it has an effect on process behavior. Therefore, with a bin width of two, and using 14 as a boundary point, we would get the class boundaries detailed in Table 184: Frequency Table - Regulatory Compliance Data.

Table 184: Frequency Table - Regulatory Compliance Data

Bin Range	Observations	Percentage
$8 \leq$ and < 10	2	3.33
$10 \leq$ and < 12	12	20.00
$12 \leq$ and < 14	14	23.33
$14 \leq$ and < 16	17	28.33
$16 \leq$ and < 18	8	13.33
$18 \leq$ and < 20	5	8.33
$20 \leq$ and < 22	2	3.33

The resulting frequency table and histogram, have seven bins, each with a width of two. The histogram is presented in Exhibit 185: Histogram of Regulatory Compliance Data.

Exhibit 185: Histogram of Regulatory Compliance Data

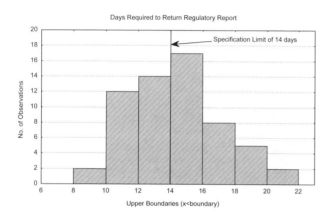

You don't need fancy statistics to tell you this process is not capable of meeting the regulatory requirements for reporting. Although the ability of a process to meet expectations (called capability) will be discussed in detail later on, it is still clear from the histogram that the process cannot meet expectations. The process is not capable of meeting the 13-day or less specification.

The company's statement that occasional lapses and human error are to blame for failure to meet regulatory requirements is simply not accurate. Rather, the system as designed and operating is incapable of meeting the 14-day requirement and will likely continue to miss the requirement as often as it meets it.

Stated differently, the process appears to be operating under chance or common cause variation with no special causes of variation present. In such circumstances, we would not expect any change in operating performance, as measured by the days-to-report metric, unless some redesign of the reporting system were to take place.

HISTOGRAM EXAMPLE 3: PER-CAPITA DEBT

The tools of data analysis, including histograms, are not just for use in analyzing organizational process data. Whenever teams are confronted with a data set, their immediate reaction should be to think about which tool would do the best job in presenting the data in a fashion that would convey some meaning.

Take the per-capita debt levels of the various states. In reviewing this data we might be interested in whether the distribution of data appeared normal, or whether special patterns are present that could tell us something about the borrowing patterns of the various states. The data set is presented in Table 186: Per-Capita Debt by State.

A quick review of the data shows that the smallest per-capita debt was in Kansas at $432. The largest was $5,916 in Alaska. These represent the *min.* and *max.* statistics respectively. The difference between these two values is the range, in this case $5,484. There are 50 states, so the number of bins should be about seven (since the square root of 50 is very close to seven).

Each bin width is approximated by the range divided by the number of bins, or in this case $5,484 divided by seven. The result is $787. Rounding this up to $800 is convenient, as is starting the first bin at $400. Our first bin, therefore, would be between $400 and $1200, the second between $1,200 and $2,000 and so forth. The frequency table arising from these bin definitions is presented in Table 187: Frequency Table for State Per-Capita Debt.

Two histograms based upon the frequency table are presented in Exhibit 188: Histograms of Per-Capita Debt. The first presents a histogram based upon a count of data – the number of states falling into each of the bins. The second histogram presents the percentages this count represents. The two histograms

Table 186: Per-Capita Debt by State

#	STATE	PCDEBT	#	STATE	PCDEBT
1	Alabama	$913	26	Montana	$2,462
2	Alaska	$5,916	27	Nebraska	$905
3	Arizona	$778	28	Nevada	$1,156
4	Arkansas	$739	29	New Hampshire	$4,970
5	California	$1,531	30	New Jersey	$2,897
6	Colorado	$892	31	New Mexi	$1,049
7	Connecti	$4,152	32	New York	$3,582
8	Delaware	$4,812	33	North Carolina	$642
9	Florida	$1,044	34	North Dakota	$1,186
10	Georgia	$733	35	Ohio	$1,091
11	Hawaii	$4,365	36	Oklahoma	$1,189
12	Idaho	$1,130	37	Oregon	$1,829
13	Illinois	$1,732	38	Pennsylvania	$1,134
14	Indiana	$969	39	Rhode Island	$5,561
15	Iowa	$704	40	South Carolina	$1,357
16	Kansas	$432	41	South Dakota	$2,331
17	Kentucky	$1,762	42	Tennesse	$508
18	Louisiana	$2,035	43	Texas	$510
19	Maine	$2,414	44	Utah	$1,102
20	Maryland	$1,824	45	Vermont	$2,707
21	Massachu	$4,417	46	Virginia	$1,208
22	Michigan	$1,212	47	Washington	$1,547
23	Minnesot	$953	48	West Virginia	$1,386
24	Mississi	$774	49	Wisconsin	$1,525
25	Missouri	$1,225	50	Wyoming	$1,476

Table 187: Frequency Table for State Per-Capita Debt

Bin #	Range for Each Bin	Count	Percent
1	> 400 and < 1200	23	46
2	>= 1200 and < 2000	13	26
3	>= 2000 and < 2800	5	10
4	>= 2800 and < 3600	2	4
5	>= 3600 and < 4400	2	4
6	>= 4400 and < 5200	3	6
7	>= 5200 and < 6000	2	4

are essentially the same and present the same pattern for analysis. One might think the two histograms are equivalent. They are close but they are not the same.

Using a histogram based upon percentages hides the actual number of measures taken. This is a variation of the old marketing trick, where some advertisement states that 80 percent of experts agree product X is the best, leaving unstated that only five such experts were consulted (and three of them were on the company payroll!). For this reason, it is best to present a histogram with the raw counts. It conveys not only the pattern but details the sample size as well. If a histogram based upon percentages would enhance the analysis, then ensure a fre-

quency table accompanies the chart. Never trust percentages presented alone.

The pattern presented by the histograms is one of a highly skewed distribution. The majority of states have per-capita debt of less than $2,000 – 72 percent of states in fact. The balance, 18 percent of states, have per-capita debts that range between $2,000 and $6,000. If someone were investigating the drivers behind per-capita debt loads of various states, this is crucial information to have.

For the "quantitatively inclined," the mean per-capita income is $1,855 while the median is $1,218. This difference between the mean and median values for the data set is typical with skewed distributions. The standard deviation, a measure of the variation in the data, is $1,408.

HISTOGRAM EXAMPLE #4: SURVEY RESULTS

This example emphasizes the use of histograms in situations where they are rarely used, but should be. In this case, we are technically using a frequency distribution as opposed to a histogram. The format is the same; what is different is that the nature of the data does not require determining the number of

Exhibit 188: Histograms of Per-Capita Debt

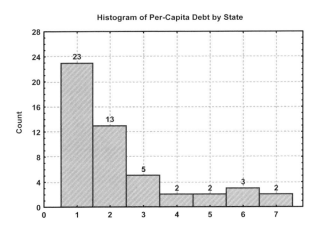

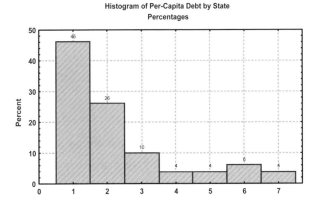

bins or bin width. A bin is created for each of the values used in the rating scale. Whether we call it a histogram or frequency distribution, what is more important is the need to use graphic techniques to display the data with its variation.

Presented in Table 189: Customer Survey Satisfaction Ratings are the results from a hypothetical survey question. The x-axis represents the question scale ranging from 1 to 5 (Very Poor to Very Good). The bins have already been defined – one bin for each rating level with five bins in all.

Table 189: Customer Survey Satisfaction Ratings

Rating	Example A	Example B
1	22	23
2	48	76
3	100	33
4	51	97
5	29	21
Sum	250	250
Average	3.068	3.068
Range	4	4

Two hypothetical sets of responses are presented. Let's assume the question was about some overall level of satisfaction with an organization's product. The sample sizes in both cases are the same, 250. So is the average result, 3.068. If we reported only the average score, we might be inclined to think that the responses in both cases were pretty much the same. But examine the frequency distributions of the data presented in Exhibit 190: Histogram of Survey Data (Example A) and Exhibit 191: Histogram of Survey Data (Example B). The histograms make it clear that these are two very different situations.

Exhibit 190: Histogram of Survey Data (Example A)

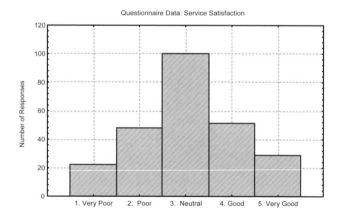

The first histogram depicts a basic normal distribution. From such a distribution we might conclude that customers were neither satisfied nor dissatisfied with the service. Of course, there is some variation – some are pleased or more than pleased with the product, others are decidedly less so.

Exhibit 191: Histogram of Survey Data (Example B)

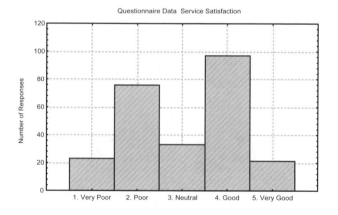

The second distribution is very different from the first. This histogram looks bi-modal, almost as if two distinct systems or processes were at work. That is very likely what is going on. Perhaps the data represents customer satisfaction results from two distinctly different products, or the same product delivered or serviced by two different methods. Perhaps the products are essentially the same, but the different distributions are really the effects of two different customer segments – one population liking the service, the second disliking it.

The crucial point here is the extent to which these types of graphical representations should be used. In short – everywhere. Never let a numerical summary statistic replace the appropriate graphical representation of the data. Statistics such as the mean, median, range, variance, standard deviation, kurtosis and skewness are all useful, but they all hide more than they reveal. Always insist on seeing the data.

CAPABILITY: CAN WE MEET EXPECTATIONS?

Capability is the ability of a process to meet expectations, typically the expectations of customers. These may be external customers receiving some product or service, or internal customers receiving some input to their process. Either way, capability is about the relationship between what the process can do and what we want it to do. Process performance or "*voice of the process*" is compared with expectations or "*voice of the customer*" to see how they match up – to determine if the process is **capable** of meeting these expectations.

Expectations related to some performance characteristic are called specifications. Specifications exist in many areas of business. Paying invoices within 30 days, acceptable levels of contamination in a chemical, minimum signal-to-noise ratios in a piece of electrical gear, pollution-control limits, and a seven-minute response time for emergency vehicles are all examples of different types of expectations defined as specifications. It is important to remember that as specifications, they are a product of the mind that created them. They are not necessarily connected to the underlying physical reality of the process.

CAPABLE AND INCAPABLE PROCESSES

Making a connection between the voice of the process and the voice of the customer is most easily accomplished by mapping the specification limits (representing the voice of the customer) on the histogram (which represents the voice of the process).

PICTURING CAPABILITY

The result of this mapping of specifications on the histogram is shown in Exhibit 192: Picturing Capability – Double- and Single-Sided Specifications. The Exhibit presents situations of double-sided specifications (top) and single-sided specifications (bottom).

Double-sided specifications occur most often in manufacturing when components are made to a specific nominal target with a specified tolerance. An example may be a manufactured steel rod with a specified diameter of 1.5 inches, plus or minus 0.1 inches.

Exhibit 192: Picturing Capability – Double- and Single-Sided Specifications

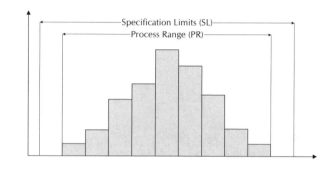

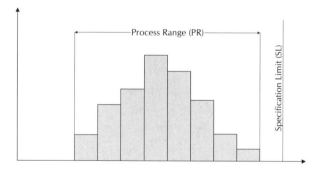

Single-sided specifications occur most frequently in service applications when some maximum or minimum serves as the specification. An example would be emergency response where vehicles are required to be at the scene of an accident within 14 minutes of notification.

In both cases, the specifications (voice of the customer), are represented by vertical lines. The position of the histogram (voice of the process) relative to these lines determines capability.

THREE CAPABILITY CONDITIONS

There are three possible relationships between actual process performance and managerial/customer expectations. The process can be performing at levels that meet, fall short of, or exceed expectations.

1. Process performance is equal to expectations

When performance equals specifications there is no room for error. The process is just able to produce results that are within expectations. Any unexpected circumstances that affect the process will result in errors or rejects – data going beyond the expectations or specifications.

These are good processes to target for improvement. Nothing is wrong, but only just. The objective should be to narrow process variation, so that the process range is smaller than the range implied by the specification limits. This provides room to accommodate those unexpected causes and conditions that arise from time to time.

Exhibit 193: Performance Equal to Expectations

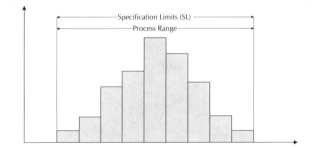

2. Process performance is less than expectations

In this case, the process is simply incapable of meeting the expectations or specifications set for it. There are values falling beyond the specifications set for the process.

This condition is far more common than most believe, because most organizational reporting cites only the average. For example, suppose management has set a standard that emergency vehicles will reach an emergency site within seven minutes of the phone call being received. Management reports indicate that average response time is five minutes. This kind of report, presenting only the average response time (the case with most such reports) would indicate that the process is good shape – after all, the average is below the upper specification limit. Without seeing the data – that is, without seeing the histogram – management may not know that despite this average, a large number of responses fail to arrive within the seven minute specification.

Processes are incapable relative to specifications for two reasons. First, the process variability or range may be greater than the range of the specification limits. A picture of this is presented in Exhibit 194: Process Less Than Expectations: Excess Variation.

Exhibit 194: Process Less Than Expectations: Excess Variation

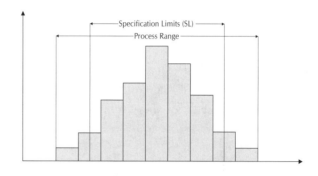

A second cause of an incapable process is where the process range is less than the spread of the specifications, but where the process has drifted off target. Process drift occurs when the process moves in one direction or the other relative to its target or nominal position. In Exhibit 195: Process Less Than Expectations – Process Drift, the process has drifted to the left (it is no longer centered between the specification limits). This has caused the process to produce results that are not acceptable, despite the fact the spread is less than the specifications.

Exhibit 195: Process Less Than Expectations – Process Drift

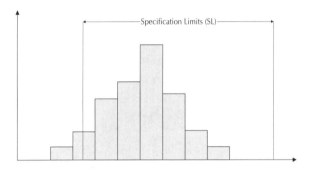

3. Process performance exceeds expectations

Congratulations! This is what quality is all about – exceeding expectations of the customer. Here, the process is easily out-performing the expectations set. This means two things:

▲ **The process is creating value.** Exceeding customer or managerial expectations means the process is creating value and delighting customers. Things are simply better than expected.

▲ **The process is robust.** Put plainly, there is room to screw up. If something begins to go wrong with the process and performance declines (in the form of increasing process range or the process drifting off target), there is room to accommodate the change and still meet expectations. People will have time to review the problems and correct them before any sub-standard product or service is produced.

Exhibit 196: Process Exceeds Expectations

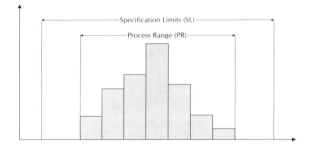

Processes that exceed expectations are usually last in line for any performance improvement efforts. Only when incapable and just-capable process have been brought to an improved level of performance capability should attention be turned to processes that are already exceeding expectations.

This does not mean that just because a process is more than capable, it cannot or should not be improved. It only means there are likely other priorities. Processes functioning beyond expectations can and should be improved. This is central to continuous improvement. Every performance level can be improved upon.

DETERMINING CAPABILITY

Determining the actual capability level of a process is a four-step procedure. These steps are:

1. **Determine Process Stability.** This is done through the control chart. A process can be said to have a defined capability only if the system is in a state of statistical control – operating under common cause variation. The control chart is required to make this assessment.

2. **Determine Process Variability.** This is done by plotting the histogram. The data used are the individual values used to create the control chart in step 1. The histogram

presents the performance profile of the data over the time period of interest.

3. **Compare Process Variation With Specifications.** This is accomplished by plotting the customer specifications on the histogram. These expectations are usually represented as vertical lines on the x-axis of the histogram. This enables a direct comparison of the specification with the data.

4. **Interpret.** If any values on the histogram lie outside the specification limits, the process is not capable of meeting expectations and will continue to produce a fraction of its output as non-conforming product. In contrast, if none of the values plotted on the histogram lies outside these specification limits, then the process is a capable one.

These four steps represent the basic and most direct approach to determining capability. The analysis is largely qualitative. It involves looking at the data and arriving at a conclusion of whether the process is capable or not. No calculations, beyond those required for the control chart, are required.

However, the *degree* of capability can also be determined. Doing so requires quantification, specifically of the distance between observed values in the histogram (voice of the process) and the specification limits (voice of the customer). There are a number of approaches to measuring this distance; however, all of them are driven by sigma (standard deviation). What differentiates various quantification methods is whether or not they transform sigma into some other form and how this is done. These methods are detailed in the section "Quantifying Capability" on page 484.

Determining Capability Example: Response Time

The first histogram example (See "Histogram Example 1: Time to Answer for Emergency Response" on page 465) concerned time to answer for incoming calls received by an emergency response department of a major municipality. In this case, an expectation set by management is that every incoming call will be picked up by an emergency response operator within 10 seconds. This represents a performance standard of the organization, for which the municipality holds the department accountable.

Can the department perform to this level? That is, can it answer incoming calls within 10-seconds? Answering this question is

the task of capability analysis. Our specification limit, to use the terms of capability analysis, is the 10-second performance standard. Notice this is a single-sided specification. There is no lower specification because in this situation, faster is better.

Step 1: Assessing stability through the control chart

The first step in determining capability is using a control chart to assess stability. Remember, without stability there is no capability. In this case, the control chart is an XmR chart, where every value taken is plotted.

The resulting control chart is presented in Exhibit 197: Individuals Control Chart of Time to Answer Data. As the control chart demonstrates, the process is in a state of statistical control and, therefore, its performance is reliable or stable enough to make some conclusions about its likely future level of performance. (All the observed values are within the control limits, indicating the system is operating solely under common causes.) This means we can proceed. If the process had no stability, there would be little use in trying to assess capability.

Exhibit 197: Individuals Control Chart of Time to Answer Data

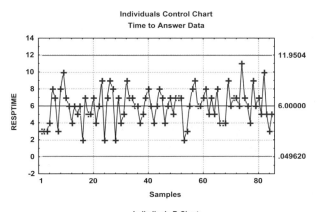

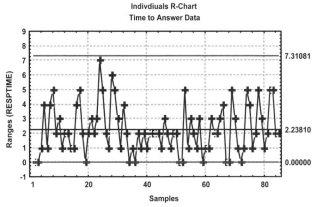

Step 2: Determine process variability through the histogram

Next is determining process variability using a histogram. The data used to create the histogram is the same data employed to create the control chart (see step 1). A different tool is being used to present the data in a different way. The control chart analyzes how stable the process has been over the period. In contrast, the histogram presents a profile of the process that emphasizes the degree of variability. The resulting histogram is presented in Exhibit 198: Time to Answer Histogram Before and After Specification Limit.

Step 3: Compare process variation with specifications

Making the comparisons between process variability and specifications is a simple matter of plotting the specification limits on the histogram. This is represented in the second histogram in Exhibit 198. In this case, the stated expectation is that all calls will be picked up with 10 seconds or less. Ten seconds, therefore, is the specification limit and it is represented as a vertical line drawn at the 10-second mark.

Step 4: Interpret

Interpretation is done by examining the relationship between the histogram and the specification limit – specifically looking for data that goes beyond the specifications. If they do, the process is not capable. In this case, some data go beyond the specification limit – a single data point at 11 seconds. As a result, we must conclude that the process is not capable of meeting the 10-second specification. Stated differently, the process will continue to go over the 10-second limit.

Hold on. Maybe the process is capable. After all, if it wasn't for that single 11-second result the process would have been capable. How do we know the 11-second result is not some anomaly?

Well, it is no anomaly. We know this because of the control chart. With the values operating in a state of control, the data plotted on the histogram represents a sort of "standard operating procedure" for the process. In other words, the 11-second result will happen again because it is a function of the current process design and construction.

This is a good example of why an assessment of capability must be initiated with the control chart. You can't tell what is

Exhibit 198: Time to Answer Histogram Before and After Specification Limit

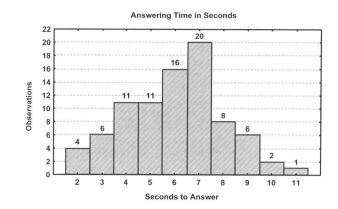

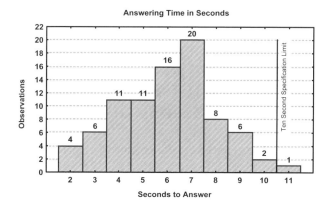

common cause and what is special cause variation without it. Once the stability of the process is confirmed, the data plotted on the histogram can be fairly assumed to be a typical set of data for the characteristics under analysis.

QUANTIFYING CAPABILITY

The capability analysis of time-to-answer data is straightforward, simple to administer and easy to interpret. It produces a simple and straightforward answer: the process is either capable or it isn't.

This response, for all its simplicity, may strike some as just a little too simple. What is missing is the natural follow-up question: "If things are 'bad,' just how bad are they?" In other words, there is often a need to quantify the degree to which the process is capable or incapable. Doing so moves the analysis beyond simply classifying capability (capable or incapable), to measuring the degree of capability or lack thereof.

Providing a measure of capability – that is, quantifying the degree of capability, allows for:

▲ **Determination of the amount of improvement required to meet customer expectations.** Capability can be used to determine or quantify the extent of a performance gap within any process or number of processes.

▲ **Comparison of different processes against a common performance metric.** The capability of two processes can be compared by their relative ability to meet customer expectations.

FOUR APPROACHES

Four basic methods to quantify the capability of a process are common.

1. **Sigma Analysis.** This method analyzes both the degree of spread (or variation) in the process and the extent to which the process is centered, measured in units of sigma.

2. **Capability Index:** This method converts the sigma analysis into an index where any value over 1.0 represents a capable process, and any value of less than 1.0 represents a non-capable process.

3. **Fraction Non-Conforming:** This converts sigma analysis into a proportion of non-conforming product. The degree

of capability, therefore, is represented by an estimate of the fraction or amount of non-conforming product that will be produced by the process.

4. **Taguchi Loss Function:** The Taguchi loss function sets up customer expectations as a continuous function (as opposed to a set of cut-off specifications), where improved process performance is usually measured in units of dollars and cents or reduced cost.

Note that *capability indexes* and *fraction non-conforming* both involve the conversions of sigma analysis into some other format. A legitimate question is, "Why bother?" If sigma analysis is the basis for two of the alternatives methods, why not just do sigma analysis and forget fraction non-conforming and capability indexes?

Why not indeed! The easiest, most straightforward approach is to simply adopt sigma analysis and forget the other two methods. Capability indexes add no information. Their sole advantage is in boiling down interpretation to a single reference index – over 1.0 is good, under 1.0 is bad.

Likewise, the fraction non-conforming method adds no information and even distorts the figures that result from converting

sigma. This is because a particular distribution must be assumed before such a conversion from sigma to fraction non-conforming can take place. The almost universal assumption is that the data are normally distributed – an assumption that is virtually impossible to verify. But fraction non-conforming speaks in a very customer/manager-oriented language, which specifies or estimates how many bad products will be made. This is rather more accessible than detailing how many sigma units we are from specifications.

These approaches are summarized in Exhibit 199: Summary of Capability Quantification Approaches, and are detailed starting with "1. Sigma Analysis" on page 492. All these approaches require finding a value for the process sigma (the standard deviation of the process) and determining the natural process limits from this value.

DETERMINING PROCESS SIGMA AND FINDING THE NATURAL PROCESS LIMITS

All the methods used to quantify capability depend upon determining a value for sigma. This is determined from the control chart. The average dispersion statistic from the control chart (either $\bar{R}$ or $\bar{s}$), is divided by a factor (either d_2 or c_4), and then

---

Table 199: Summary of Capability Quantification Approaches

Approach	Application	Statistic	Formula	Comment
Sigma Analysis	Process Range	ST	$ST = \dfrac{USL - LSL}{Sigma(x)}$	Provides results in units of sigma, which are easily converted to the original units of measure. The results make for easy interpretation, but will be confusing to those unfamiliar with process performance measurement.
	Process Centering / Single Sided	DNS	$DNS = \dfrac{T_{Min}}{Sigma(x)}$	
Capability Index	Process Range	C_p	$C_p = \dfrac{USL - LSL}{6 Sigma(x)}$	Converts sigma analysis to an index where values above or below 1.0 indicate more than capable, or less than capable, processes. Because it is an index, the results have no units of measure.
	Process Centering / Single Sided	C_{pk}	$C_{pk} = \dfrac{T_{Min}}{3 Sigma}$	
Fraction Non-Conforming	Process Range / Process Centering	$DPMO$	Normal Probability Tables	Converts sigma analysis results to an estimated number of defects (i.e. defects per million opportunities). Assumes normal distribution. Easy to communicate results.
Taguchi	Double-Sided Specifications	$EL_{(x)}$	$EL_{(x)} = k(s^2 + (\bar{x} - T)^2)$	Provides results in expected or average dollar loss per unit. Ignores "goal-post" specifications and deals with the economic impact of variation.
	Larger is Better	$EL_{(x)}$	$EL_{(x)} = k\left(s^2 + \left(\dfrac{1}{\bar{x}^2}\right)\right)$	Because it provides results in dollars it is very easy to communicate. Best when used with measured data (as opposed to attribute data).
	Smaller is Better	$EL_{(x)}$	$EL_{(x)} = k(s^2 + \bar{x}^2)$	

multiplied by 3 to get three-sigma. These formulas are presented in Table 200: Converting Control Limits to Natural Process Limits. The three-sigma value is then added to, and subtracted from, the process mean to obtain the upper and lower natural process limits.

Table 200: Converting Control Limits to Natural Process Limits*

Control Chart	Factor	Sigma for Individual Values	Natural Process Limits
XmR	None	$\dfrac{\bar{R}}{1.128}$	$\bar{R} * 2.659$
$\bar{X}, R$	d_2	$\dfrac{\bar{R}}{d_2}$	$\bar{X} \pm 3\dfrac{\bar{R}}{d_2}$
$\bar{X}, s$	c_4	$\dfrac{\bar{s}}{c_4}$	$\bar{X} \pm 3\dfrac{\bar{s}}{c_4}$

*   These formulas and a more detailed listing of Bias Correction Factors are presented in Appendix 1.

Table 201: Bias Correction Factors – Converting Control Limits to Sigma for Individual Values*

Control Chart Sub-Group Size	d_2	c_4
2	1.128	.7979
3	1.693	.8862
4	2.059	.9213
5	2.326	.9400
6	2.534	.9515
7	2.704	.9594
8	2.847	.9650
9	2.970	.9693
10	3.078	.9727
20	3.735	.9869
30	4.086	.9915
40	4.322	.9936
50	4.498	.9949
60	4.639	.9957
70	4.755	.9963
80	4.854	.9968
90	4.939	.9972
100	5.015	.9975

A table of d_2 and c_4 factors is provided in Table 201: Bias Correction Factors – Converting Control Limits to Sigma for Individual Values. These are the same d_2 and c_4 values presented earlier in Table 144: Control Chart Factors.

Why go through this calculation? Why not simply use the control limits on the control chart and use these as the natural process limits?

The answer is we can use the control limits from the control chart as the natural process limits, but only when using an *XmR* control chart or when using attribute control charts. However, when we have measured control charts with sub-group sizes beyond one ($\overline{X}$, R or $\overline{X}$, s), we need to apply the bias correction factors d_2 and c_4. Why? Because with the $\overline{X}$, R and $\overline{X}$, s charts, we are dealing with sub-group averages, not individual values. But with capability, it is the individual values we are concerned with, and the variation of individual values will always be greater than the variation of sub-group averages. The d_2 and c_4 factors essentially take this into account, and when divided into $\overline{R}$ or $\overline{s}$, determine sigma for individual values.

Let's take two examples of determining sigma for capability analysis. One involves using the Individuals (*XmR*) chart and the other an $\overline{X}$, R control chart with a sub-group size of four.

Determining natural process limits with the Individuals control chart: Time to answer data

Using the time to answer data for an emergency response department that was presented earlier, an *XmR* control chart is created. The control limits on this chart are the natural process limits for the histogram. This is shown graphically in Exhibit 202: Relationship Between Individuals Control Chart and Natural Process Limits. The histogram in this case has been plotted on its side to show how the control limits conceptually extend from the control chart to the histogram.

We can see from the control chart that the process is in a state of statistical control – operating under common cause variation. This means the process has a defined performance level, with an average time-to-answer of 6.0 seconds with an upper control limit of about 12 seconds and a lower control limit of just over zero seconds. These values also represent the upper and lower natural process limits.

Recall, however, that in this example, a specification that calls would be answered within 10 seconds was in place. Thus, the process is not capable despite the fact the process is 'in-control' – all observations are within the natural process limits.

Exhibit 202: Relationship Between Individuals Control Chart and Natural Process Limits

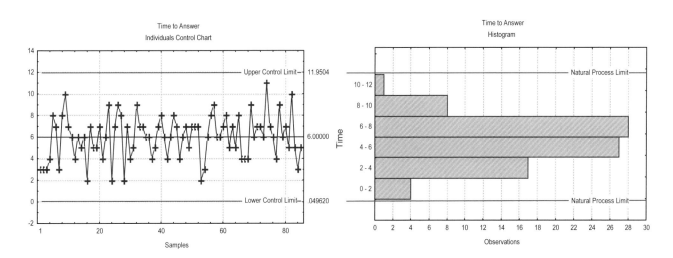

Determining natural process limits with the *x-bar, R* control chart: Service turnaround time

The situation is different with a control chart based upon subgroup averages. The control limits are no longer equivalent to the natural process limits. However, the d_2 factor enables us to accommodate this.

Take the example of a computer department analyzing the time it takes to turn around report requests from various user departments. A number of complaints has arisen about lengthy wait times beyond the 48 hours maximum time committed to by the Information Services vice-president. The vice-president in this case has noted that average response times are well below the 48-hour maximum specification. Making such observations, however, hasn't stemmed the complaints from users.

To help resolve the issue, a study is conducted of report turn-around time. Four report requests are tagged each day for 20 days. Tracking the turnaround time on each of these reports yields the data presented in Table 203: Service Department Turnaround Time. Each day is considered to be a sub-group. Because four measurements (sample reports) were taken each day, the sub-group size is four.

From this, an *X-bar, R* control chart is generated. The *X-bar* chart plots the average turnaround time for each day. On day one, this is the average of 40, 19, 35 and 32, which is 31.5. The *R* or ranges chart plots the difference between the largest and smallest values for each sub-group or day. On day one, this is the difference between 40 and 19, or 21. These control charts are presented in Exhibit 204: X-bar, R Charts of Report Turn-around Data.

From this data, it becomes easy to calculate the natural process limits. $\overline{R}$, or the average for the ranges, is divided by the factor given in Table 201: Bias Correction Factors – Converting Control Limits to Sigma for Individual Values. In this case, $\overline{R}$ is taken directly from the ranges chart. Its value is 21.55 (see Exhibit 204). The value from the table for d_2 for sub-group size

Table 203: Service Department Turnaround Time

Day sub-group	Sample				$\overline{X}$	R
	1	2	3	4		
1	40	19	35	32	31.5	21
2	41	35	23	33	33	18
3	24	15	25	30	23.5	15
4	16	34	35	29	28.5	19
5	40	32	15	33	30	25
6	18	22	23	43	26.5	25
7	10	29	27	33	24.75	23
8	30	27	29	36	30.5	9
9	27	24	41	33	31.25	17
10	34	44	33	39	37.5	11
11	50	22	35	38	36.25	28
12	18	21	25	45	27.25	27
13	29	44	34	42	37.25	15
14	37	49	39	30	38.75	19
15	44	16	11	29	25	33
16	38	52	37	29	39	23
17	44	35	40	16	33.75	28
18	16	26	13	50	26.25	37
19	32	11	21	33	24.25	22
20	18	28	27	12	21.25	16
					606	431
					30.3	21.55

Exhibit 204: *X-bar, R* Charts of Report Turnaround Data

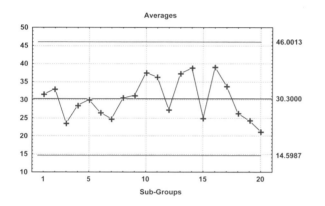

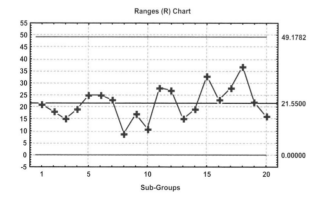

of four is 2.059. Dividing 21.55 by 2.059 yields a sigma of 10.47.

To create the natural process limits, we multiply 10.47 by three and then add and subtract this value from the process average. So, 10.47 times three is 31.41. This figure, added to the process average of 30.3 (see the averages chart) gives us an upper natural process limit of 61.71. Subtracting 31.41 from 30.3 yields a lower natural process limit of -1.11. Since the time cannot be less than zero, the lower limit can be ignored or set equal to zero. Thus, the natural process limits are zero and 61.71. Note that these values are different than the upper and lower control limits for sub-group averages.

Now to create the histogram. We have 80 observations in all. This would mean having eight or nine bins. The range between the highest observed value (52) and lowest (10) is 42. If we used eight bins, each bin would have a range or width of 42 divided by 8 or 5.25. This could be rounded to six to keep things neat and still ensure all the data is encompassed in the histogram.

Table 205: Frequency Table of Turnaround Time

Response Time	Count	Percent
7.0 < x <= 13.0	5	6.25
13.0 < x <= 19.0	10	12.50
19.0 < x <= 25.0	10	12.50
25.0 < x <= 31.0	15	18.75
31.0 < x <= 37.0	20	25.00
37.0 < x <= 43.0	11	13.75
43.0 < x <= 49.0	6	7.50
49.0 < x <= 55.0	3	3.75

Exhibit 206: Histogram of Turnaround Times

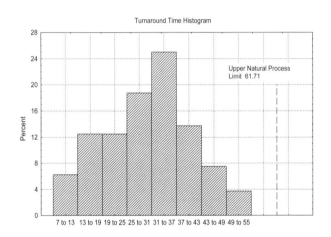

The resulting histogram is presented Exhibit 206: Histogram of Turnaround Times. The natural process limits derived from the calculation have been drawn in.

The natural process limits differ from the control chart control limits, because the latter focus on daily *averages* whereas the natural process limits focus on *individual* turnaround times. So, while the daily *average* turnaround time for the department will not likely exceed the standard of 48 hours (since the control chart limit is about 46), the turnaround on individual reports will exceed this limit on a regular basis. This is because the natural process limit (for individual reports) is far above 48 hours – 61.71 hours to be exact.

The example shows how the control chart can be used to determine the value of sigma for any characteristic, regardless of sub-group size. Once the value of sigma is known, and the natural process limits determined, the capability of the process can be quantified.

1. SIGMA ANALYSIS

Two basic measures are involved in sigma analysis. These are:

▲ **Specified Tolerance,** which is concerned with the amount of variation in the process relative to the distance between specifications. Upper and lower specifications are required for the calculation of specified tolerance.

▲ **Distance to Nearest Specification,** which focuses on the degree to which the process is centered, by determining the distance between the natural process limits and the nearest specification. Distance to nearest specification can be used with single-sided specifications (higher-is-better or lower-is-better), typical in service industry applications, as well as with double-sided specifications.

Specified Tolerance (*ST*)

Specified tolerance (*ST*) is defined as the distance between the specifications divided by sigma. This is expressed mathematically as:

$$ST = \frac{USL - LSL}{Sigma(x)}$$

Where:
USL = Upper Specification Limit
LSL = Lower Specification Limit
Sigma(x) = sigma derived from d_2 control chart factors

Six sigma represents the spread of the natural process limits for any process. So, a specified tolerance of six sigma means that the distance between the specification limits is the same as the natural process limits. This makes a *ST* of six sigma the minimum for any process to be considered capable.

An *ST* greater than six indicates that the process has some "elbow room" – there is some space between the natural process limits and the specifications. This would indicate the process is more than capable. Of course, a value of less than six indicates just the opposite, that the process is not capable of meeting specifications.

Distance to Nearest Specification (DNS)

The distance to nearest specification (*DNS*) is concerned with how close the process comes to the nearest specification limit. It takes into account that a process may not be capable when its specified tolerance (*ST*) is greater than six, but when it is also sufficiently off target to produce results beyond the specification limits. The formula is:

$$DNS = \frac{T_{Min}}{Sigma(x)}$$

Where:

T_{Min} = *the Minimum of (USL-$\overline{X}$) or ($\overline{X}$-LSL)*

$\overline{X}$ = *The Mean*

USL = Upper Specification Limit

LSL = Lower Specification Limit

Sigma(x) = sigma derived from the control chart d_2 factors

In this case, a *DNS* of three sigma units would represent the bare minimum of a capable process. A *DNS* larger than three indicates a capable process, since the distance to the nearest specification (measured in sigma units) is greater than the natural process spread of three sigma from the mean. In other words, the process is further away from danger. Likewise, a *DNS* of less than three indicates that some non-conforming product is being produced.

Example of ST and DNS calculations: Time to answer data

In our time-to-answer example for an emergency response department (See "Determining Capability Example: Response Time" on page 481 and "Determining natural process limits with the Individuals control chart: Time to answer data" on page 488), recall that the process had an upper specification limit of 10 seconds. Sigma in that example obtained from the *XmR* chart, was 1.984. With these values we can compute both

Specified Tolerance (*ST*) and Distance to Nearest Specification (*DNS*).

In the example, there was only a single upper specification limit since faster is better. In this circumstance, we would be concerned with calculating only *DNS*. However, for the purpose of demonstrating the calculations we can take the natural minimum time, namely zero seconds, to serve as the lower specification limit. In this case, the calculation becomes:

$$ST = \frac{USL - LSL}{Sigma(x)} = \frac{10 - 0}{1.984} = 5.04$$

In fact, as mentioned, only one specification limit was of real interest – the upper specification limit of 10 seconds. So using this in the *DNS* calculation, we take the distance from the mean (six seconds) to the upper specification (10 seconds) and divide by sigma.

$$DNS = \frac{T_{Min}}{Sigma(x)} = \frac{10 - 6}{1.984} = 2.016$$

Both calculations indicate the process is not capable of meeting specifications. An *ST* of 5.04 indicates that the process has excessive spread relative to specifications (specifically, the process is too wide by about one sigma). To make the process capable, we must reduce the variation in the time it takes to answer an incoming call.

Exhibit 207: Visualizing Specified Tolerance (*ST*) and Capability Index (*Cp*)

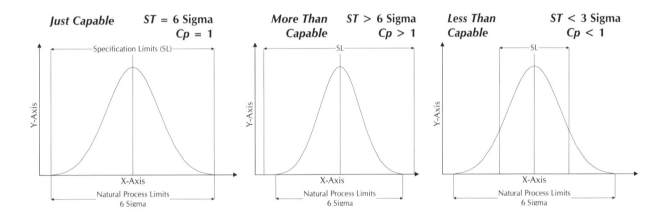

The *DNS* calculation also indicates that the process is not capable. With a *DNS* of 2.016, the process mean is simply too close to 10 seconds to prevent the occasional call from being answered past this upper specification.

This was the conclusion we reached using a qualitative approach, by mapping the specification on the histogram. At that time, we noticed an 11-second value beyond the upper specification limit of 10 seconds. We concluded that the process was not capable. Now we know the degree by which it is not capable – about one sigma.

2. CAPABILITY INDEX

Process capability indexes are simply a modification of the sigma analysis calculations. As with sigma analysis, there are two basic calculations. These are:

▲ C_p, which compares the variability of the natural process limits to the spread of the specifications. C_p is equivalent to specified tolerance with the same formula, except that sigma in the denominator has been multiplied by six to produce a value of 1.0 when the process is just capable (natural process limits equal the spread between specifications). Like *ST*, it requires an upper and lower specification limit to calculate.

▲ C_{pk}, is like C_p but takes into account the degree to which the process is centered. It is equivalent to *DNS* with the same formula, except that sigma in the denominator has been multiplied by three to produce a value of 1.0 when the process is just barely capable. Like *DNS*, C_{pk} can be used when there is only a single specification limit.

Sigma analysis and capability indexes, therefore, amount to much the same thing. Instead of a *ST* of 6.0 indicating a barely capable process, C_p produces a value of 1.0. Likewise, C_{pk} produces a value of 1.0 when the *DNS* is equal to 3.0. This is another way of saying that *ST* divided by six equals C_p and that *DNS* divided by three equals C_{pk}.

The difference is that C_p and C_{pk} are indexes where 1.0 is the "magic" number. As an index, there are no units associated with values of C_p and C_{pk}, so interpretation concerning the distance of these values from 1.0 are subjective. This is contrasted with *ST* and *DNS*, which are measured in units of sigma.

C_p Index

C_p represents process capability as the ratio between specification spread and the spread of the natural process limits or six sigma. This can be expressed mathematically as:

$$C_p = \frac{USL - LSL}{6 Sigma(x)}$$

We can see that this calculation is simply a more formal representation of the basic comparisons already highlighted. We are comparing the natural process limits to the specifications and developing a ratio from this comparison. Basically, three possibilities exist:

▲ **C_p is equal to 1.0.** Given the definition of the C_p index, C_p is equal to 1 when the spread of the natural process limits is equal to the spread of the expectations or specifications.

▲ **C_p is less than 1.0.** Here, the spread of the natural process limits is greater than the specifications. The process is simply incapable of meeting the specification set by management or the expectations of the customer.

▲ **C_p is greater than 1.** Here, the spread of the natural process limits is less than specifications. There is room to breathe. The process is robust and, to use the language of process improvement, the process is more than capable of meeting expectations.

Example of calculating C_p: Manufacturing appliance motors

Let's assume we are dealing with the manufacture of a specific component used by our customer to assemble appliance motors. The customer requires the part to have an external diameter of 72.0 mm with tolerance limits set at +/- 0.10mm. In other words, to be acceptable to our customer, the diameter of our part must be between 71.9 and 72.1 mm. These repre-

sent the "voice of the customer" and they will be represented as the specification limits our process must meet.

Exhibit 208: Customer Expectations and Process Performance

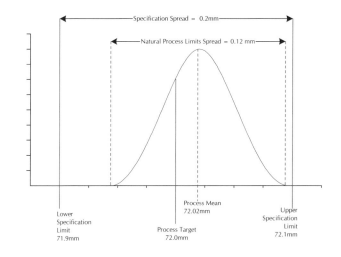

In analyzing our manufacturing process, control charts have been used to monitor process stability. The result (over the last month and a half) has been a capable process yielding parts with a mean diameter of 72.02 and a standard deviation or sigma of 0.02 mm. The three-sigma spread is therefore 72.02 +/- 0.06 or 71.96 (the lower control limit) to 72.08 (the upper control limit). What all this looks like is presented in the Exhibit 208: Customer Expectations and Process Performance.

To calculate C_p, we divide the specification spread by the spread in the natural process limits (six sigma). This would be:

$$C_p = \frac{72.1 - 71.9}{6 \times 0.02} = \frac{0.2}{0.12} = 1.67$$

Here we have a very capable process, as C_p is over one. Capable, that is, of meeting customer expectations. (Note that in this case, the *ST* would be 10.0, which is simply the calculated C_p multiplied by six.) With C_p we have an index – a score relative to 1.0. In contrast, with *ST* we have a measure of distance, which provides some additional information, namely that we have four sigma worth of elbow room in the process.

It is important to note here, however, that the calculations do not take into account how well the process is centered. Using the example above, what would happen if the spread in the natural process limits was the same, but the mean was 72.06mm? The process capability measured by C_p would still be 1.67,

indicating a more-than-capable process. But clearly, the process in this case would not capable of meeting expectations (Exhibit 209: Process Drifting With Mean at 72.06mm).

Exhibit 209: Process Drifting With Mean at 72.06mm

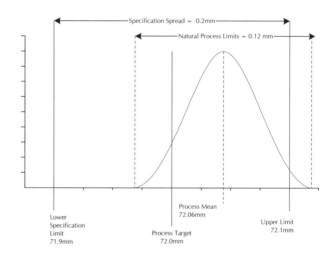

The problem here, of course, is that while process spread is relatively narrow, the process is not properly centered. Adjusting the C_p, index to take into account the degree to which the process is centered is the function of the C_{pk} index.

C_{pk} Index

C_{pk} attempts to adjust for the degree of centering within the process, thereby overcoming the problem identified with C_p. It does this by considering the worse case of two basic comparisons:

▶ The difference between the mean and the upper specification limit divided by three sigma.

▶ The difference between the mean and the lower specification limit divided by three sigma.

We are creating a ratio of the smallest distance between the mean and one of the specification limits, and three sigma. Where the index is greater than one, we can say the process is capable. Where it is less than one, the process is not capable of meeting expectations. Again, this is simply converting the *DNS* calculation to an index. The formula is;

$$C_{pk} = \frac{T_{Min}}{3Sigma}$$

Where:
T_{Min} = the minimum of (USL-$\overline{X}$) or (LSL-$\overline{X}$)
$\overline{X}$ = the Mean
USL = the Upper Specification Limit

LSL = the Lower Specification Limit
3Sigma = three sigma from the d_2 control chart factors

Using the same example, we can calculate C_{pk} for a process mean of 72.02mm and then for 72.06 mm. In this case, we need only to compare the process mean to the upper specification limit, because this will be the smallest of the two possible specification limit comparisons.

Let's examine the case for a process mean of 72.02 mm. The distance between the upper specification limit of 72.1 mm and the mean of 72.02 mm is 0.08 mm. This is divided by three sigma (0.06 mm), producing a C_{pk} of 1.33. This is greater than one, so we can say the process is more than capable of meeting specifications. (The *DNS* is 1.33 multiplied by three, or 4.0.)

However, notice that the C_{pk} is closer to 1.0 than C_p, which was calculated to be 1.67. This is because C_{pk} has taken into account that the process is a bit off target (by 0.02mm).

Now let's examine the case where the process mean is 72.06 mm. Recall that C_p indicated that the process was capable, despite it being decidedly less so from a visual inspection of the histogram (See Exhibit 209: Process Drifting With Mean at 72.06mm). The distance between the upper specification limit and the process mean is 0.04 mm. This figure divided by three sigma or 0.06 mm, is 0.67. This is less than 1.0, so we can conclude the process is definitely not capable of meeting expectations. C_{pk} has done a better job than C_p of evaluating process capability in this case, because it has taken centering into account. (Note here that the *DNS* would be 2.01, telling us that the process mean would have to be moved by a sigma unit to bring the process back to being capable.)

Time to answer data

Using the time to answer data used in calculating *DNS*, we can also calculate C_{pk}. *DNS* in this case was 2.016 (See "Example of ST and DNS calculations: Time to answer data" on page 494). C_{pk} is simply the *DNS* divided by three. So the value of C_{pk} is 0.672 (2.016 divided by 3.0).

Summary comments on process capability indexes

Process capability indexes provide a valuable way of summarizing process data in an easy-to-understand format – an index. All indexes, however, hide or destroy some of the informational content in the data by eliminating any units of measure.

Sigma analysis provides all the information of capability indexes while maintaining a standard unit of measure, sigma. Put simply, sigma analysis tells us by how much the process must be adjusted in real terms. Capability indexes do not.

To help overcome the shortcomings of C_p and C_{pk}, a guide providing a subjective interpretation of different C_p and C_{pk} values is offered. For clarity, the corresponding *ST* and *DNS* values are also provided. These are presented in Table 210: Qualitative Interpretation of Cp and Cpk.

If there is a choice, teams pursuing improvement initiatives are best advised to stick to sigma analysis over capability indexes. However, the popularity of indexes may make this difficult. In these circumstances, try to restrict the use of indexes to purposes of communication and use sigma analysis where the real work of improvement is being done.

3. FRACTION NON-CONFORMING ANALYSIS

Rather than focus on units of sigma or some index of capability, fraction non-conforming analysis focuses on the proportion or number of units that will fail to meet specifications for a

Table 210: Qualitative Interpretation of C_p and C_{pk}[*]

C_p or C_{pk} Value	Values for *ST*	Value for *DNS*	Description
2.0 or More	Over 12	Over 6	Six-sigma quality level. Beyond world class.
Between 2.0 and 1.67	Between 10 and 12	Between 5 and 6	World-class quality. Inspection can likely be eliminated.
Between 1.67 and 1.33	Between 12 and 8	Between 6 and 4	Very good quality. Reduce any existing inspection.
Between 1.0 and 1.33	Between 8 and 6	Between 4 and 3	Good quality. Inspection plans required.
Between 1.0 and 0.67	Between 6 and 4	Between 3 and 2	Poor quality. Defects and errors are built in to the system.
Less than 0.67	Less than 4	Less than 2	Very bad.

[*] This idea is adapted from Kaoru Ishikawa, Introduction to Quality Control, 3A Corporation, Tokyo, 1991. p. 238

given process. The intent is to make capability analysis a little more relevant to decision makers.

Executives may hum and haw or simply fall asleep listening to comparative C_{pk} or upon hearing that a *DNS* is 2.5. But it's pretty hard to ignore a conclusion that our process is going to produce 20,000 bad units this year or that 20 percent of everything we make is worthless trash. That is the strength of fraction non-conforming analysis. It converts capability into terms that everyone can understand and relate to.

Fraction non-conforming analysis takes one of two forms. These are:

▲ a fraction non-conforming is inferred from a sigma analysis.

▲ a sigma level is inferred from some known level of defects.

Converting the fraction non-conforming into some measure of sigma or vice versa is only possible if the nature of the underlying statistical distribution is known. If it is, the calculation is straightforward. Real world data, however, never corresponds perfectly to some theoretical distribution. Therefore, in practice, fraction non-conforming analysis is forced to impose an

Exhibit 211: The Fraction Non-Conforming, Assuming Normality

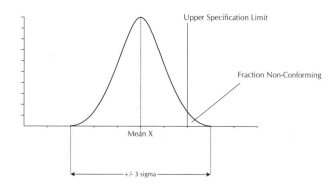

assumption upon the data. The common assumption is that the data is normally distributed.

The bottom line is to use extreme caution when converting sigma into fraction non-conforming and vice versa, or when communicating the results. Everything is based upon an assumption that, in all likelihood, cannot be verified and may likely be wrong.

Fraction non-conforming from a known sigma level

Once the assumption of normality is made, conversion of a known sigma level to fraction non-conforming is relatively simple. This is because the characteristics of the normal curve are known, including the relationship between sigma and the fraction non-conforming. These are presented in Exhibit 212: Areas Under the Normal Curve and Fraction Non-Conforming.

For example, using the table in Exhibit 212, the mean plus or minus three sigma (previously referred to as the natural process limits) will contain 99.74 percent of the data under the curve. By extension, 0.26 percent of the data will lie beyond these limits. If we had a C_p of 1.0 or a *ST* of 6.0 sigma where the specification limits exactly matched the natural process limits, fraction non-conforming analysis tells us that 0.26 percent of the parts or whatever we are making would fail to meet specifications. If we were making 10,000 parts a year, that would amount to 26 defective units annually.

For any known value for sigma, the fraction non-conforming can be read directly from any set of normal distribution tables.

Exhibit 212: Areas Under the Normal Curve and Fraction Non-Conforming

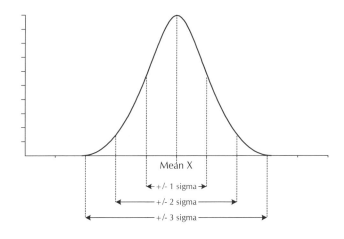

Mean X

+/- 1 sigma
+/- 2 sigma
+/- 3 sigma

Sigma	Inside	Outside
+/- 1 sigma	68.3%	31.7%
+/- 2 sigma	95.54%	4.55%
+/- 3 sigma	99.74%	0.26%
+/- 4 sigma	99.9937%	0.0063%
+/- 5 sigma	99.999943%	0.000057%
+/- 6 sigma	99.9999998%	0.0000002%

A more extensive normal probability distribution table is provided in Table 213: Sigma to Fraction Non-Conforming Table.

Table 213: Sigma to Fraction Non-Conforming Table[*]

Z Score Mean +/- Sigma	Single-Sided Probability Defect Rate	Double-Sided Probability Defect Rate	Z Score Mean +/- Sigma	Single-Sided Probability Defect Rate	Double-Sided Probability Defect Rate
0.0	0.5000000002	1.0000000000	3.0	0.0013499672	0.0026999344
0.1	0.4601721045	0.9203442089	3.1	0.0009676712	0.0019353425
0.2	0.4207403128	0.8414806257	3.2	0.0006872021	0.0013744042
0.3	0.3820886425	0.7641772851	3.3	0.0004834825	0.0009669651
0.4	0.3445783034	0.6891566068	3.4	0.0003369808	0.0006739616
0.5	0.3085375326	0.6170750653	3.5	0.0002326734	0.0004653467
0.6	0.2742530649	0.5485061299	3.6	0.0001591457	0.0003182914
0.7	0.2419635785	0.4839271570	3.7	0.0001078301	0.0002156603
0.8	0.2118553339	0.4237106679	3.8	0.0000723724	0.0001447449
0.9	0.1840600917	0.3681201835	3.9	0.0000481155	0.0000962310
1.0	0.1586552598	0.3173105195	4.0	0.0000316860	0.0000633721
1.1	0.1356661015	0.2713322030	4.1	0.0000206687	0.0000413374
1.2	0.1150697317	0.2301394634	4.2	0.0000133541	0.0000267082
1.3	0.0968005495	0.1936010990	4.3	0.0000085460	0.0000170920
1.4	0.0807567113	0.1615134225	4.4	0.0000054170	0.0000108339
1.5	0.0668072288	0.1336144576	4.5	0.0000034008	0.0000068016
1.6	0.0547992895	0.1095985789	4.6	0.0000021146	0.0000042293
1.7	0.0445654318	0.0891308636	4.7	0.0000013023	0.0000026046
1.8	0.0359302655	0.0718605310	4.8	0.0000007944	0.0000015887
1.9	0.0287164929	0.0574329857	4.9	0.0000004799	0.0000009597
2.0	0.0227500620	0.0455001241	5.0	0.0000002871	0.0000005742
2.1	0.0178643574	0.0357287148	5.1	0.0000001701	0.0000003402
2.2	0.0139033989	0.0278067978	5.2	0.0000000998	0.0000001997
2.3	0.0107240811	0.0214481621	5.3	0.0000000580	0.0000001160
2.4	0.0081975289	0.0163950577	5.4	0.0000000334	0.0000000668
2.5	0.0062096799	0.0124193597	5.5	0.0000000190	0.0000000381
2.6	0.0046612218	0.0093224436	5.6	0.0000000107	0.0000000215
2.7	0.0034670231	0.0069340461	5.7	0.0000000060	0.0000000120
2.8	0.0025551906	0.0051103813	5.8	0.0000000033	0.0000000067
2.9	0.0018658801	0.0037317603	5.9	0.0000000018	0.0000000036
			6.0	0.0000000010	0.0000000020

[*]	A more comprehensive normal probability table is presented in Appendix 3.

Using this table, we would find the sigma equal to 3.0 and move across to find the appropriate probability. The two-sided column should be used in this case, because we are assuming a part would be a defect if the critical quality characteristic was either too big or too small. In situations where smaller or larger is better, the nature of the specification is one-sided, so the single-sided probability column would be used.

Using the time to answer data, recal that the *DNS* was calculated to be 2.016. This was a single-sided specification as faster was better. To determine the fraction defective (number of calls taking longer than the 10-second specification), the nearest Z-score to 2.016 in Table 213needs to be found. This is 2.0. The corresponding defect rate (single-sided) is about 0.02275 or approximately 2.3 percent. This is the theoretical defect rate of the process. Notice this value is different from the observed defect rate of one call out of 85 or 1.18 percent (See "Histogram Example 1: Time to Answer for Emergency Response" on page 465).

Converting fraction non-conforming into sigma

As might be expected, the process of converting fraction non-conforming into sigma is simply the reverse of the process described above. We start with a count of the fraction and convert this into sigma.

For example, suppose that we are dealing with a telephone-based help desk support for a major software supplier. Owners of the software call the help line to obtain assistance with certain problems. One of the metrics deemed critical to performance is the call drop-off rate. These are the calls in which people tire of waiting for a technician to answer and eventually give up by hanging up the phone. Automatic call-recording equipment maintains data on call drop-offs.

From this data, it is determined that three out of every 1,000 incoming calls ends with the caller giving up in frustration and hanging up the phone. Thus, the call drop-off rate is 0.003 or 0.3 percent. The nature of the specification in this case is single-sided. As process performance improves, the lower the drop off-rate becomes, so smaller is better. In this case, we need to find 0.003 in the single-sided column of Table 213 and move across until we find an appropriate sigma. Using the table, we can see that the sigma is between 2.7 and 2.8. As such 2.75 is as good as estimate as any. This would imply a *DNS* of 2.75 or a C_{pk} of 0.92 (2.75 divided by 3.0).

Six sigma

A number of high-profile companies have recently adopted "six sigma" as an improvement approach or methodology. As a result, *sigma* has been in the business news lately. This in itself may be a first – where a statistical concept has obtained news-worthy status. The result has been a lot of confusion around sigma and six-sigma approaches to improvement.

Six sigma is essentially is a performance objective, and six-sigma improvement programs attempt to improve processes until they reach this level of performance.[69] These programs place considerable emphasis on estimating the level of defects per million opportunities – represented by different sigma lev-els.

Six-sigma programs, however, throw in a bit of a wrinkle. To accommodate the possibility of the process shifting over repeated cycles of operation, a "fudge factor" is built into the calculation. This fudge factor is set at +/- 1.5 sigma and is referred to as a "mean shift" within six-sigma programs.

A non-mean adjusted six-sigma performance level can be cal-culated using the double-sided column of the fraction non-con-forming conversion table. Find the defect rate corresponding to the 6.0 sigma. The rate from Table 213 is 0.000 000 002. This is usually expressed as the defect rate per one million opportu-nities (*DPMO*), which is 0.002 (the rate times one million). This translates to a C_p of 2.0.

A mean-adjusted, six-sigma performance level corresponds to the single-sided column of the table with a sigma of 4.5 (since we take into account a possible 1.5 sigma mean shift). Taking the figure directly from the table, the fraction non-conforming rate is 0.000 003 400 8, or roughly 3.4 defects per million opportunities. This is the defect rate most often associated with a six-sigma performance level.

The number of expected defects, both mean-centered and mean-shifted, for different levels of sigma and its relationship to capability indexes is presented in Exhibit 214: Six-Sigma Program Defect Rates. This is simply a summary of the defect rates presented in Table 213. It is important to note, then, that six-sigma programs make the same basic assumptions made by fraction non-conforming approaches. They assume the data is

---

69. Harry Miket, Richard Schroeder, Six Sigma, Currency Book, 2000 p. 13

normally distributed, and that a normal model best describes the operating characteristic of the process under examination.

Exhibit 214 also presents some of the implications of six-sigma analysis given that different products have different levels of complexity, defined here as either the number of parts or operations required to complete a final product. Operating at a mean-shifted, six-sigma performance level we would expect 3.4 defects per million operations. However, if the product required four such operations to complete, the expected number of products with some level of defect would equate to 14 per million constructed. If the same product required 1,024

operations, we would expect to make some 3,476 defective products for every 1 million made.

The fraction of non-conforming product, then, depends on the performance level of the process, as well as the complexity of that process or the product it produces. Fraction non-conforming or six-sigma targets do not refer to the overall product, but rather to a "single critical-to-quality characteristic."[70] The number of characteristics comprising the product or service delivered to the customer (complexity), greatly influences the product defect rate.

---

70. ibid.

Exhibit 214: Six-Sigma Program Defect Rates

Sigma	Mean Centered		Mean Shifted		PPM Defects as a Function of Number of Operations or Parts								
	Cp	Expected Defects	Cpk	Expected Defects	4	8	16	32	64	128	256	512	1024
1	0.33	317,400.000		697,700.000	991,649	999,930	1,000,000	1,000,000	1,000,000	1,000,000	1,000,000	1,000,000	1,000,000
2	0.67	45,500.000		308,700.000	771,616	947,841	997,279	999,993	1,000,000	1,000,000	1,000,000	1,000,000	1,000,000
3	1.00	2,700.000	0.50	66,800.000	241,599	424,828	669,177	890,556	988,022	999,857	1,000,000	1,000,000	1,000,000
4	1.33	63.500	0.85	6,200.000	24,570	48,537	94,718	180,465	328,362	548,902	796,510	958,592	998,285
5	1.67	0.570	1.17	233.000	932	1,862	3,721	7,429	14,803	29,387	57,910	112,467	212,286
6	2.00	0.002	1.50	3.400	14	27	54	109	218	435	870	1,739	3,476

4. THE TAGUCHI APPROACH

All this talk of comparing expectations with performance and the accompanying diagrams may remind you of the traditional "goal-post" approach to variation discussed in Chapter 2. In fact, the specification limits drawn in the histogram even look like goals posts. Well, that's pretty much what they are. The process must keep the ball (outputs) between the posts (specifications) to score points (good products). These approaches to quantifying capability have the advantage of being easy to handle and present graphically. Unfortunately, while easy to conceptualize, the goal post approach does a rather poor job of reflecting the reality of the situation.

Rather than behaving like a goal post or on-off function, expectations tend to decline continuously as the distance from the target increases. The further away we are from our expectations, the less satisfied we tend to be. The Taguchi approach recognizes this simple truth. Taguchi replaces the goal posts with a mathematical function that represents this decline in satisfaction (loss of value) as distance from the target increases.

The Taguchi loss function assumes the decline in value can be approximated using a quadratic function. A quadratic function is simply one where increasing the deviation from the ideal or target value produces increasingly larger losses in value. Specifically, the loss increases with the square of the deviation or distance from the ideal. Doubling the distance from the ideal or target would increase economic loss by a factor of four.

The formulas for the Taguchi loss function are provided for three cases:

1. **Nominal is best.** This is where some specified target value is assumed to be the ideal level for the quality characteristic measured. This situation is common in manufacturing environments where products have engineering targets to meet, such as a specific weights or dimensions. Deviations can happen in either direction from this target level. The formula for the expected loss within a process is:

$$EL_{(x)} = k(s^2 + (\bar{x} - T)^2)$$

Where:
$EL(x)$ = the expected average loss for $(\bar{x})$.
$\bar{x}$ = the mean of the process (derived from control chart)
s^2 = the variance (sigma squared)
T = the target value
k = a constant

The loss is equal to the variance added to the squared difference between the process mean and the target value, all multiplied by a constant k.

2. **Larger is better.** This is where a bigger value is better such as in the breaking strength of a material, brilliance of a television screen, or the longevity of an ink cartridge. The formula in this case is:

$$EL_{(x)} = k\left(s^2 + \left(\frac{1}{\bar{x}^2}\right)\right)$$

3. **Smaller is better.** The smaller a value is, the more value it has, such as the time required to build a product or answer an emergency phone call.

$$EL_{(x)} = k(s^2 + \bar{x}^2)$$

This is often the case in service environments where faster service (less time) is a critical characteristic. It also applies, however, when examining incidents of problems such as fraction defective, incidents of crime and the like.

Applying the Taguchi approach

The calculations are not as difficult as they may appear. Estimates of standard deviation (s) and process average $(\bar{x})$ are obtained from the control chart or from calculations of individual values derived from the histogram. The only missing value is k.

Determining k is the tricky part of the exercise regardless which of the Taguchi formulas is being used. This is because k must be estimated from empirical data.

The best way to estimate k, is find some value for the quality characteristic at which we know we have to scrap the product we are making. Because the cost of scrapping a product is usually known, this can be used to estimate k as follows:

$$k = \frac{Cost_{scrap}}{(x_{scrap} - T)^2}$$

Where:
$Cost_{Scrap}$ = the cost of scrapping the product
x_{Scrap} = the value of x at which the product must be scrapped
T = the target value

As may be evident from the calculation, an advantage of the Taguchi approach is that cost will be expressed in terms of dollars and cents. Let's face it, saying something has a C_{pk} of 0.67 is not exactly going to get management's attention. However, the Taguchi loss function speaks the language of management – money. And that tends to get everyone's attention.

Example: Deviation from target in manufacturing

Let's return to the manufacturing example used with C_p and C_{pk} calculations. The product manufactured has a target diameter of 72.0 mm. The specifications call for acceptance and rejection at +/- 0.10 mm. Let's take this example one step further. Now let's say that at these limits the product must be scrapped (x_{Scrap}) and that the cost of doing so is $670.00 ($Cost_{Scrap}$).

To find k, we substitute these values into the formula:

$$k = \frac{\$670}{0.10^2} = \$67,000$$

So k is $67,000. The other values required we know from the example. The process is operating with a mean of 72.02mm and with a standard deviation of 0.02mm. Substituting these values into our loss function provides the calculation:

$$L_{(x)} = k(s^2 + (\bar{x} - T)^2)$$

$$L_{(x)} = 67,000(0.02^2 + (72.02 - 72.00)^2)$$

$$L_{(x)} = \$53.60$$

The average loss is $53.60 for every unit we manufacture. This is the case despite the fact that process capability was calculated with a C_{pk} of 1.67, indicating the process had room to move and implying no economic loss.

How can this be? How can the relative loss be $53.60 per unit when process capability indicates we are not making any bad units? The answer is that all process capability approaches assume an on/off or good/bad approach to variation, despite the fact that variation doesn't work that way. The Taguchi approach recognizes the continuous nature of variation and the related degree of economic loss. In other words, the greater the variation, the greater the economic loss, regardless of what process capability or specifications have to say.

SUMMARY OF CAPABILITY

So where does all this leave us in determining capability? There are a number of important conclusions.

NO CONTROL (CHART), NO CAPABILITY

Capability, in any real sense, exists only when dealing with a system that is operating under common cause variation. The process is stable, in a state of statistical control with no (or very few) special causes of variation present. Since the control chart is the tool used to determine whether a system is operating under a system of chance or common causes, it follows that determining system capability must be done in conjunction with the control chart.

For those in the field trying to work through the often bewildering array of information and conflicting advice about capability, there is a simple guideline. Capability analysis must include a control chart of the data upon which the capability analysis is based. No control, no capability. No control chart, no capability analysis.

TWO DIMENSIONS TO PERFORMANCE

Improving performance is not limited to improving average response rates or getting any other performance metric closer to a target. There are always two dimensions to performance -- the degree to which performance is on target and the amount of variation present. This fundamental fact of performance is reflected in all the approaches to capability. The two-dimensional nature of performance improvement is represented graphically in Exhibit 215: Two Dimensions to Performance.

Donald Wheeler boiled this notion down to its very basics. In defining world-class quality, or for our purposes, world-class performance, he has provided the following:

"On target with minimum variance"[71]

---

71. Donald Wheeler, Understanding Statistical Process Control, SPC Press, Knoxville, Tennessee, 1992, p.146

Exhibit 215: Two Dimensions to Performance

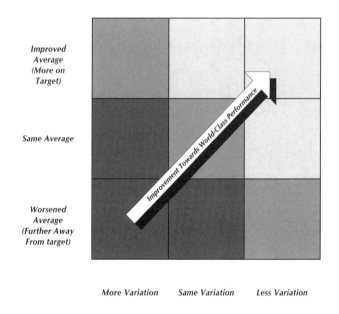

The more on target we are, the lower the variation, the greater the performance. All performance is characterized by these two dimensions. One is never enough.

TWO VOICES NEED TO BE HEARD

Teams seeking to improve performance of process or product need to listen to two voices – the *Voice of the Process* and the *Voice of the Customer*.

Control charts are the tools used to listen to the voice of the process. They provide us with critical information concerning the stability or reliability of the process, its mean (average) performance, and the amount of variation in that performance level.

Specifications and target values represent the voice of the customer. They reflect what the customer (internal or external to the organization) is demanding. They may be obtained from customer research or engineering specifications or some other source.

The two voices can be mapped on a histogram to determine capability, and a variety of quantitative techniques can be applied to determine the extent of that capability.

Capability analysis provides a vital link between these two all-important voices.

Analyzing Relationships: Tools for the Analysis of Cause and Effect

7

Run charts, control charts and histograms establish the behavior and performance of a system or process. But improvement demands going beyond analysis of performance, to the analysis of possible cause and effect relationships – to see if changing one thing yields a change or improvement in something else. To improve performance, the factors affecting performance (performance drivers) must be identified, validated and, ultimately, modified in some way.

Performance drivers go by various names: factors, explanatory variables, causal variables and root causes. Whatever the name, they are those real-world causes and conditions that have an impact upon the critical quality characteristic of interest – that is, upon performance. It could be the time of day, a particular assembly line, training levels, maintenance schedules, machine adjustment, temperature of a reaction process, or any other real-world factor.

THE SEARCH FOR PERFORMANCE DRIVERS

The theoretical model of the drivers that could be affecting some critical quality characteristic is represented through the cause and effect diagram. The possible explanatory variables or drivers are represented by the various branches of the diagram. These, in turn, lead to a specific critical performance characteristic that lies at the end of the causal relationships identified. The diagram presents the thoughts, beliefs and ideas of the team as to what could be impacting performance.

The search for performance drivers does not end with the creation of the cause and effect diagram. The diagram is, after all, nothing more than a visual map of our theory. It represents an educated guess as to where to look for performance drivers, but the map is not evidence that any such drivers have been found.

The theory represented by the cause and effect diagram must still be validated.

To validate and confirm the theory, we need data. Gathering and analyzing explanatory variable data relating to a response variable is, therefore, a way of testing the theory represented by the cause and effect diagram. If we see a relationship between the explanatory (causal) and response (effect) variable, we have evidence that the theory captures some essence of behavior and that a performance driver has been found. If no relationship emerges between a causal variable and the response variable, we have reason to believe the theory as represented by the cause and effect diagram is to some extent flawed. What was labelled a cause may not be a cause at all.

Things rarely work out so simply, though. When trying to understand what is happening, we are operating in the real world with all its attendant messiness and uncertainty. Various causes and conditions that were unexpected or unidentified (confounding factors) will confuse the results and make analysis and interpretation difficult.

Caution, therefore, is warranted. An apparent relationship between a causal and a response variable is not proof of causal effect. Other factors could be affecting our results and making it look as though some relationship exists even though it does not. Likewise, the reverse is also true. The lack of any evident relationship in an analysis is not proof the variable in question has no influence on the critical quality characteristic. It is quite possible it has such an influence, but that confounding factors have confused the results and only made it appear that no relationship exists.

For these reasons, improvement teams are well advised to remove the word 'proof' from their vocabulary. People parading some statistical analysis while declaring *"This proves it!"* need to get out of their office more for some real-world exposure. Statistical analysis proves very little. What it does is offer evidence.

Think of analyzing cause and effect and the search for performance drivers as a courtroom drama – some ultimate "who dunnit?" Evidence points in one direction, then another. New discoveries are made and new evidence introduced. Tension mounts. A surprise witness is introduced with new information. And all the while, the jury weighs each new fact, each new piece of evidence in an attempt to decide whose theory of the crime (prosecution or defence) best fits with the evidence presented. In the end, a decision is made and guilt or innocence is declared.[72]

In improvement teams, the search ends with agreement among team members on what the underlying performance drivers are and what must be changed to achieve performance improvement. There will always be uncertainty, however. Just because the team agrees that some cause is a performance driver doesn't make it so. The final test is ultimately the reality test. A change is made to some suspected cause, and the critical performance characteristic is examined to see if this change produces the desired effect. The search for cause and effect can be a cruel and difficult one.

But improvement teams are not totally unarmed in the search for cause and effect. There are tools designed to help those seeking the drivers of performance. These tools work by mapping the data associated with the two variables of interest (explanatory and response) on a single chart, in a manner that reveals underlying patterns that are evidence (not proof) of a causal relationship.

THE TOOLS

There are basically three analytical tools used to examine relationships between variables. These tools are:

▲ **Pareto Charts** are used when explanatory data is categorical and the associated response variable is counted. The different causal categories are represented across the x-axis, becoming the different bars of the Pareto chart.

▲ **Box & Whisker Plots** and their close relatives, dot plots, are used whenever explanatory variables are categorical or ordinal and the response variable is measured. Again, causal variables are represented across the x-axis while the response variable is presented along the y-axis.

▲ **Scatter Diagrams** are used when both the explanatory and the response variable consist of measured data.

Data comes in different varieties, and the tool used will depend in large measure on the data the improvement team is dealing

---

72. This cause and effect analysis as courtroom drama metaphor was first introduced to me by my business partner, Shelley McLean. She has a talent for making the business of data analysis accessible to those who normally don't like such things. I use the metaphor regularly in my seminars. The number of people I run across, often years later, that tell me about their latest search for the "guilty party" has convinced me of its appropriateness for getting people to remember the fundamentals of cause and effect analysis.

Exhibit 216: Examining Relationships - Exploring for Cause & Effect

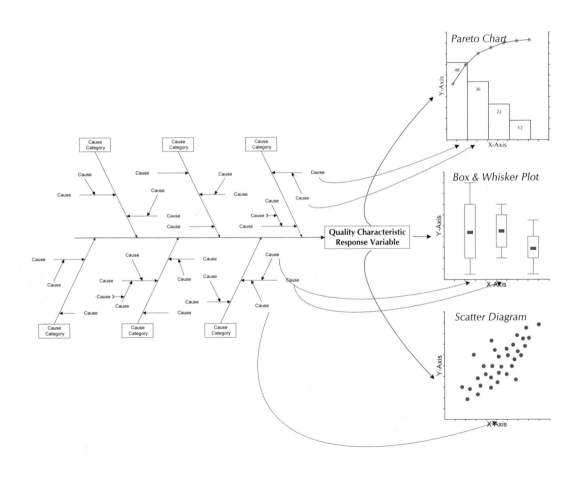

with. Categorical data places things in categories. Ordered data implies a scale, but where the units of the scale are not equal intervals apart. Both data types are common when improvement teams have stratified the data. Interval- and ratio-scaled data is usually measured data where a well-defined scale has been used – time, weight, length and temperature are all examples. Comparing the process yield with temperature of the chemical batch (both interval-scaled measures) would use the scatter diagram. Comparing process yield across three different machines (the different machines are categorical data) would use the box and whisker plot.

COMMON APPROACH TO ANALYSIS

A common approach to displaying data is used in all three tools. The explanatory variable – the variable assumed or believed to be the causal influence – is plotted along the x-axis. The performance characteristic or response variable is plotted against the y-axis. Just remember cause and effect – x and y.

This approach is consistent with that taken with run and control charts, where the factor of interest is the sub-group (usually time) presented along the x-axis, and the results or observa-tions associated with each time period are plotted against the y-axis.

PARETO CHARTS

The Pareto chart is really just a special form of frequency distribution (like the histogram), but is used with counted data that has been stratified or collected by categories.

The chart gets its name from the principle of distribution named after the Italian economist, Vilfredo Pareto. It was his observation that the distribution of wealth in Italy was uneven, and he proposed a logarithmic law of income distribution to fit the observed distribution. Subsequently, quality pioneer Joseph Juran proposed that such a distribution fits a wide range of process phenomena. This has become known as the 80/20 rule or the rule of the critical few and trivial many.

For example, companies may find that 80 percent of their profit comes from 20 percent of customers, or that 80 percent of process errors comes from 20 percent of the causes. The numbers are approximations, of course – the point is that these relationships tend not to be equally distributed. By focusing on the critical few, leverage can be gained.

The purpose of Pareto charts, then, is to help separate the trivial from the critical – to identify what is important and where activities should be focused in the process of performance improvement. By separating the important from the trivial, the Pareto chart helps identify areas of highest leverage in a system. These areas are where we get the biggest bang for our performance improvement buck.

DESCRIPTION

A Pareto chart consists of two parts. First is a bar chart showing the frequency of effect owing to each category. Second is a line representing the cumulative percentage of these effects.

Like the histogram, the Pareto chart is basically a frequency distribution where the frequency (response variable) is represented by bars. Unlike the histogram, the bottom (x-axis) in the Pareto represents specific categories, which are sorted from highest (greatest number of observations) to lowest (fewest number of observations).

Exhibit 217: Basic Pareto Chart

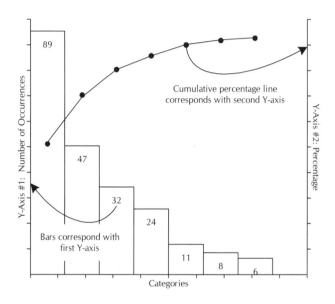

Also unlike the histogram, the Pareto chart has two y-axes. The first, to the left, represents the frequency of occurrence against which the bars are plotted. Additionally, a second y-axis is presented to the right, expressing the percentage of the total represented by each of the categories. A line is plotted against this axis. Thus, the Pareto chart tells us the actual frequency of occurrence for a particular category and the percentage of the total it represents.

For example, a company may want to present sales levels by customer types or segments. There is no implied order or importance to segments, beyond the counts associated with each. They are simply descriptions of customers. In such cases, the Pareto chart is an excellent tool to highlight the differences across segments. The different segments can be represented along the bottom axis, and sales levels presented through the height of the bars. Combining this with the percentage line immediately translates these sales figures into the proportion of the total sales volume attributable to each segment.

Two Types of Categories

The categories used to organize the data on the Pareto chart can be of two types. These are:

▲ **Content categories.** Content categories deal with different classifications within a single causal factor (a single branch on the cause and effect diagram). For example, if analyzing service problems, detailing the various types of problems encountered by customers would create a set of content categories. There is no classification of what is causing the problems, only the types of problems experienced. Note that a content category is often the result of stratification. For example, classifying service problems by the type of problem encountered is just another way of saying the problems have been stratified by type of problem.

▲ **Causal categories.** Causal categories deal with the search for the root causes of problems. The categories in this case are usually different factors (different branches of the cause and effect diagram). Using customer complaints again as an example, recording that a package was delivered late would be an example of a content category. Determining that the reason it was late was because the shipping address had been recorded incorrectly would constitute a causal category.

The Pareto "one-two punch" to root cause analysis

The two categories make a useful "one-two punch" in seeking out root causes of performance problems. The typical combination is content category analysis first, followed by causal category analysis.

Using customers complaints again as the example, the first Pareto chart would be conducted using content categories. This would identify the largest type of complaint experienced by the organization and, therefore, the area of greatest leverage. This becomes the focus of the second, follow-up Pareto. Using only the data for this type of complaint, the second Pareto would analyze the causes behind it. The one-two punch of Pareto analysis employs a principle referred to earlier – stratify first, then analyze.

Using the Pareto

The Pareto chart is a flexible and useful tool, especially when categorization or stratification of data is involved. Use the Pareto chart whenever:

▲ **You need to develop a focus on a specific problem or issue.** Pareto charts are intended to help distinguish the important few from the trivial many. In a process of continuous improvement, the trick to success is often not spreading yourself too thin. The Pareto chart highlights what is most important, and allows the team to focus on this aspect of the issue where leverage will likely be greatest.

▲ **You need to predict the impact or effectiveness of an improvement initiative.** Because the Pareto chart details the frequency of occurrence of a particular type of problem and usually the costs associated with this problem, the Pareto chart can be used to make an initial prediction about the impact of eliminating the problem or improving the situation.

▲ **You need to examine the relationship between a performance characteristic and some causal factors.** This is particularly true when the causal factors are categories and we are dealing with counted data. An example would be detailing the various causes for different types of defects in a product. In such applications, remember the one-two punch – stratify first to select the area of leverage and then analyze for causes.

▲ **You need to analyze the importance of various open-ended or qualitative data that can be categorized.** Organizations often amass great quantities of qualitative data, but it goes unused because people simply do not know how to analyze it. Customer complaints are a perfect example. Many organizations gather customer complaints and address the immediate concern or problem. But what can these complaints tell us about the system?

Plenty. Organizing these complaints into basic categories, and then tallying the number of complaints in each category provides an excellent analysis of such data. It details the frequency and nature of complaints the system is producing. Other such qualitative data includes open-ended responses on market research, employee opinion surveys and the like.

PREPARING PARETO DIAGRAMS

Pareto diagrams are easy to prepare. The are five basic steps.

1. Decide on the items to study

What is the purpose of the analysis? What do we wish to study? What data do we need? The first step involves answering these questions to fully understand what is expected of the analysis. Remember to distinguish the types of categories that are possible. If we want to know what is going on, we will create content categories to detail the nature of errors or problems. If we are seeking to understand why something is happening, we need to create causal categories for the data. The purpose of

the analysis will dictate the nature of the data and the type of categories used in the Pareto chart.

2. Stratify the data as appropriate

Stratify by different causes, type of error, nature of defect, or whatever category makes the most sense to the improvement team given the nature of the problem under analysis. A production process may involve three or more streams of production. Doing a single Pareto chart on either content or causal categories across all three streams would likely reveal little. Better to conduct a Pareto on each stream.

Remember, the purpose of the analysis is to reveal something about real-world conditions. The data, to be useful, must fairly represent those conditions. Therefore, the data should be stratified to reflect the underlying real systems and processes of interest.

3. Tally the number of occurrences in each category

Once the categories have been determined, tally or count the number of occurrences in each category. If possible, show losses in financial or monetary terms rather than simple frequency counts. This may require multiple diagrams and phases of analysis. For example, conduct an initial analysis to determine the frequency of an error, then a follow-up analysis to show the cost of these errors. These two analyses could then be combined to produce a final estimate of the financial losses resulting from the error.

4. Calculate the percentages

Once the physical counts or tallies have been completed, calculate the percentages of the total represented by each of these categories. This is done by adding up the total for all categories and then dividing this figure into the total for each category. The result is the proportion or percentage of observations attributable to the specific category.

5. Plot the chart

The Pareto chart is really two charts, a bar chart showing the counts calculated in step 3, and a line chart showing the cumulative percentages calculated in step 4. Use standard graph paper, histogram paper or, better yet, a personal computer with software capable of doing proper Pareto charts. The Pareto is a sorted chart so remember to plot the category with the most

observations first, the category with second-most observations next, and so forth.

USING AND INTERPRETING PARETO CHARTS

Here are some basic rules for using and interpreting Pareto charts:

▲ **Start with the problem yielding the largest benefits.** Overlooking the big issues is a common occurrence in organizations both large and small. Pareto is intended, in part, to overcome that tendency. Focus on the problems yielding the biggest payoff, but be sure your team has the ability to implement the changes required. Pareto charts also help provide focus to improvement efforts – to set priorities. Too often, we dilute improvement efforts by trying to fix everything. The result is we end up fixing nothing. The Pareto chart can help get teams focused on the big issue first, moving on to other issues once the first problem has been addressed.

▲ **Understand the effects of time.** Gathering data over too short a time period can bias results. Too long a time period may confuse the analysis because corrective actions may be included along the way. The Pareto, like the histogram, is intended to provide a snapshot of the process. Time and sampling approach must be taken into account before the analysis is conducted.

▲ **Do before and after diagrams.** Pareto diagrams can effectively document the impact of an improvement team's actions. Success shows – the content category that was the focus of the team's improvement effort should drop relative to other categories on the Pareto.

For example, solder defects on a circuit board may be the target of an improvement team's efforts. This is the largest type of defect experienced, accounting for roughly 40 percent of all circuit board defects. After a change is made to the set-up parameters of the solder machine, the number of overall defects declines and the proportion of solder defects falls to third place, accounting for just over 10 percent of the defects experienced with the boards. Evidence of a successful improvement initiative.

However, it may be that after the improvement effort, no change in the targeted error is observed in the Pareto chart. Such a result is not without value to the team, however.

Something has been learned, if only that the implemented improvement has had no impact. The team can now turn its attentions elsewhere, to more promising corrective actions. As such, the Pareto can help analyze where improvement efforts went wrong and serve as input to modify the cause and effect diagram.

Some patterns tend to emerge when using Pareto to document changes resulting from process improvement activities. These include:

▲ **The defects or losses in the problem area targeted for improvement suddenly decrease.** This is an indication that our quality improvement efforts are successful, and can be used to document the payoffs from the improvement effort.

However, it should be noted that changes in performance may also be a result of the attention paid to the problem, independent of our system improvement efforts (Hawthorne Effect).[73] Track performance over the longer term to ensure improvement efforts are permanent.

▲ **All sources of defect or problems begin to decline.** This indicates that our improvement focus in one area is bringing the entire system into a greater level of control or higher level of performance. As a result, benefits are accruing across the system. For example, a single causal category may produce a variety of problem types. By focusing improvement effort on this single factor, error reduction occurs across a host of problem categories.

▲ **The errors or problems in the area in which improvement efforts are focused declines, but overall defect rates remain constant.** This is an indication that the process under examination is not in a state of statistical control. Chances are the system may even be chaotic, with nothing being done the same way twice. If this happens, adopt a standardization strategy to bring consistency to the system.

73. The Hawthorne Effect refers to the results of efficiency improvement experiences at Western Electric's Hawthorne Plant over 50 years ago. Experimenters adjusted the lighting conditions in an effort to improve worker output. When they turned the lights up, output increased. When they turned the lights back down, the output went up again! The basic conclusion was that the workers were working harder because they knew people were experimenting on them.

PARETO EXAMPLE 1: ROOT CAUSE OF WORKER INJURIES

A steel company is investigating the current levels of worker injuries occurring at a pipe manufacturing plant. Beyond the concern for the safety of its employees, management believes the levels are out of line with industry standards and is concerned that worker compensation payments may soon increase. The bottom line is that management needs to reduce the level of injuries occurring on the job.

A process improvement team is formed to accomplish the task. The team begins by reviewing the types of accidents occurring to see where the biggest problems are. Fortunately, accurate safety records are kept, allowing the team to gather reliable historical data. The team decides to go back through two years' worth of workers' compensation claims to see what was going on.

The first analysis examined the type of injuries experienced at the plant. The number of occurrences, as well as the cost to the organization grouped (stratified) by type of injury, were captured and Pareto charts created. These data are presented in Table 218: Frequency Table for Pareto Chart – Worker Injuries, and the resulting Pareto charts are presented in Exhibit 219: Pareto of Injuries and Cost.

Table 218: Frequency Table for Pareto Chart – Worker Injuries

Location of Injury	Number of Time Lost Accidents	Dollar Value in Workers' Compensation Claims
Eyes	23	$94,300
Back	12	$60,000
Feet/Leg	9	$16,200
Hands	6	$10,200
Other	3	$3,600
Total Injuries	53	$184,300

From this analysis of occurrences and cost, the team decided to focus on reducing eye injuries. This was the most common type of injury experienced and also had the greatest cost to the organization. Moreover, the team felt the very nature of eye injuries, with the potential for permanent blindness, required addressing these injuries first.

If nothing else, the Pareto gave the team a focus to the improvement efforts. The first stage of improvement would

Exhibit 219: Pareto of Injuries and Cost

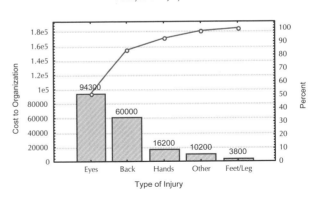

deal with reducing eye injuries. In this way, the resources available to the team can be concentrated on a specific target rather than dispersed across a host of different possibilities. Notice that the categories here are content categories. We are focused on the performance or response variable (injuries) and are analyzing the type of injuries that occur.

DRILLING DOWN FOR ROOT CAUSES

Knowing that most accidents involved eye injuries is one thing, knowing why is another. To find out what is going on, teams will often have to "drill down," conducting a Pareto on the initial Pareto, in this case analyzing only eye-injury accidents. Again, the Pareto chart was used to analyze the additional data and essentially drill down in search of potential root causes. The team wanted to know what activity employees were engaged in when the injury occurred. They went back to the records and gathered this activity data. Where the data was unavailable, employee interviews filled in the gaps.

As detailed in Exhibit 220: Pareto by Activity, most eye-injury accidents occurred while cutting operations were being performed, usually on a lathe. The categories on the Pareto are

Exhibit 220: Pareto by Activity

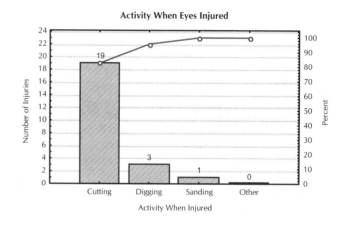

now causal. They identify what activity the employee was engaged in at the time the injury occurred.

This result was confusing to the team because the company insisted on employees wearing protective goggles during these operations. Moreover, in reading the accident reports, employees indicated that the accident occurred just as they had stopped working and were removing their goggles. This seemed unusual – so many accidents occurring in this way.

Interviews with employees, however, revealed a different story. Goggles had become so yellowed and scratched with age, it had become common practice among employees to let the goggles "accidently" slide down the nose to get a better view when doing detailed cutting work. This was never to be stated in the accident reports because it would be admitting to breaking company policy.

The replacement of existing goggles eliminated virtually all eye injuries at the plant. Moreover, management introduced a policy of giving employees the right to purchase basic personal safety equipment (goggles, safety boots, gloves, etc.) at any time without the need for prior managerial approval. At last report, expenses on such items were not significantly above the figures in other years, but accident incidents had dropped dramatically.

This provides a good example of the Pareto one-two punch. Use the Pareto on content categories first to identify areas of greatest leverage within the system. Then analyze this area of leverage by causal categories to identify root cause.

PARETO EXAMPLE 2: ANALYZING CUSTOMER COMPLAINTS

A bank regularly conducted follow-up service satisfaction surveys with its customers. These tended to rely on numerical summaries of satisfaction: *"How did you find the overall level of service on a scale of 1 to 5, where 5 means completely satisfied and 1 means completely dissatisfied?"* The organization also gathered open-ended feedback where respondents were encouraged to provide comments on specific problems or dislikes with the bank. This had produced considerable data and always made for entertaining reading. But it was generally regarded as useless information because the organization had no clear way to make sense of it all.

A performance improvement team responsible for finding ways to increase business customer satisfaction went back through the old customer survey files, to see if they could provide any useful insights on how service might be improved. The team segmented business customers and compiled the listing of customer complaints. These were placed on sticky-notes and organized into categories using an affinity charting procedure (see Chapter 8).

The number of complaints associated with each category was tallied and placed on a Pareto chart (see Exhibit 222: Pareto of Business Customer Complaints). The results were somewhat disappointing. Although some priorities did emerge, the results were not as clear as team members would have liked. The top three categories, for example, accounted for less than 60 percent of the responses. On this basis, the Pareto analysis offered only marginal help in identifying priorities for improvement.

Table 221: Business Customer Complaints by Category

Categories	Total Business	Percentage Distribution
Slow Approvals	341	22.82
Repetitive Info	214	14.32
Confusing Forms	302	20.21
Scheduling	139	9.30
Error in Set Up	226	15.13
Interest Rates	118	7.90
Branch Hours	96	6.43
Treatment	58	3.88
Total	1,494	100.00

The team, remembering that such flat distributions are often the result of mixing the data arising from different systems or

Exhibit 222: Pareto of Business Customer Complaints

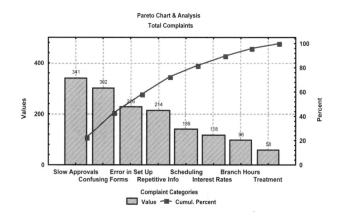

processes, decided to stratify the data. Segmenting business customers, on the basis of whether they were opening or making changes to loans accounts versus deposit accounts at the time the complaint was registered, produced more useful results. The team reasoned that the process for handling loans was very different than the process for opening or changing deposit accounts. Therefore, people's experience with the system would be different.

Fortunately for the team, records were maintained noting the type of activity or transaction engaged in. This enabled the team to stratify responses. In this case, the team decided to maintain the original set of categories. The resulting stratified Pareto charts are presented in Exhibit 223: Pareto Stratified by Deposit or Loan Complaint.

With the data segmented or stratified in this fashion, some clear priorities emerge. Those business customers engaged in changing or opening deposit accounts most frequently complained about errors experienced in the set up of their account, along with confusing forms. These two categories accounted for about half of all deposit-related complaints.

The results with loan accounts were even more dramatic. Those engaged in dealing with a loan account complained most frequently of slow approval process, repetitive information requirements and confusing forms. These three categories accounted for about 80 percent of all loan-related complaints.

Improving its position in the loan market was a high priority for the bank. Because of this, they chose to target the slowness of the approval process as the first priority. Since it could be tightly coupled with confusing forms and repetitive information requirements (often due to different forms requiring the same information), the company decided to redesign the pro-

Exhibit 223: Pareto Stratified by Deposit or Loan Complaint

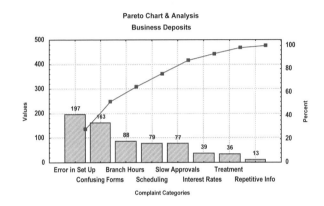

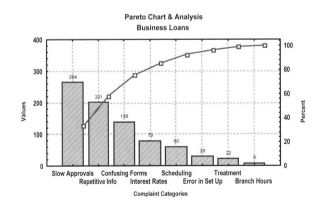

cess from scratch. The bank eliminated forms and informational requirements that added no value and removed excessive levels of approval. The result was a reduction in loan processing time of 50 percent, combined with an elimination of over 70 percent of the paper required for loan approval.

OPEN-ENDED RESPONSES

The customer complaint analysis example demonstrates a good approach to use when dealing with any type of open-ended responses to a questionnaire. Too often, the written responses to questions on customer or employee surveys consist of a long list of quotes. It is far better to get the organization involved in classifying or categorizing the responses, and then analyzing the number of responses in each category. This provides not only an indication of the nature of respondents' concerns, but some indication of how widespread these and related concerns are. In short, it provides the big picture view of the type and distribution of complaints the system produces.

BOX & WHISKER PLOTS

J.W. Tukey first introduced the box and whisker plot in his 1977 book, *Exploratory Data Analysis* (Addison-Wesley). Dr. Tukey is known in the statistical community for advocating simple graphic techniques for analyzing data, and the box and whisker plot certainly fills the bill.

The box and whisker plot attempts to preserve and present the variation in a data set, but without all the complexity of the histogram. This makes it easier to compare distributions or results where the data has been stratified by category. The box and whisker plot can also be used to represent distributions where there are limited amounts of data.

DESCRIPTION

The box and whisker plot comes in different varieties. For most applications of performance improvement, however, teams will likely use the median or quartile box and whisker plots, so we'll focus on these.

Exhibit 224: Basic Box & Whisker Plot

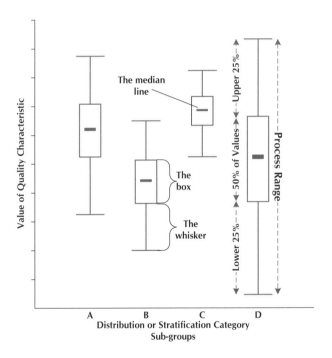

The box and whisker plot basically divides the data into four parts or quarters. Imagine ordering the data by placing the largest value at the top of the page, the second-largest value

beneath that, and so on until all the data had been ordered from largest to smallest. If we had 20 different values arranged in this way, we could draw a line after the first five values (the upper quartile) then under the next five (the median point) and then under the next five (lower quartile). This is essentially what the box and whisker plot does – order the data and then indicate where the quartiles are.

The basic box and whisker has the following components:

▲ **The median line, indicated by a horizontal line dividing the box**. Recall that the median is a measure of central tendency dividing the data into two equal halves, with half the observations falling above the median line and half below.

▲ **The "box" encloses the second and third quartile.** These quartiles make up the middle half of the observations. How the box is positioned relative to the median is an indicator of how symmetrical the distribution is.

▲ **The whiskers of the box and whisker plot enclose the highest and lowest values**. This is the range of the data set. The upper whisker contains the largest 25 percent of the values and the lower whisker contains the smallest 25 percent of the values.

▲ **Outliners are sometime used and indicated by asterisks on the box and whisker plot.** These are observations in the data that lie far outside the adjacent values. These observations are unusually far from the center of the distribution, and the team should investigate to see if they are the result of measurement error or an unusual set of conditions in the process.

The information in the box and whisker is similar to that of a histogram – both depict the central tendency and dispersion in the data. The box and whisker plot is a more concise, simplified version, making it ideal when more than two distributions need to be compared or when data is too scant to use the histogram.

This simplicity, however, also means that some of the information present in the histogram is lost in the box and whisker plot. The relationship between a distribution and the box and whisker is represented in Exhibit 225: Relationship Between a Distribution and the Box & Whisker.

Exhibit 225: Relationship Between a Distribution and the Box & Whisker

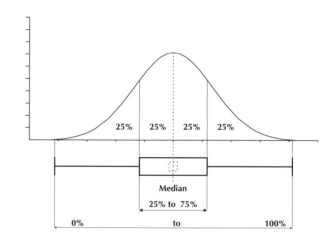

WHEN TO USE THE BOX AND WHISKER PLOT

So why not use histograms with all the additional information they present, and forget about box and whisker plots? There are a number of reasons to use a box and whisker plot:

▲ **When comparing distributions.** The simplicity of box and whisker plots allows multiple box and whiskers to be plotted on a single chart so that comparison of different distributions can be made. Try plotting four histograms on a single page and see the mess that results! Any more than two or three histograms on a single plot (some would say two is too many) and interpretation and comparison becomes difficult. The complexity of the task certainly increases considerably as the number of histograms to be compared increases. In contrast, it is easy to make comparisons among as many as 10 box and whiskers on a single plot and make sound interpretations of the data. In short, whenever you want to compare results from two or more groupings of data, consider using use the box and whisker plot.

▲ **When using relatively small data sets.** Box and whisker plots can be used to effectively display data when less than 50 data points have been gathered. Histograms generally require 50 data points, preferably more. At times, gathering this amount of data is impractical or simply impossible. When this is the case, the box and whisker plot can display the data set effectively. However, box and whisker plots should not be used when there are less than eight data points. In these cases, use a simple dot plot (discussed later in this section).

▲ **When testing theories and identifying root causes.** With a cause and effect diagram in hand, teams might want to examine or confirm the relationships theorized in the diagram. Box and whisker plots provide the capability to do so when the causal variables are categorical or ordinal in nature. Moreover, as the search for root causes continues and analysis proceeds up the causal chain represented in the cause and effect diagram, the amount of data available typically grows smaller. Using box and whisker plots means this process can continue, even when the data sets become small.

BOX & WHISKER INTERPRETATION

The strength of the box and whisker plot is its ability to compare multiple distributions even when the data is relatively scant. Interpretation, then, is largely focused on comparing the various box and whiskers plotted to identify areas of difference among them.

If the patterns of the various box and whiskers for each of the distributions or factors are similar, then there is little evidence that the differences that define the various factors analyzed have an impact upon performance. In contrast when differences in the response variable for different factors are observed on the box and whisker, there is evidence that the differences that define these factors have a causal impact upon performance.

For example, emergency response times could vary depending upon the day of the week a call is received. Each day would represent a sub-group. If the box and whisker plots for each day were similar, then we would conclude that the day of the week the call is received has little or no causal impact upon performance.

In contrast, if the various box and whisker plots were different from one another, then we would conclude that the day of the week does indeed influence response times. When we see these differences, it leads us to believe there is more than random chance operating and that the factors of interest are actually having an impact on performance.

When comparing distributions, attention must also be paid to the patterns displayed by the individual box and whiskers:

▲ **Examine the location of the median line.** Comparing the locations of the median across the different groupings of data conveys where the distributions are centered relative to one another. For example, in comparing the output of different machines, a box and whisker with a lower median point might be indicating wear on a particular machine relative to the rest.

▲ **Compare the sizes of the boxes and the lengths of the whiskers.** The size of the box and the length of the whiskers show how spread out the data is, indicating variability. By comparing the relative sizes of boxes or whiskers across categories, the relative variability of output can be estimated.

▲ **Look at the overall shape of each box and whisker.** Because the box and whisker gives a picture of the distribution of the sub-group or category it represents, you can estimate whether the data in the category appears to be normal or skewed. When the box and whisker is approximately symmetrical – the lengths of the whiskers and the two halves of the box are about equal – it suggests the data for the category is symmetrical. Where the plot extends in one direction or the other it suggests the distribution is skewed.

The Exhibit 226: Distributions Associated With Box & Whisker Patterns details some typical box and whisker patterns:

Exhibit 226: Distributions Associated With Box & Whisker Patterns

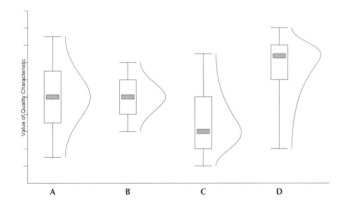

A   is a balanced, 'normal' distribution pattern. The median line is in the center of the distribution and the length of the box and the whiskers are balanced.

B   is similar to A except now the dispersion, as measured by the range, is much less.

C   is a skewed distribution where the bulk of the values are relatively low on the measured scale.

D   is also skewed, this time in the opposite direction, with the bulk of values relatively high on the measured scale.

HOW TO CONSTRUCT A BOX AND WHISKER PLOT

The nature of box plots makes them relatively tedious to complete by hand. The calculations are mathematically simple, but because they require the ordering of data, this simplicity is not reflected in actual construction.

Generally, construction of the box and whisker tends to get pretty complicated once the number of observations in each distribution exceeds 20. Ordering this amount of data and dividing it into quartiles is one of the more tiresome processes of analysis. Whenever possible, therefore, use a computer to create the box and whisker analysis for you. Any good statistical software package has the capability and you'll appreciate the time and effort saved.

Nevertheless, here is the procedure for creating the box and whisker plot.

1. Collect the data

All the values need to be recorded and classified when more than one distribution is to be compared. Capturing the classification or grouping data is critical, whether doing the construction by hand or computer. Every measurement in the response variable must have a corresponding classification so that you (or the computer) know from which distribution the data was obtained.

This means the improvement team must have an idea or a theory of what factors influence the response variable **before** the data is collected. Trying to identify possible causal relationships after data collection is difficult to impossible. Theory comes first. Data is then used to confirm or verify the theory – not the other way around.

2. Order the data from each distribution

To create the box and whisker plot, the data must be ordered or sorted so the median and quartiles can be identified. This is the tedious part of the process and there is no easy way to do it. Start with one distribution or sub-group of data. Find the smallest value in the data set and write it down on a separate piece of paper. Put a light line through the number in the data set so you don't count it twice. Now find the next-lowest number and write it down beneath the last number and so on. At the end of this process you will have a listing of all the data in order for each sub-group or category.

3. Find the median and quartiles

Once the data set has been ordered, count up the number of values you have in each data set. A handy way of doing this that facilitates calculation is to write the order in which the number appears besides the value – write down '1' beside the first number (lowest value), a '2' beside the next value and so on (see the sort position column in Table 227: Emergency Response Time Data in Seconds for an example).

The median represents the middle of the data. To find the middle data point, add one to the number of observations and divide by two. This gives you the depth or position of the median point. The equation provides an exact position when the number of data points is an odd number.

$$Depth\ of\ Median\ =\ d(\tilde{x})\ =\ \frac{n+1}{2}$$

When the number of data points is even, the position of the median will contain a decimal. In this case, calculate the average (mean) for the two values on either side of this decimal and this becomes the median. Finding the quartiles uses a similar procedure as finding the median and employs the following formulas:

$$Depth\ of\ First\ Quartile\ =\ \frac{n+2}{4}$$

$$Depth\ of\ Third\ Quartile\ =\ \frac{3n+2}{4}$$

4. Draw and label the axes

The horizontal axis generally represents the categories that define each of the distributions. These need to be clearly labeled so we know what we are comparing.

The vertical axis must contain the range of values for all the distributions or sub-groups to be analyzed. A simple rule is to make the top end of the scale about 25 percent larger than the largest value in the data. Likewise, the lower end of the scale should be about 25 percent lower than the smallest value in the data set.

5. Draw the box and whisker plots

Using the numerical calculations performed in step 3, draw the box and whisker plot for each distribution. Be careful to ensure that each box and whisker is drawn above its corresponding label on the x-axis.

Make sure the symbols of the plot are labeled clearly. The reader must know if outliners are included in the process range or have their own symbol. A clear legend lets them know.

6. Interpret the results

Interpret the results of the analysis. Do the box and whiskers plotted for each sub-group look the same or are they different? If different, how are they different? Is the median value lower or higher? Are the relative amounts of dispersion the same? Do the individual box and whiskers look balanced or skewed?

Answering these questions requires the application of the ITT – Inter-ocular Trauma Test. With proper preparation, the message in the box and whisker plot should hit you right between the eyes.

BOX & WHISKER EXAMPLE 1: EMERGENCY RESPONSE TIMES

A process improvement team is investigating the time it takes emergency response vehicles to reach emergency sites. Some staff have speculated that response time at night is worse, because of the increased demand for emergency response during these hours and the greater difficulty of driving at night.

The first task of the team was to investigate whether day and night response times were indeed different. A small, carefully selected random sample of response times from the last month was drawn to see if there is any evidence to support this theory or whether the improvement team should spend its time elsewhere. The data gathered is reproduced in the first two columns of Table 227: Emergency Response Time Data in Seconds.

Table 227: Emergency Response Time Data in Seconds

Day	Night	Sort Position	Day Sorted	Night Sorted
9	20	1	7	10
12	27	2	7	10
10	10	3	8	12
15	22	4	9	13
14	21	5	10	14
19	24	6	10	14
11	19	7	11	15
7	13	8	11	16
17	14	9	12	16
16	21	10	12	16
16	16	11	12	17
12	17	12	13	17
10	19	13	14	18
7	12	14	15	18
11	22	15	16	19
13	10	16	16	19
8	23	17	17	19
12	18	18	19	19
	26	19		20
	19	20		20
	14	21		21
	16	22		21
	20	23		22
	17	24		22
	16	25		23
	23	26		23
	18	27		24
	19	28		26
	15	29		27

This data for both sub-groups was then sorted from lowest to highest and a sort position list was added. These are displayed in the last three columns of the Table.

With the data for the two sub-groups sorted, and their sort positions documented, the basic formulas for finding the medians and quartiles can be applied. To find the median response time for daylight hours:

$$Depth\ of\ Median\ =\ d(\tilde{x})\ =\ \frac{n+1}{2}$$

$$Depth\ of\ Median\ =\ d(\tilde{x})\ =\ \frac{18+1}{2} = 9.5$$

The median is 9.5 positions down through the sorted data. To find the median in this example, we take the average of the values in the 9th and 10th positions. Both these values are 12, so the mean of these two values is likewise 12. This, then, is the median value for response time in daylight hours – 12 minutes.

For night-time hours, the position of the median is calculated as:

$$Depth\ of\ Median\ =\ d(\tilde{x})\ =\ \frac{29+1}{2} = 15$$

The median response time for night-time hours is therefore found in the 15th position. Moving down the sort order column until we come to 15, and then moving across to the 'Night Sorted' value, we get 19 minutes. This is the median response time for night-time hours. This same procedure is used to find the first and third quartiles using the appropriate formulas.

Exhibit 228: Emergency Response Times

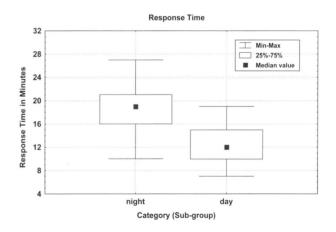

The resulting box and whisker graph is reproduced in Exhibit 228: Emergency Response Times. A review of the plot indicates there is evidence supporting the theory that daylight and night-time responses differ, at least enough to warrant further investigation. The team could begin by taking a larger sample, perhaps with a greater level of stratification to enhance the analysis and thus their ability to locate root causes of the problem.

Note that this is not hypothesis testing in the formal statistical sense. There are no tests of significance, confidence intervals and the like. Our interest is exploring for possible cause and effect relationships – searching for clues as to what could impact performance. In this case, the box and whisker has provided evidence that differences between daylight and night-time hours have a significant[74] effect upon system performance.

BOX AND WHISKER EXAMPLE 2: LEVELS OF CONTAMINANT

A company is making a decision to purchase one of two systems for production of a particular chemical. An important

consideration is the amount of contaminant produced by the process. The less contaminant the better, as product purity is an important selling point with customers.

A review team examines the two systems by running some tests and comparing the data. Ten tests are done on each process. The data from these tests is presented in the Table 229: Contaminant Data.

Each process produced similar average contaminant levels. The specific average contamination levels were calculated as:

▶ Process A = 81.2

▶ Process B = 78.3

The process improvement team, however, recognizes there is more to performance than averages. They correctly decide to plot the data from the two processes, to compare the performance levels. Using the histogram in this instance would not be appropriate because there are only 10 observations for each process, and histograms require closer to 50 observations. The solution, then, is to use the box and whisker plot. The data from Table 229 has been plotted and the results are presented in Exhibit 230: Amount of Contaminant.

---

74. Not statistically significant necessarily, but significant to the performance of the system.

Table 229: Contaminant Data

Sample Number	Parts per Million	Process
1	93	a
2	74	a
3	89	a
4	81	a
5	76	a
6	80	a
7	90	a
8	73	a
9	77	a
10	79	a
11	78	b
12	83	b
13	78	b
14	76	b
15	79	b
16	74	b
17	76	b
18	80	b
19	78	b
20	81	b

Exhibit 230: Amount of Contaminant

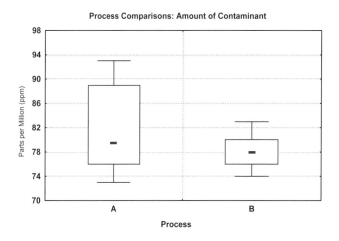

The box and whisker plot presents a much more comprehensive picture than simply comparing averages. The plot shows the median values to be about the same, but there are significant differences in the amount of dispersion.

Process A demonstrates a large degree of variation, with 50 percent of the values falling between about 77 and 89 parts per million of contaminant and a range of about 73 to 93 parts per million.

Process B presents a much 'tighter' distribution. Values here range from 74 to about 83 parts per million. From what we know about the relationship between variation and value, it is clear that process B will produce greater value than process A

– much more value than one would conclude by comparing only process averages.

THE DOT PLOT

Even when the amount of data available for each stratification level is less than eight data points, you can still present an analysis of the data through the dot plot. Teams would not usually want to rely on such scant data; however, there may be occasions when additional data is simply impossible to get. This doesn't mean that you can't use the dot plot with larger data sets – you can. But it is a particularly useful tool when data sets are relatively small.

The dot plot is organized in exactly the same way as the box and whisker plot. The various stratified groups are represented along the bottom or x-axis, and the range of values in response variable is represented along the vertical or y-axis. However, instead of drawing a box and whisker around the data, the data points themselves are plotted directly on the chart.

The example presented in Exhibit 231 uses the data from the second box and whisker chart example (see Table 229 on page 541) to present levels of contaminant for two different

Exhibit 231: Dot Plot of Contaminant

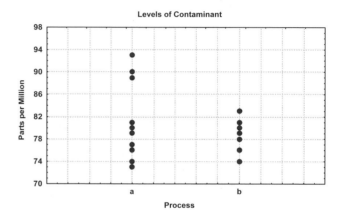

processes. Here, we had more than eight data points per stratification level (different processes). There is nothing saying we can't use the dot plot when we have more than eight data points. But we definitely should use it with eight data points or less.

The purpose and application of the dot plot are the same as the box and whisker. This example details the data for different strata or presumed causes of variation in the process. Note that while a computer is most helpful in constructing the box and whisker, a dot plot requires only graph paper and a pencil. The dot plot is simplicity itself.

LEARNING TO LOVE THE DOT PLOT

Simplicity does not mean lightweight analysis. It is no accident that Richard Feynman, the Nobel prize-winning physicist and member of the Presidential Commission investigating the Challenger disaster, used a dot plot to show the relationship between temperature and failure occurrences of "O-rings" in the solid rocket boosters.[75] Dot plots present all the data (they show all the dots) in a way that immediately conveys center tendency and dispersion associated with each category of data.

The power of the dot plot is made more evident in the Exhibit 232: Comparing the Dot Plot and Control Chart. As this exhibit demonstrates, the dot plot presents and summarizes in a single chart what the control chart takes two plots to do -- the x-bar and ranges charts. A good way to think of the control chart is as plots of the sub-group averages and ranges arising from the dot plot. Conversely, the dot plot can be thought of as

Exhibit 232: Comparing the Dot Plot and Control Chart

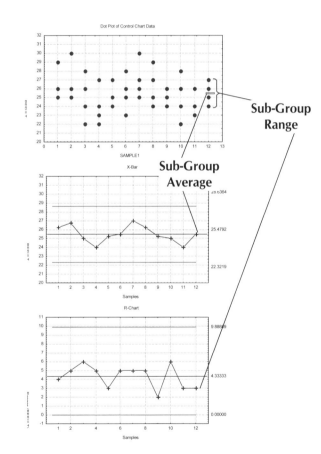

---

75. Richard P. Feynman, *What Do You Care What Other People Think?* Bantam Books, New York, NY, 1989 p.137

a plot of all the data before it is summarized on the x-bar and range control charts.

The dot plot can do more. The dots on the plot can be given different configurations or colored differently to display additional levels of stratification. A sample is presented in the Exhibit 233: Stratified Dot Plot. Here, a second factor, other than that stratified along the x-axis, is represented by different-shaped dots. This second factor has three levels, labelled Low, Medium and High. If this second factor was at low, the data point is drawn as a dot. If this second factor was at a medium level, the data point is plotted as an square. If at high, the data is plotted as a diamond.

The dot plot makes it clear that whatever this second factor is, it has an impact upon the results. At low, results were (appropriately enough) lower than at the medium or higher factor levels. Similarly, when set at high, this second factor tended to produce results that were higher than the other two settings or factor levels.

It is this ability to represent complex data that makes the dot plot so useful, especially when small data sets are involved. This makes the dot plot ideal in the analysis of experimental

Exhibit 233: Stratified Dot Plot

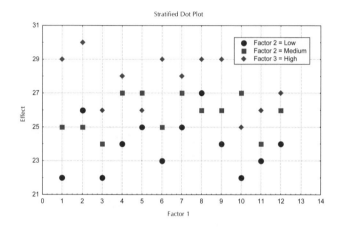

data where the number of data points are few, but the number of factors that need to be represented are often many.

SCATTER DIAGRAMS

The use of scatter diagrams in analyzing potential cause and effect relationships is about 200 years old, beginning with the advent of commercially available graph paper in the later part of the 18th century. In 1832, J.F.W. Herschel, who advocated the use of graphs as a standard tool of science, was the first to fit a curve to a scatter diagram. However, it was Dr. Kaoru Ishikawa who, in the 1950's, popularized the industrial application of scatter diagrams, calling them one of the "indispensable tools of quality control."

The scatter diagram requires plotting data points that have two measured values, with one value representing the horizontal position and the other representing the vertical. Because two values are required for each data point, collecting the data must be done in pairs – a principle called correspondence. Correspondence requires careful data-gathering methods to ensure the data pairs correspond to each other.

The scatter diagram consists of three parts. These are:

Exhibit 234: Basic Scatter Diagram

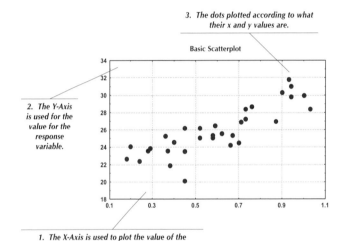

▲ **The x axis.** This is used to represent the explanatory variable or factor believed to cause the change in the response variable.

▲ **The y axis.** This is used to represent the values of the response variable.

▲ **The data points.** Data is plotted given its values for x and y. This means two values must exist for each data point, a value for x and a value for y.

By convention, the variable believed to represent the cause (the independent variable) is placed on the horizontal or x-axis. The variable believed to represent the effect or result is generally referred to as the dependent variable and is placed on the vertical or y-axis.

WHERE TO USE

The box and whisker plot (and the dot plot) are used to show relationships between two different variables, as long as the explanatory or causal variable is categorical – usually the result of stratifying the data. But what happens when the explanatory variable is measured along a scale? What if there are no categories? What do we do then?

There are two possible responses. The first is to group the explanatory (measured) data into categories and use the box and whisker plot. This is a good strategy when the stratification is reflective of real world conditions. For example, a team may be examining the relationship between time of day (measured variable) and response time to the scene of an accident. But what the team really wants to know are differences in response time between light and dark hours. In this case, we could stratify the recorded times into a daylight versus night-time classification and then use the box and whisker to compare performance. However, at times it is better to leave the data alone and adopt a second strategy – using the scatter diagram. This is particularly true when stratification to create subgroups is based on arbitrary classifications – not reflective of any real world conditions.

Too often, organizations rely upon judgment (read: bias) to establish the relationship between variables. This is evident from such statements as, "Everyone knows advertising increases sales!" or "It's obvious training increases productivity." Doing some measurement and analyzing results through the scatter diagram is seen as too complicated, time consuming or 'statistical' to be of value.

Of course, a little evidence to establish the veracity of such claims would be of value and that is where the scatter diagram comes in. Nothing does a better job of comparing two sets of measured data than the scatter diagram.

Some specific applications are:

▲ **When trying to identify potential root causes of problems.** The cause and effect diagram usually guides the process of tracking down root causes. As we have mentioned, the cause and effect diagram is a theoretical model of the causal relationships affecting some quality characteristic. Using the scatter diagram, the relationships between explanatory variables and any one of the key performance or response variables can be systematically examined, to see if any empirical evidence supports the theory represented in the cause and effect diagram. If no relationship exists, this cause can be eliminated from the diagram or in some way noted that it has been evaluated and found not have any correlation with the effect of interest. In contrast, when a correlation is discovered, we may well have found a key to improvement – a root cause.

▲ **When analyzing the correlation between two effects.** Scatter diagrams can be used to compare two effects to see if one can be used as a surrogate for the other. For example, a manufacturer of sophisticated digital cellular telephone switching networks examines the signal-to-noise ratios of all amplifiers before shipping. Signal-to-noise (S/N) ratios are measured at 0.01, 0.1, 1.0, 2.5, 5.0 and 10.0 watts of amplifier output prior to shipping, as part of a quality control program. A review of past quality data plotted on the scatter plot reveals that the S/N ratios are highly correlated at all these various output levels. In other words, a single measure of S/N at 5.0 watts would be almost as good as taking six measures at various output levels – saving time and money in the process.

▲ **When evaluating whether two causes are related.** Another application for scatter diagrams is analyzing the relationship between causes. This can be particularly useful when designing solutions (see below). For example, an improvement team may identify a relationship between a causal variable and a critical quality characteristic. Unfortunately, this causal element is beyond the direct control of the improvement team. They know what can yield an improvement; they just can't change it. The scatter diagram can be used to see if this root cause is correlated to any other causes that are within control of the team. Assuming there is a logical and empirical reason for why this second cause should affect the first, the team may have found a way to get the improvement they are looking for.

▲ **When designing solutions.** Scatter diagrams are also useful in helping teams identify effective solutions and maintain improvement gains. Analyzing relationships of cause and effect isn't beneficial only because it may identify root causes of problems. It can also help identify what is most important in maintaining process performance. Once a solution or improvement is implemented, it may well be worth the team's effort to re-evaluate the various cause and effects to see what is really important in maintaining process performance, and where the priorities for future process improvement should start.

CONSTRUCTING THE SCATTER DIAGRAM

The scatter diagram requires pairs of measurements corresponding to the variables of interest. Measurements can be any continuous variable like time, weight, volume, length or temperature. Attribute data such as defects per unit, number of transactions processed, units produced and crime rates can also be used. It is necessary that both sets of data be at least ordinal scaled.

As you might have guessed, scatter diagrams place considerable emphasis on good data collection.

SAMPLING CONCERNS

So how to get the data? What considerations should teams keep in mind?

1. **Whatever sampling procedure is used, keep the data-collection forms simple and straightforward.** Every point emphasized earlier on data gathering comes home here with a vengeance! That's because we are not collecting a single set of data, but two sets that must be carefully matched with one another. The added complexity demands greater attention to detail in the data-gathering effort.

2. **Beware of non-correspondence.** At times data may look like it is connected, but it really isn't. This is the case with many ratios that are calculated and used in business. For example, "Today's Rework" divided by "Today's Production." This may be an interesting ratio, but the fact is that today's rework is not caused by today's production; it is caused by the production in some previous time period.

3. **Keep stratification in mind.** Stratification can play a role in helping teams identify confounding factors. Confounding factors may influence the response variable and can screw up[76] or make interpretation more difficult. It pays to spend time thinking about what other variables influence the quality characteristic of interest. Try and hold these factors constant while you gather data. If this is not practical, identify and measure the factors so you can stratify the scatter plot to enhance the analysis. For example, different-colored or shaped points can be used to identify different strata or factor levels (as was used on the dot plot example, see "Stratified Dot Plot" on page 544).

4. **Use the largest sample size possible.** Scatter diagrams, like histograms, work best with larger data sets. Generally speaking, the same rules for histograms apply to scatter diagrams. Fifty paired data points will give good results. One hundred and you have it made. However, with caution, you can apply scatter diagrams with as few as 25 observations.

---

76. I don't believe "screw up" is a recognized technical term but it seems to capture the essence of things.

In designing samples for scatter diagrams, you must have:

▲ **A good theory.** Teams should know before they create the scatter diagram what type of relationship they are looking for and what the scatter diagram should look like when it is finished. It is not enough to show some correlation between two sets of data. Teams should have in mind some idea as to why they believe the data will be related.

▲ **Correspondence.** There must be a physical connection between the data points gathered. Ideally, pairs of measurements should be gathered and recorded simultaneously and be clearly linked on the check sheet.

▲ **Complete data.** If there are important factors that could confound the results, identify them at the time data is gathered and try to ensure they are captured, along with the specific data to be plotted on the check sheet. This will allow the team to stratify during the analysis.

STEPS IN CONSTRUCTING A SCATTER DIAGRAM

Creating the scatter diagram or plot consists of seven basic steps.

---

1. Set up the plot area

Assuming the data has been gathered correctly, you will have a data table with at least three columns. In the first column will be a data point identifier. In the second column will be a measurement corresponding to this data point identifier, and in the third column will be another measurement corresponding to the same data point. It is these two values that will position the data point along the x- and y-axes of the scatter diagram. Any additional columns will likely be stratification identifiers.

With the data in hand, the axes of the scatter diagram can be established. The first step is deciding which measurements will plotted against the x-axis and which will be plotted against the y-axis. Remember, the suspected cause or performance driver should be plotted on the horizontal x-axis, and the effect variable plotted on the vertical y-axis.

Knowing which variable will be plotted on which axis, the job of building the respective axes can begin. Some basic building tips are:

▲   The axes should be roughly the same lengths, creating a square plotting area. This isn't essential but it tends to make interpretation a little easier.

▲   The axes should range from the nearest round number below the lowest observed data point, to the nearest round number that is above the largest data point on each axis. This allows the data to fill the plotting area. Ensure the lowest value on the scale is less than the low value to avoid having to plot points directly on the axis.

▲   Increasing values should go from bottom to top on the vertical axis, and left to right on the horizontal axis.

▲   Provide a caption to describe the variable and its units of measure.

2. Plot the paired data

With the axes in place, the data can be plotted. Each observation is plotted at the intersection point of its corresponding x and y values. Go across the x-axis until the appropriate x-value is determined, and then move up the y-axis until the corresponding y-value is located and plot the dot.

If you are plotting a stratified scatter diagram, choose symbols that will show the different strata or sub-groups clearly and distinctly.

3. Title the chart and provide other appropriate notations

All scatter plots should have appropriate notations describing when and where the measurements were taken and by whom. If a stratified plot was made, be sure to provide a legend describing the symbols used to describe different segments or factor levels. Don't be frightened of some messiness. Good scatter diagrams are those with lots of notes, providing the necessary background for those using and interpreting the results.

4. Identify and classify the pattern of correlation

Interpretation of the scatter diagram is largely a matter of applying the ITT. The team needs to look at the plot and identify any patterns in the data. A guide to some of the more typical patterns is presented in Exhibit 235: Some Basic Scatter Diagram Patterns. Use this to make basic conclusions about the nature and strength of the correlations between the two variables in the analysis.

More formal methods of correlation analysis can also be conducted to determine the relative strength of the correlation. This includes the Pearson's correlation coefficient and the non-metric quadrant analysis, (See "Strength of Correlation" on page 553).

5. Check for potential pitfalls in your analysis

All sorts of things can impact the analysis. Consider potential confounding factors and other possible explanations for any correlation patterns. Could something else be causing the pattern? Was the data gathered correctly? Is the pattern really there or are we imposing our desire to see a pattern on the plot?

INTERPRETING SCATTER DIAGRAMS

What are we looking for when we construct a scatter diagram? The answer is correlation. Correlation is simply the degree to which a change in one variable is associated with a change in another. On the scatter diagram, this shows up as a group of points forming some sort of line. The more the points resemble a line, the stronger the correlation.

CORRELATION NOT CAUSATION

Correlation is not causation. Scatter diagrams show the relationship between two variables or the amount of correlation. This does not prove one variable *causes* the other. We can never prove through statistical analysis that any one thing causes another. All we can demonstrate is that things are correlated with one another – that is, a movement in one is associated with a movement in another. To make the causal connection, we must have a theory of the causal relationship – why a change in one thing would cause a change in another.

For example, there is a very strong relationship between hospitals and death. Most people in North America die in hospitals. Yet we would be hard pressed to say hospitals cause death. (We hope we would be hard pressed!) These two variables are associated because of the nature of the hospital business, but this association or correlation proves nothing about a causal relationship. This is correlation without causation.

On the other hand, a team may want to examine the relationship between the amount of training received and the ability to perform some task. The team would have a reason for believing that training increases ability and a strong case could be made for causality. The scatter diagram can now be used to test this theory by searching for the expected correlation. If it finds it, we have empirical evidence that supports the causal relationship. (We haven't proved anything, only supplied empirical evidence to support our theory.) If there is no correlation, we had better re-evaluate the theory or the effectiveness of our training program.

WHAT CORRELATION LOOKS LIKE – SCATTER DIAGRAM PATTERNS

Scatter diagrams display a number of patterns that are a function of both the strength and the direction of the correlation between them. The strength of a correlation is essentially the degree to which the dots on the scatter diagram can be seen as forming a line. There are a number of statistical tests for strength of the correlation, but judgment and the Inter-ocular Trauma Test (ITT) are usually sufficient to assess whether the relationship is basically strong, moderate, weak or non-existent.

If some relationship or degree of correlation exists, the direction of this correlation may also be assessed. A positive correlation is one where the value of y increases as the value of x increases, or where the value of y decreases as the value of x decreases. In both cases, the values of x and y move in the same direction.

In contrast, a negative correlation occurs when y increases as x decreases or where y decreases as x increases. Here, x and y move in different directions; an increase in one is associated with a decrease in another.

Among the various patterns we can identify are:

▲ **Strong, Positive Correlation.** The value of y clearly increases as the value of x increases.

▲ **Strong, Negative Correlation.** The value of y clearly decreases as the value of x increases.

▲ **Weak, Positive Correlation.** The value of y increases somewhat as the value of x increases.

▲ **Weak, Negative Correlation.** The value of y decreases somewhat as the value of x increases.

▲ **No Correlation.** For any value of x, y can have both large and small values. There does not appear to be any particular relationship between x and y. Look for other variables that influence x or y.

STRENGTH OF CORRELATION

Terms like "weak" and "strong" have been used to describe the degree of correlation between two variables. These assessments can be derived from simply looking at the scatter diagram and making conclusions from the ITT. Additionally, there are a number of more formal, mathematical ways to describe the strength or weakness of a correlation between two variables. Basic methods include:

▶ Pearson's Correlation Coefficient (usually denoted as R^2).

▶ Non-metric examination of quadrants.

Pearson's correlation coefficient

Pearson's R^2 statistic measures the direction and strength of correlation on a scale from -1.0 to +1.0. A zero indicates no correlation at all while a +1.0 would indicate a perfect positive correlation. In contrast, a -1.0 would indicate a perfect negative correlation.

For all practical purposes, Pearson's R^2 requires a computer to calculate. The availability of desktop computers with user-

Exhibit 235: Some Basic Scatter Diagram Patterns

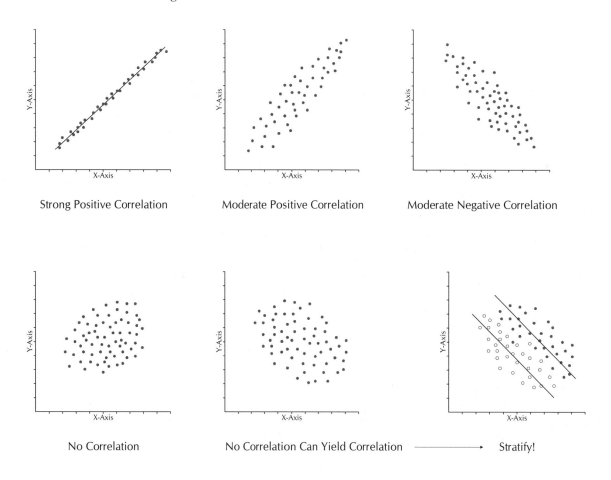

friendly software that allows for easy calculation of correlation coefficients has made this a popular technique with teams and individual analysts. Perhaps no other statistic is more abused and misinterpreted than the correlation coefficient. While the R^2 is a valuable statistic, problems arise when the analyst forgets to look at the data and interprets the R^2 statistic as some form of proof that a relationship exists.

This can be a serious error. Consider the Exhibit 236: Same Correlation - Different Reality. Here are two scatter diagrams with the same correlation of 0.91, indicating a very strong positive relationship. But look at the pattern of the data. In the first case, there is a continual pattern of correlation across the range of data. In the second case, we have one grouping of data showing no correlation at all at the bottom left-hand corner, and a single data point high and to the right. The computer doesn't understand the data – it simply fits a line and performs a calculation. In the first case, we have some evidence to believe that a correlation exists. In the second, we have no such evidence at all – despite the strong correlation coefficient.

Improvement teams working to discover cause and effect must use the tools designed for that purpose and insist on seeing the data. In this case, this means seeing all those dots on the scatter

Exhibit 236: Same Correlation - Different Reality

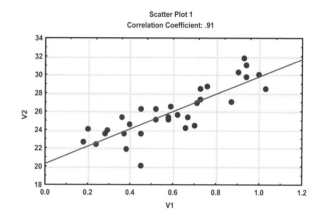

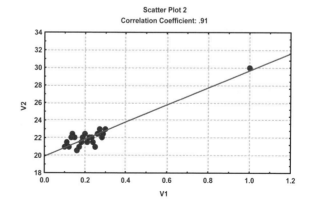

diagram. What was said for the average applies to the correlation coefficient or any other statistic – never use them in isolation of the graphical tool depicting the data. Never accept the correlation coefficient as evidence of anything without an accompanying scatter diagram.

Non-Metric Quadrant Analysis

In this regard, using the non-metric quadrant technique can be useful for establishing correlation, if only because it requires actually looking at the data as opposed to relying upon quantitative indicators. At the same time the technique allows teams to confirm, in a mathematical sense, what their judgment tells them by looking at the data.

Looking at the data is precisely what is required by this technique. Basically, it divides the scatter diagram into four quadrants. The dividing lines are the median lines for the data points. Therefore, one line divides the data points into two equally sized halves with equal numbers of points above and below. The second median line divides the data into two equally sized sets to the left and right.

Exhibit 237: Dividing the Scatter Diagram Into Quadrants details the dividing of a data set of 22 observations or data

Exhibit 237: Dividing the Scatter Diagram Into Quadrants

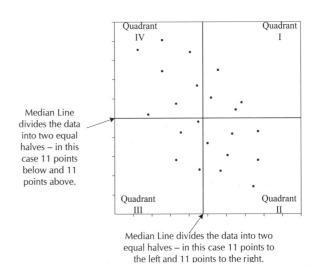

points. The median lines divide the data into 11 points above and below, and 11 points to the right and the left. This creates four quadrants in the scatter diagram. Starting at the upper right-hand corner and moving clockwise, these are labeled from I to IV. The number of points in quadrants I & III are added together to calculate *A,* and the number of points in quadrants II & IV are added together to calculate *B*.

The following procedure is then used to analyze the data:

▶ A = the number of points in Quadrant I + Quadrant III.

▶ B = the number of points in Quadrant II + Quadrant IV.

Whatever is smaller between A and B is then compared to Table 238: Correlation Test Table. If it is smaller than the Limit referenced in the table, then a relationship or correlation likely exists between the two variables.

In the example, there were 22 data points. The following calculations were performed:

A = 8 = 4 + 4 (Quadrant I + Quadrant III)

B = 14 = 7 + 7 (Quadrant II + Quadrant IV).

The smaller of these two values is A, which is equal to eight. This is compared to the Limit value in Table 238. The Limit value in the table for 22 observations is five. Since eight is greater than five, we conclude that the data provided in the example is not correlated.

Table 238: Correlation Test Table

Number of Observations	Limit	Number of Observations	Limit
1 - 8	0	51 -53	18
9 - 11	1	54 - 55	19
12 - 14	2	56 -57	20
15 -16	3	58 - 60	21
17 - 19	4	61 - 62	22
20 - 22	5	63 - 64	23
23 - 24	6	65 - 66	24
25 - 27	7	67 - 69	25
28 - 29	8	70 - 71	26
30 - 32	9	72 - 73	27
33 - 34	10	74 - 76	28
35 - 36	11	77 - 78	29
37 - 39	12	79 - 80	30
40 - 41	13	81 - 82	31
42 - 43	14	83 - 85	32
44 - 46	15	86 - 87	33
47 - 48	16	88 - 89	34
49 - 50	17	90	35

EXAMPLE: STEEL HARDENER AND THE HARDNESS OF STEEL

In making steel, a special chemical hardener is added during the process to increase the hardness of the resulting product. Like many such processes, there is a balance point or limit after which adding additional hardener will not produce sufficient economic benefit in terms of harder steel. Knowing the precise nature of the relationship between the amount of hardener added and the resulting hardness of the steel is, therefore, essential for the plant to know. The critical question is, "How much hardener should we use?"

To answer this question, the plant began what amounted to a series of experiments. Workers adjusted the percentage of hardener added, and the Testing and Acceptance Department followed up by testing the hardness of the resulting steel. The result is the data presented in Table 239: Steel Hardness Data.

From this data set a basic scatter diagram was constructed. Notice that the minimum and maximum values for the hardener were about 0.0 percent to just over 1.0 percent. From this, a scale along the x-axis was created from zero to 1.2. Likewise, the mean hardness of the steel was never less than 20.0 and

Table 239: Steel Hardness Data

Sample #	Hardener (%)	Hardness	Sample #	Hardener (%)	Hardness
1	.520	26.200	17	.520	25.100
2	.580	25.400	18	.450	23.500
3	.660	24.200	19	.730	28.400
4	.180	22.700	20	.280	23.600
5	1.000	30.000	21	.450	26.200
6	.710	26.900	22	.380	21.900
7	.870	27.000	23	.670	25.400
8	.360	25.300	24	.370	23.600
9	.620	25.600	25	1.030	28.400
10	.730	27.300	26	.290	23.900
11	.760	28.700	27	.700	24.500
12	.400	24.600	28	.580	25.100
13	.240	22.400	29	.590	26.500
14	.940	31.000	30	.200	24.100
15	.940	29.800	31	.450	20.100
16	.900	30.300	32	.930	31.800

never more than 32.0. This became the range for the y-axis. With the scales set up, the data was plotted, resulting in the scatter diagram presented in Exhibit 240: Scatter Diagram Steel Hardness.

Exhibit 240: Scatter Diagram Steel Hardness

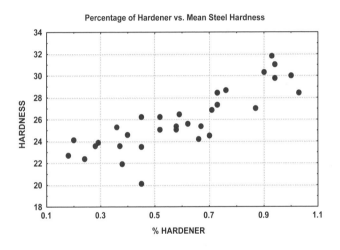

The scatter diagram tells the story. It indicates a clear and positive correlation between the amount of hardener added and the resulting hardness of the steel. You don't need any fancy statistics to tell you this, and calculating a correlation coefficient in such a case would be a waste of time. Even preparing a nonmetric quadrant analysis in such circumstances is not going to tell you anything more than you can see just from looking at the scatter diagram.

The plant in this case can now read the relationship between the amount of hardener and the resulting steel hardness right off the scatter diagram. For example, using 0.6 percent hardener, the resulting steel hardness will be about 25 to 27.

Exhibit 241: Scatter Diagram Steel Hardness With Best Fit Line

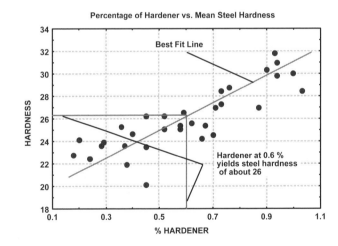

If it helps, a simple line can be drawn in that best fits the data points. Again, while it is convenient to have the computer calculate this line (and calculate an R^2 statistics as well if you like), simply 'eye-balling' the best fit line works more than well enough in most improvement applications. The result of adding such a line is presented in Exhibit 241: Scatter Diagram Steel Hardness With Best Fit Line. The exhibit also shows how fitting the line can help with determining the specific hardness level associated with the amount of hardener added, is this case at the 0.6 percent level.

POTENTIAL PROBLEMS OF INTERPRETATION

The most common mistake with regard to scatter diagrams is failing to use them. The rationale for this usually falls into one of two categories:

1. **The assumption is made that since a logical argument can be offered to explain why the two variables are related, empirical verification is not required.** Examples include Human Resources concluding that increased training will increase individual performance. Or Marketing assuming that increasing advertising expenditures will raise sales. Or the Information Services department assuming that increased computer expenditures will increase productivity. These are all examples of assuming that we know what will happen to some response variable if we make a change to a theoretical causal variable. Beware of theory without data, especially when expressed by such statements as "Everyone knows . . ." or "It is obvious that . . ." This is usually the first sign that whatever is being argued is untested, unproved and unverified. Oh, yes – and wrong!

2. **It is assumed that a numerical index, such as a correlation coefficient, provides an adequate summary of the relationship between the variables.** As we have pointed out, numerical summaries of the data are never sufficient. If the data exists within a computer and the computer says a relationship exists, take the time to push a few extra buttons and generate a scatter diagram to verify that conclusion. Never accept any "goodness of fit" test, no matter how sophisticated, without having a look at the data. Statistics augment the scatter diagram – they can never replace it.

Other Interpretation Problems

A number of potential problems and misinterpretations exist with scatter diagrams. Here are some key points to keep in mind:

▲ **Range of the Data.** Never go beyond the data. The conclusions made from any scatter diagram are only good for the range of values used in the analysis. At times, people will want to extend some correlation line beyond the range that the data supports. Many forms of forecasting are prime examples, where historical data is analyzed using some model that projects the regression results into the future.

Take another example – adding a chemical hardener during a steel-making process. As more hardener is added, the harder the steel gets. Extending this data, we could conclude that using 100 percent hardener would yield very strong steel. Such is not the case, however, as rumor has it that a little iron helps, too! Teams analyzing data must not only insist on seeing the data, but must ensure they never go beyond it.

Exhibit 242: Going Beyond the Data

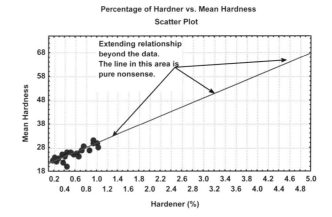

▲ **Confounding Factors.** A scatter diagram examines a potential relationship between two variables. But there are a great many variables that could be influencing the results. Some of these variables may not be included in the analysis. These are called confounding factors. The best defense in dealing with confounding factors is to create a good cause and effect diagram before the analytical work is begun. Using this tool can go a long way to ensuring that potential confounding factors are at least identified. This, in turn, can point the way to improving the analysis, especially if some means of controlling or holding confounding factors constant can be adopted.

▲ **Correlation Without Understanding.** A correlation by itself proves nothing. There must be an underlying theory relating the data or results to physical reality. In other words, there must be some understanding as to *why*. Finding correlation, without supporting theory, is pretty much meaningless.

Think of it this way. Comparing all the various causes in the cause and effect diagram with the response variable would generate a number of scatter diagrams – the same number as there are branches on the cause and effect diagram. Lets say there are 50 such branches, so 50 scatter diagrams are prepared. What is the likelihood that out of these 50 scatter diagrams, one shows some degree of correlation due to nothing other than random chance? The chances are very good. Not because there is any real-world connection, but because if enough variables are thrown into the mix, something is bound to correlate.

▲ *Stratification.* Stratification can make patterns appear in the data where none were apparent before. Stratification is carried out graphically, by coloring the data points differently or using different symbols to represent the different strata. This enables the team to examine not only the underlying relationships, but to see how these relationships vary according to different groupings of the data.

SUMMARY

Scatter diagrams are one of the most powerful tools that improvement teams can use to analyze potential cause and effect relationships. Conceptually, they are quite straightforward – relating one variable to another. Moreover, their ability to do so makes them indispensable in tracking down root causes of problems and identifying potential areas for improvement.

Yet few tools have been more abused than the scatter diagram. Aided in part by microcomputers that can easily analyze data points, plot the data, fit distributions and generate statistics, some organizations have found themselves flooded with analysis that looks or claims to be 'scientific.' The most common form of abuse is fitting the data to some form of mathematical curve and then removing the actual observations from the diagram. The result is some form of line with corresponding goodness-of-fit test that assures the reader (incorrectly) that the model is valid.

This violates one of the most important rules of measurement for performance improvement – ***always insist on seeing the data!*** If only the model is presented without the corresponding data points, throw the model/analysis out.

PERFORMING EXPERIMENTS

Experiments involve the active modification of the process in order to generate new data. So far, most of the tools and analytical techniques have been discussed within the context of passive application. That is, the tools are applied to operating process or system data in an effort to establish performance or identify possible cause and effect relationships. In contrast to this passive approach, experiments involve deliberate modification to the process, to test the impact on some performance characteristic.

This deliberate modification, usually under controlled conditions, gives experiments their power. By carefully designing what gets modified (and what doesn't), including the degree to which variables are varied and when, the investigator is able to control the impact of confounding factors. This enables those engaged in the research to reach more definitive conclusions on cause and effect relationships than is possible through a passive approach. In short, experiments improve the quality of the evidence.

TYPES OF EXPERIMENTS

Experiments are often viewed as a science unto themselves. Proper experimental design, especially sophisticated designs examining multiple factors, background variables and effects, demand a considerable level of expertise. Yet the basic principles of sound experimental design are understandable by anyone. Conceptually, experiments are nothing more than intentionally "mucking about" to see if doing so makes things better or worse.[77] Proper experimental design simply provides

---

77. "Mucking about" is another of my favorite phrases that fairly describes a technical idea in a not-so-technical way.

Table 243: Types of Experiments

Level of Sophistication	Eight Types of Experiments
Informal Methods	1. Trial and Error. Introduce a change and see what happens.
	2. Running special lots or batches. Trying to test under some controlled conditions.
	3. Pilot runs. Set up to produce a desired effect.
Formal Experimental Method	4. One-factor experiment. Using a control chart to experiment on a process.
	5. Planned comparisons. Background variables are considered in the experimental plan.
Sophisticated Experimental Designs	6. Experiment planned with two to four factors. Study to separate effects and interactions.
	7. Experiment with five to 20 factors. Screening studies.
Very Sophisticated and Complex Designs	8. Comprehensive experimental plan with multiple phases. Modelling, multiple factor levels, optimization.

a way to ensure we maximize the knowledge produced through this mucking about.

Ron Moen et. al. have identified eight basic types of experiments based upon the level of sophistication and formality demanded. These eight types of experiments are presented in Table 243: Types of Experiments.[78] Experiments need not be intense formal arrangements requiring a doctorate in statistics. They take place whenever people modify or muck about to better understand how things work. However, the power of experiments, and the extent to which they generate knowledge, increases exponentially with the level of sophistication. This is because greater sophistication provides for increased control of confounding factors and more precise measurement of the cause and effect relationship.

DESIGNING THE EXPERIMENT

More formal experimental designs require careful planning to ensure the experiment is effective at isolating confounding factors and yields clear results. To help, a 10-step approach to

78. Ronald D. Moen, Thomas Nolan, Thomas and Lloyd Provost, *Improving Quality Through Planned Experimentation*; McGraw-Hill, 1991, p.65

planning an experiment is presented, along with a Planned Experiment Documentation form. The 10 steps or components of a well-planned experiment are presented below.

1. **Process.** The specific process upon which the experiment will be conducted is clearly defined. There should be no ambiguity here. If a specific machine is going to be used, record the serial number of the machine. Be specific and clear.

2. **Objective.** These are the causal relationships we are attempting to assess. This entails answering the questions of what we think will happen to performance (a specific quality characteristic) if we make an adjustment or change in the process. In other words, it states what our theory is.

3. **Background Information.** This is a summary of current knowledge as well as why the experiment is being conducted, specifically the nature of the problem or improvement opportunity.

4. **Experimental Variables.** These are the things we will be measuring. There are three types of experimental variables:

▶ **Response or Effect Variables.** These are the measures of performance we hope to improve. These variables should show some response to changes in the factors or causal variables.

▶ **Factors or Causal Variables.** These are the variables we will be modifying or adjusting to see how doing so affects the response variable. It is essential to detail the levels or degree to which will be modifying each factor.

▶ **Background Variables/Confounding Factors.** These are the variables that may affect the results of the experiment but are not the primary factors of interest. They are, therefore, a bit of nuisance and their impact needs to be controlled in some fashion so they do not contribute to a confounding of the results.

5. **Replication.** This basically details how the experiment will be run and what features of it will be repeated. Replication may play a role in reducing the impact of background or nuisance variables.

6. **Method of Randomization.** This is a tool to help control the influence of nuisance variables, including any bias the

Exhibit 244: Planned Experiment Documentation Form

Planned Experiment Documentation	Prepared By:	Date:

1. Process

2. Objective

3. Background Information

4. Experimental Variables

   A. Response (Effect) Variables   Measurement
   1. _____   _____
   2. _____   _____
   3. _____   _____

   B. Factors (Causal) Variables   Levels
   1. _____   _____
   2. _____   _____
   3. _____   _____

   C. Background Variables   Control Method
   1. _____   _____
   2. _____   _____
   3. _____   _____

5. Replication   6. Method of Randomization

7. Design Matrix (attach copy)   8. Data Collection Forms (attach copies)

9. Planned Method of Statistical Analysis   10. Estimated cost, schedule, resources.

experimenter might have. It is used to assign factor combinations to experimental units, or to assign the order in which experimental steps will be taken.

7. **Design Matrix.** This is the precise schedule for running the experiment. It details when each run will be conducted and at what factor levels.

8. **Data-Collection Forms.** These are the specific forms to be used in recording the data for the experiment. As was the case with check sheets, these should be kept simple and easy to use.

9. **Planned Methods of Analysis.** How will the resulting data be analyzed? At a minimum, this must include a run chart of the results (effects) during the period of the experiment. Numerous other techniques can be applied.

10. **Estimated Costs and Related Resource Considerations.** What resources will be required to run the experiment? Include both financial and material costs as well as the time required of people involved.

BASIC ANALYTIC APPROACH

Analysis of experimental data can be a very complex and sophisticated process. However, a basic analytical strategy employs the same tools already discussed. Indeed, in the analysis of experimental data, it is good to remember that it is, after all, just data. As such, the seven basic tools of data analysis are the tools to use in examining the results of the experiment.

Three Basic Steps: A Survivor's Guide

A basic three-step analytical approach to analysis of experimental data can be defined.[79] These three steps represent a kind of survivor's guide for those involved in an industrial experiment. If you made it this far, analyzing the data through this basic approach will provide a sound analysis. These three steps are:

1. **Plot a run (or control) chart of the data as the experiment was actually run.** In other words, plot the data in original time order. Use symbols and labels to clearly identify factor levels.

---

79. Ronald D. Moen et al.; Improving Quality Through Planned Experimentation, McGraw-Hill Inc., New York, New York. p. 81

2. **Reorder the run chart by factor level.** This entails, in essence, creating a dot plot of the data for each factor and/or each factor level. Use of color coding to highlight stratification can help support interpretation.

3. **Remove effects of background variables.** This usually requires mathematically adjusting the data to remove the effects of background variables and then plotting the adjusted data by factor level using the dot plot or box and whisker plot.

Using run charts and control charts, dot plots and box and whisker diagrams allows the analyst to look at the data as it was created and then reorganize it to highlight special causes of variation.

Keep It Simple

The tools and techniques of experimental data analysis are many and often complex, requiring considerable skill in their application. A problem mentioned previously is the ability of powerful microcomputers, combined with sophisticated statistical analysis programs, to apply complex analytical techniques to data. This may happen whether the data supports the techniques or not. Too often, those involved in data analysis apply fancy analytical procedures, where they would have been better off to simply grab a pencil and paper and plot a run chart or dot plot.

The bottom line is '*keep it simple.*" Before applying any other analytic technique, the first steps to be done are the three basic steps outlined here. Analysis of experimental data, without these three steps, has likely gotten ahead of itself.

Example: A Single Factor Experiment

To get the idea of how to run a basic one-factor experiment, let's take an example. Here the issue is one of a manufacturing process in which a part is made that requires a high degree of precision – specifically to a dimension measured in thousandths of an inch.

Over the past few months, the control charts of this specific dimension have remained in control. The company wants to reduce the variation of this dimension, however, and will undertake an experiment on how to do this. An improvement team is formed comprised of process operators, technical engineers and a manager (the process owner). Old cause and effect diagrams are gathered and reworked into a new diagram. The team then reviews the diagram to document what has been modified in the past, and to identify likely high-impact causal factors.

This process highlighted a number of possible causes – far too many to be tested. However, the team also reached a consensus of sorts. They believed that adjusting the torque applied to a critical set-screw of the machine would reduce the level of variation currently experienced. There was a logical reason for this belief, as the set-screw in question kept a critical module of the machine aligned with a number of other components. Moreover, operators reported feeling some minute vibration in the module held by this screw. This, then, was the theory to be tested. Current specifications called for 35 pounds of torque to be applied to the screw. A Planned Experiment Documentation form (Exhibit 245) was prepared and the experiment initiated.

Design Matrix

The design of the experiment called for the factor or causal variable (set-screw torque setting) to be tested at four different

Exhibit 245: Clamp Pressure Designed Experiment Documentation

Planned Experiment Documentation	**Prepared By:** B. Preston	**Date:** 24/02/00

1. Process   Lathe process on Part # NP657. Same model lathe in operation in 8 other locations.

2. Objective   Reduce variation of part diameters as measured by the Ranges chart.

3. Background Information   While lathes produce average results that are on target, the piece to piece variation in diameter is too large. Rejection rates on parts is now approaching 15 per cent (diameters are either too large or too small. Set screw torque is team's best guess as means to reduce variation.

4. Experimental Variables

A. Response (Effect) Variables   Measurement

1. Diameter of part. (see measurement guide AB12)   Deviation from nominal in thousands of an inch
2. _____
3. _____

B. Factors (Causal) Variables   Levels

1. Primary set screw torque   25, 35, 45, 55 lb. of torque
2. _____   Note: 35 lb. is manufacturer's recommendation and our current standard
3. _____

C. Background Variables   Control Method

1. None identified
2. _____
3. _____

5. Replication
Torque adjusted every hour (8 hour day) and the experiment will be run for 4 days for a total of 32 runs. Four measures taken per run.

6. Method of Randomization
Torque setting for each run will be assigned by toss of dice.

7. Design Matrix (attach copy)
Copy attached.

8. Data Collection Forms (attach copies)
Copy attached.

9. Planned Method of Statistical Analysis
Control chart (*X-bar, R* with each run treated as a sub-group). Keep *X-bar* on target while minimizing the *R* chart.

10. Estimated cost, schedule, resources.
Start the experiment on Tuesday, Feb. 22. Cost of analysis $5,000. production slowdown costs, $32,000 (est.).

---

levels: 25, 35, 45 and 55 pounds. These are the factor levels in the experiment. These torque settings would be adjusted every hour on a random basis. The plan also called for four samples or measurements to be taken each hour. So, at approximately 15-minute intervals, a completed part would be selected as it came out of the machine and its critical dimension established with a micrometer. All together, this meant there would be eight torque adjustments per day and four measures would be taken at each setting, producing some 32 measures each day. The experiment was to be run for four days. All these elements are reflected in the design matrix presented in Table 246: Design Matrix.

The design matrix details when the different factor levels will be adjusted and by how much, in effect creating a detailed plan for the actual conduct of the experiment. For example, the first hour of the first day will be called run #1 and the torque will be set at 55 lbs. Four measurements will be taken during this run. The second hour of the first day will be run #2, and the torque setting will be set to 35 lbs. Again, four measurements will be taken.

Table 246: Design Matrix

DAY	RUN #	TORQUE	HOUR	NUMBER OF SAMPLES	DAY	RUN #	TORQUE	HOUR	NUMBER OF SAMPLES
1.000	1.000	55.000	H1	4	3.000	17.000	35.000	H1	4
1.000	2.000	35.000	H2	4	3.000	18.000	35.000	H2	4
1.000	3.000	45.000	H3	4	3.000	19.000	55.000	H3	4
1.000	4.000	25.000	H4	4	3.000	20.000	25.000	H4	4
1.000	5.000	35.000	H5	4	3.000	21.000	25.000	H5	4
1.000	6.000	55.000	H6	4	3.000	22.000	25.000	H6	4
1.000	7.000	35.000	H7	4	3.000	23.000	45.000	H7	4
1.000	8.000	35.000	H8	4	3.000	24.000	45.000	H8	4
2.000	9.000	25.000	H1	4	4.000	25.000	25.000	H1	4
2.000	10.000	55.000	H2	4	4.000	26.000	45.000	H2	4
2.000	11.000	35.000	H3	4	4.000	27.000	55.000	H3	4
2.000	12.000	45.000	H4	4	4.000	28.000	55.000	H4	4
2.000	13.000	45.000	H5	4	4.000	29.000	45.000	H5	4
2.000	14.000	25.000	H6	4	4.000	30.000	45.000	H6	4
2.000	15.000	25.000	H7	4	4.000	31.000	35.000	H7	4
2.000	16.000	55.000	H8	4	4.000	32.000	55.000	H8	4

RUNNING THE EXPERIMENT

With the design matrix prepared, the experiment was run on a specific machine, to avoid the confounding effects of different machines on study results. The basic set screw was adjusted eight times per day in accordance with the experimental design matrix. Four times per hour, measurements were taken on the difference between the nominal or target value and the actual diameters produced by the process.

The resulting data are presented in Table 247: Data Table – Single Factor Experiment. Notice that the data has been grouped by hour (the experiment treats each hour as a sub-group). Note, too, the presence of negative values. The measurements taken were deviations from the nominal or target value. So a diameter smaller than target was a negative value, while a diameter larger than target was a positive value.

ANALYZING THE DATA

To analyze the data, the three-step survival plan discussed earlier is used. It is important to remember that the objective of the experiment was to reduce the amount of variation about the target value – that is to improve the reliability of the process.

Step 1: Prepare run and/or control chart as the experiment was actually run

There are two ways to approach this. First, we could plot a run chart of all 128 data points (32 measures per day over 4 days), or we could plot the data sub-grouped by hour. Let's show it both ways.

First the data in original time order. This is presented in the run in Exhibit 248: Run Chart of Experimental Data. This chart maps out all 128 measurements as they actually occurred, in original time order. What should be seen, if the experiment was properly randomized, is common cause variation – no special cause. If some patterns were evident, it would imply that time influenced the results of our experiment and would be a confounding factor to our results.

The second approach is to plot the data through a *X-bar, R* control chart. Since four measures were taken each hour, at the same factor level, each hour can be treated as a sub-group. This follows Shewhart's principle of rational sub-grouping – that common cause variation should be captured within the sub-group so that special cause variation will show through between sub-groups. Each sub-group, therefore, corresponds to a specific run (as identified in the design matrix) and presented in the original time order. The resulting *X-bar, R* control chart is presented in Exhibit 249: Control Charts of Set Screw Experiment.

Both the run chart and the control chart tell pretty much the same story. No patterns are evident when the data is presented

Table 247: Data Table – Single Factor Experiment

DAY	RUN	TORQUE	HOUR	S1	S2	S3	S4	AVG	RANGE
1.000	1.000	55.000	H1	-1.716	1.430	-2.145	2.800	.092	4.945
1.000	2.000	35.000	H2	7.700	5.300	-11.800	13.500	3.675	25.300
1.000	3.000	45.000	H3	-1.200	1.000	-1.500	.700	-.250	2.500
1.000	4.000	25.000	H4	-2.431	13.585	-4.433	-5.577	.286	19.162
1.000	5.000	35.000	H5	-10.500	9.900	9.800	-5.900	.825	20.400
1.000	6.000	55.000	H6	-4.719	1.573	-4.576	2.002	-1.430	6.721
1.000	7.000	35.000	H7	7.600	-1.300	-6.900	-8.700	-2.325	16.300
1.000	8.000	35.000	H8	-1.700	9.500	-3.100	-3.900	.200	13.400
2.000	9.000	25.000	H1	11.011	7.579	-16.874	19.305	5.255	36.179
2.000	10.000	55.000	H2	1.287	4.862	3.575	-2.431	1.823	7.293
2.000	11.000	35.000	H3	-.700	11.000	14.500	-3.900	5.225	18.400
2.000	12.000	45.000	H4	1.200	.500	-2.100	3.800	.850	5.900
2.000	13.000	45.000	H5	-3.300	1.100	-3.200	1.400	-1.000	4.700
2.000	14.000	25.000	H6	10.868	-1.859	-9.867	-12.441	-3.325	23.309
2.000	15.000	25.000	H7	-15.015	14.157	-14.014	-8.437	-5.827	29.172
2.000	16.000	55.000	H8	1.716	.715	-3.003	5.434	1.216	8.437
3.000	17.000	35.000	H1	6.800	3.900	-7.700	2.400	1.350	14.500
3.000	18.000	35.000	H2	-8.800	1.000	-7.100	-10.000	-6.225	11.000
3.000	19.000	55.000	H3	-4.100	6.864	-3.861	4.719	.906	10.964
3.000	20.000	25.000	H4	9.724	5.577	-11.011	3.432	1.931	20.735
3.000	21.000	25.000	H5	-1.001	15.730	20.735	-5.577	7.472	26.312
3.000	22.000	25.000	H6	-12.584	1.430	-10.153	-14.300	-8.902	15.730
3.000	23.000	45.000	H7	1.600	-1.900	-2.900	-1.700	-1.225	4.500
3.000	24.000	45.000	H8	-3.900	4.800	-2.700	3.300	.375	8.700
4.000	25.000	25.000	H1	-11.297	15.730	-8.437	-3.718	-1.931	27.027

The Performance Improvement Toolkit

Table 247: Data Table – Single Factor Experiment

DAY	RUN	TORQUE	HOUR	S1	S2	S3	S4	AVG	RANGE
4.000	26.000	45.000	H2	-3.700	1.400	3.800	-2.900	-.350	7.500
4.000	27.000	55.000	H3	-5.291	2.002	5.434	-4.147	-.500	10.725
4.000	28.000	55.000	H4	2.002	-1.400	2.717	1.859	1.295	4.117
4.000	29.000	45.000	H5	.900	3.400	2.500	-1.700	1.275	5.100
4.000	30.000	45.000	H6	1.400	-2.800	1.900	1.300	.450	4.700
4.000	31.000	35.000	H7	-7.900	11.000	-5.900	-2.600	-1.350	18.900
4.000	32.000	55.000	H8	2.288	-2.717	-4.147	3.900	-.169	8.047

Exhibit 248: Run Chart of Experimental Data

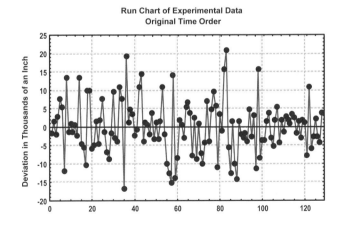

in original time order. This means that there are no special causes and that time was not a confounding factor in this experiment. That's good.

The ranges control chart, however, has highlighted an out-of-control point in run #9. Notice that this was one of the runs where pin torque was at its weakest factor level – 25 lbs. This might be expected if the set screw really is an important factor contributing to variation in production. Specifically, it might be an indication that setting the screw at such a weak level was a special cause of variation within the sub-group. Apart from this one data point, however, we can see no discernible pattern in the *X-bar* or *R* charts.

There is one more way to present the data from the experiment. Recall that the dot plot can present the same data as the two

Exhibit 249: Control Charts of Set Screw Experiment

Exhibit 250: Dot Plot of Experimental Data in Original Time Order

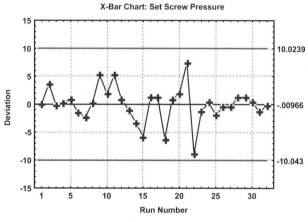

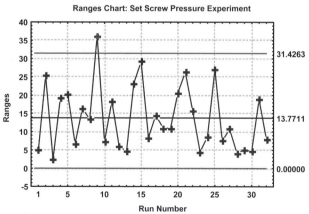

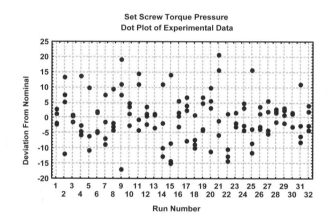

control charts – showing the data behind the calculations of averages and ranges. Such a dot plot is presented in Exhibit 250: Dot Plot of Experimental Data in Original Time Order. While all the information is captured in the dot plot, it is a little more difficult to interpret. Notice at how easy it is to overlook the extreme variation observed in run #9. It is easy to see once you know to look for it, but the ranges control chart makes it obvious.

Nevertheless, the dot plot presented in Exhibit 250 makes it clear that no special causes of variation or time-based patterns are in the results – again driving the conclusion that time is not a confounding factor in the experiment.

Step 2: Re-order the data by factor level

In step 2, we need to sort or order the data by each of the four factor levels. When the data was presented in original time order (step 1), we hoped to see no special causes of variation. This would mean that the order in which we ran the experiment had no effect on the outcome. In re-ordering the data by factor level, we now hope to see just the opposite. We would like to identify patterns or special causes, as this would indicate that the factor of interest (at the factor levels chosen) does indeed have a significant impact on the performance characteristic of interest.

Like the first step, the use of run charts, dot plots and control charts is pretty much interchangeable in step 2. Use whatever chart works best in the circumstances. Difficulties in interpretation with the dot plot, however, tend to fade once the data is ordered by factor level. Exhibit 251: Dot Plot of

Experimental Data Sorted by Factor Level, presents a dot plot of the data, but with this data sorted by the four factor levels.

Exhibit 251: Dot Plot of Experimental Data Sorted by Factor Level

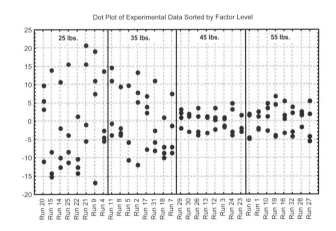

As the exhibit details, this simple plot presents a very clear picture with an obvious pattern that wasn't present in the previous dot plot. In the first plot, where data was maintained in time order, nothing was apparent through the ITT test. The order of the data as presented represented no special cause of variation. But with the data sorted by factor level, special cause is readily apparent – it is the factor levels. Now here is special cause that can be clearly seen – just by looking!

The degree of variation in the data clearly declines as set screw torque is increased from 25 pounds to 35, and finally to 45 pounds. When torque is increased to 55 pounds, it is not clear whether there is any improvement in the amount of variation. In fact, it looks as though variation may actually increase at this factor level as the screw is tightened above what might be suitable limits. In any case, the experiment makes it clear that setting the set screw to 45 pounds of torque will produce the best set of results among the various choices. It is also clear that there is little, if anything, to be gained by setting the screw beyond this amount.

Simple run charts can also be prepared of the data sorted by factor level, and they tell a similar story. In Exhibit 252: Run Charts of Average and Ranges Arising From Experimental Data Sorted by Factor Level, run charts are prepared for both the averages and ranges for each run of the experiment. This presents an easy-to-read, all-in-one picture of how the process performance changed with different factor levels.

Exhibit 252: Run Charts of Average and Ranges Arising From Experimental Data Sorted by Factor Level

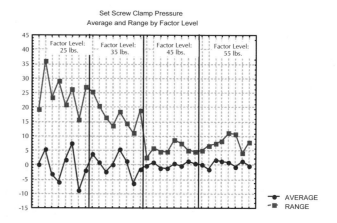

Step 3: Adjust the data for background variables and replot data by factor level

In this example, no background variables were identified in the experiment. However, let's assume that at this stage of the analysis, someone begins to call into question the validity of the experiment. They note that various factor levels were not distributed equally across the four days of the experiment. Perhaps, they argue, day-to-day differences have influenced the

Exhibit 253: Adjusting the Data for Background Variables

Day	Run	Foot Pounds	Hour	Average	Range	Adjusted Average	Adjusted Range
1	1	55	H1	0.09	4.95	-0.05	5.13
1	2	35	H2	3.68	25.30	3.53	25.48
1	3	45	H3	-0.25	2.50	-0.39	2.68
1	4	25	H4	0.29	19.16	0.14	19.34
1	5	35	H5	0.83	20.40	0.68	20.58
1	6	55	H6	-1.43	6.72	-1.57	6.90
1	7	35	H7	-2.33	16.30	-2.47	16.48
1	8	35	H8	0.20	13.40	0.06	13.58
		Day 01 Averages		0.13	13.59		
2	9	25	H1	5.26	36.18	4.72	33.28
2	10	55	H2	1.82	7.29	1.29	4.39
2	11	35	H3	5.23	18.40	4.69	15.50
2	12	45	H4	0.85	5.90	0.31	3.00
2	13	45	H5	-1.00	4.70	-1.54	1.80
2	14	25	H6	-3.32	23.31	-3.86	20.41
2	15	25	H7	-5.83	29.17	-6.36	26.27
2	16	55	H8	1.22	8.44	0.68	5.53
		Day 02 Averages		0.53	16.67		
3	17	35	H1	1.35	14.50	1.88	14.22
3	18	35	H2	-6.23	11.00	-5.69	10.72
3	19	55	H3	0.91	10.96	1.44	10.68
3	20	25	H4	1.93	20.74	2.46	20.45
3	21	25	H5	7.47	26.31	8.00	26.03
3	22	25	H6	-8.90	15.73	-8.37	15.45
3	23	45	H7	-1.23	4.50	-0.69	4.22
3	24	45	H8	0.38	8.70	0.91	8.42
		Day 03 Averages		-0.54	14.06		
4	25	25	H1	-1.93	27.03	-1.78	30.03
4	26	45	H2	-0.35	7.50	-0.20	10.51
4	27	55	H3	-0.50	10.73	-0.35	13.73
4	28	55	H4	1.29	4.12	1.44	7.12
4	29	45	H5	1.28	5.10	1.43	8.11
4	30	45	H6	0.45	4.70	0.60	7.71
4	31	35	H7	-1.35	18.90	-1.20	21.91
4	32	55	H8	-0.17	8.05	-0.02	11.05
		Day 04 Averages		-0.16	10.76		
		Grande Average		-0.01	13.77	-0.01	13.77

results. In this case, the different days become a background variable to the experiment.

Removing the effects of day-to-day variations is accomplished by adjusting the data points of the experiment by the average effect for each level of the background variable. In this case, the background variable is the day in which the experiment was run. There are four factor levels for this background vari-

able, one for each of the days. To adjust the data, the average results for each day are calculated and then subtracted from the data points to be plotted on the run chart. The overall average for the entire experiment is then added back on to this figure. This process is presented in Exhibit 253: Adjusting the Data for Background Variables.[80]

The data presented in this case are the averages and ranges for the experiment as it was originally run. The individual data have been removed, since it will be the averages and ranges that will be plotted. Notice that the average for the experimental averages and ranges is calculated at the end of each day. For example, the average of the averages for day one was 0.1 and the average for the ranges on that same day was 13.6.

To adjust the data, the daily average is subtracted from the data point to be plotted, and then the grand average for the entire experiment is added back on. So for the first run, the average was 0.09. The average for day was 0.13. Subtract 0.13 from 0.09 and you get the adjusted value of -0.04. All the data could be adjusted in this fashion and then plotted. For convenience, however, the grand average for the overall experiment is added back on to bring the measures back to their natural units. The grand average for the experiment is -0.01, so the final adjusted value is -0.05 (-0.01 + -0.04). Similarly, this process is repeated for all the averages and ranges, giving the adjusted amounts in the table.

Exhibit 254: Run Charts of Adjusted Average and Ranges Arising From Experimental Data Sorted by Factor Level

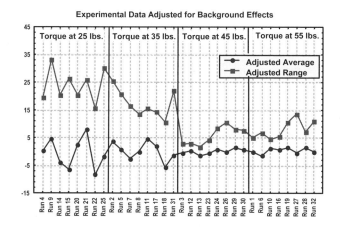

These adjusted values are then ordered by factor level and plotted. The resulting run chart of averages and ranges is presented in the exhibit. In this case, as days had little or no impact on the results, the chart is very similar to that of the averages and ranges chart produced earlier, where the data had not been adjusted for background variables.

---

80. This approach is well documented in Ronald D. Moen, et al. in Improving Quality Through Designed Experimentation, Mcgraw Hill, New York, NY 1991, pp. 88-91

ANALYSIS OF DATA ARISING FROM EXPERIMENTS

Few things can compare to the power of experiments in the pursuit of improved performance. The manipulation and control of causal factors, and the careful measurement of both factor levels and response, provide unparalleled opportunities to assess and better understand the root cause drivers of performance.

The three-step process outlined will likely prove more than satisfactory at yielding meaningful results from most real-world applications. There are, of course, a host of other techniques that apply to experimental data. ANOVA, the most popular, is discussed next. However, analysis that jumps to ANOVA or other advanced techniques has likely gotten ahead of itself. Start with the three basic steps and have a good, long look at the data first.

A NOTE ON ANALYSIS OF VARIANCE (ANOVA)

One of the more advanced techniques, and perhaps the most common statistical approach to the analysis of experimental data, is Analysis of Variance (ANOVA). While ANOVA is beyond the scope of this book, the technique does necessitate some comment if only due to its extensive use.

ANOVA, like the control chart, is designed to analyze the variance in the data by using sub-groups to rationally partition the data and the type of variation. Unlike the control chart, ANOVA applies a test of significance (F-Ratio) that, in turn, requires the experimenter to state a desired confidence level.

While ANOVA is an extremely valuable technique, all too often those sitting in front of their computers jump to ANOVA as a first step of analysis. Again, this is a mistake. The use of basic run charts and control charts, combined with other graphical tools such as dot plots and box and whisker diagrams, are usually more than capable of handling the types of real-world experiments that organizations are likely to conduct. Moreover, even when more advanced techniques are necessary, there is no substitute for performing the three steps of the survivor's guide first. If nothing else, these steps demand that the analyst actually look at the data – an essential first step to any analytical procedure.

The F-Ratio and Significance

The use of the F-ratio within ANOVA as a "test of significance" suffers from some poor wording that can lead to misinterpretation. When we say the F-ratio is 'significant,' this does not mean the finding is of any practical importance. Rather, it means our experiment was able to detect a difference between sub-groups – that is, a signal in the data (special cause) was detectable through the background noise (common cause) variation. As such, the F statistic is perhaps best interpreted as a signal-to-noise ratio.

It is also important to note that the significance test compares the calculated F-ratio to a confidence level that is established by the experimenter. "Significant" results, therefore, tell us as much about the degree of confidence of the experimenter as they do about conditions in the real world.

Summary: Analyzing Relationships

To improve performance we need to identify the drivers of performance. When processes and systems are unstable, these drivers are the special causes of variation creating the instability. When processes are stable, however, the drivers or factors influencing performance must be sought out.

It is in this later case where the tools for the analysis of cause and effect really shine. By carefully examining the system for evidence of correlation between potential drivers and critical performance metrics, the tools allow us to see underlying relationships and the often hidden patterns in the data that can reveal significant opportunities for improved performance. These same tools present the same opportunities for insight when organizations actively muck about – conduct experiments – to create or generate new knowledge.

Root cause analysis is more than people brainstorming possible causes. It is also the process of carefully examining the evidence so that verdicts are rendered and improvement is accomplished.

Creating Solutions: Tools for Generating and Analyzing Ideas

8

If all processes and systems could be improved by simply analyzing quantitative data, the world would be a simpler place. Such is not the case. Teams striving for improvement must use their own knowledge to determine where the improvement priorities lie. They must decide what to measure, interpret measurement results, identify ideas and potential solutions, and address implementation and change issues. Teams, therefore, will continually face the task of generating or eliciting the implicit knowledge that exists within the team. In short, collecting and analyzing data is only one part of the improvement process. Organizations also must continually fit new knowledge together with existing knowledge to make it relevant, meaningful and real.

Tapping into the existing knowledge of team members and structuring it in a way that is useful for making improvements can be a difficult task. A number of tools and techniques can help. Some tools are meant to elicit information or knowledge, others are designed to organize it. Some are designed to stimulate ideas among members of the team, while others are designed to elicit individual knowledge and then share it in a group setting. Different tools for different jobs. Before identifying the most appropriate tool to use, therefore, the first step is clearly defining the job at hand. Before starting the job, we must identify what it is we are trying to do.

WHAT ARE WE TRYING TO DO?

The various tools are differentiated by what they try to achieve, and the techniques or methods used to accomplish these objectives. What was true for quantitative data is true for working with qualitative data. Specifically, there are only four things we can do with data of any type. These four things are:

1. **Gather the data.** We can gather qualitative data from any number of sources or generate it through some variation of brainstorming or related technique. When generating data in team settings, we're usually trying to develop or identify as many ideas as possible, regardless of how "far out" they may seem. We are engaging people in divergent thinking. Agreement is not the goal. Diversity, creativity and comprehensiveness are the goals.

2. **Organize the data,** by grouping or sorting the data in a manner that is meaningful to the team or group responsible for its analysis. With qualitative data, organization usually means grouping the data, although grouped qualitative data can also be sorted by frequency (size of the group) or by importance (after some form or preference scoring technique has been applied).

3. **Summarize the data,** usually by representing it with a statistic (with qualitative data the statistic is usually a count or importance rating) or a qualitative summary description. In summarizing the data, we emphasize con-

vergent thinking. We're trying to get the team or group to focus on some preferred options or provide new ideas to an existing structure or model. The objective is to 'bring things together' – reducing scope and providing focus.

4. **Make conclusions,** usually by comparing the summaries with some expectation or other data.

Team leaders or facilitators must ask themselves what they are trying to achieve before they apply tools in a team setting. For example, there is a tendency to apply brainstorming – a tool emphasizing divergent thinking and data generation – no matter what the nature of the problem or issue. This can be disastrous if the team desperately needs to reach agreement on what is important or not, or requires greater structure in the information it already has at its disposal (organizing).

THE TOOLS

The specific tools used to generate and organize information are:

Table 255: Information-Generating and Organizing Tools

The Tool or Process	Data Analysis Phase	Basic Description	When to Use
1. Brainstorming	Gathering (Generating) Data	Generates a list of ideas from a group.	Best at eliciting divergent ideas. Use whenever comprehensiveness is most important.
2. Multi-voting	Summarizing Data	Uses voting to reduce items in a list the team will deal with immediately.	Use when it is important to zero in on a reduced set of alternatives or set some immediate priorities.
3. Nominal Group Technique	Gathering then Summarizing	Individual idea generation combined with group ranking of ideas generated.	Use when issue is controversial within the group or when some participants are dominating discussions.
4. Mind Mapping	Gathering and Organizing	Group idea generation concurrent with organization.	Use when you want to map out the landscape of a particular problem or issue.
5. Crawford Slip Method	Gathering then Organizing and Summarizing	Gathering and/or generating data and then organizing data into groups and providing qualitative summary descriptions.	Use when you want to organize and summarize a highly diverse data set including brainstorming output, printed material and qualitative data.
6. Affinity Charting	Gathering then Organizing and Summarizing	Individual idea generation followed by group organization and summary of data.	Use when you want to generate ideas and organize them quickly within a team setting.
7. Tree Diagram	Organizing	Organizing data into a specific hierarchical structure.	Use whenever a precise structure or organization is required of data or team ideas. Excellent in many planning applications.

▲ **Brainstorming.** Many people are familiar with this technique, used to generate a wide variety of ideas. Brainstorming sessions can focus on identifying problems or generating ideas as potential solutions.

▲ **Multi-voting.** This is a technique that rates alternatives or ideas in order to reduce the number of topics under consideration. It is commonly used after a brainstorming session to reduce the data.

▲ **Nominal Group Technique.** This technique combines elements of brainstorming and multi-voting in a structured format that minimizes group interaction during the information-generating phase. This is useful when topics are controversial or when there are significant disagreements among team members.

▲ **Mind Mapping.** This is the simultaneous generation of ideas in relation to one another, to create and organize data in a single session.

▲ **Crawford Slip Method.** This is a structured information-generating technique focusing on data reduction and classification. It is useful when combined with cause and effect diagrams.

▲ **Affinity Diagrams/Charting.** This organizational method uses information from brainstorming or other idea-generating sessions and organizes it in related groupings.

▲ **Tree Diagrams.** This is a hierarchical arrangement of data in which information is arranged into successive layers of detail.

Table 255: Information-Generating and Organizing Tools links the specific tools with the three basic objectives. Each of these tools or techniques is discussed in detail. Teams should feel free to use the technique they are most comfortable with, or to seek help using a technique they feel would be useful in certain circumstances.

BRAINSTORMING

Brainstorming can be used by one person working alone on a problem, by a small team, or by large groups. It is a useful and flexible process that can help a variety of creative ideas. Unfortunately, brainstorming is a much-abused technique as well. There is a tendency for teams to engage in some form of brainstorming exercise, no matter what the nature of the problem is, or the issue to be resolved. The result is usually an abundance of information without any relevance.

WHEN TO USE BRAINSTORMING

Brainstorming is most useful when seeking to encourage and obtain variety, creativity and comprehensiveness – in other words, when divergent thinking is the objective. For example, it can be used when:

▲ You need to emphasize creativity over any other objective.

▲ There is no straightforward solution to a problem or when traditional approaches have not proved useful.

▲ Expertise exists within many people in the group, or where the nature of the issue being explored demands a variety of expertise from many types of people, making everyone's participation essential.

▲ You need to generate possible "causes" when constructing a cause-and-effect diagram.

▲ When comprehensiveness is important – you want to ensure all possibilities have been identified.

Exhibit 256: Brainstorming Output

Shipping Space not Organized
Lot of Confusion With New Hires
Equipment Getting Old
Shipping Not Seen As Important -- No Training
Bad Light
Labels Are Shoddy
Company Policy on Using All Carriers
Constant Breakdowns of Moving Equipment
Additional Training in Space Management
Manual Shipping Request Forms Are Terrible
Customers Always Want It Now

Sales Do Not Find Out When Really Needed by the Customer
Shipping Forms Take Too Long to Complete
Use One Carrier
Sometimes Only New People in Department
Spreading the Work Around Different Carriers Doesn't Work
Summer Vacations Not Coordinated
Computer Old
Supposed to Balance Our Ordering Through Different Carriers But Sometimes Not The Best Carrier to Use.

Computer System Not Integrated With Company
Sometimes Not Enough Staff -- No One Answers Phone
Only One Bar Code Reader
Sales Over Promise Delivery Dates
Paper Labels Are No Good
Put Bar Codes & Descriptions on Same Label
Require More Shelving
Only One Dock, Line-Up's
Who Is Answering the Phone?
Use Plastic Labels Not Paper

Environment is Dismal
Everything Always Has "Now" Priority
Hot During Summer, Cold in Winter
Inventory System Out of Date, Slow
Labels Become Fouled (Dirty, Torn, etc.)
Manual Shipping Orders
Bar Codes & Descriptions on Different Labels
New People Not Trained (Learn by Doing)

GUIDELINES TO BRAINSTORMING

There are several varieties of brainstorming, but the basic guidelines of generating ideas are the same. These guidelines are:

▲ **Be creative and imaginative.** Wild ideas are fine! At times, ideas only seem wild when evaluated in the context of conventional organization thinking. Often, these same organizational conventions are the source of the problem.

▲ **Generate as many ideas as possible.** Be more concerned about quantity than about quality of ideas during the brainstorming process. Time can be used after the session to evaluate or rate the ideas. However, the main brainstorming session should be used to get everything out.

▲ **Everyone participates.** There are no "observers" in brainstorming. Some participants will display reluctance to join in and not everyone will participate to the same degree. But everyone present is expected to participate and contribute to the proceedings to the extent they feel comfortable.

▲ **Build on previous ideas.** Modifying of other people's ideas, or your own, is great. The process is called hitchhik-

ing or bootstrapping. But whatever it's called, all participants should feel free to use someone else's comments in helping clarify or build their own thoughts.

▲ **Do not criticize or evaluate during the brainstorming period.** People become inhibited or defensive when criticized, and they may self-censor their other ideas during the session. These unexpressed ideas might just be the ones to solve the problem, or serve as the jumping-off idea for the eventual solution proposed by someone else.

▲ **Keep a record.** Use a flip chart to record all ideas and keep them visible. Usually, this means taping flip chart pages to the wall as you go. This visibility helps others to bootstrap or combine ideas to produce new ideas.

Brainstorming is a technique designed to ensure that all, or at least a wide range of problems or solutions have been identified. It allows people to be as creative as possible – to generate ideas rather than analyze. Its free- form approach can generate enthusiasm in a team as well as information overload.

GENERAL SEQUENCE OF EVENTS

A brainstorming session usually proceeds along four basic process steps.

1. Review the subject of the brainstorming session

The better defined the topic or question is going into the brainstorming session, the more focused and useful the results tend to be. Some sample going-in questions might be:

▶ What can we do to reduce customer frustration when line-ups are long?

▶ How can transaction processing time be reduced?

▶ What is causing the rise in customer complaints?

▶ What are all the potential causes affecting emergency response times?

Be prepared to discuss and refine the question. Before the actual generation of ideas, it is important that those participating share a common understanding of the question or issue that serves as the focus of the session.

2. Let people think about the issue

Don't jump right in and demand people generate a bunch of ideas immediately. Give the team a minute or two to think about the question or issue. Sometimes the silence in a room can work wonders. Be patient.

3. Invite people to call out their ideas

Use a facilitator to encourage people to call out their ideas, writing them down on a flip chart as you go. Remember, there is no discussion or evaluation of the ideas as they come up (see the guidelines). Building on the ideas of others is fine, however. One person may call out an idea and another adds to it. When this building process happens, write down both ideas separately on the flip chart paper.

4. Post the flip chart pages

As flip chart pages are filled, post them on a wall so that the team can look at them. Team members can only build on ideas if they can see them. To do that, the ideas generated must be in plain view of everyone participating. Keep going until the well runs dry – that is, until no one can identify any more ideas.

These four steps comprise the basics of any brainstorming process. A number of variations, however, can be used to enhance the productivity of the exercise.

VARIATIONS TO ENHANCE CREATIVITY AND "BUST" BARRIERS

A number of variations can be used in brainstorming to enhance creativity and "bust" barriers in thinking patterns. Some suggested variations include:

▲ **Goal Reversal.** Brainstorming sessions often focus on some positive objective or goal, such as improving customer service. Reversing the goal – say, making customer service terrible – can stimulate creative thinking. This is particularly useful when people are a little worn-out or on the tired side. Coming up with ideas to slow production, produce poorer quality, decrease productivity and anger customers is generally a lot more fun than the traditional approach to brainstorming. For this reason, consider conducting a regular brainstorming exercise and then combining it with the goal reversal version when the team is running out of steam. It's a good way to energize people and develop some new ideas at the same time.

▲ **Metaphors.** Metaphors can be used to great effect to enhance creativity. Asking whether the situation or problem at hand is like any others seen before can help drive a session forward.[81] These situations can be listed on the flip chart. Discussion should then focus on the implications of assuming the two cases are similar or the same.

The choice of metaphor need not be directly related to the subject at hand. For example, when brainstorming ideas to speed up service delivery, a team might choose to ask how the current delivery system is like the Mississippi River. Remember, the intent here is to stimulate divergent thinking – there will be time for evaluation later.

▲ **Alternative Perspectives.** This approach involves looking at the problem through the eyes of others to gain fresh perspectives. The range of alternative perspectives is limitless. Asking how your customers see the problem is one such approach. However, the use of perspective, as was the case with metaphors, need not be so directly related to the problem at hand. What would Attila the Hun do in this

---

81. Technically, these are similes, not metaphors. The distinction, it turns out, is important to book editors and English teachers – one of which I'm married to.

situation? How would the Internal Revenue Service approach the problem?

NOW WHAT?

Brainstorming is a great technique to generate information. But the results of the brainstorming session, by themselves, are usually too disjointed and too numerous to deal with. It is divergent thinking, after all, so it should be disjointed. This means some form of data classification or reduction is usually required following the brainstorming session. Multi-voting can be used to reduce the ideas identified, while affinity charting and tree diagrams are among the most commonly used approaches to organizing or providing some structure for the output.

MULTI-VOTING

Multi-voting, as the name implies, is a voting procedure. It is typically used following a brainstorming session, to select the ideas the team considers most important or relevant to the problem or issue at hand. It is, therefore, a technique designed to reduce the amount of data a team must handle, rather than to make any final decisions. It is called multi-voting because individuals are given multiple votes that they can use to reduce the range of options or alternatives.

USES OF MULTI-VOTING

Multi-voting quickly reduces the amount of data or ideas that the team must handle. There is only limited discussion before the vote. Because it is a voting procedure, the results may not reflect the consensus position of the group. Be careful, therefore, to apply multi-voting only when in the preliminary stages of reducing information. Stay away from applying any voting procedure when final decisions must be made, especially on contentious issues. In these situations of higher risk, decision techniques using evaluative criteria should be used.

Use multi-voting when:

▲ **You need to get an idea of where the team stands on a current issue, but you do not want to engage in a formal decision-making process.** Multi-voting is a good technique for helping team leaders manage the conflict that emerges when dealing with issues. Using the multi-voting technique allows the leader or facilitator to gauge the state of affairs without formally committing to a final decision process.

▲ **You need to reduce the data set that a team must deal with coming out of a brainstorming session.** Brainstorming sessions produce a lot of information, but no organization or priority setting of this information. When some initial priorities must be established, multi-voting provides an excellent mechanism to focus on what the team, as a whole, feels is important.

GENERAL SEQUENCE OF EVENTS

Multi-voting usually follows a basic five-step procedure. These five steps are:

1. Generate and organize a list to vote on

This can come from a number of sources. Data produced by a brainstorming session is the most common "list" for a multi-voting procedure, but there are other sources. For example, a list of customer complaints could be reduced to a more limited set of target improvement areas through a multi-voting procedure.

2. Number the list

Make sure that the entire list is visible and clearly numbered so that each item on the list has its own unique identifier. At this point, if the entire group agrees that two ideas on the list are the same, they may be combined.

3. Allocate the votes

A good rule to follow is that each person will have a number of votes equal to about one-third the number of items on the list. This is often referred to as the n/3 rule. For example, if there are 70 items on the list, each team member will have about 24 votes. In the exhibit following, there are 37 alternatives. Each team member, therefore, would have received 12 votes.

4. Conduct the vote

Voting can be done a number of ways. All are effective. Teams can choose whatever approach they feel is appropriate.

▲ **Ballot**. This maintains secrecy since no one on the team knows how the others have voted. Ask team members to write down on paper the numbers of the items on the list they think are most important. Remember point 3 – team members are limited in the number of votes they cast to one-third the number of items on the list. The facilitator then records the votes on the flipcharts.

▲ **Show of Hands.** The facilitator calls out the number for each item on the list. People vote by raising their hands. The facilitator counts the hands and records the number of votes on the flipchart.

▲ **Post the Dots.** This method uses colored dots available through stationery stores. The appropriate number of dots is distributed to each team member. Team members then post these next to the items on the flipchart as votes. The facilitator then totals these votes. Exhibit 257: Reducing the Data From a Brainstorming With a Voting Procedure presents a typical listing of alternatives, where team members have "posted their dots" as a means of voting for their preferred alternative.

5. Tally the results and repeat as necessary

After the vote, the facilitator tallies the results and writes down on the flipchart the number of votes each item received. Items on the list that didn't receive many votes are removed. The vote is then conducted again until the remaining items on the

Exhibit 257: Reducing the Data From a Brainstorming With a Voting Procedure

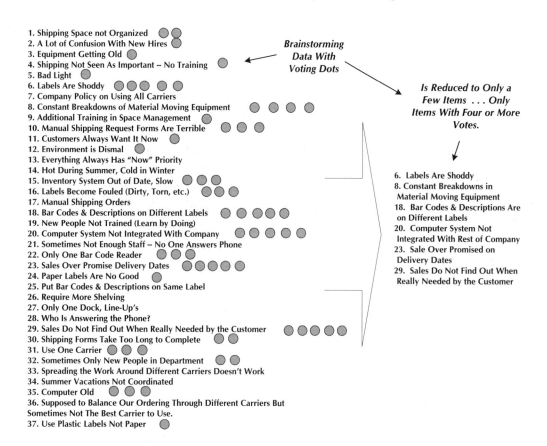

1. Shipping Space not Organized
2. A Lot of Confusion With New Hires
3. Equipment Getting Old
4. Shipping Not Seen As Important -- No Training
5. Bad Light
6. Labels Are Shoddy
7. Company Policy on Using All Carriers
8. Constant Breakdowns of Material Moving Equipment
9. Additional Training in Space Management
10. Manual Shipping Request Forms Are Terrible
11. Customers Always Want It Now
12. Environment is Dismal
13. Everything Always Has "Now" Priority
14. Hot During Summer, Cold in Winter
15. Inventory System Out of Date, Slow
16. Labels Become Fouled (Dirty, Torn, etc.)
17. Manual Shipping Orders
18. Bar Codes & Descriptions on Different Labels
19. New People Not Trained (Learn by Doing)
20. Computer System Not Integrated With Company
21. Sometimes Not Enough Staff -- No One Answers Phone
22. Only One Bar Code Reader
23. Sales Over Promise Delivery Dates
24. Paper Labels Are No Good
25. Put Bar Codes & Descriptions on Same Label
26. Require More Shelving
27. Only One Dock, Line-Up's
28. Who Is Answering the Phone?
29. Sales Do Not Find Out When Really Needed by the Customer
30. Shipping Forms Take Too Long to Complete
31. Use One Carrier
32. Sometimes Only New People in Department
33. Spreading the Work Around Different Carriers Doesn't Work
34. Summer Vacations Not Coordinated
35. Computer Old
36. Supposed to Balance Our Ordering Through Different Carriers But Sometimes Not The Best Carrier to Use.
37. Use Plastic Labels Not Paper

Brainstorming Data With Voting Dots

Is Reduced to Only a Few Items ... Only Items With Four or More Votes.

6. Labels Are Shoddy
8. Constant Breakdowns in Material Moving Equipment
18. Bar Codes & Descriptions Are on Different Labels
20. Computer System Not Integrated With Rest of Company
23. Sale Over Promised on Delivery Dates
29. Sales Do Not Find Out When Really Needed by the Customer

list represent a reasonable number that the teams feels it can work with. In the example, an arbitrary vote total of four was selected. This resulted in six priorities for the team.

MIND MAPPING

Mind mapping promotes a free association of ideas like brainstorming, but does so in a manner that provides a preliminary structure as the data is generated. This creates a visual map of the "mind" of the group or team. This structure can then be reworked to refine the organization of the data. Mind mapping taps the divergent properties of brainstorming to allow for wild ideas, and for individuals to build upon the ideas of others. But mind mapping also makes the building process visible by drawing lines that link similar ideas.

The results resemble cause and effect diagrams with their branch-like organization. But unlike cause and effect diagrams, mind map branches radiate from a central core in all directions, in what initially looks like a haphazard manner. Like cause and effect diagrams, the branch-like effect can help contribute to the brainstorming effort. Making things visible helps people build on the ideas of others, while also making gaps apparent.

Exhibit 258: Sample Mind Map

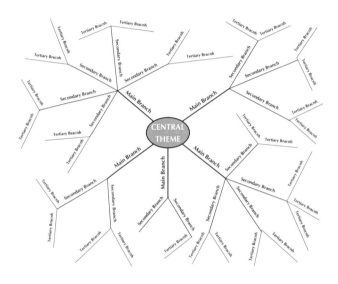

Rarely does mind mapping happen in a single pass. Usually, after the first map is created, it is analyzed and a second map is then created to arrive at the finished product.

USES OF MIND MAPPING

Mind mapping has some definite advantages, especially when working in large groups. The use of a single map within a large group can create a focus for the group, keeping people's attention on the task. However, mind maps are not restricted to large groups. Use mind mapping whenever:

▲ there is a need to map or scope out some issue, problem or theme. This is particularly useful when trying to understand the breadth of some issue that seems too large to really get a handle on.

▲ a large group of diverse participants, each with his or her own perspectives on a problem, needs to create a shared understanding of the problem from all the various perspectives.

▲ analyzing all the various ways one could approach the resolution of some issue or pursue some goal.

▲ trying to understand the complexity of the environment and the factors that contribute to some condition or effect having an influence upon the organization, especially in planning or strategic planning applications.

GENERAL SEQUENCE OF EVENTS

Mind mapping is done on a single large sheet of paper. The process can generate as much data as brainstorming, so we do mean a LARGE piece of paper! With improvement teams or small groups, a smaller sheet of paper eight feet long and four feet wide will do nicely. With larger groups, you'll need larger sheets of paper. I have used mind mapping with groups as large as 100, and in that case the paper measured five feet wide and over 20 feet long. Whatever the final size, this sheet of paper needs to be securely fastened to a wall so all participants can see it.

1. Define the central issue

Write the motivating focus or central issue on a flip chart. It is important that everyone understands this focus in much the same way, so take some time to discuss it and be prepared to re-write if necessary. When everyone agrees on the central issue, write it down in the center of the large sheet of paper posted on the wall. Make sure it is in large capital letters and easy to read from anywhere in the room. Enclose it in a box of some form.

2. Begin the mind mapping

Now the mind mapping process begins. Team members call out a word or brief phrase that relates to the central focus or issue. As they call out the word, it is noted on the sheet in large block letters, and then connected by an arrow to either the central focus or a related word placed elsewhere on the page. As things become more complex, participants involved in calling out words or phrases can also identify the specific branch or area where they believe the word or phrase should be connected. As the process moves along, the entire team becomes involved in a process of divergent thinking with simultaneous organization, in a very open and freewheeling environment.

3. Keep on going

Continue the process until the team is completely out of ideas. By the time they are, you will have what appears at first glance to be quite a mess on your hands. That's okay. Give the team members a chance to look for an underlying structure of the map elements and their connections. Patterns do emerge. As people examine the map, additional ideas will come forward. As they do, record them on the diagram.

4. Create a second map

As the team examines the map for underlying structures, certain elements of the map will make up related clusters or groupings. Some of these will be readily apparent from the original map and the connecting lines, while others may be harder to see. The facilitator circles these clusters with marker pens of different colors – each color representing a different cluster or group. As clusters are identified, a descriptive word or phrase is developed to define the grouping, and this phrase is written on a second mind map. Continue the process until all the elements are grouped and the major groups are recorded on the new map.

5. Fill in the detail

Once the major headings have been recorded on the second mind map, the detailed elements can then be filled in. Connections between the data elements may be re-defined by the team as the map is prepared.

Mind mapping's unique combination of idea/data generation with organization makes it a highly effective technique. But it is also demanding. You are doing both idea generation and idea organization in the same session.

Here are some suggestions to help things along:

▲ **Give yourself and the team plenty of time.** The demands of mind mapping mean you should give yourself plenty of time to conduct the session. Completing an initial map will take at least an hour, probably more. And that is just the initial map. To reconstruct and organize the map will take longer than this, probably over two hours. Naturally, the time involved will vary considerably depending upon the nature of the problems or issue, the number of people participating and so on.

▲ **Schedule a break after completing the initial mind map.** The completion of the initial mind map represents a natural break point in the exercise. Make use of this to schedule a break for those participating. The facilitator should encourage participants to review the mind map during the break and to discuss the results. Often, this more relaxed review yields additional material for the map and helps the group find the underlying structure.

Mind mapping, like brainstorming, can generate a great deal of information, often more than the team or group can effectively handle. For this reason, multi-voting can be used to help reduce the number of options or to set priorities. The best approach is to provide participants with paper dots or other types of stickers and let them post these votes where they think most appropriate. The facilitator can then tally the votes and circle the priorities.

EXAMPLE: HELPING PEOPLE LIVING WITH HIV/AIDS

As part of a process to redesign the method of service delivery to people living with HIV/AIDs, including redesigning the organization of agencies and funding practices, a major planning conference was held. Participants included agencies, funding organizations, government representatives, health officials and those suffering with the disease. Part of the conference design included an assessment of the current environmental conditions affecting those living with HIV/AIDS. With close to 100 participants, reaching agreement on what this environment looked like might prove difficult.

Mind mapping, however, was the perfect tool in these circumstances. First, a very large piece of paper (20 feet by five feet) was posted on the wall. Tables and chairs were then oriented toward what was to become the mind map. From here, the facilitator drew the central theme for the session, and invited people to call out what they saw as the major factors of influence affecting the theme. What resulted was the initial tumble presented in Exhibit 259: Initial Tumble.

From this initial tumble or mapping, the team started to analyze the map. Areas that seemed similar or were related were circled and arrows drawn to connect them (see Exhibit 260: Reworking the Initial Tumble). Lots of discussion in this phase of the process was encouraged. Soon the group had a pretty big mess on its hands, but a mess that was relatively easy to redraw.

The final results are presented in Exhibit 261: Final Mind Map. It is a much simpler and easier to grasp map than the initial tumble. This is because in the first mind mapping round, emphasis was placed on the free-form nature of the exercise – the brainstorming component. Efforts were made at classifying or linking branches as the brainstorming occurred, but the emphasis was on idea generation, not organization. Classification of ideas took a back seat.

In the second round, however, idea generation takes a back seat and classification and organization drive the process. The result is that data elements are combined, summarized or otherwise modified to paint a consistent picture of the landscape that is the focus of the team's efforts.

The group also arranged the map to reveal what they saw as a continual process or cycle (reflected in the diagram by the arrows indicating the flow of the cycle). Those affected by HIV/AIDS cause a community response which, in turn, influences public policy and so forth.

The team used this interpretation to help develop a long-term strategy for change, including a resetting of funding priorities within the health system.

The example shows how effective mind mapping can be at capturing an enormous amount of data, usually qualitative in nature, and rework this data into an organized format that still reflects the often unstructured nature of the reality or problem being addressed.

Exhibit 259: Initial Tumble

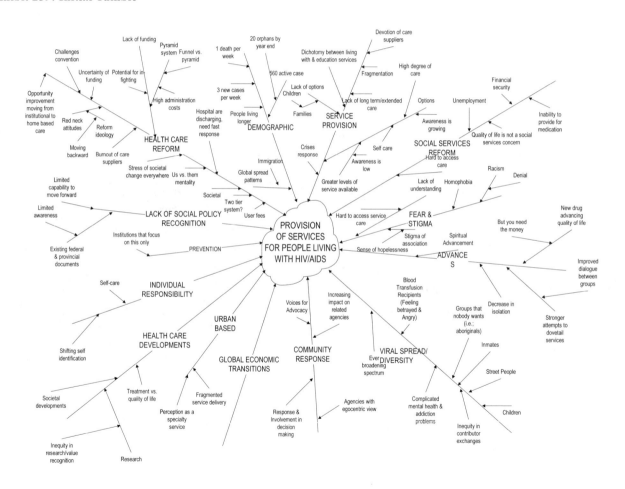

Exhibit 260: Reworking the Initial Tumble

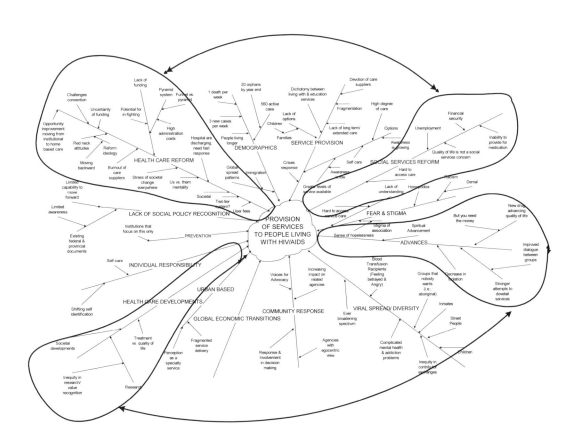

Exhibit 261: Final Mind Map

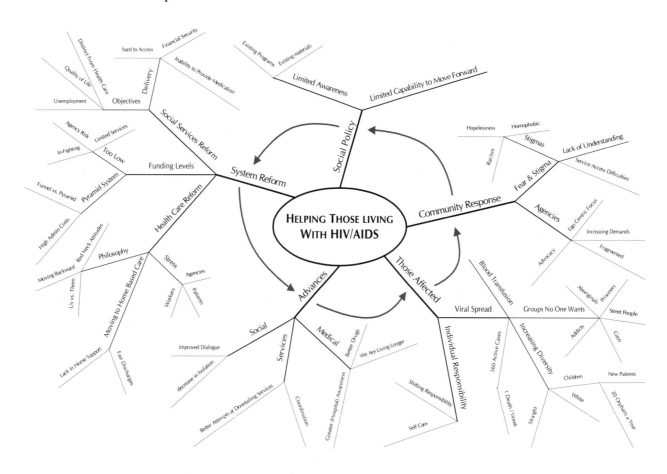

NOMINAL GROUP TECHNIQUE

The nominal group technique (NGT) attempts to initially generate and then reduce information in a single session. In this regard, it is not unlike combining a brainstorming session with some multi-voting. The technique is called nominal, because the initial idea-generating phase and the subsequent voting (data reduction) are done without discussion among team members. Idea generation and voting are both done in silence. Team members work more as individuals, but within a group setting.

USES OF THE NOMINAL GROUP TECHNIQUE

The "no-discussion" aspect may seem like a disadvantage to the technique, but it is very useful when the team is stuck in some form of disagreement or when highly controversial or emotionally charged issues are at hand. In these circumstances, the lack of interaction helps keep people focused on the issues and away from individual positions.

The nominal group technique is also useful when the team leader wants to encourage participation from everyone. At times, team members may become intimidated or withdraw from the issues at hand, especially if one or two vocal individuals are dominating discussions. NGT limits the extent to which this 'domination' can occur and, as a result, facilitates the gathering of a more diverse and representative set of views.

GENERAL SEQUENCE OF EVENTS

Eight steps define the general sequence of events of the nominal group technique.

1. Define the task

Like with brainstorming, the task for the NGT group should be clearly defined. Post it on the wall and be prepared to discuss the issue before beginning the session proper. Make sure everyone in the room has a shared understanding of the topic (what will be discussed), and the task (how the NGT process will work).

2. Generate the ideas

Unlike the brainstorming session, idea generation is done on an individual basis. Team members are asked to write down all their ideas on a piece of paper. No discussions at this point are permitted. Generally, about 20 minutes is allocated for this process. While the number of ideas an individual can generate starts to diminish after about five to 10 minutes, the quality of ideas generated tends to rise over time, so give people the time to think.

3. List the ideas

The facilitator goes around the table and asks each team member to read one idea on his or her list, recording the idea on a flip chart as the process proceeds. Other team members may "piggy-back" or add to the ideas as they are called out. These ideas are also recorded. As each page of the flip chart becomes full, it is removed from the easel and posted on the wall. Lots of ideas means you will need lots of wall space, so be prepared. The process continues until all the ideas have been recorded. Again, there is no discussion or evaluation of ideas at this point, just a listing of everything team members have produced.

4. Discuss the ideas for clarity

Once all the ideas have been recorded, the team is encouraged to discuss them but only for the purposes of clarification. This is not a time for debate over the ideas' merits or a time to judge the validity of the ideas. Discussion is focused on clarification as a means to enhance understanding. However, everyone on the team is invited to contribute to this understanding. At this point, the facilitator numbers the ideas on the flip chart paper so that they are clearly visible to all participants in the session.

5. Make individual rankings

Individuals are next asked to rank the various alternatives. Each participant is given between four and 10 cards. The number depends upon the number of ideas. Use four cards if the number of items or ideas is less than 20. Try using about five or six cards when the list is between 20 and 35 items, and seven or eight cards when the list is between 35 and 50 items. For anything over 50 items use nine or 10 cards.

On each card, each participant writes down the number of the idea (from the flip chart) on the upper left-hand corner of the card. In the centre of the card, each participant writes down a few words that describe the issue. Lastly, each participant's

Exhibit 262: Ranking Cards

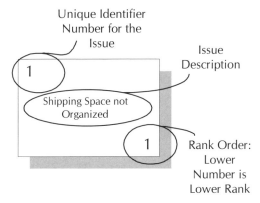

ranking is placed in the lower right-hand corner of the card. This is an obligatory ranking, so if six cards were handed out, the participant would rank the most important item as a six and write this number down in the lower right-hand corner. The next most important item would receive a five and so on until all six cards are completed.

6. Tally the results

When every participant is finished with his or her rankings, the cards are collected by the facilitator and the results tabulated.

This is most easily done if, during the individual rankings step, the facilitator has prepared a tally or checksheet for the answers. The format of this sheet is simply two columns, with the number of the item listed to the left and the blank column to record the results on the right. The facilitator records the votes in the columns and totals the results. The items with the greatest number of votes and highest scores comprise the group's selection.

The results can also be displayed through a Pareto chart. This can be quickly sketched on flip chart paper to summarize the items receiving votes.

7. Discuss the results

Ranking items will rarely produce a consensus, although it may move the team closer to consensus. Take some time to discuss the results. If a greater degree of consensus can be achieved, wonderful. Ideas should be recombined and another vote taken. If consensus is not possible, the team should proceed based on the results of the initial vote. Either way, the nominal group technique has generated as much agreement as possible.

8. Document

Results of any team session such as this should be saved, at the very least for future reference. Better yet, have the flip charts and the voting checksheet typed up and circulated to team members. This serves as a valuable reference for the team. Invariably, team members will ask how they got to where they are. "Why are we working on this priority?" "Who made this decision?" It is helpful in such circumstances to go back to the decision points of the team and remind ourselves of how we got to where we are.

SUMMARY OF NGT

The nominal group technique is deceptively simple and very effective. If the team needs to reduce the information it has or set some immediate priorities, NGT fits the bill nicely. This is especially so when the group is facing contentious issues or when a few members have tended to dominate the discussions.

CRAWFORD SLIP METHOD (CSM)

The Crawford slip method (CSM) was developed in the late 1920's by Dr. C. Crawford of the University of Southern California. It uses individual "slips" of paper (hence the name) as a data generating and organizing tool.

The method limits team member interaction during the idea-generating phase, but emphasizes interaction during idea classification. Of all the techniques discussed, it is often the most efficient means of generating ideas and organizing them quickly into categories.

USES OF CSM

The Crawford slip method excels when the team is confronted with a mix of data – some quantitative, some qualitative, some generated by team members, some generated from outside the team. Pieces of factual or quantitative data can be cut and pasted onto the slips and combined with qualitative data. Conclusions, observations and recommendations from outside sources can be cut out of articles or reports and likewise transferred to cards or slips. These slips are then 'worked' together, allowing the team to recombine what it knows in new and different ways. A couple of sample applications:

▲ In developing a strategy for a large bank, managers gathered qualitative and quantitative data from internal records, consultants, studies, branch reports and industry studies. All this was cut and pasted onto cards. To this was added their own opinions on what was happening in the industry, and the directions that needed to be pursued. The resulting cards (over 6,000) were then grouped using the CSM, to build a comprehensive situation appraisal of the bank and the business environment in which it found itself.

▲ A major North American municipality needed a strategy to address issues of homelessness. Research from other jurisdictions located all over the world was gathered to identify possible "best practices." In addition, the municipality conducted some of its own field research, including a homeless count and a series of focus groups with social service agencies and not-for-profits. At the end of a year's worth of work, they had mountains of information but no real way to makes sense of it. To resolve this situation, they brought together over 100 stakeholders to work with the data. Information gathered was transferred to cards and participants at the homeless conference were asked to add to this collection with their own thoughts and ideas. Then, breaking into working groups, the cards were grouped using the Crawford slip method. The result was a comprehensive assessment and strategy that guided activity for over three years.

In short, the Crawford slip method is a great way to organize and makes sense of large amounts of data, especially when the data represents a mix of data types and sources.

GENERAL SEQUENCE OF EVENTS

The Crawford slip method follows a basic six-step process:

1. Define the task or issue

The team leader or facilitator defines the issue or objective at hand. It is important that everyone has a clear understanding of what this issue is all about, so devote some time to ensure there is clarity.

2. Distribute the slips

Slips of paper about four inches by three inches are distributed to team members. Stationery and office supply stores sell index cards of this size and they are ideal, especially when other factual information is to be combined with the printed brainstorming ideas of team members. If the slips are to be handled on a vertical surface, sticky-notes of similar size work well. There is no limit to the number of slips each member may have.

3. Generate the ideas

Team members are given some time to write down their ideas on the slips of paper – one idea per slip. Idea generation is done in silence – no discussion among team members at this stage. Like the nominal group method, enough time should be allocated so more interesting ideas have the opportunity to emerge. The time varies, but 20 minutes is usually a good minimum.

If printed factual information is to be combined with the ideas generated by the team, such information can be distributed at this point. Participants in the process may read the data and paste it to a slip so that it can be worked with the rest of the data and ideas.

Exhibit 263: Idea Slips

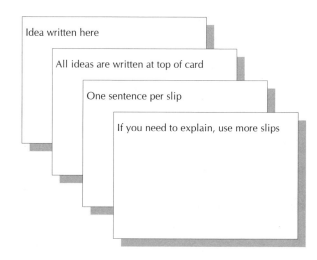

4. Sort the ideas

The ideas generated can be posted to the wall (if sticky-notes were used) or simply spread out across a table when using index cards. The team as a whole then attempts to sort the slips into some general categories. Lots of discussion is encouraged here. However, there can be a tendency for the team to become dominated by certain individuals who want to impose the structure as they see it. If this begins to occur, apply a no-talking rule (see also affinity charting) for a limited time. This will place people on a more equal playing field and promote greater participation and involvement by all concerned.

5. Consolidate the categories

Once the ideas are sorted into various categories, these categories are then grouped into some larger topic areas. The idea is to reduce the entire list initially produced on paper slips to anywhere between three and 10 broad headings. Each of these headings, of course, may have sub-groupings. Use different-colored and sized (slightly larger) cards to represent a group header and mark clearly on the card what the topic is. At the end of the process, the team will have all its data organized into a logical set of topics relevant to the original task or issue.

The Crawford slip method is like a combination of the nominal group technique (where people write down their ideas independently) and affinity charting (where ideas are recorded directly on sticky-notes or index cards for eventual organization). Because of this, the CSM is extremely efficient and provides a smooth flow between the generation and organization of ideas.

Exhibit 264: Classification Cards

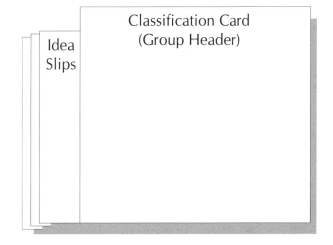

6. Summarize the ideas on each classification card

The last step is to interpret what all this information means to team members – how specifically, does it impact or relate to the task or issue as defined in step 1? In short, conclusions need to be drawn and the question "What does it all mean?" needs to be answered.

This requires the team to go through the cards associated with - sub-groups (lowest level group) first and summarize the information. This summary is written down on the appropriate classification card. Then the team moves on to the next level, summarizing the summaries and writing the conclusions down on the classification card. The process continues until every classification card has the conclusions of the team written upon it.

SOME HELPFUL HINTS

Here are some hints to help the process along:

▲ **All members participate.** Everyone is expected to contribute ideas and help with the task of sorting.

▲ **One sentence or idea per slip.** Keep your ideas straightforward and easy to understand. Long paragraphs are not used, nor is technical jargon.

▲ **Sort and re-sort.** As the sorting/categorization process proceeds, members are encouraged to discuss progress and break apart or re-name old categories or create new ones. Consensus on the categorization is the goal.

The Crawford slip method works extremely well, but it can produce a lot of frustration at the sorting/categorization phase. Team members, facilitators and leaders must be aware of this going in and be prepared to deal with problems as they arise.

If the team has serious difficulty with grouping, use a pre-existing model as a starting point, such as the 6-M's. As is the case with using the Ishikawa diagram, the team can become stalled at trying to find major groupings. If this happens, applying an arbitrary classification scheme as a starting point will help get things going.

An arbitrary approach is less than ideal, because we are searching for groupings that have meaning for the team as opposed to some existing structure. However, simply compelling the team to use a pre-defined grouping will often stimulate the creativity to generate a unique grouping or classification scheme by the time the process is completed. In other words, an existing model may be used to start the classification. But that doesn't mean the team should restrict itself to that classification scheme once things get going.

AFFINITY DIAGRAMS

The affinity diagram is an organizational tool developed in the 1960's by Jiro Kawakita. It takes large amounts of unstructured or verbal data – often the output of a brainstorming session – and groups the data elements based upon perceived affinity among the elements. By organizing the data, the affinity charting process helps us better understand complex problems or see old issues in new ways.

Exhibit 265: Basic Affinity Diagram

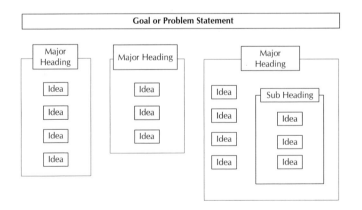

Despite affinity charting's focus on providing structure and organization to data, the tool involves more of a creative process than a logical/linear one. This is because it relies on high levels of participation, achievement of consensus and intuitive knowledge. This is facilitated by having the grouping process done in silence. The process can be frustrating to some, but the silent procedure compels individuals to think about what is going on, and participate through the movement of cards. Moreover, the whole process helps facilitate the building of teams, especially toward a shared understanding of how others see things.

USES OF AFFINITY DIAGRAMS

Affinity diagrams are useful whenever teams are confronted with large amounts of unstructured or verbal data. Some specific areas of application include:

▲ When the facts are difficult to comprehend or fail to present any immediately apparent pattern or meaning.

▲ When you want to organize a lot of data resulting from a brainstorming or similar session.

▲ When thoughts are unclear and disorganized. At times, the thinking of teams is all over the map. Affinity diagrams can help get things organized and providing a focus.

▲ When you need to create some consensus on the meaning of opinion or unstructured data.

▲ When you need to generate some preliminary organization before using the data in an Ishikawa or tree diagram.

▲ When you want to organize the results of open-ended questions from a customer or employee survey.

▲ When there is a need to look at an existing problem in a completely new way. Affinity charting is an ideal tool for re-combining components of some issue into a new organization, and therefore into a new way of seeing it.

PREPARING AFFINITY DIAGRAMS

Preparing or creating an affinity diagram involves six basic steps:

1. Select the subject

The first step in affinity diagramming is to clearly define the subject. What is the problem we are addressing? What is the existing understanding of the subject we wish to see anew? Everyone engaged in the process must share an understanding of the subject. Spend a little time for discussion and clarification to make sure this common understanding is in place.

2. Gather the data

Next, gather the data to be used. If the data originated from a brainstorming session, this task has already been done. However, one strength of affinity charting is its ability to deal with all forms of verbal or qualitative data regardless of the source. Sources of verbal/qualitative data that are suitable for organization through an affinity diagram would include:

▲ **Brainstorming exercise.** Brainstorming generates considerable verbal data from teams or groups of people.

▲ **Interviews.** Teams may gather the opinions of people through on-site interviews or focus group sessions.

▲ **Individual thoughts.** Individuals on the team or elsewhere in the organization can, through reflection and recall, list their thoughts or ideas about the subject matter.

▲ **Literature reviews.** Historical data or facts, and published studies and opinions are all forms of data that, when captured, can be analyzed through affinity diagramming.

▲ **Direct observation.** Team members may wish to gather observational data on how some process functions or the problems experienced by front-line staff. The resulting notes can then be used within the affinity diagram.

▲ **Surveys.** Information arising from open-ended questions on employee or customer surveys is also an good source of verbal data.

In short, any form of verbal or qualitative data can be analyzed using the affinity diagram. The appropriate collection method is dependent upon the nature of the subject matter. It is also important to note that the data to be analyzed does not necessarily have to come from only one of many potential sources. Affinity charting can use data from two, three or all of the sources mentioned above at the same time.

3. Transfer the data to cards

The next step is transferring the data to a format that facilitates construction of the diagram. The standard format is three inch-by-five inch cards (sticky-notes are ideal for this procedure). Use only one idea or thought per card. Print as large as possible so that the idea on each card is clearly visible. Be clear and concise. Three to ten words per card should do it.

To avoid ambiguity, try to use a simple verb-noun construction to create a statement with some meaning. Phrases like "computer department" are meaningless. What about the computer department? A verb-noun structure helps produce clarity. "Slow report turn-around time in the computer department" says a lot more than the original formulation of the statement. It leaves no doubt what was on the mind of the originator of the data.

4. Group the cards

Begin grouping the cards of a similar nature. This is done on the basis of group feeling or intuition, rather than according to any pre-existing categories. Remember, the cards are not being classified, but grouped. Throughout the procedure, all members of the team participate. Each member of the team should feel free to move or adjust any card at any time. We are trying to achieve a consensus on the grouping and consensus takes time. However, a key feature of affinity charting is that no talking or discussion is permitted during the procedure. Communication takes the form of moving the cards. Individuals are compelled to think about what others are trying to say by moving the cards the way they are.

If working on a flat surface, be sure it is large enough for the group to gather around and work with the cards. Using a wall is preferred for this procedure. It provides a larger work area and gets people out of their chairs (and off their respective duffs!). If there is a white board (dry-erasable board), try using it as the surface on which the sticky-notes will be placed. An alternative is to tape a large piece of butcher paper on the wall to accommodate the sticky-notes.

Continue to arrange the cards until four to ten groupings are created. Don't worry if some cards simply refuse to be grouped. The key to deciding if you are finished or not is agreement among team members that the groupings reflect the thinking of the team. As the team is working in silence, this agreement is generally reflected with heads nodding in agreement.

5. Label the cards

With the cards grouped, the facilitator should read back the cards to the team and ensure there is agreement among team members. Groupings are then given a label. This label is written on another card, known as a header card, which is then posted at the top of the grouping. The label must convey the full meaning of the grouping, but not in ambiguous terms. Use three to five words that will be clear to anyone reading the diagram.

6. Draw the affinity diagram

Draw lines around each grouping, making it clear which cards belong to which group. If groupings are somewhat related, place them next to each other and connect by lines. You may want to create another header card to describe how these groupings are related.

The ability of affinity charting to organize data makes it an ideal tool to link brainstorming output with other more analytical tools, such as Ishikawa diagrams, tree diagrams, matrix and deployment tools and flowcharting. The affinity diagram can be seen as an intermediate step between data generation and final organization.

EXAMPLE: AFFINITY CHARTING SHIPPING PROBLEMS

An example of how to use affinity charting to organize brainstorming output is provided in the shipping problem discussed earlier (See "Brainstorming" on page 584). The data was transferred from the flipcharts to sticky-notes so they could be easily re-arranged using a wall as the work surface. (See Exhibit 266: Transferring Brainstorming Data to Cards.) There were 37 ideas generated in the brainstorming session so 37 cards were required to transfer the data.

The cards or sticky-notes were then used to build the affinity diagram within the team setting. As the affinity diagram details, three basic problem areas emerged. The components of each problem area were also broken down through the arrangement of the cards. For example, physical elements of the shipping system were sub-grouped as facility, technology, equipment and labelling problems, each of which was detailed by the type of issues the team had identified. From this charting, specific strategies to reduce problems in each of the three areas could be addressed, or a single area could be targeted for improvement. The final affinity diagram is presented in Exhibit 267: Affinity Diagram of Shipping Problems.

PARALLEL PROCESSING AFFINITY

An interesting variation of affinity charting can be used when dealing with larger groups. Divide the group into smaller teams of between five and 10 individuals. Each team is presented with the same data on sticky-notes or cards. Working independently, these smaller teams create their own affinity charts.

When all teams have completed the task, each team presents their results to the group at large. This can be the foundation for some fascinating discussion, as participants attempt to understand the affinities produced by each team. In turn, this discussion can provide the foundation for a larger affinity chart as the entire team attempts to create consensus on the various affinities.

Exhibit 266: Transferring Brainstorming Data to Cards

Results of Brainstorming Session → Are Transferred to Sticky-Notes

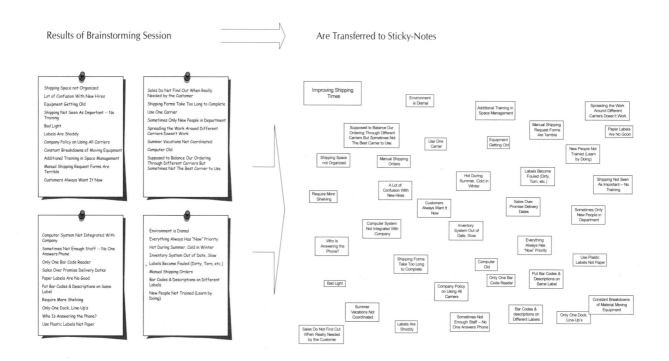

Exhibit 267: Affinity Diagram of Shipping Problems

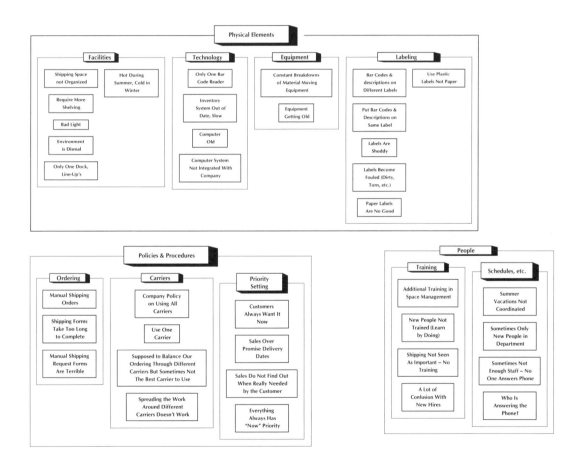

TREE DIAGRAMS

Tree diagrams are among the most effective means for organizing large amounts of qualitative data or information. They arrange such data in hierarchical levels according to some logical structure.

By hierarchically ordering the data, tree diagrams present (to extend the metaphor) a "forest *and* the trees" graphical representation of the implementation plan, issue or problem under analysis. We can see at a glance, for example, how all the elements of a plan relate to the primary objective or mission of that plan. This ability to present both the big picture, as well as all the smaller elements contributing to it, in a clear logical format is the real strength of the tree diagram.

The representation is linear in its presentation, revealing a nice, logical picture. Such a picture, however, may be inappropriate when the underlying reality that the diagram is intended to represent is non-linear. Where these non-linear relationships are important and need to be depicted, other organizational/analytical tools can be used, especially the relationship diagram.

Exhibit 268: Basic Tree Diagram Structure

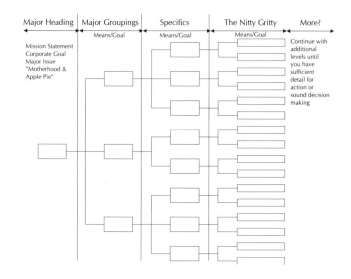

APPLICATIONS

Change and improvement plans tend to be linear. Subsequently, tree diagrams have found broad application in analyzing and organizing the plans and intentions of people – as opposed to analyzing situations in which people actually find themselves. Basically, tree diagrams can be used whenever:

▲ There is a need to organize the information resulting of from brainstorming or a similar session that produces a large amount of data.

▲ There is a need to move from "motherhood" pronouncements, such as those typically coming out of mission statements, into specific plans and action-items upon which organizational units and people can work.

▲ Specific corporate objectives need to be translated into meaningful initiatives and actions for the organization.

▲ Specific details on how something should be done, to achieve a specific end or objective, need to be made explicit.

▲ Additional structure to the results of affinity charting, mind mapping or force field analysis needs to be provided.

▲ A sequence of tasks required to address a key issue or problem needs to be identified.

▲ You want to make an Ishikawa diagram a little more comprehensible or accessible. (Some people find the Ishikawa

a little confusing, but it can be easily translated into a tree diagram which has a more organized appearance.)

When used in planning applications, tree diagrams also have a cascading effect. In Exhibit 268, we have three major groupings representing the *means* to accomplishing the major goal. But these same *means* act as *goals* or *ends* to the next level, specifics, which are the *means* to accomplish the major groupings/initiatives. This cascading of *goals* to *means* which, in turn, become the next set of *goals*, is a particular feature of tree diagrams that facilitates the "roll-down" of action plans to different layers in the organization.

THE GENERAL SEQUENCE OF EVENTS

As with other information-generating and organizing tools, tree diagrams are a team activity. Successful creation of the diagrams demands comprehensiveness and accurate logical relationships. So make sure the people who are involved in the process and understand it are there to help. The steps involved in creating the tree diagram are:

Exhibit 269: From Vision Statement to Metrics

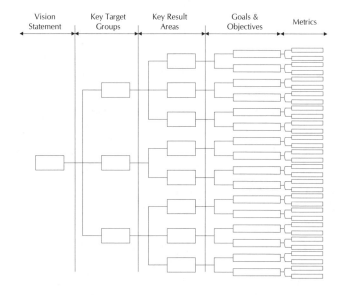

1. Choose the goal or problem statement

The goal or problem statement is the start of the tree diagram. The first task of the team is to identify and agree on this goal statement. If used to organize the results of a brainstorming session, the goal or problem statement will be closely related to the original question that drove the brainstorming process.

Similarly, when an affinity diagram has been built, the header card is typically used as the goal statement. Subsequent groupings in the affinity diagram can then be used as the basis for a tree diagram.

If an affinity diagram is especially large, you may choose to create a number of tree diagrams rather than tackle everything at once. These tree diagrams could then be considered separately or recombined later to form one large tree. The route you take depends upon the nature of the issue under consideration and the requirements of the team.

When the tree diagram focuses on action-planning or implementation, the goal statement should be restated if problem-oriented data is being used. A problem statement used to drive a brainstorming session, such as "Why is Customer Satisfaction Declining?" should be rephrased as "Means to Improve Customer Satisfaction." This action-oriented goal statement makes it easier for the team to focus on positive routes to improvement.

Whatever goal or problem statement is adopted, it is written down on the far left-hand side of the working area, preferably on a large sheet of paper posted on a wall where it is visible to everyone.

2. Create the major headings

The next step is creating a comprehensive set of means or major headings that will accomplish the goal statement or fully describe the issue under analysis. If working with data from an affinity diagram, header cards can be used to define the major tree diagram headings. However, if no previous attempts at organizing efforts have been done, tree diagram headings can be created through a brainstorming process or by the facilitator probing the team for their thoughts.

The key is – *don't be afraid to start*! The first draft is not written in stone. The team can decide to go back at any time and re-state the major tree diagram headings. In fact, some time should taken to reflect on the tree diagram and make changes. You are not trying to create perfection – only trying to get a handle on the logical structure in the data.

With the goal statement written at the far left of the working area, (flipchart, paper sheet, etc.) the tree diagram moves from the general to the specific in a left-to-right direction. Although flip chart paper or a large white board can be used, the use of cards or sticky-notes is recommended. Items on sticky-notes can be moved or adjusted, headings created and removed and so forth. Creating the tree diagram is a team activity so anticipate and encourage discussion.

3. Complete the tree diagram

Completing the tree diagram means taking existing data and placing it at different levels within the diagram. The facilitator needs to continuously probe the team to ensure each level of the tree is comprehensive and there are logical connections between the components at different levels.

As the tree takes shape, gaps in the teams' knowledge will appear. Where these gaps exist, brainstorming can be used to generate new knowledge. This, in turn, can be roughly grouped through an affinity diagram and then brought into the tree diagram. This process can be repeated as often as necessary until the tree diagram is complete.

The process of "filling-in" the tree continues, using a variety of techniques. But how do you know when you are finished? Two rules apply, and they work well as a means of moving towards completing a comprehensive diagram.

▲ **Comprehensiveness Rule**. Is each level of the tree diagram comprehensive? It should cover all the possible means or ways to the higher-level component to which it is connected.

▲ **Sufficiency Rule**. Is sufficient detail present to make the analysis relevant to the decisions or actions required? Keep going until the detail is meaningful to someone, or requires action of someone.

4. Review the tree diagram

Once the tree diagram is completed, its comprehensiveness should be reviewed along with its underlying logic. This needn't happen right away. Usually after a session of creating the tree diagram, team members will be a little worn out. In these circumstances, it is worthwhile to post the tree diagram at a location where it will not be disturbed but where it is accessible to team members (the team "war room" if available, is usually ideal). There, team members can visit the chart and analyze it when they have the energy. Hand-written notes can be added to the tree diagram along with comments, suggestions, additions and proposed modifications.

After a week, the team can reconvene to consider the suggestions and modify the tree diagram where appropriate.

EXAMPLE: USING A TREE DIAGRAM TO PLAN IMPROVEMENT

A major oil and gas company used tree diagrams to help analyze improvement opportunities designed to maximize the economic value of oil and gas producing fields. This is a classic example of tree diagram application. The company wanted to maximize the economic value of the fields (corporate objective or ends), and the tree diagram analyzed all the possible ways in which this value could be enhanced.

The initial tree diagram created is presented in Exhibit 270: Initial Planning Tree Diagram. The gray area in the tree diagram was highlighted because it was seen as an area requiring additional detail. This supports the observation that teams should provide a level of analysis appropriate for the decisions or actions under consideration.

This doesn't mean all branches of the tree diagram must be or should be taken to the same level of detail. Where one branch has been sufficiently detailed – stop! Don't waste your

Exhibit 270: Initial Planning Tree Diagram

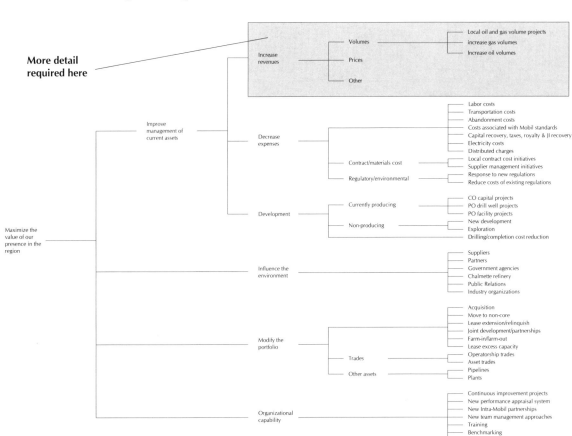

Exhibit 271: Expanding Detail to Increase Revenue

Use Brainstorming to Fill In Tree Diagram Gaps

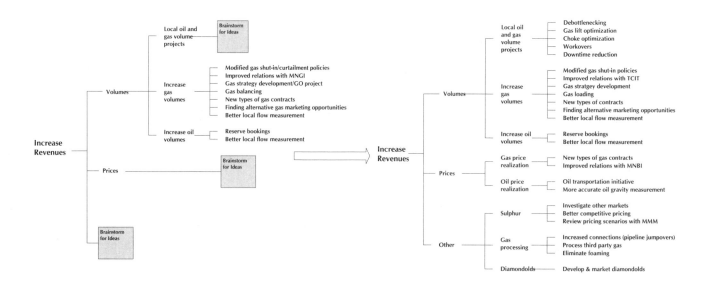

resources providing more information than necessary. By the same token, just because you have reached the sufficient level of detail with one branch of the tree, don't assume that enough detail exists for all branches.

In the example, the improvement team decided that it had to pursue the potential for additional revenues. In so doing, it expanded upon the gray areas of the tree and provided additional

tional detail (see Exhibit 271: Expanding Detail to Increase Revenue).

The tree diagram explicitly links what must be done to accomplish some higher-order goal – in this case, to maximize the value of the company's properties. All too often, executive management sets corporate objectives that are important for the organization, but that are obscure and meaningless to employees in the front lines.

The failure of organizations to follow up on the corporate directions set by executive management is not so often a problem of commitment or communication, but rather a failure of understanding and alignment. Employees want to support the organization and create value, but they do not see or understand how their specific activities contribute to accomplishing the goal. By presenting a logical and hierarchical linkage between these lofty corporate goals and the specific tasks of the employee, the tree diagram helps create and support the understanding necessary for employees to see that changes they make contribute do organizational goals.

In the case of our oil and gas company, the tree diagram shows precisely how a specific activity – say de-bottlenecking –

increases volume, which in turn increases revenues. This all improves the overall level at which the company manages its current assets and that, in turn, creates value.

USING THE TREE DIAGRAM TO DRIVE BRAINSTORMING

The example also provides some ideas as to how the tree diagram can be used to drive additional brainstorming. A large number of ideas can arise out of a brainstorming session. The intent is to ensure comprehensiveness. Because the data is unstructured, however, it is often difficult to see whether all the bases have been covered or not.

By taking the results of the brainstorming and organizing the input in a tree diagram, (sometimes also using affinity charting as an intermediate step), the team can quickly assess which areas are weak in terms of detail and which areas are strong. Weak areas can then become the focus of additional brainstorming activity.

Exhibit 272: Using Trees to Drive Additional Brainstorming

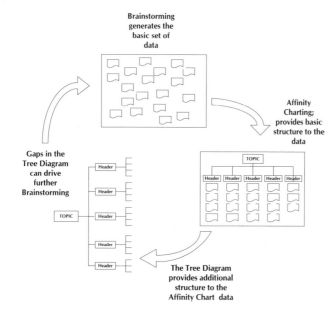

SUMMARY: WORKING WITH IDEAS

Qualitative data, by its very nature, is often the most meaning-ful to decision makers. For the most part, people feel more comfortable with words than with numbers. Yet, qualitative data is often characterized as being unscientific (whatever that means) or too 'fuzzy' to deal with. It isn't. It just requires a different set of tools to help provide meaningful analysis.

Qualitative and opinion data do lack the 'hard-fact' nature of quantitative data, but they are still data. In using the tools and techniques discussed in this chapter, we tap into the tacit knowledge of people and share and combine it with other knowledge in a manner that contributes to an improved understanding of the issues and opportunities that confront the organization.

For the most part, working with qualitative and opinion data involves organizing the data so that an improvement team can reach some agreement on "what it all means." Data-reduction techniques, such as multi-voting and nominal group technique, address this objective by setting priorities – identifying what is or is not important. Data-organization techniques organize and group the data, allowing the team to make initial conclusions about its underlying structure for the purpose of interpretation. Proper application of the correct tools will help ensure this type of data is analyzed in a way that makes it most effective for the purposes of performance improvement.

8. Creating Solutions: Tools for Generating and Analyzing Ideas

Making Decisions: Tools for the Evaluation of Alternatives   9

Decision-making tools are designed to help teams reach conclusions about the data that has been collected, organized and analyzed, and come to agreement on alternative actions. Sooner or later in any improvement process, decisions must be made and priorities set. This is where a lot of team breakdowns occur. Vested interests, hidden agendas, and personal biases all tend to surface when it comes down to making a decision.

Decision-making tools provide a means for helping teams make the decisions that must be made, while minimizing the dysfunctions that can occur. In general, decision-making tools and techniques are designed to accomplish three objectives:

▲ **Generate Commitment.** Decisions are of little value if no one is willing to support them. Commitment is about having the support of those that must carry out the decision or are affected by it. Decisions without support may be beautiful and elegant solutions to a problem, but they will wither on the vine from a lack of implementation. A reasonable but less-than-perfect decision with widespread support will at least get implemented and have some positive effect on the organization.

▲ **Improve the Quality of Decisions.** Of course, we do not want mediocre decisions. Fortunately, team-based decisions tend to be of higher quality than those resulting from some autocratic source, simply because of the variety of perspectives teams bring to the decision-making process. The application of specific decision tools adds to this improved quality, by ensuring different perspectives are accommodated and by limiting sources of bias in the decision-making process.

▲ **Timeliness.** Most teams working to improve processes are under some form of time constraint. But even when time is not an issue, taking too long to reach conclusions can frustrate people and tire the group. Decision tools and techniques help move the team along – overcoming the 'analysis paralysis' that occurs so often when it comes to making a decision.

DECISION METHODS

A variety of decision methods exists and organizations tend to use them all depending upon circumstances. We can classify the basic types as *autocratic, democratic, consensus, and unanimous.*

AUTOCRATIC

Autocratic decisions are made by one individual. The reason one individual "makes the call" may be due to technical expertise or simply due to an autocratic approach by the manager or supervisor. Consultation with others is not sought. While this approach can result in very timely decisions, the decisions also tend to suffer from a lack of support.

DEMOCRATIC

We are all familiar with this form of decision making – it is the basis for running our government. Democratic decision making tends to use simple voting or ranking techniques to elicit the preferences of team members. The bottom-line is that the choice or the alternative with the most votes wins. While this generates involvement by those affected by the decision, it can also create win-lose situations and a constituency of the disaffected that may work to undermine the decision made.

CONSENSUS

Consensus decision making uses many of the same techniques of the democratic approach. But rather than stop after the vote, the consensus process continues to work with the team to generate a solution that all can support. Notice that this does not mean that all agree that the decision made is the best that can be done. It only means everyone agrees that the decision is good enough to warrant the support of all involved. Consensus decisions generate win-win situations and tend to create greater levels of support and commitment.

Table 273: Decision Methods

Method	Examples	Commitment	Quality	Timeliness
Autocratic	Driving a car. Driving demands the driver make instantaneous decisions. Manager makes a decision based on his or her technical competence. Trial by judge only.	The decision process does not seek out nor require general commitment or support.	May be high or low depending upon the nature of the decision. Technical experts may make high quality decisions if technical considerations are paramount. All too often, however, decision makers assume technical considerations are paramount only to find out differently after the fact.	Can be very quick since no level of agreement or support is required. However, this is not always true. Sometimes decision makers linger extensively over the decisions to be made or suffer from analysis paralysis. In such circumstances team-based decision making can actually speed decision making.
Democratic	Elections in democracies or other democratic organizations. Team needs a quick decision on some matter of minor importance to the overall project so a team vote is taken.	People at least have an opportunity to voice their preferences. Commitment will reside with the majority. The creation of win-lose situations, however, can create dissatisfied minority.	Brings a variety of perspectives to bear on the decision, enhancing decision quality. Technical considerations may be lost in the range of perspectives sought out.	Usually very quick, only marginally slower than autocratic methods and on occasion actually faster than autocratic methods.
Consensus	A committee comprised of opposing political forces attempts to hammer out a compromise solution to a specific problem. Team decides to focus on a specific area to improve the quality of a product.	Team members all support the decision made creating a win-win environment. Commitment higher than autocratic or democratic methods with no disenfranchised groups.	Produces high quality decisions that accommodate both technical and organizational requirements.	Best classified as moderately fast, as the need to make the decision quickly is balanced off against the need to generate commitment.
Unanimous	Jury decisions of guilt or innocence.	Highest level of commitment possible. "Fake" unanimity is created when team members agree solely for the sake of reaching a decision.	Usually produces high quality decisions. However, the need to achieve consensus can encourage "group think," yielding the camel-designed-as-a-race-horse syndrome.	Takes the longest time to reach a decision. Boredom and frustration can yield fake unanimity.

UNANIMOUS

A unanimous decision is one where all team members agree that the decision made is the best for everyone. Achieving unanimity is often difficult, requiring a considerable amount of time to accomplish. Nevertheless, there may be situations where the team believes the added time and effort is worth the result. In our system of justice, for example, individual freedom and proof beyond a reasonable doubt are deemed important enough that juries are required to make unanimous decisions of guilt. Where the issue is fundamental or especially difficult, teams may decide to require unanimity in the decision.

COMPARATIVE DECISION METHODS

Before decisions are made, teams should agree on the level of commitment they need for the decision and adopt the most appropriate method. Experience indicates that in most team based improvement initiatives, consensus decision making usually represents the best combination of advantages among the decision method alternatives available. Therefore, if the team cannot agree on the decision method to use, adopt the consensus approach.

TYPES OF DECISION TOOLS & TECHNIQUES

Decision tools and techniques consist of two broad categories: tools to elicit preferences of team members (Preference Decision Methods), and tools to evaluate alternatives against specified criteria (Evaluative Decision Methods).

▲ **Preference Decision Tools.** What do we mean by preferences? Simply, it means that members of the team are asked to state what decision alternative they prefer. The reasons for these preferences are implicit, although they may be discussed and shared with other members of the team. Ultimately, preference decision methods entail the rating or ranking of alternatives.

▲ **Evaluative Decision Tools.** Evaluation tools differ from preference tools in that they explicitly state the criteria by which the decision shall be made. Because of this, evaluation tools better encompass both technical and organizational considerations in the decision-making process. Also, because they tend to focus first on identifying the criteria by which a decision will be made, evaluation tools are very effective in removing personal bias and hidden agendas from the process.

Preference decision methods are typically used when the team is still in the early stages decision making, taking stock on what team members think or reducing the number of alternatives under consideration. When it comes to making the final decision, or when the decision is of significant importance, evaluative decision tools are preferred.

PREFERENCE DECISION TOOLS

Preference decision tools are best used as an information gathering technique, to assess how much agreement exists between team members. They provide a quick way for team leaders and facilitators to determine the current thinking on the team, assess the current situation among team members and the strength of differences of opinion if any.

For example, in selecting which problem to work on first between two alternatives, a team could conduct a quick vote to assess where the team believes their first priority should be. Let's say there are nine team members and seven of them (a clear majority) prefer to work on Problem A. Once this is known, the other two team members might feel comfortable about taking on Problem A as well. In other words, they would prefer to work on problem B, but can support working on problem A first. This is a classic example of using preference techniques to move toward a consensus.

In contrast, a vote simply to choose between the two alternatives could lead to a clear and strongly felt division among team members, perhaps where five members prefer Problem A and four prefer Problem B. A post-vote discussion indicates the division among team members is strongly held. Making a decision, by whatever method at this point, would be divisive. The team should gather additional information, identify additional problems or perhaps reframe the problems presented.

Use preference decision tools whenever:

▲ **You want to reduce a list of options.** When there are a great many alternatives for consideration, preference techniques can be used to help reduce the number. Rather than deciding what single alternative will be selected, preference techniques can be used to decide which alternatives will not be pursued (at least at this time), reducing the remaining alternatives to a manageable few.

▲ **You want to generate information.** This amounts to taking stock of where the collective thinking of the team is in terms of the decision to be made. Where agreement is high, the team may want to move ahead to an evaluative method to reach the final decision. But where there is little agreement among team members, further discussion, data gathering or reframing of the issue or alternative may be appropriate.

▲ **The decision is of low importance or impact.** Preference methods can also produce decisions, but only when the nature of the decision is of low importance or impact.

Typical applications in decision-making include:

▲ **When the team needs to identify likely root causes of a problem**. After completion of a cause and effect diagram, teams must decide where they believe the root cause(s) of the problem lies. Usually, this list does not have to be boiled down to a single cause. Rather, the team may identify a few areas in which to gather data and do additional research. Preference methods are ideal in such circum-

stances because they require only the reduction of alternatives, not the selection of a single issue or solution.

▲ **When the team is selecting a problem to work on.** A team may have a number of possible problems or priorities and be experiencing difficulty deciding which ones to pursue first. Preference methods can help move the team toward a final selection by reducing the set of alternatives . In this way the tool serves as a basis of discussion as to why team members prefer certain problems as priorities over others.

▲ **When the team is creating a list for further analysis.** Generally, evaluative decision methods are more complex and time consuming than preference methods. Anything that helps reduce the number of possible alternatives before applying the evaluative tools, therefore, saves time and effort. Preference techniques are well suited to this task. By reducing the number of alternatives prior to using an evaluative decision process, preference techniques reduce the amount of work required in the evaluative process.

▲ **When the team is seeking to create a list of alternatives rather than reach a single decision.** Not all decisions require the selection of one thing. Many circumstances require the generation of a list of the top four or five options. For example, a team is seeking to identify the top five issues facing the department or affecting the efficiency of a particular process. Preference techniques are well suited to separating the top five or so issues from the rest of the pack.

▲ **When the team is seeking to weigh or prioritize some options.** At times, the objective is not to reduce a list of alternatives, but rather to create a weighting for all the alternatives that exist. For example, criteria-based decision methods often require the weighting of evaluation criteria. Preference methods are well suited to this task.

There are three basic types of preference decision-making tools:

▲ **Voting Methods**, where each person votes for his or her preference, with each person having one or a limited number of votes.

▲ **Rating Methods**, where each person rates the degree of preference associated with each alternative against some scale.

Table 274: Preference Decision Methods

	Voting	Rating	Ranking
Basic Description	Each member casts a vote or votes for their preferred choice.	Each member rates the alternatives against a scale.	Each member of the team rank orders the alternatives from highest to lowest.
Strengths	Very simple and easy to conduct in large groups. When multiple votes are used, can effectively reduce a range of alternatives.	Very simple and easy to conduct in large groups. Produces a set of weights for a set of alternatives	Simple and easy to administer. Compels team members to choose among alternatives — ranking some higher than others.
Weaknesses	Success usually dependent upon the number of votes given each participant and the number of voting rounds conducted.	Can produce a lot of alternatives all with the same, or very close to the same, weight.	Can introduce artificial scarcity (forcing choice without reason) in the decision making process.
Use When	Want a quick summation of where the team stands.	Need to produce an initial set of importance weights or priorities for alternatives.	The underlying reality supports the forced ranking approach.

▲ **Ranking Methods,** where each person orders the alternatives from most to least preferable.

VOTING METHODS

Most of us are familiar with voting in elections. In team settings, the principles are the same – each person votes for his or her most preferred choice.

Voting methods may differ, however, according to how the actual voting procedure is carried out. For example, a show of hands may be suitable for most situations. But when a subject is controversial, a secret ballot may be preferred so that team members may vote their preference without undue influence or pressure from others.

WHEN TO USE VOTING METHODS

Like all preference techniques, voting methods are rarely used to reach a final decision. Typically they are used whenever:

▲ **An extensive list or range of alternatives is before the team and there is a need to reduce this list to a more workable size.** Simply reducing the size of a list or the number of alternatives is an ideal application of voting techniques.

▲ **The size of the group is very large.** When a large group is faced with the task of alternative reduction or selecting a few priorities from a more extensive list, voting techniques are efficient and effective.

▲ **There is a need to ascertain the state of affairs within the team.** At times, there is a need not to select a particular option, but to judge the state of the team and assess the degree of consensus that exists. In such circumstances, the efficiency of voting techniques allows the team to make this assessment before moving to the process of reaching a final decision.

BASIC PROCEDURE

Generally, voting follows a six-step procedure:

1. List all alternatives

A clear list of the alternatives that team members are being asked to consider is required. All alternatives should be posted in clear view of the team, using flip chart paper or similar means. Make sure to leave plenty of room between the alternatives to allow for clarifying remarks.

Remember that the tools described throughout this book all work together! Creating the alternatives may come from background research, brainstorming and an affinity charting exercise. Team members may be trying to identify the most likely cause from a cause and effect diagram. The source of the alternatives is less important than the fact that the team believes the list is comprehensive.

2. Clarify alternatives

The facilitator should check with team members to ensure everyone actually understands what they are voting on. Any confusion and questions need to be addressed. Clarifying remarks can then be noted in point form under each alternative. Moreover, the discussions may identify additional alternatives for the list, which will also have to be added and clarified.

3. Conduct the voting

Once the clarification is completed and team members understand the options, the voting is conducted. This is usually done through a show of hands. The facilitator simply asks how many

prefer option one, option two and so on down the list, recording the number of votes each alternative receives.

Secret voting can also take place using ballots. In this case, the facilitator clearly numbers each alternative and asks team members to write down the number of the alternative they prefer. These ballots are returned to the facilitator who records the tally.

4. Eliminate "unpopular" alternatives

Items receiving few or no votes can usually be eliminated from consideration by the team. Before doing so, the facilitator should ask if any team members have any objections to removing the alternative, which ensures consensus of the team.

5. Continue discussing the remaining alternatives

The final step in a voting procedure is not necessarily reaching a final decision, but rather deciding upon a reduced set of alternatives – what should stay and what should go. Thus, the vote in this case does not end discussion; it simply gives the discussion greater focus.

6. Repeat steps 3 through 5

These steps can be repeated if the remaining list of alternatives is still too large. Repeat voting can work to continually reduce the options available until a list small enough for an evaluative decision method is identified, or until consensus on a single alternative is reached.

EXAMPLE: IDENTIFYING CAUSES OF SHIPPING ERRORS

To see how voting techniques work in practice, consider the following example. An improvement team has been given the task of 'fixing things' in the Shipping Department where significant levels of shipping errors are occurring. As expected, customer complaints concerning these errors are on the rise.

The improvement team wants to move quickly, to fix what it can now and then move on to do more in-depth analysis before making longer-term improvements. A brainstorming session is conducted with participants from the Shipping Department, Sales, Information Systems and Accounting. The intent of the brainstorming session is to identify likely sources of error to target for improvement.

The list produced through the brainstorming exercise is presented. Nineteen likely sources of problems are identified. This is much too big a list for the team to tackle, so a voting exercise is conducted to reduce the number of areas to a workable size. Notice in this application that there are no decisions being made. The team is simply trying to set some priorities about what to tackle first.

In a simple voting approach, each team member has one vote. The items with the most votes become the priorities for the team. The results of the voting procedure are presented in Exhibit 276: Results of a Simple Voting.

In the example, only three issues received votes, with one issue receiving two votes. So, this would result in the following priorities:

▶ Inventory System Out of Date/Slow

▶ Shipping Not Seen as Important

▶ Computer System Not Integrated With Rest of Company

There are some problems with this approach, however. As the exhibit details, when there are a large number of issues and the

Table 275: Possible Causes of Shipping Problems

Potential Sources of Error in Shipping
Shipping Space not Organized
Equipment Getting Old
Shipping Not Seen As Important
Shipping Area Has Poor Ergonomics
Constant Breakdowns of Material Moving Equipment
Additional Training in Space Management
Manual Shipping Request Forms Are Confusing
Inventory System Out of Date, Slow
Labels Become Fouled (Dirty, Torn, etc.)
Manual Shipping Orders
Bar Codes & Descriptions on Different Labels
New People Not Trained (Learn by Doing)
Computer System Not Integrated With Company
Sometimes Not Enough Staff
Only One Bar Code Reader
Require More Shelving
Only One Dock, Line-Ups
Sales Do Not Find Out When Really Needed by the Customer
Multiple Carriers, Multiple Work

Exhibit 276: Results of a Simple Voting

OPTIONS: Likely Causes of Shipping Errors	Shelley	Bob	Sean	Marc	TOTALS
1. Shipping Space not Organized					
2. Equipment Getting Old					
3. Shipping Not Seen As Important			✓		1
4. Shipping Area Has Poor Ergonomics					
5. Constant Breakdowns of Material Moving Equipment					
6. Additional Training in Space Management					
7. Manual Shipping Request Forms Are Confusing					
8. Inventory System Out of Date, Slow	✓	✓			2
9. Labels Become Fouled (Dirty, Torn, etc.)					
10. Manual Shipping Orders					
11. Bar Codes & Descriptions on Different Labels					
12. New People Not Trained (Learn by Doing)					
13. Computer System Not Integrated With Company				✓	1
14. Sometimes Not Enough Staff					
15. Only One Bar Code Reader					
16. Require More Shelving					
17. Only One Dock, Line-Up's					
18. Sales Do Not Find Out When Really Needed by the Customer					
19. Multiple Carriers, Multiple Work					

team is relatively small, having one vote per person is restricting. Some team members may feel there is no difference between two areas, but cannot express this in the voting procedure because they have only a single vote. Therefore, some important opportunities for improvement may be missed entirely.

For these reasons, simple voting procedures are more efficient and effective when:

▲ **The number of people doing the voting is relatively large.** At times, large meetings have 20 or more participants. In these circumstances, one person- one vote is useful because of its simplicity.

▲ **The number of team members is close to the number of items on the list.** If there are only seven or eight items on the list and about the same number of team members, one person - one vote works well and can be used to identify priorities.

However, the times when these conditions are present are relatively rare. For these reasons, multi-voting is a more common option.

MULTI-VOTING

Muti-voting is a variation of simple voting that assigns multiple votes to each participant and encompasses multiple rounds of voting, depending on the number of alternatives and the degree to which they must be reduced.

Each team member is assigned a number of votes depending on the number of items. Typically, each participant receives one vote for every three items on the list. This is called the N/3 procedure, since each person receives a number of votes equal to the number of alternatives (N) divided by three.[82]

For example, when deciding among 37 different issues, each team member would be assigned about 12 votes. These 'votes' can take different forms. A typical technique is to hand out color-coded file markers (small dots used to mark files of different subjects). Each participant is given his or her share of votes (dots) and asked to post them beside the alternatives listed on flip chart paper and posted on the wall. Team members can assign their votes any way they want. Some may place all their votes beside one issue, if they feel strongly about it. Others may chose to divide their votes with one vote going to each alternative. The method is up to the individual. At the end of the process, the votes are tallied and the alternatives receiving no or few votes are eliminated from the list.

---

82. Another approach to determining the number of votes each participant receives is to use the square root of N, rather than N/3. I find using the square root a little more robust in varied situations (i.e. when dealing with a very large number of alternatives).

In addition, multiple rounds of voting may be conducted. Once the first set of items is reduced from the list, a discussion on the remaining items with the team and another round of voting is conducted. The number of votes assigned each individual again uses the one vote for every three items on the now- reduced list, meaning each person will receive fewer votes than they did initially.

EXAMPLE OF MULTI-VOTING

In the previous example, a team had identified 19 possible areas for improvement in a shipping department. Using multi-voting to reduce these to a manageable set of priorities, each team member would receive about six votes (19 divided by three). Exhibit 277: Multi-Voting, shows how the same team members allocated their votes.

There are the same four team members. With each person receiving six votes, there should be 24 votes in all. This procedure allows individual team members to allocate their votes however they see fit. Shelley has allocated her six votes to three alternatives, each of which she weighted equally at two votes each. Bob spread his six votes across six different alter-

Exhibit 277: Multi-Voting

OPTIONS: Likely Causes of Shipping Errors	Shelley	Bob	Sean	Marc	TOTALS	% DIST.
1. Shipping Space not Organized						
2. Equipment Getting Old						
3. Shipping Not Seen As Important			✓✓		2	8.3
4. Shipping Area Has Poor Ergonomics						
5. Constant Breakdowns of Material Moving Equipment						
6. Additional Training in Space Management						
7. Manual Shipping Request Forms Are Confusing		✓			1	4.2
8. Inventory System Out of Date, Slow	✓✓	✓	✓		4	16.7
9. Labels Become Fouled (Dirty, Torn, etc.)	✓✓	✓	✓	✓	5	20.8
10. Manual Shipping Orders		✓			1	4.2
11. Bar Codes & Descriptions on Different Labels	✓✓	✓	✓	✓	5	20.8
12. New People Not Trained (Learn by Doing)						
13. Computer System Not Integrated With Company			✓	✓✓	3	12.5
14. Sometimes Not Enough Staff						
15. Only One Bar Code Reader						
16. Require More Shelving						
17. Only One Dock, Line-Up's						
18. Sales Do Not Find Out When Really Needed by the Customer		✓		✓	2	8.3
19. Multiple Carriers, Multiple Work				✓	1	4.2
TOTALS	6	6	6	6	24	100.0

natives. Sean placed two votes for his first choice and then one vote each for four alternatives – a strategy also used by Marc.

In a multi-voting procedure, those alternatives receiving votes would be selected to move on to the next round of voting. If the team had reduced the alternatives sufficiently, no additional rounds of voting would be required. However, if the objective is to reduce the list of items to the top two or three, additional rounds would be required.

Between rounds of voting, the team should discuss why people voted the way they did. The purpose, at a surface level, is to try and convince other team members to vote they way you voted. However, such a discussion is really aimed at improving understanding. It gives team members a chance to challenge assumptions, examine supporting logic and data, and generally provides an opportunity to learn. During these discussions, team members may want to combine or add new alternatives to help clarify things as their shared understanding grows. This is entirely appropriate.

SIMPLE RATING

With rating procedures, participants assign a numerical value that represents the degree of preference they have for a particular option. For example, a scale of 1 to 9 may be selected, with 1 representing an alternative not at all important to the team member while 9 represents an extremely important alternative. The facilitator or team leader tallies these ratings.

Rating procedures differ from voting procedures in that voting restricts the amount of preference that can be allocated among the alternatives in the form of the number of votes distributed. Rating methods impose no such restrictions. If a team member decides that all alternatives are worthy of a 9 rating, they are free to distribute a 9 to every alternative. As a result, rating procedures can result in numerous ties between alternatives, or scores where only a few points separate the highest-rated from lowest-rated alternatives. For this reason, rating procedures are not recommended when the group is trying to narrow a list of alternatives. The procedure may not be able to generate any meaningful differences.

WHEN TO USE RATING METHODS

The best time to use rating methods is when the objective is to assign weights or degrees of importance to alternatives. In other words, we are not trying to reduce the set of alternatives but are interested in scoring then. Use rating methods when:

▲ **You need to weigh the criteria used to reach an evaluative decision.** Evaluative decision-making techniques compare alternatives across various decision criteria. These criteria can be weighted according to their importance to the team. The fastest and easiest way to obtain these weights is to use a rating procedure. Notice that none of the criteria is being removed. They will all play a role in making the decision. They are only being weighted such that some criteria will count more in the decision than others.

▲ **You need to weigh the relative importance, impact or performance of an issue or action.** Another evaluative decision method compares the importance of an alternative against performance – the importance/performance matrix. Plotting where the alternatives are on the matrix requires a scoring across these two dimensions. Here, rating methods are ideal. They allow team members to quickly score the importance or performance of any number of options. These scorings, in turn, are used to plot the alternatives on the matrix.

BASIC PROCEDURE

The basic procedure to rating a list of alternatives involves six steps:

1. List the alternatives

The first step is to clearly list all the alternatives on a large piece of flip chart paper or numerous sheets of flip chart paper taped together. Usually, the options are listed down the left side of the paper leaving plenty of space to the right. (This will be used later to tally individual ratings.)

2. Clarify alternatives

The facilitator should check with team members to ensure everyone actually understands what they are voting on. Any confusion and questions need to be addressed. Clarifying remarks can then be noted in point form under each alternative. Moreover, the discussions may identify additional alternatives for the list that will also have to be added and clarified.

3. Define the scale

Once the clarification is completed and team members understand the options, the scale upon which the rating will be based must be defined. The first step is deciding upon a scale to be used. This is really up to the team; however, a 1 to 9 or a 1 to 10 scale is typically used. In creating the scale, attach relevant descriptors to at least every other number in the scale to provide a meaningful reference point for making the ratings. Some sample descriptors are provided in Table 278: Nine-Point Rating Scale and Descriptors.

Table 278: Nine-Point Rating Scale and Descriptors

Scale	Importance Descriptors	Scope Descriptors
9	Extremely Important	Strategic
8		
7	Very Important	Tactical
6		
5	Important	Operational
4		
3	Somewhat Important	Local / departmental
2		
1	No Importance Whatsoever	None

Debating the merits of various scales in team-based rating situations can be a time waster – time that could be better spent elsewhere. If the team is bogging down on discussions about which scale to use or which scale is best, adopt a nine-point scale. It will likely work fine. Remember, though, that the descriptors attached to the numbers should be relevant to the options being rated. This will serve to facilitate discussion after the ratings have been assigned and provide a more meaningful rating procedure.[83]

4. Conduct the ratings

With the options and scale clearly defined, the team can proceed to rate the alternatives. Generally, team members first rate the alternatives privately. The facilitator then asks each member of the team to call out his or her ratings. These are marked down on the flip chart. The process continues until every team member has called out his or her ratings for all the alternatives. The totals for each alternative are then calculated. If desired,

---

83. One of the more interesting things in working with groups is how often discussions become bogged down on simple, as opposed to complex, issues. Deciding upon a scale is a good example. I have seen teams discuss such items at length, carefully debating the use of seven- versus nine- versus five-point scales, while significant decisions concerning the adoption of a new procedure take place in only a few minutes. It should be the other way around. Don't let yourself get bogged down on the simple stuff – save time for the stuff that matters. That's why we recommend simply adopting the nine-point scale as the default scale if things become bogged down on this topic.

these totals can be normalized to a percentage score by dividing the overall total into the total for each alternative.

5. Discuss the results and re-conduct the ratings

As a general rule, do not accept the initial rating as the final result. It is wise to conduct at least two ratings, with a discussion of the initial results between the first and second rounds. Team members should be prepared to explain and discuss why they voted the way they did. The purpose here is not so much to defend one's point of view as to increase the shared understanding among team members.

With the discussion complete, the second round of rating is conducted and the results tallied. These become the absolute or raw weights for the various alternatives before the team.

6. Calculate the distributional percentage

The last step in rating alternatives, especially when the ratings are to be used to weigh criteria or alternatives, is calculating the distributional percentage of the raw weights. This calculation of the distributional percentage does not change the results – it simply converts them into a more usable form.

To calculate the distributional percentage, total the results for all the alternatives. Then, divide this total into the results for each alternative. Multiply this result by 100 to convert to a percentage. The result is the percentage importance of a specific alternative relative to all the other alternatives (the total of all alternatives will total 100 per cent plus or minus a small fraction attributable to rounding).

EXAMPLE: SHIPPING DEPARTMENT PROBLEMS

Using the same Shipping Department example referred to for voting procedures, we can see how ranking systems work. Each team member is compelled to consider and rate every item on the list.

In this example, the totals from all the ratings have been totalled. This grand total (389) has then been divided into the totals for each option to produce a percentage result. In most instances, these percentages are easier to work with than the rating totals.

Exhibit 279: Rating Shipping Department Problems, provides a good example for how to set up the flipchart paper to record the results of the rating process. The only changes might be to

Exhibit 279: Rating Shipping Department Problems

OPTIONS: Likely Causes of Shipping Errors	Shelley	Bob	Sean	Marc	TOTALS	% DIST.
1. Shipping Space not Organized	2	2	6	5	15	3.9
2. Equipment Getting Old	6	8	6	6	26	6.7
3. Shipping Not Seen As Important	1	2	8	2	13	3.3
4. Shipping Area Has Poor Ergonomics	2	2	3	6	13	3.3
5. Constant Breakdowns of Material Moving Equipment	6	2	5	6	19	4.9
6. Additional Training in Space Management	4	3	5	6	18	4.6
7. Manual Shipping Request Forms Are Confusing	5	6	2	5	18	4.6
8. Inventory System Out of Date, Slow	7	8	2	5	22	5.7
9. Labels Become Fouled (Dirty, Torn, etc.)	9	8	8	9	34	8.7
10. Manual Shipping Orders	6	7	7	2	22	5.7
11. Bar Codes & Descriptions on Different Labels	9	9	9	9	36	9.3
12. New People Not Trained (Learn by Doing)	3	2	3	4	12	3.1
13. Computer System Not Integrated With Company	7	7	7	9	30	7.7
14. Sometimes Not Enough Staff	2	3	2	3	10	2.6
15. Only One Bar Code Reader	4	6	7	7	24	6.2
16. Require More Shelving	5	4	1	3	13	3.3
17. Only One Dock, Line-Up's	5	5	7	1	18	4.6
18. Sales Do Not Find Out When Really Needed by the Customer	7	7	7	8	29	7.5
	4	5	1	7	17	4.4
TOTALS					389	100.0

enlarge the paper. This would provide more room to write any explanations of the alternatives, and space to list the results of the second round of rating that should follow discussion of the first round's results.

SIMPLE RANKING

With simple ranking, each person in the team orders the alternatives from most preferred or important, to least preferred or important. A summary ranking is then calculated to create an overall rankings for the team. Ranking, like voting, restricts the allocation of preference. All alternatives cannot be 'top-ranked' a 9 as was the case with rating procedures. Ranking compels an ordering of preference. Participants can only rank one alternative as first choice, one alternative as second choice, one as third choice and so on.

Ranking has certain advantages over simple voting and rating procedures. One advantage is the method by which participants are required to evaluate the alternatives. The process of making direct comparisons and asking which is better tends to produce useful insights and discussion. We can ask "Why did you rank alternative F as more important than alternative C?" Participants often see this as a little more relevant and meaningful than asking "Why did you rate alternative C as 6 but alternative F as a 7?" In short, the ranking compels us to evaluate alternatives on a very specific and objective basis – namely the other alternatives being considered. This process of making direct comparisons and asking which is better tends to produce more thought-provoking discussions than simple voting or rating procedures.

A second advantage to ranking is that it results in a broad distribution of preference. It is possible under voting and rating procedures to have all the alternatives rated the same, or at least have two or more alternatives tied for first place. This is not the case with ranking. Ranking forces one alternative to be in first place, a second in second place, and so forth. As such, ranking methods impose a fundamental constraint on the process – there can be no ties and only one winner. This is the forced constraint characteristic of ranking.

WHERE TO USE

Due to the forced constraint characteristic of the procedure, ranking should only be used when it reflects the nature of the underlying reality. In other words, if the set of alternatives is such that we must have one over the other, then ranking makes sense. But if no forced choice is required, then ranking should not be applied because it introduces an artificial constraint that is not reflected in the reality of the situation.

Ranking Gone Wild

The misuse of ranking techniques has become epidemic. This misuse takes the form of applying ranking techniques when the underlying reality makes no requirement of forced choice or order.

Take the use of forced ranking of employee performance – only so many receive a 'very high' rating, so many a 'high' rating and so forth. Forcing the numbers into ranks or predetermined proportions is simply lying with statistics. The reason is because the constraint is imposed by the measurement system (the ranking procedure), not by the underlying reality. After all, it is quite possible that all employees did an exceptional job last year.

The situation is worse in the educational environment where institutions demand that teachers "force rank" or distribute marks. This is the process of destroying children through a process of applied ignorance. To add insult to injury, at least one school district of which I am aware requires teachers to rank the learning ability of students at the beginning of the school year. Stupidity knows no bounds.

Forced choice is not a requirement when weighing decision criteria because no criteria are being selected or eliminated. Ranking methods, therefore, should not be used in such circumstances. In contrast, when a list of alternatives consists of different options or ways of performing a function, only one of which can be adopted, ranking becomes a far more appropriate tool.

Use ranking whenever:

▲ There is a natural constraint among the alternatives that supports the use of the ranking procedure.

▲ Different concepts are being evaluated and only one can be implemented.

▲ Teams need to make a choice and where the direct comparison among alternatives is desirable.

▲ The team must set some priorities because there are insufficient resources to do everything.

BASIC RANKING PROCEDURE

The basic ranking procedure is similar to the process used for the other preference techniques. There are six basic steps:

1. List the alternatives

The alternatives need to be clearly listed on some flip chart paper and posted where all can see. Every alternative should have a unique identifying number. If the number of alternatives is more than 20 items (some would say more than 10 items) it becomes difficult to rank alternatives. Because of this, provide each team member with a set of cards equal to the number of options available. As the facilitator lists the options, participants can write down the issues on the cards – one issue per card. These will be used to conduct the rankings.

2. Clarify the alternatives

Each alternative should be briefly described by the facilitator. Participants are free to ask questions for clarification but not to engage in arguing the merits of any particular alternative. Team members may choose to write down any key clarifications on their cards if they so choose.

3. Rank the alternatives

If cards are not being used, each team member should record each alternative on a piece of paper along with its unique number. If the total number of alternatives is 12, then the first-

Exhibit 280: Creating the Ranking Cards

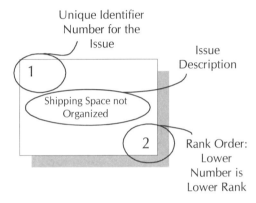

Exhibit 281: Ranking the Cards

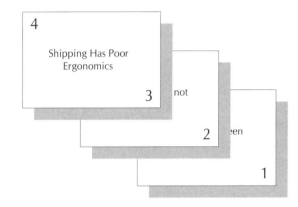

ranked alternative is given a ranking of 12, the second-place alternative an 11 and so on.

If cards are being used, it is often convenient to have each participant first place his or her cards in one of three piles – an important pile, an in-between pile and an unimportant pile. Then ask each participant to sort each pile. Finally, the piles are combined to produce the overall ranking. Ask each participant to then write down the order of the ranking, with highest number indicating the highest-ranking card, in the bottom right-hand corner of the card. If 30 cards are being sorted, the most

important card at the top of the pile would get a 30, the second-most important card a 29 and so on.

4. Tally the results

The facilitator then tallies the results on a large sheet of flip chart paper in a similar format as that used for rating procedures. Usually this is done in full view of the rest of the team. Each participant can call out the number of his or her first-ranked alternative, the second and so forth. At times, obtaining the results confidentially may be appropriate – especially if the issue is particularly 'hot' or controversial. In these circumstances, use cards and simply have participants return their sorted cards to the facilitator. Schedule a coffee break so the facilitator can record the results on the flip chart paper.

5. Discuss the results

Like with rating procedures, teams should be reluctant to accept the results of the initial rankings. Be prepared to discuss the initial results. Again, the purpose is not to defend individual rankings, but rather to gain understanding and insight into how others see the problem and what other considerations have guided their rankings.

6. Re-conduct the rankings

Lastly, the team re-conducts the rankings and interprets the results. Changes in the way people rank alternatives may arise out of the discussions. Indeed, that is the whole point of having the discussion. It allows people to share information and perspectives in a manner that enhances their consideration of the problem. Re-conducting the rankings allows the team members to reflect on these discussions in their rankings.

EXAMPLE: RANKING POTENTIAL AREAS OF SHIPPING PROBLEMS

Exhibit 282: Ranking the Importance of Shipping Problems depicts how a ranking procedure may be applied to the same set of options regarding shipping problems. There are 19 problem areas, so the ranking procedure required each team member to award 19 points to their highest priority, 18 points to the second-highest priority and so on. In the example, problem #13 (computer system not being integrated with the rest of the company) was ranked as most important or the highest priority.

Ranking is an appropriate tool in this case because the improvement team simply would not have the time, money and staff to address all these issues at once. In practice, the team might choose one of three alternative strategies:

▲ **Select the top three or four priorities resulting from the ranking procedure.** Since the team has limited resources, it restricts its choice to the top few priorities determined through the ranking procedure and proceeds. Unfortunately, at times even selecting two or three priorities can spread the team's resources too thin.

Exhibit 282: Ranking the Importance of Shipping Problems

OPTIONS: Likely Causes of Shipping Errors	Shelley	Bob	Sean	Marc	TOTALS	% DIST.
1. Shipping Space not Organized	2	6	11	12	31	4.1
2. Equipment Getting Old	14	17	10	13	54	7.1
3. Shipping Not Seen As Important	1	1	19	2	23	3.0
4. Shipping Area Has Poor Ergonomics	3	5	7	11	26	3.4
5. Constant Breakdowns of Material Moving Equipment	13	3	9	10	35	4.6
6. Additional Training in Space Management	4	4	8	8	24	3.2
7. Manual Shipping Request Forms Are Confusing	12	14	6	9	41	5.4
8. Inventory System Out of Date, Slow	17	18	5	7	47	6.2
9. Labels Become Fouled (Dirty, Torn, etc.)	19	16	17	16	68	8.9
10. Manual Shipping Orders	11	13	16	1	41	5.4
11. Bar Codes & Descriptions on Different Labels	18	15	18	15	66	8.7
12. New People Not Trained (Learn by Doing)	5	2	4	6	17	2.2
13. Computer System Not Integrated With Company	16	11	15	19	61	8.0
14. Sometimes Not Enough Staff	6	7	3	4	20	2.6
15. Only One Bar Code Reader	10	12	13	14	49	6.4
16. Require More Shelving	9	8	1	5	23	3.0
17. Only One Dock, Line-Up's	8	10	12	3	33	4.3
18. Sales Do Not Find Out When Really Needed by the Customer	15	19	14	18	66	8.7
19. Multiple Carriers, Multiple Work	7	9	2	17	35	4.6
TOTALS					760	100.0

▲ **Select the top priority and work from there.** Generally, this is more effective than pursuing the top three or four priorities. Picking the top priority and dealing with it requires a high degree of improvement focus. When the problems or issues in this area have been dealt with, the team can proceed to the next area and so on. This approach also demands a fair amount of discipline. It is generally difficult for people, teams included, to select one priority and stick with it.

▲ **Select the top priority and an additional two or three priorities that are directly related to it.** This is a type of mixed strategy. The top priority becomes the target of the improvement effort (computer not integrated with rest of the company), but other related priorities are also included. In our example, these may be the confusing manual request forms, having a single bar code reader and the like. In short, the team proceeds with the top priority and then asks itself what other areas will likely be impacted by addressing this issue.

Regardless of the basic strategy, however, the ranking process produces some clear results. In this case, "Labels Become Fouled" was a clear priority, accounting for 68 of the 760 ranking scores tabulated. Notice, too, that distributional percentages are calculated (the total for each option divided by the overall total of 760). Thus, 68 out of 760 yields 8.9 percent, meaning that "Labels Become Fouled" accounted for 8.9 percent of all ranking scores assigned by the team.

EVALUATIVE TOOLS AND TECHNIQUES

Preference decision methods are fine for generating information and weighing or narrowing alternatives. But at some point decisions – and important ones at that – must be made. They can include what process to improve first, what improvements to introduce, what marketing theme to use and so forth. Evaluative decision techniques help teams make these decisions.

Evaluation tools differ from the simple preference methods, in that they require the team's identification of, and agreement on, the set of criteria against which decision alternatives will be compared. The criteria are explicit in evaluative methods, but they are implicit or unknown in preference techniques.

For example, in a ranking procedure, one team member may rank an alternative higher than another. But there is no explanation for why they did so. Evaluative techniques, however, require the team to be explicit about the criteria against which alternatives will be judged. This explicit *a priori* identification of criteria is the fundamental distinguishing characteristic of evaluative methods.

There are four basic evaluation methods that are commonly used. They are:

▲ **Pugh Concept Evaluation Matrix.** This is used to help select from among a number of conceptual improvement alternatives. For example, it can be used in trying to decide which of three alternative product designs to implement or adopt. It is particularly useful when selecting from alternative means of providing a specific function within a product or process design.

▲ **Analytical (Data) Matrix.** This method is used to help identify the impact associated with different alternatives across two dimensions. These dimensions are usually, but not always, associated with the costs and benefits of the alternatives being evaluated. These matrix diagrams are typically applied when analyzing emerging issues, identifying customer requirements or helping to establish priorities.

▲ **Criteria Evaluation/Rating Technique.** This is used to help team members make final decisions from a limited number of options. It is perhaps the most common of the evaluative techniques, since it can handle virtually all decision situations in a relatively straightforward manner.

Table 283: Evaluative Decision Tools

Decision METHOD	Description	Applications	Strengths/Weaknesses
Pugh Concept Evaluation Matrix	Alternatives are rated as better, worse or equal relative to a reference concept.	When certain design concepts must be selected. For example, the best power source for a new watch or deciding on the best process design to deliver some service to customer.	Very simple and straightforward, making it easy to explain and conduct, including in larger group settings.
Analytical (Data) Matrix	Alternatives are plotted on a data matrix or scatter diagram, graphically positioning them relative to two performance dimensions.	When alternatives can be evaluated across two basic dimensions. Examining the costs and benefits, strengths and weaknesses, importance versus performance, effectiveness and efficiency and so on.	Graphical format that conveys a lot of information in an easy to understand and interpret format. Limited to two dimensions or criteria.
Criteria Evaluation	Alternatives are rated against weighted criteria within a matrix format. The weights and scores are then multiplied to yield a weighted rating score.	Most widely used decision method and suitable to a variety of applications. If you are not sure what to use, this is probably the technique to employ.	Explicitly details all the criteria: how they are weighted and how all the alternatives performed against them on a single matrix. Produces interval-scaled data indicating the priorities.
Analytical Hierarchy Process	Same as above but rather than using ratings to establish weights and scores, uses a series of pair-wise comparisons.	Especially useful when the decision is especially complex, the cost of error is great, or the importance of the decision is especially high. Examples are decisions requiring major capital outlays, or those of strategic importance to the organization or of major significance to customers.	Produces the highest quality of results. Paired comparisons make optimum use of human judgment, and normalizing the paired comparison produces ratio-scaled data. Complex and time consuming.

When you are not sure what evaluative decision approach to use, use criteria evaluation.

▲ **Analytical Hierarchy Process (AHP)** AHP is used when quality of the decision is paramount, or the number of evaluative criteria and options are few and well defined, or when ratio-scaled data are required for input to deployment tables. AHP requires pair-by-pair rankings of all evaluative criteria as well as for every option against every criteria, making the process time consuming and the calculations complex. Nevertheless, AHP is the best approach to use in conditions of high risk or importance.

PUGH CONCEPT SELECTION MATRIX

The Pugh concept selection matrix is a tool for evaluating new concepts and comparing them to existing and/or world-class benchmarks. Originally developed by Stuart Pugh at the University of Strathclyde, Glasgow, the concept selection matrix was used initially to evaluate alternative concepts related to engineering design. Its ease of use and simplicity, combined with its ability to deal with complex evaluative situations, has resulted in its appeal and use spreading far beyond the engineering applications for which it was originally designed.

The Pugh concept selection matrix allows a number of alternative concepts to be evaluated simultaneously against a great many criteria. Moreover, the evaluation takes place against a reference concept with which the team is already familiar, or whose performance characteristics are already known. This typically provides for a more grounded, real-world evaluation framework than is offered by alternative approaches.

For example, a team may be considering three alternative means of powering a watch. The current design uses a small traditional battery. However, two new types of batteries could replace the current one, albeit at a higher cost. Moreover, the use of kinetic energy could also be considered as the third new alternative. The design team must compare these alternatives to the existing power method, to determine which concept offers the greatest potential for obtaining performance improvement while maintaining or improving customer satisfaction. The Pugh concept selection matrix helps structure the comparison of alternatives against a real-world reference concept with which team members are familiar – the existing battery. Moreover, a wide range of criteria can be accommodated, from cost to operating reliability to product appeal. This helps the team better understand how alternatives will, or will not, improve upon existing performance.

BASIC DESCRIPTION

The Pugh concept selection matrix looks like a basic matrix or table. By convention, the alternative concepts are listed across the top of the matrix to create the columns. The existing process is designated as the "datum." It is a reference point – the baseline or benchmark against which the alternative concepts are compared. As such, the datum concept is not rated. But the alternative concepts are rated on the basis of their strength or weakness relative to this datum. The datum or reference concept is usually placed in the last column of the matrix.

The criteria against which the various alternatives will be evaluated are listed down the side to create the rows of the matrix. Additionally, three rows are placed at the bottom of the matrix for totalling the scoring.

The intersection points of the matrix are filled with three symbols. A plus sign indicates the alternative concept is superior to the reference concept for this criterion. A minus sign indicates

Exhibit 284: Basic Pugh Concept Evaluation Matrix

Evaluation Criteria	Concept A	Concept B	Concept C	Existing Process
Criterion 1	-	+	+	D
Criterion 2	-	+	+	A
Criterion 3	+	+	-	T
Criterion 4	-	+	S	U
Criterion 5	+	-	+	M
Total (+)	2	4	3	
Total (s)	0	0	1	
Total (-)	3	1	1	

the alternative concept is inferior to the reference concept. And an 's' indicates the alternative and the reference concepts are essentially the same relative to the specific criterion.

For example, in Exhibit 284: Basic Pugh Concept Evaluation Matrix, Concept A is judged to be inferior to the reference concept for Criteria 1, 2 and 4 but superior to the reference concept for Criteria 3 and 5. The number of strengths and weaknesses associated with each alternative concept is then tabulated and totalled at the bottom of the matrix. In the exhibit, Concept B would likely be preferred as it has four positive scores and only one negative score relative to the reference concept or datum.

WHERE TO USE THE PUGH MATRIX

In the process of trying to make improvements, teams can generate a host of new ideas. From new product features to process enhancements, improvement is about finding new and often innovative ways of doing things.

During this process, teams must at some point decide between alternative approaches and new innovations or the existing way of doing things. The enthusiasm with which ideas are developed can often blind teams to fundamental flaws or problems with a new concept. Improvement or product redesign teams owe it to themselves to stop and ask the important questions. "Is this new process really better than the existing one?" "How do I define better – is it more cost effective, does it provide better customer service?" "Will this new idea actually perform better than the best-in-class alternatives currently used by the competition?"

Pugh concept selection matrices are designed to give teams the opportunity to review alternatives as well as ask and answer these types of questions. Use the Pugh concept selection matrix whenever:

▲ **The team is trying to decide on a new way to do things.** This involves improvements or changes to an existing process where there are a number of alternatives under consideration. Because there is a reference concept against which alternatives can be evaluated – usually the existing process – the Pugh concept selection matrix is a quick way to determine, through the judgment of the team, whether the alternatives will actually produce an improvement over the existing way of doing things.

▲ **The team is trying to decide among alternative product design concepts.** This might include, for example, what type of power source to use for a watch. Batteries, solar power, kinetic energy, mechanical winding – perhaps a small fusion reactor. The Pugh concept selection matrix allows teams to explicitly compare the strengths and weaknesses of each approach against a reference concept – likely the power source being used now – to see if alternatives offer any significant improvement to the overall product.

▲ **The team wants to benchmark an existing or proposed process or product against some existing competitive**

process or product. The straightforward method of superior, inferior, or same comparisons allows teams to benchmark against best-in-class competition even when comparative data is sparse. Usually, there is sufficient knowledge within the team to make these simple straightforward comparisons. The result can be an excellent initial approximation of the comparative strengths and weaknesses of the competition.

▲ **A quick method to evaluate a host of design alternatives is required in a large team setting.** The Pugh concept selection matrix is a simple tool to explain and administer in larger team or group settings. Mathematical calculations require nothing more than an ability to add. This simplicity gives it a significant advantage over other evaluative decision methods in larger group settings.

CREATING THE MATRIX

Creating a Pugh concept selection matrix can be done in six steps. These are:

1. Define the evaluation criteria

The first step is defining the set of criteria against which the

alternatives will be evaluated. This can be done using brainstorming techniques and affinity diagrams. These techniques, especially when combined with tree diagrams, can produce a comprehensive list of criteria.

At times, the criteria may be pre-defined for the team. For example, a team may be redesigning the process in response to a corporate directive to make operations more efficient. In such circumstances, management may have pre-defined corporate priorities such as customer satisfaction, and cost and cycle time for delivery. These priorities can then be used in the matrix as the evaluation criteria.

In short, there are no pre-set rules for defining the criteria to be used. Different circumstances demand different approaches. If the team is having trouble identifying the important criteria, a listing such as Kaoru Ishikawa's quality characteristics is an excellent foundation to at least get people thinking. Pay attention to customer requirements so that the expectations of those paying the bill are not lost. Also, consider basic requirements in such areas as business, legal, social, environmental, and safety regulations. How well a redesigned process or product will meet these requirements must be taken into account.

The criteria selected may be weighted or unweighted. Generally, Pugh concept selection matrices are applied without weighting the criteria. But at times, weighting may be important, especially if some criteria clearly do out-weigh others in terms of their importance to customers or the priorities of the organization.

2. Define the alternatives

Usually, by the time teams are ready to use the Pugh matrix, the alternatives have already been well defined. What is important at this stage, however, is that all team members share a common understanding of the alternatives being evaluated. This means, at a minimum, having some discussion about the alternatives. Team members with concerns or questions can then raise them to the group for clarification or resolution.

Once a shared level of understanding has been created, the alternatives are listed across the top of the selection matrix. The last column is reserved for the reference concept, referred to as the 'datum.' When teams are redesigning a process, the reference concept is the process being redesigned or replaced. A team could also be creating a product or process designed to surpass the competitors' or reach some "best-in-class" bench-

mark standard. In these cases, the reference concept would be the process or product we are trying to surpass.

3. Evaluate each process concept

With the initial two steps completed, we have essentially created a large matrix with evaluation criteria down the side and alternative concepts across the top. Now each concept is evaluated against the criteria.

Each concept is rated by how it compares to the reference concept for each of the criteria. A scoring method using +, - and s is used. A + means the alternative is better than the reference concept in the evaluation criteria. A - means it is not as good as the reference concept, and an s means it is essentially the same as the reference concept.

While this scoring is straightforward for an individual, it can be a little more complex in a team environment. If the facilitator is not worried about strong personalities affecting the team scoring, an open discussion format can be used. The facilitator or team leader simply goes through the matrix, asking the team to decide on whether a +, -, or s is most appropriate.

This process can bog down, however. An alternative is to ask individual team members to allocate their evaluations. This can be done by having individuals come up to the flipchart and mark their individual evaluations, or by having them prepare their evaluations privately and then have them call them out one at a time with the facilitator recording the results. With either approach, the resulting matrix will have a number of +'s, -'s and S's in each cell. Two steps are now required:

▲ **Summarize the results in each cell by counting which symbol outnumbers the rest.** If a cell has 6 +'s, 2 -'s and one S, the facilitator simply draws a circle around the evaluations and writes in a big +. This is continued for every cell in the matrix until each cell is designated as either a +, a - or an S for same.

▲ **Facilitate discussion on why people voted the way they did.** Once the summary is completed, ask people to explain why they voted the way they did. This is an opportunity for people to change their minds, discuss implications and try to change the opinions of others.

Evaluations may not always rely on human judgment. In engineering applications, for example, empirical data can be used to drive the evaluation process. For example, criteria such as tensile strength, battery life, corrosion resistance and the like can be empirically measured, with the results producing a rating within the matrix.

4. Tabulate the results

Tabulation of results is straight-forward. The number of +'s, -'s and S's are totaled at the bottom of each column (for each alternative concept). The process with the most +'s becomes the candidate process upon which to base the more detailed redesign.

In Exhibit 284: Basic Pugh Concept Evaluation Matrix, Concept A received two +'s and three -'s. Concept B received four +'s and only one -, while the third and last alternative had three +'s, one -, and one S. In this example, concept B would be selected.

If the Pugh matrix has weighted criteria, these weights are multiplied by the content of the cell to produce a total. Exhibit 285: Weighted Criteria in Pugh Matrix provides a modified example where the criteria are weighted. In this example, Concept A has two + or positive ratings, one in the ergonomics and safety criterion and the other in capital costs criterion. The weightings for each of these criteria is seven. So the total weighted number of +'s is 14, seven for the first criterion and seven for the second. These weighted scores are presented in the shaded portion of the Pugh matrix in the exhibit.

Exhibit 285: Weighted Criteria in Pugh Matrix

Evaluation Criteria	Criteria Importance (optional)	Concept 1	Concept 2	Concept 3	Existing Process
Service Reliability	6	-	+	+	D
Service Speed	9	-	+	+	A
Ergonomics & Safety	7	+	+	-	T
Operating Cost	4	-	+	S	U
Implementation - Capital Costs	7	+	-	+	M
Total (+)		2	4	3	
Total (s)		0	0	1	
Total (-)		3	1	1	
Weighted Total (+)		14	26	22	
Weighted Total (s)		0	0	4	
Weighted Total (-)		19	7	7	

5. Discuss and revise

The process of comparing alternatives with the reference standard, including discussing strengths and weaknesses, can lead to additional insight. For this reason, teams should return to the matrix to review the alternatives to see if any changes can be made to the various conceptual designs.

Examine the candidate concept and brainstorm ways to change it so that the - or s criteria become +. Examine the other concepts to see if you can incorporate their best ideas into the candidate concept. If your examination results in modifications to the candidate concept, evaluate it again on the matrix.

For example, in the exhibit, Concept 2 is ahead on both a weighted and unweighted basis. Its only shortcoming relative to the reference concept is in the criterion of capital cost. This is the same criterion where the other alternatives scored positively. A key question, then, is whether there is anything the team can borrow or adapt from these alternative concepts that could be applied to Concept 2. This would improve this Concept 2's performance relative to high capital costs.

6. Compare concept to benchmarks

So far, the basis of comparison has been the existing process or product with the organization. Once a concept is selected and revised, the Pugh concept selection matrix can be used to compare the redesigned product or process with competitors' or best-in-class alternatives. These new 'benchmarks' become the new reference concept or datum.

Exhibit 286: Using the Pugh Matrix to Compare Against World-Class Benchmarks

Evaluation Criteria	Existing Process		Redesigned Process		Best in Class Benchmark	
	Evaluation	Values	Evaluation	Values	Evaluation	Values
Service Reliability	-	79%	-	84%	D	92%
Service Speed	-	Mean 8.2 Minutes	S	Mean 6.9 Minutes	A	Mean 7.0 Minutes
Ergonomics & Safety	S	Moderate (3)	S	Moderate (3)	T	Moderate (3)
Operating Cost	-	$2,450 / Transaction	+	$1,800 / Transaction	U	$2,000 / Transaction
Implementation Capital Costs	+	$75,000 (upgrading)	+	$245,000	M	$325,000
Total **+**	1		2			
Total **S**	1		2			
Total **-**	3		1			

The existing and redesigned processes are then evaluated against the benchmark to establish how the improvements identified by the team 'stack up.' How the new design compares can be summarized in three ways:

▲ **The redesign fails to match the performance of the world-class reference concept.** The organization will have to suffer in second place or go back to the drawing board.

▲ **The redesign matches the performance of the world-class benchmark.** The organization has managed to at least catch the competition.

▲ **The redesign surpasses the world-class benchmark.** In effect, the redesign effort has allowed the organization to gain some degree of competitive advantage.

A sample of a possible comparative matrix is provided in Exhibit 286: Using the Pugh Matrix to Compare Against World-Class Benchmarks. In this version of the Pugh matrix, the world-class benchmark is the reference concept. The matrix also includes the basic performance measures that provide the source of the evaluation. In the example, the redesign is slightly better than the world-class reference standard, and certainly a great deal better than the existing process.

ANALYTICAL (DATA) MATRIX

The analytical matrix is basically a scatter plot, where the x- and y-axes represent the two basic decision criteria against which various alternatives will be evaluated. Usually, these criteria are some measures of organizational effort (cost) on the x-axis, and potential return or impact (benefit) on the y-axis. Each decision alternative is plotted on the matrix by its respective effort and impact scores.

The analytical matrix is a versatile tool and can be used to help teams deal with a host of decision-making and priority-setting problems. Moreover, by reducing the decision criteria to two, the analytical matrix simplifies representation of the issues and can provide for effective communication of complex decisions.

A basic analytical matrix is pictured in Exhibit 287: Basic Analytical Matrix. The components of the matrix are:

1. **Horizontal Axis.** This usually represents the dimension of an organizational effort. This can be some measure of cost, time or number of man-hours required to accomplish the alternatives. Team evaluations can be used if empirical data is not available or not possible to obtain. Single measures are not required. Multiple measures can be combined

into a single figure that can then be represented on the matrix.

Exhibit 287: Basic Analytical Matrix

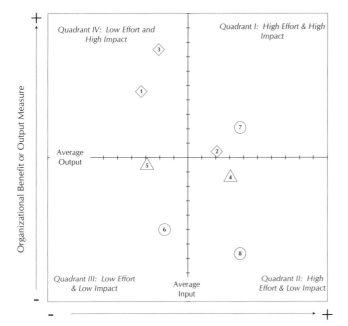

2. **Vertical Axis.** This usually represents the dimension of an organizational benefit. This can be measures of revenue, customer satisfaction, market share or a rating of the team's expectations of benefit accruing as a result of some improvement initiative. Here, too, single measures are not required. Multiple measures (indexes) can be combined and represented on the matrix.

3. **Data Points.** These represent the alternatives being considered. They are plotted on the matrix according to their effort/benefit scores. Data points can also be stratified – given different shapes or colors to represent different types or classifications of data. In the exhibit, they are represented by circles, diamonds and triangles.

4. **Average Lines.** These can be either median lines (dividing the data into two equal halves) or mean lines calculated from the scores. Either way, they divide the matrix into quadrants. These quadrants are then used to provide interpretation to the data.

The result is basically a scatter plot. However, we distinguish the analytical matrix from the scatter plot as two distinct tools based on their purposes. The scatter diagram is reserved for empirical data analysis, specifically for finding possible correlations or relationships between a pair of variables. This requires special considerations such as a minimum of 50 data points, the need for carefully designed sampling procedures, and rules for interpretation of correlation.

The analytical (data) matrix is intended for use on judgment or summary data. Finding correlation is not the intent here – helping to classify and prioritize alternatives is. As such, the matrix can be applied with far fewer than 50 data points, and no special sampling procedures are required.

WHERE TO USE THE ANALYTICAL MATRIX

The analytical matrix is a versatile and flexible tool. It can be used to analyze, prioritize and make decisions for any set of alternatives, where the evaluative criteria can be boiled down to two basic dimensions. This does not mean, however, that the number of evaluative criteria needs to be restricted to two items.

For example, a measure of organizational effort could be created from an index of capital investment plus man-hours plus elapsed time. So three evaluative criteria can be combined to create one dimension – organizational effort. The same holds for organizational benefit. This could be made up of some index that includes revenue enhancement, the length of time that the increased revenue stream would flow and so on.

Broadly speaking, the analytical matrix has been applied in four basic applications, characterized by the dimensions against which choices are evaluated. These standardized applications are: effort/impact matrix, importance/performance matrix, efficiency/effectiveness matrix and the issues analysis matrix.

▲ **Effort/Impact Matrix.** The effort/impact matrix is used to analyze alternative concepts, ideas, innovations and other organization sources of potential improvement. The x-axis is scaled for the degree of organizational effort. The y-axis represents the potential impact. Ideas or concepts are then plotted on the matrix according to how they scored across each of these dimensions. These alternatives can relate to any potential process or product improvement opportunity.

▲ **Importance/Performance Matrix.** In this case, the matrix is used to analyze customer perceptions about the importance of various product or process characteristics, compared with the ability of the organization to deliver those characteristics. Here the x-axis represents the importance to the customer, while the y-axis represents how well the customer perceives this characteristic being delivered.

▲ **Efficiency/Effectiveness Matrix.** This matrix compares the performance of a process with two of the fundamental performance dimensions. One dimension is effectiveness, which deals with the degree to which the process is meeting objectives or customer requirements. The other dimension is efficiency, which deals with how well the process is functioning, particularly in relation to the inputs consumed to produce the output that it does.

▲ **The Issues Analysis Matrix.** This is used to analyze issues that could possibly affect an organization. The dimensions are usually some measure of likelihood of occurrence (x-axis), against potential impact should it occur (y-axis). The issues analysis matrix is typically used in planning applications where teams are concerned with the impact of potential environmental changes on the organization.

CREATING THE ANALYTICAL MATRIX

Creating the analytical matrix is done in six basic steps. These are:

1. Identify the alternatives

Usually, by the time the effort/impact matrix is applied, the team usually has a well-defined set of alternatives. This may not always be the case. Brainstorming, combined with affinity charting and tree diagramming, can help fill in the gaps and provide a comprehensive picture of the alternatives.

An important addition to the simple identification of alternatives is the classification of alternatives. This is an option in the process but a useful one where appropriate. Essentially, we are applying Ishikawa's stratification technique to enhance the analysis. For example, if using a tree diagram to arrange alternatives or issues, major branches of the tree could become the classifications. Likewise, if doing affinity charting, the affinity groupings would become the classifications. These classifications can be represented by different-shaped points on the matrix.

2. Decide on the two dimensions

How will effort and impact be determined? What are the important dimensions to be considered? The answers to these questions will determine the dimensions used. For the most part, these are likely pre-set depending upon the basic type of evaluation being conducted, and will usually fall into one of the four categories already described.

The scales used to measure each dimension are usually set at 1 to 10 or 1 through 100. However, there is no requirement to standardize any specific scale. When empirical data is being used, it is generally good practice to use a scale that reflects the actual measurements taken. That way, nothing is hidden from those using the matrix.

3. Score the alternatives

With the alternatives clarified and the dimensions of evaluation clear, the team can now score the various alternatives. There must be two scores for each alternative, one for each dimension. There are three basic ways to gather these scores. These are:

▲ **Team consensus on each score.** This involves facilitating the group to agree on the scoring for each dimension for each alternative. This takes some time but it can be very productive, with such sessions usually involving a high degree of interaction among team members debating the characteristics of each alternative. The downside, of course, is that particularly strong-willed or forceful individuals may dominate the scoring.

▲ **Individual scoring.** As an alternative, individuals may score the alternatives in a team setting or completely removed from the meeting. The scores are then tabulated and the averages for each are used as the scores. With such a process, it is advisable to have at least two rounds of scoring so that differences can be discussed.

▲ **Empirical data is used.** The analytical data matrix is not used only to present judgment data – empirical data may be used as well. For example, actual costing data could be used to measure organizational effort, or projected revenue streams to gauge organizational benefit. The analytical data matrix can also be used to summarize consumer or employee responses to questionnaires, especially across importance/performance dimensions.

Exhibit 288: Scoring the Alternatives details a typical scoring type of worksheet. The alternatives, nine in all, are presented in

Exhibit 288: Scoring the Alternatives

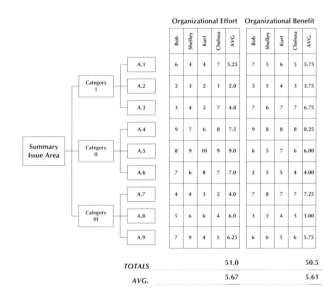

	Organizational Effort					Organizational Benefit				
	Bob	Shelley	Kurt	Chelsea	AVG	Bob	Shelley	Kurt	Chelsea	AVG.
A.1	6	4	4	7	5.25	7	5	6	5	5.75
A.2	2	3	2	1	2.0	3	5	4	3	3.75
A.3	3	4	2	7	4.0	7	6	7	7	6.75
A.4	9	7	6	8	7.5	9	8	8	8	8.25
A.5	8	9	10	9	9.0	6	5	7	6	6.00
A.6	7	6	8	7	7.0	2	5	5	4	4.00
A.7	4	4	3	2	4.0	7	8	7	7	7.25
A.8	5	6	6	4	6.0	3	2	4	3	3.00
A.9	7	9	4	5	6.25	6	6	5	6	5.75
TOTALS					51.0					50.5
AVG.					5.67					5.61

a tree diagram. These are labeled A.1 through A.9 on the tree. The tree diagram has also grouped the alternatives into three groups labeled Category I, II and III. These represent three different types of solution categories.

Attached to the tree is a table to summarize the scoring given by four team members, as well as the resulting averages. The first part of the table deals with the organizational cost dimension, the second part with the benefits. Notice that at the bottom of the table, the averages have been totaled and an overall average (mean) is calculated. These averages will be used to place the lines delineating the four quadrants of the matrix. Instead of the mean, teams can also use the median.

4. Create the matrix

The matrix can be drawn on flipchart paper or created on a computer. The facilitator needs to create the scales with the same scale used to evaluate the alternatives. In our example, a scale of 1 through 10 was used, so this scale is used to create the data matrix. Once the matrix is created, the lines representing the averages are drawn in.

5. Plot the scores

Now the scores of the individual alternatives are plotted. If facilitating in a team setting, the facilitator may wish to use sticky-notes for this purpose. This will make it easier to change the plot if another round of scoring is to be undertaken. Each note should be clearly labelled for the alternative it represents. In the exhibit, this could be done using the alternative identifier A.1, A.2 and so on.

Also, remember Ishikawa's stratification principle. Use different symbols to represent different types of improvement opportunities or issues. In the example, Category I, II and III alternatives can be represented by different shapes. If using sticky-notes, use different colors to represent the different categories.

6. Make your conclusions/decisions

As the example shows, alternative A.7 provided the highest returns for the lowest cost comparing both organizational effort and organizational benefit. This was followed closely by alternative A.3. Based on this analysis, these two alternatives represent the best choices for the team.

However, interpretation of the analytical data matrix need not be so direct or simplistic. If stratification has been part of the process, look for patterns in the data. In the exhibit, Category I,

Exhibit 289: Completed Analytical Matrix

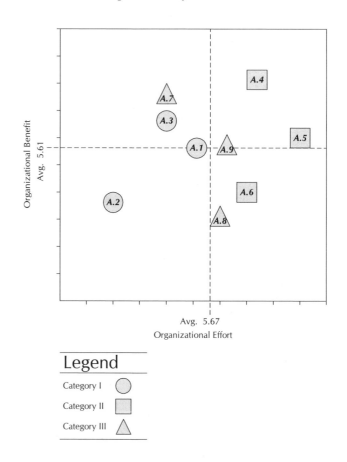

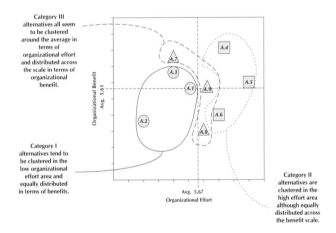

II and III alternatives do seem to form some basic patterns. If this is the case, the team should discuss the implications.

Exhibit 290: Looking for Patterns Through Stratification

Category III alternatives all seem to be clustered around the average in terms of organizational effort and distributed across the scale in terms of organizational benefit.

Organizational Benefit
Avg. 5.61

Category I alternatives tend to be clustered in the low organizational effort area and equally distributed in terms of benefits.

Avg. 5.67
Organizational Effort

Category II alternatives are clustered in the high effort area although equally distributed across the benefit scale.

For example, if the grouping of alternative solutions is closely related to one another, such that implementing one solution would reduce the cost of implementing the others, the team may decide to implement all the alternatives in the group, rather than just the one.

The same holds true when confronted with a common set of issues. If grouped together by common cause, it may be advantageous to address the issues comprising the group rather than dealing with each issue separately. This applies despite the fact that no one issue of the group scored highest on the matrix.

The bottom line is to avoid simplistic approaches to interpretation and stratify where possible. Doing so will make the analytical data matrix more relevant and useful – helping to drive discussions and proceed toward a final decision.

THE EFFORT/IMPACT MATRIX

Interpretation of the results for this matrix depends in large measure on how the various points fall relative to the four quadrants. These quadrants and their respective interpretations are:

▲ **Quadrant I: High Effort & High Impact.** Alternatives located within this quadrant will have a high impact on the organization. Unfortunately, they will also require considerably high levels of organizational effort. They represent alternatives of relatively high risk and high return.

▲ **Quadrant II: High Effort & Low Impact.** These alternatives should be dropped from the list. Not only do they fail to promise relatively significant levels of benefit or impact, they require a lot of effort in the process.

▲ **Quadrant III: Low Effort & Low Impact.** These alternatives require very little effort, but they don't promise too much in return. If the team is seeking some "easy hits," some early success before tackling larger or more detailed improvement efforts, this can be an effective place to start.

▲ **Quadrant IV: Low Effort & High Impact.** Points located in this quadrant represent our Number 1 improvement priorities. We can gain relatively large impact or benefit from a relatively modest improvement effort.

When interpreting the matrix, remember that the measures of importance and effort are relative. All the characteristics, for example, may have a high impact. It is just that some will have a higher impact than others. By dividing the matrix into quadrants, we force a classification of high and low that may emphasize differences that are not so apparent in the data itself. Therefore, if you plot deviations from the average, make sure you also accompany this with a plot of actual values. That way,

Exhibit 291: Effort/Impact Matrix of Oil Company Revenue Opportunities

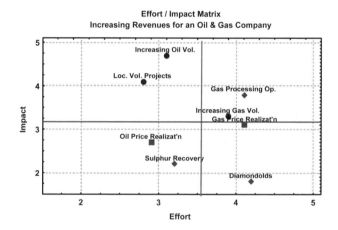

team members can gain an appreciation of the actual data as well as the standardized data.

In Exhibit 291: Effort/Impact Matrix of Oil Company Revenue Opportunities, revenue enhancement opportunities for a specific oil and gas area are presented. The simplest and most direct route to enhancement entails undertaking those projects associated with increasing the flow of oil in existing streams, followed closely by undertaking local volume projects. Notice that these two alternatives fall into the same grouping, along with increasing gas volumes, although this later alternative has a higher-effort / lower-impact profile. As a result of this analysis, the organization in question developed an oil volume strategy and focused its resources appropriately.

IMPORTANCE/PERFORMANCE MATRIX.

The sequence of steps in preparing the importance/performance matrix is essentially the same as creating the effort/impact matrix. Generally, the importance/performance matrix is applied when evaluating which core processes should become the initial focus for improvement, and when summarizing customer evaluations of performance characteristics of products and service.

In the case of customer evaluations, data may be the result of team judgment or it may be empirical, arising from consumer research. If the data is to be empirical, survey respondents must be presented with the complete set of quality characteristics. They should be asked to rate the importance of the characteristic and how well the organization performs in providing the

characteristic. The average response, stratified as appropriate, is then used to plot the data on the matrix.

When core processes are being evaluated, the evaluation is usually part of the strategic planning process at a high level in the organization. As such, the scoring is usually the result of judgment supported by internal reports and measures.

Here's a guide to interpreting the four quadrants of the importance/performance matrix;

▲ **Quadrant I. High importance and performance.** Characteristics in this quadrant are relatively important to the customer and are being done well from the customer's point of view. There is a level of congruency here.

▲ **Quadrant II. High importance and low performance.** A problem area. It is important to the customer, but we are not delivering to the level expected. This is a key target for improvement, and resources should be reallocated so that the characteristic can be delivered in some improved fashion. Items in this quadrant are generally the Number 1 priority for improvement.

▲ **Quadrant III. Low importance and low performance.** Our organization or product does not do a relatively good job of delivering on this characteristic. But, thankfully, this characteristic isn't all that important to the customer. Items in this quadrant represent a low priority for improvement.

▲ **Quadrant IV. Low importance and high performance.** The good news is that we are strong in delivering on this quality characteristic. The bad news is that the customer doesn't care all that much. This, too, is a strategy for improvement, especially in considering allocating fewer resources to the function or characteristic – perhaps reallocating them to items in quadrant II.

In Exhibit 292: Importance/Performance Matrix of Customer Requirements for Telephone Repair, the results of a customer survey are presented. Customers were asked to rate their preferences for certain characteristics for a telephone repair service. In this case, we want to see which areas are particularly important to the customer and where our performance may be lacking. In the exhibit, this problem area is clearly dependability. In a typical application, this would become the focus of the improvement effort.

It is important to note that such a summary evaluation of various performance characteristics should never take place in iso-

Exhibit 292: Importance/Performance Matrix of Customer Requirements for Telephone Repair

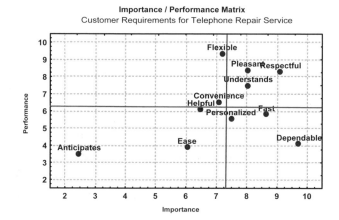

lation of other data analysis. Histograms and other data-analysis techniques would first be applied to consumer research data, in addition to providing a summary through the analytical data matrix. Only through the use of histograms and other tools can useful stratifications and interpretations of the data be made.

In this regard, however, the analytical matrix can be used to compare how different customer segments view the importance/performance characteristics of any product and service. Different matrices, for example, can be prepared for different segments. How different customer segments view the same characteristic also can be presented on a single matrix. Different matrices would then be prepared for each performance characteristic.

EFFECTIVENESS/EFFICIENCY MATRIX

The effectiveness/efficiency matrix is used to evaluate the performance of a process across these two vital dimensions. Effectiveness is concerned with outputs – specifically, how well process outputs meet corporate objectives, stakeholder requirements or customer expectations. Efficiency is focussed on the ratio of inputs used to obtain these outputs. Efficiency is usually placed on the horizontal axis, effectiveness on the vertical.

Here are some notes on interpretation:

▲ **Quadrant I. Effective and Efficient.** Here is a process doing all we can ask of it. As such, it would represent the lowest order for improvement.

▲ **Quadrant II. Efficient but Not Effective.** Here is a good candidate for redesign. The process is very good at mini-

mizing the resources for a given level of output, but these outputs are not well regarded. The key strategy in such a situation is too see if the process can be reconfigured to produce a redesigned output, without serious change to its existing method of functioning.

▲ **Quadrant III. Ineffective and Inefficient.** This is lowest of the low. The process produces outputs that are not congruent with demands and, moreover, produces these outputs in a way that wastes resources. Processes in this quadrant are the first targets for improvement.

▲ **Quadrant IV. Effective but Not Efficient.** Here, the process is producing what we ask of it, but just not doing so in a manner that maximizes the use of resources. Efficiency strategies such as attacking waste, using statistical process control techniques and related strategies need to be applied.

The efficiency/effectiveness matrix is an excellent tool to use in corporate level strategy sessions, especially after completing a critical process map. With the critical processes identified, the next stage in driving a strategic-level improvement will be targeting those critical processes most in need of improvement.

This analytical matrix can help by placing all these critical process on a single map.

The placement of the various processes involved also provides some indication of the type of improvement strategy that needs to be employed. Processes that are both ineffective and inefficient are good candidates for major redesign or re-engineering. Processes that are inefficient but effective are good candidates for refinement strategies, or for a cross-function team focused only on process operations since no redesign of output is required. Ineffective but efficient processes are candidates for cross-function redesign teams that have expertise in product design and customer requirements.

In Exhibit 293: Efficiency/Effectiveness Matrix of Finance Department Core Processes, the review of the processes in the finance department led to just such a strategic approach to improvement. Despite the year-end process being classified as both inefficient and ineffective, the team decided to focus its initial efforts on processes that were effective, but inefficient. The logic was, that approach would give the team some initial experience at improvement. That would enable them to leverage greater levels of resources in the future, for the larger improvement effort required to improve the year-end process.

Exhibit 293: Efficiency/Effectiveness Matrix of Finance Department Core Processes

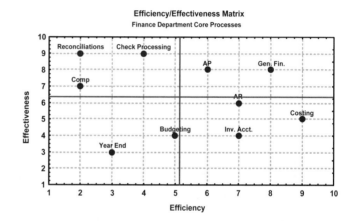

With efficiency/inefficiency areas addressed, the department next year turned its attention to highly efficient but ineffective processes, specifically its costing process and general inventory accounting. Here, the department was good at its processes but producing results of marginal benefit to the organization. The year's theme became effectiveness and these areas were targeted for improvement.

Lastly, in year three, year-end closing was addressed, taking into account the revisions made in the previous two years.

ISSUES ANALYSIS MATRIX

The issues analysis matrix focuses on setting priorities for emerging problems or issues. This matrix is usually associated with strategic planning applications, where the intent is to assess the nature of the external environment and its impact on the organization.

The two dimensions of the analysis are usually the likelihood of occurrence and the impact upon the organization. Interpretation is as follows:

▲ **Quadrant I. High Likelihood and Impact.** These constitute the first priority of the team. Members believe that the issue or problem will arise and that when it does, the impact on the organization or performance will be large.

▲ **Quadrant II. High Likelihood and Low Impact.** Issues here will likely occur, but they will have less of an impact on the organization. The key issue here is exactly how much of an impact the issue will have. The team needs to detail the nature of the impact to a greater degree, before specific action is committed to dealing with the issue.

▲ **Quadrant III. Low Likelihood and Low Impact.** These are at the bottom of the priority scale. The team believes there is relatively less chance the issue will arise and, even if it does, the impact will be relatively small as well.

▲ **Quadrant IV. Low Likelihood and High Impact.** These are items the team believes are not likely to come about, but if they do they could give rise to significant problems. These issues must be examined against those in Quadrant II to see where priorities should be placed.

In Exhibit 294: Likelihood/Impact Matrix of Issues for Regional Bank, various issues relating to a medium-sized regional bank are analyzed. The executive of the bank had struggled with this set of issues previously. Unfortunately, the executive team believed all the issues were important and tried to address them all simultaneously. Almost two years later, little progress had been made on any of the issues identified.

To help the situation, the analytical data matrix was prepared using the analysis provided by the executive team and the board of directors. From the analysis, three clear priorities

Exhibit 294: Likelihood/Impact Matrix of Issues for Regional Bank

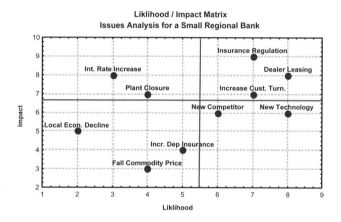

By focusing on the top three issues, the bank developed a two-year strategic plan targeted at improving its position in each of these areas. Improvement teams were chartered for each area, and given the resources required to study the problems and recommend solutions.

The high degree of focus and commitment resulted in a clear strategic direction for the organization. The analytical data matrix presented in the exhibit was, in fact, used to communicate to employees why the organization was taking the directions it was. The matrix was used in various communication sessions to explain certain decisions and changes to the bank's operations. They included the acquisition of an insurance brokerage business, and the establishment of a dealer finance and leasing area targeted at providing improved service to automotive dealers.

emerged – addressing insurance deregulation, dealer leasing and increasing levels of customer turnover.

It is important to mention that none of this analysis means that the other issues are not important to the organization. The analytical data matrix simply forces issues into prioritized quadrants. As such, all the issues may be important – the matrix helps only to set the priorities.

CRITERIA RATING TECHNIQUE

The criteria rating technique is the workhorse of decision methods. It is a flexible tool that can be used in almost any decision situation. As such, it is best applied in the variety of day-to-day decision situations that improvement teams face.

The criteria rating technique uses a matrix to compare various decision alternatives against evaluative criteria. Typically, the alternatives are placed along the top of the matrix, creating the set of columns. Evaluative criteria are placed along the sides of the matrix to create the rows. The intersection points record the rating given each alternative relative to the criteria.

Usually, these intersection points contain both the team ratings and the weighted rating that was derived from multiplying the rating by the weighting for the respective criteria. At the bottom of the matrix, the totals for the ratings, the weighted ratings and the percentage distributions are presented.

WHEN SHOULD THE CRITERIA RATING TECHNIQUE BE USED?

The criteria rating technique is a good, all-purpose decision-making tool. It is simple enough to apply in actual team settings, but is also effective in helping individuals resolve issues and set priorities. The technique can be used whenever the team is forced to make a decision from a set of well-defined alternatives, but where no reference concept or datum alternative exists. (If a datum or reference concept exists, then consider using the Pugh concept selection matrix.)

Exhibit 295: Basic Criteria Rating Matrix

Decision Alternatives / Decision Criteria	Weighting	Alternative A		Alternative B		Alternative C		Alternative D	
Criteria 1	9	3	27	1	9	3	27	5	45
Criteria 2	7	5	35	2	14	3	21	2	14
Criteria 3	8	2	16	5	40	3	24	5	40
Criteria 4	2	4	8	2	4	2	4	2	4
Criteria 5	5	1	5	5	25	5	25	2	10
Criteria 6	9	3	27	4	36	5	45	7	63
Criteria 7	3	3	9	3	9	1	3	4	12
Total Score		21		23		22		27	
Weighted Score		127		137		149		188	
% Distribution (Weighted)		21.1		22.8		24.8		31.3	

Teams will find the criteria rating matrix useful when:

▲ **The team must make a decision from a small list of well-defined alternatives, produced from a larger list that was reduced using preference techniques.** This is a typical pattern with improvement teams. A long list of potential solutions is identified, which is then reduced to a set of the most promising alternatives through the use of multi-voting or a similar preference technique. Sub-teams are then assigned to flesh out what the reduced list of alternatives looks like in some detail. With this detail added, the team can then evaluate the alternatives against a set of criteria through the criteria rating matrix.

▲ **The team not only needs to make a decision, but also needs to clearly document the rationale or logic behind the decision.** Criteria-based evaluative decision methods make the assumptions or logic behind the decision explicit. They document what the team believed to be important (the criteria), the scope or range of possibilities to be considered (the alternatives), how the team saw each alternative performing across the criteria (the scoring), and the final set of conclusions represented by the tabulations in the matrix. Criteria rating matrices produce not only a decision, but also a decision that can be clearly communicated and documented.

▲ **There are possible divisions in the team lined up along possible alternatives.** It happens to the best of teams. Divisions form, with one side favoring one alternative, another faction favoring a different alternative. If the division is left too long, each side begins to identify more with the alternative than the overall mission of the team. Differ-

ences can also be political. The selection of one alternative may be perceived as a victory for one department over another. In these situations, the application of the criteria rating matrix can help shift the focus to what is best for the organization, by moving the focus off the divisive agendas and onto the criteria and how the alternatives stack up.

While the criteria rating technique is the workhorse of decision-making techniques, this doesn't mean it is the best tool in all circumstances. The tool suffers from all the weaknesses associated with ratings generally. First of all, it may produce numerous ties or alternatives that score very closely. Second, ratings can be rather nebulous things – what does a four really mean when compared to a five? For this reason, clear descriptions must be prepared for the rating scale to be used. If alternatives are well defined and a reference standard is available, consider using the Pugh concept selection matrix instead. Lastly, when the decision is of major importance, or involves considerable risk, consider using the analytical hierarchy process instead (discussed next). Its system of paired comparisons overcomes many of the issues associated with ratings, although the trade-off is greater complexity.

CREATING THE CRITERIA RATING MATRIX

Reaching a decision using the criteria rating matrix is a seven-step process. To help us through the process, we'll use an example of selecting a specific computer supplier.

1. Start the session and list the alternatives

Like other evaluative, criteria-based tools, the list of alternatives will likely be familiar to the team. This matrix should not be used with a brand-new set of alternatives freshly created from a brainstorming or similar exercise. In such circumstances, a preference technique such as multi-voting is preferred. If that has been done, we should now have a reduced list of alternatives that include some descriptive detail – enough detail to allow team members to picture the alternatives clearly and evaluate across criteria.

Each alternative should be briefly reviewed in a team setting to ensure everyone shares the same understanding of the various alternatives presented. It is helpful to have a blank criteria rating matrix prepared in advance, either on an overhead transparency or on a large piece of flip chart paper.

2. Determine the decision criteria

The next step is to decide on the decision criteria against which the decision evaluations will be made. These may have been determined already, perhaps from the marketing research department (what's important to the customer) or from an executive improvement team (what's important to the organization). Even when criteria are provided in this manner, however, it may be appropriate to provide additional detail to create a more comprehensive set of criteria.

For example, reducing cost is usually an organizational objective and, therefore, a possible decision criterion. But what kind of cost? Long-term or short-term? How are capital outlays vs. operating expenses to be traded off? Calculating cost looks straightforward but it is rarely as simple as we would like to believe. The same holds true for other possible decision criteria. Make sure the criteria are clear enough so that a reasonable evaluation can be made. If they are not, break them out using a tree diagram or another such data-organization technique, to ensure there is clear understanding and a that valid assessment against criteria is possible.

3. Determine the weight of each criterion

Each criterion is assigned a weight representing its relative importance. Several techniques are available for determining these weights. Easiest among these is to use any of the preference techniques to assign a numeric weighting to the criterion. Team members can be given voting dots to be placed beside the criterion of their choice for example. These are then tallied to provide a numeric weighting. An example of the first-round criteria weighting is presented in Exhibit 296: Initial Weighting of Decision Criteria.

Whatever system is used to determine the weighting, it is usually convenient to covert the values to a percentage weighting score. This is done by totaling up the weights and then dividing this total into the weight associated with each criterion. The result will be a set of weighting scores totaling 100 percent.

When the first set of weights is determined, some discussion of the results is required. The team should agree that the weights represent the relative importance of the various criteria. If there is substantial disagreement, each side should be given an opportunity to express its case. The rating procedure is then conducted again. Sometimes the disagreement comes from a criterion that is too broadly defined – each side is interpreting it differently. In such cases, break the criterion in two and conduct the weighting exercise again. An example might be costs. One group sees the cost as being small, the other as being large. The first group, however, is thinking of operating costs while the other is thinking of capital or acquisition costs. In this circumstance, both capital cost and operating cost criteria should be created.

Exhibit 297: Revised Criteria Weights for Six-Member Team, presents the results from conducting the criteria weightings a second time. Again, the distributional percentages for each criterion are calculated. Using these percentages as the weights, as opposed to the actual ratings, will not affect the results and are usually easier to understand. It is easier, for example, to talk about capital cost representing 9.1 percent of the importance among all criteria than saying it scored 40 out of a possible 438 points.

4. Establish the scale

With the criteria now weighted, the next step is determining the scale to be used in rating the alternatives against the criteria. Any scale will work, as long as the same scale is used throughout. The most common are 9- or 10-point scales, where higher

Exhibit 296: Initial Weighting of Decision Criteria

Decision Criteria		Team Members						Results	
		Jim	Rhonda	Tim	Bob	Shelley	Sean	Total Score	Percentage Score
Low Cost	Capital Cost	5	7	8	9	5	7	**41**	**9.2**
	Operating Cost	3	7	8	8	5	7	**38**	**8.5**
Simple Technology	PC Based	9	8	9	7	9	8	**50**	**11.3**
	Modifiable Code	7	2	3	2	7	7	**28**	**6.3**
Fast Implementation Time	Time to Install	4	5	2	3	8	6	**28**	**6.3**
	Training Time	6	6	2	4	5	8	**31**	**7.0**
End User Satisfaction	Ergonomics	8	7	7	5	7	8	**42**	**9.5**
	Graphic Display	8	9	3	6	7	8	**41**	**9.2**
	Minimum Space	3	3	2	6	3	6	**23**	**5.2**
	Processing Speed	9	9	8	6	9	9	**50**	**11.3**
Extent of Existing System Modification	Hardware Modifications	2	6	6	3	7	9	**33**	**7.4**
	Software Modifications	6	6	6	5	7	9	**39**	**8.8**
TOTAL								**444**	**100.0**

Exhibit 297: Revised Criteria Weights for Six-Member Team

Decision Criteria		Jim	Rhonda	Tim	Bob	Shelley	Sean	Total Score	Percentage Score
		Team Members						**Results**	
Low Cost	Capital Cost	6	7	8	7	5	7	**40**	**9.1**
	Operating Cost	4	7	8	8	7	7	**41**	**9.4**
Simple Technology	PC Based	9	8	9	7	9	8	**50**	**11.4**
	Modifiable Code	7	4	3	2	7	7	**30**	**6.8**
Fast Implementation Time	Time to Install	4	5	3	3	6	6	**27**	**6.2**
	Training Time	4	5	2	4	5	5	**25**	**5.7**
End User Satisfaction	Ergonomics	8	6	7	5	7	8	**41**	**9.4**
	Graphic Display	8	9	6	6	7	8	**44**	**10.0**
	Mininum Space	3	3	2	4	3	5	**20**	**4.6**
	Processing Speed	9	9	8	7	9	9	**51**	**11.6**
Extent of Existing System Modification	Hardware Modifications	2	6	6	3	7	5	**29**	**6.6**
	Software Modifications	6	7	6	6	7	8	**40**	**9.1**
TOTALS								**438**	**99.9**

numbers indicate stronger performance relative to the specific criterion.

When creating the scale, it is critical to ensure a clear description is provided with the numbers. There should be no confusion about how to interpret a one versus a three. Take time to define just what the numbers in the scale mean and post this explanation for the team to see.

5. Conduct the ratings

The actual process of conducting the rating can be a little complicated in a team setting. It is one thing to have one person rate an alternative against some criteria, and quite another to have seven people do it. Two approaches are common.

▲ **Nominal Method.** The most common method is to have individuals first prepare their individual ratings, then 'go around the table' asking team members to call out their ratings. These are recorded in a table or in each cell of the matrix. Once everyone's ratings have been recorded, the ratings can be summed or averaged to produce the rating for each cell. If this approach is taken, a second round of rating needs to take place preceded by a period of discussion to clarify the individual reasoning behind the ratings.

▲ **Consensus Method.** As an alternative, the team may prefer to reach consensus as they proceed, agreeing in turn on the various ratings assigned to each alternative against each criterion. Thus, the team rates each alternative across the criteria as a group. This requires greater effort but also yields greater quality and levels of understanding and commitment. This approach works better when the number of alternatives and/or criteria are few.

With either approach, the rating process is ended when all alternatives have been rated across the criteria.

6. Calculate and discuss the results

The facilitator or team leader must next calculate the weighted results for each cell in the matrix. This is done by multiplying the rating assigned each cell (in step 5) by the weighting for the criteria associated with the cell (determined in step 3). The resulting weighted score is recorded in the right-hand corner of each cell. In Exhibit 298: Criteria Rating Matrix, the highlighted cell has the alternative CyberTech rating a 3 against the capital cost which is weighted a 9.1. The resulting weighted score for this cell is therefore 27.3 (3 times 9.1).

It is these weighted scores that are used to provide an overall evaluation of the alternative. Add the weighted scores up for each column, recording the totals at the bottom of the column. These values represent the criteria-weighted scores of each alternative. The alternative with the highest score represents the selection or decision of the team.

Again, some level of discussion is warranted, especially if the results are in dispute or divisions are present in the team. Discussion of the results usually takes the form of different viewpoints trying to demonstrate to the 'other side' why they rated things they way they did. This keeps the focus where it should be – on the logic underlying the ratings, and away from pre-defined agendas. This can help diffuse tensions by narrowing argument and discussion to the rationale behind the decision, rather than the decision itself.

With the final weighted scores totaled, a percentage distribution is also calculated. This is done by dividing the weighted totals for each alternative by the grand total for all the alternatives. The result is the distributional percentage represented by the weighted score for each of the alternative. Note that calculating the distributional percentage does not change the results, it simply makes the scoring a little easier to communicate. In this case, the first alternative, Systech, was the clear choice for the team, with a rating of 647 out of a total of 2975.5 points or 21.7 percent of all rating points.

7. Wrap up the criteria rating technique session

Once the alternative is agreed to by the group – that is, a level of consensus has been achieved – the session is over. Ensure that the results and figures recorded on the matrix are clear enough for typing. Facilitators or team leaders should try to circulate results as quickly as possible after the session.

Having made a decision, something else needs to follow – some form of action! Before team members leave, ensure that job assignments, including communications, are assigned to team members and that the next steps to be undertaken and the next team meeting are clear to all.

SUMMARY COMMENTS ON THE CRITERIA RATING TECHNIQUE

The criteria rating technique is a useful tool for improvement teams or any other organizational group trying to reach a decision on a matter of some importance. Perhaps its greatest

Exhibit 298: Criteria Rating Matrix

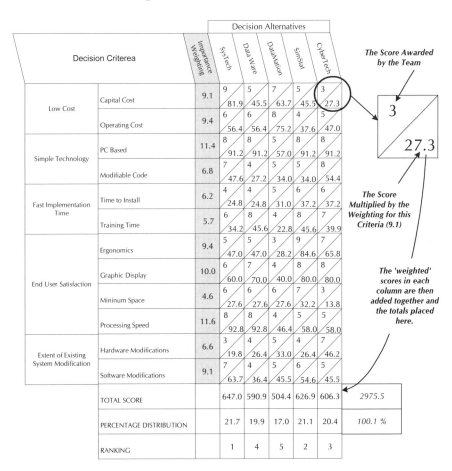

Decision Criterea		Importance Weighting	SysTech	Data Ware	DataMation	SimStat	CyberTech
Low Cost	Capital Cost	9.1	9 / 81.9	5 / 45.5	7 / 63.7	5 / 45.5	3 / 27.3
	Operating Cost	9.4	6 / 56.4	6 / 56.4	8 / 75.2	4 / 37.6	5 / 47.0
Simple Technology	PC Based	11.4	8 / 91.2	8 / 91.2	5 / 57.0	8 / 91.2	8 / 91.2
	Modifiable Code	6.8	7 / 47.6	4 / 27.2	5 / 34.0	5 / 34.0	8 / 54.4
Fast Implementation Time	Time to Install	6.2	4 / 24.8	4 / 24.8	5 / 31.0	6 / 37.2	6 / 37.2
	Training Time	5.7	6 / 34.2	8 / 45.6	4 / 22.8	8 / 45.6	7 / 39.9
End User Satisfaction	Ergonomics	9.4	5 / 47.0	5 / 47.0	3 / 28.2	9 / 84.6	7 / 65.8
	Graphic Display	10.0	6 / 60.0	7 / 70.0	4 / 40.0	8 / 80.0	8 / 80.0
	Mininum Space	4.6	6 / 27.6	6 / 27.6	6 / 27.6	7 / 32.2	3 / 13.8
	Processing Speed	11.6	8 / 92.8	8 / 92.8	4 / 46.4	5 / 58.0	5 / 58.0
Extent of Existing System Modification	Hardware Modifications	6.6	3 / 19.8	4 / 26.4	5 / 33.0	4 / 26.4	7 / 46.2
	Software Modifications	9.1	7 / 63.7	4 / 36.4	5 / 45.5	6 / 54.6	5 / 45.5
TOTAL SCORE			647.0	590.9	504.4	626.9	606.3
PERCENTAGE DISTRIBUTION			21.7	19.9	17.0	21.1	20.4
RANKING			1	4	5	2	3

Decision Alternatives

The Score Awarded by the Team

3

27.3

The Score Multiplied by the Weighting for this Criteria (9.1)

The 'weighted' scores in each column are then added together and the totals placed here.

2975.5

100.1 %

strength is the degree to which it can help a team stay focused on what is important (the criteria, and evaluation against the criteria), while directing focus away from possible private agendas and positions.

A second strength of this approach, and of evaluative tools generally, is the documentation they provide for the future. This is the basis of organizational learning. Documenting why we made the decisions we did provides future improvement efforts with insight and understanding that is otherwise unavailable.

Consider the savings in time and effort if improvement teams had access to background documentation as to why previous decisions were made the way they were. Unfortunately, for whatever reasons, the core logic behind decisions is rarely captured. The result is that new teams must expend considerable time and energy trying to understand and second-guess why certain decisions were made.

An interesting test for organizations is to pick any major decision made by the organization about five years ago. Then, try to find out why the specific alternative was selected. A good bet is that no one knows or can remember. This is as revealing a measure as any of a failure to learn and of knowledge lost.

ANALYTICAL HIERARCHY PROCESS (AHP)

The analytical hierarchy process (AHP) is the most complex of the decision-evaluation methods described. This reason alone has limited its use, especially in team settings. This is unfortunate, because AHP is also the most rigorous of the decision methods, bringing sound measurement practice to the exercise and application of human judgment.

The analytical hierarchy process grew out of the work of Dr. Thomas Saaty. Despite the AHP's rigor, Dr. Saaty makes it clear the process is intended to enhance our understanding and improve our thinking.

"The central purpose of all explanation is understanding, not playing with the numbers. The question then is, what is the connection of our understanding, judgment, and feeling with numbers and how do these numbers reflect the strength of our

feelings? . . . we offer the reader a new tool for this purpose, that of using mathematics to understand our own feelings and help us in the process of decision making."[84]

On the surface, the analytical hierarchy process and especially the decision matrix that results from it looks much like the criteria rating matrix. In fact, the two processes are a lot alike. The difference between them is how the weightings of the criteria and the ratings of alternatives against these criteria are determined. In the criteria rating matrix, preference-setting techniques – usually group based ratings – tend to be used. In the analytical hierarchy process, a much more methodical process of paired comparisons is employed, combined with a scale that elicits the strength of the comparison. It is this comparative ranking and rating approach that gives the AHP its rigor and complexity.

WHERE TO USE AHP

As problems and decisions become more complex or more important to the organization, use of the analytical hierarchy process becomes more appropriate. While the mathematical manipulations demanded by the process may have been daunting in the past, these calculations have been considerably simplified by personal computer software designed specifically for this purpose and related tools such as spreadsheets. Nothing compares with the AHP for evaluating complex situations and providing a foundation for sound decision making.

The downside is that, for all practical purposes, the technique cannot be applied within a team setting. The rating procedure and mathematical manipulations are simply too complex and time consuming. (Although some group-based computer software has recently been introduced to help overcome this limitation.) Usually, the team sets up the evaluation criteria and clarifies the alternatives. The paired comparison rating procedure is then conducted by individuals whose results are forwarded to someone, or a sub-team is assigned the task of performing the analysis. The team is then brought back together to discuss the results.

84. Thomas L. Saaty,; Mathematical Methods in Operations Research; Dover Publications, 1988; p. 415

Despite its complexity, the AHP should be used whenever:

▲ **The decision is some sense a final decision representing the culmination to a milestone or key element in the project.** These types of decisions usually affect the direction the team will take in some fundamental way. As such, it is worthwhile to take some extra time analyzing the decision options.

▲ **The complexity of the decision is high.** This complexity often requires a carefully thought-out method of weighing the evaluative criteria and analyzing the options according to those criteria. The analytical hierarchy provides this function through a meticulous process of paired comparison judgments. It simply does a better job of capturing human judgment in such complex situations.

▲ **The impact of the decision is high, and where making a mistake could be costly for the company or the project team.** When the cost of error is high, it makes sense to spend extra effort in the decision-making process to help ensure good decisions are made. The analytical hierarchy process, because of its rigorous approach, produces better quality decisions.

▲ **There is a need to create ratio-scaled data from human judgment.** Voting, rating, ranking and related techniques are all capable of producing an estimate of what items or alternatives are more important to the team than others. The criteria evaluation matrix can even produce a rough measure of the interval (degree of preference) among alternatives. However, only the analytical hierarchy process can produce ratio-scaled data from human judgment. Ratio-scaled data is data that allows for comparisons such as A is twice as good as B, or that alternative X involves half the organizational effort of alternative Z. If such data is required and is based on human judgments, the AHP is the tool --the only tool – to be used.

▲ **There is a mixture of measurement and judgement data to be used in making a decision.** One of the strengths of the AHP is the ability to reduce measurements (such as cost, market share, revenue projections, customer satisfaction measures) and judgment data (such as management perceptions of risk) to a common scale that allows for comparison. In short, the AHP is the best technique when there is a mix of data inputs to the decision.

GENERAL SEQUENCE OF EVENTS

Applying the AHP process to decision making generally consists of five steps. These are: Problem Statement, Problem Decomposition, Comparative Judgments, Comparative Evaluations and Synthesis of Priorities. These phrases are taken directly from Dr. Saaty's work.[85] For the most part, these steps correspond to: defining the purpose of the analysis; defining the decision criteria; scoring or weighting the criteria; scoring the alternatives; and lastly, calculating the results. We have added a final last step, of actually making the decision. These steps are described in detail.

1. Define the purpose (problem statement)

Like all decision methods, the first step is to clearly define the problem or issue to be resolved. In the AHP, this problem or issue must be reduced to a single sentence that captures the essence of what we are trying to achieve. Statements might be:

▶ Maximize satisfaction with new car purchase

▶ Minimize construction costs

▶ Ensure maximum customer satisfaction

▶ Select the best computer system

▶ Purchase the most economic machine

▶ Identify the priorities for a community's social services program

Part of arriving at this problem statement involves identifying the various alternatives. Remember, by the time the AHP is being used, the team has been at work on the problem for some time. This means the fundamentals of the problem, and the decision to be made, are already well understood. The AHP is used to tap into this understanding to reach the best decision possible.

For the purpose of explaining the technique, we will use the same decision situation discussed with the criteria rating technique – which technology to acquire. In this case, we could phrase the problem statement as *"Which computer system best meets the needs of our company?"*

---

85. ibid

2. Identify the criteria (problem decomposition)

The single problem statement is then broken down into its constituent parts. In this case, these parts define what we mean by *"best meets the needs of our company."* A number of approaches can be used to help teams identify these constituent parts, including some of the group process tools already discussed. For example, the team could use a brainstorming session to elicit a comprehensive set of ideas, combined with affinity diagramming to organize these ideas into meaningful categories.

Let's assume we managed to identify five basic components of "best meets the needs of our company." These are:

▶ Low Cost

▶ Simple Technology

▶ Fast Implementation Time

▶ End User Satisfaction

▶ Extent of Existing System Modification

This is the same set of criteria used with the criteria rating matrix. The AHP can further breakdown each of these criteria into additional levels. This process can be repeated any number of times, producing a very complex set of evaluative criteria existing on many levels.

The appropriate level of detail to be used in analyzing the problem is best left up to the team. As one would expect, the more complex the decision, the more detailed the analytical hierarchy. As in most things, teams are advised to try and keep the analysis as simple and practical as possible, given the nature of the particular decision. In other words, don't seek complexity in the decision-making process. But also don't simplify to the point where important considerations are missing.

It is important for teams to remember that, no matter what level of detail is decided upon, the analysis must be comprehensive. The components of the problem statement that make up the criteria must take into account all the important considerations. Comprehensiveness, then, involves carefully considering the breadth or scope of the criteria used, and ensuring that all major factors are taken into account. When it comes to details, the concern is the relative depth of the analysis, which depends on the desires of the team and the nature of the decision to be made.

Exhibit 299: Problem Decomposition – Establishing the Criteria

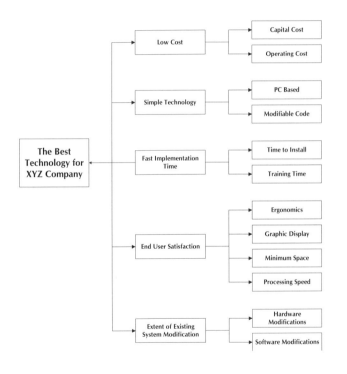

If Exhibit 299: Problem Decomposition – Establishing the Criteria reminds you of a tree diagram, you're right – that's

exactly what this is. Recall that tree diagrams are the best way to represent a hierarchy and that's exactly what we are creating here – an analytical hierarchy.

3. Weight the criteria (comparative judgments)

At this point, we have identified and organized our evaluation criteria in much the same way as we did for the criteria-ranking process. It is at this point – where we determine the relative importance of each of the criteria – that things take a dramatically different turn. The criteria-rating technique used some form of voting procedure to establish the weights. The AHP will use a mix of comparative judgments and ratings to establish the weights of each criterion.

In conducting the process, the criteria at the highest end of the hierarchy is ranked and rated first. When all the criteria at this level are completed, the next level of the hierarchy is ranked and rated, and so on down the hierarchy or tree diagram until the process has been completed for all the criteria in the hierarchy.

This process of comparisons can best be represented in a matrix. In our example, with five criteria, the matrix would look like the one in Table 300: Generic AHP Matrix. The criteria are presented in both the horizontal and vertical axis of the matrix.

Using the first part of this matrix, each criterion is compared with every other criterion using a nine-point scale. The diagonal line is always equal to 1 since each criterion is equal to itself. The score, by convention, is used to examine the element in the row relative to the element in the column.

▶ **If the row element is more important than the column element,** the number will be somewhere between 1 and 9 depending on the judgment of the individual or team doing the evaluations.

▶ **If the row element is less important than the column element,** the inverse of the scoring weight is used — that is, 1 over the rating. This produces scores such as 1/5 or 1/9.

Table 300: Generic AHP Matrix

		Matrix for Comparisons and Ratings					Matrix for Normalizing Scores					Matrix for Final Calculation of Results	
		#	#	#	#	#	#	#	#	#	#		
												Total	Total; (%)
#		1											
#			1										
#				1									
#					1								
#						1							
	Totals						1	1	1	1	1		100

Table 301: AHP Nine-Point Rating Scale

Rating	Description
9	Extreme
8	
7	Very Strong
6	
5	Strong
4	
3	Moderate
2	
1	Equal

Shaded cells are those where the values are predetermined once the ranking and ratings are completed for the other cells. They will be the inverse of the corresponding cell above the diagonal of 'ones.'

This is easier to see when applying the matrix to our actual example. The Table 302: Weighting the First-Level Criteria presents the complete AHP matrix for our five decision criteria at the highest level of the hierarchy. Now it becomes easier to see why we began our matrix with a 1 in the intersection point of identical criteria – the same criteria have the same importance.

When applying the scale to the criteria, we work across in rows. In the example, we ask ourselves: "How much more important is End User Satisfaction (row item) over Low Cost (column item)." Let's assume our conclusion was that End User Satisfaction is much more important than Low Cost. In fact, the difference is extreme so we would place a 9 at the intersection point, where End User Satisfaction is the row item and Low Cost is the column item. This automatically determines what the value will be in the corresponding intersection point, where Low Cost is the row element and End User Satisfaction is in the column. It will be the reciprocal of 9 or 1/9.

This process of pair-wise comparisons continues until all elements of the matrix are completed. Once the initial scoring matrix is completed, four basic calculations are performed.

▲ **The scores for each column are totaled.** In the example, the total score for Low Cost is 21, Simple Technology is 16.2, Fast Implementation Time 9.0, End User Satisfaction 1.62, and Current System Integration is 7.4.

▲ **The scores in the first matrix are normalized in the second.** The scores in the second matrix are simply the scores in the first matrix, divided by their respective column total calculated in the initial matrix. For example, the first value in the initial matrix is 1 – the intersection of Low Cost with itself. In the second matrix, 1 is divided by the column total 21 to yield a score of 1/21 or approximately 0.05. Likewise, the intersection of Low Cost (row) with Simple Technology (column) is 1/5 which, divided by its column total of 16.2, yields a score in the second matrix of 0.01 (see Exhibit 302: Weighting the First-Level Criteria).

▲ **The normalized scores in each row of the second matrix are then added together to produce a row total.** These row totals are the absolute weights associated with each decision criteria. In our example, these totals are 0.27 for Low Cost, 0.51 for Simple Technology, 0.48 for Fast

Implementation Time, 2.83 for End User Satisfaction and, finally, 0.92 for Current System Integration.

▲ **These row totals are then totaled and normalized.** In the example, the total of all these scores is 5.0. This total is then used to normalize the weights in the Percentage column. Each row total is divided by the grand total (in this case 5.0) to produce a final normalized score or percentage weight for each of the criteria.

At this point, we have a set of ratio-scaled weightings for the first-level criteria in our analytical hierarchy. If we only had one level in our hierarchy, we could use these weights to evaluate the decision alternatives. However, such is not the case. We also have a secondary set of criteria beneath the first.

Table 302: Weighting the First-Level Criteria

	Score (Initial Matrix)					Normalized Scores (Second Matrix)					Totals	Percentage
	Low Cost	Simple Tech.	Fast Implement-ation Time	End User Satisfaction	Current System Integration	Low Cost	Simple Tech-nology	Fast Implement-ation time	End User Satisfact-ion	Current System Integration		
Low Cost	1	1/5	1	1/9	1/5	0.05	0.01	0.11	0.07	0.03	0.27	5.33%
Simple Technology	5	1	1	1/9	1/5	0.24	0.06	0.11	0.07	0.03	0.51	10.13%
Fast Implementation Time	1	1	1	1/5	1	0.05	0.06	0.11	0.12	0.14	0.48	9.58%
End User Satisfaction	9	9	5	1	5	0.43	0.56	0.56	0.62	0.68	2.83	56.64%
Current System Integration	5	5	1	1/5	1	0.24	0.31	0.11	0.12	0.14	0.92	18.33%
Totals	21.00	16.20	9.00	1.62	7.40	1.00	1.00	1.00	1.00	1.00	5.00	100.00%

Table 303: Evaluating the Second-Level Criteria Using Generic AHP Matrices

Low Cost Criteria	Capital Cost	Operating Cost		Capital Cost	Operating Cost		Totals	Percentage
Capital Cost	1	1/3		0.25	0.25		0.50	25.00%
Operating Cost	3	1		0.75	0.75		1.50	75.00%
Totals	4.00	1.33		1.00	1.00		2.00	100.00%

Simple Technology	PC Based	Modifiable Code		PC Based	Modifiable Code		Totals	Percentage
PC Based	1	9		0.90	0.90		1.80	90.00%
Modifiable Code	1/9	1		0.10	0.10		0.20	10.00%
Totals	1.11	10.00		1.00	1.00		2.00	100.00%

Fast Implementation Time	Time to Install	Training Time		Time to Install	Training Time		Totals	Percentage
Time to Install	1	3		0.75	0.75		1.50	75.00%
Training Time	1/3	1		0.25	0.25		0.50	25.00%
Totals	1.33	4.00		1.00	1.00		2.00	100.00%

End User Satisfaction	Ergonomics	Graphic Display	Minimum Space	Processing Speed		Ergonomics	Graphic Display	Minimum Space	Processing Speed		Totals	Percentage
Ergonomics	1	1/3	5	1/5		0.11	0.07	0.23	0.12		0.53	13.30%
Graphic Display	3	1	7	1/3		0.33	0.22	0.32	0.20		1.07	26.76%
Minimum Space	1/5	1/7	1	1/9		0.02	0.03	0.05	0.07		0.17	4.17%
Processing Speed	5	3	9	1		0.54	0.67	0.41	0.61		2.23	55.77%
Totals	9.20	4.48	22.00	1.64		1.00	1.00	1.00	1.00		4.00	100.00%

Extent of Existing System Modification	Hardware	Software		Hardware	Software		Totals	Percentage
Hardware	1	1/5		0.17	0.17		0.33	16.67%
Software	5	1		0.83	0.83		1.67	83.33%
Totals	6.00	1.20		1.00	1.00		2.00	100.00%

To weight these criteria, we repeat the process for the second-level criteria, calculating the paired comparisons for criteria within each primary criteria grouping. For example, under Low Cost we had two secondary-level criteria: Capital and Operating. These two items are compared in the same way as the original five first-level criteria were compared, using the same method of calculations. The complete set of AHP matrices for all the second-level criteria is shown Table 303: Evaluating the Second-Level Criteria Using Generic AHP Matrices.

The scores obtained for these secondary criteria are called "local" scores because they are local to their respective primary-level criteria. For example, Capital Cost constitutes 25 percent of the importance within the Low Cost category, while Operating Cost makes up the remaining 75 percent. To determine the global weights – that is, how important these scores are relative to all the other second-level criteria – we first take the weight determined for the primary-level criteria (Low Cost). We multiply this by the local scores recorded for the second-level criteria associated with it, Capital Cost and Operating Cost. Therefore, the global scores are:

▶ Capital Cost = (25%) × Low Cost (5.33%) = 1.33%

▶ Operating Cost =(75%) × Low Cost (5.33%) = 3.99%

Therefore, in reaching a decision about which alternative technology to adopt, Capital Cost carries exactly 1.33 percent of the weight. Operating cost is three times as important at 3.99 percent. The complete set of decision criteria with all weights is presented in the Table 304: Evaluation Weightings of Criteria. For each second-level criteria, the first percentage provided is the local weight derived from the previous calculations. The second number is the global percentage used to actually weight decision alternatives.

4. Evaluate the options (comparative evaluations)

The next step is actually evaluating the various alternatives. The process used is similar to that used to establish the weightings for the various criteria. The same 9-point scale is used with the same method of comparison. But instead of doing a pair-wise comparison of criteria, we conduct a pair-wise comparison of the alternatives relative to each of the criteria. This, like the process of establishing criteria weights, can be quite complex and time consuming.

In our example, we have 12 criteria against which to compare our decision alternatives. We also have five decision alternatives: systems provided by Systech, Data Ware, Datamation,

Table 304: Evaluation Weightings of Criteria

Primary Level	Secondary Level	Local Level	Global Level
Low Cost 5.33%	Capital Cost	25.00%	1.33%
	Operating Cost	75.00%	4.00%
	Sub-total	100.00%	5.33%
Simple Technology 10.13%	PC Based	90.00%	9.12%
	Modifiable Code	10.00%	1.01%
	Sub-total	100.00%	10.13%
Fast Implementation Time 9.58%	Time to Install	75.00%	7.18%
	Training Time	25.00%	2.39%
	Sub-total	100.00%	9.58%
End User Satisfaction 56.64%	Ergonomics	13.30%	7.53%
	Graphic Display	26.76%	15.16%
	Minimum Space	4.17%	2.36%
	Processing Speed	55.77%	31.59%
	Sub-total	100.00%	56.64%
Current System Integration 18.33%	Hardware Modifications	16.67%	3.05%
	Software Modifications	83.33%	15.27%
	Sub-total	100.00%	18.33%
Totals		100.00%	100.00%

SimStat and Cyber Tech. This means we will need to produce 12, five-by-five AHP matrices, one for each criterion. For example, our first criterion was Operating Cost. We need to conduct a pair-wise comparison of every alternative against every other alternative for this specific criteria. Then we conduct a pair-wise comparison of every alternative against every other alternative against the next criteria, Capital Cost. We continue until pair-wise comparisons have been conducted across all alternatives for every criteria.

So what does all this look like? Well, the next two pages present the complete set of 12, five-by-five AHP matrices. Don't panic! It is not as bad as it looks. Okay, maybe it is. But remember, AHP isn't usually used in team settings, at least not without some technology to help things along. For the most part, participants will have time in their own working environments to evaluate the alternatives, with a specific group or individual assigned the task of computing results. To be frank, this is also a pretty complex example. If you can figure your way through this one, you can probably handle just about anything that comes your way in the real world of performance improvement. The amount of work involved in pair-wise comparisons goes up exponentially with the number of alternatives or criteria involved. Finally, while there is a lot of number

Exhibit 305: Pairwise Comparisons of Decision Alternatives

Capital Cost	SysTech	Data Ware	DataMation	SimStat	Cyber Tech		SysTech	Data Ware	DataMation	SimStat	Cyber Tech		Totals	Percentage
SysTech	1	5	3	5	7		0.53	0.35	0.62	0.49	0.37		2.36	47.28%
Data Ware	1/5	1	1/3	1/5	3		0.11	0.07	0.07	0.02	0.16		0.42	8.46%
DataMation	1/3	3	1	3	7		0.18	0.21	0.21	0.29	0.37		1.26	25.15%
SimStat	1/5	5	1/3	1	1		0.11	0.35	0.07	0.10	0.05		0.68	13.51%
Cyber Tech	1/7	1/3	1/7	1	1		0.08	0.02	0.03	0.10	0.05		0.28	5.60%
Totals	1.88	14.33	4.81	10.20	19.00		1.00	1.00	1.00	1.00	1.00		5.00	100.00%

Operating Cost	SysTech	Data Ware	DataMation	SimStat	Cyber Tech		SysTech	Data Ware	DataMation	SimStat	Cyber Tech		Totals	Percentage
SysTech	1	1	1/3	3	3		0.18	0.14	0.15	0.27	0.32		1.06	21.23%
Data Ware	1	1	1/3	1	1		0.18	0.14	0.15	0.09	0.11		0.67	13.31%
DataMation	3	3	1	3	4		0.53	0.43	0.44	0.27	0.43		2.10	42.07%
SimStat	1/3	1	1/3	1	1/3		0.06	0.14	0.15	0.09	0.04		0.48	9.53%
Cyber Tech	1/3	1	1/4	3	1		0.06	0.14	0.11	0.27	0.11		0.69	13.85%
Totals	5.67	7.00	2.25	11.00	9.33		1.00	1.00	1.00	1.00	1.00		5.00	100.00%

PC Based	SysTech	Data Ware	DataMation	SimStat	Cyber Tech		SysTech	Data Ware	DataMation	SimStat	Cyber Tech		Totals	Percentage
SysTech	1	1	3	1	1		0.23	0.23	0.23	0.23	0.23		1.15	23.08%
Data Ware	1	1	3	1	1		0.23	0.23	0.23	0.23	0.23		1.15	23.08%
DataMation	1/3	1/3	1	1/3	1/3		0.08	0.08	0.08	0.08	0.08		0.38	7.69%
SimStat	1	1	3	1	1		0.23	0.23	0.23	0.23	0.23		1.15	23.08%
Cyber Tech	1	1	3	1	1		0.23	0.23	0.23	0.23	0.23		1.15	23.08%
Totals	4.33	4.33	13.00	4.33	4.33		1.00	1.00	1.00	1.00	1.00		5.00	100.00%

Modifiable Code	SysTech	Data Ware	DataMation	SimStat	Cyber Tech		SysTech	Data Ware	DataMation	SimStat	Cyber Tech		Totals	Percentage
SysTech	1	5	3	3	1		0.35	0.26	0.36	0.37	0.35		1.69	33.73%
Data Ware	1/5	1	1/3	1/5	1/5		0.07	0.05	0.04	0.02	0.07		0.26	5.13%
DataMation	1/3	3	1	1	1/3		0.12	0.16	0.12	0.12	0.12		0.63	12.65%
SimStat	1/3	5	1	1	1/3		0.12	0.26	0.12	0.12	0.12		0.74	14.75%
Cyber Tech	1	5	3	3	1		0.35	0.26	0.36	0.37	0.35		1.69	33.73%
Totals	2.87	19.00	8.33	8.20	2.87		1.00	1.00	1.00	1.00	1.00		5.00	100.00%

Time to Install	SysTech	Data Ware	DataMation	SimStat	Cyber Tech		SysTech	Data Ware	DataMation	SimStat	Cyber Tech		Totals	Percentage
SysTech	1	1/2	1/3	1/3	1/5		0.07	0.04	0.05	0.15	0.04		0.35	7.02%
Data Ware	2	1	1	1/4	1/5		0.14	0.09	0.14	0.12	0.04		0.52	10.37%
DataMation	3	1	1	1/4	1		0.21	0.09	0.14	0.12	0.19		0.74	14.76%
SimStat	3	4	4	1	3		0.21	0.35	0.55	0.46	0.56		2.12	42.49%
Cyber Tech	5	5	1	1/3	1		0.36	0.43	0.14	0.15	0.19		1.27	25.35%
Totals	14.00	11.50	7.33	2.17	5.40		1.00	1.00	1.00	1.00	1.00		5.00	100.00%

Training Time	SysTech	Data Ware	DataMation	SimStat	Cyber Tech		SysTech	Data Ware	DataMation	SimStat	Cyber Tech		Totals	Percentage
SysTech	1	1/5	1	1/9	2		0.06	0.06	0.11	0.02	0.29		0.54	10.74%
Data Ware	5	1	1	3	1		0.30	0.28	0.11	0.62	0.14		1.46	29.27%
DataMation	1	1	1	1/5	1		0.06	0.28	0.11	0.04	0.14		0.64	12.78%
SimStat	9	1/3	5	1	2		0.55	0.09	0.56	0.21	0.29		1.69	33.78%
Cyber Tech	1/2	1	1	1/2	1		0.03	0.28	0.11	0.10	0.14		0.67	13.42%
Totals	16.50	3.53	9.00	4.81	7.00		1.00	1.00	1.00	1.00	1.00		5.00	100.00%

Exhibit 306: Pairwise Comparisons of Decision Alternatives (continued)

Ergonomics	SysTech	Data Ware	DataMation	SimStat	Cyber Tech	SysTech	Data Ware	DataMation	SimStat	Cyber Tech	Totals	Percentage
SysTech	1	1/3	3	1/5	1	0.10	0.03	0.25	0.07	0.26	0.71	14.22%
Data Ware	3	1	3	1/7	1/3	0.29	0.09	0.25	0.05	0.09	0.77	15.33%
DataMation	1/3	1/3	1	1/3	1/2	0.03	0.03	0.08	0.12	0.13	0.40	7.98%
SimStat	5	7	3	1	1	0.48	0.60	0.25	0.37	0.26	1.97	39.37%
Cyber Tech	1	3	2	1	1	0.10	0.26	0.17	0.37	0.26	1.16	23.10%
Totals	10.33	11.67	12.00	2.68	3.83	1.00	1.00	1.00	1.00	1.00	5.00	100.00%

Graphic Display	SysTech	Data Ware	DataMation	SimStat	Cyber Tech	SysTech	Data Ware	DataMation	SimStat	Cyber Tech	Totals	Percentage
SysTech	1	1/5	1	1/9	1/7	0.04	0.01	0.05	0.07	0.03	0.21	4.12%
Data Ware	5	1	1	1/9	1/5	0.22	0.06	0.05	0.07	0.04	0.44	8.84%
DataMation	1	1	1	1/7	1/9	0.04	0.06	0.05	0.08	0.02	0.27	5.34%
SimStat	9	9	7	1	3	0.39	0.56	0.37	0.59	0.67	2.58	51.55%
Cyber Tech	7	5	9	1/3	1	0.30	0.31	0.47	0.20	0.22	1.51	30.15%
Totals	23.00	16.20	19.00	1.70	4.45	1.00	1.00	1.00	1.00	1.00	5.00	100.00%

Mininum Space	SysTech	Data Ware	DataMation	SimStat	Cyber Tech	SysTech	Data Ware	DataMation	SimStat	Cyber Tech	Totals	Percentage
SysTech	1	1	1	1/3	3	0.16	0.16	0.16	0.15	0.20	0.83	16.50%
Data Ware	1	1	1	1/3	3	0.16	0.16	0.16	0.15	0.20	0.83	16.50%
DataMation	1	1	1	1/3	3	0.16	0.16	0.16	0.15	0.20	0.83	16.50%
SimStat	3	3	3	1	5	0.47	0.47	0.47	0.45	0.33	2.21	44.18%
Cyber Tech	1/3	1/3	1/3	1/5	1	0.05	0.05	0.05	0.09	0.07	0.32	6.31%
Totals	6.33	6.33	6.33	2.20	15.00	1.00	1.00	1.00	1.00	1.00	5.00	100.00%

Processing Speed	SysTech	Data Ware	DataMation	SimStat	Cyber Tech	SysTech	Data Ware	DataMation	SimStat	Cyber Tech	Totals	Percentage
SysTech	1	1	5	3	3	0.35	0.27	0.45	0.32	0.35	1.75	35.01%
Data Ware	1	1	1	3	3	0.35	0.27	0.09	0.32	0.35	1.39	27.74%
DataMation	1/5	1	1	1	1	0.07	0.27	0.09	0.04	0.12	0.59	11.74%
SimStat	1/3	1/3	3	1	1/2	0.12	0.09	0.27	0.11	0.06	0.65	12.92%
Cyber Tech	1/3	1/3	1	2	1	0.12	0.09	0.09	0.21	0.12	0.63	12.60%
Totals	2.87	3.67	11.00	9.33	8.50	1.00	1.00	1.00	1.00	1.00	5.00	100.00%

Hardware Modifications	SysTech	Data Ware	DataMation	SimStat	Cyber Tech	SysTech	Data Ware	DataMation	SimStat	Cyber Tech	Totals	Percentage
SysTech	1	1/2	1/3	1	1/7	0.07	0.06	0.06	0.10	0.08	0.36	7.27%
Data Ware	2	1	1	1	1/5	0.14	0.12	0.17	0.10	0.11	0.64	12.77%
DataMation	3	1	1	2	1/3	0.21	0.12	0.17	0.20	0.18	0.88	17.62%
SimStat	1	1	1/2	1	1/5	0.07	0.12	0.09	0.10	0.11	0.48	9.63%
Cyber Tech	7	5	3	5	1	0.50	0.59	0.51	0.50	0.53	2.64	52.71%
Totals	14.00	8.50	5.83	10.00	1.88	1.00	1.00	1.00	1.00	1.00	5.00	100.00%

Software Modifications	SysTech	Data Ware	DataMation	SimStat	Cyber Tech	SysTech	Data Ware	DataMation	SimStat	Cyber Tech	Totals	Percentage
SysTech	1	3	2	2	3	0.38	0.33	0.33	0.41	0.38	1.83	36.61%
Data Ware	1/3	1	1	1/3	1	0.13	0.11	0.17	0.07	0.13	0.60	11.93%
DataMation	1/2	1	1	1	1	0.19	0.11	0.17	0.21	0.13	0.80	15.94%
SimStat	1/2	3	1	1	2	0.19	0.33	0.17	0.21	0.25	1.14	22.89%
Cyber Tech	1/3	1	1	1/2	1	0.13	0.11	0.17	0.10	0.13	0.63	12.62%
Totals	2.67	9.00	6.00	4.83	8.00	1.00	1.00	1.00	1.00	1.00	5.00	100.00%

crunching going on here, a spreadsheet program and a half-hour of time are all the resources needed to ease the computational load.

5. Calculate the results (synthesis of priorities)

The next step is to combine the results of steps 3 and 4 in reaching some final conclusions. Saaty called this "synthesizing the priorities." Step 3 calculated the overall or global importance for every criterion. Step 4 calculated the relative performance of all the decision alternatives for each alternative. Step 5 involves simply multiplying the results – adjusting how each decision alternative scored in each criterion based on the importance of that criterion. This is done the same way as the multiplication of weights and ratings in the criteria rating matrix. The calculations for our technology selection example are presented in Exhibit 307: Calculating the Results.

The format of the analytical hierarchy matrix is also the same as that used in the criteria rating technique. Criteria are presented in rows, along with their associated weights. These weights are used to adjust the evaluative scores obtained through the pair-wise comparisons of decision alternatives. The results for each decision alternative are then summed

down the column to produce a percentage weight for the alternative.

A key product of all this effort is the nature of the numbers produced. The result is a set of normalized ratio-scaled weights for each decision alternative. Ratio-scaled data, remember, is the highest order of data. Rather than being able to say that one thing simply ranks or rates higher than another, we can say by how much more it does so. In fact, we can even make observations based on evaluations or criteria used, for example, that the SimStat product is more than twice as good as the Datamation alternative for our company. Likewise, we can evaluate other ratios. How much better is SimStat over SysTech? Because the data we have produced is ratio-scaled, we can calculate ratio differences. In this case, they are:

▶ Percentage Difference =((SimStat-SysTech)/SysTech)

▶ Percentage Difference =((26.37-23.64)/23.64)

▶ Percentage Difference = 11.5 percent

So, given the criteria used, the SimStat alternative represents a better than 10 percent improvement over SysTech. This kind of data assists the decision-making process. It is one thing to

Table 307: Calculating the Results

Primary Level Criteria	Secondary Level Criteria	Global Weights	SysTech		Data Ware		DataMation		SimStat		Cyber Tech	
Low Cost	Capital Cost	1.33%	47.28%	0.63%	8.46%	0.11%	25.15%	0.34%	13.51%	0.18%	5.60%	0.07%
	Operating Cost	4.00%	21.23%	0.85%	13.31%	0.53%	42.07%	1.68%	9.53%	0.38%	13.85%	0.55%
Simple Technology	PC Based	9.12%	23.08%	2.10%	23.08%	2.10%	7.69%	0.70%	23.08%	2.10%	23.08%	2.10%
	Modifiable Code	1.01%	33.73%	0.34%	5.13%	0.05%	12.65%	0.13%	14.75%	0.15%	33.73%	0.34%
Fast Implementation time	Time to Install	7.18%	7.02%	0.50%	10.37%	0.75%	14.76%	1.06%	42.49%	3.05%	25.35%	1.82%
	Training Time	2.39%	10.74%	0.26%	29.27%	0.70%	12.78%	0.31%	33.78%	0.81%	13.42%	0.32%
End User Satisfaction	Ergonomics	7.53%	14.22%	1.07%	15.33%	1.15%	7.98%	0.60%	39.37%	2.97%	23.10%	1.74%
	Graphic Display	15.16%	4.12%	0.62%	8.84%	1.34%	5.34%	0.81%	51.55%	7.81%	30.15%	4.57%
	Minimum Space	2.36%	16.50%	0.39%	16.50%	0.39%	16.50%	0.39%	44.18%	1.04%	6.31%	0.15%
	Processing Speed	31.59%	35.01%	11.06%	27.74%	8.76%	11.74%	3.71%	12.92%	4.08%	12.60%	3.98%
Current System Integration	Hardware Modifications	3.05%	7.27%	0.22%	12.77%	0.39%	17.62%	0.54%	9.63%	0.29%	52.71%	1.61%
	Software Modifications	15.27%	36.61%	5.59%	11.93%	1.82%	15.94%	2.43%	22.89%	3.50%	12.62%	1.93%
Total		100.00%	23.64%		18.10%		12.69%		26.37%		19.19%	

know one alternative is better than another. It is a whole different thing to know how much better.

6. Make the decision

The last step is to actually make the decision. Groups are bound by the results of the analysis, but should take the results as a set of facts to be discussed. Discussion can then be based on the criteria used, the resultant weightings and scorings. In short, the discussion should focus on the components of the analysis and not the results, per se. This is important because it helps keep the discussion exactly where it should be – on why things turned out the way they did, not on defending positions. Most people have their personal preferences for one alternative or another. The process of decision making can often turn into a process of people defending their positions instead of analyzing the logic behind them. The use of AHP, especially when the stakes (and often personal emotions) are high, helps remove this defensiveness and keep team members on track.

Nevertheless, in this case, given the criteria established by the group and the preferences gathered, the best alternative is Sim-Stat, which is at least 10 percent better than its nearest rival.

SPECIAL SITUATIONS

The example provided has focused on the application of the analytical hierarchy process in situations where human judgments were used throughout. However, a big advantage to AHP is its ability to handle a diversity of data or measurement types, and convert them all to a common and comparable scale. This allows for criteria as diverse as cost (measured in dollars) and physical appearance (measured in the evaluative impressions of a panel of judges) to be used alongside one another. This is because AHP converts these two sets of measures into a common ratio scale.

Handling Diverse Measures of Performance

To see how the analytical hierarchy process works in comparing diverse measurements, let's take an example of evaluating four alternative designs (A, B, C, D) for a new software product. The critical decision is which design to go with. The performance criteria are:

▶ Revenue (measured in dollars)

▶ Cost (measured in dollars)

▶ Simplicity (evaluated on a seven-point scale)

▶ Speed (measured in seconds of response time)

To understand how AHP can handle these diverse kinds of measures, we need to first reflect on the type of numbers we get when the whole process is finished. Because the data is normalized at every stage of the process, the final result is always a set of numbers adding to 100 percent. Once this is understood, converting different types of scales becomes easy. All we have to do is convert everything to a distributional percentage – that is, a set of numbers totalling 100 percent for each of the criteria. Let's look at each set of criteria:

▲ **Revenue.** Revenue is a result of measurements or counts where the more there is, the better. Conversion to a distributional percentage is straightforward. The revenue associated with each strategy is totaled and this total is divided into the amounts associated with each strategy. This conversion is presented in Table 308: Converting Measurements (More is Better) to a Distributional Percentage.

In the example, the first alternative design has a potential revenue stream of $100 million dollars compared with $130 million for design B and so on. The total revenue for all four alternatives equals $390 million. This $390 million, divided into the $100 million revenue stream for

Table 308: Converting Measurements (More is Better) to a Distributional Percentage

| Revenue (millions) | Design Alternative | | | | |
	A	B	C	D	Totals
Est. Value	$100	$130	$70	$90	$390
Normalized	0.256	0.333	0.180	0.231	1.000

design A, equals the 0.256 presented in the 'Normalized' row of the table for this design alternative. This calculation is done for each of the design alternatives, producing the set of normalized values presented in the table.

▲ **Costs.** Like revenue, costs are data resulting from a measurement or count. But with costs, the situation is that the less there is, the better. To adjust our calculations for this situation, the inverse of the cost (the cost divided into 1.0) is calculated first. These inverse values are used to calculate normalized values. These calculations are presented in Table 309: Converting Measurements (Less is Better) to a Distributional Percentage. The normalized results are consistent with the 'smaller the better' nature of this criterion. Notice that the lowest-cost design alternative in this case (Alternative C) has the highest normalized value of 0.339.

Table 309: Converting Measurements (Less is Better) to a Distributional Percentage

Costs (millions)	Design Alternative				Totals
	A	B	C	D	
Est. Value	$70	$100	$50	$65	$285
Inverse	0.014	0.010	0.020	0.015	0.059
Normalized	0.237	0.169	0.339	0.254	1.000

▲ **Simplicity.** The simplicity of the various designs was evaluated through human judgment, rather than through a measurement. Nevertheless, these evaluations can be treated like any measured value and converted into a normalized priority rating – a distributional percentage. In this case, the scale used by the experts was a nine-point scale, with 9 being extremely simple and 1 being extremely difficult. The ratings for each of the design alternatives and the normalized conversions are presented in Table 310: Converting Rating Judgments to a Distributional Percentage.

Note here as well that the scale reflected a 'more is better' direction where greater simplicity was associated with a higher number. Had the scale been reversed or simplicity been undesirable, the inverse of the ratings would first be

Table 310: Converting Rating Judgments to a Distributional Percentage

Ratings (9 Point Scale)	Design Alternative				Totals
	A	B	C	D	
Est. Value	8	5	7	5	25
Normalized	0.32	0.2	0.28	0.2	1.000

calculated (as was the case with costs), and then the distributional percentage calculated on these values.

▲ **Speed.** With speed, we go back to a measured value, although not financial as was the case with costs and revenues. Speed is measured in seconds of response time. So, the greater the time, the worse the performance of the design since faster response time is better. This is a "fewer the better" situation requiring the calculation of inverses prior to normalizing the values. These are presented in Table 311: Converting Physical Measurements (Speed) to Normalized Values.

With the values for the four alternatives all converted to a normalized scale, we can proceed with development of the analytical hierarchy. From here, the weights of the four criteria must be established and then the alternatives evaluated. To establish

Table 311: Converting Physical Measurements (Speed) to Normalized Values

Time (seconds)	Design Alternative				
	A	**B**	**C**	**D**	**Totals**
Est. Value	9	5	12	11	37
Inverse	0.111	0.200	0.083	0.091	0.485
Normalized	0.229	0.412	0.172	0.187	1.000

the relative importance of the criteria, a pair-wise evaluation is performed within a typical AHP matrix. The results are presented in Table 312: Evaluating the Importance of the Criteria.

As the table details, revenues are deemed to be most important, accounting for roughly 0.555 or 55.5 percent of the importance represented by all criteria. Speed is evaluated to be least important, with about six percent of the importance across criteria.

With criteria weightings and local priorities calculated, we can combine the work into a single matrix and conduct the evaluation. The resulting AHP table is presented in Table 313: Resulting AHP Table.

The table presents the evaluation along with all the data that went into it. This includes the actual measurements and ratings for each alternative within each criteria (upper portion of each cell). Also presented are the local priorities (how each alternative fared within the criteria, in the middle of each cell), as well as the global priority scores (the results of multiplying the global importance weights for each criteria by the local priority weights for each alternative, in the lower portion of each cell). These global priority scores are then summed under each alternative to create the overall total priority for each alternative.

In this example, the best alternative would appear to be B with an overall score of 0.267 or 26.7 percent, if you prefer. But the scoring is very tight. Alternative A is a close second with a score or priority weight of 25.3 percent. This serves to illustrate some of the advantages of using AHP. First, by converting the various types of data (revenues, costs, ratings, time measured in seconds) to a common normalized scale, it really does allow decision makers to compare apples with oranges. The relative importance of a five-second response time can be compared with the relative importance of a nine-second response time, or with the relative importance of a $100 million dollar development cost. Also, by visually presenting the concluding analysis with all the data, decision makers can focus on and examine the assumptions and weightings that went in to the analysis. This brings focus to where it belongs – on the data and issues rather than on pre-defined positions and agendas.

Table 312: Evaluating the Importance of the Criteria

	Relatives Judgment (Raw Scores)				Normalized Judgment Scores				Row Total	Normal-ized Row Total
	Revenues	Cost	Simplicity	Speed	Revenues	Cost	Simplicity	Speed		
Revenues	1	3	5	7	0.597	0.643	0.543	0.438	2.220	0.555
Cost	1/3	1	3	3	0.199	0.214	0.326	0.188	0.927	0.232
Simplicity	1/5	1/3	1	5	0.119	0.071	0.109	0.313	0.612	0.153
Speed	1/7	1/3	1/5	1	0.085	0.071	0.022	0.063	0.241	0.060
Totals	1 2/3	4 2/3	9 1/5	16	1.000	1.000	1.000	1.000	4.000	1.000

Table 313: Resulting AHP Table

Criteria	Global Importance		Design A	Design B	Design C	Design D
Revenue	55.5%	$ millions	$100	$130	$70	$90
		local priority	0.256	0.333	0.18	0.231
		global priority	0.142	0.125	0.100	0.128
Cost	23.2%	$ millions	$70	$100	$50	$65
		local priority	0.237	0.169	0.339	0.254
		global priority	0.055	0.039	0.079	0.059
Simplicity	15.3%	rating	8	5	7	5
		local priority	0.32	0.2	0.28	0.2
		global priority	0.049	0.031	0.043	0.031
Speed	6.0%	seconds	9	5	12	11
		local priority	0.229	0.412	0.172	0.187
		global priority	0.007	0.012	0.005	0.005
Totals	100.0%	Overall Priority	0.253	0.267	0.226	0.223

SUMMARY: USING DECISION TOOLS

It would be fair to say that many of the decision-making methods described in this chapter have found far more application at the operating levels of organizations than at senior levels. There are likely many reasons for this, but I suspect that at the heart of the matter is a general reluctance to use the tools due to what might be called the "heroic" model of management.

The heroic model sees the manager as some form of white knight, ready to take on the evil black prince (otherwise known as an issue requiring a decision). The heroic manager's only weapons are superior judgment and decision-making skills. In the strong version of this model, the skills are innate – something the manager is born with and, therefore, cannot be taught under any circumstances.

Thus, the model becomes a self-serving justification for why the individual is a manager or leader and others are not. The higher up the hierarchy one goes, the more entrenched this idea becomes. Tied to this is the notion that what is important is not necessarily making good decisions, but simply making any decision.[86]

Using some form of decision-making 'tool' in the context of this model, then, could only be interpreted as an admission of managerial incompetence. After all, only incompetents would need some form of tool to help them along. In other words, real managers don't need decision tools.

Wrong. As we have seen, decision-making tools don't make decisions for people. They bring together the judgments of those with knowledge relevant to the issues or solutions being decided upon. They compel these individuals to be explicit about what has gone into their thinking and about the importance of these factors in their deliberations. (The more formal the tool, the greater the degree to which those involved must be explicit in how they arrived at their conclusions.) The tools, therefore, are really about collective wisdom and the sharing of information with others. There is certainly nothing incompetent about doing that. In fact, using these tools is the sign of a real leader, someone who has the ability to make the sound decisions rather than just any decision.

---

86. I have heard this repeated far too often in organizations. If the purpose is truly to make any decision rather than good decisions, why not hire a six-year-old to make them? It will cost the organization less and the decisions will get made quickly, far more quickly than if some actually gave some consideration to the various alternatives presented. The reason I suspect (and hope) is that we realize that making a good decision is more important than making any decision.

Management & Planning Tools: 10
From Intention to Implementation

Management and planning tools are designed to help teams deal with issues of implementation. They help define objectives and explore the means by which they will be accomplished. Improvement teams can analyze the process through visual mapping techniques and statistical analysis, develop alternative designs and decide upon which is the most practical. But sooner or later, product or process improvement teams must take actions to ensure the chosen alternative is actually implemented, in place and working. These tools are all about helping teams accomplish this implementation.

Discussion of management and planning tools also brings us full circle. Application of management and planning tools is not limited to the planning and implementation of the teams' improvement efforts. They can also be applied at the very beginning of the improvement effort, when the team is just beginning to plan and organize itself. Thus these tools can be used to help move the recommendations of the project team forward (near the end of the improvement project cycle) or the activities of the project team itself (at the beginning of the improvement project cycle).

THE TOOLS

The six tools discussed here each have their own application. However, all the tools are designed to help managers and teams deal with the problem of moving from the world of ideas to the world of substance – moving from intention to implementation. The six tools are:

▶ Force Field Analysis

▶ Responsibility Charting

Table 314: Summary of Management and Planning Tools

Management & Planning Tool	Purpose	Description
Force Field Analysis	Analyze the forces in an organization working to support or resist a change.	Organizes brainstorming data graphically, presenting a picture of the forces working for or against a change. Typically applied whenever a team needs to analyze the prospects for change and develop strategies to overcome barriers.
Responsibility Charting	Analyzes the relationship between what needs to be done and who should do it.	A matrix that relates resources, usually people or departments, to the tasks to be accomplished. Most often used by teams for planning the assignment of responsibilities during an improvement project.
GANTT Charts	Shows how time is deployed to various organizational or improvement project tasks.	Used by teams to analyze the time it will take to complete a project and examine the implications. GANTT uses a matrix to analyze the relationship between task and time, through the use of bars and basic symbols.
Program Evaluation & Review Technique (PERT)	A technique used to help teams assess the level of uncertainty surrounding single-point estimates.	PERT produces a 'likely' estimate of the parameter in question, but also compels the team to elicit high and low estimates for the parameter. Most often used in conjunction with GANTT charts to estimate the time required to complete tasks. PERT can be used to estimate any parameter where empirical data is scant.
Relationship Diagram	Used to analyze complex non-linear systems in a logical manner.	Maps out the various system components and then connects these, using arrows to highlight the causal relationships. Especially appropriate when analyzing a complex system and/or when there is a need to separate driving forces from effects.
Matrix Diagrams	Compares the relationship between two or more sets of information.	Different types of matrices can be used to compare two, three or four sets of data. A common coding scheme is used to weight the degree of relationship existing between the various information sets.

- ▶ GANTT Charting and Arrow Diagrams

- ▶ Program Evaluation & Review Technique (PERT)

- ▶ Relationship (Inter-relationship) Diagram

- ▶ Matrix Diagrams

These tools and their applications are described in Table 314: Summary of Management and Planning Tools.

FORCE FIELD ANALYSIS

Force field analysis is a tool designed to help teams identify and analyze the forces acting to support or resist a proposed change. It presents a graphical representation of these forces.

It is easy for an organization to charge a team with some noble task such as "fix the inventory system." But it is quite another matter to support the set of recommendations that come back. It is not unusual for teams to find their recommendations have only moderate or mixed support in the organization, despite the best efforts at creating the charter, scoping out the project and

ensuring involvement and representation of affected departments.

The originator of force field analysis, Dr. Kurt Lewin,[87] recognized that ability or inability of organizations to implement change goes beyond simple pronouncements such as "people resist change." In fact, in many instances, history demonstrates quite the opposite. Our world is one of constant change. So why do companies find it so difficult to move plans into action, to actually implement change? To help answer this question, Dr. Lewin proposed that the potential for change is better thought of as existing within a field of forces. Some forces support or drive the change while others resist, restraining the possibility of change.

If the forces supporting the change are greater than those opposing it, change will come about. The rate of change will be determined by the relative strength of the forces at work. A large number of forces supporting the change, operating against a small number of resisting forces, will see change

---

87. Dr. Kurt Lewin immigrated to the United States from Germany in the 1930's. A psychologist, he contributed to the fields of social and organizational psychology and was one of the early pioneers in addressing issues of organizational change and equilibrium.

occur rapidly. Where the forces are nearly in balance, the change will happen much more slowly, if at all.

Of course, the opposite condition also exists. At times, the forces resisting the change will be equal or greater in number and strength than the forces supporting the change. In this case, change will not come about or the organization may actually regress.

WHAT THE FORCE FIELD DIAGRAM LOOKS LIKE

The force field diagram is a simple way of representing these forces. It consists of a single vertical line representing the current position of the organization – where it stands today. This line is usually placed in the center of the diagram. The objective or change sought is represented as a statement, and is positioned at the extreme right side of the diagram. (See Exhibit 315: Basic Force Field Diagram).

Arrows representing the forces at work are then drawn as pushing against the vertical line. Arrows representing the forces supporting or driving the change are drawn as pushing the cur-

Exhibit 315: Basic Force Field Diagram

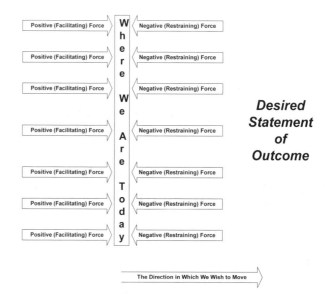

rent vertical line toward the objective – that is, toward the right. Those arrows representing the restraining forces are drawn on the right side of the vertical line, pushing the line (current position) away from the objective.

Each of the arrows is labeled with a descriptor of the force at work. Arrows may also be weighted as to their strength, by numbers placed on the diagram or by the size of the arrow drawn.

WHEN TO USE

Use force field analysis whenever you want to better understand the acceptability of proposed improvements within the organization. In other words, use the tool when you want to assess the prospects for proposed and desirable change. Specifically, use it:

▲ **Before a team begins working on a particular problem and wants to know which forces are supporting the team's efforts and which are working against.** Doing so can go a long way in helping teams better identify appropriate representation in the team, as well as significant issues that will have to be addressed during the project.

▲ **When the team is planning to implement a solution and needs to understand what forces within the organization are likely to work for and against the proposed changes.** Analysis of the forces working for and against different alternative solutions can become part of the decision criteria in selecting a specific option. Moreover, once

an alternative has been selected, analysis of forces can help smooth the path to implementation.

In short, force field analysis can be used whenever a team wishes to analyze the prospects for change, or as a preliminary step in determining what actions can be taken to improve the likelihood of change. Thus, the force field diagram can be used as an initial step in developing a plan for change, a strategy that will help the changes come to fruition.

PROCEDURE

The force field diagram is a simple and straightforward tool to summarize verbal or qualitative data arising from the team. The diagram should take about an hour to an hour and a half to complete. There are five basic steps:

1. State a desired action or outcome

Word the description as simply and plainly as possible and try to be specific. Vaguely worded statements can lead to extensive listings of forces that have little to do with the real concern or action you're trying to address. Clearly stated, the desired action or outcome is written on the right side of a flip chart or similar paper posted on the wall. Then, draw a long vertical line in the center of the paper, representing the organization's current position or state of affairs.

2. Brainstorm all the negative or restraining forces working against the change

Write them on the right side of the vertical line, with arrows pointing left, toward the line and away from the objective. Starting with negative forces is usually easier than identifying positive forces supporting change. For whatever reasons, people seem to identify the negatives easier – perhaps it's our fondness for solving problems! Whatever the reason, having a list of negatives usually makes it easier to brainstorm the positives, the next step in the process.

As the brainstorming of restraining forces continues, represent each idea with an arrow pointing to the left along the right-hand side of the vertical line. Place similar ideas near to one another if possible.

3. Brainstorm the forces working to support the change

Write these ideas on the left side of the vertical line, with arrows pointing right, towards the objective. At times, teams may have difficulty in identifying these positive forces. The facilitator can help by getting team members to focus on a specific negative, and then asking them to identify any positive forces that may be working against this negative. This can be done for each negative identified in the force field analysis.

A caution, however. At times, this procedure may force the issue to an extent where team members feel obligated to come up with some positive forces, even when they do not feel such influences exist. Before starting the procedure, caution the team that the technique is intended to help prompt ideas, not to force responses.

4. Review the forces and modify the diagram

Once the diagram is completed, the facilitator or leader should ask the group to review it. The first step is checking for completeness, to ensure all the forces supporting or restraining the change effort been identified. If not, add them.

The second step is to combine ideas. Are some forces really the same thing but simply worded differently? If so, combine them. Also check for those forces that the team doesn't believe are significant. A lot of ideas emerge during brainstorming, but because the basic brainstorming procedure does not permit criticism, not all ideas or forces identified will be seen as valid or significant. Now is the time to remove them from the diagram – but only if everyone agrees.

5. Analyze the results

The first step in the analysis of the force field diagram is examining the final product to find any general conclusions or patterns. How do the numbers of restraining and supporting forces look? Are the numbers overwhelming to one side or the other? Does the diagram present a general conclusion? All these questions should be asked of the group and any observations noted on a flip chart.

However, the analysis can go further. Simple voting procedures can be used to gather the team's collective perception of the strength of the various forces identified. One approach may be to provide team members with a limited number of votes that can be placed beside the various forces on the diagram.

These can then be counted to determine each of the force's relative strengths.

Regardless of the techniques used, remember that the force field diagram is intended to help us understand the situation. It is not sufficient, therefore, to simply complete the diagram and walk away. Conclusions need to be made.

INTERPRETATION & CHANGE STRATEGY

Interpretation of the force field diagram requires the team to make some basic conclusions about the outcome of the exercise. If the forces are in balance – the same number of forces are working for the change as are against it – change will not occur. Likewise, change is impossible if the number of forces working against the change is greater than those working for it. Only when the forces working toward the desired outcome are greater than the restraining forces will there be an opportunity to move in the desired direction.

In conducting a force field analysis, remember that the forces identified represent conditions the team believe exist – an appraisal of the existing situation. These forces are deemed to represent the existing operating reality, but this reality can be changed. That is the function of a change strategy.

Whenever the forces working against the improvement are greater than the forces working to support the proposed change, the team has three options.

1. **Reduce the forces working against the change.** The number of forces or the impact of these forces can be reduced. For example, employee fear surrounding the introduction of a new process or method of manufacture is common. This can be addressed by providing employees training in the new methods. Doing so eliminates the fear and, as a result, much of the resistance to change.

2. **Increase the forces working for the change.** Positive forces for change also can be increased, either through increasing their number or impact. Every idea will have its supporters and positive points. How can these be increased? A team proposing a new training system may note that the new system should be more effective. But it may increase its positive points by noting that the old system is getting staid and boring and will have to be changed anyway. Or, perhaps that the new system will present

some job challenge and breathe some fresh air into the training department. While the fundamental force might be improved effectiveness, additional positive forces can be identified or established to push along the improvement change.

3. **Adopt another alternative.** At times, teams may have to accept that the resistance to a proposed change is simply too great. Every idea has its time and the times may simply not be right for your proposal. Perhaps there are alterna-

tives that are nearly as good, but which will not generate the negative resistance like the preferred proposal. At such times, teams may decide to go with the less-than-ideal approach that also involves less organizational turmoil and resistance.

Whatever approach is adopted by the team, watch for points of leverage. Leverage points are those where a small influence can make a big difference. These will likely be forces rated relatively important by the team. But leverage points could also be a number of relatively unimportant forces that, when taken together, represent considerable influence.

The design of strategy must address the potential benefits and the required effort. Addressing the one big restraining force may be the obvious way to go, but this strategy may require resources the team does not have. Removing a large number of less important restraining forces may be an easier route in such circumstances.

EXAMPLE: ANALYSIS OF SOLE-SOURCE SUPPLIER

As an example, let's look at the situation of a process improvement team of a large multinational oil and gas company. The company wanted to reduce its oil field surface construction costs and the time required to get such facilities up and running.

The team responsible for the task of analyzing the current process concluded that the existing competitive bid process, combined with excessive interference on contractors, was driving costs and time lines beyond what they could and should be. They redesigned the construction process, to cut costs 10 to 15 percent and reduce time-lines by more than 30 percent. A critical component of the redesigned process was the use of a sole-source supplier for construction.

However, just redesigning a process was not enough. The team realized their proposal was radical, at least within the culture of their organization. There were deep-seated beliefs about the value of competition between suppliers, and the need to keep "on top" of contractors to ensure quality of work.

Exhibit 316: Force Field Analysis of Sole Source Supplier

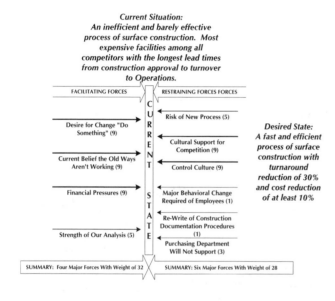

Current Situation:
An inefficient and barely effective
process of surface construction. Most
expensive facilities among all
competitors with the longest lead times
from construction approval to turnover
to Operations.

FACILITATING FORCES	RESTRAINING FORCES FORCES
	Risk of New Process (5)
Desire for Change "Do Something" (9)	Cultural Support for Competition (9)
Current Belief the Old Ways Aren't Working (9)	Control Culture (9)
Financial Pressures (9)	Major Behavioral Change Required of Employees (1)
	Re-Write of Construction Documentation Procedures (1)
Strength of Our Analysis (5)	Purchasing Department Will Not Support (3)

Desired State:
A fast and efficient
process of surface
construction with
turnaround
reduction of 30%
and cost reduction
of at least 10%

SUMMARY: Four Major Forces With Weight of 32	SUMMARY: Six Major Forces With Weight of 28

The team's assessment of the current situation was analyzed using a force field diagram. The numbers on the diagram indicate the strength of the forces involved as estimated by team members. As the analysis indicates, the team felt the forces supporting a change were stronger than those restraining it – but only marginally so. Moreover, the facilitating forces were perceived by team members to be general in nature. They sup-

ported the need to "do something" rather than back the specific recommendations of the team. In contrast, the forces restraining change were seen as more specific and concrete and as a result, more relevant to decision makers.

From this analysis, a basic change strategy was developed. The team recognized the need to be much more explicit in detailing the costs of the current way of doing things. In short, the team had to show precisely how much the old philosophies of control and competition were costing the organization, instead of skirting the issue as originally planned. Moreover, they had to show precisely how the new approach would save money. The team felt this would leverage current corporate concerns about the state of financial results and the need to do something significant.

The team also realized the revised strategy would work only to reduce the restraining factors, not eliminate them. So the team also proposed to implement the proposed change on a small scale and in a relatively low-risk area. This allowed the performance improvement team to reduce the perceived risk on the part of the executive team.

In the end, the strategy worked. The company decided to initially pursue a single-source supplier relationship for surface construction of gas processing facilities only. This was deemed to be a low-risk area and outcomes could be easily compared with results elsewhere in the company. As it turned out, the new arrangement significantly reduced surface construction time and cost. The sole-source supplier model was adopted company-wide within 18 months.

RESPONSIBILITY CHARTING

Responsibility charting provides a visual map of how human resources are deployed or assigned to different tasks or roles. Basically, responsibility charts detail who is doing what.

Responsibility charts are really just a matrix or table. By convention, resources such as people, team members or organizational units such as departments are placed across the top of the table. Activities, such as task assignments or specific jobs, are placed down the side. A coding system is then defined to describe the nature of the relationship (intersection point of the

Exhibit 317: Basic Responsibility Chart

Who / What	Dept. A	Dept B.	Dept. C	Dept. D	Dept. E	Dept. F
Task 1	R	C	A	C		I
Task 2	I	C		A	R	C
Task 3			R			I
Task 4	R	C			I	
Task 5	R		C		I	
Task 6				R	A	I
Task 7		C	C			R
Task 8	R				C	I
Task 9	C	A		I	I	R

Responsibility charts can use a variety of coding schemes. All are used to convey additional information about the nature of the relationship between the people or departments assigned to a task, and the various tasks that are to be accomplished. These coding schemes can be very detailed, involving different types of code letters conveying specific responsibility levels or roles. Other schemes can be quite basic, simply indicating with a check mark who should be involved and who shouldn't.

The level of description regarding the resources or the tasks associated with the project can vary as well. In some cases, the resources may be entire departments or divisions of a company. In others, responsibility assignments may be delineated at the individual level. The same variation in detail can occur in listing the tasks to be performed. In some cases, the tasks will be quite general in nature; in others, very specific. In summary, the level of detail required is completely dependent upon the circumstances the team is in, and on the application to which the responsibility chart will be applied.

WHERE TO USE THE RESPONSIBILITY CHART

Not every team needs to complete a responsibility chart. Teams that meet frequently or have limited individual assignments outside of team meetings rarely require responsibility charting. As the frequency of meetings declines or the length and complexity of individual or sub-team assignments increases, however, responsibility charting becomes more useful. Responsibility charting, therefore, should be used whenever the complexity is such that the team may become confused as to who is responsible for what, who is to be consulted before going ahead, which approvals are required and so forth.

Examples of specific applications include:

▲ **A large project team breaks down into smaller task forces to handle separate pieces of a common problem.** The responsibility chart makes it clear which task forces are handling which specific problem components, and the degree of communication and coordination required between various groups at different stages of the problem-solving process.

▲ **A company decides to set up a preferred supplier relationship, reducing the number of suppliers from 20 to one or two.** In redesigning its purchasing process, the company creates a detailed responsibility chart. It clarifies who is to do what by when, to ensure a smooth flow of delivered product and serve as an ongoing source of documentation for future reference.

▲ **When analyzing a process, an improvement team needs to document who actually is doing what at different stages of the process.** The team uses a responsibility chart to document and detail existing roles and responsibilities, as an aid to further analysis. This is then used to help construct a resource deployment flowchart.

▲ **In creating a new process, the process improvement team decides to use a responsibility chart to help employees understand what their new responsibilities will be.** The resulting chart not only becomes part of the process documentation and a valuable reference point for employees, but can serve as a training device for new employees. As a communications tool, the responsibility chart is unparalleled in its ability to identify "who is who in the zoo" and "what they are supposed to do."

▲ **The set of relationships in a complex system needs to be documented.** Beyond their analytical applications, responsibility charts can be used to document who is to do what – acting as an easy-to-read reference. For example, a large construction project may require numerous approvals and sign-offs for authorizing everything from basic design to the color of the flooring tile. Who needs to see what, approve or otherwise okay some facet of construction in order to proceed? Who should at least be aware of decisions made?

The responsibility chart can be used whenever there is a need to clarify who does what. It clarifies the roles and responsibilities within the organization, either for purposes of planning and documentation or for process analysis and improvement.

CREATING THE RESPONSIBILITY CHART

Creating the responsibility charting usually follows a six-step procedure:

1. Identify the process steps or tasks to be accomplished

First, the tasks that need to be accomplished must be identified. How this is done depends upon the application.

Where the responsibility chart is used to document the responsibilities pertaining to an existing process, the tasks can be obtained from process documentation, flowcharts or block diagrams. In these cases, responsibility charts can provide a useful addendum to the existing documentation. This chart can display responsibilities for task accomplishment to a greater level of detail and in more understandable graphical form.

Where the chart is used by a process team to plan some improvement effort, the team will likely need to brainstorm process steps, then create a top-down or planning version of a process flow chart from scratch. When this is completed, the steps identified in the process flow are listed in a logical (usually time-based) order along the vertical axis of the matrix.

When the task responsibilities are being created from scratch, time will have to be allocated for returning to the chart, to add additional tasks that became apparent during the balance of the process. Perfection – complete and comprehensive identification of all tasks – will not happen the first time around. If the brainstorming process bogs down, move on and be prepared to come back to task identification.

2. Identify the responsibility areas

Responsibility areas are any individual or organizational unit – people, teams, sub-teams or departments – capable of taking on accountability or responsibility for some task. It is critical during the identification of responsibility areas that stakeholders are identified – even those that may not appear to be directly involved. The goal here is comprehensiveness. It is little trouble to remove a column from the analysis if no responsibility linkages are made. But forgetting some individual or group can produced serious consequences. At a minimum, teams seeking to improve processes need to consult with their customers and

suppliers. Where and when these consultations take place must be noted on the responsibility chart.

3. Adopt a coding scheme

There are a variety of coding schemes used by organizations to classify the nature of the relationship between resources and tasks. These include using simple check marks to indicate some level of involvement, as well as the RACI, RASIN and RIDS schemes. These coding structures are detailed in Table 318: Responsibility Chart Coding Schemes. The responsibility chart does not always use a coding scheme, however. In some circumstances, it may be advantageous to write in the specific component or sub-task that will be performed by the individual(s) involved.

Whatever approach is adopted, team members must review and understand the definitions or descriptions of the various codes. Responsibility charting works best when team members understand the codes and their implications in task assignments. For this reason, organizations may wish to adopt a standardized coding scheme. Then, as improvement teams come and go, the language of roles and responsibilities stays the same.

Table 318: Responsibility Chart Coding Schemes

Coding Scheme	Symbol	Meaning
Check Mark	✓	Involved
RACI	R	Responsible (one per task)
	A	Approval
	C	Consulted before decisions are made
	I	Informed of decisions and progress
RASIN	R	Responsible (one per task)
	A	Approval
	S	Support, helps with task accomplishment
	I	Informed of decisions or progress
	N	Needs to be consulted
RIDS	R	Responsible and accountable for the work (one per task)
	I	Informed, must be informed or consulted as to progress and decisions.
	D	Does the work
	S	Supports and provides some assistance in the conduct of the work

4. Define the relationships

This step involves going through each square of the matrix and assigning codes to reflect the nature of the responsibility between task and organizational unit. In assigning these codes, the team may consider empirical data, such as current roles and responsibilities arising from analysis of flowcharts and other 'mapping' tools, or the opinions of team members as to who should and should not be involved with the various tasks under analysis.

Every box of the matrix does not need to be filled in and shouldn't be. Filling in every box would indicate that everyone has some level of involvement in every task or assignment. There would be little delegation and a lot of general confusion concerning who is to do what. It is, therefore, quite alright and preferable to have some boxes of the matrix empty.

Deciding what code should go where may compel teams to deal with uncomfortable issues. We cannot simply take everyone's opinion, add them up in each cell and create an average, as we can for some decision matrices. Rather, the team must go through the matrix cell by cell and agree on the appropriate level of responsibility.

This can be a slow and sometimes agonizing process. Because of this, it is often advantageous to go through the process the first time relatively quickly, getting team members' initial impressions. This creates an initial approximation of the responsibility structure, which in turn serves as a foundation for further discussion.

5. Review the assignments

When the first draft of the responsibility chart is complete, the team needs to review the responsibility assignments and ensure that things make sense. In this regard, the responsibility chart serves as a foundation for further and more detailed discussions. Questions like "Do we really need marketing involved in all eight tasks?" or "Shouldn't we get the user group involved in Step 12?" come to the surface, are discussed in the group setting, and decided upon.

Be prepared, therefore, to make revision upon revision with lots of crossed-out assignments, rewritten codes and the like. Lesson 1 in creating the responsibility chart is to make it big – leave lots of room for the changes that are sure to come.

Some key points to watch for:

▲ **Look for tasks where no one is responsible.** This takes the form of a blank column. If no one is responsible for the work or no one is assigned to the task, the task will not get done. Some assignments need to be made.

▲ **Look for departments or individuals that have nothing to do.** These take the form of blank columns. Are these people or departments not required or is their experience simply not being used? The team needs to decide what the role of such people or departments in the improvement project is to be and make the appropriate assignments.

▲ **Look for situations where one person or area is responsible for just about everything.** Their work-load is probably too great, which will likely result in delays and missed assignments or deadlines. Look around for people having relatively less to do and get them involved to help spread the work-load.

▲ **Where a RACI, RASIN or RIDS coding scheme is used, make sure that only one person is responsible for each task.** Multiple responsibility usually means no responsibility. Decisions need to be made and responsibility assigned. This is the area where egos tend to get bruised. Team leaders and facilitators must be aware of the possibility that issues will arise around concerns of who will be in charge of what.

▲ **Be careful when one individual has all the final approvals, but someone else is doing all the work.** Also, try to keep approvals down to a few crucial task-completion points. If approvals are involved for every step, little work will get done.

6. Finalize the chart

Once agreement around the roles and responsibilities has been achieved, the results must be documented and finalized. A final version of the chart needs to be created. The existing version will likely be marked up with revisions arising out of the discussions. Now is the time to create a new chart with the agreed roles and responsibilities filled in. Other special data may be included at this time, such as due dates.

Once the final version is completed, it must be distributed to team members and others affected by the responsibility assignments. Responsibility charting isn't much use if no one knows about it!

EXAMPLE: IMPROVEMENT TEAM RESPONSIBILITIES

A team is looking to organize its activities. Given responsibility for examining the purchasing process, the team's first tasks are defining the process, creating the charter and beginning the effort to document, through flowcharting, the existing process. It quickly becomes apparent, however, that given the scope of the assignment, the job is much larger than first anticipated.

To get things moving, the team uses responsibility charting with a RACI coding scheme, to try and assess what kind of demands the project will be making on individual team members and to clarify who will be doing what. The result is the responsibility chart presented in Exhibit 319: Responsibility Chart for Improvement Team.

EXAMPLE: SOLE-SOURCE SUPPLIER RELATIONSHIPS

Responsibility charting can be used to document the way things are supposed to work on much larger scales.

Exhibit 319: Responsibility Chart for Improvement Team

Project Activities/Plan		Pat (Project Sponsor)	Shelley (Project Leader)	Robert (Quality Support)	Marc	Kurt	Chelsea (Team Support)	Barb	Randy
Define Project	Gather Information		R	I					
	Understand Project		R	C	C	C	C	C	C
	Develop components		R	I	I	I			I
	Identify Buy In						R		
	Recognize Barriers		A	R	C	C	I	I	I
	Finalize Scope	A	R	I	I	I	I	I	I
Organize Project	Establish Relationships		R				I		
	Define Resources		R	I			I		I
	Establish Measures & Accountability			R					
	Establish Project Plan	A	R		C	C		C	C
	Establish Communications Mechanisms	C	C					R	
Understanding the System	Execute Project Plan		R	I	I	I	C	I	I
	Document Existing Processes			R	I	I		C	C
	Define Measurement Plan		C	R	I	I			
	Process Performance Analysis			R	I	I			
	Causal Analysis		I	I	R	C	I	C	C
	Communicate Activities		C				R		I
Redesigning the System	Develop Alternative Solutions		R		C	C	I	C	C
	Finalize Alternatives		R		C	C	I	C	C
	Decide on Best Alternative	A	R	I	C	C	I	C	C
Implementing the changes	Implement	A	R	C	C	C	C	C	C
	Share learnings	I	C	I	I	I	R	I	I
Acting on the Learning	Standardize	R	C	C				I	I
	Share Successes	C	C	I			C	R	

Exhibit 320: Responsibility Chart for Sole Source Supplier

Companies / Activities	West Coast Engineering			Universal Construction		Marker Oil and Gas	
Roles →	Project Manager	Design Team	Assurance Team	Project Manager	Build Team	Assurance	Operations
Part A: Project Planning							
1. Scope Plan	R	I	N	N		N	A
1.1. Work Breakdown Structure	R	N	N	N		A	C
1.1.a. Civil	A	S		I	N		
1.1.b. Structural	A	S		I	N		
1.1.c. Mechanical	R	S		N		A	
1.1.d. Pipe	R	S		N		A	
1.1.e. Electrical	R	S		N		A	
1.1.f. Instrumentation	R	S		I		A	N
1.1.g. Insulation	R	S		I			N
1.1.h. Paint and Finish	R	S		N			N
1.2 Drawings	R	S	R	I	S	A	C
1.2.a. Flow Sheets	A	S	R	I	I		I
1.2.b. Detail Drawings	A	S	R	I	I		I
1.2.c. Vendor Drawings		S	N	I	I	A	I
1.2.d. As Builts	A	S	N	I	I		I
1.3 Specifications	S					A	R
1.3.a Client	N			N		R	A
1.3.b. Engineering	R		N	I		A	N
1.3.c. Contractor	N			R		A	I
1.3.d. Vendor	N	I	N	R	N	A	I
2. Resource Plan							
2.1 Labor	A		R	S	N	N	I
2.1.a. Staff		I					
2.1.b. Direct Hire				A	R	N	I
2.1.c. Sub Contract				A	R	N	I
2.2. Material			A	R	N		
2.2.a. Client Office	I					A	R
2.2.b. Modules	N	N	R	N	I	A	
2.2.c. Bulk Material	A			R	S		
2.2.d. Field Material	A			R	S		
2.3. Tools & Equipment	I		N	A	N	N	
2.3.a. Temporary Field				A	R		
2.3.b. Job Owned				A	R		
2.3.c. Sub Contracts	N			R		A	N

In one case, an oil and gas company had adopted a sole-source supplier relationship for the engineering and construction of the oil company's surface gas facilities. The sole-source supplier relationship was a major departure for both the contracting company and the engineering firm. To help design how the new process would work, the two companies created a responsibility chart of their relationship. It detailed who was responsible for what, who needed to be informed and who required input or sign-off before construction decisions were made. The result is presented in part in Exhibit 320: Responsibility Chart for Sole Source Supplier.

The chart was an instant success. It quickly became the "quick and dirty" reference for both parties. As new projects were undertaken, the basic chart was hauled out and used to drive discussion about whether the new project required any special considerations or changes. Project start-up meetings of this type were greatly facilitated by the documented set of responsibilities.

GANTT CHARTING

GANTT charts, like responsibility charts, are a special form of deployment chart presented as a table or matrix. Rather than deploying people to a specific task, GANTT charts deploy time. They present not *who* will do what, but rather *how long* each task will take, including when it starts and finishes.

The time scale under consideration is presented across the top of the chart. As was the case with responsibility charting, the GANTT chart lists tasks or what will be accomplished down the side of the matrix. Colored bars are then used to convey the amount of elapsed time the specific task assignment will take. Elapsed time is the time it takes between starting a specific task and completing the same task. A task may take two weeks of elapsed time, but require only a few hours of actual effort.

Exhibit 321: Basic GANTT Chart

Task Name	Time Period 1	Time Period 2	Time Period 3	Time Period 4	Time Period 5	Time Period 6	Time Period 7
Task 1							
Task 2							
Task 3							
Task 4							
Task 5							
Task 6							
Task 7							
Task 8							
Task 9							
Task 10							

WHERE TO USE

Like with responsibility charts, not all teams will use GANTT charts. As the number or complexity of the tasks requiring completion increases, or as the importance of time increases, so too does the applicability and usefulness of GANTT charts. You may want to use the GANTT chart whenever:

▲ **A process improvement team has been given a substantial project to complete (i.e. analyze the inventory system) within relatively tight time-lines.** In such circumstances, the team may want to create a GANTT chart, and perhaps a responsibility chart as well, detailing how much time can be allocated to each activity to meet the deadlines set for the improvement effort.

▲ **A process team wants to plan out the implementation time-line of a set of recommendations.** All the required changes are identified. The team details the projected time period it believes it will take to see the improvements implemented by the various departments affected.

▲ **The relationship between time and task is a concern.** Time is a precious resource. It is also difficult to deal with. Unlike other resources, it can't be stored or placed in inventory to be conveniently withdrawn when we need it. Therefore, we need to manage it carefully. Whenever teams have a concern about how time is being used, consideration should be given to the GANTT chart as a tool to help us improve our understanding.

In short, GANTT charts can be used whenever the team needs to get a handle on the relationship between what must be done and the time required or allocated to do it.

PROCEDURE FOR CREATING THE GANTT CHART

The procedure for creating the GANTT chart usually consists of six steps:

1. List the tasks that need to be accomplished

A complete listing of the tasks to be accomplished is detailed down the left side of the chart. This information can come from brainstorming sessions, especially when combined with some organization tools such as affinity or tree diagramming. It can also come from documentation or existing plans of action.

Whatever the source, make sure team members are clear as to what each task actually involves. A common mistake when GANTT charting is to leave task descriptions vague and open to interpretation. If there is any confusion about what is entailed by a certain task, break the job out to an additional level of detail. This not only clarifies the task, it also improves the resulting time estimates.

Try to maintain a time order in the tasks, starting at the top of the chart with what will likely be the first task and putting the last task at the bottom. This will make the resulting analysis and presentation of the GANTT chart easier to read and comprehend.

2. Mark the time calendar across the top

The calendar is the basic time-line within which the team is expected to work. Divisions between days, weeks, months or any other appropriate time scale should be clearly marked.

So how long should the time scale be? Well, this obviously depends on the project. Most people will have an expected completion time frame for the project which serves as a valuable starting point. However, you will want to add some time, at least 30 percent, to this estimated completion date. Things always take longer than first approximations. The GANTT chart, by breaking down the project into tasks and clearly defining the time required to complete each, will likely highlight the need for additional time to complete the entire project.

3. Review each task and estimate the time required

Start with the task at the top of the list and work down. A couple of approaches can be used here. The most common is to get feedback from team members on what they feel the required time will be. Discussion is useful in bringing a reality test to the estimates. The facilitator should encourage this discussion until the team comes close to agreement. There are some additional approaches as well:

▲ Team members can call out their respective estimates of the time required. These are written down on a flip chart beside each task until every team member has provided a time estimate for every task. The facilitator may take the average of these estimates to arrive at an initial approximation of the estimated time for the task. However, discussion around the discrepancies among the various estimates will be required later. Make sure to record the various estimates as well as the 'average,' so there is a basis for discussion later on.

▲ Individuals responsible for the completion of tasks (possibly determined through a responsibility chart) are asked to estimate the time required. This may be done over the course of a few days. These estimates are then brought back into a team setting, posted on flip chart paper and discussed.

▲ Past empirical data is used to provide the estimates or at least a baseline that can be used to "reality check" the estimates. How long has it taken other teams in similar projects to complete similar tasks for their areas? Has the team had experience estimating project time before and, if so, how close were the estimates? A little reality checking can go a long way in moving estimates from optimistic projections to well- grounded figures.

▲ Program Evaluation and Review Technique (PERT) is used to provide probability estimates of the time required. A more detailed discussion of the PERT estimation procedure follows later in this chapter.

As the estimates are provided, by whatever means, the team facilitator or team leader begins to build the GANTT chart.

This can be done on a large piece of paper posted on a wall and by using sticky-notes to mark the beginning and end of each task. Alternatively, a large white board can be used to display results as the process moves down the list.

Either way, these initial results are temporary. Like with the responsibility chart, a team discussion of the estimates will prove useful. The process of discussing why the estimates turned out the way they did, or why team members estimated the time differently, can add considerable clarity to the various tasks or activities identified on the chart. At times, the discussion will highlight missing tasks or redundancies between two tasks. When this occurs, the facilitator needs to modify the GANTT chart "on-the-fly" so all team members can see the changes. In turn, this will require revised time estimates.

The value of the process, then, comes as much from the discussion as from the time estimates themselves. This is why creating the GANTT chart should not be assigned to some lone individual with expertise in project management software. While this can create fast (and attractive) GANTT charts, it loses the benefit of the group discussion where much of the value of the process is located.

4. Identify dependencies

As the team moves down the list, it will become clear that some tasks cannot start until others tasks have been completed or at least reached some final stage. These are called dependencies. The most common dependency occurs when a task cannot be started until some other task is completed. Dependencies are identified by lines connecting the bars of the GANTT chart. They are useful in allowing the team to see how changes in one project area will affect other areas. Some areas or tasks can be quickly identified as 'critical' to the overall project because a great many other tasks depend upon their completion. These critical tasks can be highlighted with a colored marker and managed with a little more attention than other activities.

5. Review and discuss

The GANTT chart, including its dependencies, should be reviewed by the entire project team. Is the scheduling realistic? Are some people overloaded with a lot of tasks all occurring at the same time? Are there some critical tasks that need to be done on time in order for many other tasks to be completed?

The team must discuss and review all these questions. The answers will require revisions. This means that the same rules for responsibility charting apply to GANTT charting. Make sure you have room to write notes, make revisions, cross things out and so forth to facilitate the review process. Discussions usually result in times being added, then reduced, then added again – often all on the same task! Be prepared. Flexibility and space are the key ingredients to developing GANTT charts in a team setting. As much as all this discussion and revision is time consuming, it is also a fundamental requirement of creating realistic GANTT charts.

6. Finalize the chart

Once the revisions have been made, a final good copy is required. Start a second chart for this purpose; the facilitator should carefully describe the estimates and special notes as each task is written down. Final questions and clarifications can be sought by team members at this point. Once completed, circulate the chart.

USEFUL TRICKS AND ENHANCEMENTS

GANTT charting grew out of the project management discipline and is often associated with complex engineering and construction applications. It is a sophisticated tool with a host of special features, most of which go beyond the requirements of process improvement teams. Don't add complexity just for the sake of doing so – keep it as simple as you can! With this caution in mind, there are some enhancements teams may find useful:

▶ tracking actual versus planned time

▶ detailing tasks for improved time estimates

▶ presenting high-low estimates

1. Tracking actual versus planned time

A useful enhancement to the GANTT chart is tracking the estimated time associated with various tasks versus actual time it takes to complete the task. The difference between planned and actual time can be represented in one of two ways. These are:

▲ The first method uses two bars for each task. A solid bar presents the original time estimates for a particular task. Immediately beneath this, a second bar is (often colored differently) maps the time actually taken. This second bar is constantly updated as work progresses on the task.

▲ The second method uses an 'empty' or blank bar to represent planned time. This is then 'colored-in' as progress is made toward completing the task.

Tracking actual time versus budgeted time is a way to identify those areas of the plan that are proving to be more difficult than expected, which helps the team make adjustments to ensure things are completed on time. Perhaps more resources need to be allocated to the task, maybe a few extra hands to help out. Or perhaps the task will simply take longer than expected and the team will have to live with it. Either way, the GANTT chart provides an effective means to feed this information back to the team, in an easily understood and structured format.

The danger in tracking estimated versus actual time is in having the process become a tool to allocate blame if things run over schedule. It is okay to identify a specific area of the project as more difficult than expected. But it's totally unacceptable to simply interpret this as "Bob didn't get his task completed on time." Perhaps no one could have completed this portion on time, or perhaps Bob demonstrated near super-human ability in getting as much done as he did. Remember, most problems lie with the system, not with the individual.

Teams need to maintain focus on the bigger picture – completing the project and not wasting time by allocating blame.

2. Detailing tasks for improved estimates

The GANTT chart is intended to help teams estimate the time it will take to complete tasks associated with a project. These time estimates will improve the more a task is broken down into sub-tasks or activities. One of the reasons teams and individuals generally underestimate the amount of time required to complete a task is that they forget all the various activities or sub-tasks that will require completion. To get a better handle on the time it will take to complete a task, break down the task into all its specific activities or sub-tasks. Estimate the time required for each of these, then add these figures together to get total task time. Use this procedure especially for the larger or more vague tasks.

The effectiveness of this technique was demonstrated on one occasion when a team leader was scheduling the next team meeting. This meeting's purpose was to have each team member present the findings resulting from his or her individual assignments. The team leader immediately said he thought the meeting would take about three hours. However, one individual quickly asked how long each presentation should take. The team leader replied that about half an hour would be appropriate. The individual pointed out there were eight presentations, so at least four hours would be required, and even that would not include time for breaks or any additional work needed to summarize and bring results together. The team decided to book off the entire day.

This example shows how easy it is for teams or individuals to underestimate the resources (including time) required to complete even the most basic tasks. So, when in doubt, break down the tasks into smaller units and re-estimate the resource or time requirements.

3. Tracking high-low estimates

This enhancement may be the most useful. GANTT charts are usually prepared without having a lot of empirical data to support the time estimates made in the chart. Usually, we are relying upon the experience and good guesswork of the team. The problem is that for all this experience, it is still a guess. People generally, experts included, tend to be overconfident in their ability to make such estimates.

A partial solution to this problem of making estimates from scant data is to ask for three estimates – a most likely estimate of time as well as a high and low estimate. In other words, the procedure asks people to estimate not only the time they believe a task will take, but also the time it will take if everything goes well and the time it will take if everything goes poorly. The details of this approach are presented in the Program Evaluation and Review Technique (PERT) presented next. These high-low estimates can be presented within the GANTT chart, allowing teams to see the range of possibilities.

PERT: *Estimating Time (or Just About Anything Else)*

What is it about people that they so often underestimate how long it will take to complete a specific task? And it is just not time. Experienced employees and managers routinely underestimate the amount of resources, from people to dollars, it will take to complete just about anything.

The reason, in part, may be overconfidence. When forced to make judgments with relatively scant data, people tend to be overconfident in their judgments. We always feel we can do something better or faster or with fewer problems than the last time we tried. But this overconfidence can be disastrous to teams that have to deal with tight time-lines or budgets.

The PERT three-estimate approach can help overcome these overly optimistic forecasts. PERT stands for Program Evaluation and Review Technique. PERT attempts to determine the time a task should take by mathematically manipulating three estimates produced by an individual or the team. The mathematics is derived from a set of assumptions about underlying statistical distributions of such estimates. But the value of the technique is in getting people to think about the possibility that things may not go as planned. PERT encourages people to think statistically (accept variation) rather than become married to a single-point estimate.

WHEN TO USE PERT

PERT should be used by teams whenever there is a need to estimate a numerical value that could vary with circumstances, and where conditions of scant empirical data forces use of judgment or guesswork. Some application examples are:

▲ **A team needs to estimate the time it will take to complete an analysis of a problem.** Anyone who has worked for a team knows things always take longer than expected. An individual that needs to be interviewed is on vacation, the cost figures that were supposedly in the computer aren't, and so forth. When teams are required to figure out how long things will take, PERT can provide a way to furnish a more realistic estimate.

▲ **Trying to estimate some parameter where historical or empirical data is scant.** Although preferable, gathering historical data to help estimate some parameter is not always possible. For example, what is the mean time-to-failure rate of the space shuttle or any new piece of equipment? NASA had estimated a probability of failure in the space shuttle at one in 100,000 (prior to the Challenger disaster), while others involved in the program had estimates as high as one in 100. PERT can assimilate different estimates into a probability distribution that recognizes the underlying uncertainty of the estimate. What will levels of sales be for a new product? How fast can a new plant be brought on stream? What is the probability that an exploratory drilling program will yield two significant "hits" on oil and gas reserves?

▲ **A team needs to estimate the final costs associated with some new strategy or acquisition.** Anyone experienced with installing a new computer system (hardware or software), implementing a new process, building a new facility and the like will know that final costs are always more than originally estimated. Some surprises always spring up. Indeed, cost underestimation is so well known that many companies simply add an obligatory 10 to 20 percent to their best estimate – the "fudge factor." A better approach is to use PERT to produce a complete distribution for final costs that accommodates the likely, as well as the disaster, scenarios.

While traditionally used to estimate time in association with GANTT charts, PERT can and should be used whenever some numerical estimate is required but empirical data is scant. Teams needing to estimate time, revenue flow, final project cost, production rate or other such variables would benefit by taking a little uncertainty into account when making their estimates — in short, they would benefit from using PERT.

A word of caution here, however. PERT is not a substitute for real world empirical data. It should only be used whenever gathering empirical data is impossible, and the team needs to guard against the overconfidence that comes from making single-point judgments.

Making a PERT Estimate

Here's how it works. Rather than asking the individual to make a single estimate, ask three questions:

▲ **What is your most pessimistic estimate?** This is the unlikely but potential time a task would take if everything goes wrong. This estimate is represented by '*b.*'

▲ **What is your most optimistic estimate?** That is, how long will it take if everything goes perfectly? This is represented by '*a.*'

▲ **What is your most likely estimate?** This is the time the task will take if everything goes normally, meaning some things will go right and some things will not. This is represented by '*m.*'

It is advisable to pose the questions in this order, with the most likely estimate last. This is because we want the individual to think about the distribution of possibilities before asking him or her to estimate the most likely time. Estimating the most

likely time first can increase anchoring effects. This is where the optimistic and pessimistic estimates become 'anchored' to the result the individual feels is most likely – limiting the range of these estimates. We are trying to avoid these effects when using PERT, emphasizing instead the possible range in order to challenge the overconfidence in our thinking.

The Basic Formulas

Now for the calculations. The equations presented below provide estimates of some key numerical descriptors arising from the three-point estimates. Formulas are provided for the expected (mean) value, the range, the variance and the standard deviation.

▶ Expected time: $t_e = (a + (4 \times m) + b) \div 6$

▶ Range: $R = b - a$

▶ Variance: $s^2 = ((b - a) \div 6)^2$

▶ Standard Deviation: $s = ((b - a) \div 6)$

For example, suppose we came up with the following estimates for the time required to complete a project.

▶ Optimistic: (a) = 2 weeks

▶ Pessimistic: (b)= 10 weeks

▶ Most Likely: (m) = 3 weeks

The expected time for the project would then be:

$$t_e = (a + (4 \times m) + b) \div 6$$
$$t_e = (2 + (4 \times 3) + 10) \div 6$$
$$t_e = 4$$

So, the time we would expect this project or task to be completed would be about four weeks. Notice that this is a full week longer than our 'most likely' estimate. For planning purposes, we would use the expected time rather than the most likely estimate simply because the expected time takes into account some of the uncertainty.

Dispersion

The next set of calculations involves those relating to dispersion. The first of these should be familiar – it is the range. Recall that the range is simply the high estimate less the low estimate. In this case, the range is:

$$R = b - a$$
$$R = 10 - 2$$
$$R = 8$$

If there is a simpler calculation around, I don't know what it is! But for all its simplicity, it may be the most useful. It tells us immediately what the expected worst- and best-case scenarios are – essential information when time is of the essence. Yes, eight weeks is quite the range. But, it is still a more useful way of looking at the situation, because it takes into account the uncertainties of the estimates.

The variance and the standard deviation, two other measures of dispersion, can also be estimated. Caution is warranted when interpreting these statistics within PERT. The calculations for standard deviation and variance in this case assume an underlying statistical distribution. That's a big assumption, one that is not likely to hold up under scrutiny. These calculations may be useful or insightful, but users should be aware of their limitations.

To calculate the standard deviation, the calculations are:

$$s = ((b - a) \div 6)$$
$$s = ((10 - 2) \div 6$$

$s = 1.33$

The variance is simply the square of the standard deviation, or in this case $(1.33)^2$ or 1.77.

We now have a probabilistic estimate of the time it will take to complete a project or specific task, assuming a specific underlying statistical model.

WHAT ARE THE CHANCES?

We can apply these estimates further, to estimate the probability of completing the project on time or on budget. Let's assume that for the example given above, we are working to a five-week deadline. What is the probability that this deadline will be met?

On the face of it, the chances look pretty good, given that our most likely estimate is three weeks and our expected time from the PERT calculation is four weeks. The equation used to provide the answer is:

$$Z = \frac{Ts - Te}{\sqrt{\sigma^2}}$$

T_s is the deadline time we are interested in, in this case the five weeks. T_e is our estimated time or four weeks. The denominator is the square root of the variance or the standard deviation, which is 1.33. So Z in this case is equal to $1 \div 1.33$ which is 0.752.

With the Z score calculated, we can now estimate the chances we will meet our deadline. Using a table of normal probabilities (See "Appendix 3: Normal Probability Table" on page 851) look to find a Z score close to 0.752. The table located in Appendix 3 provides Z scores to two digits – 0.75 should be close enough for our purposes. The corresponding probability value is 0.2266 or 22.66 percent. This is the probability we will *not* complete the project within the five weeks (nearly a one-in-four chance, in other words) based upon the judgment of those providing the estimates. Alternatively, the probability we will complete the project within the five weeks is 0.7734 or 77.34 percent.

Be careful with interpretation

A great deal of caution is warranted concerning interpretation. Your estimates are just that, estimates. Gathering multiple estimates, calculating standard deviations and using normal probability distributions give the appearance of scientific fact when they are just the best guesses of those involved that further assume some normal distribution that in all likelihood doesn't apply. Serious problems can occur when people forget the assumptions and treat the estimates as facts, (i.e. there is a specific probability the project will be completed in five weeks as opposed to the team estimating the probability of completing the project in five weeks).

However, as long as the very real limitations of the procedure are understood, using the calculations can help provide a little insight into the uncertain nature of the task and of our estimates. Looking at estimates that recognize uncertainty is certainly superior to pretending that no uncertainty exists.

APPLYING **PERT** TO MULTIPLE TASKS

The PERT approach can also be applied with greater sophistication, to estimate the times for several tasks that make up a project. PERT estimates are made for each task, and these are added together to produce the estimates for the project overall.

Table 322: PERT Estimates on Multiple Tasks

Task	Estimates a - m - b	Expected Time T_e	Variance s^2
Complete Start-Up	1 - 3 - 4	$(1+12+4) \div 6$ $= 2.83$	$(4-1) \div 6 =$ 0.25
Initial Process Review	5 - 8 - 15	8.67	2.78
Flowcharting of Key Processes	10 - 20 - 30	20	11.1
Data Collection	15 - 25 - 35	25	11.1
Data Analysis	5 - 7 - 14	7.83	2.25
Process Redesign(s)	10 - 14 - 25	15.16	6.25
Recommendations	5 - 7 - 10	7.16	0.69
TOTAL	51 - 74 - 133	86.65	34.42

The example given in the table involves the time estimates in days to complete a small process improvement project. Note how the PERT estimates are completed for each phase of the project. The expected times and variances are calculated using the usual PERT formulas. The results are then summed at the bottom of the table to give the total expected time and the variance associated with the project.

It is important that the variances be used when dealing with multiple tasks. Standard deviations are not additive, meaning they cannot be calculated for each step and then summed up to provide a total. If you want to know the standard deviation for the project, add the variances for the various tasks and then take the square root of the result.

These probability estimates can also be highlighted on a GANTT chart. They are often represented as whiskers, in much the same way as the range of observed values was represented on the box and whisker plot.

EXAMPLE: USING PERT TO ESTIMATE REVENUES

PERT is a technique originally designed to include elements of uncertainty (probability) when estimating time for the completion of complex projects. However, including uncertainty is valuable regardless of what is being estimated.

Consider the estimated revenue flow from the introduction of a new product or service. Typical approaches make use of best guesses as to what the revenue sources will be. In many organizations, this has more to do with politics than sound business judgment. Those favoring the new product will estimate high, so that revenues will justify the cost of introduction and production. Those against the new product will estimate revenue relatively low, making the product uneconomical. Using PERT to estimate likely or middle-of-the-road conditions can help balance these perspectives and provide a rough, and certainly more realistic estimate of likely revenues and costs.

Take the example of a small regional bank that is estimating revenue flow accruing from the introduction of a new product offering. The product in this case is insurance, sold as protection for borrowers. If, for any reason, the borrower cannot make payment, the insurance covers the amount owing on the loan. By introducing the product, the bank would receive about $50 in commissions from the insurance company for each policy sold. However, what is unknown is the percentage of borrowers taking out loans that would purchase the insurance. The cost of implementing the product offering and operating the program in the first year is approximately $200,000, with annual costs thereafter of about $50,000.

The bank gathered some basic 'guesstimates' from its various senior managers on what the level of insurance take-up would be. Using the PERT approach, the new product team synthesized the results around the three critical estimates of high, low and most likely. The results are presented in Table 323: PERT Estimates of Revenue Flow.

Table 323: PERT Estimates of Revenue Flow

	Volume	Revenue
Loan Assumptions	25,000	$50 per take-up
Likely Estimate of Volume	2,000 or 8 percent of total loan volume	$100,000
Low Estimate of Volume	1,500 or 4 percent of total loan volume	$75,000
High estimate of Volume	10,000 or 40 percent of total loan volume	$500,000

Using these estimates, the new product team quickly calculated a likely revenue level, and determined the probability of failing to cover the cost of the first year's operation. Here are the team's calculations:

Likely revenue is estimated to be:

$$Volume_{est} = (a + (4m) + b) \div 6$$
$$Volume_{est} = (10,000 + (4 \times 2,000) + 1,500) \div 6$$
$$Volume_{est} = 19,500 \div 6$$
$$Volume_{est} = 3,250$$

This volume, times the average commission per sale, equalled $50 times 3,250, or $162,500. This is the estimated level of revenue per year. With a $200,000 start-up cost, the first year would see a loss. After that, the profits would start to flow.

What are the chances that the organization will not recover its costs in the first year? To answer this we first calculate the assumed standard deviation for volume. This is:

$$Volume_{std.dev} = (a - b) \div 6$$
$$Volume_{std.dev} = (10,000 - 1,500) \div 6$$
$$Volume_{std.dev} = 1,417$$

Notice that we have replaced the usual *(b - a) ÷ 6* with the formula *(a - b) ÷ 6*. This is done to get a positive value and doesn't affect the result. With time, the pessimistic number (b) is larger, whereas with revenues it is the optimistic number that is larger.

We use this value in the equation for determining the Z-score, where T_e is our expected estimate (3,250). T_s is the target level or 4,000 units (since this volume, times $50 per sale, will yield the $200,000 break-even point for the cost of operating the program in the first year). The divisor is the standard deviation or 1,417.

$$Z = \frac{Ts - Te}{\sqrt{\sigma^2}}$$

Z = (4,000 - 3,250) ÷ 1,417 or about 0.53.

Looking this value up in the Z-Score table (see Appendix) yields a probability of 0.7019 or 70.19 percent. So the chance we will recover our first year's expenses in year one is a little less than 30 percent.

The real value in using PERT in this type of application is not arriving at a specific number, however. The value is that PERT gets decision makers thinking in terms of probabilities. In this example, the value comes from accepting the probability that we will not recover first-year costs, but the profit picture looks pretty good once these set-up costs are taken care of.

Moreover, just looking at the distribution arising from the estimates has value. Notice how close the most likely estimate was to the low estimate, and how very much higher the high-side estimate was from everything else. Those doing the estimating seemed to be saying that while they believed sales would be relatively low at about 2,000, the product had limited downside risk at this level (the low estimate was 1,500 units, only 500 below the most likely estimate), while the upside potential was very large indeed.

SUMMARY: USING PERT

The PERT approach can be used with estimating virtually anything. Examples include calculating sales estimates for a totally new product, the cost savings attributable to some improvement initiative, the probability of new component failure, or the time required to complete a project. Whenever teams are seeking to break free of single-point estimates and provide a more realistic, probable range of possibilities, the PERT approach provides a good way to do so.

However, it must be emphasized that PERT does not produce empirical data and is no substitute for it. It is used when teams are trying to make some estimates where gathering empirical data is impractical or impossible. PERT should never be considered a substitute for physically taking measurements from a process.

RELATIONSHIP DIAGRAM

The relationship diagram (also called the inter-relationship diagram) is a visual representation of the causal, sequential or logical connections among the components of a complex issue or system. While these connections are 'logical,' they needn't be linear.

For example, consider a small system with four components called A, B, C, and D. Component A may have a causal arrow flowing to Component B, which in turn has a causal arrow flowing to Component C. But Component C may also have an arrow that flows to Component D, which in turn flows back to Component A. The relationship is causal or logical, but the circular flow-back structure indicates it is also non-linear/complex.

The relationship diagram is designed to handle these types of non-linear flows, making it useful when trying to map or represent complex real-world conditions. The relationship diagram essentially fills the gap left by tree diagrams, which are good at mapping linear relations between components, but poor at representing non-linear relations. This makes tree diagrams more useful in planning applications where cause and effect relationships are linear, and usually expressed as goals and the means to achieve them.

While our plans may be nice and linear, the real world is anything but. The relationship diagram allows teams to break out of the linear thinking patterns or methods of analysis, and graphically represent the real world with all its messiness and complexity.

WHAT DOES IT LOOK LIKE?

All this means is that by the time you complete the relationship diagram, you, too, will have a mess on your hands! First appearances of the relationship diagram can be confusing. The diagram is usually completed on a large piece of paper (flip chart or similar paper posted on a wall) covered with boxes representing all of the system's components, each of which is connected by one or more arrows, representing the direction and strength of the causal relationship.

Exhibit 324: Basic Relationship Diagram

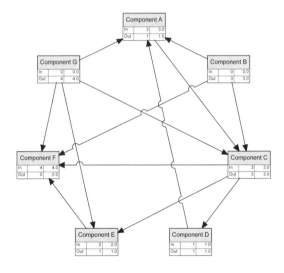

This works well when the system is relatively small, but it can become very confusing when the number of components becomes large. Nevertheless, the relationship diagram is the only tool capable of capturing the inherent messiness or complexity of a real-world system with all its underlying relationships. To help facilitate understanding and analysis, larger and more complex relationship diagrams usually combine the diagram with a matrix model of the relationships. This matrix model translates the components and relationships into a table format, to ease both interpretation and some of the computations involved in analyzing the resulting data.

WHEN TO USE AN RELATIONSHIP DIAGRAM

Don't use the relationship diagram to map out a neat logical plan – tree diagrams are far more useful in these areas. Use the relationship diagram whenever you are trying to represent real-world conditions or issues. Specifically, use the relationship diagram whenever:

▲ **The team is trying to properly frame an improvement opportunity.** One of the initial steps in preparing for any improvement effort is properly framing the issue or improvement opportunity. Framing attempts to define an issue or opportunity in an unbiased way. It's not about tak-ing an accounting perspective, or a marketing perspective, but rather involves a systems perspective that allows the team to approach the problem from a fresh viewpoint. At the same time, the frame provides a scope and shared understanding of what the issue or opportunity is all about. The relationship diagram can help develop this frame by providing a visual map of the system, allowing the team to define its own perspective and locate its boundaries or scope of inquiry.

▲ **The team believes the problem or issue at hand is really only a symptom.** A strength of relationship diagrams is their ability to help locate and identify 'drivers' or root causes of issues, and separate them from the effects or symptoms. As improvement efforts proceed, the team may get the feeling they are attacking only a symptom and missing the root cause of a problem. When this situation occurs, using the relationship diagram can help separate the wheat from the chaff. It can highlight likely drivers and provide focus to further improvement efforts.

▲ **The system is sufficiently complex that relationships among components are difficult to determine or under-stand**. The relationship diagram provides a structured and

methodical approach to identifying and representing rela-tionships in a complex system. The approach can be a little tedious for teams or individuals wishing to rush ahead and get to the root of the problem. Unfortunately, it is this ten-dency to rush ahead that can get teams into trouble, ending up in long meetings where everyone has a different opin-ion about what the relationships are in the system. These meetings rarely go anywhere beyond the thinly disguised surrender (expressed in the form of a conclusion) that "We are dealing with a very complex issue here!" So what? Nobody said improvement was easy. If the system is com-plex, we need some form of tool to help us deal with it – the relationship diagram.

PROCEDURE

Creating the relationship diagram assumes that the basic com-ponents of the system to be analyzed are known. This may have been accomplished through the use of process mapping, affinity charting, tree diagrams, cause and effect diagrams or many of the other tools described thus far. The key is that by whatever means the components have been identified, they are known and accepted by the team. The purpose of the relationship diagram is to help the team explore and analyze the inter-relationships among these components.

1. Create the cards for system components

For each system component, label a sticky-note or similar card with the name or description of the component. Ensure that only one system component is on each card, and number the cards for ease of analysis later on. The numbering does not imply any order or importance. These cards are then posted on a large piece of flip chart paper or preferably a large white-board, usually in random fashion so that the entire surface of the paper or whiteboard is covered.

2. Draw the relationship arrows

Now comes the messy analytical part. Start with card Number 1 or, in the case of Exhibit 325: Post the Cards, with the card labelled Component A. Ask if this card influences any other cards and, if it does, draw an arrow from this card to the cards it influences. It is usually easiest to proceed systematically; for example, compare card Number 1 with card Number 2, then move to card Number 3, and so on until card Number 1 has been compared to all other cards. Then move on to card Num-

Exhibit 325: Post the Cards

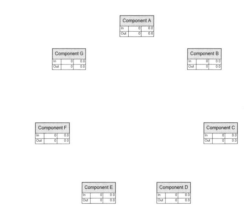

ber 2 and compare it systematically with all other cards. Continue until the team has worked its way through all the cards.

Do not allow two-way causal influences – that is, an arrow that goes from card Number 1 to Number 2 and then directly back from Number 2 to card Number 1. These sorts of influences are indications of missing components. Try to find the component that is missing and then add it to the diagram. In this case, an intermediate card (call it card Number 3) should be added. Card Number 2 may cause card Number 3, which then flows back to Number 1. The net effect may be a circular flow, but the nature of this flow should not be direct.

Be ready for the mess. Soon you will have a mass of cards and arrows everywhere. Don't be intimidated – the use of a matrix later on will ease the analysis. At this stage, it is more important to follow the arrows from card to card and ensure the team is in agreement with the underlying logic and structure.

3. Identify key or critical system components

Identifying critical system components is done by identifying those cards that have the greatest number of arrows leading in or out. In different-colored ink, the facilitator may mark on each card the number of incoming arrows and then, again in a different color of ink, the number of outgoing arrows. Those components with the highest numbers of arrows in total are deemed critical to the functioning of the system.

There are two other classifications we can consider:

Exhibit 326: Drawing the Relationship Arrows

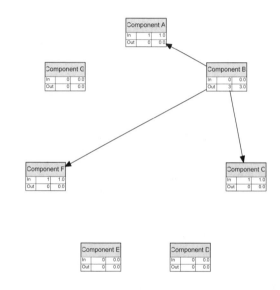

▲ **Drivers** are system components with higher numbers of outgoing arrows. Drivers are generally thought of as root or underlying causes within the system and, therefore, an area of focus when seeking to make system improvements.

▲ **Effects** are system components with relatively high numbers of incoming arrows. Effects are generally thought of as key system outputs or influences, whether they're intended or unintended. They tend not to be the cause of problems, but they may be ideal areas in which to identify quality characteristics and develop a measurement plan since they represent the cumulative effect of a great many system elements.

With these three types of system components identified (critical, drivers and effects), teams can proceed with a logical improvement strategy. They can focus improvement initiatives on the drivers and measure the result of these changes on the effects.

4. Create a matrix model of the inter-relationships

This step is usually done in concert with step 3 and is optional. The matrix can help with interpretation when the inter-relationships are complex or numerous. Creating the matrix involves listing system components down the side as well as across the top of a matrix. Arrows are then drawn in the direction of the causal, sequential or logical relationship. If an element heading

Exhibit 327: Completed Diagram

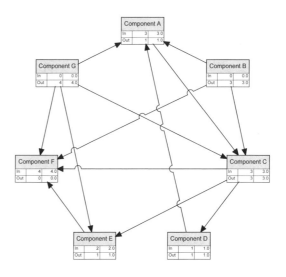

a vertical column influences an element in a horizontal row, the arrow would point to the row element in the intersection of the matrix. If the row element influences the column, the arrow would point up toward the column element. In other words, the arrows indicate the direction of causality.

Exhibit 328: Creating a Matrix Model of the Relationships

	Component A	Component B	Component C	Component D	Component E	Component F	Component G	In	Out	Total
Component A							←	1	0	1
Component B										0
Component C				↑ ←					1	1
Component D			←					1		1
Component E										0
Component F										0
Component G								0	1	1

Number of arrows pointing up.

Number of arrows pointing to the left

Scoring

This relationship is shown both ways, once on the lower part of the chart and once on the upper part of the chart (below and above the diagonal)

A minimum of three additional columns are added at the end of the matrix. One column is labelled 'IN', one labelled 'OUT', and one is labelled 'TOTAL'. The number of in and out arrows are then added up across the columns and entered in the appropriate row. For each row, arrows that point to the row heading count as 'IN.' Arrows that point up to a column heading count as 'OUT." Those components with the highest 'OUT' numbers are drivers of the system. Those components with the highest "IN" arrows are effects. And those with the highest 'totals' are critical components of the system.

5. Interpret the results

The team needs to review the completed diagram and matrix to ensure the conclusions mesh with their own collective experi-

Exhibit 329: Completed Matrix Model

	Component A	Component B	Component C	Component D	Component E	Component F	Component G	Scoring In	Scoring Out	Scoring Totals
Component A	▨	←⌐	↑	←⌐			←⌐	3	1	4
Component B	↑	▨	↑			↑		0	3	3
Component C	←⌐	←⌐	▨	↑	↑	↑	←⌐	3	3	6
Component D	↑		←⌐	▨				1	1	2
Component E			←⌐		▨	↑	←⌐	2	1	3
Component F		←⌐	←⌐		←⌐	▨	←⌐	4	0	4
Component G	↑		↑		↑	↑	▨	0	4	4

ence. It is important to avoid basing conclusions strictly on the basis of the number of arrows, whether they're in, out or total. The results need to be consistent with the experience of the team. Where the conclusions do not mesh, the team needs to review why. Are we forgetting some important influences? Do some system components seem overly important given the team's experience? Do others seem under-valued?

The key is to ensure that during the review, team members explore the reasons why some things are out of sync with the collective experience of the team. It is not sufficient to simply add arrows to make things balance with the way everyone

thought they should. After all, it is quite possible the analysis is telling the team something new, perhaps something more in tune with reality than the prevailing collective experience.

WEIGHTING RELATIONSHIPS

An enhancement to the basic procedure is to use different-colored lines or lines of different thickness (appearance) to indicate the strength of the causal influence from one component to the next. Usually these lines take on three values, indicating weak, medium and strong relationships. The weighting scheme is up to the analyst or team. However, the most common scheme uses 1, 3, 9 scale, corresponding to Low, Medium and High weighting values.

Exhibit 330: Relationship Diagram With Weighted Relationships

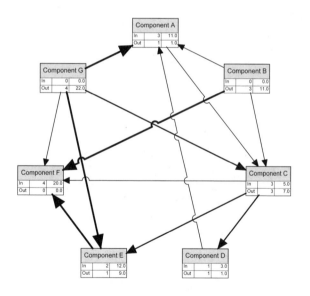

These weightings can be used to modify interpretation of the diagram and the matrix of inter-relationships. The number of in or out arrows is multiplied by their weight to get a weighted score for each component. Interpretation is then carried out, using these weighted scores, the same way the basic diagram was interpreted.

EXAMPLE: SOCIAL SYSTEM ANALYSIS

A project team is given responsibility to redesign the system of HIV/AIDS funding in a government jurisdiction. In doing so, the team must examine the current system of funding, including everything from funding for research to that for emergency housing, drugs and physician services.

A part of the analysis examines the system in general, to see what some of the drivers might be in the whole funding system. The result of the analysis is presented in Exhibit 333: Social System Analysis Using Relationship Diagram. The analysis highlighted the largest driver as people's prevailing notions and attitudes concerning HIV/AIDS. This result produced the understanding that speaking to the community at large with a single voice was essential if programming was to be effective.

Exhibit 331: Weighted Matrix Diagram

	Component A	Component B	Component C	Component D	Component E	Component F	Component G	Scoring: In	Out	In (Weighted)	Out (Weighted)	Total Weighted
Component A		↵	↑	↵			↵	3	1	11	1	12
Component B	↑		↑			↑		0	3	0	11	11
Component C	↵	↵		↑	↑	↑	↵	3	3	5	7	12
Component D	↑		↵					1	1	3	1	4
Component E			↵			↑	↵	2	1	12	9	21
Component F		↵	↵		↵		↵	4	0	20	0	20
Component G	↑		↑		↑	↑		0	4	0	22	22

Exhibit 332: Matrix Model of HIV/AIDS

Caring For People With HIV/AIDS

	No New HIV Cases	Legislation Protecting Against Discrimination	Improved Quality of Life	AIDS Patients Living Longer	Catastrophic Drug Plan	Home Care Physicians List	Housing	Funding Levels	Research	People's Attitudes & Beliefs	Coordinated Approach	Multiple Disciplinary	Responsive	Public Advocacy & Education	IN	OUT	TOTAL	IN (W)	OUT (W)
No New HIV Cases	■								↵					↵	2	0	2	18.0	0.0
Legislation Protecting Against Discrimination		■	↑				↑			↵					1	2	3	3.0	4.0
Improved Quality of Life		↵	■		↵	↵	↵	↵	↵	↵			↵		8	0	8	28.0	0.0
AIDS Patients Living Longer				■					↵						1	0	1	3.0	0.0
Catastrophic Drug Plan			↑		■					↵					1	1	2	9.0	9.0
Home Care Physicians List			↑			■									0	1	1	0.0	3.0
Housing		↵	↑				■			↵					2	1	3	12.0	1.0
Funding Levels			↑					■		↵					1	1	2	9.0	3.0
Research	↑		↑	↑					■	↑					0	4	4	0.0	22.0
People's Attitudes & Beliefs		↑	↑		↑		↑	↑	↵	■				↵	2	5	7	10.0	31.0
Coordinated Approach											■	↑		↑	0	2	2	0.0	12.0
Multiple Disciplinary											↵	■			1	0	1	3.0	0.0
Responsive			↑										■		0	1	1	0.0	1.0
Public Advocacy & Education	↑									↑	↵			■	1	2	3	9.0	18.0

Exhibit 333: Social System Analysis Using Relationship Diagram

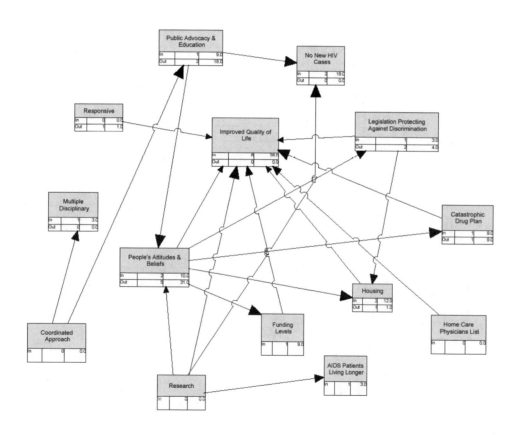

The outcome was the creation of a coordinating council, and an expansion of core processes to include funding for public education and awareness, in addition to some of the more "medical" funding allocations

MATRIX DIAGRAMS

Matrix diagrams are used to show and analyze the relationship between two or more dimensions to a problem, issue or improvement opportunity. In a typical application, one set of elements is laid out across the top of the matrix while the second set is presented along the side. Special symbols are then used at the intersection points, to detail the nature and strength of the relationship between the element in the row and the element in the column.

We have already presented some specialized types of matrix diagrams, although not referred to them as such. For example, the responsibility chart is really just a matrix diagram. Activities were presented along the side (the rows), and departments or individuals were presented across the top (making up the columns). A specialized set of symbols defined the nature of the relationship. Likewise, the Pugh concept selection matrix is

a specialized application of the matrix diagram where criteria and concepts are compared using the + or – symbol set. Even the GANTT chart is a specialized form of matrix diagram, with tasks or activities mapped along the side and time mapped out across the top of the matrix. Again, a specialized set of symbols (bars representing time) is used to characterize the relationship between task and resources.

These examples of specialized applications should make it clear how useful and flexible matrix diagrams are. Indeed, matrix diagrams are among the most useful tools for comparing one 'thing' with another.

WHERE TO USE MATRIX DIAGRAMS

Matrix diagrams are used to compare or analyze the relationship between any two sets of characteristics or factors in order to better understand the relationship between them. Some typical examples include:

▲ **When analyzing cause-and-effect relationships.** An example is comparing the types of errors occurring in a process or product with the root cause or process step that is creating the error. The matrix diagram makes it possible to see patterns and relationships, and helps identify improvement priorities.

▲ **In the design or redesign of products and services being delivered to customers.** Specific requirements or needs of the customer (usually referred to as "demanded quality" elements) are presented along the side of the matrix, creating the rows. Specific design or engineering characteristics of the product are presented across the top, creating the columns. In this case, the relationship between specific measurable product characteristics can be analyzed relative to the needs and priorities of the customer.

▲ **When seeking to create alignment of corporate direction.** High-level corporate goals and directional priorities can be presented along the side of the matrix. The supporting goals and objectives of departments, divisions and work groups can be presented across the top. The use of the matrix in this fashion allows for analysis of the supporting corporate efforts, and assessment of the degree to which they support the overall corporate mission.

▲ **Whenever objectives and the methods used to achieve these objectives need to be examined.** Objectives are used to define the rows of the matrix, while the methods or strategies used to achieve these objectives are detailed in the columns. This comparison between end and means allows the team to look for gaps in the strategy, and to identify activities or strategies that are failing to support, or perhaps working at cross purposes to, the overall direction and objectives of the organization.

▲ **When analyzing the different requirements or needs of different customer segments.** Customer segments could be used to make up the rows of the matrix, while a comprehensive listing of demanded quality characteristics creates the columns. The pattern of relationship between customer segment and product characteristic can be used to better understand the needs of different segments, and to create and design better-performing, more robust product designs.

TYPES OF MATRICES

Any matrix is limited by the flat surface of the paper or computer screen upon which it is presented. A flat surface presents information in two dimensions, the vertical and the horizontal. This might lead you to expect that all matrices are two-dimensional, having a vertical (y) and a horizontal (x) axis. Such is not the case, however. Some rather ingenious ways of formatting and combining matrices allow us to go beyond the "two-factor" boundary. There are numerous combinations of matrices, but we can identify five generic types: the L-type matrix, T-type, Y-type, X-type and the C-type.

L-TYPE MATRIX

This is the most basic of the matrix types, consisting of one set of rows and one set of columns. The most common applications of this type of matrix are examining the relationship between effects and their causes, and comparing goals and the means by which these goals are achieved.

T-TYPE MATRIX

The T-type matrix is the combination of two L-type matrices. With an L-type matrix, we could compare factor A with factor B. With the T-type, factor C can be thrown into the mix. Specifically, the T-type matrix allows factor A to be compared with factor B and factor C. Notice, however, that the arrangement of the matrix does not allow B and C to be compared or analyzed directly with each other.

Exhibit 334: Basic L-Type Matrix

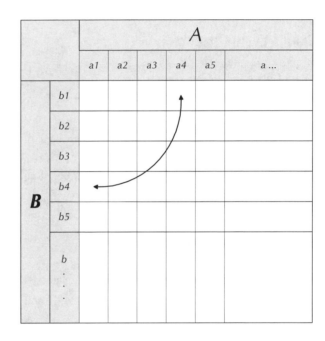

The T-type of matrix is excellent for the analysis of process in which types of errors, the cause of the errors, and the location (usually in terms of process step) are all to be examined. Another application is comparing specific product features with customer segments, including where the product feature gets used.

Y-TYPE MATRIX

The Y-type matrix makes up for the shortcoming of the T-type matrix, by allowing a full comparison of three factors. But this additional relational ability comes at a cost. The cost is the added complexity, meaning the Y-type matrix can be a little difficult to read and interpret. Moreover, this complexity seems to grow exponentially as the number of elements associated with each factor grows.

X-TYPE MATRIX

The X-type matrix combines four L-type matrices detailing the correspondences between A and B, B and C, C and D and D and A. Because of its layout, the X-type matrix is actually less confusing to use than the Y-type. However, the range of applications for which it is suitable is limited. Usually, it is easier to work with a series of L-type or T-type matrices than trying to handle everything in a single matrix design.

Exhibit 335: T-Type Matrix

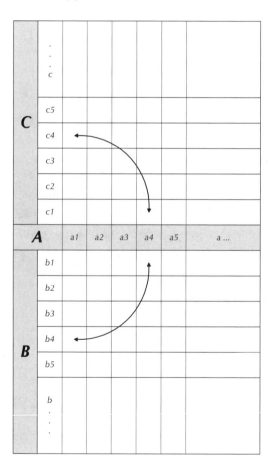

Exhibit 336: Y-Type Matrix

Exhibit 337: X-Type Matrix

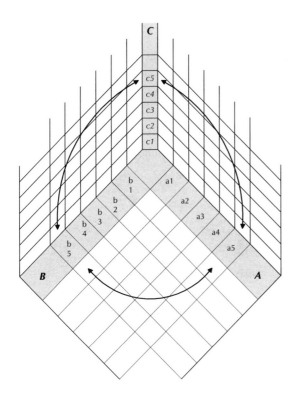

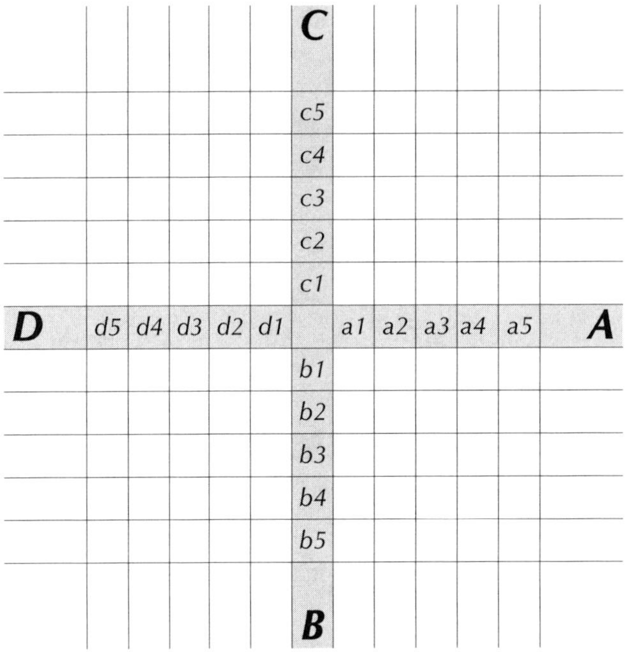

While the X-type matrix's applications may be few, where the matrix works, it works very well. Ryuji Fukuda has recently proposed a management methodology built partly upon the X-type matrix.[88] His Policy/Objectives matrix links the long-term direction priorities of the organization with its more specific set of objectives. The matrix also displays the specific targets that detail the measurable data associated with the objectives and, lastly, the overall effects all of this has on corporate performance.

Other similar methodologies have employed the X-type matrix to simultaneously compare inputs, management functions, activities, or means and outputs to a host of specific applications.

C-TYPE MATRIX

The C-type matrix (not shown) attempts to capture the relationship between three L-type matrices in three-dimensional space. This makes the matrix among the most difficult to read and interpret. It is best represented in the form of a cube.

As this survey of matrix types indicates, all the different types of matrices presented are really just variations of the L-type matrix. They add additional L-type matrices and place them wherever useful to the purposes of the analysis. The best type

---

88. Fukuda, Ryuji; Building Organizational Effectiveness, Productivity Press, Portland Oregon 1994

of matrix, therefore, is the one that most suits the analytical needs of the team using it.

CREATING THE MATRIX DIAGRAM

Creating the matrix diagram involves five basic steps. These are:

1. **Specify the problem,** which includes identifying the scope of the problem used to define the dimensions of the matrix.

2. **Detail each of the dimensions** – that is, define the set of elements that will be used to build the rows and columns of the matrix.

3. **Complete the relationships,** by assigning the appropriate symbols to the intersection points among the various rows and columns of the matrix.

4. **Conduct the scoring,** by adding the values of the various symbols applied in step 3.

5. **Analyze the results,** by making a qualitative and a quantitative analysis of the results and drawing conclusions.

1. Specify the problem

The first step in preparing the matrix diagram is to clearly specify the problem or situation to be understood. This requires identifying the purpose of the diagram, the two (or more) dimensions that will be linked through the matrix, and the underlying or supporting logic that supports this linkage. These diagrams are intended to help deal with the real world. As such, there should be logical reasons as to why dimensions are being linked through the matrix. These reasons need to be made explicit.

For example, suppose the team wishes to link different customer segments to specific customer requirements. The team believes it makes sense to do so. Believing is not enough, however. The underlying logic supporting the matrix's application of the matrix to these two dimensions should be clear. In this case, the supporting logic is simply that different types of customers tend to have different types of needs. The purpose of the diagram is to better understand and satisfy the various types of customers we have, by better understanding how their requirements are alike and how they differ.

Part of this step involves deciding on the appropriate matrix format. If the problem is defined and its dimensions are understood, the type of matrix to be used may be self-evident. In our customer segments-customer requirements example, two basic dimensions are identified and, therefore, the L-type matrix is appropriate. As the complexity and number of dimensions grow, the appropriate matrix may not be so clear. Because the difficulties in interpreting the matrix increase with added dimensions, care needs to be taken as to how the data will be presented.

With a problem of four dimensions, an X-type matrix can be used. But so can a T-type matrix along with an additional L-type. Which approach will be easier to interpret and deal with? The answers will depend on the nature of the specific problem with which the team is dealing. There are no fixed rules dictating how the matrix diagram(s) should be used. However, a useful guideline is to use the simpler matrices first and move on to more complex variations only if a combination of simpler tools fails to prove useful.

At times, there may be an implied direction to the relationship between column and row. Again, using customer segments and requirements as an example, is it more likely that different customer segments drive different needs, or more likely that different needs drive different segments? If the team is using existing customer segments to better understand requirements, then we would have good reason to suspect that different customer types drive different requirements. In this case, place the customer segments along the vertical axis so they define the rows of the matrix.

In contrast, the team may be trying to define different customer segments based upon their needs. In this case, customer requirements is the driver, literally defining the segments that will be created. So, customer requirements would be placed on the vertical axis, defining the rows of the matrix.

Whatever the relationship, the team needs to consider whether there is a direction implied by the dimensions in the matrix. If there is, try to be consistent about where the drivers are located. If this is impossible, then at least clearly define each dimension, noting the implied drivers in the diagram.

2. Detail the dimensions

Once the dimensions of the matrix diagram have been defined, the various components of each dimension need to be identified. If we are analyzing customer segments, then what segments are we going to use? Or, say we are comparing company competency requirements with components of a introductory management training program. All the management competencies demanded, and all of the training components, need to be spelled out in detail if the analysis is going to be complete.

Because of this detail, matrix diagrams usually involve the use of other tools to aid in the generation and organization of data. Most important among these is the tree diagram. To ensure comprehensiveness, it is sound practice to complete a tree diagram for each of the dimensions to be analyzed within the matrix diagram.

The objective in taking this approach is to ensure we are comprehensive in the analysis. Where key components are missing, there will be errors in the analysis, and the likelihood of incorrect interpretation increases. However, there's also the question of how much depth is required. We need to be comprehensive for the level of detail required, but there are no rules for defining what level of detail is appropriate. This depends on the nature of the problem being analyzed and the level of detail required to yield useful results to decision makers or product/ process designers.

3. Complete the relationships

With the dimensions of the matrix defined and detailed, the team must now complete the relationship between the components of each dimension within the diagram. Classifying the nature and strength of the relationship is usually done through a set of standardized symbols. These standardized symbols are presented in Table 338: Matrix Symbols & Weights.

There are two ways in which the nature and strength of the relationship can be defined: the judgment or the empirical method.

▲ **Judgment.** The simplest and most direct approach to establish the relationships within the matrix is to tap the judgment of the team or experts in the field. This can be done by requiring consensus of those participating in the project and going through each of the matrix intersection points one by one. If consensus is too difficult, a process of voting can also be used. Team members place votes on where they feel the strongest relationships exist. A rule is

then applied to divide the cells of the matrix into four groups. Those cells with the highest number of votes are labeled "strong." The next-highest grouping is labeled "medium." The next highest is labeled "low," and the last grouping is labeled "none." These descriptors correspond to the basic classification and symbol scheme presented. Any of the decision methods described in Chapter 8 will work well for this step. Simpler approaches should be applied to initial uses of the matrix diagram. More sophisticated approaches are appropriate as the importance or difficulty of the problem increases.

▲ **Empirical Methods.** Team or human judgment isn't the only way of establishing the strength of the relationship between two dimensions. Empirical measures also can be used. Research of opinion data, for example, can spell out the strength of the relationship between various segments and their respective requirements. A matrix comparing types of blemishes found on a painted surface with the different colors and manufacturers of paint could also use the matrix to compare these values, based on actual empirical data collected at the time of inspection.

4. Conduct the scoring

Once the relationships have been completed for the dimensions of the matrix, the basic scores for each component of each dimension should be tallied. Different values are associated with each symbol. The actual values can be modified by the team, but traditionally a 9, 3 and 1 scoring system is used. These can be used to help drive discussions concerning issues of importance and the like.

Table 338: Matrix Symbols & Weights

Correlation	Symbol	Weight
None		0
Weak	△	1
Medium	○	3
Strong	◉	9

Again, using the customer requirements/segments matrix as an example, a requirement with a very high score would be one shared by most or all of the segments using the product. In contrast, a requirement with a very low total score would be one that seems to serve no specific segment or does so to a very small degree. This may correspond to a product feature that can be easily eliminated from the design with little market penalty.

5. Analyze the results

Once the matrix is complete, the team needs to analyze the results. The first step is to take a look at the numbers. What components of each dimension scored highly and why? The numbers are not written in stone, however. Their purpose is to help drive discussion as much as anything.

The team also needs also to take a look at the matrix for any underlying patterns or anomalies. For example, are there any blank rows or columns? Blank rows or columns are a sign of wasted resources or unmet requirements. Take the example of required managerial competencies and training program components, with competencies forming the rows and training components making up the columns. A blank row would be a required competency with no supporting training component (unmet need). Likewise, a blank column would be a training component that does support any required management competency (wasted resources). These are clearly anomalies within the system that need exploring. It may be due to a simple error in establishing the relationship or it may be an accurate reflection of waste.

Once the matrix has been reviewed for blank rows and columns, patterns in the data can be explored. Sometimes, sorting or re-sorting the matrix can help in this regard. Does sorting either rows or columns create groupings in the relationships? And if so, what does this re-sort tell us about the dimensions under study? For example, if we're examining customer segments and requirements, can groups be created that tell us something about the behavior of customers across segments, or about affiliations among segments that were unrecognized before?

Again, we have to be careful about establishing hard and fast rules. Teams need to use their understanding of the situation and the problem being addressed by the matrix to help judge how to best approach the analysis. However, looking for blank rows and columns and re-sorting are two good initial strategies.

EXAMPLE: ANALYZING THE REQUIREMENTS OF DIFFERENT CUSTOMER SEGMENTS

A good example of the application of the L-Type matrix is the analysis of customer segments and their requirements of financial services. The financial institution in this case identified six basic customer segments. These were based on whether the customer was an individual or family (called a retail customer), a business customer, or an institutional customer (a large corporation or public sector institution). The customer groups were further segmented as to whether they were essentially depositors or borrowers.

These customer groups were then compared to the bank's predefined set of service quality characteristics used to assess corporate performance. These were derived using the SERVQUAL[89] model of service quality. In essence, this process was used to identify how important the various characteristics were to different customer groups.

---

89. Valarie A. Zeithaml, A. Parasuraman, Leonard L. Berry, Delivering Quality Service, The Free Press, New York, NY, 1990

Exhibit 339: Customer Segments and Bank Quality Characteristics

			Matrix Scoring Codes: △ = 1, ○ = 3, ● = 9	MARKET SEGMENT						TOTALS
				RETAIL ACCOUNTS		BUSINESS ACCOUNTS		INSTITUTIONAL ACCOUNTS		
				Retail Depositors	Retail Borrowers	Business Depositors	Business Borrowers	Institutional Depositors	Institutional Borrowers	
SERVICE QUALITY CHARACTERISTICS	TANGIBLES	Range of Products		○	△	○	△	○	△	12
		Interest Rates on Deposits		○		○		○		9
		Interest Rates on Loans			○		●		●	21
		Service Charges		△		○	△	●	○	17
		Branch Appearance		△	△	△		△		4
		ATM Locations		○						3
		Availability of Parking		○						3
		Hours of Operation		○		△				4
		Location of Branches		●		○		△		13
		Days of Service		○	△	△				5
	RELIABILITY	Easy to Read Statements		●	○	○	○	○	○	24
		Understandable Forms		○	△		○	△	△	9
		Accurate Record Keeping		●	●	○	●	●	●	48
	ASSURANCE	Financial Stability		●	△	○	△	○	△	18
		Deposit Insurance		○		○		○		9
		Ability to Solve Problems		△	△	○	●	●	○	26
	RESPONSIVENESS	Prompt Teller Service		○		○				6
		Prompt Loan Service			●		●		○	21
	EMPATHY	Friendly Professional Service		○	●	△	●	△	△	24
		Community Involvement		△		△		○	○	8
	TOTALS			70	39	35	54	49	37	284

The results, presented in Exhibit 339: Customer Segments and Bank Quality Characteristics, were surprising. Traditionally, the bank had targeted retail customers, but over the last two years was actively pursuing the business and institutional markets. But, as the matrix diagram makes clear, very little of what the bank considered important (the corporate set of quality characteristics) was relevant to these new markets. This sent a clear message to the bank's executive team – we still think like a retail bank, despite our efforts to appeal more to business customers. (Note that the number of points corresponding to retail depositors – 70 – is considerably larger than the score for the next largest group, business depositors.) This highlighted a need not only to change programs, but to change the way the bank thought of itself, and redesign programs and services in a fashion more geared to the new customer targets.

The bank had also relied upon its superior deposit insurance as a means of attracting customers, emphasizing this characteristic in its advertising. Yet the analysis made it clear that such insurance was important only to a small segment of the customer base, and was completely irrelevant to borrowers. In short, the matrix visually depicted just how unimportant this characteristic was in the overall scheme of things.

What did emerge as critical was the importance of accurate record keeping and easy-to-read statements across all segments. All customers wanted accurate maintenance and communication of balances and transactions. So, the analysis made it clear that all customer segments equated the performance of the bank with this quality characteristic – a basic characteristic using the Kano model, as it turned out.

EXAMPLE: ANALYZING PERFORMANCE PROBLEMS

T-type matrices have found extensive application in the analysis of process performance problems. The dimensions of the matrix are usually the outcomes experienced, the various process steps involved and the causes or errors occurring within the process yielding the effects or outcomes. In this example, the problem being analyzed was the process used by the staff scheduling department of a long-term care facility for the elderly.

Scheduling caregivers had been a long-standing problem within the organization, and indeed is a problem faced by many organizations involved with providing 24-hour care. Recently,

Exhibit 340: Scheduling Process and Problems

Outcome matrix (top) — column totals: Late Scheduling Alerts (9), Incorrect Employee Data (27), Failure to Forward Alerts (9), Data Base Reliability (1), Delays in Data Transfer (3), Failure to Log Process Closure (4), Data Entered in Incorrect Fields (1)

Outcome	Late Scheduling Alerts	Incorrect Employee Data	Failure to Forward Alerts	Data Base Reliability	Delays in Data Transfer	Failure to Log Process Closure	Data Entered in Incorrect Fields	Total
A. Staff Placed at Wrong Location		◉						9
B. Staff Placed at Wrong Time		◉						9
C. Inappropriate Staff Allocation			△					1
D. Resolution Failure	◉		◉	○				21
E. Wrong Staff Paid					○			3
F. Missing Paychecks		◉				△	△	11

Process Step matrix (bottom) — column totals: 21, 21, 9, 7, 15, 36, 12

	Process Step	Late Scheduling Alerts	Incorrect Employee Data	Failure to Forward Alerts	Data Base Reliability	Delays in Data Transfer	Failure to Log Process Closure	Data Entered in Incorrect Fields	Total
Exception Capture	1. Gather Data From Employee	◉	◉						18
	2. Enter Data Into Data base		◉				◉		18
	3. Forward Alert to Scheduling	◉		◉					18
	4. Transfer Data to Scheduling System	○			○	◉		△	16
	5. Confirm Resolution with Leader								0
	6. Log Entry	○					◉		10
Search Implementation	1. Prioritize Search Requests				△				1
	2. Initiate Search								0
	3. Log Responses						◉		9
	4. Enter Resolution				△				1
	5. Adjust Schedule/Rotation								0
	6. Log Resolution						◉		9
Adjustment Communication	1. Generate Update Notice								0
	2. Forward Notice to Leader					○			
	3. Log Acceptance of Resolution						◉		9
	4. Prepare Data for Payroll Input		◉	△				△	11
	5. Verify Coding		◉	△				△	11
	6. Approve Transfer					○			3

however, problems in this organization had increased and the number of staff complaints was rising. To address the issue, management conducted a basic process review of how people were scheduled in the organization. The resulting documentation of process steps, causes and net effects were captured and mapped out using a T-matrix diagram (see Exhibit 340: Scheduling Process and Problems).

Looking at the general pattern of correlation, the diagram makes it clear that the majority of causes affecting performance of the system are highly correlated with early process steps. Moreover, the analysis also clearly shows that the majority of negative outcomes or problems are due to the first three causes identified (Late Scheduling Alerts, Incorrect Employee Data, and Failure to Forward Alerts). These two conclusions made a course of action for improvement clear. The organization had to address the "Exception Capture" area of the process, to reduce or eliminate the possibility of the first three causes occurring.

This was the strategy pursued; the front end of the data entry process was redesigned, including significantly greater levels of error trapping in the redesign of the data input. Moreover, transfer of data was made easier, to reduce the delays in alerting Scheduling of exceptions to be addressed.

SUMMARY: MANAGEMENT & PLANNING TOOLS

Management and planning tools are designed to help integrate significant amounts of data into a simple graphic that makes it easier to see the system as a whole. This, in turn, makes it easier to identify gaps and redundancy in whatever effort is under analysis. In most cases, this amounts to analyzing relationships such as:

▲ the relationship between tasks and people (role and responsibility chart)

▲ the relationship between tasks and time (GANTT chart)

▲ the complex relationship among causes and effects or system elements generally (relationship diagram)

▲ the relationship between system elements (matrix diagrams).

Therefore, when teams are thinking about what is to be done and the resources required to accomplish it, using some form of management/planning tool is usually a good first step. It will help visualize and clarify the set of relationships that needs to be considered.

Organizational Alignment: The Tools and Techniques of Deployment

Too often, organizations work in ways where the activities of one unit fail to support the activities of another – or worse, where units work at cross-purposes, diminishing the performance of the individual units and the organization overall. This is the organizational equivalent of failing to "get your act together." Organizational alignment is about getting everyone working together in a way that supports the overall direction or purpose of the organization.

TWO DIMENSIONS OF ALIGNMENT

All organizations, and the systems and processes within them, exist to produce value. Any organization, or process within an organization, that fails to add value contributes no social or economic benefit and, therefore, has no reason for existence. Adding value is the purpose of any organization. Alignment is the process of bringing the activities of the organization in line with this purpose.

Organizational alignment has two dimensions. The first of these is horizontal and deals with value creation for customers. Clearly, organizations must create value for customers because the customer is the one that pays for the product or service. As has been noted earlier: no customers, no value added and, indeed, no business. The second dimension is vertical and deals with owners. It is not enough to provide value to the customer; in fact, this is only the first step. Value to the customer must be achieved in a manner that also provides value or return to the owners of the business as well.

The organization and its processes lie at the core of these two dimensions to value. Value must be created for the customer in a fashion that creates value for the shareholder. This concept is represented in Exhibit 341: Two Alignment Objectives.

Exhibit 341: Two Alignment Objectives

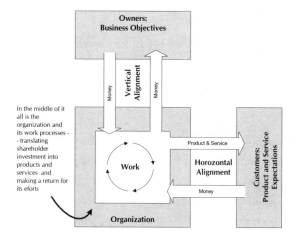

In creating value for both customer and owner, we must likewise create alignment in two basic dimensions, depending on whether we are aligning to the needs of owners or the needs of customers. In this regard we can speak of both vertical and horizontal alignment.

▲ **Vertical alignment** is concerned with the organizational direction and ensuring that the various divisions, departments and functions are aligned in such a way to support this direction and related business objectives. The technique used to provide this vertical alignment is usually referred to as ***Policy Deployment***.

▲ **Horizontal alignment** is concerned with aligning the organization with the needs and requirements of the customer, ensuring that everything from supply and design to manufacture and distribution support these customer expectations. The approach here is usually called ***Quality Function Deployment***.

A basic comparison of the two deployment applications is presented in the table. Despite the two applications, the essential purpose – alignment – is the same. As a result, the basic tool used in both applications is also the same – the deployment chart.

Table 342: Comparison of Policy and Quality Function Deployment

	Policy Deployment	Quality Function Deployment
Ends or Objectives	Business Goals and Objectives	Customer Demands and Expectations
Means or Methods	Specific activities or actions	Product or Service Characteristics
Target Group	Owners and Managers	Customers and Consumers
Direction	Vertical	Horizontal
Typical Applications	Organizational Planning	New Product Design
	Implementation of Improvement Initiative	Product or Service Re-Design
	Implementation of Strategy	Customer Segmentation
Key Tool	Deployment Chart: *Policy / Objectives Chart*	Deployment Chart: *House of Quality*

THE DEPLOYMENT CHART

The deployment chart provides a visual map of how each component of the organizational system contributes to higher-order purposes. These purposes may be the needs and expectations of owners or the requirements of the customer. Either way, the deployment chart explicitly links goals and objectives on the one hand, with the means used to achieve them on the other. This makes the deployment chart a key tool in overcoming one of the basic failings of traditional planning methods – separation of the ends from the means.

Ends and means can be separated conceptually, but not in practice. In the real world, goals that don't clearly specify the means to achieve them are simply a wish list. Likewise, strategies that don't have any objectives are meaningless activities literally designed to go nowhere. Effective planning requires consideration of both ends and means. Decisions made about one element can be reflected upon in relation to its impact on other elements. This is true whether considering the expectations of customers or owners.

The deployment chart's explicit and visual linkage, between *what* is demanded and *how* it is to be obtained, allows for critical review and creation of alignment. Moreover, the chart provides a clear 'line of sight' across organizational units and levels, allowing people to see and understand how they contribute to the bigger organizational picture.

ADVANTAGES OF DEPLOYMENT CHARTS

Deployment charts compel consideration of both the ends and the means by explicitly linking both in a matrix. This explicit linkage creates a performance model that details not only how the organization defines performance, but also how it proposes to obtain this performance level.

This approach has five basic benefits. They are:

1. **Keeps the organization grounded.** Plans where ends and means are separated tend to end up as "blue sky" pronouncements that have little connection to the operating reality in which they must be accomplished. Explicitly linking objectives to the means by which they will be achieved keeps the objective- setting process grounded, by compelling teams and decision makers to consider the 'hows' – the specific activities that will see the plan come about.

2. **Keeps organizational activities, and their relationships to one another, visible.** Use of a graphically based tool to explicitly connect ends and means lets everyone with a stake in the organization see what needs to be done to accomplish the objectives. Equally important, the tool allows everyone to see precisely how his or her involvement (at any level) impacts the bigger picture.

3. **Provides a visual map linking the activities of the organization's employees or teams with the outcomes the organization want to achieve.** All too often, employees have an understanding of their job, but they lack an understanding of how they connect to the bigger picture – where their job fits in. Deployment charts make these connections visible, by detailing precisely how each job fits into the larger scheme of things. Thus, the clerk in accounts receivable can see how he or she impacts sales and customer satisfaction. As such, the deployment chart provides a "line of sight" for those in the front lines --allowing them to see how what they do affects overall business objectives and/or customer satisfaction. This same line of sight is

also extended to senior management levels, allowing executives to see how their decisions impact on operating levels as well as customer satisfaction.

4. **Serves as a translation device between organizational boundaries.** Every level or functional division of the organization contains people that speak and look at things differently than people in other levels or functional areas. Accounting speaks a different language than production. Production sees things differently than marketing. And customers speak a different language and see things differently than people within the organization.

Customers may want cars that start quickly – a quality characteristic. But such definitions are too loose for engineering. What is meant by quickly? Ten seconds, 15? And at what temperature? It takes longer in the cold. Engineers must translate the customers' requirements into operational terms that can be designed and measured, so they're reflected in the product or service.

Similar problems exist between organizational levels. As Joseph Juran has pointed out, senior management tends to speak a different language (finance) than the organiza-

tion's middle management (people and process), and different again from the front-line levels of the organization (production or service delivery).[90] Deployment charts can serve as the link that spans these boundaries, effectively translating the language of one level into the language of the other.

5. **Compels identification of the value drivers.** Deployment charts compel the explicit definition of what creates value for customers and for owners. Further, they demand that the key value drivers are likewise defined and their relationships detailed. In short, deployment charts detail how the organization adds value or how it proposes to increase value added. As value represents the purpose of a process or system, this is a way of saying that deployment charts demand that organizations are explicit about their purposes and the means by which these are achieved.

---

90. This point is made in a number of Joseph Juran's writings. See Juran, Joseph; Managerial Breakthrough, McGraw Hill Inc. 1995

WHAT DOES THE CHART LOOK LIKE?

The basic deployment chart looks like a number of matrices and tables all placed on the same chart. This is in fact what it is. What defines the deployment chart is the specific set of components (matrices and tables) and how they are combined to present a comprehensive picture of ends and means. There are five basic components to a deployment chart. These are:

▲ **The Ends Table,** a detailed and usually hierarchically ordered set of objectives. The ends represent *what* the organization wants to achieve or what customers expect. By convention, these are arranged vertically on the left side of the deployment chart, creating the rows of the correlation matrix.

▲ **Planning Matrix,** which highlights the measurable objectives associated with each of the 'ends.' The matrix provides numerical indicators of the current and/or planned performance levels for each of the ends identified. These performance levels may be contrasted with past performance levels, or with the performance levels of competitors.

▲ **The Means/Hows Table,** the set of strategies, methods or ways by which the organization proposes to reach the ends

Exhibit 343: Basic Concept of Deployment Chart

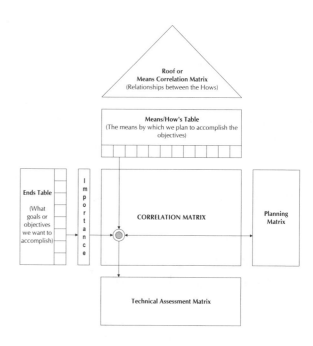

defined. These are also arranged hierarchically. The means are arranged horizontally across the top of the deployment chart, creating the columns of the correlation matrix.

▲ **Evaluative or Technical Assessment Matrix,** which highlights current performance measures relating to the means of the matrix. These measures can include engineering standards, process performance measures, design specifications and the like. This matrix is located at the bottom of the deployment chart.

▲ **The Correlation Matrix.** The central matrix at the core of the diagram provides the explicit linkage or correlation between the ends we want to accomplish (specified in the ends table) and the means by which we propose to get there (as detailed in the means table). Symbols are used at appropriate intersection points within the matrix to represent the nature and strength of the relationship between the ends and the means. By convention, the correlations within this matrix are described as High, Medium, Low or None, with corresponding numerical values of 9, 3, 1 or zero. The result is a highly detailed map of the relationship or correlation between our efforts and the ends we hope to achieve.

Other structures can be added to this basic deployment chart. These include:

▲ **Roof or Means Correlation.** This matrix presents how the various means are related to one another, highlighting strategies or design components that support or work against them. This room is triangular -shaped and located at the very top of the chart – hence its reference as the roof.

▲ **Side Roof or Ends Correlation** (not shown in Exhibit 343) can be added as well. Like the means correlation, the side roof is triangular, but it is located at the left side of the diagram. This matrix details how the various ends relate to each other, highlighting objectives or ends that are either mutually supportive or working against one another.

▲ **Graphical Analysis Rooms** (not shown in Exhibit 343) take the data provided in either the planning or the technical assessment matrix, and present it in a graphical format to support analysis and decision making.

Adding additional rooms or matrices need not be restricted to these rooms. Complex deployment maps can be constructed to align customer requirements for a complex product such as an automobile, down to the design specifications for specific materials and individual component designs.

CREATING A BASIC DEPLOYMENT CHART

The process of building the deployment charts can vary significantly, depending on the purpose of the analysis and the focus of the analytical effort. In some cases, the purpose is to translate general consumer demands for a specific product into a more clearly defined set of product or engineering specifications. In such cases, extensive use of brainstorming or other qualitative data-generating techniques may be used. In other cases, creation of the deployment chart can be used to drive sophisticated statistical experiments. In these circumstances, construction of the matrix is likely to be driven by empirical data that provides direction to the experiment. The bottom line is that the construction procedure is dependent upon the application, because the range of applications of deployment charts is so varied.

Nevertheless, we can describe a basic process for building a deployment chart. The steps outlined here are meant as a generic approach to using this tool. They're a guide to construction that ultimately must be flexible enough to meet the specific requirements of your situation.

1. Define the ends we want to accomplish

Construction of the deployment matrix begins with the ends or objectives we hope to accomplish. When designing a new product or service, these ends would be a set of customer needs or requirements. In planning applications, the ends would be the higher-order or corporate-level goals and objectives that our process or function is intended to meet. Regardless of the application, defining precisely what it is we intend to accomplish is the essential first step.

As might be expected, the origin of these ends is varied. They might be presented to a project team as "givens," such as a set of corporate objectives. Or they might come out of a brainstorming exercise where the data has been organized by an affinity or a tree diagram. The origin of the ends will, therefore, depend on the specific application as well as the circumstances in which the improvement team finds itself.

While the source of the data for the ends may vary, comprehensiveness and clarity are a constant. Because this tool is used to help design new products and services, it is important that the full range of customer or corporate requirements is known and incorporated into the analysis. If this is not done, we will be designing or redesigning according to a subset of requirements, where the missing components could be critical for success. At the same time, the search for comprehensiveness cannot be reduced to a set of vague, generic statements designed to cover all the bases. The requirements must be broken down into clear and concrete statements that are not open to broad and varied interpretation.

For this reason, the ends are usually analyzed and presented in a table version of a tree diagram. The higher-order 'ends' lie to the left and the lower-order, specific ends are located to the right. The resulting hierarchy of ends or ends table is then displayed so that the broad objectives are acknowledged as well as the more specific items that define them within the overall deployment chart.

Also included with the ends are some numerical indicators that detail the relative importance of the various ends or requirements. Any number of techniques can be used here. Customer requirements may be weighted using customer research data. Management objectives could be weighted through preference techniques (see preference and criteria-based decision making methods).

Exhibit 344: The 'Ends' or Requirements Table

ENDS	A. High Level End	1. End
		2. End
		3. End
	B. High Level End	1. End
		2. End
	C. High Level End	1. End
		2. End
		3. End
	D. High Level End	1. End
		2. End

At times, the research may simply not be available or possible to obtain. In these circumstances, the team only has two choices – weight all the requirements equally or use their own experience to provide the weightings. If the team decides to use their own experience, a rating or voting system can be employed to provide the weightings in relatively short order.

Some prefer to place these importance ratings in the planning matrix (discussed next). This is fine. The location of these importance figures is not so critical as having the importance specified.

Whatever the approach, obtaining some indication of the relative importance of various ends to be pursued is important. It compels decision makers to deal with the inevitable trade-offs that occur when real world planning takes place.

2. Complete the planning matrix

The planning matrix is where the quantitative data associated with the ends are located. Generally, there are a number of components to the planning matrix that will vary depending upon the application. Typical quantitative data or controls include:

▲ **Current performance.** Importance of the ends is one-half of the equation, and this is delineated when the ends are first defined. Performance is the other half. In quality

function deployment (QFD) applications, performance is most often defined as the levels of customer satisfaction associated with each of the customer requirements. Data might come from customer surveys, or perhaps from feedback from frontline staff on largest sources of customer frustration and complaints. In policy deployment, performance may be described as the satisfaction levels of senior management with the performance of the organization in each of the major key result areas, or it may consist of specific performance data. Whatever the application, the planning matrix requires the team to identify some measure of performance for each of the major 'ends' that the organization is expected to accomplish.

▲ **Competitive performance.** Our organization is not the only one where performance needs to be analyzed. There is also the performance of our competitors. If customer satisfaction measures were used to establish the performance of our organization for each of the ends in the analysis, similar research can be used to establish the satisfaction of customers with our competitors. Likewise, if specific corporate performance measurement metrics were used (i.e. return on capital deployed, number of safety incidents, financial margin), corresponding perfor-

Exhibit 345: Building the Planning Matrix

The ends or requirements
defined in step 1

The Planning Matrix

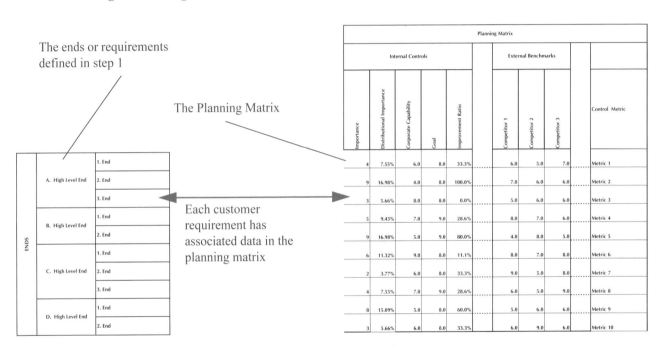

Each customer
requirement has
associated data in the
planning matrix

Planning Matrix										
	Internal Controls						External Benchmarks			
Importance	Distributional Importance	Corporate Capability	Goal	Improvement Ratio		Competitor 1	Competitor 2	Competitor 3		Control Metric
4	7.55%	6.0	8.0	33.3%		6.0	5.0	7.0		Metric 1
9	16.98%	4.0	8.0	100.0%		7.0	6.0	6.0		Metric 2
3	5.66%	8.0	8.0	0.0%		5.0	6.0	6.0		Metric 3
5	9.43%	7.0	9.0	28.6%		8.0	7.0	6.0		Metric 4
9	16.98%	5.0	9.0	80.0%		4.0	8.0	5.0		Metric 5
6	11.32%	9.0	8.0	11.1%		8.0	7.0	8.0		Metric 6
2	3.77%	6.0	8.0	33.3%		9.0	5.0	8.0		Metric 7
4	7.55%	7.0	9.0	28.6%		6.0	5.0	9.0		Metric 8
8	15.09%	5.0	8.0	60.0%		5.0	6.0	6.0		Metric 9
3	5.66%	6.0	8.0	33.3%		6.0	9.0	6.0		Metric 10

ENDS

A. High Level End	1. End
	2. End
	3. End
B. High Level End	1. End
	2. End
C. High Level End	1. End
	2. End
	3. End
D. High Level End	1. End
	2. End

mance metrics should be gathered for competitors. Notice that gathering comparative performance data for both our organization and that of competitors enables the identification of a performance gap – the difference between our performance and that of our competitors.

▲ **Goals.** For each end or requirement, numerical goals may also be included in the matrix. These goals are usually expressed in the same numerical scale as the performance levels were expressed. This allows for the direct comparison of current versus desired performance, as well as the development of an improvement ratio (next step). The creation of goals within the planning matrix is in no way intended to be an arbitrary goal-setting exercise equivalent to that found within traditional management practice. Just the opposite. Goals are set within the planning matrix so the implications of our plans and expectations can be assessed. In the real world, there will be trade-offs between the benefits and organizational costs that will force a revision and rethinking of the initial goals set.

▲ **Improvement ratio.** The improvement ratio is simply the goal divided by the current level of performance (current levels of satisfaction or performance expressed by either customers or senior management). The larger the goal relative to the current level of performance, the larger will be the improvement ratio. The ratio is a measure of the degree of improvement required in different performance areas; it is not a measure of the degree of difficulty associated with this improvement. The improvement ratio answers a simple question: "Compared to our expectations or the expectations of our customers, where do we need to improve the most?"

▲ **Degree of difficulty.** The degree of difficulty is a rough measure of the amount of organizational effort required to accomplish the change. Degree of difficulty or organizational effort is used rather than cost, because the considerations to be included go beyond simple financial cost. Cultural change is an example. A redesign in product or process may be possible, but it may be totally out of keeping with organizational norms. In such cases, the degree of organizational effort or degree of difficulty may far outstrip the financial costs associated with the implementation. Teams assessing the degree of difficulty, therefore, must keep in mind all the resources required to see the change implemented. They range from financial resources and employee time, to organizational learning and re-learning of behavior.

A standard measure for estimation of organization difficulty is the three-point scale:

▶ No significant effort required: 0

▶ Moderately difficult effort required: 2

▶ Difficult, significant effort required: 5

Other rating techniques can be used as well. The three-point scale is common because it allows for quick calculation of values and can be used to easily calculate a benefit-cost ratio.

▲ **Benefit-Cost ratio.** The benefit-cost ratio is simply the improvement ratio divided by the degree of difficulty. In a sense, the ratio 'discounts' the resulting improvement by the amount of organizational effort required to see the improvement come about.

▲ **Raw & Normalized Weights.** The raw weight is the value of the specific end or requirement. It is calculated by multiplying the benefit-cost ratio by the importance weight. The result is a numerical value that reflects the amount of improvement required (the goal divided by the current performance). The value is also discounted by the amount of organizational effort required to bring about the change. And, it's adjusted by the requirement's importance to the customer or senior management (depending upon the application). In short, the raw weight is a summary statistic or value that helps the team focus on what is important in the real world of trade-offs and competing objectives.

The normalized weights are simply the percentages of the total of all the weights that are represented by the specific end or requirement.

3. Define the means by which we propose to accomplish the ends

With the ends clearly defined, along with their quantitative data or respective controls in the planning matrix, the means we propose to accomplish these ends must now be spelled out. What is meant by "means" varies according to the application. They might be specific product design features, process characteristics or service elements. They can be anything we are using to deliver the requirements identified, or that help translate the language of customers or management into more operational terms.

Defining the means is often referred to as the technical response. We are defining how we propose to respond to the needs of the customer or the requirements of the organization in our own 'technical' language. The ends are stated in the language of the customer or executive management. But the means are stated in the language of the organization or department that is creating the plan, whether it's in the language of the designer, engineer or manager.

Teams will likely use some basic information-generating tools to elicit this information. Brainstorming, affinity charting and the like can be used to generate ideas and critical response variables or design characteristics. These can then be grouped, refined, modified and generally re-worked to the point where an agreed-upon set of means has been identified.

As was the case with identifying the ends, the means are usually presented in some hierarchical form. General or global statements go at the top, with specific details presented in the lower levels of the tree. These detailed design characteristics represent the set of technical characteristics that will be deployed throughout the design to meet the specified requirements. They will also be measurable, because performance along these characteristics must be evaluated in analyzing how well customer or corporate requirements are met.

So how far should we go? How many means should be identified and how much detail is required? Again, there are no hard and fast rules. Specifics will vary with the type of application. But there are two basic criteria that apply here:

▲ **Is the list complete?** This is the comprehensiveness criterion. Have we covered all the bases and ensured that the scope or range of activities identified fully encompasses all the elements required to deliver the "ends?" That is, can we deliver the expectations of executive management or customers?

▲ **Is the list sufficient?** We need sufficient level of detail for the results to provide useful information. If we are redesigning a process, the team must define the level of information it requires to analyze and understand the process it is improving. If creating a new product, what level of detail is required at this stage of the product design effort? The level of detail provided must be sufficient for teams involved in the improvement effort to make decisions and change or improve designs.

Experience also provides some guidelines on the appropriate level of detail. Generally speaking, a means hierarchy should be limited to a maximum of three levels. This limit was not arrived at through any sophisticated analysis. Rather, it's from the simple observation that more than three levels tends to produce charts of such complexity that the visual/explicit linkages between the ends and the means become more obscure and difficult to follow. The benefits of using the deployment chart, therefore, tend to diminish. After all, the objective of the exercise is to make these linkages clear.

So what do teams do when the three-level limitation is not sufficient? The answer is to create multiple charts, with the first chart providing scope to a high order of detail. Then roll this

Exhibit 346: Means Table Added to Create the Correlation Matrix

			Direction of Improvement	1. Mean ↓	1. Mean ↓	1. Mean ↓	1. Mean ↓	1. Mean ↑	1. Mean ↓	1. Mean ↑	1. Mean ↓	1. Mean ↓	1. Mean ↓	1. Mean ↓	1. Mean ↓	1. Mean ↓		Importance	Distributional Importance	Corporate Capability	Goal	Improvement Ratio	
				A. High Level Mean					B. High Level Mean				C. High Level Mean										
ENDS	A. High Level End	1. End																4	7.55%	6.0	8.0	33.3%	
		2. End																9	16.98%	4.0	8.0	100.0%	
		3. End																3	5.66%	8.0	8.0	0.0%	
	B. High Level End	1. End																5	9.43%	7.0	9.0	28.6%	
		2. End																9	16.98%	5.0	9.0	80.0%	
	C. High Level End	1. End																6	11.32%	9.0	8.0	11.1%	
		2. End																2	3.77%	6.0	8.0	33.3%	
		3. End																4	7.55%	7.0	9.0	28.6%	
	D. High Level End	1. End																8	15.09%	5.0	8.0	60.0%	
		2. End																3	5.66%	6.0	8.0	33.3%	

Means or How the Whats are to Accomplished — MEANS — Internal Controls — Plannir

Ends or What is to be Accomplished

down to a new deployment chart that provides additional levels of detail. This is called roll-down and is discussed in a following section of this chapter.

4. Define the relationship between the ends and the means

With the customer or corporate requirements listed down the side and the means to get there listed across the top, a matrix is created. The set of intersecting points is then analyzed one at a time to determine the nature and strength of the relationship between the ends and the means.

The strength of the relationship or correlation is usually expressed symbolically and with an assigned weighting. There are four basic weightings: strong, medium, weak and none. The weightings and symbols match those used in matrix diagrams and are Table 347: Deployment Chart Symbols & Weights. There are two basic ways in which these weightings can be determined.

1. **Team or expert experience.** The most basic approach to establish weightings is simply use the judgment of members of the team or experts in the field. Usually, opinions are gathered from a number of individuals, using a rating scheme to assign numerical values to the various relationship points. The first approximation of weightings is obtained by adding up the scores obtained for each intersection point. The difference between the highest score

Table 347: Deployment Chart Symbols & Weights

Correlation	Symbol	Weight
None		0
Weak	△	1
Medium	○	3
Strong	◉	9

and the lowest (the range of the data) is then calculated. This range is then divided into quartiles. The lowest quartile is assigned no relationship between the ends and the means. The second-lowest quartile scores are assigned a weak relationship status with a weight of 1. Points in the top quartile are assumed to be a strong relationship with a weighting of 9. Once this first approximation is completed, the chart is then reviewed by the team and reality-tested against their experience. Adjustments and modifications are made until there is consensus among team members.

2. **Empirical methods.** Empirical data can also be used to drive or create the correlation matrix. Some relationships between the means and customer or corporate requirements might already be known from past research. If not, an initial correlation matrix can be used to design new research in order to establish the validity of the expert judgments. The most sophisticated research in this regard is the application of controlled experiments. The demanded quality items become the response variables for the experiment. The means become the factors under study in the experiment, as well as some of the background variables that will be controlled. Once the experiment is designed, the relationship judgments of the team or experts can be tested by examining how the demanded or desired quality characteristic varies with controlled changes in the factors in the experiment. This results in empirical data that can be used to redefine the correlation matrix.

Once these relationships have been recorded within the correlation matrix, a quick review is required. Specifically, those building the matrix should look for any blank rows or columns. A blank row means there is something required but we have no means of delivering it. This may represent reality or it may be we have simply failed to identify all the means. Similarly, a blank column is a means or activity that has no corresponding purpose. Perhaps we have simply failed to identify all the requirements or ends.

If blank rows or columns are found, the team should review the ends and means tables just to ensure all the bases have been covered. If something is missing at this point, add it. If the means and ends tables seem complete, but there are still blank rows or columns, proceed with the next steps. This is an indication that what is missing (be it an end or means) really is missing and not simply a function of failing to describe the system adequately.

5. Complete the technical assessment (evaluative) matrix

Like the planning matrix, the technical assessment matrix is largely comprised of quantitative data, in this case, numerics associated with the means. The evaluative matrix usually has a number of standardized components.

▲ **Importance of the means.** The importance of the means does not use the judgments of the team or empirical data from customers, as was the case with the importance lev-

Exhibit 348: Filling in the Correlation Matrix

			Direction of Improvement →	A1 (↓)	A2 (↓)	A3 (↓)	A4 (↓)	A5 (↑)	B1 (↓)	B2 (↑)	B3 (↓)	B4 (↓)	B5 (↓)	C1 (↓)	C2 (↓)	C3 (↓)	Importance	Distributional Importance	Corporate Capability	Goal	Improvement Ratio
ENDS	A. High Level End	1. End		◉													4	7.55%	6.0	8.0	33.3%
		2. End					△										9	16.98%	4.0	8.0	100.0%
		3. End												○			3	5.66%	8.0	8.0	0.0%
	B. High Level End	1. End			◉		○		△								5	9.43%	7.0	9.0	28.6%
		2. End															9	16.98%	5.0	9.0	80.0%
	C. High Level End	1. End							△								6	11.32%	9.0	8.0	11.1%
		2. End															2	3.77%	6.0	8.0	33.3%
		3. End							○		○		◉				4	7.55%	7.0	9.0	28.6%
	D. High Level End	1. End														△	8	15.09%	5.0	8.0	60.0%
		2. End									△			○	△		3	5.66%	6.0	8.0	33.3%

Means or How the Whats are to be Accomplished — MEANS: A. High Level Mean, B. High Level Mean, C. High Level Mean; Internal Controls. Ends or What is to be Accomplished.

els set for the various ends. Rather, the importance of the means is determined by the demanded quality weights and the strength of the correlation defined in the correlation matrix. For each corresponding means, the strength of the correlation with a specific quality characteristic is multiplied by the weight for that quality characteristic. This is done for every quality characteristic, and the results totaled beneath the column of the corresponding means. These scores are then converted into percentages.

This process determines the importance of each and every means by the degree to which it supports the set of demanded quality characteristics (customer or corporate requirements). In other words, with deployment charts, the importance of any means or technical response is only that to which it supports the ends demanded.

This is critical in understanding the power of deployment charts. The importance of a strategy, design element, department, process or any other means to an end is only as strong as the degree to which the specific means supports the accomplishment of the end and the relative importance of that end. It doesn't matter what the engineer or senior management thinks is important – the importance is established by the objectives we want to achieve.

▲ **Performance measures.** Once each of the means is identified, a specific performance measure must be identified for each. These performance measures must specify:

▶ **The metric to be used.** This is the specific indicator of performance for the specified means.

▶ **The measurement process.** This is the process and units to be used in establishing performance, including when the measurement takes place, how it will be measured, who will measure and so on.

▶ **The direction of improvement.** There are three basic directions of improvement for any measure: more is better, less is better, and nominal. This is a crucial consideration. Often, performance measures are created without much thought about what it means when the measure goes up or down. A clear direction for improvement must be associated with every measure, and the logic behind these directions must also be well understood and shared within the organization.

▲ **Benchmark performance measures.** The next step in assessing performance is identifying how competitors perform in the same area. The technique used to gather this information is often referred to as competitive benchmarking. The technical assessment matrix of the deployment chart provides a specific set of areas to benchmark that are explicitly linked to ends or objectives. Because of this,

Exhibit 349: Adding the Technical Response Matrix

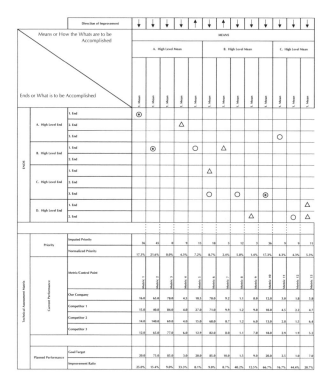

teams that have been encouraged to "Get out there and benchmark our performance!" are well advised to complete the deployment chart first. It can provide direction to the benchmarking efforts and a method of integrating the results.

These benchmarking efforts do not necessarily require a formal benchmarking exercise with the team visiting various competitive or best-in-class organizations. Not all organizations have access to benchmark data or the resources to engage in a formal benchmarking effort. Here again, team judgment can be used as a substitute. In many circumstances, teams will discover that considerable implicit knowledge exists within their organization, including knowledge about how well competitors perform in certain areas. A meeting of sales people, counter staff, design engineers, marketing specialists and front-line staff can often produce a significant knowledge base about the performance of competitors. Facilitation and voting techniques (already discussed) can be used to help the group develop a comparative assessment of how our organization compares with others. The results can then be incorporated into the technical assessment matrix.

▲ **Target setting.** Like with the planning matrix, targets may also be set in the technical assessment matrix. These are usually derived from the benchmark data. The assessment matrix will have already produced a calculation of the relevant priorities – that is, how important each means is in its ability to support a customer or executive requirement. Moreover, the benchmark data also reveals how well we stand relative to others. These two vital pieces of information can then be used to help teams set the improvement targets or goals for each means. The team needs to decide whether the organization should aim to outperform the competition in the selected area, to match the competition or to concede leadership to others.

▲ **Calculate the degree of difficulty.** Like with the planning matrix, estimates of degree of difficulty or organizational effort may also be included in the technical assessment matrix. By including the cost of achieving the targets for each of the means, teams can conduct a sound cost-benefit analysis for each mean included in the matrix.

6. Analyze and interpret the results

With the correlation, planning and technical assessment matrices completed, results of the deployment chart can be analyzed

and interpreted. The deployment chart presents an explicit model of the relationship between what we want to achieve and how we propose to achieve it. With this model, we can examine the relationships between these ends and means, as well as additional elements within the various rooms, or add-on matrices. Analysis of the deployment chart takes place in two dimensions:

Qualitative Analysis, which involves reviewing the data produced and identifying any patterns or surprises. This stage is essentially the same as the ITT – simply looking at the data to see what hits you. At the very least, this requires examination of the correlation matrix for:

▲ **Blank rows or delivery gaps.** A blank row represents a requirement that is not being met. Without any corresponding means to achieve the objective, the requirement or demanded quality has no way of being delivered – a delivery gap. If the product, service or process is to meet the demands of the company or its customers, a product characteristic or service element will have to be added.

▲ **Blank columns or redundant delivery.** A blank column indicates there is a means component which is serving no useful purpose, at least in terms of the specified demanded

Exhibit 350: Putting It All Together: Overall Deployment Chart

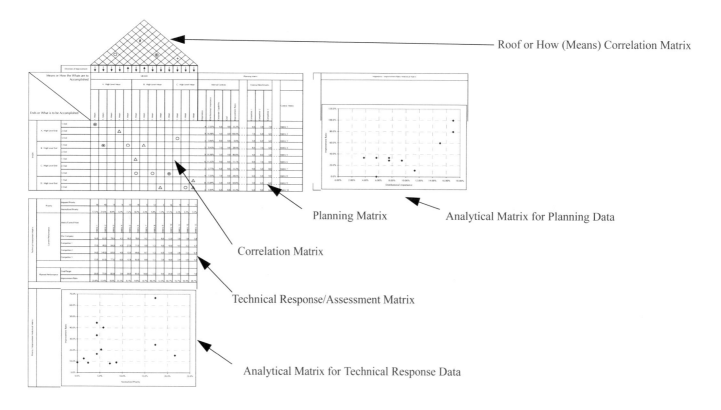

Roof or How (Means) Correlation Matrix

Planning Matrix

Analytical Matrix for Planning Data

Correlation Matrix

Technical Response/Assessment Matrix

Analytical Matrix for Technical Response Data

quality. We are doing or delivering something no one wants. This may be the result of a missing customer or corporate requirement, in which case it needs to be identified and added to the deployment chart. Or, the blank column may be indicating a feature or task that, in fact, is serving no useful purpose – providing no value. In this case, this means component is a good candidate for elimination.

▲ **Patterns in the correlation.** Beyond blank rows and columns, attention should be paid to examining the deployment chart for any special patterns in the correlation matrix. There is no way to define what these patterns might be in advance; it requires knowledge of the subject matter combined with an application of the ITT. Perhaps the bulk of the correlation lies with just one or two means, which indicates we are putting too many of our eggs in one basket. Perhaps the correlation suggests that different means are related to some degree, reflecting different aspects of the same strategy. Whatever the pattern might be, improvement teams need to look at the data to see if any patterns reveal themselves.

Quantitative analysis, which involves the plotting of results using some of the data analysis and decision-making tools

already mentioned. The most common of these are Pareto charts and analytical matrices. In conducting this review, comparisons usually focus on:

▲ **Importance/Performance Analysis,** which compares the importance of an end or means with the current level of performance exhibited by the organization.

▲ **Performance Gap Analysis,** which analyzes the difference between current organizational performance levels and those of competitors.

▲ **Performance Planning Analysis,** which examines current performance levels and the goals established by the organization.

▲ **Importance/Effort Analysis,** which compares the degree of effort required to achieve a level of performance improvement with the importance of the characteristic being improved.

All of these evaluations can be conducted for both planning matrices and technical assessment matrix measures.

POLICY DEPLOYMENT:
CREATING VERTICAL ALIGNMENT

Policy deployment or Management by Policy (to distinguish it from Management by Objectives) is one translation of the Japanese term "hoshin kanri." Hoshin is translated as "policy" or "targets and means," and kanri is translated as "management," "planning" or "control." Putting the two concepts together conveys the message of linking the targets and the means (the objectives and the strategies/initiatives) through a systematic process of management planning. Doing so is intended to bring about alignment among the various functions and levels within the organization and the overall purpose of the organization.

Policy deployment, therefore, is concerned with the degree of "fit" between the activities of the organization and the objectives it hopes to accomplish. What is happening in the front lines or on the shop floor should support the broad corporate goals and objectives that the organization wishes to pursue. If this is not the case, the organization is literally wasting its effort. In short, there needs to be alignment among the various levels and functions of the organization so that all organiza-

tional efforts work toward the overall mission of the organization.

In policy deployment, the ends are the set of management or organizational expectations. They may begin at any level – the higher the better. This may mean starting with the basic mission of the organization, or with a single all-encompassing improvement initiative for the year. The means of the deployment chart encompass all the strategies, initiatives or actions designed to see these corporate objectives accomplished.

WHERE TO USE THE POLICY DEPLOYMENT CHART

The policy deployment chart can be applied in a number of ways depending on the specific application. Applications can include organizational-wide strategic planning efforts, departmental planning activities, the planning associated with specific improvement initiatives, or any other activity where alignment between ends and means is deemed to be important. Some specific examples would include:

▲ **A company wants to know how departmental activities contribute to corporate performance.** Having created a corporate scorecard detailing key result areas and performance metrics and targets, a regional bank wanted to examine how its various departments and departmental activities contributed to corporate results. It defined and mapped these activities against the key result areas through a deployment chart to see where and how these activities were adding value now and where there was a basis for planning improvements. The ends in the deployment chart were the corporate key result areas and the planning matrix consisted of the corresponding metrics. The means of the deployment chart were the current range of departmental activities.

▲ **Ensuring performance improvement team's activities stay focused on primary objectives.** A process improvement team has been given the task of improving the order-handling process. Four objectives have been stated for the improvement effort. They are: improve customer access to the order desk; reduce the cycle time between the customer order and the actual shipment of the product; reduce the number of shipping errors; and reduce the overall cost of order handling. The team now has two tasks. The first is to better define the set of measures it will use to define performance in this improvement effort, and the second task is to examine how different improvement initiatives can support the objectives listed. The deployment chart supports both tasks. The ends of the deployment chart become the objectives set for the improvement effort. The planning matrix component of the chart establishes each of the measures. The corresponding means in the chart are the various improvement initiatives that can be used. The two ends and means are linked in the correlation matrix, allowing the team to see precisely how and to what degree different initiatives will contribute to the overall objectives.

▲ **Linking required organizational competencies with training program design.** An organization has defined the set of competencies it requires of its managers in the future. The human resources department has been asked to review the current management training program, to assess the degree to which current training supports these newly defined competencies. Where appropriate, human resources has been assigned the task of redesigning the current courses to improve the development of these competencies. Deployment charts are used to link the ends (competencies) with the current strategies or means for developing these competencies (training program components). From this analysis, gaps in the current training program are identified. The information is used to redesign the training program to enhance development of the desired competencies.

▲ **A municipal government embarks on an effort to improve the quality of life within the community.** Specific quality of life objectives are stated. The city administration now wants to examine its current set of programs and activities against this new set of objectives, to better understand how its current programming supports the quality of life among the citizenry. Administrators use the deployment chart to compare the quality of life objectives (ends) with the city's current programming levels and funding (means) as the basis for redesigning the system.

In each example, the organization's requirements become the 'ends' in the deployment chart. The challenge of the department or improvement team is to deploy its resources and strategies in such a way that they make the greatest contribution to the corporate direction.

EXAMPLE: IMPROVING BANK PERFORMANCE

The policy deployment chart in this example depicts the strategic plan of a medium-sized community bank. The bank's performance improvement team had defined a set of key result areas with accompanying measures used to determine corporate performance. As part of the planning effort, the bank wanted to clarify where it stood relative to others operating in the same industry (benchmarking) as a way of setting realistic corporate performance targets. Equally important, the bank's team needed to decide on a set of strategies designed to achieve these performance objectives. Deployment charting was used to help drive the planning process and to provide ongoing control for the plan.

Integrating the Bank's View of Performance

The bank had already defined and was using a set of key result areas as its corporate scorecard of performance. These key result areas were: Financial Performance, Customer Satisfaction, Employee Satisfaction, and Growth & Development.

Within each of these areas, a number of specific measurable objectives had also been defined.

To integrate the bank's definition of performance, the existing set of key result areas with accompanying objectives were placed into the 'ends' component of the deployment chart. In addition, corresponding performance data was entered into the planning matrix.

Completing the Planning Matrix

Next, the planning matrix was completed. The bank already had details on its current performance, and these were placed in the matrix in the current performance column. The organization also gathered some basic corporate benchmark data to provide a basis of comparison with the bank's own current performance level, and to define the extent of the performance gap between itself and other competitors. The results of this analysis (top three performers) were placed in the competitors' section of the planning matrix.

This analysis in turn drove board and executive considerations relative to improvement objectives. These objectives were entered into the 'Goal' column of the planning matrix. The

level of improvement implied by these objectives was calculated and presented in the 'Improvement Ratio' column.

Crafting Strategy

With the planning matrix defined, the organization had a complete reference for the outcomes it wanted to accomplish. What it didn't have was the strategy designed to get them to these new, planned levels of performance.

A number of strategies were proposed by management, far more than could be fully implemented by the bank. As an aid to decision-making, all these strategies and their supporting actions were mapped across the top of the deployment chart. Once this was done, the intersection between the ends (key result ares) and the means (strategic initiatives) were examined. These intersections were then coded using the standard symbols. This allowed the executive team to examine how certain strategies supported the set of corporate objectives and the degree of this support. It also allowed for redundancies to be identified – those strategies providing the same or similar net effect on the key result areas. Where such redundancies existed, resources would likely be wasted by pursuing both strategies – one strategy needed to be selected. Likewise, the degree of fit among various strategies could also be deter-mined. This ensured that the final set of strategic alternatives were fully capable of achieving the results that the organization wanted.

The deployment chart drives management to more clearly define and consider issues of alignment. This includes align-ment between goals and strategies, as well as alignment among various strategies. How will the strategic initiatives yield the improvement in key result areas? If they fail to contribute, then it's best to eliminate such strategies from the available options. Is the set of means sufficient to the task – will it provide the results demanded? If not, other strategies or components to existing strategies will have to be added. Are all the means necessary? Did some strategies fail to support or support only in a minor fashion the results desired? If so, could they be eliminated without impacting the corporate direction?

The process of asking and answering these questions forces consideration of the trade-offs that need to be made when craft-ing strategy. Organizations can never do all they desire. Focus and discipline are required. Objectives may have to be modi-fied if the organization has insufficient means to bring about results. Likewise, some means may be added and others

dropped, as trade-offs are made between what we want to achieve and the amount of effort and resources required to accomplish it.

At the end of the bank's process, the performance improve-ment team was left with three specific strategies: the Operating Margin Initiative, the Market Re-Positioning Initiative and the Customer Loyalty Initiative. Each of these strategies had a number of programs associated with them. Together, they were assessed to be the best set of strategies most likely to take the bank in the direction it wanted to go. These policy initiatives, combined with the previous work done, created the basic deployment chart presented in Table 351: Policy Deployment - Planning and Correlation Matrix Completed.

It is the concise and visual nature of the deployment chart that makes it such a useful tool, not only for planning purposes, but also for communicating the plans. In essence, the chart pro-vides a clear line of sight between "what" and "how." For example, how does the Operating Margin Initiative contribute to the market share objective? Answer: it doesn't. Look at the matrix. There are no intersecting points between the two, indi-cating that this initiative does nothing – and indeed isn't intended – to improve share. Rather, this strategic initiative is

Exhibit 351: Policy Deployment - Planning and Correlation Matrix Completed

		A. Operating Margin Initiative			B. Loans Process Improvement Initiative			C. Relationship Banking Initiative				Importance	Corporate Capability	Goal	Improvement Ratio	Competitor 1	Competitor 2	Competitor 3	Control Metric
		1. Operating Expense Reduction	2. Operating Income Improvement	3. Forms Review	1. Loans Administration System	2. Loans Processing Streamlining	3. Legal Requirements Review	1. Branch Upgrade Program	2. Relationship Training Initiative	3. Relationship Process Design	4. Marketing Campaign								
A. Financial Performance	1. Revenue		◉									10	4.5%	5.5%	22.2%	4.8%	3.9%	3.8%	(Interest Margin + Operating Revenue) / Assets
	2. Profitability	◉	◉									15	1.1%	2.6%	136.4%	1.8%	0.9%	1.0%	Income Before Taxes / Assets
	3. Internal Efficiency	◉		○	○	◉	○					5	3.4%	2.9%	14.7%	3.0%	3.0%	2.8%	Operating Expenses / Assets
B. Growth	1. Loan Growth			△	○	○	△	△			○	15	11.8%	13.0%	10.2%	12.0%	14.0%	10.0%	(Loans Current Over Loans Previous) - 100
	2. Deposit Growth							○			○	15	10.5%	13.0%	23.8%	9.0%	11.0%	11.0%	(Deposits Current Over Deposits Previous) - 100
	3. Market Share							○			○	10	22.5%	25.0%	11.1%	24.0%	18.0%	14.0%	Average for Deposits and Loans
C. Customer Satisfaction	1. Satisfaction							△	◉	◉		10	7.2	8.0	11.1%	N/A	N/A	N/A	Yearly Customer Survey on 9 point scale
	2. Customer Turnover							△	◉	◉		10	2.5%	2.0%	20.0%	N/A	N/A	N/A	Customer Accounts Transferred Out / Average Number of Customer Accounts
D. Employee Satisfaction	1. Satisfaction							○	△	△		10	7.5	8.0	6.7%	N/A	N/A	N/A	Yearly Employee Survey on a 9 point scale
	2. Employee Turnover							△	△	△		5	1.5%	1.0%	33.3%	N/A	N/A	N/A	Number of Employees Leaving / Average Number of Employees

designed to impact the financial objectives of the organization. Market share objectives will be most greatly influenced by the Relationship Banking Initiative, specifically the Branch Upgrade and Marketing Campaign components of that strategy.

The Technical Assessment Matrix

The next step in building the bank's deployment chart was detailing the technical assessment matrix. In the same way the planning matrix provides the performance 'controls' for each component of the ends, so the technical assessment matrix provides the control measures for each of the means – the strategic initiatives and their associated components. The means present how the organization will pursue its goals. The technical assessment matrix answers how much change will be required.

For the most part, these performance measures are similar to the measures presented in the planning matrix. For example, the technical assessment matrix, where possible, identifies comparative performance measures of other banks. There are also current performance levels as well as planned levels of performance. There is one significant difference between the two matrices, however. The importance of the various means is not established by executives directly, as is the case with the various key result areas. Rather, the importance is 'inputted' or calculated from the matrix. The importance of a strategy (or a means) is determined by the extent to which it is correlated with the ends required by the organization and the importance of those ends. The calculations involved have already been included. However, note that the importance for a means in any deployment chart is determined solely from these calculations. Doing so ensures that the relative priority placed upon any strategy is in alignment with the end results desired by the organization.

Exhibit 352: The Technical Assessment Matrix is Added (Planning Matrix Not Shown)

With the technical assessment matrix completed, the organization now has its first clear outline of the organization's strategy and the amount of change required by this strategy. In short, what needs to be done, and to what degree, have been specified.

Building On With Managerial Tools

Specifying what needs to be done is never enough. Other equally important implementation questions remain. Who will take responsibility for these tasks? When do they need to be completed? These are very real concerns that need be addressed if plans are to move from paper to practice, from intention to implementation.

To assist in implementation, other managerial tools are added to and embedded in the deployment chart. Placed below the technical assessment matrix are a responsibility chart and a GANTT chart. They detail who will be involved and take responsibility for each of the means, and provide a time-line for when the various projects supporting the strategy will be initiated and completed.

Exhibit 353: Adding the RACI and GANTT Charts

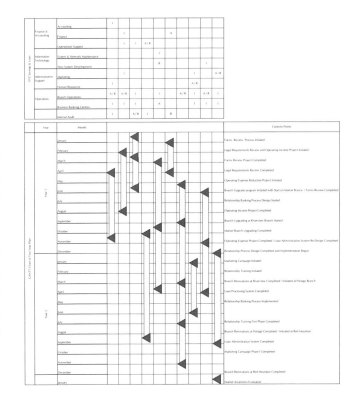

The Big Picture: Detailing the Plan

Once assembled, the elements of the deployment chart detail all the components of the bank's plan. This enables anyone to track how each component of the plan affects every other component. We can quickly see how a two-month delay in completing branch renovation work will impact the timing of profitability objectives (not at all). At the same time, we can also see that failing to meet deadlines for the Loan Processing Streamlining Project (due for completion in April, with Information Technology having accountability) will have some serious impacts on meeting the Internal Efficiency objectives.

As the chart in the exhibit also indicates, it's best to have the chart printed in a very large format. The bank in question laminated large copies of the chart for those that wanted them. The charts were quickly posted on walls throughout the bank. They were usually covered in marker-pen notes updating each chart with the latest information or 'to do' items. In short, the deployment charts gave employees what they so often need yet so often fail to receive. It presented a clear picture of where the organization was going, and its strategy for getting there. The chart also provided employees with a clear assignment of responsibilities that not only detailed what was expected of

Exhibit 354: The Big Picture: Completed Deployment Chart

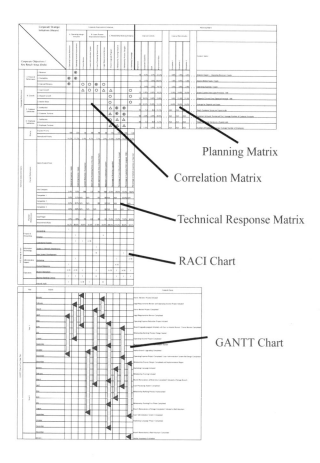

Planning Matrix

Correlation Matrix

Technical Response Matrix

RACI Chart

GANTT Chart

people, but also showed how individuals could contribute to the big picture.

QUALITY FUNCTION DEPLOYMENT: CREATING HORIZONTAL ALIGNMENT

Customer effectiveness is concerned with the degree of fit between what our customers want and the specific design or characteristics of the products we are delivering. Customers have their unique set of expectations for the products they purchase. These must be understood and built into the product if the organization is to grow market share and profit. This is what being customer-driven is all about – ensuring that what the customer wants or expects drives what the organization does. This is what is meant by "customer-in" thinking.

Bringing the voice of the customer into the design of a product or process is called *quality function deployment (QFD)*. The objectives or ends we want to accomplish are the customer requirements for the product. The means of the deployment

chart are the specific technical product characteristics we use to help deliver those customer requirements.

WHERE TO USE QFD

Quality function deployment helps to ensure that the voice of the customer is heard in the design or redesign of products and processes. The degree of complexity associated with the QFD process varies. Some applications, such as in the design of automobiles, are extremely complex and require considerable experience and expertise in the technique.

Complexity, however, isn't required. Any organization can benefit from examining the relationship between customer demands and the specific characteristics of product or service provided by the organization. Indeed, any organization that fails to conduct such an analysis is not likely to be around long. QFD provides a structured and focused approach for making precisely this type of analysis, and does so in a way that contributes directly to identifying improvement priorities. The application may be basic or complex. What matters is that an explicit analysis of the relationship between customer requirements and product characteristics is done.

Some examples of applications include:

▲ **The Emergency Medical Services (EMS) Department of a major metropolitan area has decided to review its operations.** In doing so, the department started with an extensive analysis of "customer" requirements under different circumstances. Customer segments were defined by the nature of the emergency rather than by any socio-demographic means. The needs of each segment and its relative priority or importance were then detailed using medical and other data (i.e. how important is having the right service show up at the door versus having anybody get there, but quickly?). These needs became the demanded quality characteristics (ends) of the department. The basic structure of the department, including locations, personnel deployments, technology and core processes became the means of the matrix. The result was a comprehensive analysis of how the organization was structured to deliver upon the demanded ends. From this, the organization built an improvement plan based upon a qualitative analysis of the correlation matrix that highlighted numerous 'delivery gaps' – ends with little or no correlating means.

▲ **A regional bank develops a comprehensive customer service model built upon the SERVQUAL[91] model.** The critical dimensions of service quality are tangibles, reliability, responsiveness, assurance and empathy. The bank then measures its performance against those of its competitors and identifies two major weaknesses – business loan application time and accessibility. By examining how these weaknesses relate to its core processes (the means of the deployment chart) the bank develops key initiatives for overcoming these weaknesses, including a revised loan application procedure, a new application processing technology, revised loan application standards and an enhanced web-based banking system for customers.

▲ **A major oil and gas company is undertaking an effort to redesign all of its service stations across the country.** Before the company does so, it conducts a major research effort to find out what characteristics of gas stations are important to different customers. Affinity charting is used to sort this data into a meaningful set of demanded quality characteristics, complete with importance weightings. Specific design characteristics of gas stations are then

---

91. See Valarie A. Zeithaml, et al., Delivering Quality Service, The Free Press, New York, NY., 1990

identified – some 120 characteristics are organized into five major groups. The correlations between these design characteristics and the customers' demanded quality elements are then compared to guide the redesign effort of the company's stations nation-wide.

▲ **A software developer is designing a new breakthrough product aimed at dramatically improving functionality and ease of use.** A complete set of user requirements is created to detail customer expectations. These expectations are compared, using a deployment chart, with all the critical characteristics of the new software program. The deployment matrix provides a method of benchmarking performance characteristics of the new program with major competitors' products. The chart also helps target improvement areas that will likely have the biggest impact on users, and areas to highlight as major selling features of the new program.

▲ **A manufacturer of 'downhole' drilling pipe to the oil industry reviews the major causes of downhole failures and their resulting costs to the drilling industry.** With the objective of minimizing these costs ('ends' in the deployment chart are the sources of failures), the company redesigns its sales practices and pipe classification meth-

ods for different applications. The result is fewer warranty claims and improved reputation for drilling.

EXAMPLE: REDESIGNING THE SERVICE AND REPAIR FUNCTION

An example of the effective application of quality function deployment is provided by a project to redesign the service and repair function of a major utility company. In this case, management wanted the redesign of service processes and the improvements to have maximum impact with customers.

So, at least an attempt was being made to become driven by customer expectations. However, anyone who has been involved in an improvement team knows this type of such improvement effort usually ends up in endless arguments about who is the customer, what the customer wants, and what changes would likely have the greatest effect. This effort is further complicated when different perspectives are represented on the team. The human resources representative argues for the need for HR solutions, the information technology director argues for technology- based solutions and so on.

QFD was used to help minimize these dysfunctions, while keeping clearly in view the business objective of maximizing the positive impact of improvements on customers.

What Does the Customer Want?

Like many improvement efforts, the team quickly found there was far more data available than had previously been thought. The marketing department had done some research not long ago into the service expectations of customers. Rather than re-invent the wheel, the improvement team adopted these findings as the 'going-in' definitions of what customers wanted.

This data became the "whats" of the deployment chart. The data was not complete. Additional research from both primary and secondary sources filled in some of the blanks. The team had answered relatively quickly the question of what the customer wanted. Moreover, the team had organized these objectives in a way (within the deployment chart) that was designed to facilitate effective alignment of service processes to meet these ends.

Completing the Means

Next step was examining the service delivery system to see how it compared to the set of customer requirements. The team wanted to see how aligned business activity was with customer expectations. Three basic functions of the service and repair area were identified. These were:

▲ **Call Answering & Scheduling**, which was responsible for taking customer repair requests and scheduling the arrival time of the service technician. This area also created the service order within the department's data base.

▲ **Service Operations,** which was responsible for visiting the customer's residence, determining the nature of the trouble and making the necessary repairs.

▲ **Closing & Billing,** which was responsible for preparing and mailing the invoices, and collecting and accounting for payments.

These functions were listed across the top of the deployment chart. Under each function, specific performance characteristics were identified. For example, under Call Answering & Scheduling, characteristics such as customer hold time, the call drop -off rate and the time required to actually schedule the

Exhibit 355: What the Customer Wants and Associated Planning Matrix

Good Service			Importance	Distributional Importance	Corporate Capability	Goal	Improvement Ratio		Competitor 1	Competitor 2	Competitor 3	Control Metric
	A. Fast	1. Quick to Handle Call	3	4.00%	7.0	8.0	14.3%		8.0	6.0	8.0	Ratings on Customer Survey (9point Scale)
		2. Short Time to Wait Before Service	6	8.00%	6.0	8.0	33.3%		6.5	7.0	5.5	Ratings on Customer Survey (9point Scale)
		3. Problem Resolved Quickly	9	12.00%	7.5	8.0	6.7%		7.0	7.0	8.0	Ratings on Customer Survey (9point Scale)
	B. Reliable	1. Problem Resolved	9	12.00%	7.0	9.0	28.6%		7.0	5.5	6.0	Ratings on Customer Survey (9point Scale)
		2. Problem Doesn't Return	9	12.00%	8.0	9.0	12.5%		7.0	8.0	7.0	Ratings on Customer Survey (9point Scale)
	C. Convvient	1. Easy to Get a Hold Of	6	8.00%	8.0	8.0	0.0%		8.0	7.5	8.0	Ratings on Customer Survey (9point Scale)
		2. Time Scheduled is Convenient	9	12.00%	7.0	8.0	14.3%		6.5	7.0	7.5	Ratings on Customer Survey (9point Scale)
		3. Personnel Arrive When Scheduled	9	12.00%	7.5	9.0	20.0%		8.0	7.0	5.0	Ratings on Customer Survey (9 Point Scale)
	D. Friendly	1. Treat Me as Important	7	9.33%	7.0	8.0	14.3%		7.0	5.5	6.0	Ratings on Customer Survey (9 Point Scale)
		2. Polite & Professional	8	10.67%	7.0	8.0	14.3%		7.5	6.0	6.5	Ratings on Customer Survey (9 Point Scale)

appointment were considered as important characteristics. Together, these functions and characteristics created the set of means for the deployment chart. They detailed how the department functioned in meeting customer requirements.

Examining the Correlations

With the means added to the chart, the correlation matrix could be filled in. This was done entirely through a brainstorming exercise among selected department members. Participants were asked to discuss the relationship between the various performance characteristics listed across the top of the chart and the various customer requirements along the side. In less than half a day, the team completed its assessment, coming to a general level of consensus concerning the nature and strength of the relationships between ends and means. The result of this effort is presented in the QFD chart.

With the chart completed, the team had a clear picture of what performance characteristics had the greatest impact upon customer satisfaction. Moreover, the deployment chart permitted further analysis on what areas of customer satisfaction would be impacted and to what degree, given different service delivery process improvements. Lastly, by providing a structured approach, the chart focused team efforts on content and substance, rather than on arguing specific points of view.

Completing the Technical Assessment

With the ends, means, planning matrix and correlation matrix completed, the team next moved to the technical assessment matrix. The first order of business was calculating the importance of the various service and repair delivery performance characteristics.

Remember, importance here is a calculated value derived from the correlation between the performance characteristic and the various customer requirements. Calculating this importance or priority level accomplishes two things:

▲ **It ensures that improvement priorities are driven by customer requirements.** The nature of the calculation ensures that the sole determinant of priority is the degree to which the performance characteristic supports improvement in customer satisfaction.

▲ **It eliminates or at least reduces the arguments around priority setting.** These arguments typically take place when teams meet to decide where to place their improvement focus. As mentioned earlier, such 'discussions' tend to be non-productive and too often end up with each team member arguing for his or her pet improvement project.

There is more to the technical assessment matrix than importance, however. The team also gathered some benchmarking data comparing the technical performance of competitors to their own organization's performance. From this, goal or target performance levels were set and the improvement ratios calculated.

Exhibit 356: QFD Chart - Planning Matrix Correlation Matrix Completed

Customer Requirements			1. Time to Answer	2. Hold Time	3. Call Drop Off Rate	4. Time to Schedule	5. Appointment Hit Rate	1. Time to Appointment	2. Problems Resolved of First Visit	3. Number of Return Visits	4. Late Arrivals	5. Reschedules	1. Quick Billing	2. Accurate Billing	3. Re-Billing Rate	Importance	Distributional Importance	Corporate Capability	Goal	Improvement Ratio	Competitor 1	Competitor 2	Competitor 3	Control Metric
Good Service	A. Fast	1. Quick to Handle Call	⊙	⊙	⊙	○										3	4.00%	7.0	8.0	14.1%	8.0	6.0	8.0	Ratings on Customer Survey (9point Scale)
		2. Short Time to Wait Before Service				△	⊙									6	8.00%	6.0	8.0	33.3%	6.5	7.0	5.5	Ratings on Customer Survey (9point Scale)
		3. Problem Resolved Quickly						○	⊙	⊙			○			9	12.00%	7.5	8.0	6.7%	7.0	7.0	8.0	Ratings on Customer Survey (9point Scale)
	B. Reliable	1. Problem Resolved							⊙	⊙						9	12.00%	7.0	9.0	28.6%	7.0	5.5	6.0	Ratings on Customer Survey (9point Scale)
		2. Problem Doesn't Return								⊙						9	12.00%	8.0	9.0	12.5%	7.0	8.0	7.0	Ratings on Customer Survey (9point Scale)
	C. Convient	1. Easy to Get a Hold Of	○	○	○											6	8.00%	8.0	8.0	0.0%	8.0	7.5	8.0	Ratings on Customer Survey (9point Scale)
		2. Time Scheduled is Convenient					⊙									9	12.00%	7.0	8.0	14.3%	6.5	7.0	7.5	Ratings on Customer Survey (9point Scale)
		3. Personnel Arrive When Scheduled									⊙	⊙				9	12.00%	7.5	9.0	20.0%	8.0	7.0	5.0	Ratings on Customer Survey (9 Point Scale)
	D. Friendly	1. Treat Me as Important					△						○	⊙		7	9.33%	7.0	8.0	14.1%	7.0	5.5	6.0	Ratings on Customer Survey (9 Point Scale)
		2. Polite & Professional							○	○	⊙	⊙	○	⊙		8	10.67%	7.5	8.0	14.3%	7.5	6.0	6.5	Ratings on Customer Survey (9 Point Scale)

Completing the "Roof"

While working on the technical assessment component of the deployment chart, the team also examined the degree to which various performance characteristics supported one another or were working at cross purposes. This analysis was completed in much the same fashion as for the correlation matrix, by gathering and documenting the opinions and insights of team members.

Adding on Analytical Matrices

The team also conducted some preliminary analysis on the relationship between the importance of various customer

Exhibit 357: Adding On the Technical Assessment Matrix (Planning Matrix Omitted)

		Direction of Improvement	↓	↓	↓	↓	↑	↓	↑	↓	↓	↓	↓	↓	↓
		Technical Response	Service Delivery Process												
			A. Call Answering & Scheduling					B. Service Operations					C. Closing & Billing		
Customer Requirements			1. Time to Answer	2. Hold Time	3. Call Drop Off Rate	4. Time to Schedule	5. Appointment Hit Rate	1. Time to Appointment	2. Problems Resolved of First Visit	3. Number of Return Visits	4. Late Arrivals	5. Reschedules	1. Quick Billing	2. Accurate Billing	3. Re-Billing Rate
Good Service	A. Fast	1. Quick to Handle Call	⊙	⊙	⊙	○									
		2. Short Time to Wait Before Service				△		⊙							
		3. Problem Resolved Quickly						○	⊙	⊙			○		
	B. Reliable	1. Problem Resolved							⊙	⊙					
		2. Problem Doesn't Return								⊙					
	C. Convvient	1. Easy to Get a Hold Of	○	○	○										
		2. Time Scheduled is Convenient					⊙								
		3. Personnel Arrive When Scheduled									⊙	⊙			
	D. Friendly	1. Treat Me as Important					△				○	⊙			
		2. Polite & Professional							○	○	⊙	⊙		○	⊙
Technical Assessment Matrix	Priority	Imputed Priority	45	45	45	15	88	81	186	267	174	216	27	24	72
		Normalized Priority	3.5%	3.5%	3.5%	1.2%	6.8%	6.3%	14.5%	20.8%	13.5%	16.8%	2.1%	1.9%	5.6%
	Current Performance	Metric/Control Point	Time to Answer Call in Seconds	Average Holding Time in Seconds	Percentage of Calls Hanging Up After Being Placed on Hold	Average Time in Minutes to Agree Upon Appointment	Customer Adjustment Rate	Time in Hours Between Call Time and Appointment Scheduled	Percentage of Problems Resolved on Initial Visit	Average Number of Visits per Ticket	Percentage of On Time Arrivals (20 Minute Window)	Percentage of Visits Rescheduled	Elapsed Time in Days Between Sign Off & Billing	Percentage of Customer Concerns / Rework	Percentage of Bills Requiring Re-Issue
		Our Company	16.0	65.0	1.7%	4.5	18.5%	78.0	92.0%	1.07	79.0%	12.0%	3.0	1.5%	0.5%
		Competitor 1	15.0	40.0	N/A	4.0	N/A	71.0	90.0%	1.20	85.0%	10.0%	N/A	N/A	N/A
		Competitor 2	14.0	140.0	N/a	4.0	N/A	68.0	85.0%	1.15	60.0%	13.0%	N/A	N/A	N/A
		Competitor 3	12.0	65.0	N/A	6.0	N/A	82.0	87.0%	1.14	69.0%	18.0%	N/A	N/A	N/A
	Planned Performance	Goal/Target	10.0	40.0	1.0%	3	10.0%	60.0	1.0	1.0	85.0%	5.0%	2.5	1.0%	0.1%
		Improvement Ratio	37.5%	38.5%	41.2%	33.3%	45.9%	23.1%	3.3%	2.8%	7.6%	58.3%	16.7%	33.3%	80.4%

requirements and the planned improvement ratios. The numbers for this analysis were taken directly from the planning matrix and plotted using the analytical matrix tool.

Recall that the analytical matrix divides the resulting plot into four quadrants. The upper- right hand area reflected those customer requirements of high importance, and which required the greatest level of improvement from the service and repair department.

A similar analysis using the same tool was performed on the technical assessment data, again using inputted importance and improvement ratios.

Summary

The resulting deployment chart is presented in the following exhibit. It details what the customer wants, precisely how the service and repair department will deliver these results, and areas where technical performance must change to improve customer satisfaction. The chart also sets priorities for improvement efforts.

Exhibit 358: The Completed Quality Function Deployment Matrix

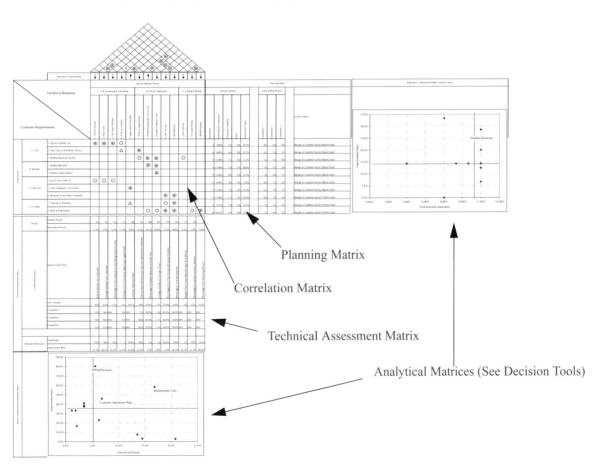

Planning Matrix

Correlation Matrix

Technical Assessment Matrix

Analytical Matrices (See Decision Tools)

HELPFUL SUPPORTING TOOLS

Deployment charting does not exist in isolation. It can and should be used with a variety of other tools to help enhance the technique's usefulness. Four such tool are discussed here. These are:

▲ **Voice of the Customer Tables** provide a useful way to gather customer expectations or requirements, for eventual inclusion in the deployment chart.

▲ **Pareto Charts** are used to graphically present single-dimension data arising from the planning matrix or the technical assessment matrix.

▲ **Analytical Matrices** provide an enhanced analytical capability to any deployment chart, by graphically representing two-dimensional data arising from the deployment chart.

▲ **Run Charts** offer a graphical presentation of competitor and benchmarking data, in a manner that enables quick understanding of competitive position and the extent of the performance gap.

VOICE OF THE CUSTOMER TABLES

In deployment charts, especially those applied to quality function deployment, a great deal depends on establishing an initial set of demanded quality characteristics – the essence of what the customer wants. These characteristics will guide all that follow. So how does one go about defining what it is the customer wants?

The process of defining customer wants or requirements is called the voice of the customer (VOC) process. A number of approaches can be used to define the VOC. These include empirical customer research, the experience of team members, or some combination of both. Wherever possible, some empirical research should be used. After all, we are trying to capture the voice of the customer. That voice can be very hard to hear if you're not actively listening and making notes.

Regardless of the source of data, a typical process for organizing the data – and ultimately presenting this data in the deployment chart – can be outlined. Specific steps will vary with the application, but a basic outline is provided below.

A Typical Voice of the Customer Process

Capturing the voice of the customer uses some of the tools we have already discussed, such as affinity charts, tree diagrams and basic data-gathering tools. The basic process includes:

▲ **Gathering research data, especially customer verbatims or comments from open-ended questions.** These comments do not necessarily have to come from formal questionnaires. Most organizations have people who are involved in gathering feedback from customers – sometimes whether they want it or not! Your sales people, complaint department, help functions and the like undoubtedly have a lot of information on what customers are asking for. Occasionally, this information will even be captured and filed, although it most likely will go unused. Old marketing research is also a great source for information, if one is careful to recognize that requirements change over time. However, it is often surprising to see so many organizations ask for open-ended responses from customers, yet have no idea what to do with these responses once they are received. The bottom line here is that teams should feel free to dig around a little. Chances are that someone in your organization knows what it is customers want. They have just never acted on the information.

▲ **Converting these verbatim customer comments into reworded, single-meaning statements.** This is a difficult step that should be approached with caution, since so much bias can creep into this act of translation. What we are trying to do is create a set of statements, each with a single, clear and concise meaning that reflects what the customer told us. For example, one customer statement might be to "add more tellers during lunch hour." A reworded statement tries to communicate a single idea of what the customer actually wants – in this case, likely "faster service between 12:00 and 1:00 p.m."

The difference between recording and sorting data verbatim, versus converting customer comments into re-worded single-meaning statements, is the difference between *providing customer data* and *understanding customer needs*. The role of analysis is not to just to provide more information, but to also provide some insight into what is going on in the mind of the customer.

▲ **Conducting an affinity charting exercise on the reworded data.** The first step in doing the affinity charting is to take the re-worded data and move it onto a set of cards (see affinity charting). This can be done by writing each re-worded single-meaning statement on sticky-notes, so the exercise can be done on a vertical surface such as flip-chart paper on a wall. Your personal computer can make this task easier. If the re-worded statements are captured on computer, print the data on mailing labels and place these on the sticky-notes. This saves a lot of writing time and ensures the re-worded data is captured for later use or possibly in other applications. Regardless of how the cards are created, they are then organized using the usual affinity charting method.

▲ **Finalizing the Voice of the Customer hierarchy.** There are no laws about the number of demanded quality levels or elements to be represented in the voice of the customer table, which will be the input to the ends in the QFD charts. Generally speaking, try to keep things simple. A good rule of thumb is to try and organize the demanded quality elements into no more than four levels. This means reworking the affinity diagram or creating a tree diagram, based on an initial affinity with three basic levels beyond the goal statement.

▲ **Determining the priorities to the customer.** Determining the priorities to the customer is really a two -step process. The first step is classifying the type of demanded quality. The second step is prioritizing the weight or importance to the customer.

As the process proceeds, results are documented in the voice of the customer tables (discussed next). This process can be a fair amount of work. The results are worth it. Too often, companies, organizations, departments and improvement teams charge ahead with some idea for improvement, assuming they know what the customer wants. All too often their assumptions are unfounded. A voice of the customer process does not eliminate these sorts of errors. But the process does force a more formal and objective consideration of that age old question: "What does the customer want?"

COMPLETING THE VOICE OF THE CUSTOMER TABLES

Voice of the customer tables (VOCT) are a convenient method to capture and record all the data arising out of a voice of the customer process. These tables are very similar to the voice of the process tables used to document processes. Both tables deal with answering who, what, when, where, why, how and how much. In the VOCT, these questions are applied to customers requirements as opposed to process issues.

Like with voice of the process tables, voice of the customer tables have two parts. The first part deals with describing customers and their needs. This data will define the "what" component of the deployment chart. The second part deals with specific performance measures related to these demands. As such, data in the second part of the VOCT will find its way into the planning matrix component of the deployment chart.

Part 1: VOCT 5W-2H Analysis

In the VOCT, the first question to answer is "who?" Answering this question involves customers, an essential step that will continue to drive the rest of the process. Different customers want different things. What a long- haul trucker demands of a service station is very different from what the average driver requires. Major corporate accounts require a different approach than occasional buyers. It is important, therefore, that customers be segmented and their salient characteristics captured, so that the differences among customers segments are reflected throughout the analysis.

With customers segmented we can move forward. For each segment, the analysis asks: "What, precisely do they want? When and where do they want it? Where do they want or use the product? And why do they want it? Is it a matter of convenience or a matter of limited time or both? How do they use the product and how much of it do they use?"

Answering who, what, when, where, why, how and how much during the process of reviewing, analyzing, and grouping data will go a long way in adding clarity to your thinking and to the resulting analysis. Filling in the columns of the VOCT provides a convenient way to ensure that all the questions have been asked, and our understanding of customer needs is sufficient to move forward with deployment charting techniques.

Part 2: Identifying Performance Characteristics

The second part of the VOCT deals with the specific performance characteristics demanded by the customer. These will eventually find their way to the planning matrix of the deployment chart. In this part of the table, the team:

▲ **Identifies the demanded quality characteristics or elements.** These are transferred directly from Part 1 of the

Exhibit 359: Voice of the Customer Table (Part 1)

Product or Service:

ID	Customer Characteristics Who	Voice of the Customer			Use											Demands	
		Actual	Why		What		When		Where		How						
			IE	Data	IE	Data	IE	Data	IE	Data	IE	Data				Statements	Characteristics

Prepared By: Date:

Exhibit 360: Voice of the Customer Table (Part 2)

Project:

ID	Demanded Quality	Quality Characteristic	Function	Reliability	Other

Prepared By: Date:

VOCT and are general statements of what is being demanded by the customer.

▲ **Defines specific performance characteristics associated with the demanded quality elements.** This is a more rigorous definition of the demanded quality elements, and provides a way to operationalize the measurements.

▲ **Clearly states what must be accomplished (function).** These are usually presented using the verb- noun technique, and they translate in very simple and direct terms precisely what must be done or provided for the customer.

▲ **Clearly states the degree of reliability required by the customer.** If the demanded quality characteristic is an absolute necessity, chances are it is a basic characteristic (using the Kano model of characteristic types).

Summary: Voice of the Customer Tables

With all this data completed, an improvement team can be reasonably sure that it has addressed what it needs to answer the question: "What does the customer want?" The team also has answered the question in a fashion where the results can be integrated into a deployment chart.

Voice of the customer tables needn't be reserved for customers, however. They also have application in policy deployment. In such applications, we might refer to them as "voice of management" tables. The idea is to clarify and define the set of managerial, executive board expectations for a specific process, product or function.

Doing so can provide clarity to improvement team efforts. The importance of having this clarity is familiar to anyone who has served on an improvement team, where the team flounders in its inability to answer such questions as: "What does management want us to do?" and "What results are we to achieve?" and the infamous "Why are we here?"

PARETO CHARTS

Deployment charts tend to produce or present a lot of numerical data. Improvement ratios, importance and priority measures, and similar numerical data tend to fill the planning and technical assessment matrices. At times, the amount of data can be a little overwhelming.

Single-dimensional data (data recorded for a single variable) can easily be presented using Pareto charts. The steps in creat-

Exhibit 361: Using the Pareto With the Deployment Chart

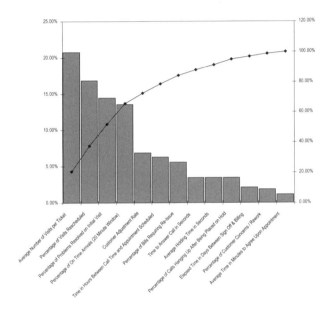

In the exhibit, importance data is presented from the technical assessment matrix in the earlier QFD chart example for utility service and repair. As the Pareto chart makes clear, Average Number of Visits per Repair Ticket has the highest importance.

ANALYTICAL MATRICES

Much of the power of deployment charts is derived from their ability to relate information about one set of data with another. For example, measures associated with a specific objective can be related back to the means employed to accomplish the objective. Likewise, information associated with a specific means or strategy can be correlated with the objective that the means was created to accomplish.

Analytical matrix applications fit well with deployment charts, because the analytical applications are also intended to relate two pieces of information at a time. Some of the more common sets of analysis that use the analytical matrix with the deployment charts are:

▲ Comparing the importance and performance measures of the planning matrix.

ing the Pareto chart are detailed in Chapter 6 and need not be repeated here. A quick example, however, would be using the Pareto chart to present the imputed importance of various alternative strategies or the importance of customer characteristics.

Exhibit 362: Using the Analytical Matrix

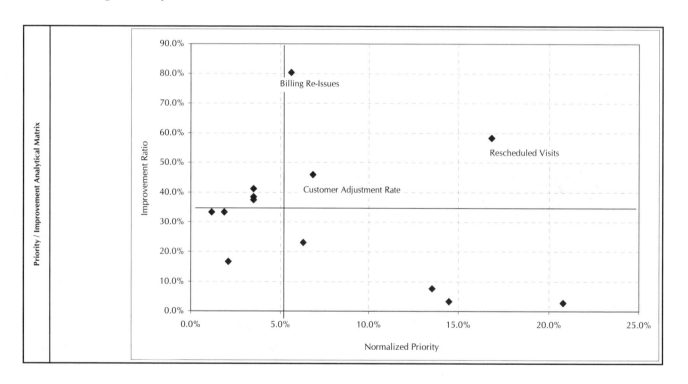

▲ Comparing the importance and improvement ratios in the planning matrix.

▲ Comparing the imputed importance with the level of organizational effort in the technical assessment matrix.

▲ Comparing imputed importance with the improvement ratio in the technical assessment matrix.

This is only a partial list, however. The most appropriate set of analytical matrices will be determined by the specific application for which the deployment chart is being used.

Exhibit 362: Using the Analytical Matrix presents the matrix used to relate the importance of, and the amount of improvement needed in, each of the areas of the service and repair function. The upper right quadrant in this case highlights areas of greatest impact on customers (distributional importance) and also having the greatest gap between current performance and corporate goals (improvement ratio).

RUN CHARTS

Run charts are typically used to present benchmarking data that compares the performance of competitors with our own. These are not typical run charts, as the data is not in time order. Nevertheless, the run chart does an excellent job in presenting this type of comparative data.

A basic example, again making use of the earlier QFD example, presents the data arising from the planning matrix. The competitors' data and our own performance is presented as a basic run chart (with lines plotted for each organization). The set of goals established for ourselves is represented in this case as triangles without any connecting line.

Exhibit 363: Run Chart of QFD Benchmarking Data

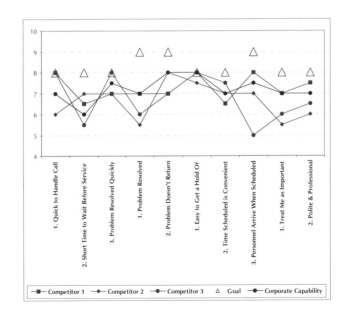

The chart in this case quickly conveys the areas where we are currently outperforming and under-performing the competition. It also shows where we have targeted for the greatest relative improvement.

CREATING AN ALIGNMENT SYSTEM

Deployment charts can be used in a variety of applications, wherever it is useful to create organizational alignment and effectiveness – which is just about everywhere. The versatility of deployment charts means that more often than not, they are up to the task. Using deployment charts for planning and improvement applications, however, only begins to tap their power.

Some organizations apply deployment charts as an integrated planning methodology. Numerous deployment charts are related to one another, to create a comprehensive picture of objectives and strategies throughout the organization. Virtually any component or activity of an organization can be represented in this fashion. Likewise, multiple deployment charts

can provide a comprehensive approach to product design, moving from customer requirements right down to part design.

Two approaches to combining and relating multiple deployment charts have evolved. They are:

▶ Four Phase Model

▶ Akao's Matrix of Matrices Approach

FOUR PHASE MODEL

The four phase model may now be the most widely used multiple deployment chart approach in North America. It has been championed by the American Supplier Institute (ASI) and the author behind much of its development, Donald Clausing. The model, originally developed for use in manufacturing applications, uses language to describe the various components of the system that is in accordance with its manufacturing model. It need not be so. The four phase model is extremely flexible and easy to use. It is easily adapted to virtually any type of planning application.

The basic idea behind the four phase model is the concept of "roll down." Roll down provides increasing level of detail by

Exhibit 364: Basic Concept of Roll Down

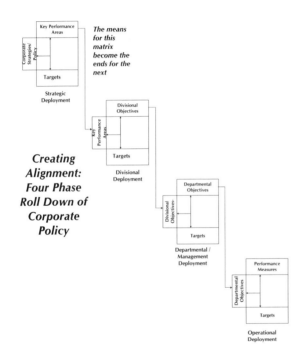

Creating Alignment: Four Phase Roll Down of Corporate Policy

met. In turn, this set of hows can then be rolled down to become a new set of ends and the process repeats itself. This process is illustrated in Exhibit 364: Basic Concept of Roll Down.

The nature of these roll downs will depend upon the specific application to which the deployment chart is being applied. The only rule is that the higher-order hows become the next level's ends. In this manner, activities, tasks, components and parts at the lowest levels of the organization are linked with the highest-order objectives of the organization. This linkage goes to the very heart of creating alignment across organization levels and organization functions, or between the organization and its customers.

This process is called the four phase model because, in its original application of automobile manufacturing, four specific levels were identified as all that can and should be required to roll down to a suitable level of detail. This is as good a rule as any in guarding against over-analysis.

rolling down a specific path where the hows of the deployment chart become the ends for the next level down. A new set of hows is then defined that details how these new ends will be

AKAO'S PLANNING SYSTEM: THE MATRIX OF MATRICES APPROACH

Dr. Yoji Akao is one of the early developers of quality function deployment and of the deployment chart as a tool for business and management planning. So, it should not be surprising that the system described by Dr. Akao is highly developed and very complex, but is capable of handling virtually any planning situation.

The Akao system proposes extensive use of matrices for everything from the highest-order planning right down to parts design. The system encompasses everything in between, including technology design, failure mode and effects analysis, system and sub-system analysis, reliability deployment and so on. This system of planning was later simplified for use in the United States by Bob King into a set of 30 matrices, themselves organized in a matrix (hence the matrix of matrices).[92] Later, this set of 30 was further reduced to 17 matrices to simplify the approach. The 30 matrices are presented in Exhibit 365: Matrix of Matrices.

---

92. Bob King, Better Designs in Half the Time, GOAL/QPC, Salem, N.H.

The matrix of matrices approach is not intended to be applied in a rigid fashion where each and every matrix needs to be completed. Rather, the intent is to present the full range of possibilities, to show how matrices could be connected to build a comprehensive planning system. The approach represents a menu of options, allowing the user to select those matrices most appropriate to the analysis at hand.

SUMMARY: CREATING ALIGNMENT WITH DEPLOYMENT TOOLS

The challenge of creating alignment is a significant one. Too often, the organizational response is simplistic, consisting of the one-day executive retreat in the woods to craft the plan. What emerges are blue-sky pronouncements that are long on vision and expectations and short on specifics – such as how the expectations will be met.

Setting expectations is only half the job (or less). Deployment charts explicitly detail the *how* behind the *what*. Specifically,

Exhibit 365: Matrix of Matrices[*]

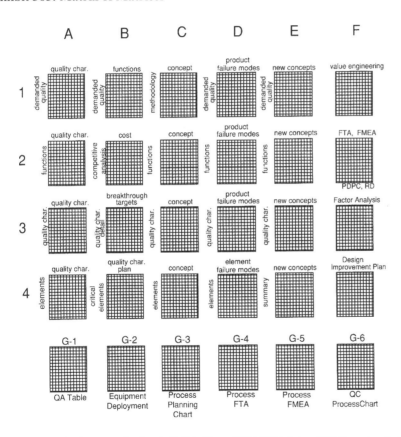

*Source: Bob King, Better Designs in Half the Time, GOAL/QPC, Salem, N.H. Reproduced with Permission.

they show the linkages between objectives specified as either customer or management expectations, and the set of activities, tasks and actions designed to deliver those expectations. In so doing, they allow management and employees to develop a line of sight between their respective responsibilities and tasks, and the higher order end-states desired by the organization.

Building Systems of Improvement: Key Considerations for Performance-Based Organizations

12

The tools and techniques presented are effective methods for understanding organizational issues and problems, and taking action to improve performance. Data-analysis tools, process maps, management and planning tools, decision techniques and information-generating and organizing techniques are all useful in helping individuals better understand and resolve performance issues.

Using the tools as stand-alone pieces to accomplish specific tasks, however, is the bare minimum. It is the starting point for organizations seeking to improve organizational performance. As familiarity with the performance improvement toolkit grows, organizations can and should begin combining the tools into systems of analysis and improvement. These systems can be used to build leverage, increasing the value of each tool by linking multiple tools into a systematic approach for address-

ing organizational issues and continuously driving organizational performance improvement. To put it plainly, there must be a method of improvement that describes "the way things get done around here."

BUILDING A PERFORMANCE IMPROVEMENT CULTURE

"The way things get done around here" is a good summary of what organizational culture boils down to. The way things are done is, in turn, a reflection of what the organization knows and how it uses this knowledge to define its purpose and its actions. Knowledge and culture are bound together – you are what you know.

THE PURSUIT OF KNOWLEDGE

Building a performance culture, then, starts with the pursuit of knowledge. We started this book noting that some organizations outperform others because they *know how to*. Knowledge is the fundamental driving force behind any form of performance improvement. You can't do it if you don't know how.

Despite the importance of knowledge, less attention is paid to its development than to other factors of production. Perhaps this is because knowledge is so difficult to see, count or measure. But it is no less real, and its impact on performance is certainly no less important than any other contributor to the business or to improvement.

This lack of attention manifests itself in lightweight approaches to knowledge generation that yield more lip service than learning. Superficial approaches are characterized by:

▲ **Substituting individual training for knowledge generation.** Organizations may rightly be proud of their high level of commitment to training and development, but individual learning is not equivalent to organizational learning. Organizational learning demands the addition of practical application in real-world situations. It entails the sharing of knowledge obtained, as well as the documenting of best practice so the knowledge can be deployed throughout the organization – redefining the way things are done. Organizational learning demands greater discipline in applying or testing new knowledge, and ensures that the knowledge, where appropriate, becomes standardized.

▲ **Substituting employee involvement for knowledge generation.** Knowledge is more than just whatever people believe. A few hundred years ago, most people would have told you the world was flat, resting on the back of a giant turtle. They were wrong. Elaborate theories, ideas or beliefs are no substitute for knowledge. There needs to be some real-world analysis and experimentation of the idea to validate it. Likewise, simply getting 10 employees in a room to brainstorm problems and possible solutions doesn't mean that the ideas identified represent either the real problems or practical solutions. This is a start, but it is only a process of gathering tacit knowledge. For organizational learning to occur, these ideas must be validated and the results made part of the explicit knowledge base of the organization. Getting people together and involving them in the improvement effort is a fundamental component to organizational performance improvement. But it is not, in and of itself, organizational learning.

As important as individual training and development and employee involvement are, they are not enough. There must be more for organizational learning to occur – there must be knowledge.

CHARACTERISTICS OF A PERFORMANCE CULTURE

So what are the characteristics of a performance culture? How do we move from the lightweight approaches of learning to real knowledge generation and performance improvement? We can identify six basic characteristics that describe performance-based cultures. These are cultures where knowledge generation results in the constant improvement to product and process. These six characteristics are:

1. PROBLEMS ARE PURSUED

Generating knowledge starts with a problem. In every organization, every society, every family – indeed in virtually every group of *homo-sapiens* that can be defined – one member of the group is dissatisfied with something. It may be the method of allocating the weekly allowance or the method of allocating capital expenditures for the year. The problem can be virtually anything, but to paraphrase Gilda Radner: "There's always something."

It's that "something" that drives people and organizations to figure out how to beat the problem. This is a roundabout way of saying that problems suffer from bad press. In traditional organizational cultures, problems are perceived to be mundane and uninteresting, or something associated only with operations as opposed to the more interesting and "sexy" world of strategy. Problems are to be relegated to the lowest of endeavors. I once met a vice-president of a large company that claimed he didn't want his people to be "problem solvers" but rather "visionaries." Indeed, the world would be a much easier place if we could just "envision" our way to success.

Such is not the case, however. Solving problems is anything but mundane – it is the driver of creativity. Performance-based organizations understand this. They are constantly seeking out new problems because they see such problems as opportunities for improvement.

Learning organizations that are starved for problems create their own. This may seem crazy – after all, why create problems for yourself? Well, if problems are opportunities for improvement, then creating problems represents an active approach to knowledge generation and improvement. The day the organization stops asking questions, and stops identifying or creating problems for itself to overcome, is the day performance improvement dies.

2. EXPERIMENT AND EMPIRICISM RULE

To generate knowledge, organizations must accept a method of separating fact from fiction. Traditional organizations use managerial judgment as the basic criterion for determining reality. All too often this amounts to little more than the application of bias and prejudice masquerading as experience. The prevailing ideas of the organization are used to evaluate reality, resulting in stagnation.

Performance-based organizations, on the other hand, use some form of the PDSA cycle. They submit their ideas and theories to the reality test. No matter how modified the cycle is for specific organizational contexts, the fundamentals of *plan* the improvement, *do* the experiment, *study* the results, and *act* on the conclusions must be present if any meaningful learning is to result. This is because the PDSA cycle defines the right sequence – having a theory validated by experiment and data rather than the other way around. Trying to work the cycle in reverse, using theory and beliefs to validate real-world findings, is 14th century thinking.

Knowledge-generating organizations place reality above ego. If someone's pet theory about how best to do something turns out to be false, then the best action is to drop the theory and accept the cold hard judgment of fact. We are all guilty, to some degree, of placing our pet notions, theories or beliefs above reality. In doing so, we don't create or guard knowledge. We invent myths and defend legends. We allow untested and unverified methods to rule over us.

It is reality that rules whether we like it or not. And because it does, we cannot advance knowledge in any meaningful sense without experimenting, without getting our hands dirty in the real world. Organizations must try things – not just anything, but well-thought out experiments for which we have good, rational reasons to believe will improve performance.

Such experiments may not be, and probably won't be, the formal, double-blind controlled experiment of the medical researcher. Rather, they will be the real-time testing of ideas in the field, as part of the continuing effort at improving performance. Organizations are, after all, complex places. A new manufacturing process, an enhanced telephone answering system, or a new process for handling customer complaints cannot usually be tested in isolation or in some laboratory. This comes down to what Dr. Jiro Kawakita referred to as "field science."[93] Field science does not differ in principle from any other form of science. What does differ is where this science occurs – where it is conducted. For most organizations, this will be in the field, in the real world in which organizations must operate.

All organizations, whether they realize it or not, are engaged in a continuous process of generating knowledge. Every change, every enhancement, every new product or service, every new development is an experiment and an opportunity for learning. Some organizations make much better use of these experiments and learn more. Sometimes these changes can be structured in a way that certain confounding factors are controlled, making evaluation of the changes easier. At other times, such controls are impossible and the organization will rely on other methods, such as sub-grouping of data, stratification and run and control charts, to evaluate the impact of change and draw meaningful conclusions for the organization.

3. FEAR OF FAILURE IS TEMPERED

Not all initiatives that are intended to improve performance succeed. Sometimes they fail, and fail miserably. But if such initiatives were driven by the honest desire to make improvements, then the experiment can be evaluated with an eye to enhancing learning and organizational knowledge. Traditionally managed organizations don't care what was learned. Their only response in the face of failure is to hunt for the guilty and allocate the blame.

---

93. Dr. Kawakita is the originator of affinity charting. For a discussion of field science as distinguished from experimental and speculative science see; Building Organizational Fitness, Ryuji Fukuda, Productivity Press, Portland, Oregon, 1997. pp. 108-110

Performance-oriented organizations know that some failure is inevitable, and it represents the beginning of understanding and learning. "Why did it fail?" isn't a lead-in to seeking guilty parties. It is the first step in understanding the root causes of the performance problem, in identifying what assumptions didn't hold, and what expectations we held but didn't see come to fruition.

This same form of questioning should take place with successes as well. Did things turn out because of our theory or in spite of it? Did things happen the way in which we thought they would or did success emerge from some other factor that at the time we thought relatively unimportant? These types of questions drive real learning from both success and failure.

The key to building an organization capable of continually generating knowledge is ensuring that people have the opportunity to experiment. This does not mean that individuals should engage in any change they want, or that anyone should seek failure. Improvement initiatives must be carefully designed, well considered and properly conducted. The opportunity to fail is not to be taken as an excuse for having a sloppy method. If organizations get into the habit of punishing failure,

however, experimentation will dwindle. Learning will cease, and innovation and improvement will die.

4. INFORMATION AND IDEAS FLOW

Learning requires an exchange of information, including the free flow of findings and results of experiments, whether they succeed or fail. Information, however, is power. As a result, there are implicit rewards for holding onto and restricting the flow of information in traditional organizational cultures. This limits organizational learning and the leveraging impact that comes with sharing acquired knowledge.

Most of us are aware of the requirement to publish in academic/scientific circles. The requirement even has its own slightly macabre motto: "Publish or Perish." Yet few of us are aware of the immense importance of publishing in the advancement of science. Without publishing, there would be no learning. Anyone could hold any ideas they wanted, without submitting those ideas to the reality test, and to the expert judgment of one's peers. Knowledge would never advance.

When scientists are compelled to publish, others working in the field immediately seek to validate or disprove the findings or conclusions arrived at in the experiment. Others may build on the ideas developed, extending them into more useful or productive avenues. In short, the flow of ideas creates a cycle of learning that, in turn, drives knowledge generation. Publish or perish doesn't just apply to academics, but to the status of knowledge within organizations. Failing to publish – that is, failing to communicate what has been learned to the rest of the organization – represents a horrendous loss of knowledge and a waste of resources.

Does your organization report the results of its new experiments in this completely honest fashion? A new product is introduced and sales are disappointing. Is there an honest review of the situation in the company newsletter or does the communications staff immediately seek to put a positive spin on the situation? Is the job of communications conveying the facts or a cover-up? You could probably think of many such situations in your organization where the purpose of communication is to build morale by bending the truth and, in the process, kill any chance of real learning and improvement taking place.

Performance-oriented organizations have teams of people in discussion. But this is not done just to get together to talk. They are coming together to talk about the latest successes or failures. They are discussing the roots of those results, how they might be adapted in their own work groups. In short, teams are coming together to ensure that ideas and information flow. In the process, they facilitate the deployment of those ideas throughout the organization. It is the only way to engage the organization in problem solving, and the only way that lessons learned can be deployed.

The job of communication is to covey information – not cover it up!

5. IMPROVEMENTS ARE STANDARDIZED

It is not enough to learn. The learnings or knowledge must be applied and become standardized into "the way things are done around here." Traditional organizations, however, suffer from an inability to implement. Studies may be done, plans produced and people prepared. But nothing really changes, or the changes that do occur are pale imitations of the original improvement objective.

What is going wrong? In traditional organizational cultures:

▲ **Symbols of improvement are manipulated.** Posters are posted, minor structural changes are made, jobs are given new titles, slogans are trumpeted, task forces are struck, and speeches are delivered. Change, it seems, is everywhere. But nothing really changes. The work gets done the same way as it always has and the results are just as poor.

▲ **People affected are not involved.** To become "the way things are done around here," changes made must be adopted by people. If those affected are not involved, the pace of that adoption – if it occurs at all – will be slow. Moreover, the nature of the change itself will likely be less than ideal. It will have been made without the involvement, and therefore without the knowledge and commitment of those most familiar with what is being changed.

▲ **Gains are lost.** Sometimes, improvements are made and change introduced, but the organization quickly falls back to the old ways of doing things. The gains made are lost. The reasons may be many – a failure to gain commitment of people affected, a lack of organizational discipline or simply a lack of effort. Whatever the reason, the lost gains represent a waste of knowledge, of knowing how but failing to use it.

Performance-oriented organizations recognize that any improvement to the way things are done represents the 'state of the art,' the new best way to do something. To add value, however, the new best way needs to be adopted by as much of the organization as is appropriate. This is the task of standardization, to ensure every part of the organization is doing things the best way the organization knows how to. When organizations standardize, they 'hard-wire' the performance gains into whatever processes are at work.

6. THERE IS A SYSTEM OF KNOWLEDGE GENERATION AND IMPROVEMENT

Knowledge doesn't just happen – you have to work at it. Ask any child in school or recall your own school days. Did the learning always come easily or was some work involved? Learning takes effort. This is especially so when we speak of organizational learning. Generating knowledge doesn't just happen because your employees are learning. Effort must be expended to translate the implicit knowledge of the individual into the explicit knowledge of the organization. It is this explicit knowledge that allows for the sharing of information among employees, which in turn allows others to add to, and further refine, the knowledge base.

This means performance-oriented organizations must have a system for learning – for generating knowledge. The nature of this system will vary, but whatever its specifics, it will have components that support the characteristics just described. Specifically, such systems typically:

▲ **Have mechanisms in place that encourage the pursuit of new problems.** Problems are not hidden behind the veil of corporate communications. They are discussed and debated openly. Where problems are not immediately apparent, the organization conducts experiments in an attempt to create new problems (opportunities) to conquer. The systems in place may consist of formal and ongoing benchmarking efforts designed to highlight areas of comparative weakness, or they may be staff surveys designed to identify perceived problems. The methods or combination of methods vary. In all cases, however, problems are sought out, prioritized and pursued.

▲ **Have adopted a corporate improvement model based upon the PDSA cycle.** Performance-oriented cultures use this cycle in whatever form, driving home the need to rely on data and apply sound analytical procedures in corporate decision making. Analytical tools such as control charts, histograms and scatter diagrams are not just used, they are expected and demanded at every level of the organization, from board reporting to operations management. Moreover, this improvement model is applied to every improvement initiative, to provide a consistent framework for organizational improvement initiatives and a basis for the communicating and sharing of knowledge.

▲ **Have processes that support experimentation and the removal of fear**. Everywhere one looks in a performance-based organization, people are trying out new ideas, evaluating new concepts. Systems supporting such efforts include allocating informal improvement time to every job or group of jobs. Teams are provided with experimental resources intended to do nothing other than prove or disprove certain improvement ideas. Equally important, however, are the things that one doesn't see. Systems designed to punish failure are missing. This includes most forms of performance management and incentives targeted at the individual. Systems that pit employees against one another or force-rank individual performance will destroy opportunities for experimentation and risk taking.

▲ **Have mechanisms that support honest communication and the exchange of ideas**. Communication systems are designed to communicate honestly, to providing real feedback on how things are going with the organization generally and improvement/change initiatives specifically. Newsletters are actually read and used by employees. Improvement teams use the organization's intra-nets to provide information and receive feedback and help. People are talking and talking is encouraged. Failures are actually acknowledged and discussed. Moreover, the organization actually encourages discussion of failure with an eye to sharing the learnings that result. In short, communication processes are designed to encourage the free and honest flow of ideas, with the goal of improvement as opposed to spin-doctoring.

▲ **Are consumed with the need to implement.** Organizational leadership walks the talk. Managers are out on the floor because they insist on observing the changes that have taken place, as well as understanding the way things are done now. Organizational systems support making changes. They are designed with the need for flexibility, because they know however things are done now will probably be different in six months. This often translates into staying focused on the 'gemba' – the 'heart and soul' of the business – and refusing to let organizational constraints get in the way of a good idea.

THE COMPONENTS OF IMPROVEMENT

In Chapter 1, five basic components of improvement were identified as critical to the new management of performance. Together, these components comprise an informal model of the pieces that come together to create effective improvement or a knowledge-generating culture. Here, we revisit these components and examine the implications from all we have discussed.

PURPOSEFUL

Dr. Deming was fond of saying, "A system without an aim is not a system!" All organizations and any improvement efforts therein must have an aim, a purpose. Such purposeful activity requires:

▲ **Leadership.** Somewhere in the organization, someone must be willing to state what they believe to be the problems or opportunities of the organization, develop a consensus for change and begin the process of making things better. This is the task of leadership. Indeed, the first task of leadership is to lead. Whether defining and stating what others already hold true, or identifying wholly new problems and opportunities, for improvement to be purposeful the leadership must be there to help clarify purpose and give direction to the improvement effort.

▲ **Focus.** In trying to do everything, organizations usually end up accomplishing nothing. Peter Scholtes talks of pursuing problems in a manner that is "an inch wide and a mile deep." This means solving problems by clearly defining a well-targeted issue and pursuing it to whatever depths are required to see its resolution. In contrast, mile-wide and inch-deep strategies characterize a lightweight approach to improvement. Superficial approaches try to do everything, with insufficient resources or effort to be effective in any area. You can't do everything. So pick one thing and do it well.

▲ **Planned activity.** Purposeful activity is planned activity. Improvement is not about giving free reign to do whatever anyone wishes. Purpose demands intelligence. Purposeful activity is intelligently planned, and skillfully conducted. It is built upon a foundation of existing knowledge, and framed in a logical and rational sequence of activities that are both essential and sufficient to the task.

▲ **Disciplined activity.** Purposeful activity is disciplined activity. Too often, organizations begin to pursue improvement only to get sidetracked by some new management fad with its requisite promises of great things to come. Or perhaps some new priority quickly pulls organizational attention away from the original task. Purposeful activity requires the discipline to stick to it, to see things through to their completion, and only then turn attention to some new task or issue.

CUSTOMER DRIVEN

Organizations must pay attention to a wide variety of stakeholders in the business, from shareholders to employees to suppliers. But performance improvement demands that improvement be customer driven. Why? Because it is the customer that pays for it. At the end of every business process is a customer that is making decisions about whether to give up his or her cash to purchase our products. Increasing performance means increasing the willingness of our customers to buy. Being customer driven requires:

▲ **Customer-in philosophy.** High-performing organizations attempt to bring the customer into the business, establishing a relationship that enhances understanding of needs and ultimately reduces marketing effort. In contrast, traditional organizations hold fast to a product-out philosophy. It views the customer as the enemy – something to be out-maneuvered and sold to. The last thing such organizations would want to do is bring the 'customer-in' where the customer would quickly learn just how much disdain they're held in. Being customer driven means staying close to the customer, truly understanding their requirements and producing products and services that meet or exceed those requirements. The result is a demand 'pull' rather than a sales 'push.'

▲ **Value.** Being customer driven requires an understanding of value. Specifically, value is whatever the customer says it is and is willing to pay for. Improving value added, therefore, is an effort to improve whatever the customer says is important to them. Traditional organizations believe value can be improved or enhanced without attention to customer needs. This inevitably becomes translated into cost-cutting exercises. There is nothing wrong with reducing costs; indeed, it is important and vital to do so.

But doing so, without paying attention to what the customer is willing to pay for and wants to pay for, is suicidal.

PROCESS FOCUSED

Where do we place the focus of our improvement efforts? It would be fair to say that organizations are split on the issue. Conventional thinking places the focus of the improvement effort on the individual – on people, in other words. This is because such organizations have confused the means by which improvement happens (people) with the focus or target of the improvement effort (process).

Performance-oriented organizations keep the focus on the process. They know that for any performance measure, the process is responsible for 80 percent to 95 percent of the outcome. Individual effort makes up the balance. Organizations that focus improvement on people, therefore, are focusing on areas where leverage is minimal. In contrast, keeping the focus on the process ensures that leverage is maximized, giving the organization the best return for its improvement effort.

Keeping the focus on process requires:

▲ **Systems thinking.** Systems thinking looks across time, individuals, events and places to construct a big picture representation of what is happening. In contrast, localized thinking focuses on a specific time, individual, event or place. The difference is critical. Organizations dominated by localized thinking look for individuals to blame (or reward), and ask "What happened?" and "Who is responsible?" Organizations characterized by systems thinking ask "How does this happen?" and "How do we ensure this doesn't happen again?"

▲ **Going to the gemba.** All processes are not created equal and no bill of rights exists for processes. The most important processes are gemba processes – the ones that go to the heart and soul of the organization. This is where the performance-based organization places its first priority. It focuses on the gemba processes that, by definition, are most directly connected to customer value. Next are those process responsible for supporting the gemba. These are the processes that will work to improve gemba processes or facilitate their operation. Performance-oriented organizations place management processes last in line for service. Moreover, much of the focus of improvement in this regard involves limiting the impact of management processes on gemba-supporting processes. The bottom-line is: performance-oriented organizations focus on and go to the gemba whenever possible.

▲ **Appreciating variation.** Every system and process produces variation. This is the reality of every process that exists, natural or man-made. It is this reality that shapes and limits our understanding of process behavior and performance. No process can be understood without appreciating and understanding variation. Indeed, the fundamental tools required to interpret any process performance measure are used precisely because they make the variation visible.

SCIENTIFIC METHOD

How should organizations pursue improvement? What method should they use? The answer to this is straightforward – the scientific method. This approach may appear dry, cold or mechanistic. It is, of course, nothing of the sort. The scientific method is a means to separate fact from fiction. It helps us establish the veracity of ideas as we pursue and perhaps find some truth. Performance-oriented organizations are characterized by:

▲ **Fact over fashion.** In the choice between the latest management fad or fashion and the simple truth, performance-based organizations choose truth. There is a reluctance to pursue the latest and greatest fad, especially when the preachings run contrary to established and tested knowledge. In contrast, poorly managed organizations are forever flipping from one fashion to the next. One year it's TQM (Total Quality Management), then BPR (Business Process Re-Engineering) and then it's TCS (Total Customer Satisfaction). No wonder Dr. Deming referred to all these acronyms as "alphabet soup." Scientific method demands discipline. It requires careful examination of the world, the development of understanding, and the supremacy of fact over fashion.

▲ **Reliance on data.** The scientific method relies on data. To play on an old saying, "In God we trust, all others use data!"[94] To which we can only reply: "Amen." Organizations that fail to use data will be guided by mistaken impressions, bad judgment, management myths and bias.

Reliance upon data also demands the use of the right data-analysis tools. Using data is not a matter of simply stating numbers. The right tools must be used to derive appropriate interpretation and meaning from the numbers.

▲ **Use of an improvement model, based upon the PDSA cycle.** Scientific method is first and foremost a method – a way of doing things. This way of doing things is embedded in the organizational culture of performance-oriented organizations. A part of this embedding process is adopting a model of improvement. Doing so gives the organization a common framework or reference that serves as a basis of understanding and communication. The details of the model are not as important as its underlying structure. We have proposed our own seven-step model, but there are others just as sound. What is important is that the underlying model's structure be based upon the PDSA cycle, which is nothing more than an elaboration of the scientific method applied to organizations.

---

94. I have seen this quote referenced many times with the source usually listed as "unknown." Any help to attribute this to the original author would be greatly appreciated.

PEOPLE-BASED

Performance-based organizations understand that people are the means by which results are accomplished. The focus of improvement is upon the processes and systems that produce results. The means by which this improvement comes about, however, is people. People-based improvement, therefore, is all about:

▲ **Development over improvement.** People are developed, not improved. Performance-based organizations develop their people through training, expanded work experience and the assigning of new and challenging work. In so doing, they develop the capabilities of their people to improve the organization's processes and products. Conventional organizations try to improve the person. They measure and manipulate their people to try and get them to do more. Performance appraisals, performance incentive schemes, performance-based pay, and performance management plans are all signs of traditional approaches that seek to improve rather than develop people.

▲ **Understanding individuals.** Performance cultures make the effort to appreciate their people as individuals. They see them not as simple cogs in an industrial wheel, but rather as the means by which the organization can continue to learn, improve and grow. Part of this involves understanding what really motivates people. Non-learning organizations believe motivation comes down to money. Performance organizations know better. They understand that people want to do good work and will do so if given the opportunity. They also know that most people want to help and contribute to the organization – they want to use not just their hands, but their brains as well. In fact, real improvement can't happen any other way.

▲ **Teamwork.** Processes are the focus of the improvement effort, but these processes tend to run across a variety of organizational boundaries. Improving a process, therefore, requires teamwork. It involves bringing together those that know the current process and have a stake in improving it. Teams themselves are a form of organization, and organizations exist because of the fact that we can accomplish more within such structures than we can as lone individuals. People can accomplish far more as teams of individuals working toward some improvement objective, than they can as lone individuals pursuing the same goal.

ACCELERATED CYCLE LEARNING

Improvement is itself a process. Like with any other process, organizations must work constantly at improvement. Leading performance-oriented organizations are no longer content with simply improving. They are beginning to improve how they improve. In short, they are working to accelerate the learning cycle.

Like all processes, knowledge generation and application takes time. The less time it takes, the more efficient the process and the greater the value added. If the improvement cycle time is reduced, value added improvements happen earlier. More importantly, the organization learns at an ever- increasing pace, allowing it to stay ahead of the competition.

THE PACE OF IMPROVEMENT

Measurement is a key component of establishing the performance of any system or process. This holds true for the process of improvement as well. If we are going to improve the process of improvement, we need to measure the process itself. We need an improvement measure.

The concept of half-life works well as such a measure. Many of us have heard of the concept in dealing with issues of radioactive decay. When we hear that the half-life of some nuclear material is 1,000 years, that's how long it will take for half of its radioactivity to disappear. The concept needn't be restricted to nuclear material, however; it could also be applied to ice cream. The half-life of ice cream is the length of time it takes half of your ice cream to melt if you leave it outside the freezer. The measure of half-life is simply the time it takes for half of anything being measured to disappear.

This idea can be extended to measuring the pace of continuous improvement. For example, suppose we are working to improve the performance of a production process. A key measure is the number of defects occurring per thousand units produced. If we are successful in our improvement efforts, the defect rate should fall. But if we are continuously improving, the defect rate should continue to fall at a constant or near-constant rate of improvement. The extent to which it does can be measured as the length of time it takes to see the number of defects reduced by 50 percent – the defect rate half-life.

Exhibit 366: Concept of Half-Life

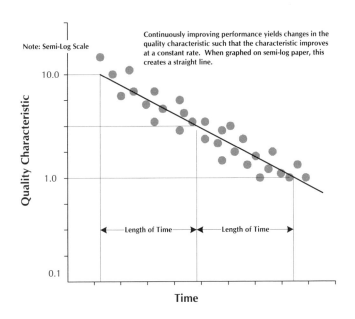

Note: Semi-Log Scale

Continuously improving performance yields changes in the quality characteristic such that the characteristic improves at a constant rate. When graphed on semi-log paper, this creates a straight line.

Of course, the concept applies beyond defects. It can be the length of time it takes sales or profits to double, for example, or the time it takes to reduce costs by 50 percent. The idea of half-life can be extended to any of these areas as a means of measuring the pace of improvement.

Several empirical examples of this concept are presented by Arthur Schneiderman in "Setting Quality Goals."[95]

ACCELERATING IMPROVEMENT

Measurement by itself doesn't improve anything, or course, and it alone will certainly not accelerate the improvement process. So how is this done?

Accelerated cycle learning is an organized, systemic approach to improvement that is designed to dramatically cut the cycle time associated with the PDSA cycle. The specific characteristics of the process are situationally dependent. They depend upon the peculiarities of the specific organizational circumstances within which accelerated cycle learning will apply. Nevertheless, all accelerated cycle learning shares certain fundamental characteristics. These are:

▲ **A single target for improvement is selected and focus is demanded.** The focus of the improvement effort is well defined, with clear and specific boundaries. Where possi-

---

95. Arthur Schneiderman, "Setting Quality Goals", Quality Progress, April 1988, p. 55

ble, a single critical performance characteristic is selected as the indicator of improvement success.

For example, the improvement focus might be on inventory levels. Within this focus, average dollar value of inventory at month's end might be defined as the single performance characteristic.

▲ **People are brought together in a gathering of implicit knowledge.** Once the improvement area is defined, people with an interest in, stake in and knowledge of the system to be improved are brought together in the same room. This can mean a lot of people, but getting them all together is essential. In essence, this group holds a conference to assess the current state of knowledge, discuss possible root causes of problems, and share likely improvement scenarios.

Naturally, there is never agreement on the best possible solution, or on root causes for that matter. Fortunately, agreement isn't required. The conference only needs to select the top three to 10 possible solutions for one common problem. For each possible solution, an improvement team comprised of conference participants is assigned. Their task is to implement their improvement idea on a

small scale in their particular part of the company. This may be a geographical location, a department, or defined in some other fashion that makes sense given the nature of the improvement initiative.

▲ **Multiple (usually parallel) improvement initiatives are employed.** Each improvement team returns to its part of the company and immediately implements its improvement initiative. As a result, the company would have anywhere from three to 10 teams working in parallel, testing out alternative solutions to a common problem. The result is a comprehensive corporate effort to improve one well-defined aspect of the operation. It is an effort that is simultaneously testing various alternative theories as to the best way to solve the problem.

These are not competitive initiatives. In fact, any notion of competitiveness among the teams will destroy the process. Where teams want to "win," data validity becomes suspect, the learning questionable. Rather, the teams must see themselves as engaging in a cooperative process of discovery. They are exploring alternative solutions in a true scientific enterprise of learning what works best, where and why.

▲ **Measuring is done constantly.** From start to finish, measurements are taken constantly to provide immediate feedback to each improvement team. This often means establishing temporary measurement systems necessary to get the data required. Standard tools (see the seven basic data-analysis tools) such as run charts and control charts are used exclusively.

Measurement is critical, because the measured results will determine what solution will be adopted by the organization. This is a rigid application of the reality test. Whatever solution presents the best results is considered to be the best solution.

▲ **The conference is reconvened for reporting.** When the experiments are done, the conference is reconvened with all teams participating. The results achieved by each improvement team are presented and discussed. The critical piece of this reporting is the performance analysis obtained through the measurement program. In addition, however, it is important to understand why things turned out the way they did. For learning to occur, we need to do more than decide upon a winning strategy. We need to understand why things happened the way they did.

The learning that occurs within this follow-up conference has another purpose – to facilitate implementation of the objectively preferred strategy. This allows each team returning to its part of the organization to understand how the best improvement strategy was implemented, including problems experienced along the way.

▲ **Best solutions are implemented quickly.** Each team participating in the follow-up conference is also responsible for implementing the best improvement strategy in their part of the organization. This enables the rapid deployment of knowledge. In short, organizational learning and standardization are embedded in the process. This ensures that not only does learning take place, but the entire organization benefits immediately from the learning that occurs.

HOW FAST?

A critical decision in accelerated cycle learning is determining how much time needs to be allocated to conducting the field trials or experiments of the various alternative improvement ideas. Put simply, how fast can the process be done?

For organizations first starting out, a good rule of thumb is to reduce the cycle time by two orders of (time-based) magnitude.

For example, an improvement project focused on improving monthly inventory levels would set the time required for the experiments by reducing the implied time scale (months) by a factor of two. So the scale is compressed from months to weeks and from weeks to days. In this case, measurements would be taken daily and the length of the experiment would be appropriate to this level of measurement – perhaps 25 to 50 days. (Remember, the control chart requires a minimum of 20 to 25 points so this would be a minimum for the experiment. This time frame can be doubled to 50 days to give the experiment a chance to work, and the new process a chance to cycle around a second time.) The bottom line of accelerated cycle learning is simple – make improvements faster.

PERFORMANCE: IT'S ABOUT KNOW HOW

We started this book talking about *know how* and we end it the same way. Some organizations out-perform others because they know how. In the battle for markets in the 21st century, organizations that know how to identify and produce what the customer wants better than anyone else will win the battle.

In doing so, the winners will have engaged all their employees in the effort. There will be no room for the lightweight approaches to improvement. Performance improvement will come from real effort guided by real knowledge.

All workers are knowledge workers.

Appendix

APPENDIX 1: BIAS CORRECTION FACTORS FOR ESTIMATING SIGMA

Unbiased estimates of standard deviation can be obtained from the equations below and by obtaining values for c_4, d_2 and d_3 from Table 367: Bias Correction Factors.

Unbiased estimator of sigma based on standard deviation

$$s_x = \frac{s}{c_4} \ or \ \frac{\bar{s}}{c_4}$$

Unbiased estimator of sigma based on the range

$$s_x = \frac{R}{d_2} \ or \ \frac{\bar{R}}{d_2}$$

Unbiased estimator of the Sigma of R

$$s_R = \bar{R} \times \frac{d_3}{d_2}$$

APPLICATIONS

Bias correction factors are typically used in capability analysis, specifically when estimating the natural process limits. Natural process limits require the determination of sigma from the control chart. There is, however, a problem. Measures of dispersion (R or s) from the control chart are based on sub-group averages, whereas natural process limits are based on individual values.

The bias correction factors provide a solution. They provide the means by which R or s from the control chart is converted into an estimate of sigma for individual values.

Table 367: Bias Correction Factors

Sub-group Size	d_2	c_4	d_3
2	1.1280	0.7979	0.8525
3	1.6932	0.8862	0.8884
4	2.0590	0.9213	0.8798
5	2.3260	0.9400	0.8641
6	2.5340	0.9515	0.8480
7	2.7040	0.9594	0.8332
8	2.8470	0.9650	0.8198
9	2.9700	0.9693	0.8078
10	3.0780	0.9727	0.7971
11	3.1730	0.9754	0.7873
12	3.2580	0.9776	0.7785
13	3.3360	0.9794	0.7704
14	3.4070	0.9810	0.7630
15	3.4720	0.9823	0.7562
16	3.5320	0.9835	0.7499
17	3.5880	0.9845	0.7441
18	3.6400	0.9854	0.7386
19	3.6890	0.9862	0.7335
20	3.7350	0.9869	0.7287

Table 367: Bias Correction Factors

Sub-group Size	d_2	c_4	d_3
21	3.7780	0.9876	0.7272
22	3.8190	0.9882	0.7199
23	3.8580	0.9887	0.7159
24	3.8950	0.9892	0.7121
25	3.9310	0.9896	0.7084
30	4.0860	0.9915	0.6927
35	4.2130	0.9927	0.6799
40	4.3220	0.9936	0.6692
45	4.4150	0.9943	0.6601
50	4.4980	0.9949	0.6521
60	4.6390	0.9957	0.6389
70	4.7550	0.9963	0.6283
80	4.8540	0.9968	0.6194
90	4.9390	0.9972	0.6118
100	5.0150	0.9975	0.6052

APPENDIX 2: CONTROL CHART FACTORS

Table 368: Control Chart Factors contains control chart factors for the XmR, $\overline{X}$, R and $\overline{X}$, s control charts for sub-group sizes 1 through 25.

For sub-group sizes larger than 25, the following formulas can be used to derive the appropriate factor.

FACTORS FOR USE WITH THE $\overline{X}$, R CHART

Calculate A₂

A_2 is used to determine three sigma for the $\overline{X}$ chart based on Ranges ($\overline{X}$, R).

$$A_2 = \frac{3}{d_2 \times \sqrt{n}}$$

Calculate D₃

D_3 is used to determine the lower control limit for the ranges of the R chart.

$$D_3 = 1 - \frac{3 \times d_3}{d_2}$$

Calculate D₄

D_4 is used to determine the upper control limit for the ranges of the R chart..

$$D_4 = 1 + \frac{3 \times d_3}{d_2}$$

FACTORS FOR USE WITH THE $\overline{X}$, s CHART

Calculate A_3

A_3 is used to calculate three sigma for the $\overline{X}$ chart based on standard deviations ($\overline{X}$, s).

$$A_3 = \frac{3}{c_4 \times \sqrt{n}}$$

Calculate B_3

B_3 is used to determine the lower control limits for the s chart.

$$B_3 = 1 - \left(\frac{3}{c_4} \times \sqrt{1 - (c_4)^2} \right)$$

Calculate B_4

B_4 is used to determine the upper control limits for the s chart.

$$B_4 = 1 + \left(\frac{3}{c_4} \times \sqrt{1 - (c_4)^2} \right)$$

Table 368: Control Chart Factors

Sub-Group Size (n)	Individuals (XmR Chart)		Control Chart for Averages ($\overline{X}$, R Chart)			Control Chart for Averages ($\overline{X}$, s Chart)		
	3 sigma of X-chart	Upper control limit of R-chart	3 sigma of $\overline{X}$-chart	Lower control limit for Ranges chart	Upper control limit for Ranges chart	3 sigma for $\overline{X}$-chart	Lower control limit for s-chart	Upper control limit for s-chart
			A_2	D_3	D_4	A_3	B_3	B_4
1	2.659	3.267	-	-	-	-	-	-
2	-	-	1.880	-	3.268	2.659	-	3.267
3	-	-	1.023	-	2.574	1.954	-	2.568
4	-	-	0.729	-	2.282	1.628	-	2.266
5	-	-	0.577	-	2.114	1.427	-	2.089
6	-	-	0.483	-	2.004	1.287	0.030	1.970
7	-	-	0.419	0.076	1.924	1.182	0.118	1.882
8	-	-	0.373	0.136	1.864	1.099	0.185	1.815
9	-	-	0.337	0.184	1.816	1.032	0.239	1.761
10	-	-	0.308	0.223	1.777	0.975	0.284	1.716
11	-	-	0.285	0.256	1.744	0.927	0.321	1.679
12	-	-	0.266	0.283	1.717	0.886	0.354	1.646
13	-	-	0.249	0.307	1.693	0.850	0.382	1.618
14	-	-	0.235	0.328	1.672	0.817	0.406	1.594
15	-	-	0.223	0.347	1.653	0.789	0.428	1.572
16	-	-	0.212	0.363	1.637	0.763	0.448	1.552
17	-	-	0.203	0.378	1.622	0.739	0.466	1.534
18	-	-	0.194	0.391	1.608	0.718	0.482	1.518
19	-	-	0.187	0.403	1.597	0.698	0.497	1.503
20	-	-	0.180	0.415	1.585	0.680	0.510	1.490
21	-	-	0.173	0.425	1.575	0.663	0.523	1.477
22	-	-	0.167	0.434	1.566	0.647	0.534	1.466
23	-	-	0.162	0.443	1.557	0.633	0.545	1.455
24	-	-	0.157	0.451	1.548	0.619	0.555	1.445
25	-	-	0.153	0.459	1.541	0.606	0.565	1.435

APPENDIX 3: NORMAL PROBABILITY TABLE

The normal probability table provides an area (probability) under the normal curve responding to area 'B'. The scores are standardized, meaning they provide corresponding probabilities for a normal curve whose mean is equal to 0.0 and whose standard deviation is equal to 1.0. .

Exhibit 369: Area Under the Normal Curve for Z-Scores

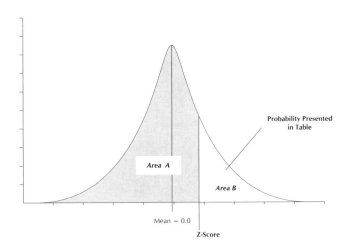

APPLICATIONS

There are two basic applications in the *Performance Improvement Toolkit* for which a table of standardized normal probabilities are required. These are:

▲ Program Evaluation and Review Technique (PERT), discussed starting on page 733. PERT is used to make probabilistic estimates from human judgment, typically where empirical data is scant. The distance between these estimates and specified targets can be converted into a Z-score. Using Table 370, these Z-Scores can be converted into probabilities allowing a term to estimate the chances of meeting some project deadline or revenue forecast.

▲ Quantifying Process Capability, discussed starting on page 484. Capability determines the distance between the process mean and a specified target such as a customer requirement. Using Table 370, capability estimates can be converted into estimated levels of fraction non-conforming.

Table 370: Standardized Normal Probabilities

Z Score	Probability	Z Score	Probability	Z Score	Probability	Z Score	Probability
0	0.5000000000						
0.01	0.4960106211	0.26	0.3974319427	0.51	0.3050257194	0.76	0.2236272209
0.02	0.4920216462	0.27	0.3935801859	0.52	0.3015317708	0.77	0.2206498761
0.03	0.4880334735	0.28	0.3897388141	0.53	0.2980559435	0.78	0.2176953690
0.04	0.4840465011	0.29	0.3859081823	0.54	0.2945984893	0.79	0.2147638174
0.05	0.4800611267	0.3	0.3820886425	0.55	0.2911596550	0.8	0.2118553339
0.06	0.4760777474	0.31	0.3782805434	0.56	0.2877396824	0.81	0.2089700255
0.07	0.4720967599	0.32	0.3744842304	0.57	0.2843388082	0.82	0.2061079938
0.08	0.4681185603	0.33	0.3707000455	0.58	0.2809572638	0.83	0.2032693348
0.09	0.4641435437	0.34	0.3669283271	0.59	0.2775952757	0.84	0.2004541391
0.1	0.4601721045	0.35	0.3631694101	0.6	0.2742530649	0.85	0.1976624920
0.11	0.4562046358	0.36	0.3594236256	0.61	0.2709308475	0.86	0.1948944734
0.12	0.4522415297	0.37	0.3556913012	0.62	0.2676288340	0.87	0.1921501576
0.13	0.4482831771	0.38	0.3519727603	0.63	0.2643472298	0.88	0.1894296138
0.14	0.4443299674	0.39	0.3482683225	0.64	0.2610862348	0.89	0.1867329057
0.15	0.4403822885	0.4	0.3445783034	0.65	0.2578460437	0.9	0.1840600917
0.16	0.4364405267	0.41	0.3409030144	0.66	0.2546268456	0.91	0.1814112251
0.17	0.4325050665	0.42	0.3372427629	0.67	0.2514288244	0.92	0.1787863537
0.18	0.4285762907	0.43	0.3335978518	0.68	0.2482521584	0.93	0.1761855202
0.19	0.4246545799	0.44	0.3299685798	0.69	0.2450970206	0.94	0.1736087623
0.2	0.4207403128	0.45	0.3263552412	0.7	0.2419635785	0.95	0.1710561122
0.21	0.4168338659	0.46	0.3227581259	0.71	0.2388519940	0.96	0.1685275974
0.22	0.4129356133	0.47	0.3191775190	0.72	0.2357624236	0.97	0.1660232400
0.23	0.4090459268	0.48	0.3156137013	0.73	0.2326950183	0.98	0.1635430573
0.24	0.4051651756	0.49	0.3120669487	0.74	0.2296499237	0.99	0.1610870614
0.25	0.4012937262	0.5	0.3085375326	0.75	0.2266272797	1	0.1586552598

Table 370: Standardized Normal Probabilities

Z Score	Probability	Z Score	Probability	Z Score	Probability	Z Score	Probability
1.01	0.1562476547	1.26	0.1038347468	1.51	0.0655217368	1.76	0.0392038578
1.02	0.1538642439	1.27	0.1020423808	1.52	0.0642555096	1.77	0.0383635227
1.03	0.1515050200	1.28	0.1002726336	1.53	0.0630083833	1.78	0.0375379306
1.04	0.1491699712	1.29	0.0985253944	1.54	0.0617801926	1.79	0.0367269040
1.05	0.1468590808	1.3	0.0968005495	1.55	0.0605707709	1.8	0.0359302655
1.06	0.1445723276	1.31	0.0950979821	1.56	0.0593799505	1.81	0.0351478382
1.07	0.1423096856	1.32	0.0934175725	1.57	0.0582075625	1.82	0.0343794454
1.08	0.1400711246	1.33	0.0917591982	1.58	0.0570534371	1.83	0.0336249108
1.09	0.1378566096	1.34	0.0901227340	1.59	0.0559174033	1.84	0.0328840585
1.1	0.1356661015	1.35	0.0885080517	1.6	0.0547992895	1.85	0.0321567132
1.11	0.1334995566	1.36	0.0869150208	1.61	0.0536989229	1.86	0.0314427001
1.12	0.1313569271	1.37	0.0853435082	1.62	0.0526161302	1.87	0.0307418449
1.13	0.1292381608	1.38	0.0837933781	1.63	0.0515507373	1.88	0.0300539739
1.14	0.1271432015	1.39	0.0822644926	1.64	0.0505025693	1.89	0.0293789140
1.15	0.1250719888	1.4	0.0807567113	1.65	0.0494714509	1.9	0.0287164929
1.16	0.1230244582	1.41	0.0792698915	1.66	0.0484572063	1.91	0.0280665389
1.17	0.1210005414	1.42	0.0778038884	1.67	0.0474596590	1.92	0.0274288813
1.18	0.1190001661	1.43	0.0763585552	1.68	0.0464786323	1.93	0.0268033499
1.19	0.1170232562	1.44	0.0749337428	1.69	0.0455139490	1.94	0.0261897756
1.2	0.1150697317	1.45	0.0735293005	1.7	0.0445654318	1.95	0.0255879898
1.21	0.1131395091	1.46	0.0721450753	1.71	0.0436329029	1.96	0.0249978252
1.22	0.1112325011	1.47	0.0707809127	1.72	0.0427161847	1.97	0.0244191152
1.23	0.1093486168	1.48	0.0694366564	1.73	0.0418150990	1.98	0.0238516942
1.24	0.1074877621	1.49	0.0681121483	1.74	0.0409294680	1.99	0.0232953977
1.25	0.1056498391	1.5	0.0668072288	1.75	0.0400591136	2	0.0227500620

Table 370: Standardized Normal Probabilities

Z Score	Probability	Z Score	Probability	Z Score	Probability	Z Score	Probability
2.01	0.0222155248	2.26	0.0119105882	2.51	0.0060365747	2.76	0.0028901245
2.02	0.0216916245	2.27	0.0116037563	2.52	0.0058677603	2.77	0.0028028721
2.03	0.0211782008	2.28	0.0113038111	2.53	0.0057031470	2.78	0.0027180034
2.04	0.0206750946	2.29	0.0110106273	2.54	0.0055426460	2.79	0.0026354615
2.05	0.0201821478	2.3	0.0107240811	2.55	0.0053861705	2.8	0.0025551906
2.06	0.0196992035	2.31	0.0104440502	2.56	0.0052336346	2.81	0.0024771362
2.07	0.0192261061	2.32	0.0101704140	2.57	0.0050849541	2.82	0.0024012444
2.08	0.0187627012	2.33	0.0099030531	2.58	0.0049400459	2.83	0.0023274629
2.09	0.0183088356	2.34	0.0096418496	2.59	0.0047988286	2.84	0.0022557401
2.1	0.0178643574	2.35	0.0093866874	2.6	0.0046612218	2.85	0.0021860256
2.11	0.0174291159	2.36	0.0091374516	2.61	0.0045271466	2.86	0.0021182698
2.12	0.0170029619	2.37	0.0088940289	2.62	0.0043965255	2.87	0.0020524243
2.13	0.0165857472	2.38	0.0086563075	2.63	0.0042692823	2.88	0.0019884417
2.14	0.0161773253	2.39	0.0084241771	2.64	0.0041453418	2.89	0.0019262755
2.15	0.0157775507	2.4	0.0081975289	2.65	0.0040246306	2.9	0.0018658801
2.16	0.0153862796	2.41	0.0079762554	2.66	0.0039070761	2.91	0.0018072110
2.17	0.0150033693	2.42	0.0077602509	2.67	0.0037926074	2.92	0.0017502246
2.18	0.0146286788	2.43	0.0075494110	2.68	0.0036811545	2.93	0.0016948780
2.19	0.0142620681	2.44	0.0073436327	2.69	0.0035726488	2.94	0.0016411295
2.2	0.0139033989	2.45	0.0071428147	2.7	0.0034670231	2.95	0.0015889381
2.21	0.0135525343	2.46	0.0069468569	2.71	0.0033642110	2.96	0.0015382639
2.22	0.0132093388	2.47	0.0067556608	2.72	0.0032641476	2.97	0.0014890676
2.23	0.0128736783	2.48	0.0065691295	2.73	0.0031667693	2.98	0.0014413109
2.24	0.0125454202	2.49	0.0063871672	2.74	0.0030720134	2.99	0.0013949564
2.25	0.0122244334	2.5	0.0062096799	2.75	0.0029798186	3	0.0013499672

Table 370: Standardized Normal Probabilities

Z Score	Probability	Z Score	Probability	Z Score	Probability	Z Score	Probability
3.01	0.0013063077	3.26	0.0005571219	3.51	0.0002240969	3.76	0.0000849834
3.02	0.0012639426	3.27	0.0005377977	3.52	0.0002158162	3.77	0.0000816499
3.03	0.0012228379	3.28	0.0005190951	3.53	0.0002078219	3.78	0.0000784397
3.04	0.0011829598	3.29	0.0005009959	3.54	0.0002001049	3.79	0.0000753486
3.05	0.0011442758	3.3	0.0004834825	3.55	0.0001926562	3.8	0.0000723724
3.06	0.0011067538	3.31	0.0004665376	3.56	0.0001854674	3.81	0.0000695072
3.07	0.0010703626	3.32	0.0004501443	3.57	0.0001785299	3.82	0.0000667491
3.08	0.0010350715	3.33	0.0004342863	3.58	0.0001718356	3.83	0.0000640944
3.09	0.0010008508	3.34	0.0004189477	3.59	0.0001653768	3.84	0.0000615394
3.1	0.0009676712	3.35	0.0004041129	3.6	0.0001591457	3.85	0.0000590806
3.11	0.0009355045	3.36	0.0003897667	3.61	0.0001531349	3.86	0.0000567147
3.12	0.0009043226	3.37	0.0003758946	3.62	0.0001473372	3.87	0.0000544383
3.13	0.0008740986	3.38	0.0003624821	3.63	0.0001417457	3.88	0.0000522484
3.14	0.0008448059	3.39	0.0003495154	3.64	0.0001363534	3.89	0.0000501418
3.15	0.0008164187	3.4	0.0003369808	3.65	0.0001311538	3.9	0.0000481155
3.16	0.0007889117	3.41	0.0003248652	3.66	0.0001261406	3.91	0.0000461668
3.17	0.0007622602	3.42	0.0003131558	3.67	0.0001213076	3.92	0.0000442927
3.18	0.0007364404	3.43	0.0003018400	3.68	0.0001166487	3.93	0.0000424907
3.19	0.0007114286	3.44	0.0002909058	3.69	0.0001121581	3.94	0.0000407581
3.2	0.0006872021	3.45	0.0002803412	3.7	0.0001078301	3.95	0.0000390925
3.21	0.0006637385	3.46	0.0002701349	3.71	0.0001036594	3.96	0.0000374913
3.22	0.0006410161	3.47	0.0002602757	3.72	0.0000996405	3.97	0.0000359523
3.23	0.0006190137	3.48	0.0002507526	3.73	0.0000957684	3.98	0.0000344732
3.24	0.0005977105	3.49	0.0002415553	3.74	0.0000920380	3.99	0.0000330518
3.25	0.0005770865	3.5	0.0002326734	3.75	0.0000884446	4	0.0000316860

Table 370: Standardized Normal Probabilities

Z Score	Probability	Z Score	Probability	Z Score	Probability	Z Score	Probability
4.01	0.0000303738	4.26	0.0000102283	4.51	0.0000032444	4.76	0.0000009692
4.02	0.0000291131	4.27	0.0000097804	4.52	0.0000030949	4.77	0.0000009223
4.03	0.0000279021	4.28	0.0000093512	4.53	0.0000029520	4.78	0.0000008776
4.04	0.0000267389	4.29	0.0000089400	4.54	0.0000028154	4.79	0.0000008350
4.05	0.0000256217	4.3	0.0000085460	4.55	0.0000026849	4.8	0.0000007944
4.06	0.0000245489	4.31	0.0000081687	4.56	0.0000025602	4.81	0.0000007556
4.07	0.0000235188	4.32	0.0000078072	4.57	0.0000024411	4.82	0.0000007187
4.08	0.0000225297	4.33	0.0000074610	4.58	0.0000023272	4.83	0.0000006836
4.09	0.0000215802	4.34	0.0000071295	4.59	0.0000022185	4.84	0.0000006501
4.1	0.0000206687	4.35	0.0000068121	4.6	0.0000021146	4.85	0.0000006181
4.11	0.0000197938	4.36	0.0000065082	4.61	0.0000020155	4.86	0.0000005877
4.12	0.0000189542	4.37	0.0000062172	4.62	0.0000019207	4.87	0.0000005588
4.13	0.0000181484	4.38	0.0000059387	4.63	0.0000018303	4.88	0.0000005312
4.14	0.0000173753	4.39	0.0000056721	4.64	0.0000017439	4.89	0.0000005049
4.15	0.0000166335	4.4	0.0000054170	4.65	0.0000016615	4.9	0.0000004799
4.16	0.0000159218	4.41	0.0000051728	4.66	0.0000015828	4.91	0.0000004560
4.17	0.0000152391	4.42	0.0000049392	4.67	0.0000015077	4.92	0.0000004334
4.18	0.0000145843	4.43	0.0000047156	4.68	0.0000014360	4.93	0.0000004118
4.19	0.0000139563	4.44	0.0000045018	4.69	0.0000013676	4.94	0.0000003912
4.2	0.0000133541	4.45	0.0000042972	4.7	0.0000013023	4.95	0.0000003716
4.21	0.0000127766	4.46	0.0000041016	4.71	0.0000012400	4.96	0.0000003530
4.22	0.0000122230	4.47	0.0000039145	4.72	0.0000011806	4.97	0.0000003353
4.23	0.0000116922	4.48	0.0000037355	4.73	0.0000011239	4.98	0.0000003184
4.24	0.0000111834	4.49	0.0000035644	4.74	0.0000010699	4.99	0.0000003024
4.25	0.0000106957	4.5	0.0000034008	4.75	0.0000010183	5	0.0000002871

Table 370: Standardized Normal Probabilities

Z Score	Probability	Z Score	Probability	Z Score	Probability	Z Score	Probability
5.01	0.0000002726	5.26	0.0000000722	5.51	0.0000000180	5.76	0.0000000042
5.02	0.0000002588	5.27	0.0000000684	5.52	0.0000000170	5.77	0.0000000040
5.03	0.0000002456	5.28	0.0000000647	5.53	0.0000000161	5.78	0.0000000037
5.04	0.0000002331	5.29	0.0000000613	5.54	0.0000000152	5.79	0.0000000035
5.05	0.0000002213	5.3	0.0000000580	5.55	0.0000000143	5.8	0.0000000033
5.06	0.0000002100	5.31	0.0000000549	5.56	0.0000000135	5.81	0.0000000031
5.07	0.0000001992	5.32	0.0000000520	5.57	0.0000000128	5.82	0.0000000030
5.08	0.0000001890	5.33	0.0000000492	5.58	0.0000000121	5.83	0.0000000028
5.09	0.0000001793	5.34	0.0000000466	5.59	0.0000000114	5.84	0.0000000026
5.1	0.0000001701	5.35	0.0000000441	5.6	0.0000000107	5.85	0.0000000025
5.11	0.0000001614	5.36	0.0000000417	5.61	0.0000000101	5.86	0.0000000023
5.12	0.0000001530	5.37	0.0000000395	5.62	0.0000000096	5.87	0.0000000022
5.13	0.0000001451	5.38	0.0000000373	5.63	0.0000000090	5.88	0.0000000021
5.14	0.0000001376	5.39	0.0000000353	5.64	0.0000000085	5.89	0.0000000019
5.15	0.0000001305	5.4	0.0000000334	5.65	0.0000000080	5.9	0.0000000018
5.16	0.0000001237	5.41	0.0000000316	5.66	0.0000000076	5.91	0.0000000017
5.17	0.0000001173	5.42	0.0000000299	5.67	0.0000000072	5.92	0.0000000016
5.18	0.0000001112	5.43	0.0000000282	5.68	0.0000000068	5.93	0.0000000015
5.19	0.0000001053	5.44	0.0000000267	5.69	0.0000000064	5.94	0.0000000014
5.2	0.0000000998	5.45	0.0000000252	5.7	0.0000000060	5.95	0.0000000013
5.21	0.0000000946	5.46	0.0000000239	5.71	0.0000000057	5.96	0.0000000013
5.22	0.0000000896	5.47	0.0000000226	5.72	0.0000000053	5.97	0.0000000012
5.23	0.0000000849	5.48	0.0000000213	5.73	0.0000000050	5.98	0.0000000011
5.24	0.0000000804	5.49	0.0000000201	5.74	0.0000000047	5.99	0.0000000011
5.25	0.0000000762	5.5	0.0000000190	5.75	0.0000000045	6	0.0000000010

The Performance Improvement Toolkit

Bibliography

Aguayo, Rafael. Dr. Deming: *The American Who Taught the Japanese About Quality*. Fireside Books, New York NY, 1990

Akao, Yoji (Editor), *Quality Function Deployment.* Productivity Press, Cambridge Massachusetts, 1990

Akao, Yoji (Editor), *Hoshin Kanri.* Productivity Press, Portland Oregon, 1988

Asaka, Tetsuichi; Ozeki Kazuo, *Handbook of Quality Tools*. Productivity Press, Cambridge MA, 1990

ASQ Statistics Division. (Galen C. Britz, Donald W. Emerling, Lynne B. Hare, Roger W. Hoerl, Stuart J. Janis, Janice E. Shade), *Improving Performance Through Statistical Thinking*. Quality Press, Milwaukee, Wisconsin, 1999

Box, George E.P., Hunter, Willian G., Hunter, J. Stuart, *Statistics for Experimenters*. John Wiley and Sons, New York NY, 1978

Burdock, Eugene I., Sudilovsky, Abraham, Gershon, Samuel, *The Behavior of Psychiatric Patients: Quantitative Techniques for Evaluation*. Marcel Dekker Inc., New York and Basel, 1982

Carlzon, Jan, *Moments of Truth*. Harper & Row, New York, 1989

Casti, John L. *Complexification*. Harper Collins, New York NY, 1994

Casti, John L. *Searching for Certainty.* William Morrow and Company, New York NY, 1990

Cohen, Lou. *Quality Function Deployment*. Addison Wesley, Reading, Massachusetts, 1995

Delavigne, Kenneth T., Robertson, J. Daniel. *Deming's Profound Changes*. PTR Prentice Hall, Englewood Cliffs NJ, 1994

Deming, Edwards, *Out of the Crisis*. MIT Center for Advanced Engineering Study, Cambridge MA, 1992

Deming, Edwards, *The New Economics*. MIT Center for Advanced Engineering Study, Second Edition, Cambridge MA, 1994

Deming, W. Edwards. *Sample Design in Business Research*. John Wiley & Sons, New York NY, (Wiley Classic Library Edition) 1990

DeYong, Camille F., Case, Kenneth E. "*Linking Customer Satisfaction Attributes with Process Metrics in Service Industries.*" Quality Management Journal, Volume 5, Issue 2, 1998

Dixon, J. Robb, Nanni, Alfred J., Vollmann, Thomas E., *The New Performance Challenge*. Business One Irwin, Homewood, Illinois, 1990

Drucker, Peter F. *Managing for Results*. Harper & Row, New York NY, 1964

Drucker, Peter F. *Management*. Harper & Row, New York NY, 1974

Epstein, Marc J. and Birchard, Bill, *Counting What Counts*. Perseus Books, Reading, Massachusetts, 1999

Eureka, William E., Ryan, Nancy E., *The Customer Driven Company.* ASI Press, Dearborne MI, 1988

Feynman, Richard P. *Surely You're Joking, Mr. Feynman.* Bantam Books, New York NY 1985

Feynman, Richard P. *The Meaning of It All.* Addison Wesley, Reading MA, 1998

Feynman, Richard P. *The Pleasure of Finding Things Out.* Perseus Books, Cambridge MA, 1999

Feynman, Richard P. *What Do You Care What Other People Think?* Bantam Books, New York NY 1989

Forsha, Harry I. *The Pursuit of Quality Through Personal Change.* ASQC Quality Press, Milwaukee WI, 1992

Fukuda, Ryuji, *Building Organizational Fitness.* Productivity Press, Portland Oregon, 1997

Gitlow, Howard S., Gitlow, Shelly J.; *The Deming Guide to Quality and Competitive Position.* Prentice-Hall Inc., Englewood Cliffs, New Jersey, 1987

Harrington, James H., *Business Process Improvement.* McGraw Hill, 1991

Harry, Mikel and Schroeder, Richard. *Six Sigma.* Currency, New York NY, 2000

Hillier, Frederick S. and Lieberman, Gerald J. *Operations Research.* second edition Holden Day Inc. San Francisco CA, 1974

Imai, Masaaki. *Gemba Kaizen.* McGraw Hill, New York NY, 1997

Ishikawa, Kaoru. *Introduction to Quality Control.* 3A Corporation, Tokyo Japan, 1991

Johnson, H. Thomas, *Relevance Regained.* The Free Press, New York, NY, 1992

Joiner, Brian L. *Fourth Generation Management.* McGraw Hill, New York NY, 1994

Joiner, Brian L., Gaudard, Marie A., "*Variation, Management and W. Edwards Deming.*" in the Practical Guide to Quality. Joiner Associates Incorporated, Madison WI, 1993

Juran, J.M. *Juran on Quality by Design.* The Free Press, New York NY, 1992

Juran, J.M. *Managerial Breakthrough.* McGraw Hill, New York NY, (International Edition) 1995

Kaplan, Robert S. and Norton, David P. *The Balanced Scorecard.* HBS Press, Boston Massachusetts, 1996

Kohn, Alfie. *Punished by Rewards.* Houghton Mifflin Company, Boston Massachusetts, 1993

Lareau, William, *American Samurai.* Warner Books, New York, NY, 1991

Latzko, William J., Saunders, David M., *Four Days With Dr. Deming.* Addison-Wesley, Reading MA, 1995

Lawton, Robin L. *Creating a Customer-Centered Culture.* ASQC Quality Press, Milwaukee Wisconsin, 1993

Moen, Ronald D.; Nolan, Thomas W.; Provost, Lloyd P., *Improving Quality Through Planned Experimentation.* McGraw Hill, New York NY, 1991

Neave, Henry R. *The Deming Dimension*. SPC Press, Knoxville Tennessee, 1990

Ozeki, Kazuo. Asaka, Tetsuichi. *Handbook of Quality Tools*. Productivity Press, Cambridge MA, 1990

Paulos, John Allen. *A Mathematician Reads the Newspaper*. Basic Books, New York NY, 1995

Petersen, Donald J. and Hillkirk, John. *A Better Idea*. Houghton Mifflin Company, Boston, 1991

Pfeffer, Jeffrey. *The Human Equation*. HBS Press, Boston Massachusetts, 1998

Rummler, Geary A. and Brache, Alan P. *Improving Performance*. Jossey-Bass, San Francisco, 1990

Saaty, Thomas L. *Mathematical Methods of Operations Research*. Dover Publications Inc., New York NY, 1988

Saaty, Thomas L., *Decision Making for Leaders*. RWS Publications, Pittsburgh, PA, 1995

Schneiderman, Arthur , *"Setting Quality Goals."* Quality Progress, April 1988

Scholtes, Peter R., *The Leaders Handbook*. McGraw Hill, 1998

Scholtes, Peter R., *The Team Handbook*. Joiner Associates Inc., Madison WI, 1988

Smith, Gerald. *Quality Problem Solving*. ASQ Quality Press, Milwaukee WI. 1998

Tufte, Edward R. *The Visual Display of Quantitative Information*. Graphics Press, Cheshire, Connecticut, 1983

Walton, Mary, *Deming Management at Work*. G.P. Putnam's Sons, New York, NY, 1990

Walton, Mary, *The Deming Management Method*. Perigree Books, New York, NY, 1986

Watson, Gregory H., *"Cycles of Learning: Observations of Jack Welch."* Six Sigma Forum Magazine, Vol.1, No.1, November, 2001, Wilwaukee, WI

Weisbord, Marvin R. *Productive Workplaces*. Jossey-Bass, San Francisco, 1987

Wheeler, Donald J., Chambers, David S., *Understanding Statistical Process Control*. Second Edition, SPC Press, Knoxville Tennessee, 1992

Wheeler, Donald J., *Understanding Variation*. SPC Press, Knoxville Tennessee, 1993

Wilson, Paul F., Dell, Larry D. and Anderson, Gaylord F. *Root Cause Analysis*. ASQ Quality Press, Milwaukee, WI, 1993

Zeithaml, Valarie A., Parasuraman, A. and Berry, Leonard L. *Delivering Quality Service*. The Free Press, New York NY, 1990

Index

About the Author

Robert Gerst is a principal and a co-founder of the Converge Consulting Group. He has consulted for over 15 years with such organizations as Hewlett-Packard, Mobil Oil, Nortel Networks, Canadian Pacific Railway, Shell Oil, Telus, Chevron, Carewest, Nova Chemicals and AT&T Canada as well as a number of government agencies and departments. In addition, his consulting work with non-governmental organizations supported the development of a number of community foundations in Canada, the successful redesign of AIDS/HIV funding and the development of a community strategy for addressing homelessness in Calgary, Alberta, where he currently lives.

Robert received his graduate degree in management from the University of Alberta. He is currently a member of the American Society for Quality (ASQ), the American Association for the Advancement of Science (AAAS) and the American Statistical Association (ASA).